SO-BVC-871

HISTORICAL DICTIONARIES OF U.S. DIPLOMACY

Jon Woronoff, Series Editor

Historical Dictionary of United States– Southeast Asia Relations

Donald E. Weatherbee

Historical Dictionaries of
U.S. Diplomacy, No. 7

The Scarecrow Press, Inc.
Lanham, Maryland • Toronto • Plymouth, UK
2008

SCARECROW PRESS, INC.

Published in the United States of America
by Scarecrow Press, Inc.
A wholly owned subsidiary of
The Rowman & Littlefield Publishing Group, Inc.
4501 Forbes Boulevard, Suite 200, Lanham, Maryland 20706
www.scarecrowpress.com

Estover Road
Plymouth PL6 7PY
United Kingdom

British Library Cataloguing in Publication Information Available

Library of Congress Cataloging-in-Publication Data

Weatherbee, Donald E.
  Historical dictionary of United States–Southeast Asia relations / Donald E.
Weatherbee.
    p. cm. — (Historical dictionaries of U.S. diplomacy, no. 7)
  Includes bibliographical references.
  ISBN-13: 978-0-8108-5542-7 (cloth : alk. paper)
  ISBN-10: 0-8108-5542-9 (cloth : alk. paper)
  1. Southeast Asia–Foreign relations–United States–Dictionaries. 2. United
States–Foreign relations–Southeast Asia–Dictionaries. I. Title.
  DS525.9.U6W44 2008
  327.7305903–dc22   2007046902

Contents

Editor's Foreword

Although U.S. relations with Southeast Asia are relatively recent—indeed the very concept of Southeast Asia is fairly new—they have become increasingly important, and quite rapidly. This has occurred for good and bad reasons. The worst of all conceivable reasons was engagement with Vietnam directly, and Cambodia and Laos indirectly, in the Vietnam War, which tore apart the region and the United States for nearly half a century. The more recent war on terror, in which Southeast Asia has become a second front, involved Muslim-majority states whose views are not always compatible with the United States. A more positive aspect of U.S. relations has been the emergence of dynamic trading and market economies across the region, including America's old nemesis in Indochina. Beneath the negative overtones of conflict, the basic thrust of the current relationships in Southeast Asia is positive. If anything, Washington is buying into one of the more successful parts of the globe, which, in addition, lies across strategic sea lanes and close to major powers with which the United States will have to contend in the future.

This *Historical Dictionary of United States–Southeast Asian Relations* deals with a varied group of 11 countries, ranging from vast Indonesia to the Brunei ministate, including highly developed Singapore and steadfastly backward Burma, with countries (and within them communities) of different races, religions, and cultures. Yet, better than most developing regions, the Southeast Asian nations have been collaborating with one another through regional organizations and both individually and collectively with the only remaining superpower. This relationship is traced in this volume in a chronology that covers more than a century and a half and is put into a logical framework in the introduction. The dictionary itself then looks into the crucial details, with entries on notable people, both American and Asian; significant political parties; military groupings and organizations; and the major events that shaped American–Southeast Asian relations. The list of acronyms and abbreviations at the front is another important addition. Finally, the bibliography at the end makes it easier for readers to follow up on specific areas of interest.

This volume was written by Donald E. Weatherbee, who has been following Southeast Asian affairs for more than four decades. He was long a professor of Southeast Asian politics and international relations at the University of South Carolina and has taught and held research grants at other universities and institutes in the United States, Europe, and Southeast Asia. Dr. Weatherbee has a lengthy scholarly bibliography, beginning with his 1966 book *Ideology in Indonesia: Sukarno's Indonesian Revolution*. His most recent book is *International Relations in Southeast Asia: The Struggle for Autonomy*. He has been editorially active on the journals *Asian Affairs* and *Asian Survey*. He has worked with the Asia Society on Southeast Asian issues and is currently on the Board of Advisors of the United States–Indonesia Society. Dr. Weatherbee's teaching, research, and writing focusing on Southeast Asian international relations, and this latest addition to our series of Historical Dictionaries of U.S. Diplomacy, benefits from his insightful and also balanced view of the United States in Southeast Asia.

Jon Woronoff
Series Editor

Preface

Since 1950, when in pursuit of the strategy of the containment of communism, the United States became fully engaged as the predominant Great Power actor in the Southeast Asian region, the United States has had official relations with the governments of 11 independent states. All but one of them—Thailand—achieved sovereign status only after the end of World War II. Added to these states in which the United States has been diplomatically represented, there were three governments not recognized by the United States but that had a significant impact on regional international relations affecting American national interests. Since 1950, there have been 11 American presidents served by 18 secretaries of state and 21 assistant secretaries of state for East Asian and Pacific Affairs. In the countries hosting American embassies, U.S. interests have been represented by 152 ambassadors and, in the absence of an ambassador, 19 chargé d'affaires. At this senior level of officialdom, the American establishment has interacted with a host of Southeast Asian presidents, prime ministers, and foreign ministers. Obviously, from this abundance of possibilities, not every individual can have, nor necessarily deserves, an entry in the dictionary that follows. The same is true for nonofficial or nondiplomatic individuals and agencies that have been part of the fabric of the region's relations with the United States. Nor can all bilateral or multilateral political, strategic, economic, cultural, or other transactions that make up the totality of U.S.–Southeast Asian relations be given an entry.

In compiling this *Historical Dictionary of United States–Southeast Asia Relations*, the author was faced with the task selecting entries while still being comprehensive within the allotted space. The entries that have been selected are based on the author's appreciation of the relative significance of these persons, issues, events, and institutions in shaping the course of U.S. bilateral and multilateral relations in the region. It is understood that different analysts might pick different entries. Suggestions for items to include or delete in possible future editions are welcomed. The Vietnam War, and in its extensions to Cambodia and Laos the Second Indochina War, had great impact on American–Southeast Asian relations. This is reflected in numerous entries. The work, however, is not about the war itself. For war planning, strategy, tactics, generals, combat units, and battles, Edwin E. Moïse, *Historical Dictionary of the Vietnam War*, is recommended.

For transliterations and alphabetizing of Southeast Asian personal and place names, the author has adopted that which has been customary in U.S. official usage. For the country that most of the world now knows as Myanmar, the United States still insists on Burma. Therefore, in most citations in this work, Burma it is.

The author would like to acknowledge the patient guidance and suggestions he received from Jon Woronoff, the series editor. The author is especially indebted to Prof. Epsey Cooke Farrell of Seton Hall University's Whitehead School of Diplomacy, who carefully read every entry for content and style. She helped improve the manuscript immeasurably.

Acronyms and Abbreviations

ACP	ASEAN Cooperation Plan
ADB	Asian Development Bank
AFP	Armed Forces of the Philippines
AFPFL	Anti-Fascist People's Freedom League (Burma)
AFTA	ASEAN Free Trade Area
ANS	Armée Nationale Sihanoukiste (Sihanouk National Army) (Cambodia)
ANZUS	Australia—New Zealand—United States pact
APCSS	Asia Pacific Center for Strategic Studies
APEC	Asia-Pacific Economic Cooperation
APFTA	Asia-Pacific Free Trade Area
APT	ASEAN Plus Three
ARF	ASEAN Regional Forum
ARVN	Army of the Republic of Vietnam
ASEAN	Association of Southeast Asian Nations
ASG	Abu Sayyaf Group (Philippines)
BIA	Burma Independence Army
BNA	Burma National Army
BPP	Border Patrol Police (Thailand)
BSPP	Burma Socialist Program Party
CARAT	Cooperation Afloat Readiness and Training
CAT	Civil Air Transport
CAVR	Comissão de Acolhimento, Verdade e Reconciliação de Timor-Leste (East Timor Commission for Reception, Truth, and Reconciliation)
CDCF	Cambodia Development Cooperation Forum
CGC	Consultative Group for Cambodia
CGDK	Coalition Government of Democratic Kampuchea
CGI	Consultative Group for Indonesia

CIA	Central Intelligence Agency
CIDG	Civilian Irregular Defense Group (Vietnam)
CIG	Central Intelligence Group
CINCPAC	Commander in Chief Pacific Forces
CNRT	Conselho Nacional de Resistência Timorense (National Council of Timorese Resistance)
CPC	Country of Particular Concern
CPK	Communist Party of Kampuchea
CPP/NPA	Communist Party of the Philippines/New People's Army
CSCAP	Council for Security Cooperation in the Asia-Pacific
CSI	Container Security Initiative
CSIS	Center for Strategic and International Studies
DCI	Director of Central Intelligence
DDP	Deputy Director of Plans (CIA)
DEA	Drug Enforcement Agency
DK	Democratic Kampuchea
DLG	Defense Liaison Group (Indonesia)
DMZ	demilitarized zone
DNI	Director of National Intelligence
DRL	Democracy, Rights, and Labor (State Department Bureau of)
DRV	Democratic Republic of Vietnam
DSCA	Defense Security Cooperation Agency
EAEC	East Asian Economic Caucus
EAEG	East Asian Economic Group
EAFTA	East Asian Free Trade Area
EAI	Enterprise for ASEAN Initiative
EAP	East Asian and Pacific Affairs (State Department Bureau of)
EAP/MLS	EAP Office of Mainland Southeast Asia
EAP/MTS	EAP Office of Maritime Southeast Asia
EAS	East Asia Summit
EASI	East Asia Security Initiative
ECA	Educational and Cultural Affairs (State Department Bureau of)
EDSA	Epifano de los Santos Avenue (Philippines)
EEC	European Economic Community

ETAN	East Timor Action Network
EU	European Union
Falintil	Forças Armadas le Libertação Nacional de Timor-Leste (National Armed Forces for the Liberation of East Timor)
FANK	Forces Armées Nationales Khmères (Khmer National Armed Forces) (Cambodia)
FAR	Forces Armées Royale (Royal Armed Forces Laos)
FBI	Federal Bureau of Investigation (United States)
FDI	foreign direct investment
FMF	foreign military financing
FMS	foreign military sales
FPDA	Five Power Defence Arrangement
Fretilin	Frente Revolucinária de Timor Leste Independent (Revolutionary Front for the Independence of East Timorr)
FSO	Foreign Service Officer
FTA	free trade agreement
FTO	forcign terrorist organization
Funcinpec	Front Uni National pour un Cambodge Indépendent, Neutre, Pacifique et Coopératif (National United Front for an Independent, Neutral, Peaceful, and Cooperative Cambodia)
FUNK	Front Uni National du Kampuchea (National United Front for Kampuchea) (Cambodia)
G-77	Group of 77 (United Nations)
GAM	Gerakan Aceh Merdeka (Free Aceh Movement) (Indonesia)
GATT	General Agreement on Tariffs and Trade
GESTAPU	Gerakan September Tiga Puluh (30 September Movement) (Indonesia)
GOC	Good Offices Committee (Indonesia)
GRUNK	Gouvernament Royal d'Union Nationale du Kampuchea (Royal Government of the National Union of Kampuchea) (Cambodia)
GSP	Generalized System of Preferences
G/TIP	Office to Monitor and Combat Trafficking in Persons (State Department)

ICC	International Criminal Court
ICCS	International Commission of Control and Supervision
ICK	International Conference on Cambodia
ICP	Indochinese Communist Party
ICSC	International Commission for Supervision and Control
IFI	international financial institutions
IGGI	Intergovernmental Group on Indonesia
IMET	International Military Education and Training
IMF	International Monetary Fund
INCSR	*International Narcotics Control Strategy Report*
INL	International Narcotics and Law Enforcement Affairs (State Department Bureau of)
INR	Intelligence and Research (State Department Bureau of)
INTERFET	International Force in East Timor
IPR	intellectual property rights
ISA	Internal Security Act (Malaysia)
ISF	International Stabilization Force (East Timor)
JCET	Joint combined exchange training
JCRC	Joint Casualty Resolution Center
JCS	Joint Chiefs of Staff
JI	Jema'ah Islamiyah
JIM	Jakarta informal meetings (I and II)
JPAC	Joint POW/MIA Accounting Command
JSOTF–P	Joint Special Operations Task Force–Philippines
JTF–FA	Joint Task Force–Full Accounting
JUSMAAG	Joint U.S. Military Assistance Advisory Group
KIA	killed in action
KMT	Kuomintang
KNU	Karen National Union
KOSTRAD	Komando Cadangan Strategis Angkatan Darat (Indonesian Army Strategic Reserve Command)
KPNLF	Khmer People's National Liberation Front
KR	Khmer Rouge
LPDR	Lao People's Democratic Republic
LPRP	Lao People's Revolutionary Party
MAAG	Military Assistance Advisory Group
MACV	Military Assistance Command, Vietnam
MBA	Military Bases Agreement (Philippines)

MDT	Mutual Defense Treaty (Philippines)
MEDT	Military Equipment Delivery Team (Cambodia)
MFN	most favored nation
MIA	missing in action
MILF	Moro Islamic Liberation Front
MLSA	Mutual Logistics Support Agreement (Philippines)
MNLF	Moro National Liberation Front
MNNA	Major Non-NATO Ally
NAM	Nonaligned Movement
NEP	New Economic Policy (Malaysia)
NGO	nongovernmental organization
NLD	National League for Democracy (Burma)
NLF	National Liberation Front (Vietnam)
NSAM	National Security Action Memorandum
NSC	National Security Council
NTR	normal trade relations
ODA	official development assistance
ODP	Orderly Departure Program
OEF	Operation Enduring Freedom
OES	Oceans and Environmental and Scientific Affairs (State Department Bureau of)
OIC	Organization of the Islamic Conference
OPM	Organisasi Papua Merdeka (Free Papua Organization) (Indonesia)
OSI	Open Society Institute
OSS	Office of Strategic Services
PAP	People's Action Party (Singapore)
PARU	Police Arial Reinforcement Unit (Thailand)
PAVN	People's Army of Vietnam
PEO	Program Evaluation Office (Laos)
Permesta	Perjuangan Semesta Alam (Total Struggle) (Indonesia)
Philcag	Philippine Civic Action Group
PICC	Paris International Conference on Cambodia
PKI	Partai Kommunis Indonesia (Indonesian Communist Party)
PKO	peacekeeping operation
PLAF	People's Liberation Armed Forces (Vietnam)
PM	Political-Military Affairs (State Department Bureau of)

PMC	post-ministerial conference (Association of Southeast Asian Nations)
PNTR	permanent normal trade relations
POW/MIA	prisoners of war/missing in action
PRC	People's Republic of China
PRG	Provisional Revolutionary Government of South Vietnam
PRK	People's Republic of Kampuchea
PRM	Population, Refugees, and Migration (State Department Bureau of)
PRRI	Pemerintah Revolusioner Republik Indonesia (Revolutionary Government of the Republic of Indonesia)
PSI	Proliferation Security Initiative
REDI	Regional Emerging Disease Intervention Center
RVA	Republic of Vietnam
SARS	severe acute respiratory syndrome
SEAC	Southeast Asia Command
SEACAT	Southeast Asia Cooperation against Terrorism
SEANWFZ	Southeast Asia Nuclear Weapons Free Zone
SEARCCT	Southeast Asian Regional Center for Counterterrorism
SEATO	Southeast Asia Treaty Organization
SLORC	State Law and Order Restoration Council (Burma)
SNC	Supreme National Council (Cambodia)
SOCPAC	U.S. Pacific Special Operations Command
SOFA	status of forces agreement
SOG	Studies and Observation Group
SPDC	State Peace and Development Council (Burma)
SRV	Socialist Republic of Vietnam
TAC	Treaty of Amity and Cooperation in Southeast Asia
TIFA	trade and investment framework agreement
TPA	trade promotion authority
TRIPS	Trade-Related Aspects of Intellectual Property Rights
TWEA	Trading with the Enemy Act
UMNO	United Malays National Organization
UN	United Nations
UNAMET	United Nations Assistance Mission in East Timor
UNCI	United Nations Commission on Indonesia
UNDP	United Nations Development Program

UNHCR	United Nations High Commissioner for Refugees
UNMISET	United Nations Mission in Support of East Timor
UNMIT	United Nations Integrated Mission in Timor Leste
UNODC	United Nations Office of Drug Control
UNOTIL	United Nations Office in Timor Leste
UNTAC	United Nations Transitional Authority in Cambodia
UNTAET	United Nations Transitional Administration in East Timor
UNTEA	United Nations Temporary Executive Administration (West New Guinea)
USAID	United States Agency for International Development
USDLG	United States Defense Liaison Group (Indonesia)
USINDO	United States–Indonesia Society
USIP	United States Institute of Peace
USOM	United States Operating Mission
USPACOM	United States Pacific Command
USSR	Union of Soviet Socialist Republics
USTR	United States Trade Representative
UXO	unexploded ordnance
VFA	Visiting Forces Agreement (Philippines)
WCI	War Crimes Issues (State Department, Office of)
WHO	World Health Organization
WSAG	Washington Special Actions Group
WTO	World Trade Organization
ZOPFAN	(Southeast Asia) Zone of Peace, Freedom, and Neutrality

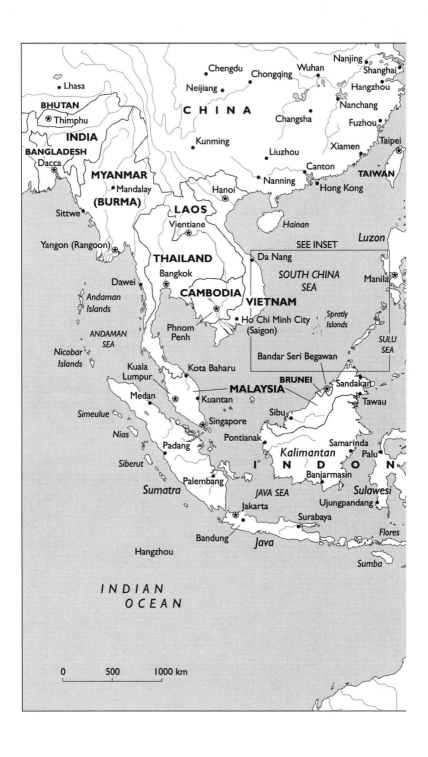

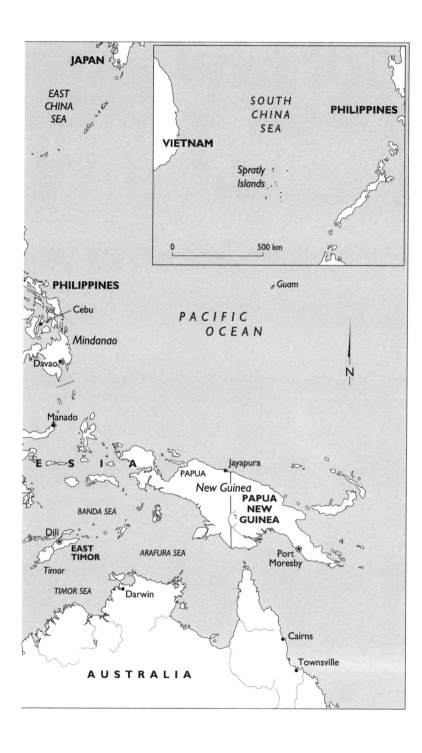

Chronology

1833 March: The Roberts Treaty of Amity and Commerce between the United States and Siam, the first between the United States and an Asian country, signed.

1845 January–June: USS *Constitution* calls at ports in Southeast Asia during a circumnavigation.

1850 June: Treaty of Friendship, Commerce, and Navigation between the United States and Brunei obtained by Joseph Balestier.

1856 May: Townsend Harris negotiates an "unequal" treaty with Siam, replacing the 1833 Roberts Treaty.

1882 October: First U.S. diplomat with rank of minister presents his credentials to the king of Siam.

1898 May: At the outbreak of the Spanish–American War. Admiral George Dewey sails into Manila Bay to seize the city from the Spanish. **June:** Philippine nationalists declare independence in convention at Malolos. **December:** Spain cedes the Philippines to the United States in the Treaty of Paris.

1902 July: End of the Philippine "insurrection" against the American occupation proclaimed.

1905 August: Taft–Katsura Agreement initialed. In it, Japan disclaims designs on the Philippines in return for American acknowledgment of Japan's sphere of interest in Korea.

1908 November: Root–Takahira Agreement signed. In it, Japan and the United States agree to respect each other's territorial possessions.

1916 August: Jones Act adopted by U.S. Congress as the organic law for the Philippines; it promises eventual independence for the islands.

1920 December: New Siam–United State treaty signed, eliminating extraterritoriality and other unequal burdens on Siamese sovereignty.

1921–1922 November–February: Washington Naval Conference convened by the United States with an American goal of limiting Japanese naval expansion and strategic threats to the Philippines and Hawaii.

1934 March: Framework for granting Philippine independence established in the Tydings-McDuffie Act, providing for a self-governing Commonwealth and a 10-year transition to independence.

1935 November: Commonwealth of the Philippines formally established. Manuel Quezon inaugurated as Commonwealth president.

1941 July: General Douglas MacArthur recalled to active duty as commander of U.S. Armed Forces in the Far East. **December:** World War II in the Pacific begins with Japanese attacks on Pearl Harbor and Manila.

1942 January: Thailand declares war on the United States, but the United States refuses to recognize it. **March:** General MacArthur, along with the president and vice president of the Philippine Commonwealth, departs the Philippines for Australia. **April:** American and Filipino forces surrender to the Japanese.

1943 October: Japanese-sponsored Republic of the Philippines established, with José Laurel as president.

1944 October: General MacArthur and president of the Philippine Commonwealth Sergio Osmeña return to the Philippines with the landings on Leyte.

1945 August: Japan surrenders, ending World War II. Indonesia, with Sukarno as president, proclaims its independence from the Netherlands. The United States accepts Thailand's declaration of peace. **September:** Ho Chi Minh proclaims the Democratic Republic of Vietnam. The Lao Issara movement, led by Prince Phetsarat, declares the independence of the Kingdom of Laos from France.

1946 February: Ho Chi Minh sends a letter to President Harry S. Truman seeking U.S. support in Vietnam's independence struggle. **July:** Bell Act (Philippine Trade Act) ratified by the Philippines, establishing the terms of the postcolonial relationship with the United States.

Philippines independence proclaimed. **December:** First Indochina War begins with an attack by the Viet Minh on the French in Hanoi.

1947 **March:** Truman Doctrine announced, setting the U.S. Cold War policy course. Philippine Senate ratifies the Military Bases Agreement. **August:** United Nations Good Offices Committee in Indonesia established, with members from Australia, Belgium, and the United States, to mediate the Dutch–Indonesian colonial war.

1948 **January:** Cease-fire agreement between Indonesia and the Netherlands signed on board the USS *Renville*. **March:** First U.S. ambassador to Burma presents his credentials.

1949 **December:** The Netherlands transfers sovereign authority to Indonesia. First U.S. ambassador presents his credentials to Indonesian President Sukarno.

1950 **February:** United States recognizes the State of Vietnam and the kingdoms of Cambodia and Laos as the French formally transfer sovereignty. **June:** First American minister accredited to U.S. legations in the State of Vietnam, the Kingdom of Laos, and the Kingdom of Cambodia. **August:** Unitary Republic of Indonesia proclaimed with Sukarno as president.

1954 **January:** Berlin "Big Four" meeting agrees to a conference on Korea and Indochina. **May:** Battle of Dien Bien Phu ends with the French surrender. **July:** Geneva Conference on Indochina negotiates the Geneva Accords, which closed the First Indochina War. **August:** U.S. representation in Vietnam, Laos, and Cambodia raised to embassy status. **September:** Southeast Asia Collective Defense Treaty, establishing the Southeast Asia Treaty Organization (SEATO), signed in Manila.

1955 **February:** First meeting of the SEATO Council held. **April:** Asian-African Conference held in Bandung, Indonesia. **September:** Laurel-Langley Agreement revising U.S.–Philippines economic relations concluded. **October:** Following a referendum deposing head of state Bao Dai, the State of Vietnam becomes the Republic of Vietnam under President Ngo Dinh Diem.

1956 **February:** From China, King Sihanouk declares Cambodia's neutrality and rejects SEATO.

1957 **March:** President Sukarno declares martial law in Indonesia. **November:** First Laos coalition government formed despite U.S. objections to inclusion of the Communist Pathet Lao.

1958 **February:** PRRI-Permesta regional revolts begin in Indonesia. **May:** Central Intelligence Agency contract pilot Allen Pope shot down over Ambon in East Indonesia, exposing CIA's covert support to the PRRI-Permesta rebels. **July:** United States suspends assistance to Laos, hastening collapse of the coalition government and the emergence of a rightist government.

1959 **July:** United States takes first military combat casualties in Vietnam. **August:** Sukarno announces a Guided Democracy in Indonesia. **October:** Bohlen-Serrano Agreement revises the U.S.–Philippines Mutual Defense Treaty and the Military Bases Agreement. **December:** With U.S. and Thai backing, Phoumi Nosavan seizes power in Laos from the neutralists. General Vang Pao, leader of the Laotian Hmong minority, reaches an agreement with the U.S. Central Intelligence Agency for support in the secret war in Laos.

1960 **June:** President Dwight D. Eisenhower makes a state visit to the Philippines. **August:** Kong Le coup establishes a neutralist government in Laos, beginning the Laotian crisis. **December:** Rightist general Phoumi Nosavan, backed by the United States, overthrows Laos's neutralist government. In South Vietnam, the National Front for the Liberation of South Vietnam (NFLSV) is formally established as the political face of communist opposition.

1961 **January:** President John F. Kennedy inaugurated. **May:** Geneva Conference on the Laotian crisis convened. **June:** At a Vienna summit meeting, U.S. President Kennedy and Chairman Premier Nikita Khrushchev agree to support a neutral and independent Laos. **October–November:** Taylor-Rostow mission sent to Vietnam by President Kennedy. **November:** President Kennedy authorizes an expansion of the U.S. military role in Vietnam.

1962 **February:** Military Assistance Command, Vietnam (MACV) established. **March:** Rusk-Thanat communiqué bilateralizes for the United States and Thailand their SEATO obligations. **June:** Second Laos coalition government formed. **July:** Geneva Accords ending the

Laotian crisis signed. **August:** Indonesia–Netherlands "Treaty of New York" (Bunker Agreement) on the transfer of authority in West New Guinea signed.

1963   **April:** Laos's second coalition government collapses. **May:** United Nations (UN) transfers administrative authority in West New Guinea to Indonesia. **August:** Washington authorities send a message to the American embassy in Saigon expressing no objection to the removal of Ngo Dinh Diem. **September:** Indonesia begins "confrontation" with Malaysia. **November:** A U.S.-backed military coup overthrows President Ngo Dinh Diem, who is killed. President John F. Kennedy is assassinated, and President Lyndon B. Johnson is sworn into office. Cambodia's Prime Minister Norodom Sihanouk suspends all U.S. economic and military assistance.

1964   **August:** An alleged attack on U.S. naval vessels in the Tonkin Gulf leads to the first American air attacks on North Vietnam. Congress approves the Tonkin Gulf Resolution, which gives the president authority to widen the war.

1965   **March:** First U.S. combat forces deployed to South Vietnam and sustained bombing campaign against North Vietnam begins. **April:** Diplomatic relations between the United States and Cambodia severed. **September:** Abortive coup in Indonesia leads to a military intervention that ends Sukarno's presidency and begins the rise of Suharto. United States and the Philippines exchange notes that start the 25-year clock on the expiration of the Military Bases Agreement.

1966   **March:** Presidential authority in Indonesia transferred to General Suharto. **October:** President Johnson holds summit meeting in Manila with the leaders of American allies in Vietnam. He visits U.S. forces in Vietnam and makes state visits to Thailand and Malaysia.

1967   **March:** General Suharto named Indonesia's acting president. **August:** Indonesia, Malaysia, the Philippines, Singapore, and Thailand issue the Bangkok Declaration, establishing the Association of Southeast Asian Nations (ASEAN). **September:** Nguyen Van Thieu elected president of the Republic of Vietnam.

1968   **January:** People's Army of Vietnam (PAVN) and Viet Cong launch the Tet offensive. Ambassador Chester Bowles travels to Phnom

Penh to discuss resumption of U.S.–Cambodia relations. **March:** General Suharto elected president of Indonesia. President Johnson announces that he is willing to negotiate with the Democratic Republic of Vietnam (DRV) and will not seek reelection. **April:** DRV agrees to peace talks with the United States. **May:** Initial meetings between the United States and the DRV in the Paris peace negotiations opened. **December:** Unrestricted air war against North Vietnamese and Pathet Lao targets in Laos begins.

1969   January: President Richard M. Nixon inaugurated. The first session of the Paris peace talks under the Nixon administration held. **March:** Secret bombing of Cambodia begins. **May:** West New Guinea becomes Indonesia's 26th province. **June:** Formation of the Provisional Revolutionary Government of South Vietnam (PRGSV) announced. President Nixon meets South Vietnam president Nguyn Van Thieu on Midway Island and announces the initial withdrawal of American troops from Vietnam. Diplomatic relations between the United States and Cambodia restored. **July:** President Nixon meets Thieu again in Vietnam and makes state visits to the Philippines, Indonesia, and Thailand. In a meeting with the press on Guam, he outlines what later came to be known as the Nixon Doctrine.

1970   February: Kissinger–Le Duc Tho secret talks on ending the Vietnam War settlement begin in Paris. **March:** Coup in Cambodia led by General Lon Nol ousts Norodom Sihanouk as head of state. **April/May:** Major U.S. military incursion into Cambodia. **June:** U.S. Senate votes to repeal the Tonkin Gulf Resolution. **December:** Church-Cooper amendments, barring the use of U.S. troops in Cambodia, Laos, and Thailand, passed by Congress.

1971   November: ASEAN declares a Southeast Asia Zone of Peace, Freedom, and Neutrality (ZOPFAN) that is not recognized by the United States.

1972   February: President Nixon makes his historic trip to China. **September:** President Ferdinand Marcos of the Philippines declares martial law to begin a presidential dictatorship. **October:** Secretary of State Henry Kissinger and DRV negotiator Le Duc Tho agree to a draft for the Paris Peace Agreement. This is rejected by Republic of Vietnam president Thieu. **December:** DRV delegation walks out of the Paris

Peace talks in protest against the "Christmas Bombings" of Hanoi and Haiphong.

1973 January: Paris "Agreement on Ending the War and Restoring the Peace in Vietnam" signed. **February:** In a secret message to Vietnam prime minister Pham Van Dong, President Nixon indicates the terms of postwar U.S. economic assistance. A cease-fire is put in place between the Lao government and the Pathet Lao. **March:** Withdrawal of U.S. forces from Vietnam officially completed. **August:** Congress orders a halt to bombing in Cambodia. **September:** Laos protocol leading to the formation of the third coalition government agreed to.

1974 April: Pathet Lao–dominated third coalition government formed. **August:** President Nixon resigns and Vice President Gerald Ford sworn in as president.

1975 March: Thailand prime minister Kukrit Pramoj terminates U.S. base rights and calls for the withdrawal of U.S. forces. **April:** Americans evacuated from Cambodia, and Khmer Rouge forces occupy Phnom Penh. Republic of Vietnam's president Thieu resigns. Americans evacuated from Saigon by helicopter. Republic of Vietnam surrenders to the Democratic Republic of Vietnam. **May:** American ship *Mayaguez* seized by Khmer Rouge forces and President Ford orders the use of force to free the crew. American trade embargo in force for North Vietnam extended to all of Vietnam and Cambodia. **June:** All U.S. assistance to Laos terminated. **December:** Monarchy abolished in Laos and the Lao People's Democratic Republic (LPDR) established. President Ford, in Indonesia and the Philippines, reasserts American commitment to the security of the region, a position he reinforces in announcing his Pacific Doctrine in Hawaii. Immediately following the Ford visit, Indonesia invades East Timor.

1976 January: East Timor incorporated into Indonesia as its 27th province. Democratic Kampuchea established. **February:** SEATO disbanded after 21 years. ASEAN states sign the Treaty of Amity and Cooperation in Southeast Asia (TAC), to which the United States does not adhere. **July:** North and South Vietnam unified in the Socialist Republic of Vietnam (SRV). **November:** United States vetoes Vietnam's admission into the United Nations.

1977 **March:** President Jimmy Carter dispatches the Woodcock Mission to Vietnam in an initial attempt to get cooperation on the POW/MIA issue. **September:** Vietnam admitted into the United Nations.

1978 **December:** Vietnam invades Cambodia, beginning the Third Indochina War.

1979 **January:** People's Republic of Kampuchea installed in Phnom Penh by Vietnam. **February:** China invades Vietnam in a campaign lasting until March, to punish it for the Cambodia invasion. **July:** First official dialogue between a U.S. secretary of state and ASEAN foreign ministers takes place.

1981 **July:** United Nations International Conference on Kampuchea convened. Its "declaration" establishes the framework for what a decade later became the comprehensive settlement of the Third Indochina War.

1982 **June:** ASEAN-, United States-, and China-backed Coalition Government of Democratic Kampuchea (CGDK) formed to resist the Vietnamese invasion and occupation of Cambodia.

1983 **August:** Philippine Senator Benigno "Ninoy" Aquino, returning from the United States, assassinated at the Manila airport, beginning the political crisis that ended the rule of Ferdinand Marcos.

1984 **March:** United States opens an embassy in Brunei. **April:** President Ronald Reagan cancels his visit to the Philippines as a sign of American concern about the murder of Benigno Aquino. To soften the blow to Marcos, he also cancels a planned Indonesian stopover.

1985 **February:** First U.S.–Laos joint search mission for Americans missing in action (MIA) goes into the field.

1986 **February:** Corazon Aquino sworn in as president of the Philippines. Former president Marcos goes into exile in Hawaii. **May:** President Reagan travels to Bali, Indonesia to meet with ASEAN ministers and President Suharto.

1987 **August:** General John Vessey undertakes his first mission to Vietnam as a Special Envoy to discuss humanitarian issues.

1988 **August:** The military junta's violence against civilian protesters begins the estrangement of the United States from Burma.

1989 July–August: Secretary of State James Baker makes the opening statement for the United States at the Paris International Conference on Cambodia (PICC), convened to attempt a settlement of the Third Indochina War. **November:** First Asia Pacific Economic Cooperation (APEC) ministerial meeting takes place. **December:** In support of President Corazon Aquino, the U.S. intervenes against a coup attempt in the Philippines.

1990 August: Indonesia and China resume diplomatic relations. **September:** Secretary of State James Baker meets Vietnamese Foreign Minister Nguyen Co Thach in New York to discuss normalization of relations.

1991 September: Philippines Senate rejects the new U.S.–Philippines basing agreement. **October:** Paris International Conference on Cambodia (PICC) ratifies the UN Security Council–backed Comprehensive Political Settlement in Cambodia, ending the Third Indochina War. **November:** Indonesian troops fire on protesting mourners in East Timor in what is called the Dili Massacre, prompting U.S. restrictions on military assistance to Indonesia.

1992 June: President George H. W. Bush makes an official visit to Singapore. **August:** American diplomatic representation in the Lao People's Democratic Republic upgraded to an ambassador. **November:** Withdrawal of U.S. forces from the Philippines completed.

1993 July: In a speech in Japan, President William J. Clinton calls for a Pacific Community. **September:** United States establishes diplomatic relations with the restored Kingdom of Cambodia. **November:** First APEC leaders' summit hosted by President Clinton at Blake Island, Washington.

1994 February: U.S. trade embargo against Vietnam lifted. **July:** Inaugural meeting of the ASEAN Regional Forum (ARF) takes place, with Secretary of State Warren Christopher absent. **November:** President Clinton travels to Indonesia for the APEC leaders' meeting, hosted by Indonesian President Suharto, at which Bogor Declaration is issued, calling for free and open trade in the Asia-Pacific region. Following the APEC meeting, President Clinton makes state visits to Indonesia and the Philippines.

1995   January: Vietnam and the United States announce that they will open liaison offices. **May:** U.S. economic and humanitarian assistance to Laos resumed. **July:** United States and the Socialist Republic of Vietnam establish full diplomatic relations. **December:** At an ASEAN summit, the leaders declare Southeast Asia to be a nuclear weapons free zone (SEANWFZ), which is not recognized by the United States.

1996   November: President Clinton attends the APEC leaders meeting in the Philippines and makes a state visit to Thailand.

1997   May: United States imposes economic sanctions on Burma because of its failure to restore democracy and its human rights record. **July:** Thailand's Central Bank floats its currency, the baht, sparking the 1997–1998 Asian financial crisis. In a quasi coup in Cambodia, Hun Sen expels Norodom Ranariddh as coprime minister, leading to a temporary suspension of U.S. assistance and ASEAN diplomatic intervention.

1998   May: President Suharto of Indonesia resigns and is succeeded by President B. J. Habibie.

1999   February: Indonesian president B. J. Habibie announces a referendum on the future of the Indonesian province of East Timor. **May:** Philippine Senate ratifies the U.S.–Philippines Visiting Forces Agreement (VFA). **August:** In a UN Security Council–supported and UN-monitored referendum, the people of Indonesia's East Timor province vote for independence from Indonesia. This is followed by widespread Indonesian army–backed violence. **September:** The international community intervenes in Indonesia's East Timor province through a UN Security Council—approved International Force for East Timor (INTERFET), led by Australia with American over-the-horizon support.

2000   July: United States and Vietnam sign a bilateral trade agreement, a necessary step for normal trade relations. **November:** President Clinton attends the APEC leaders' meeting in Brunei and makes an official visit to Vietnam.

2001   January: In a quasi-coup in Manila, Gloria Macapagal-Arroyo is sworn in as president of the Philippines. George W. Bush inaugurated as president of the United States. **September:** Terrorist attacks in New York on the 11th lead to the U.S. war on terror.

2002 January: United States deploys Joint Task Force 510 to the Philippines. **May:** East Timor achieves independence. **August:** Secretary of State Colin Powell announces the ASEAN Cooperation Plan (ACP). The United States–ASEAN Joint Declaration for Cooperation to Combat International Terrorism issued. **October:** Bali bombings bring Indonesia directly into the war on terror. President Bush announces the Enterprise for ASEAN Initiative.

2003 January: The U.S.–Singapore free trade agreement (FTA) signed, becoming the model for future American FTA negotiations in Southeast Asia. **July:** President Bush signs the Burmese Freedom and Democracy Act, expanding the economic sanctions placed on Burma. **October:** President Bush attends the APEC leaders' meeting in Thailand. He travels as well to Singapore, the Philippines, and Indonesia to enlist their assistance in the war on terror.

2004 December: A tsunami brings massive destruction to the coasts of Sumatra in Indonesia and the Andaman Sea coasts of Thailand. The United States responds immediately with the dispatch of humanitarian relief efforts.

2005 June: Vietnam prime minister Phan Van Khai visits the United States. **July:** Secretary of State Condoleezza Rice fails to attend the ASEAN Ministerial Meeting as a sign of U.S. unhappiness over the prospect of Burma assuming the chair of the organization. **November:** President Bush meets in a first mini-summit with ASEAN leaders at the Busan, South Korea, APEC leaders' meeting. President Bush and the Southeast Asian leaders release the "Vision Statement" on the ASEAN–United States Enhanced Partnership.

2006 July: "Framework Document" for the ASEAN–U.S. Enhanced Partnership released. **August:** ASEAN–United States Trade and Investment Framework (TIFA) signed. **September:** Military coup in Thailand forces the United States to suspend security assistance. **November:** President Bush attends the APEC leaders' meeting hosted by Vietnam and meet in a mini-summit with ASEAN leaders on the sidelines. He also makes working visits to Singapore and Indonesia. **December:** The U.S. Congress accords Vietnam permanent normal trade relations status.

2007 **June:** President Nguyen Minh Triet makes the first visit to the United States by a post–Vietnam War Vietnamese head of state. **July:** Secretary of State Condoleezza Rice cancels her attendance at the ASEAN Ministerial Meeting and the ASEAN Regional Forum. The White House postpones the planned U.S.–ASEAN summit meeting celebrating the 30th anniversary of the ASEAN–U.S. dialogue. **September:** President Bush attends Sydney Australia APEC meeting and invites the ASEAN leaders to a 2008 U.S.–ASEAN summit meeting at his Crawford, Texas, ranch. He also announces that the U.S. will accredit an Ambassador to ASEAN. **December:** U.S. officials at an ASEAN–U.S. dialogue indicate there will be no Texas summit because of Bruma's September crackdown on dissidents and ASEAN's unwillingness to challenge Burma on violations of human rights.

Introduction

OVERVIEW

In contrast to Northeast Asia, with China, Japan, and Korea, it is only relatively recently that Southeast Asia has been viewed in terms of a geopolitical region within which American interests could have a diplomatic coherency transcending the individual territorial units making up the region. The states of the region are Brunei, Burma, Cambodia, East Timor, Indonesia, Laos, Malaysia, the Philippines, Singapore, Thailand, and Vietnam. United States policy in Southeast Asia and the diplomacy advancing it are defined by the regional and bilateral U.S. interests that the policy supports. In the ranging of those interests, security interests have historically had primacy. Southeast Asia is geostrategically important to the United States. Freedom of the sea lanes of communication that connect Northeast Asia to the Western Pacific through the South China Sea and the straits leading to the Indian Ocean and beyond has been vital for U.S. naval posture as well as seaborne commerce. Access to the resources and markets of Southeast Asia, especially as the developing countries of the region have become important American trading partners, has added vital economic interests for the United States in the region. Since the end of the Cold War and the transformation of the strategic environment in Southeast Asia, nontraditional foreign policy issues such as democratization and human rights have been added to the American regional agenda for Southeast Asia.

Historically, in pursuit of its interests the United States has sought to promote a peaceful and orderly region to which it has full political, economic, and strategic access. The underlying continuity of American policy in the region has been the determination to win and maintain its presence in the region in competition with other extraregional Great Powers that would limit the U.S. role. In the 20th century, the challengers were

Japan (through 1945), and, in the post–World War II period, the USSR (through 1991). In the early years of the 21st century, the People's Republic of China is now emerging as an important political and economic player in Southeast Asia and a possible future challenger to American interests. In the historical Great Power competition, the United States has broadly brushed its policies and presence in Southeast Asia as contributing to the maintenance of the regional balance of power. In fact however, after 1945 the American notion of balance of power in Southeast Asia came to mean a preponderance of American power. American dominance was criticized by local nationalists as a form of hegemony or even neoimperialism. Classic balance-of-power tactics were employed by the United States, such as diplomatically forging formal and informal alliances and alignments with local actors, providing economic and military assistance to build up their capabilities, and, where necessary, employing military force. American diplomatic activity was supported by the covert operations of the Central Intelligence Agency (CIA). In looking to the future, however, the political and military tools wielded by the United States during the Cold War seem less useful in shaping a U.S.–Southeast Asia–China balance.

The competition of Great Power interests in Southeast Asia has meant that at least up to the collapse of the Soviet Union, in the search for security American diplomacy was centered on conflict. The geostrategic regional notion of Southeast Asia itself was a product of conflict. During World War II in the Pacific the Allies' counteroffensive strategy against Japan's forceful incorporation of the region into its Great East Asian Coprosperity sphere included the creation in 1943 of a Ceylon (Sri Lanka)–based Southeast Asia Command (SEAC) to carry the war against Japan to continental Southeast Asia. After the defeat of Japan, Great Power competition in the region was connected to successive conflicts in France's colonies and protectorates in French Indochina: Vietnam, Laos, and Cambodia. Indochina served as a pivotal conflict zone for American-dominated U.S.–Southeast Asian relations over a span of four decades. The American perception of a central issue of the containment of communism emerged as early as 1947 and still had vitality in 1991.

The First Indochina War (1946–1954) was the French efforts after the defeat of Japan to restore sovereignty in the Indochinese states in the face of nationalist and communist demands for independence. The

United States supported France materially and financially as part of its policy of containing in Southeast Asia the global threat presented to the United States by communist expansion. The Second Indochina War, or America's Vietnam War, with its extensions into Laos and Cambodia, brought Southeast Asia sharply into focus for the American public. Domestic political controversy raged between 1965 and 1975 over the human and economic costs of the use of American force to support South Vietnam (Republic of Vietnam [RVN]) against Soviet- and China-backed North Vietnam (Democratic Republic of Vietnam [DRV]). American diplomacy in Southeast Asia during the Second Indochina War was centered on mobilizing support for American military policy. The Third Indochina War began in 1978 with the Vietnamese invasion and occupation of Cambodia (Kampuchea). The United States supported its frontline-state ally Thailand and the other noncommunist Southeast Asian states that felt threatened by a seemingly aggressive USSR-backed Vietnam. The Third Indochina War did not end until 1991, with the United Nations (UN)–endorsed Comprehensive Political Settlement on the Conflict in Cambodia.

Beginning in 1967, and beneath the Great Power political overlay of conflict, noncommunist Southeast Asian states outside the Indochinese battlefields created the Association of Southeast Asian Nations (ASEAN), an autonomous structure for regional cooperation overarching their deep political, economic, ethnic, and cultural differences. ASEAN grew from its core five—Indonesia, Malaysia, the Philippines, Singapore, and Thailand—to include by 1999 Brunei, Burma, Cambodia, Laos, and Vietnam. With the exception of newly independent (2002) East Timor, through ASEAN, a geopolitical/geoeconomic Southeast Asian region is now coterminous with the geographic region. Although Washington increasingly deals with ASEAN on a multilateral level, within ASEAN, the individual member states remain independent sovereign actors. A future integrative process might lead to functional delegations of sovereignty to an ASEAN supranational authority, but until then U.S. relations in the region will continue primarily to be with the national states of Southeast Asia as the sovereign state actors.

The collapse of the Soviet Union, ending of the Cold War, and peaceful integration of the Indochinese states into ASEAN in the 1990s marked a new era for U.S. relations in Southeast Asia. The strategic imperatives of the Cold War gave way to new emphasis on economic interests in investment and markets and the political concerns of democracy and human rights. After 11 September 2001, however, security took priority again when Washington declared Southeast Asia to be the second front in the war on terror. The United States has not been unmindful of Southeast Asian concerns that the war on terror has diverted American attention from the long-term implications of China's rise as a regional Great Power. Since 2002, the United States has raised its own economic and political profile in the region to reassure the ASEAN countries that it will continue to be an active participant in the regional balance of power, although that future balance may no longer be on the basis of U.S. preponderance.

In order to establish a degree of historical continuity in which to place the discrete entries that follow in the dictionary, it may be useful to survey some of the principal issues and events that have informed Washington's policy makers in decision making about Southeast Asia. This is organized within a framework of main periods in U.S. diplomatic history in Southeast Asia: pre–World War II; decolonization and the onset of the Cold War, 1945–1954; the Vietnam War (Second Indochina War), 1954–1975; the interwar period, 1975–1978; the Third Indochina War and the ending of the Cold War, 1979–1991; the second interwar period, 1991–2001; and the war on terror and the rise of China, 2001–.

THE UNITED STATES IN SOUTHEAST ASIA TO WORLD WAR II

When World War II in the Pacific broke out on 7 December 1941 with the Japanese attack on Pearl Harbor, Thailand, known until 1938 as Siam, was the only sovereign nation in Southeast Asia with which the United States could have diplomatic relations. Only Siam had escaped the imposition of 19th-century Great Power imperial rule that dominated elsewhere in Southeast Asia. Although territorially nibbled away at its margins by European powers, Siam's independence was a function of a balance of imperial power that buffered a possible collision in the center of continental Southeast Asia between the expansive ambitions of the French in Indochina and the British in Burma, Singapore, and Malaya. In addition to the British and French on the continent, the

Philippine and Indonesian archipelagoes were the imperial possessions of Spain and the Netherlands, respectively. When the U.S. flag appeared in Southeast Asia on American merchant ships in the 1830s, it was only in Siam that the United States could find a relatively open door of equal opportunity for its commercial and political interests in the region in competition with the established European powers. In 1833, a Treaty of Amity and Commerce was negotiated between the Kingdom of Siam and the United States of America, preceding the first U.S. treaty with China by 11 years and Japan by 24. An American consul was named in Bangkok in 1856 and a consul general was named in 1881, who two years later became America's first minister-plenipotentiary in Southeast Asia.

Elsewhere in the region, American representation was by consuls and consuls general appointed to further and protect U.S. interests and citizens in territorial domains ruled from Europe. The modest interests that the American official establishments sought to promote were largely commercial, involving agents of American private trading houses working at a competitive disadvantage against the colonial monopolistic and protected enterprises. Another class of Americans for whom consular officials had responsibilities was protestant missionaries, who found the "heathen" population of Southeast Asia ripe for conversion. American Baptists were in Burma by 1813 and Presbyterians in Siam less than 20 years later. The first American consul in Thailand was a Presbyterian missionary. While the Christian message was largely ignored by Buddhists and adherents to other great religious traditions, it did resonate with ethnic minority groupings like the Karens and Shans, producing unexpected political consequences in the 20th century.

It was not until the very end of the 19th century that the interests of American merchants and missionaries in European colonial realms in Southeast Asia were overlaid for the first time by geopolitical interests. These were derived from sovereign possession of America's own territorial domain in Southeast Asia by virtue of conquest of the Philippines in 1898. Although a by-product of the Spanish–American War with its focus on Cuba and Puerto Rico, for some American imperialists the prize was the Philippines. Shut out of the scramble for spheres of influence in China by Japan, Russia, Great Britain, and France, American imperialists saw the Philippines as at least a second-best base from which to pursue U.S. interests in East Asia. American opinion, as reflected in Congress, was sharply divided on annexing the Philippines. President William McKinley reconciled imperialism and anti-imperialist idealism by appealing to a civilizing mission and "contingent necessity"; that is, if the United States did not keep the Philippines, another country would step in and America would have no future role in a Great Power balance in East Asia.

Before American rule could be fully imposed in the Philippines, the U.S. Army had first to quell a Filipino nationalist armed resistance, called by the United States an "insurrection." Once in place, the colonial administration reflected America's democratic political impulse. From the outset, U.S. rule was directed to Philippine self-government, and in the 1916 Jones Act to eventual independence. The 1934 Tydings-McDuffie Act established the framework for independence, creating a Commonwealth of the Philippines for a 10-year transition to independence. The political dynamic of the first half-century of Philippine–American relations was one of tension between Philippine nationalists, who wanted faster and greater political empowerment, and American governors general, who defended U.S. sovereign interests.

Possession of the Philippines made the United States a geostrategic actor in East Asia. The U.S. Navy's Asiatic Squadron, which after 1908 became the Asiatic Fleet, replaced the Spanish at Cavite in Manila Bay and in Subic Bay. The American naval presence on the Chinese coast was deployed from the Philippines. As a player in the East Asian power game, the United States was faced with the strategic problem of defending the Philippines. From the end of the Russo–Japanese War in 1904, the possible enemy was seen as an expansionist Japan. The United States sought through diplomacy—the Taft-Katsura Agreement (1905) and Root-Takahira Agreement (1908)—to win Japanese assurances of respect for American Pacific territories. After World War I, the United States sought to limit Japan's strategic reach in the Pacific through naval disarmament—the Washington Conference (1922) and London Conference (1931). Even as Japan became more and more powerful in the 1930s, Congress was unwilling to build up American defenses west of Hawaii to match what military planners and war-gamers saw as the growing threat to the Philippines. Efforts led by General Douglas MacArthur to strengthen Philippine defense capabilities were too little, too late in a U.S. Pacific war strategy that essentially sacrificed the Philippines for the defense of Hawaii. But the Japanese threat was not directed just at the Philippines. The vast natural resources of the other imperial domains in Southeast Asia were tempting targets for resource-poor Japan and its war machine. American economic sanctions on Japan because of its widening war in China made Japan's search for alternatives even more necessary. The defeat of the Netherlands and France by Germany in Europe, as well as Great Britain being under siege, left the European nations' Southeast Asian imperial realms strategically vulnerable.

When war came, despite heroic efforts by American and Filipino defenders, the Philippines was surrendered to the invading Japanese after a last stand on the Bataan Peninsula and the fall of the bastion of Corregidor Island on 6 May 1942. American commander General MacArthur and the president and vice president of the Philippine Commonwealth were evacuated, vowing to return. The French, British, and Dutch imperial possessions also rapidly came under Japan's sway. Thailand, although not attacked or occupied, but threatened, declared war on the United States. Washington ignored the declaration, dealing through the Office of Strategic Services (OSS) with the exiled Thais of the Free Thai resistance and their links inside of Thailand. Recovering from the surprise shock and speed of the Japanese assault, the United States and its allies quickly regrouped and began to plan their counteroffensive. From Australia, Gen. MacArthur's Southwest Pacific Command began its island-hopping campaign backstopped by U.S. naval and air superiority. From headquarters in Kandy, Ceylon, the British-led Southeast-Asia Command (SEAC) took the war to the Japanese in Burma and was preparing amphibious landings in Malaya when the war ended in August 1945. British and U.S. intelligence and special operations forces operated to support anti-Japanese guerrilla activities behind the lines. Many of the later U.S. State Department and Central Intelligence Agency officials with Southeast Asia responsibilities got their introduction to the region in the OSS or military intelligence. MacArthur's forces returned to the Philippines in October 1944, although Japanese resistance did not end until spring 1945.

DECOLONIZATION AND THE ONSET OF THE COLD WAR IN SOUTHEAST ASIA

The totality and speed of the Japanese expulsion of European and American power from Southeast Asia in 1942 had a profound psychological and political impact. It demonstrated that Asians could beat the West at their own game, undermining colonialism's racist underpinning of the white man's superiority. It also fed nationalist aspirations that had been growing among the indigenous elites in the colonies. Although under heavy-handed control and directed to Japanese war ends, in Burma, Indonesia, and the Philippines, Japan's rule was indirect through indigenous "autonomous" governments. In Indochina, Japan ruled indirectly through French administrators loyal to the German puppet Vichy regime until 1944, when Tokyo interned the French and ruled directly. In Malaya and Indochina, anti-Japanese guerrilla movements with strong communist cores had postwar agendas that did not include the return to colonial rule. In the Philippines, anti-Japanese guerrilla forces also included communists, whose program for American-promised postwar independence was not that envisioned by Washington or the Philippine Commonwealth's leaders.

Although secondary to the major concerns of American planning for the postwar era, the future political order in Southeast Asia was addressed. President Franklin D. Roosevelt was unsympathetic to British, French, and Dutch intentions to restore the status quo ante. Initially the American officials seemed wedded to the war aim of self-determination for dependent peoples enshrined in the Anglo–American 1941 Atlantic Charter. The example brandished by the United States was its promise of independence for the Philippines. An American notion of a kind of international trust system to administer a transition to independence for the rest of Southeast Asia fell on deaf European ears. As the war came to an end, American idealism adjusted to the realities of European opposition and the fact that the United States might be left to pick up the economic and political burden of weak states in a region far from America's primary concerns. Moreover, Washington needed the cooperation of its European allies for the reconstruction of Europe and its defense against the Soviet threat. The Europeans accommodated the American position to the degree that the shape of empire would be restructured to give greater self-government in a framework of commonwealth or association with the sovereign power, but still less than independence.

The U.S. promise to the Philippines was fulfilled on 4 July 1946. The legal framework for Philippine independence was encumbered by economic and political entanglements designed to guarantee American economic and political interests in the new republic. Denounced by Filipino critics as neocolonialism, the special position of the United States was a matter of almost continuous diplomatic negotiations and modifications over 45 years. For Philippine nationalists and the political Left, the most egregious symbol of the derogation of Philippines' sovereignty was the retention by the United States of military bases in the Philippines and the inapplicability of Philippine legal jurisdiction on them. Elsewhere in Southeast Asia, nationalists were unwilling to settle for less than full independence. The Dutch returned to the Netherlands East Indies to find an Indonesian Republic, proclaimed on 17 August 1945, prepared to defend its independence forcefully. The Dutch were determined to fight to restore sovereignty under the queen. The colonial war in Indonesia became the UN Security Council's first test. In the face of Burmese resistance, an economically strapped British socialist government had to abandon a plan for gradual self-government for Burma as a British Commonwealth dominion and accept in 1947 Burmese independence. As an imperial territory, Burma had been devalued by the partition of India into the two independent states of Pakistan and India. The economic, political, and strategic logic of British decolonization also led to the independence of Malaya. In Indochina, communist-backed resistance groups and noncommunist nationalists allied in rebuffing French efforts to enlist Vietnam, Laos, and Cambodia in an amorphous French Union that would leave them less than fully independent.

In the first years of President Harry S. Truman's administration, the United States took little notice of events in Southeast Asia outside of its responsibilities in the Philippines. A war-weary American public had little interest in or enthusiasm for involvement in Southeast Asia's colonial affairs. For Truman, Indochina was a French problem. It was only when colonialism, nationalism, and communism became linked to the expansion of the influence of the Soviet Union through Southeast Asia's communist parties and movements that the United States began to view its interests in Southeast Asia through a geostrategic lens. Monolithic communism with its Russian state agency replaced Japan as the Great Power enemy of American interests. While Japan's threat was confined to East Asia, the Soviet Union's regional threat was a flank of the global threat to what the United States was ideologically defining as the Free World. In 1947, communist-led insurgencies and uprisings in the Philippines, Indonesia, Malaya, Burma, and the Indochinese states seemed proof of the Soviet intentions. What the 1947 Truman Doctrine had identified in general terms as a totalitarian (meaning communist) challenge to global peace and security, and hence American security, was manifest in Southeast Asia. The Chinese communist victory and establishment of the People's Republic of China in 1949 heightened Washington's perception of the threat to Southeast Asia. Washington stubbornly refused to separate China's interests in Asia from the Soviet Union's for another decade until the Sino–Soviet split became obvious to all.

The American response to the perceived threat of communist expansion in Southeast Asia was the local application of the global strategy of containment. The full array of American diplomatic, political, and economic instruments of power was mobilized to contain the spread of communism in Southeast Asia. The logic of containment, elegantly spelled out by longtime State Department Russian specialist George Kennan, was given policy primacy in Southeast Asia. The security of the Free World nations of Southeast Asia was considered to be indivisible. A threat to one was a threat to all. This was given a geostrategic formulation in the "domino theory," which posited that if Vietnam fell to communism, the other nations of the region would fall like a row of dominoes, with consequences for the security of Japan, Australia, New Zealand, and beyond. Although the use of the domino analogy is attributed to President Dwight D. Eisenhower, the sequential strategic threat to Southeast Asia and beyond in the event of communist victory in Vietnam had already been stated in the Truman administration. Containment of communism and its Great Power backers, the Soviet Union and China, was the overriding American interest in Southeast Asia for 40 years. It underpinned U.S. bilateral relations in the region, whether friend, foe, or neutral. American assistance programs were geared to containment. The CIA moved behind the scenes in the service of containment. Finally, in Vietnam, the United States went to war in the name of containment.

When Truman handed off to Eisenhower in 1952, the major test for containment in Southeast Asia was Vietnam. The British and Commonwealth forces were winning the war against the communist insurgency in Malaya. Under international pressure, the Dutch had been forced to transfer sovereignty in Indonesia. One of the reasons for American support of Indonesia in its struggle for independence had been the new republic's success in crushing a communist uprising. The multiple low-intensity insurgencies in Burma, communist and ethnic, were not viewed as threatening the region. The United States had given strong economic and military backing to the Philippines, much of it wasted, in the successful struggle against the Hukbalahap insurgency. The French, however, were losing in Indochina. Communist leader Ho Chi Minh's Viet Minh forces were becoming stronger, with a military assistance pipeline running to China, and behind China, the Soviet Union. The French were looking for both increased American support and a way out. The Eisenhower administration wanted the French to stay the course but was unwilling to commit American forces to the fight. By 1954, domestic French politics made its disengagement from colonial wars a requirement. The United States reluctantly agreed to participate in an international conference in Geneva that ended with the Geneva Accords. The agreements called for a temporary partition of Vietnam between the Democratic Republic of Vietnam and the Republic of Vietnam until an election, promised for 1956, for a unified Vietnamese government was held. Independent Laos and Cambodia were theoretically neutralized. With the ending of the First Indochina War, the stage was set for the Second Indochina War.

SOUTHEAST ASIA, AND THE SECOND INDOCHINA WAR, AMERICA'S VIETNAM WAR: 1954–1975

Already a major supporter of the RVN government headed by President Ngo Dinh Diem, Washington was determined that South Vietnam not be lost to communism. Financial and military assistance poured into the country, and the American military replaced the French military training presence. The U.S. supported politically the Diem government's unwillingness to participate in national elections. Washington did not believe free elections would be allowed in the DRV, and in the background there was concern that in an election Ho Chi Minh might prevail nationally. American regional diplomacy sought political recognition and support for the Diem government in a legitimate South Vietnamese state. As it became clear that the political terms of the Geneva settlement were not going to be implemented, DRV-sponsored Viet Cong guerrilla warriors in the South began an insurgent war against the southern government, with the United States becoming increasingly involved in the defense of the RVN.

From the American perspective, the French defeat in Vietnam opened a strategic window of opportunity into Southeast Asia for the Soviet Union and China. To help close the window, Secretary of State John Foster Dulles brought to Southeast Asia, even if in diluted fashion, the strategy of collective defense and forward deterrence represented in Europe by the North Atlantic Treaty Organization (NATO). The parties to the 1954 Southeast Asia Collective Defense Treaty (the Manila Pact) recognized that aggression against one would be a threat to all and that they would consult to meet the common danger. Only the Philippines and Thailand in Southeast Asia were signatories and members of the Southeast Asia Treaty Organization (SEATO), although the Indochinese states of Cambodia, Laos, and "free" Vietnam were placed under the SEATO security umbrella. In addition to the United States and the Southeast Asian states, the other members were Australia, France, Great Britain, New Zealand, and Pakistan. Unlike NATO, SEATO had no military teeth. For Washington, however, SEATO provided a multilateral regional framework for the forward deployment of American power as part of an Asian alliance system running through Asia and the Pacific. The real defense capabilities came in the U.S. bilateral hub-and-spoke alliance system that in Southeast Asia included the Philippines, with its U.S. bases, and Thailand, where in the 1962 Rusk–Thanat communiqué it was understood that the SEATO commitment was bilateral as well as collective.

By the end of the 1950s and the Eisenhower administration, the Cold War battle lines and international structures were firmly established in Southeast Asia. The front was in Indochina. In addition to the insurgent warfare in Vietnam, in Laos the forces of the communist Pathet Lao movement, supported by the Viet Minh, menaced the noncommunist royal government supported by the United States. Cambodia, under Prince/Prime Minister Norodom Sihanouk, tried to maintain precarious neutrality under pressure from Thailand and the two Vietnams. As the deepening involvement of the United States and the Soviet Union threatened to escalate the political tensions in the region in a zero-sum game of allegiances, some Southeast Asian states sought alternatives to choosing sides in the Cold War. In 1955, Indonesia hosted the Asian-African Conference in the city of Bandung. Although U.S. allies Thailand, the Philippines, and South Vietnam were among the 29 nations invited, the conference agenda was driven by the themes of neutralism, anti-imperialism, and peaceful coexistence. In addition to Indonesia, Burma and Cambodia were prominent Southeast Asian promoters of what became known as the Bandung Principles. These became formally institutionalized in the 1961 Belgrade conference, which established the Nonaligned Movement (NAM). For the United States, nonalignment and neutralism on the part of a Southeast Asian state was equated with opposing the Free World and to be resisted, marginalized, or undermined.

Although Vietnam was the main Cold War battlefield, by the early 1960s the situation in Laos had become critical as the Pathet Lao forces threatened coup-prone noncommunist governments. Thailand saw the advance of the Pathet Lao toward the Thai–Lao Mekong River border as a direct threat and pressed the United States for assistance. President Eisenhower, handing off the Indochina problem to incoming president John F. Kennedy, argued that Laos was the key to the future of Southeast Asia. He warned Kennedy that if Laos fell the United States would have to write off the whole area to the Soviet Union and Communist China. President Kennedy reacted by beefing up the American military presence in Thailand and threatened direct U.S. intervention in Laos. This was matched by an expansion of Soviet and DRV assistance to the Pathet Lao. As the United States and the USSR seemed ready to collide in the 1961–1962 Laos crisis, Cambodia's Sihanouk, fearful of a Cold War spillover, proposed a way out. A second Geneva Conference was convened, which in 1962 reestablished Laotian neutrality in the framework of a short-lived rightist-neutralist-Pathet Lao coalition government. Although a U.S.–USSR confrontation was avoided, the domestic struggle in Laos continued. The United States, working through the CIA, supported the ethnic Hmong forces of General Vang Pao in the "secret war" against the Pathet Lao and their Viet Minh allies. The DRV's interests in Laos were more direct than just support of the Pathet Lao. The major supply line from North Vietnam to the Viet Cong in the south, the so-called Ho Chi Minh trail, ran through Laos.

President Kennedy was as committed as his predecessor to the defense of South Vietnam. There was to be no Laos solution there. Even as he upped the American ante with a massive infusion of U.S. military advisors in November 1961, he, like Eisenhower before him and President

Lyndon B. Johnson after him, was frustrated by the undemocratic and corrupt RVN government. In 1963, the United States signed off on an anti-Diem military coup that ended with Diem's murder. A succession of military leaders was no better able to carry out reform than Diem had been. Johnson succeeded to the presidency in 1963 after Kennedy was assassinated. In 1965, Congress, in the Tonkin Gulf Resolution, gave President Johnson a blank check to use whatever force was necessary to defeat communism in Southeast Asia. The burden of the war in Vietnam shifted from the Army of the Republic of Vietnam to the U.S. military. Eventually, American forces were joined by units from SEATO allies Australia, New Zealand, the Philippines, and Thailand, as well as South Korea. The structure of the war changed from insurgent to conventional as the DRV's People's Army moved into South Vietnam in what Secretary of State Dean Rusk called "aggression from the North." Washington carried the war to Laos and Cambodia in heavy bombing intended to interdict the enemy supply lines. A 1970 Cambodian coup led by General Lon Nol overthrew Sihanouk. Washington backed the new regime as it fought the communist Khmer Rouge forces, who were supported by the DRV forces from their Cambodian sanctuaries.

While the United States poured its political, diplomatic, material, and military resources into the containment of communism in Indochina, a different threat was emerging in Indonesia. Indonesia's president Sukarno presented another challenge to the American-dominated status quo in Southeast Asia. He translated Indonesia's principled nonaligned position into a struggle against imperialism and neocolonialism. From 1957, his "guided democracy" legitimated a political role for the Indonesian Communist Party, which by 1964 seemed ready to come to power peacefully. In 1958, the Eisenhower administration clandestinely supported a failed anti-Sukarno Indonesian rebellion. This only hastened the radicalization of Sukarno's foreign policy. Under Kennedy, Washington sought to mollify Sukarno by diplomatically supporting Indonesia's claim to the Netherlands' New Guinea. Sukarno explicitly allied Indonesia in his proclaimed Jakarta–Phnom Penh–Hanoi–Beijing–Pyongyang axis in a struggle against Western imperialism. Indonesia's closest target was the federal state of Malaysia, which in 1963 brought together already independent Malaya and the British territories of Singapore, Sarawak, and Sabah. Sukarno's undeclared war to "crush Malaysia" had the full backing of the Indonesian Communist Party, which saw a chance to build a volunteer armed force with weapons from China. The uneasy balance between the communists and the anticommunist military with Sukarno at the fulcrum was suddenly and violently broken in late 1965, when a communist-backed coup was met by a military countercoup that led to the destruction of the Indonesian Communist Party and stripped power from Sukarno. The threat of communism in Indonesia outflanking the American line of containment in Indochina was ended.

The escalation of the war in Indochina and the political upheaval in Indonesia were behind the effort in 1967 to structure a multilateral framework within which the anticommunist governments of Indonesia, Malaysia, the Philippines, Singapore (independent in 1965), and Thailand could cooperate. The aim was to shape a regional environment in which Indonesia could be peacefully reintegrated and the consequences of the Second Indochina War mediated. The product was the Association of Southeast Asian Nations (ASEAN). The goal of insulating the region from any spillover of the Cold War and the "Hot War" in Indochina was made explicit in ASEAN's 1971 Zone of Peace, Freedom, and Neutrality (ZOPFAN). In the United States, growing domestic political opposition to the war essentially had driven President Johnson from office and led to the election of Richard Nixon who, with his National Security Advisor and later Secretary of State Henry Kissinger, significantly altered the Great Power status quo in Southeast Asia. The 1969 Nixon Doctrine placed primary responsibility for a threatened nation's defense on that nation itself. This prompted friends and allies in Southeast Asia to reassess the integrity of the U.S. security umbrella in the region.

In 1972, the Great Power balance was turned upside down by the Nixon visit to China and the beginning of the Sino–American reconciliation process. Following the U.S. lead, Malaysia, Thailand, and the Philippines recognized the People's Republic of China (PRC) despite China's insistence that state-to-state relations were separate from communist party-to-party relations and support for communist insurgencies in Southeast Asia. United States–DRV peace negotiations, which had begun in 1969, were successfully concluded in the 1973 Paris Agreement ending the Vietnam War. The North–South war in Vietnam continued, but the United States was no longer fighting. The prospect of an American geostrategic disengagement from Indochina as the result of the Paris peace agreement ending an American military role in Vietnam forced the ASEAN states to address a future with a communist Indochina and continuing domestic communist insurgencies in the absence of a firm American shield.

THE INTERWAR INTERREGNUM: 1975–1978

In April 1975, communist governments came to power in South Vietnam, Laos, and Cambodia. As the communist armies rolled south in Vietnam, last-minute efforts to give new assistance to the crumbling RVN government by the administration of President Gerald Ford, who succeeded after Nixon resigned as a result of the Watergate scandal, were rebuffed by Congress. Within nine months, South Vietnam was united with the North in the Socialist Republic of Vietnam (SRV). Existing U.S. economic sanctions against the DRV were extended by the Ford administration to all of Vietnam. The United States did not have diplomatic relations with the new Vietnamese government. Washington insisted that normalization of relations had to be preceded by the resolution of prisoner of war/missing in action (POW/MIA) issues. After President Jimmy Carter came to office in 1977, a tentative initiative to open a humanitarian dialogue with Vietnam was scuttled because of concerns within the administration that this would set back normalization of relations with China. The Chinese viewed the growing USSR presence in the SRV in the context of Sino–Soviet tension and warned the United States against Soviet aims in Vietnam.

The situation was different for the United States in Laos. Even though the new Lao People's Democratic Republic (LPDR) was primarily oriented toward Vietnam, the United States did not break relations with it. A low-profile American embassy under a chargé d'affaires was maintained in Vientiane with minimum programs and contacts. The primary U.S. interest in communist Laos was the POW/MIA issue. Cambodia was a special case. The United States had no political contacts with postwar Cambodia. The Lon Nol government was swept away by the triumphant Khmer Rouge (KR), with Prince Sihanouk as a figurehead leader. Sihanouk soon fled into Chinese and North Korean exile as the true nature of Democratic Kampuchea (DK) revealed itself. The Khmer Rouge imposed a harsh domestic rule that has been characterized as national self-genocide. Hundreds of thousands of Cambodians perished at the hands of the KR, and thousands more escaped as refugees to Thailand and Vietnam. Tension mounted between Democratic Kampuchea and Vietnam, both in terms of traditional geoethnic rivalries and as surrogates in the Sino–Soviet conflict. The SRV and its Russian backers saw the PRC seeking to strategically penetrate the SRV rear through Chinese support to DK.

The ASEAN states held out an olive branch to the SRV by advancing its ZOPFAN as a framework for peaceful coexistence in Southeast Asia. At its 1976 Bali Summit, ASEAN drew up the Treaty of Amity and Cooperation in Southeast Asia (TAC) as a normative framework for interregional relations. Through 2006, the TAC has been accepted by all of ASEAN's major dialogue partners except the United States. Vietnam initially showed extreme hostility toward ASEAN, denouncing it as a reactionary tool of Washington. Hanoi countered ZOPFAN by demanding a ZOPGIN, a Zone of Peace and Genuine Independence. This would have meant the termination of all foreign military alliances and bases. Rather than dealing with ASEAN as a grouping, Vietnam worked bilaterally to establish normal relations with the individual member states. Thailand's 1975 unilateral termination of U.S. base rights was an important step toward normalizing Thailand–Vietnam relations. Also on the regional agenda was the flood of refugees from Vietnam, the so-called boat people.

Despite the widely held opinion that the United States had suffered a defeat in Indochina, the Ford administration tried to reassure the ASEAN states that America would remain a power in the region. Ford himself traveled to Southeast Asia in 1975 to demonstrate that commitment. Returning from the trip, he announced his Pacific Doctrine, in which he guaranteed a U.S. presence in support of ASEAN. The forceful American military response in May 1975 to the Cambodian seizure of the U.S. merchant vessel *Mayaguez* was used by Ford to prove that there was no "Vietnam syndrome" operating to inhibit America's defense of its security interests. While the ASEAN nations were focused on a potential regional threat from Vietnam, the strongest local military power in Southeast Asia, American attention was concentrated on growing Soviet influence in the SRV, signified by the 1978 Vietnam–USSR alliance and Russian basing in Vietnam.

Although the U.S. bases in the Philippines were vital for American forward deployment in Southeast Asia, Indonesia became the key state in the evolving American strategic view of the regional balance of power.

Indonesia under President Suharto seemed a bastion of anticommunist political stability and the natural leader of ASEAN. Although there were no formal security ties between the United States and Indonesia, a close security partnership was developed. In furtherance of that, Washington turned a blind eye politically to the Indonesian invasion and annexation of the former Portuguese overseas territory of East Timor shortly after Ford and Kissinger met with Suharto in Jakarta in December 1975. For a quarter of a century issues of human rights and self-determination for East Timor irritated U.S.–Indonesian bilateral relations.

Much of the work that Ford and Kissinger had done to allay the concerns of Southeast Asian leaders about U.S. staying power seemed at first undone by the Carter administration. Candidate Carter had denounced the power politics of the Nixon–Kissinger–Ford foreign policy. Previous administrations in their containment policy had basically ignored the political quality of the domestic regimes of America's friends and allies. The corruption and human rights abuses of the Marcos dictatorship in the Philippines were offset by the need for the bases. The American anticommunist alliance with Thailand had politically enabled Thai military dictatorships. Prime Minister Lee Kuan Yew, the authoritarian leader of Singapore's government, was a strong booster of American policy in Southeast Asia. Military-led Indonesia had become the lynchpin of the American strategic thinking. In contrast, Carter promised that democratic values and human rights would be paramount in his approach to foreign policy. This was viewed with alarm in capitals throughout the region. The institutionalization of a human rights agenda in the Carter administration led to policy conflicts within the administration between advocates of a principled stance in opposition to domestic policies in the Philippines, Singapore, and Indonesia and officials who deemed American security interests to have the first priority. In Southeast Asia itself, U.S. policy seemed in disarray and the American commitment to the security of the region downgraded.

THE THIRD INDOCHINA WAR AND THE ENDING OF THE COLD WAR: 1979–1991

In December 1978, Vietnam invaded Cambodia, expelling the Khmer Rouge and installing a Vietnam-sponsored People's Republic of Kampuchea (PRK). Vietnam's invasion and occupation of Cambodia was a shock to ASEAN. The Vietnamese–Cambodian clash was the culmination of the bitter and complex relationship between erstwhile communist comrades in arms but also traditional ethnic enemies that was complicated by their competitive Chinese and Soviet alliances. It put an end to ASEAN's hope for normal relations with communist Indochina. In ASEAN eyes, the first Southeast Asian domino had fallen to aggressive Vietnamese expansionism. It made the Thai–Cambodian border ASEAN's strategic frontier with a seemingly threatening Vietnam. ASEAN viewed the PRK as an illegitimate product of Vietnamese military aggression. Its policy response was to demand the withdrawal of Vietnamese forces and Cambodian political self-determination. This agenda was internationalized in UN General Assembly resolutions. ASEAN's diplomatic offensive against what the Vietnamese considered an irreversible fait accompli was given military teeth in its backing of a Khmer resistance force that from refugee bases in Thailand carried out a low-intensity war in Cambodia against the Vietnamese and the PRK. The political and military contest over the future of Cambodia—the Third Indochina War—dominated Southeast Asian diplomacy for more than a decade.

For the United States, the Vietnamese invasion of Cambodia added further justification to its policy of isolating the SRV. Washington added compliance to ASEAN's demands on Vietnam to leave Cambodia to its list of conditions for the normalization of Vietnam's relations with the United States. American diplomacy strongly supported ASEAN in the United Nations and other international fora. The Carter administration, jolted not just by Vietnam but particularly by the Soviet invasion of Afghanistan, put American security interests in Southeast Asia back on the front burner. Of particular importance to ASEAN, and especially Thailand, was an explicit American commitment to Thailand's defense if Vietnam should invade. The course set by Carter for the United States in the Third Indochina War was continued during the subsequent administration of Ronald Reagan. The U.S. position was complicated by the fact that the internationally reviled Khmer Rouge provided the backbone of the armed Khmer resistance. The KR's role was diplomatically disguised in the 1982 Coalition Government of Democratic Kampuchea (CGDK), which occupied the Cambodian seat in the UN. Washington's support to the resistance was financial and material.

The United States was allied with China in supporting the ASEAN position on Cambodia. China was the major source of lethal assistance for the Khmer resistance. China seemed intent on bleeding Vietnam, which some analysts saw as only driving Vietnam deeper into dependence on the Soviet Union. The Soviet presence, particularly its navy, loomed ever larger in American threat perceptions. In the Philippines, the United States could no longer ignore the Marcos government's systematic human and political rights abuses as opposition to his regime threatened American interests. In 1986, the Philippines seemed poised for civil violence as Marcos clung to power in the face of a People's Power revolution. With the future of the bases at stake, Washington intervened to persuade Marcos to step down and go into Hawaiian exile. A sputtering American–Vietnamese dialogue on normalization of relations produced some movement on the POW/MIA question, but the roadmap the Reagan administration presented Hanoi still had Cambodia as an important marker.

Although American power was in the background during the Third Indochina War, the United States was not a critical player in the diplomacy that ended it. At the regional level, ASEAN's position was transformed by Thai Prime Minister Chatichai Choonhaven, who opened extra-ASEAN bilateral negotiating channels to Phnom Penh and Hanoi. The decisive players, however, were China and the USSR. In May 1989, the PRC and USSR leaders agreed to a framework of détente that included a decoupling of the Sino–Soviet relationship from the Third Indochina War. With the basic Great Power connection to the conflict no longer shaping strategy, a consensus on a settlement emerged. A final Comprehensive Political Settlement of the Cambodia Conflict was fashioned by the UN Security Council's five permanent members and adopted in the October 1991 session of the Paris International Conference on Cambodia (PICC).

The emphasis placed by the USSR and the PRC on their respective economies and social development led to a restructuring of the Cold War Great Power strategic triangle in Southeast Asia. The collapse of the Soviet Union and the weaknesses of its successor state Russia meant that there was no longer a Soviet threat to be contained by the United States. After 1991, Vietnam, Cambodia, and Laos were no longer surrogates for Great Power conflict. The Cold War strategic line that ran between the ASEAN states and Indochina had been erased. China normalized its relations with Vietnam in 1991. Vietnam, Laos, and Cambodia became members of ASEAN. The United States (1978), China (1996), and Russia (1996) became official dialogue partners of ASEAN. The Cold War was over.

A SECOND INTERWAR PERIOD: FROM GEOSTRATEGIC TO GEOECONOMIC INTERESTS: 1991–2001

The disappearance of the old Soviet Union as a significant strategic presence in Southeast Asia left the United States and China to refashion their political relations with the countries of the region in support of interests divorced from Cold War and Third Indochina War alliances and alignments. The Cold War environment in Southeast Asia was characterized by polarizing political conflict. The post–Cold War environment that began to emerge in the 1990s was one of growing economic interdependencies among the ASEAN nations and between them and their extraregional partners. The political competitions of the Cold War were succeeded by the economic competitions of globalization. The United States has been at the center of this as the most important single market and source of foreign direct investment for Southeast Asian nations. At both the bilateral and multilateral levels of negotiation and agreement, the United States has promoted trade and investment liberalization. One of the most important issue areas to emerge has been the U.S. defense of intellectual property rights (IPR). President William Clinton offered in 1993 his vision of a Pacific Community built on security, democracy, and economic growth. The assumption was that security would be guaranteed by unchallenged U.S. power, democracy by expanding civil societies in economically developing countries, and economic growth through liberal market economies. Up to 1997, the economic model seemed to be working. Even the failing command economies of the socialist states turned to the market. The Asian financial crisis of 1997–1998 abruptly interrupted the surging economic progress that had been experienced in Southeast Asia. China's and Japan's responses to the bursting of bubble economies in Southeast Asia were viewed as more timely than that of the United States.

A wider multilateral setting for Southeast Asian economic cooperation was found in the Asia-Pacific Economic Cooperation (APEC) intergovernmental consultative mechanism. Established in 1989, APEC in 1994 set a goal of free and open trade in the Asia-Pacific region by 2010 for its developed economies and 2020 for the developing economies. Although not originally an American inspiration, APEC was given its momentum by President Clinton's hosting of the first APEC summit. Within ASEAN, Indonesia's president Suharto had to overcome the objections of Malaysia's prime minister Mahathir Mohammad to bring ASEAN into APEC's framework. Mahathir had urged an alternative regionalist program that would have excluded the United States from an East Asian Economic Group (EAEG). Although Suharto prevailed, the EAEG proposal was the initial move toward a more exclusive regionalism embodied in the ASEAN plus three grouping of ASEAN, China, Japan, and South Korea. The launching of the East Asia Summit (EAS) in 2005 also excluded the United States but included Australia, New Zealand, and India. The United States also objects to proposals for an East Asia Economic Community. It insists on a loose, inclusive Pacific basin regionalism that does not draw a line through the middle of the Pacific Ocean.

In terms of regional security, the ASEAN states sought to reduce the residual Great Power military footprints in the region through strengthening the declaratory ZOPFAN with the 1995 treaty for a Southeast Asia Nuclear Weapons Free Zone (SEANWFZ). The United States ignored this as it had its ZOPFAN antecedent. Washington did relax its resistance to regional multilateral security initiatives by agreeing to participate in the ASEAN Regional Forum (ARF), a loose consultative grouping that does not constrain U.S. core alliance relations in the region. The ARF first met in 1994. The U.S. strategic profile in Southeast Asia had already been reduced when the Philippine Senate in 1991 refused to ratify a new U.S. bases agreement. The American bases had been a key element in the Cold War American security presence in Southeast Asia. Although Washington was able to negotiate access and facilities agreements to pick up some of the functions of the Philippine bases elsewhere in the region, the most visible evidence of American power and commitment in Southeast Asia was lost. Progress toward normalization of U.S.–Vietnam relations signified a new kind of commitment to the region. The pace of negotiations accelerated in the administration of President George H. W. Bush as the Third Indochina War wound down, and culminated in diplomatic relations in 1995 in the Clinton administration.

The ending of the Cold War gave greater attention to human rights advocacy, which has been expanded to include religious rights. The American–Indonesian bilateral security relationship received new scrutiny. With the Cold War strategic imperatives no longer operating, Indonesia's political and human rights records assumed a new priority for U.S. foreign policy. In response to the unprovoked killing by Indonesian soldiers of civilian demonstrators in East Timor in 1992, Congress put in place the first of a series of limitations on U.S. military-to-military relations with Indonesia. These were expanded in the aftermath of the brutal attacks on East Timorese civilians by Indonesian army–backed militias following the UN-sanctioned Timorese vote for independence in 1999. It was to Burma, however, that the harshest U.S. measures were directed, in an effort to unseat the military junta in power since 1988 and restore democracy. A wide range of economic sanctions effectively cut Burma off from the U.S. economy. First declared by President William Clinton in 1997, the sanctions have been renewed and expanded annually. The United States opposed ASEAN's 1997 admission of Burma, and Burmese membership has complicated U.S.–ASEAN relations. American efforts to enlist other nations in a sanctions regime against Burma have only been partly successful and have been totally unsuccessful as far as Burma's ASEAN partners are concerned. China has become the Burmese junta's patron, and Chinese and Indian competition for Burma's energy resources underwrite the Burmese economy, notwithstanding American sanctions.

With security considerations no longer monopolizing the American post–Cold War agenda in Southeast Asia, nontraditional foreign policy issues assumed greater prominence in U.S. bilateral and multilateral relations in Southeast Asia. As Southeast Asia has been globally integrated, in addition to human rights, other nontraditional international interests such as the eradication and interdiction of narcotics production and trafficking in persons, gender, labor rights, environmental issues, and pandemic diseases, to name a few, have been placed on the American diplomatic plate in Southeast Asia. As the new century began, however, security again leapt to the fore.

THE WAR ON TERROR AND THE RISE OF CHINA: 2001–

After the 11 September 2001 terrorist attacks on the United States, Southeast Asia became a second front in the U.S. war on terror, because the region was the home to radical Islamic groups, such as Indonesia-based Jema'ah Islamiyah (JI), with ties to al-Qaeda. The United States has carried out an intensive diplomatic campaign at the bilateral and ASEAN multilateral level of relations to mobilize its allies and friends in a common battle against terrorists. This was complicated by the American linkage of the war on terror to the Iraq War. Muslims throughout the region became sympathetic to the charge made by radical Islamists that the United States was making war on Islam. The domestic reaction in Muslim-majority Malaysia and Indonesia limited how far political leadership in those countries can go in cooperation with the United States. The Philippines, Thailand, and Singapore, America's traditional allies in Southeast Asia, contributed to the "coalition of the willing" in the toppling of Saddam Hussein's regime in Iraq.

The most direct U.S. assistance in the regional war on terror went to the Philippines, where it became a vital partner in the Philippine counterterrorism efforts against the Abu Sayyaf Gang and other radical Muslim separatists. Philippine president Gloria Macapagal-Arroyo was the first ASEAN leader to contact President George W. Bush after 9/11 to pledge assistance. A new Visiting Forces Agreement with the Philippines allowed the U.S. military to reestablish close military-to-military relations with the Armed Forces of the Philippines (AFP), which had been in abeyance since the 1991 termination of the Military Bases Agreement. Since 2002, uniformed American Special Forces elements have been in the field as advisors to the AFP in the war on terrorism in the Philippines' Muslim south. Indonesia has also been a strategic center of the Southeast Asian front. JI had tentacles throughout the region. Terrorist bombings in Bali in 2002 energized the Indonesian government, which, with American and Australian support in the background, had made serious inroads into the JI's capabilities by 2006. A new confidence in the bilateral U.S.–Indonesian security relations came with the 2005 waiver of the last of the East Timor–related congressional restrictions on military-to-military relations. Both countries by 2006 could speak of a strategic partnership.

Even as the United States was enlisting Southeast Asian allies in the war on terror, concerns were being raised in the region about the perceived neglect of America's broader, longer-range interests. Many observers saw China's heightened economic and political profile in Southeast Asia as challenging the fundamental basis of U.S. strategic policy in the region since the end of World War II. China's "peaceful rise" has been most conspicuous in a pattern of bilateral and ASEAN economic arrangements that have linked China's economic development to its partners in Southeast Asia. Southeast Asia also is wary about China's growing military power, despite Chinese disclaimers of its peaceful attention. China's new economic prominence has caused the United States to refocus on Southeast Asia as an interest area in its own right, not just as a theater of the war on terrorism. The Bush administration has pursued an agenda designed to deepen American economic ties in the region by moving from bilateral trade and investment framework agreements (TIFA) to free trade agreements (FTA), and in 2006 an ASEAN–United States Enhanced Partnership that has as an ultimate goal a United States–ASEAN free trade agreement. In 2007, the Bush administration was reconsidering the historical American refusal to adhere to the Treaty of Amity and Cooperation in Southeast Asia. President Bush also announced that the United States would name an ambassador to ASEAN, thus giving the regional organization a new diplomatic identity for the United States.

ASEAN has adapted to China's own Great Power ambitions by both engaging it and hedging and balancing with its own ties to the United States. ASEAN does not want to be forced to choose between them. It seeks to promote a strategic environment that is not a threat to the interests of either China or the United States. Proactive U.S. policy and diplomacy across all areas of international activity, not just security, have the potential to ensure that the United States will remain a significant actor in Southeast Asia, able to defend its interests in the emerging new distribution of power. This may be one in which for the first time since the defeat of Japan in World War II, American power may be not predominant, but rather a participant in a balance of power in which ASEAN itself has the option to shape the dynamic.

The Dictionary

– A –

ABDULLAH BADAWI (1939–). Prime minister of Malaysia since October 2003, when his predecessor, **Mahathir Mohammad**, stepped down, Abdullah won his own overwhelming electoral mandate in 2004. By education a religious scholar, he had previously been minister of education, minister of defense, minister of foreign affairs, deputy prime minister, and minister of the interior. Abdullah's style as prime minister was in sharp contrast to that of Mahathir, who seemed to go out of his way to offend American political sensibilities. Although affirming that relations with the United States were cordial, Abdullah, like Mahathir, had few value or ideological affinities with America. A proponent of what is called Islam Hadhari (Civilizational Islam), in contrast to the domestic Islamic fundamentalist opposition party, Abdullah, again like Mahathir, attributed great importance to Malaysia's involvement in the **Organization of the Islamic Conference (OIC)** and **Nonaligned Movement (NAM)**. He also has been credited with originating the vision for an **East Asia Summit (EAS)**. In 2004, he met President **George W. Bush** at the White House and in 2006 at the **United Nations (UN)**. He also engaged with Bush at the 2005, 2006, and 2007 **Association of Southeast Asian Nations (ASEAN)**–United States mini-summits on the sidelines of the **Asia–Pacific Economic Cooperation (APEC)** heads of states' meetings. *See also* WAR ON TERROR.

ABRAMOWITZ, MORTON I. (1933–). A career Foreign Service Officer, Morton Abramowitz was ambassador to **Thailand** (1978–1981) during the **refugee** outflow from **Cambodia** and the Vietnamese "**boat people**." In recognition of his humanitarian efforts, he received the

State Department's Distinguished Service Award and the President's Award for Distinguished Federal Service. After serving in Bangkok, he was nominated to be ambassador to **Indonesia**, but for reasons Jakarta did not explain, the Indonesian government did not agree to accept him. It is thought that a paper originating in the Defense Department or **Central Intelligence Agency (CIA)** accusing Abramowitz of being too liberal and too close to President **Jimmy Carter** was given to the Indonesians. There is also reason to believe that the Thai leadership back-channeled their Indonesian counterparts with some negatives. Finally, it was also charged that the Indonesians refused him because he was Jewish. Yet **Paul Wolfowitz**, who was also Jewish, later became an ambassador to Indonesia. Abramowitz, rather than going to Indonesia—**John Holdridge** got the post—became director of the State Department's Bureau of Intelligence and Research (INR) and then assistant secretary of state for INR, 1985–1989. In that post, he provided important input into the change in U.S. policy of support for the **Ferdinand Marcos** administration in the **Philippines**. After a tour as ambassador to Turkey, Abramowitz retired in 1991. Since then he has been a prolific commentator on U.S. Asian policy from positions at the Carnegie Endowment, the Council on Foreign Relations, and the Century Foundation. In 2006, the American Foreign Service Association presented Abramowitz with its lifetime award for contributions to American diplomacy.

ABU SAYYAF GROUP (ASG). The Abu Sayyaf ("Bearer of the Sword") Group is a splinter group of Islamic extremists with **al-Qaeda** and **Jema'ah Islamiyah (JI)** links operating in Mindanao Island and the Sulu Archipelago in the southern **Philippines**. It has connections to other Muslim insurgent groups like the **Moro Islamic Liberation Front (MILF)** and the **Moro National Liberation Front (MNLF)** claiming to represent the **Moro** people (**Bangsamoro**), the Muslim population of the Philippines' southernmost Islands. The ASG is one of the three Southeast Asian groups on the U.S. **Foreign Terrorist Organization (FTO)** list. The ASG's alleged links to al-Qaeda and JI have made it a major target in the American **war on terror**. The ASG's origin was with the Filipino Muslim *mujahidin* (Holy Warriors), who fought with the Taliban against the USSR in Afghanistan in the 1980s. Its founder was Abdurajak Janjalani, who preached a virulent **Wahabist** ideology. Abdurajak was killed in a shootout in 1998. He was succeeded by his younger brother, Khadaffi Janjalani, who was killed in late 2006. The ASG is responsible for terrorist attacks, banditry, and kidnapping, including in 2001 two American missionaries, one of whom was killed in a rescue attempt. In November 2001, President **George W. Bush** announced U.S. support for the Philippine government's campaign against the ASG. Since the resumption of joint U.S.–Philippine military exercises in 2002 after the signing of a new **Visiting Forces Agreement (VFA)**, the United States has provided training and intelligence for the Philippine military in the field against the ASG. The U.S. Pacific Special Operations Command (SOCPAC) created an American **Joint Special Operations Task Force–Philippines (JSOTF–P)** operating in the Philippine army's Southern Command to give continuity to the coordinated counterterrorist effort against the ASG.

ACHESON, DEAN G. (1893–1971). Dean Acheson was U.S secretary of state from 1949 to 1953. Previously he had served as undersecretary of state (1945–1947), in which post he helped implement the **Truman Doctrine** and Marshall Plan. As secretary of state during President **Harry S. Truman**'s elected term, he managed America's diplomatic response to the transfer of power in **China** from the nationalists to the communists and the outbreak of the Korean War. He resisted U.S. direct involvement in the Chinese civil war. In a famous speech to the National Press Club in January 1950, he defined the U.S. "defensive perimeter" in the Western Pacific, mentioning only the great chain of islands—the Aleutians, Japan, the Ryukyus, and the **Philippines**. Because he did not mention Korea, this was later interpreted by Republican opponents as an invitation to North Korea to invade South Korea. Acheson favored American assistance to the French in their colonial war in Indochina—the **First Indochina War**. He laid the foundation for the future American security role in Southeast Asia when he stated that "it is a fundamental decision of American policy that the United States does not intend to permit further extension of Communist domination on the continent of Asia or in the Southeast Asia area."

AGENCY FOR INTERNATIONAL DEVELOPMENT (USAID). The United States Agency for International Development is the bureaucratic framework for the delivery of programmed economic and technical aid to over 100 nations eligible for U.S. official development assistance (ODA) and humanitarian aid. The administrator of USAID is concurrently the **State Department**'s Director of U.S. Foreign Assistance, with a rank equivalent to deputy secretary of state. The United States is the largest single ODA donor in the world, with an FY 2006 appropriated budget of over $9 billion. Since 11 September 2001, U.S. ODA has been closely tied to the **war on terror**. In USAID's "Policy Framework for Bilateral Aid," the agency's goals are stated to be promoting democratization, strengthening fragile states, supporting strategic states, and providing humanitarian relief. **Indonesia** is currently the recipient of the lion's share of American bilateral ODA in Southeast Asia. The FY 2007 budget request was $158 million, a 31 percent increase over FY 2004. The FY 2007 budget request numbers for the other Southeast Asian states with bilateral aid programs are the **Philippines**, $60.6 million; **Cambodia**, $47.4 million; and **East Timor**, $13.3 million. Historically, the Philippines and the pre-1975 **Republic of Vietnam (RVN)** were the largest beneficiaries of the flow of U.S. ODA. In 2007, the United States pledged $190 million to be administered by USAID over five years for development projects in the southern Philippines as a stimulus to the peace process in that troubled region. USAID's *Green Book* gives country breakdowns in actual and constant dollars of ODA from the inception of a bilateral ODA relationship. In addition to bilateral programs, there are regional programs aimed at transnational issues such as vulnerable populations, **refugees**, and **pandemic disease**. The South and Southeast Asia FY 2007 budget request for region-wide programs was $54 million, a nearly 100-percent increase over FY 2004.

AGUINALDO, EMILIO (1869–1964). Emilio Aguinaldo was a **Philippine** nationalist and military leader in the 1896–1898 Philippine revolt against Spain. Forced into exile, he returned with the Americans in 1898, allying with them in the Spanish–American War against the common Spanish enemy. When U.S. imperial intentions became clear, the Philippine nationalists, from their seat in the provincial city of Malolos in Central Luzon, declared Philippine independence on 12 June 1898. Aguinaldo was elected Philippine president at a January 1899 constitutional convention. Aguinaldo was a skilled guerrilla leader and led an armed struggle against the Americans, known respectively from Filipino or American perspectives as either the Philippine War of Independence or the Philippine "insurrection." It was only after Aguinaldo's capture in 1901 and his oath of loyalty to the United States, secured by military governor of the Philippines General **Arthur MacArthur**, that the insurgency petered out. Aguinaldo never reconciled with the United States. He is a Philippine national hero and is considered by Filipinos to be the country's first president. Philippine Independence Day was changed in 1962 from 4 July to the 12 June date of the Malolos declaration of independence.

AIR AMERICA. This was a **Central Intelligence Agency (CIA)** proprietary company that was an important asset in the **secret war** in **Laos**. Air America was a successor to the CIA's **Civil Air Transport (CAT)**. It was Air America's capacity with both fixed and rotary wing aircraft to get in and out of short and rough landing sites that kept CIA-backed General **Vang Pao**'s force of ethnic **Hmong** in the field against the **Pathet Lao** and **Viet Minh**. Air America also extracted downed American airmen. In April 1972, the agency decided it no longer had a need for its own lift capacity. The last Air America flight out of Laos was in June 1974, and the company went out of business in 1976. Air America and other CIA-held aviation companies like Southern Air Transport were accused of facilitating the Southeast Asian drug trade that helped finance local warlords and paramilitary groups.

ALBRIGHT, MADELEINE K. (1937–). When she was sworn in as secretary of state in 1997, Madeleine Albright became the first woman to hold the post and the highest-ranking woman ever in the government of the United States. Prior to becoming President **William J. Clinton**'s second secretary of state, succeeding **Warren Christopher**, she had served from 1993 in Clinton's first term as American permanent representative to the **United Nations**, a cabinet-level post. Albright had an academic background, holding a Columbia University Ph.D. and an Eastern Europe–Russia special area of interest. She had been shaped intellectually by her father, Joseph Korbel, a distinguished professor of international relations and founder of the Graduate School of International Studies at the University of Denver. Korbel was also mentor to Secretary of State **Condoleezza Rice**. Secretary Albright's agenda for Southeast Asia reflected President Clinton's general Asia strategy of deeper and broader security and economic contacts.

During her tenure she attended all of the **Association of Southeast Asian Nations (ASEAN)** postministerial conference (PMC) meetings with ASEAN's foreign ministers and **ASEAN Regional Forum (ARF)** sessions, in succession in **Malaysia**, the **Philippines, Singapore**, and **Thailand**. Coming into office, she immediately had to manage the diplomacy of the Southeast Asian **financial crisis of 1997–1998**. She also diplomatically supported the administration's **human rights** policies toward **Burma**, seeking unsuccessfully to isolate Burma from ASEAN and using the ARF meetings as a bully pulpit. She created a stir on the sidelines of the November 1998 **Asia–Pacific Economic Cooperation (APEC)** meeting in Kuala Lumpur when she met with the wife of imprisoned Malaysian politician **Anwar Ibrahim**. His wife, Dr. Wan Azizah, had become the leading figure in the Malaysian Justice Party, which opposed Prime Minister **Mahathir Mohammad**. In March 1999 in **Indonesia**, as part of the effort to further a peaceful democratic transition in **East Timor**, Albright met with East Timorese resistance leader **Xanana Gusmão** while he was under house arrest in Jakarta. She also continued the Clinton administration's efforts to firm up newly normalized relations with **Vietnam**. Her first trip to the region in June 1997 was to meet with the Vietnamese leadership. At that time she laid the cornerstone for a new American consulate in Ho Chi Minh City (previously Saigon). She returned two years later to open the consulate.

ALI SASTROAMIDJOJO (1903–1975). An Indonesian statesman and politician, Ali Sastroamidjojo was **Indonesia**'s first ambassador to the United States (1951–1953) and twice Indonesia's prime minister (1953–1955 and 1956–1957). He came to the prime minister's office after the fall of the previous government, which had been secretly negotiating a **mutual security agreement** with the United States. Ali, a radical nationalist, was determined to demonstrate Indonesian independence and importance, and in the face of American disapproval opened diplomatic relations with both the Soviet Union and the People's Republic of **China**. He was also a co-convener of the 1955 **Asian–African Conference**, with its twin agendas of anti-imperialism and nonalignment.

AL-QAEDA. The principal enemy in the American **war on terror** has been al-Qaeda, led by Osama bin Laden. The Southeast Asian front of that war has focused on al-Qaeda's links to indigenous Southeast Asian Islamic radicals and terrorist groups, including **Jema'ah Islamiyah (JI)**, the **Abu Sayyaf Group (ASG)**, and the **Moro Islamic Liberation Front (MILF)**. The ideological link is fundamentalist Islam's **Wahabism**, with the centrality of *jihad* (holy war). The historical link is the armed resistance to the 1979 Soviet invasion and occupation of Afghanistan. The senior leaders of the Southeast Asian *jihadists* received indoctrination and training as *mujahidin* (Holy Warriors) in Afghanistan. After the defeat of the Russians, the triumphant Taliban hosted al-Qaeda and its terrorist training camps. Al-Qaeda operatives forged personal links with their Southeast Asian counterparts, like **Hambali** and **Omar al-Faruq**, who provided the human nexus linking al-Qaeda's global *jihad* to the local and regional struggles of Southeast Asia's radical Islamic movements. The common enemies are the United States and secular Western culture.

ANDERSON, BENEDICT R. O'G. (1936–). From his **Cornell University** post and its Modern Indonesia Project, Benedict Anderson was a major academic figure in contemporary Indonesia studies. He was a trenchant critic of **Indonesia**'s **Suharto** regime and American support for it. A lead author of a 1971 "white paper" rebutting the Indonesian official view of the 1965 **Indonesian coup**, Anderson became a frequent and forceful public commentator on the Suharto government's **human rights** record and U.S. policy toward Indonesia.

ANWAR IBRAHIM (1947–). Anwar Ibrahim was **Malaysia**'s deputy prime minister and finance minister as well as the assumed heir apparent when, in 1998, Prime Minister **Mahathir Mohammad** sacked and arrested him on what turned out to be bogus charges of corruption and sexual misconduct. Anwar had disagreed with Mahathir on how to handle the **financial crisis of 1997–1998** and had advocated political reform and greater democratic opening in Malaysia. His arrest and mistreatment under Malaysia's Internal Security Act (ISA), followed by punitive prison terms, made Anwar a cause célèbre for democracy advocates worldwide. The official position of President **William J. Clinton**'s administration was that it was "outraged" by the treatment of Anwar and that Malaysia's poor **human rights** record was an obstacle in U.S.–Malaysian relations. The bilateral relationship was particularly strained after American vice president Al Gore, in Kuala Lumpur for the 1998 **Asia–Pacific Economic Cooperation (APEC)** summit, seemed to encourage pro-Anwar demonstrators, whom he called the "brave people of Malaysia," to continue their calls for freedom, democracy, and reform. Anwar's fate was shoved to the background after 9/11 when Malaysia became an ally of the United States in the **war on terror** and Prime Minister Mahathir was welcomed to the White House by President **George W. Bush**. After Mahathir stepped down as prime minister in 2003, Anwar was legally and politically rehabilitated by the **Abdullah Badawi** government. Upon release from prison, Anwar accepted in 2005 a visiting professorship at the Johns Hopkins Nitze School of Advanced International Studies in Washington, D.C. Returning to Malaysia as head of the Foundation for the Future, he reentered politics as advisor to the opposition Justice Party.

AQUINO, BENIGNO, JR. (1932–1983). When president of the **Philippines Ferdinand Marcos** carried out his 1972 "constitutional coup," his most prominent political opponent was Senator Benigno "Ninoy" Aquino. As the democratic alternative in Philippine politics, Aquino was Marcos's political nemesis and would likely have been elected president if the scheduled 1973 elections had not been derailed by martial law. He was arrested, tried by a military court on trumped up charges of treason and murder, and sentenced to death. Imprisoned for the next seven years, he became the rallying point for the anti-Marcos democratic opposition and international **human rights** activists. In 1981, Aquino was allowed to leave for the United States, ostensibly for a heart bypass operation. From a Boston base, he worked to mobilize both Filipino and American opposition to the Marcos regime. Although coolly received by the administration of President **Ronald Reagan**, he had congressional champions, particularly Representative **Stephen Solarz**, who chaired the House Foreign

Affairs Subcommittee on Asia and the Pacific. In August 1983, believing Marcos to be seriously ill, despite warnings Aquino returned to the Philippines to be in place for a transition. Upon his 21 August 1983 arrival at Manila International Airport (now Ninoy Aquino Airport), he was escorted off the plane by security forces and shot to death on the tarmac. His martyrdom became a cause underpinning the spreading and deepening opposition to the regime that was catalyzed by the emergence of his wife, **Corazon Aquino**, as the unlikely heroine of the **EDSA revolution** that toppled the Marcos regime.

AQUINO, CORAZON (1933–). Catapulted into politics by the 1983 murder of her husband **Benigno Aquino,** Corazon "Cory" Aquino took her husband's place as the symbol of democratic resistance to the **Ferdinand Marcos** regime. She was a daughter of the Cojuangco family, among the wealthiest of the Filipino oligarchs. Convent educated, she was deeply religious. As Benigno "Ninoy" Aquino's wife, she had always been in the background until thrust into the limelight by his assassination. In the opposition's activism leading up to the 7 February 1986 snap elections called by Marcos, once Cory Aquino announced that she would run for president, she became the people's choice. The government's fraudulent manipulation of the outcome of the election led to the Catholic Church–supported "people's power" **EDSA revolution**, which with military defections and U.S. pressure, forced Marcos to leave for exile in Hawaii. On 25 February 1986, Cory Aquino was sworn in as president. One of the achievements of her presidency was the drafting of a new, democratic constitution designed to prevent another Marcos-like figure from seizing power. The centerpiece was a presidential term limit of one six-year term. During her six-year term there were seven failed coups, the most serious being the **Honasan coup** of December 1989, in which the United States directly intervened in her support. She personally was favorably disposed toward the United States but had to balance this with the nationalist anger at the United States for its long record of support for the Marcos regime. When it was time for the ratification of the new **Military Bases Agreement** in 1991, she backed it but did not have the necessary Philippine Senate votes to secure it. On leaving office in 1992, the former president remained largely in the background, only to reemerge in 2006 in opposition to President **Gloria Macapagal-Arroyo**'s perceived retreat from the democratic safeguards of the 1987 "Aquino constitution."

ARMACOST, MICHAEL H. (1937–). A veteran U.S. diplomat, Ambassador Michael Armacost arrived in the **Philippines** in 1982 to promote an American policy of steadfast support for the government of **Ferdinand Marcos**. When he left in 1984 to become undersecretary of state for political affairs, the basis for that support had been seriously eroded. The tipping point was the murder of Marcos's democratic rival, **Benigno Aquino**, in 1983. Even though Ambassador Armacost continued to communicate to Marcos that the United States would not intervene in support of his rivals, his relationship with the government cooled. Despite a warning from the Philippine Foreign Ministry that it would be considered an unfriendly act, Armacost attended Aquino's funeral mass. He returned to Washington as undersecretary of state, from which position he counseled support for **Corazon Aquino**'s anti-Marcos political movement. Armacost and his Manila successor as American ambassador, **Stephen Bosworth**, argued that American national interest would be best served by a democratic Philippines. Armacost's last diplomatic posting was as ambassador to Japan, from 1989 to 1993.

ARMITAGE, RICHARD L. (1945–). One of the most decorated officials in the U.S. government, Armitage's last post was as deputy secretary of state from 2001 to 2005 in President **George W. Bush**'s administration. A significant part of his career was Southeast Asia centered. He graduated from the U.S. Naval Academy in 1967. After serving on a destroyer off the Vietnamese coast, he had three combat tours in riverine forces. In 1973, he moved to the defense attaché's office in the Saigon embassy and then on to the Defense Intelligence Agency in 1975. In 1981, he was named deputy assistant secretary of defense for international security affairs responsible for East Asia and the Pacific. From 1983 to 1989, he was assistant secretary, in which role he spearheaded U.S.–Pacific security policy as well as the **POW/MIA** question. In 1989, President **George H. W. Bush** designated Armitage presidential special negotiator for a new **Military Bases Agreement (MBA)** in the **Philippines**. The MBA was successfully concluded but was rejected by the Philippine Senate in 1991. In 2006, Armitage was tipped as the U.S. government official who blew Valerie Plame's **Central Intelligence Agency (CIA)** cover, in a leak that seriously embarrassed the Bush administration.

ARROYO, GLORIA MACAPAGAL (1947–). Daughter of **Diosdado Macapagal**, the Philippine president defeated by **Ferdinand Marcos** in the 1965 election, Gloria Macapagal-Arroyo was elected vice president of the **Philippines** in 1998. The same election made **Joseph Estrada** president. He was a hugely popular actor running on a different party ticket. In 2001, she was sworn in as president after a quasi-constitutional coup swept Estrada from office, in what has been called **EDSA** II or the second people's power revolution. Arroyo won election to the presidency in her own right in 2004 by defeating actor Ferdinand Poe Jr., widely considered a surrogate for Estrada, by more than a million votes. After the election, Arroyo's administration was weakened by evidence of corruption and allegations of significant electoral fraud by her camp. Opinion polling in 2007 depicted her as the most distrusted and disliked president in Philippine history.

Beleaguered by threats of military coups, the **Communist Party of the Philippines/New People's Army (CPP/NPA)** continuing insurgency, and **Moro** separatism and terrorism in the southern Philippines, President Arroyo sought to strengthen her wounded legitimacy by a closer embrace of the United States. She made it clear that the strategic relationship with the United States was fundamental to the Philippines. In 2001, she traveled to Washington to celebrate the 50th anniversary of the U.S.–Philippine **Mutual Defense Treaty (MDT).** She was the first Asian leader to call President **George W. Bush** after the 11 September 2001 terrorist attacks. The Philippines joined the international coalition in the **Iraq War** with a small military unit. Whatever initial Washington qualms there may have been over the irregularity of Arroyo's assumption of the presidency, they were overcome by her promise of a stable and friendly Philippines and ally in the **war on terror**. American appreciation of her role was amply demonstrated by the warmth of her reception in Washington in May 2003 on a state visit.

President Arroyo's standing with the American administration was slightly tarnished when she unilaterally withdrew the Philippine contingent from Iraq in July 2004 as the condition for the release of a kidnapped Filipino worker. Her democratic credentials were undermined by her declaration of a state of emergency in early 2006 as civilian and military pressure to force her from office increased in an effort to unleash an **EDSA** III "people's power" revolt. American–Philippine relations were further strained by an espionage case in which secret American views on Philippine politics were given to Arroyo's opponents. In 2006, she was criticized by both the United-States and Philippine nationalists for what appeared to be her ambivalence toward a criminal proceeding under the U.S.–Philippine **Visiting Forces Agreement (VFA)**. Despite Washington's misgivings about the democratic quality and **human rights** failings of her government, particularly accusations of military extrajudicial killings, Arroyo's continued assertion that the foundation of Philippine foreign policy is the strategic alliance with the United States controlled the trajectory of the bilateral relationship in the war on terror.

ARTICLE 98 AGREEMENTS. *See* INTERNATIONAL CRIMINAL COURT.

ASEAN COOPERATION PLAN (ACP). Secretary of State **Colin Powell** announced the ASEAN Cooperation Plan in August 2002. It was a U.S.-funded initiative to strengthen the **Association of Southeast Asian Nations (ASEAN)** secretariat; build regional capacity to address transnational challenges like the **war on terror, trafficking in persons**, and **pandemic and infectious diseases** including AIDS, SARS, and avian flu; and foster economic integration. More than 20 projects have been undertaken at a cost of more than $9 million. It is coordinated by the U.S. **Agency for International Development (USAID)** and brings together a mix of U.S. government agencies, state governments, nongovernmental organizations (NGOs), and academic and private sector actors.

ASEAN PLUS 3 (APT). This is the consultative grouping of the 10 members of the **Association of Southeast Asian Nations (ASEAN)** and **China**, Japan, and South Korea. Begun in 1997 and institutionalized in 1999, APT meetings regularly take place at summit, ministerial, and senior official levels, with the goal of deepening East Asian political, economic, and social cooperation. In its exclusion of the United States, the APT format has some resemblance to former Malaysian prime minister **Mahathir Mohammad**'s stillborn **East Asian Economic Group (EAEG)**.

ASEAN REGIONAL FORUM (ARF). The ASEAN Regional Forum is a foreign ministerial meeting of states in the Asia Pacific region. In addition to the 10 members of the **Association of Southeast Asian Nations (ASEAN)**, the members are ASEAN's 10 official dialogue partners (Australia, Canada, **China**, the European Union, India, Japan, New Zealand, Russia, South Korea, and the United States) plus Bangladesh, **East Timor**, Mongolia, North Korea, Pakistan, Papua New Guinea, and Sri Lanka. The ARF ministerial meeting follows the ASEAN annual foreign ministers' meeting and postministerial conferences (PMC) with its dialogue partners. ARF's purpose is to foster dialogue on issues of regional peace and security and to make contributions to confidence building and preventive diplomacy. For the United States, ARF provides an additional diplomatic arena in which to address regional issues of political and security interest such as the **war on terror**, weapons of mass destruction, and transnational crime.

American participation in ARF was a result of President **William J. Clinton**'s reversal of long-standing U.S. reluctance to multilateralize its security policy in the region. The inaugural ARF was held in Bangkok on 25 July 1994, at which U.S. Secretary of State **Warren Christopher** was missing. Beginning with the ninth ARF in 2002, military and defense officials from the member states meet the day before the foreign ministers. In an organizational innovation, the official "Track I" governmental level of ARF is linked to unofficial "Track II" nongovernmental ARF support groups through the **Council for Security Cooperation in the Asia–Pacific (CSCAP)**. The ARF is often criticized as just another "talk shop." In order to give it a more concrete focus, moving away from "seminars to actual cooperation," the United States proposed at the 14th ARF meeting in 2007 the formation of an ARF-sponsored joint disaster relief force. The U.S. initiative, however, was thrust into the background by the absence of Secretary of State **Condoleezza Rice** from the session. She had also skipped the 2005 session.

ASEAN–UNITED STATES ENHANCED PARTNERSHIP. On 18 November 2005, following a meeting between President **George W. Bush** and seven heads of government from the **Association of Southeast Asian Nations (ASEAN)** attending the annual **Asia–Pacific Economic Cooperation (APEC)** Summit meeting in Busan, South Korea, a "Vision Statement on the ASEAN–U.S. Enhanced Partnership" was released. It called for the ASEAN foreign ministers and economic ministers to develop with the American secretary of state and the **United States Trade Representative (USTR)** a plan of action for the implementation of the partnership. It envisioned a comprehensive and action-oriented intensification of U.S.–ASEAN cooperative activities in all sectors of international relations: political, security, economic, and social. Discussions to this end had been underway since the announcement of the U.S. **Enterprise for ASEAN Initiative (EAI)** and the **ASEAN Cooperation Plan (ACP)** in 2002 and were accelerated in June 2005 at the official ASEAN–U.S. dialogue meeting, followed by the September 2005 meeting between ASEAN foreign ministers and Secretary of State **Condoleezza Rice**.

Following the announcement of the "Vision Statement," U.S. officials and ASEAN counterparts worked on developing a program of action to deepen the ASEAN–U.S. relationship. On 27 July 2006, a "Framework Document" for a plan of action was ceremonially signed by Secretary Rice and the ASEAN foreign ministers. A month later, the first fruits of the "enhanced partnership" were realized with the signing of an agreement by USTR Susan Schwab and her ASEAN ministerial counterparts to work toward the conclusion of an ASEAN–U.S. regional **trade and investment framework agreement (TIFA)** as the first step toward a regional **free trade agreement (FTA)**. Although the explicit goals of the enhanced interaction are functional and technical, the background is political. For both ASEAN and the United States, the strategic context is the balance of power in the region. Of ASEAN's major dialogue partners, only the United States did not have an overarching political/economic framework within which its various activities could be given regional policy integration. The major concern on both the U.S. and ASEAN sides was the perception that the United States, in its concentration on the **war on terror**, was allowing China to undermine the U.S.'s soft-power presence in the region.

ASIA FOUNDATION. The Asia Foundation, established in 1954 and headquartered in San Francisco, is a grant-seeking/grant-giving non-profit organization that has operated to promote democracy, governance capabilities, and civil society in the Asian region. In addition to grants from private foundations, corporations, and individuals, the Asia Foundation is also funded for specific programs by multilateral development agencies such as the **Asian Development Bank (ADB)** and receives specific program funding from the U.S. **Agency for International Development (USAID)** and the **State Department**. It also receives an annual appropriation from Congress. Of the major U.S. private foundations and other nongovernmental organizations (NGOs) operating in Southeast Asia, the Asia Foundation's programs are the most obviously complementary to U.S. official developmental goals in the region. The foundation has representative offices and programs in six Southeast Asian countries: **Cambodia**, **East Timor**, **Indonesia**, the **Philippines**, **Thailand**, and **Vietnam.** The largest Southeast Asian programming by the foundation is in Indonesia, where its current emphasis on Islam and civil society includes support for over 30 Muslim NGOs. Although not directly related to the **war on terror**, the effort is to help give Islam a key role in Indonesia's democratization.

ASIA PACIFIC CENTER FOR STRATEGIC STUDIES (APCSS). Created in 1995 and based in Honolulu, Hawaii, the Asia–Pacific Center for Strategic Studies is tasked by the **United States Pacific Command (USPACOM)**. The APCSS offers courses, conferences, and outreach programs on regional and global security issues of concern for executive level military and civilian officers of the national defense establishments of the countries of the Pacific Basin region. In its first decade it had 3,000 professional course alumni and nearly 7,000 conference participants.

ASIA–PACIFIC ECONOMIC COOPERATION (APEC). This is an intergovernmental forum of 21 "member economies" established at a November 1989 ministerial meeting in Canberra, Australia, to promote economic growth in the Asia Pacific region. The founding members were the then six **Association of Southeast Asian Nations (ASEAN)** members: Australia, Canada, Republic of Korea, Japan,

New Zealand, and the United States. To these have been added Chile, People's Republic of **China**, Hong Kong, Mexico, Papua New Guinea, Peru, Russia, Taiwan, and ASEAN member **Vietnam**. ASEAN members **Cambodia, Laos**, and **Burma** are not APEC members, nor is **East Timor**. APEC's secretariat is headquartered in **Singapore**. Organizationally, it is a form of loose regionalism without binding commitments, and decision making is by consensus. APEC's membership is frozen until at least 2010, which leaves out not only four Southeast Asian states but also, and significantly for East Asian regionalism, India.

Since 1993, APEC's annual ministerial meeting has been accompanied by a leaders' meeting. The first APEC summit, held at Blake Island, Washington, in November 1993, symbolized America's structural commitment to regionalism as enunciated in President **William J. Clinton**'s earlier call for a **Pacific Community**. The Blake Island "vision" was one of "stability, security, and prosperity" for the peoples of the Asia Pacific. This was followed in 1994 by the Bogor, **Indonesia** summit hosted by President **Suharto**. Indonesia's endorsement of APEC's "open regionalism" was a rebuff to Malaysian prime minister **Mahathir Mohammad**, who had proposed an alternative **East Asian Economic Group (EAEG)** that would exclude the United States and other non-Asia–Pacific basin nations. The **Bogor Declaration** set APEC's goal as free and open **trade** and **investment** in the Asia Pacific region by 2010 for industrialized economies and 2020 for the developing economies. APEC's original agenda has been expanded to include counterterrorism, transnational crime, narcotics, and disease. Washington considers the APEC summit to be the highest level U.S. presidential commitment to East and Southeast Asian regionalism since it is excluded from the **East Asia Summit (EAS)**.

ASIA–PACIFIC FREE TRADE AREA (APFTA). A new Japan-backed effort to build an **East Asian Free Trade Area (EAFTA)** that would exclude the United States led President **George W. Bush** at the 2006 **Asia–Pacific Economic Cooperation (APEC)** summit to push the organization to study the creation of an Asia–Pacific Free Trade Area. This would build on the existing APEC's **Bogor Declaration** on free trade and open regionalism as opposed to the exclusionary regionalism. The APEC leaders agreed to commission a feasibility study.

ASIA SOCIETY. The Asia Society is America's largest educational and cultural institution dedicated to strengthening and deepening relations between Asia and the United States. Founded in 1956 by John D. Rockefeller III, the Asia Society is headquartered in New York, with centers in Washington, Houston, Los Angeles, San Francisco, Hong Kong, Shanghai, Manila, Melbourne, and Mumbai. Although nongovernmental, Asia Society platforms are used frequently for major addresses by senior ministers and heads of state visiting the United States. It is also a venue for American officials to speak to policy issues.

ASIAN–AFRICAN CONFERENCE (BANDUNG CONFERENCE). Meeting in the Indonesian city of Bandung in April 1955, leaders from 29 African and Asian countries gathered in a search for peaceful coexistence in a world threatened by Great Power conflict. Although the countries represented different security orientations— pro-Western, communist, neutralist—they did have the political cement of anti-imperialism. From Southeast Asia, the **Philippines**, **Thailand**, and **Republic of Vietnam (South Vietnam)** were linked to the United States through the **Southeast Asia Treaty Organization (SEATO)**. **Indonesia** and **Burma** were neutralists. The **Democratic Republic of Vietnam (North Vietnam)** was communist, and **Laos** and **Cambodia**, although passive protocol states under SEATO, were neutralist-inclined. President **Dwight D. Eisenhower**'s administration viewed the Bandung conference darkly, suspecting the motives of its primary sponsors, Nehru of India, **Sukarno** of Indonesia, **Sihanouk** of Cambodia, and **U Nu** of Burma, all of whom were out of favor in Washington.

The final communiqué of the Bandung Conference called for economic, cultural, and political cooperation among the peoples of Africa and Asia. It condemned colonialism as an evil and called for self-determination of all dependent peoples. It gratified host country Indonesia by specifically supporting Indonesia's claim in the **West New Guinea dispute**. The most lasting achievement of the conference was the setting forth of 10 principles for peaceful coexistence, known as the **Bandung Principles**, which, together with the Charter of the **United Nations**, form the normative bedrock, if not the reality, of Southeast Asian international relations. The conferees finessed the problem of Great Power alignment in Bandung principle number five, "respect for the right of each nation to defend itself singly or collectively in conformity with the Charter of the United Nations," by adding the codicil principle six, "abstention from the use of arrangements of collective defense to serve the particular interests of any of the big powers." At Bandung, the seeds were laid for the 1961 Belgrade meeting that launched the **Nonaligned Movement (NAM)**. The Bandung Conference's importance to Indonesia has been signified by two anniversary Asian–African conferences, in 1985 and 2005.

ASIAN DEVELOPMENT BANK (ADB). The Asian Development Bank, established in 1966, is a multilateral development lending institution headquartered in Manila, the **Philippines**. It has 66 member countries—47 regional states and 19 outside the region, including the United States. Its project lending totals more than $5 billion a year. Its largest single project loan ever of $1.2 billion was made in 2007 for a highway linking Hanoi in Vietnam to Kunming in China's Yunnan Province. The United States and Japan are the largest financial backers of the ADB. Each has capital subscriptions of $15.781 million, which gives them each 12.942 percent voting power. Japan has always provided the president of the ADB. American interests in the ADB are represented on the ADB Board of Directors through the U.S. Directors Office, headed by an American ambassador. It is the task of the U.S director to see that U.S. views are expressed and reflected in ADB decisions. In more recent years, these views have come to include environmental and other nontraditional criteria for lending.

ASIAN VALUES. In the 1990s, under attack from the United States and other Western liberal democracies on issues of political and **human rights**, there emerged in Southeast Asia a cultural defense or justification of "soft-authoritarianism" in which so-called Asian values were invoked. It was claimed that these values, emphasizing social harmony, political order, respect for authority, consensus, and the collective good, underpinned economic development in Southeast Asia. The intellectual drive for the Asian values debate came from **Singapore** academics and officials and seemed to reflect Prime Minister **Lee Kuan Yew**'s vision of Singapore's economic and political requirements.

ASSOCIATION OF SOUTHEAST ASIAN NATIONS (ASEAN). The Association of Southeast Asian Nations was established on 8 August 1967 by the **Bangkok Declaration** issued by the foreign ministers of **Indonesia**, the **Philippines**, **Singapore**, and **Thailand**, and the deputy prime minister of **Malaysia**. It is the highest-level regional multilateral structure with which the United States engages in Southeast Asia. Its original stated purpose was to promote regional cooperation in functional economic, social, cultural, technical, scientific, and administrative spheres in order to further the common goal of a prosperous and peaceful community of nations in Southeast Asia. From the ASEAN core five, the grouping has expanded to a Southeast Asia inclusive 10, not including prospective member **East Timor**. **Brunei** joined at independence in 1984, **Vietnam** became a member in 1995, **Laos** and **Burma (Myanmar)** in 1997, and **Cambodia** in 1999. The expansion of ASEAN has not been without problems. What are called the CLMV countries (Cambodia, Laos, Myanmar, and Vietnam) do not share many of the political and economic commonalities that originally united the founding members.

ASEAN is organized as a voluntary association of sovereign nations in which decision making is by consensus. Its chair rotates annually among the ASEAN states by alphabetical order. ASEAN escaped a diplomatic crisis when Myanmar (Burma) gave up its turn to be chair for 2006 in the face of a threatened U.S. and European boycott of the postministerial meetings with ASEAN's dialogue partners because of Burma's **human rights** record. The Philippines, next in alphabetical line, took its place. At their November 2007 summit meeting, the ASEAN heads of state adopted a new Charter of the Association of Southeast Asian Nations conferring legal personality on ASEAN as an intergovernmental organization. The ASEAN charter was an effort to translate the norms and values of the organization into rules. Although the charter espouses democracy and human rights, there are no compliance mechanisms and the core commitments to sovereignty and noninterference in the affairs of members suggest that no real change in the operational code will take place.

ASEAN is loosely structured with no central executive authority. Under the new charter the supreme policy-making body is the ASEAN Summit of heads of states. It will meet biannually and if necessary on an ad hoc basis. Below the summit, an ASEAN Coordinating Council comprised of the ASEAN foreign ministers will manage ASEAN affairs in general and coordinate the work of three ASEAN Community Councils: the ASEAN Political-Security Community Council, the ASEAN Economic Community Council, and the ASEAN Socio-Cultural Community Council. The community councils will have under their purview the relevant ASEAN Sectoral Ministerial Bodies such as the ASEAN finance ministers, environmental ministers, health ministers, etc. The work of ASEAN is supported by a secretariat headed by the ASEAN Secretary-General, who is appointed for five years with ministerial rank on a basis of alphabetical rotation. Surin Pitsuwan, a former Thai foreign minister, took office on 1 January 2008,

Although politics and security were not expressly mentioned in the Bangkok Declaration as areas of cooperation, ASEAN's creation was the political reaction of the noncommunist states of Southeast Asia to the prospect of a widening sphere of communist influence in **Indochina**, the Sino–Soviet struggle, and their own domestic communist insurgencies. The collective political and security aspects of ASEAN were explicitly addressed in the 1971 Kuala Lumpur Declaration of a Southeast Asia **Zone of Peace, Freedom, and Neutrality (ZOPFAN)** that in 1991 also embraced a **Southeast Asia Nuclear Weapons Free Zone (SEANWFZ)**. The organization's political underpinning was further highlighted in its 1976 Bali Summit's Declaration of ASEAN Concord calling for political solidarity and coordination of positions, as well as the **Treaty of Amity and Cooperation in Southeast Asia (TAC)**, which is basically a Southeast Asia nonaggression treaty. ASEAN's capacity as a political/security collective was demonstrated in the **Third Indochina War**—Vietnam's invasion and occupation of Cambodia—when the grouping insisted on Vietnamese withdrawal and self-determination by the people of an independent and neutral Cambodia. Working in concert with the United States and **China**, ASEAN words were backed by coordinated diplomacy and material support for the **Khmer resistance** forces politically united in the ASEAN-sponsored **Coalition Government of Democratic Kampuchea (CGDK)**.

With the resolution of the Cambodia problem in 1991, the ending of the Cold War, and full normalization of its member nations' relations with the People's Republic of **China**, ASEAN returned to the functional interests of the Bangkok Declaration with a series of intra-ASEAN economic and cooperation schemes, such as an ASEAN Free Trade Area (AFTA), ASEAN Framework Agreement on services, ASEAN Investment Area, and ASEAN Currency Swap Agreement. ASEAN has also negotiated or is negotiating broad, comprehensive strategic frameworks for free trade with China, Japan, India, and Australia and New Zealand. A pattern of East and Southeast Asian economic integration is emerging in the **ASEAN Plus 3 (APT)** grouping of ASEAN plus China, Japan, and South Korea.

ASEAN has become a Southeast Asian regional diplomatic caucus in which the members have a minimum consensus on policy positions from which to engage their external interlocutors. Although most significant policy decisions and transactions are directed to and implemented in bilateral settings, the regionalist context represented by ASEAN has become a very important part of international relations and diplomacy in Southeast Asia. The United States has consistently affirmed its strong national interest in promoting relations with ASEAN as a force for stability and prosperity in Southeast Asia, even though ASEAN's image has been tarnished in the West by its inability to effect democratic change in Burma. The structured framework for ASEAN's regionalist relations with external partners is the official ASEAN plus 1 dialogue process, in which issues of common interest are discussed.

The United States is one of the 10 official dialogue partners of ASEAN. The others are Australia, Canada, China, the European Union, India, Japan, New Zealand, Russia, and South Korea. Each of the dialogues is coordinated by one ASEAN country. For the decade 2000–2009 the dialogue coordinators for the United States have been or will be Vietnam, 2000–2003; Thailand, 2003–2006; and Singapore, 2006–2009. Since 2000, the dialogues with the Western partners have included the issues of democracy and human rights in Burma. The dialogues take place at different levels of interaction. The primary consultations take place in a postministerial conference (PMC) immediately following the ASEAN Foreign Ministers Meetings. The PMC has two parts: an ASEAN plus 10 and then 10 ASEAN plus 1 sessions. These meetings are ordinarily attended by the American secretary of state. There was consternation in 2005 when Secretary of State **Condoleezza Rice** absented herself as a sign of disapproval about Burma's upcoming chairmanship of ASEAN. She sent her deputy secretary instead. Rice smoothed it over in September 2005, when she met the ASEAN foreign ministers in New York at the **United Nations**. The PMC is followed by the security-focused **ASEAN Regional Forum (ARF)**. There is a functional U.S.–ASEAN dialogue at the assistant secretary of state level that alternates between Washington, D.C., and the capital of the ASEAN dialogue coordinator. Among other items, the dialogue reviews aspects of ASEAN—U.S. cooperation in various programs and initiatives, including the 2002 **ASEAN Cooperation Plan (ACP)** and **Enterprise for ASEAN Initiative (EAI)**. An intensification of U.S.–ASEAN cooperation is envisioned in the plan for an **ASEAN–United States Enhanced Partnership** announced in November 2005. One of the fruits of the Enhanced Partnership was the signing of an ASEAN–U.S. **trade and investment framework agreement (TIFA)** in August 2006. Since 11 September 2001 the **war on terror** has become a significant area of U.S.–ASEAN dialogue and cooperation. This was formally enunciated in the 2002 ASEAN–United States Joint Declaration for Cooperation to Combat International Terrorism.

The one area of ASEAN activity with external partners that the United States has not been part of is ASEAN's formal summitry. The annual ASEAN Summit has been expanded to include ASEAN plus 1 summits with China, Japan, India, Russia, and South Korea. This became the core of the first **East Asia Summit (EAS)** in 2005, which also included Australia and New Zealand. All of ASEAN's summit partners are signatories to the TAC. The United States is not. The American president has other opportunities to meet with ASEAN counterparts in bilateral visits or on the sidelines of international gatherings. President **George W. Bush** met with the seven ASEAN heads of government at the 2005 **Asia–Pacific Economic Cooperation (APEC)** meeting in Busan, Korea, which is where American enhanced partnership with ASEAN was unveiled, and again at the 2006

APEC summit in Hanoi, Vietnam and the 2007 APEC summit in Sydney, Australia. The United States now views these informal summits as an annual adjunct to the APEC gathering even though they do not include all of the ASEAN leaders.

A new urgency has entered U.S. policy toward ASEAN as a result of the perception that China is gaining greater influence in Southeast Asia, challenging historic American primacy. Both the American reluctance to sign the TAC and its uncompromising stance toward Burma—an ASEAN member—have acted as a brake on U.S. regional relations, in contrast to ASEAN's other partners, particularly China. The American insistence that ASEAN is important for U.S. policy in Southeast Asia was again thrown into doubt in mid-2007 when Secretary Rice skipped the PMC dialogue and the ARF. A formal U.S.–ASEAN summit had been projected in 2007 to commemorate the 30th anniversary of the ASEAN–U.S. dialogue but was postponed by the United States. In both cases the reason given was preoccupation with issues in the Middle East. President Bush sought to regain some of the lost ground in his meeting with his ASEAN counterparts on the sidelines at the 2007 APEC summit in Sydney, Australia. He took the opportunity to announce that the United States would name an ambassador to ASEAN. President Bush also invited the ASEAN leaders to a U.S.–ASEAN summit to be held in Texas in 2008. It was suggested in late 2007 that his invitation might be withdrawn following the Burmese junta's September crackdown on monks and democratic protesters.

AUNG SAN (1915–1947). Bogyoke (General) Aung San is **Burma**'s national hero. He was a pre–World War II nationalist activist against British colonial rule. Fearing arrest by British authorities, Aung San slipped away to Japan in 1941 for military training. He was the leading figure of the "Thirty Comrades," who formed the core of the Burma Independence Army (BIA). Returning to Burma with the Japanese invaders, Aung San became a major general in the renamed Burma National Army (BNA) and minister of war in the Japanese-sponsored Burmese government. Recognizing that the puppet government had no real independence, Aung San broke with the Japanese, and in March 1945 took the Burmese army into revolt in alliance with the returning British. After the war, he became the leader of the

Anti-Fascist People's Freedom League (AFPFL), the mass nationalist party. Elections swept the AFPFL with Aung San at its head into control of the government that was preparing to take power when Great Britain relinquished sovereignty in 1947. One month before independence, Aung San was shot to death in a cabinet meeting, supposedly at the instigation of a political enemy. His assassination made him a political martyr whose legacy as the father of the nation has been appropriated by his daughter, **Aung San Suu Kyi**.

AUNG SAN SUU KYI (1945–). Iconic symbol of Burmese resistance to the ruling military junta, the **State Peace and Development Council (SPDC)**, Aung San Suu Kyi became the touchstone for the post-1988 American economic sanctions regime against **Burma**. She is the daughter of General **Aung San**, the Burmese nationalist hero who was assassinated in 1947 on the eve of Burma's independence. Her status as the daughter of the martyred Aung San gave her initial domestic political prominence. Internationally, it was her steely resolve to defy the junta and refuse to give up the cause of democracy or to go into exile that made her a **human rights** celebrity. She was the 1991 Nobel Peace Prize winner and has been awarded a U.S. Presidential Medal of Freedom.

In 1988, Aung San Suu Kyi was living in London. She completed her university education in Great Britain and was married to distinguished British academic Michael Aris, with whom she had two sons. She returned to Rangoon that year to take care of her ailing mother, where she was caught up in the popular uprising against the junta. She became the leading figure in the **National League for Democracy (NLD)** and led the NLD into the 1990 elections that had been forced on the junta. The NLD won the elections, and the junta responded with a crushing martial law regime. Aung San Suu Kyi was placed under arrest and imprisoned until 1995, was rearrested in 2000–2002, was released and rearrested again in 2003, and was moved from prison to remain under house arrest. While she was a prisoner of conscience, her husband died of cancer, and she herself has had major health problems. The suppression of democracy and continued detention of Aung San Suu Kyi not only prevent normal bilateral relation between the United States and Burma, but have also negatively affected U.S relations with the **Association of Southeast**

Asian Nations (ASEAN), of which Burma is a member. The fate of Aung San Suu Kyi was thrust again into the global limelight by the 2007 antijunta demonstrations by Buddhist monks. In December 2007, the U.S. House of Representatives voted unanimously to award her the Congressional Gold Medal.

AVIAN FLU. *See* PANDEMIC AND INFECTIOUS DISEASES.

– B –

BA'ASYIR, ABU BAKAR (1938–). A fiery Indonesian Islamic cleric, Abu Bakar Ba'asyir is the alleged spiritual leader of the radical Islamic terrorist movement **Jema'ah Islamiyah (JI)**, which was the main target of the **war on terror** in Southeast Asia. Born in East Java, **Indonesia**, Ba'asyir's radical message calling for an Islamic state led to jail in the 1970s under Indonesian President **Suharto** and then years of exile in **Malaysia** until the 1998 fall of Suharto. Many of the JI terrorists had attended Ba'asyir's Islamic boarding school in Central Java. Although claiming that the JI did not even exist, Ba'asyir publicly praised al-Qaeda's attacks against the United States and other Western targets. As a senior member of the Indonesian Mujahidin Council, he had a national platform for his radical message. Under heavy pressure from the United States, Australia, and other Western powers, Indonesia arrested Ba'asyir shortly after the October 2002 **Bali bombings** and put him on trial for treason. He was found guilty in 2003, although the further charge of leading JI was not proven.

To the astonishment and dismay of the United States and Australia, the treason conviction was overturned by a higher court. Indonesia rearrested him in connection with the Bali bombings and other attacks. In the second trial, he was found guilty of being involved in an "evil conspiracy" in giving his approval to bombings even if he was not directly involved. After serving 25 months of a 30-month sentence, he was released on 14 June 2006 to reclaim his post as chair of the Indonesian Mujahidin Council and his advocacy of an Islamic state. The 2002 conspiracy conviction was overturned by the Indonesian Supreme Court in 2006, effectively clearing

Ba'asyir of any involvement in the terrorist attacks. Foreign and Indonesian intelligence officials still believe Ba'asyir is the inspiration of JI. Ba'asyir's supporters argue that he has been persecuted by the Indonesian government acting on behest of the United States. Indonesian prosecutors blamed the U.S. refusal to allow Indonesian investigators to interrogate captured JI terrorists **Omar al-Faruq** and **Hambali** for the weakness of their case against Ba'asyir.

BAKER, JAMES A., III (1930–). James Baker was one of the most influential officials in the administrations of Presidents **Ronald Reagan** and **George H. W. Bush**. He was Reagan's White House chief of staff (1981–1985) and then secretary of the treasury (1985–1988). President Bush named him secretary of state (1989–1992) and then his chief of staff (1992–1993). As secretary of state, backed by Assistant Secretary of State for East Asian and Pacific Affairs **Richard Solomon**, he promoted a peaceful settlement of the **Third Indochina War**, endorsing the diplomacy that led to a **comprehensive political settlement of the Cambodia conflict**. Baker made the opening statement for the United States at the July 1989 **Paris International Conference on Cambodia (PICC)**. He also furthered the process of **normalization of relations with Vietnam**, meeting with the Vietnamese foreign minister **Nguyen Co Thach** in October 1991, presenting him with a "road map" to normalization.

Baker deemed the **Association of Southeast Asian Nations (ASEAN)** to be one of the most constructive and successful regional groupings in Asia or Africa. He attended the annual ASEAN post-ministerial conferences (PMC) from 1989 to 1992, successively in **Brunei, Jakarta, Singapore**, and Kuala Lumpur. Baker was a proponent of liberalized **trade** in East Asia and strongly opposed Prime Minister **Mahathir Mohammad** of **Malaysia**'s idea of an **East Asian Economic Group** that would exclude the United States to rival the U.S.-backed **Asia–Pacific Economic Cooperation (APEC)** format.

BALESTIER, JOSEPH B. (1785–1852). Commissioned as the first American consul in **Singapore** from 1837 to 1852, Joseph Balestier was appointed by President Zachary Taylor in 1849 as a special diplomatic agent to secure U.S. interests in **Siam (Thailand)**, Cochin China (Annam [**Vietnam**]), and various principalities in the East Indies. Taylor credentialed Balestier as his envoy and minister to "South Eastern Asia." This may be the earliest American geopolitical designation of the region as such. In Siam his task was to persuade the king to abide fully by the terms of the 1833 **Roberts Treaty**. The Siamese ignored his overtures, and it was not until the **Harris Treaty** of 1856 that the U.S. relationship was put on a par with the British. In Annam, Balestier delivered a letter to the emperor from President Taylor. In it, Taylor apologized for the use of weapons by the U.S. frigate *Constitution* at Tourane (Danang) in 1845. The president warned, however, that if the emperor did not accept the apology and acted vengefully, the United States would make war on him. Balestier was no more successful in negotiating a commercial treaty with the Annamite ruler than **Edmund Roberts** had been 15 years earlier. He was more successful in **Brunei**, where he obtained a U.S.–Brunei Treaty of Friendship, Commerce, and Navigation in 1850, something the captain of the *Constitution* had been unable to do five years earlier. *See also* BALESTIER TREATY.

BALESTIER TREATY, 1850. This was the Treaty of Friendship, Commerce, and Navigation between the United States and the Sultanate of **Brunei** negotiated by American special diplomatic agent **Joseph Balestier**, the U.S. consul in **Singapore**. This followed the failed effort by the captain of the U.S. frigate *Constitution* to secure a treaty in 1845 and the Anglo–Brunei treaty of 1847, in which the sultan promised no concessions to any other power beyond what had been secured by Britain. Any Bruneian hopes that the Americans might balance the British or the predatory demands of James Brooke, the "White Raja" of Sarawak, were not realized.

BALI BOMBINGS. On 12 October 2002, bombs went off at two nightclubs at Kuta Beach on the island of Bali, **Indonesia**'s tourist mecca. The clubs were crowded with young people and 202 were killed, the majority Australian. This was the first, and perhaps the most shocking, of the bomb attacks or threats of attacks on Western targets in Indonesia by radical Islamist terrorists linked to the shadowy network of the **Jema'ah Islamiyah (JI)**. The Bali blast demonstrated to Indonesia not only that it was not immune to terrorism, but also that it was at the epicenter of the Southeast Asian front of the

war on terror. The Indonesian government had previously shrugged off efforts to prod it to greater counterterrorism measures and international cooperation. Shocked by the Bali bombings and spurred by Australia and the United States, the Indonesian government investigated, arrested, and tried the perpetrators. In the context of American policy, the Indonesian government took great pains to distinguish between its pursuit of the Bali bombers and a wider alliance with the United States in the broader global confrontation. Good police work, with foreign assistance, led to the arrest and conviction of the actual bombers. The alleged mastermind and JI's spiritual leader **Abu Bakar Ba'asyir** was cleared of the charges.

BALIKATAN. Translated into English as "Shoulder to Shoulder," Balikatan is the name of annual **Philippine**–U.S. military exercises designed to enhance joint/combined planning, combat readiness, and interoperability. Based on the 1951 U.S.–Philippine **Mutual Defense Treaty (MDT)**, Balikatan began in 1991. It was suspended in 1995 after the legal framework for U.S. forces in the Philippines was put in doubt by the rejection of a new U.S.–Philippine **Military Bases Agreement (MBA)** and a status of forces agreement (SOFA). It recommenced in 2001 after the signing of a U.S.–Philippine **Visiting Forces Agreement (VFA)**. Balikatan is the largest of the more than 30 annual military exercises carried out between the United States and the Philippines. In addition to the directly military operations, the program includes civic action and humanitarian activities. The military aspects have been redirected from conventional warfare to the **war on terror**.

BALL, GEORGE W. (1909–1994). George Ball, undersecretary of state from 1961 to 1966, was one of the first senior American officials to question the wisdom of the U.S. military escalation in **South Vietnam**. Ball was a protagonist in the American support of the 1963 **Diem coup**. The **State Department** cable to the American ambassador in Saigon, 24 August 1963, expressing no objection to a coup, was sent on Ball's authority as acting secretary of state during Secretary of State **Dean Rusk**'s absence from Washington. Ball's second thoughts about the war after President **John F. Kennedy**'s assassination were conveyed in memos he sent to Rusk, Defense Secretary

Robert McNamara, and National Security Advisor **McGeorge Bundy**. Ball brought his reservations directly to President **Lyndon B. Johnson** in 1965. His particular concern was that an aggressive American posture would trigger Chinese and even Soviet intervention. His dovish stance did not change policy and he was essentially sidelined. He was briefly U.S. ambassador to the United Nations in 1968, but left government service to assist the presidential campaign of the Democrat nominee Hubert Humphrey.

BANDUNG CONFERENCE. *See* ASIAN–AFRICAN CONFERENCE.

BANDUNG PRINCIPLES. The final communiqué of the 1955 **Asian–African Conference** held in Bandung, **Indonesia**, set forth 10 principles by which nations could live with each other in peaceful cooperation. These are known as the Bandung Principles. They are an expanded version of the 1954 "Five Principles of Peaceful Coexistence" agreed to by **China** and India. The key principles are mutual respect for territorial integrity and sovereignty, nonaggression, mutual noninterference in internal affairs, equality of races and nations, and peaceful settlement of all disputes. Although the historical record shows that the Bandung Principles have been routinely violated in Southeast Asia, they have been at least the declaratory normative basis for Southeast Asia's bilateral and multilateral relations, referenced inter alia in the 1971 Kuala Lumpur Declaration on a Southeast Asian **Zone of Peace, Freedom, and Neutrality (ZOPFAN)**, the 1976 Declaration of ASEAN Concord, and the 1976 **Treaty of Amity and Cooperation in Southeast Asia (TAC)**.

BANGKOK DECLARATION. This is the founding document of the **Association of Southeast Asian Nations (ASEAN)** issued in Bangkok, Thailand, on 8 August 1967 by the foreign ministers of **Indonesia**, the **Philippines**, **Singapore**, and **Thailand**, and the deputy prime minister of **Malaysia**. It called for cooperation in economic, social, cultural, technical, scientific, and administrative fields in order to promote regional peace, progress, and development. Although political and security cooperation were not mentioned, the Bangkok Declaration was a response to both the need to reintegrate post-Sukarno

Indonesia into the region and the uncertainties of the **Indochina** states' future, then engulfed in the **Second Indochina War**. The Bangkok Declaration was not a treaty and put no legal obligations on its members. The organizational structure it laid out was voluntary and did not affect national sovereignty. As ASEAN developed, expanded, and became more structured, the need for a more formal constitutional foundation prompted in 2006 the drafting of an ASEAN Charter to give ASEAN legal personality.

BANGSAMORO. This is translated variously as the "Moro people" or "Moro nation." It is a term demographically embracing the Muslim population of the southern Philippines and politically captures the separatist goals of a Moro state promoted by the **Moro National Liberation Front (MNLF)** and the **Moro Islamic Liberation Front (MILF)**.

BAO DAI (1913–1997). Chief of state of the French-sponsored **State of Vietnam** (1950–1954), Bao Dai was the central figure in the "Bao Dai solution" that hoped to provide a nationalist alternative in **South Vietnam** to **Ho Chi Minh** in **North Vietnam**. Bao Dai was the last emperor of Annam, the French protectorate in Central Vietnam. His rule was proclaimed in 1925 but he ascended the throne only in 1932. He collaborated with the Japanese in their 1944 takeover of **Indochina** and in 1945 abdicated his throne in favor of the **Democratic Republic of Vietnam (DRV)**. He was named the DRV's "supreme advisor" but in 1946 went into self-imposed exile to lead a playboy life on the French Riviera. What Bao Dai brought to the French when they negotiated for his return in 1949 was the legitimacy of traditional indigenous authority, unlike the foreign communism of the **Viet Minh**. Unfortunately for France and the United States, which quickly recognized "His Majesty," as head of state, Bao Dai had neither nationalist credentials nor popular support. He was deposed in 1955 by his strong prime minister **Ngo Dinh Diem** through a referendum. In the run-up to the referendum, while Bao Dai stayed in Paris, Diem's government portrayed him as a debauched, corrupt, pro-French relic of the feudal past. Diem won with more than 98 percent of the vote. Bao Dai remained in French exile. *See also* GULLION, EDMUND A.

BELL ACT, 1946. Originally introduced by Congressman C. Jasper Bell, this legislation, the Philippine Trade Act of 1946, provided for free trade between the United States and the **Philippines** until July 1954. From 1954 to 1974 a graduated tariff regime would be in place. At the end of the regulated period, a normal tariff regime would go into effect. Quotas were applied to certain classes of Philippine exports to the United States, the most important being sugar, rice, and tobacco products. The Philippine currency, the peso, was tied to the dollar at a fully convertible fixed rate that could only be changed by agreement with the United States. A "parity" clause gave American citizens the same rights as Philippine citizens in natural resources development and exploitation and public utilities enterprises. Viewed by Filipino economic nationalists as a kind of neocolonialism, the Bell Act was revised by the 1955 **Laurel–Langley Agreement**.

BELL ECONOMIC SURVEY MISSION, 1950. Responding to a request for increased economic assistance from Philippine President **Elpidio Quirino**, U.S. president **Harry S. Truman**, concerned about misuse of American assistance, dispatched Daniel W. Bell, a former undersecretary of the treasury, to lead an economic mission to the **Philippines**. Its task was to survey the situation and make recommendations on how the Philippines could help itself and how the United States could assist. The mission coincided with the high point of the **Hukbalahap** communist revolt. The Bell report recommended that a program of supervised grants amounting to $250 million over five years be offered conditioned on basic economic, fiscal, and land reforms; a deal to which Quirino agreed in November 1950.

BENSON, GEORGE (1925–2007). A career U.S. Army officer, West Point class of 1945, for more than a decade Colonel George Benson was a critical link between the U.S. embassy in **Indonesia** and the leaders of the Indonesian military in the last years of the government of President **Sukarno** and the formative years of the **Suharto** regime. Benson's first tour (1956–1959) was as assistant army attaché, and after the illness of his superior, essentially the acting attaché. Seconded to the **State Department**, he returned to Jakarta from 1962 to 1965 as a special assistant to the ambassador, at that time **Howard P. Jones**. While giving guidance on civil–military relations, Benson was an important channel to senior Indonesian army leaders. He had a close personal relationship with Lt. General Achmad Yani, the army chief of staff, who had been a classmate of Benson at the U.S. Army Staff and Command School. Yani was one of the generals killed in the 1965 **Indonesian coup**. Benson had left Indonesia at the time of the coup, having been selected for the National War College. Immediately after the coup, he was called to work for Assistant Secretary of State for East Asia and the Pacific **William Bundy** as the United States formulated its policies toward the new, army-led Indonesian government. After commanding a brigade in Vietnam, Col. Benson had a third tour in Indonesia (1969–1972) as the defense attaché, the senior U.S. military officer in the embassy. After retirement he represented Pertamina, the Indonesian national oil company, in its Washington office. Pertamina was led by another Indonesian army friend, Gen. Ibnu Sutowo.

BHUMIBOL ADULYADEJ (KING RAMA IX) (1928–). Ninth king of **Thailand**'s Chakri dynasty, King Bhumibol Adulyadej, or Rama IX, was born in the United States, where his parents were students, and educated in Switzerland. He came to the throne unexpectedly in 1946 at the age of 18 after the mysterious death of his brother, King Ananda. He is the longest serving monarch in the world. For more than 60 years he has been a figure of continuity and stability in the often politically tumultuous Thai state. During his reign, he has conferred legitimacy on military and civilian governments alike, rarely but deftly intervening only in crises that threaten the foundation of the state and monarchy itself. His visits to the United States highlighted the warmth of the Thai–U.S. alliance in the **Second Indochina War**. In a June 1967 state visit to the United States, he met with President **Lyndon B. Johnson** and senior officials to press the United States on its security guarantee and the terms for committing Thai forces to the war in **Vietnam**.

BISSELL, RICHARD M. JR (1910–1994). Working with **Central Intelligence Agency (CIA)** head **Allen Dulles** and Deputy Director of Plans (DDP) **Frank Wisner**, Richard Bissell was a major strategist of the clandestine effort of the United States to overthrow the government of President **Sukarno** of Indonesia from 1955 to the 1958

U.S.-supported **PRRI-Permesta** regional rebellions. Bissell, who had served in the **Office of Strategic Services (OSS)**, was a postwar protégé of **Averell Harriman** and was Marshall Plan administrator in West Germany and then Director of the Economic Cooperation Administration (ECA). Bissell was brought into the CIA by Wisner to coordinate interagency intelligence and run the U-2 program. Dulles selected Bissell to replace Wisner as DDP in 1959 ahead of Wisner's deputy **Richard Helms**, who remained as Bissell's deputy until Bissell's departure from the CIA in 1962 after the Bay of Pigs disaster. Helms then succeeded as DDP. Following the CIA, Bissell headed the Institute for Defence Analysis. His autobiography is *Reflections of a Cold Warrior: From Yalta to the Bay of Pigs*.

BOAT PEOPLE. This is the term used to describe the million or more Vietnamese and ethnic Chinese in **Vietnam** who fled the country between 1975 and 1979. Many did travel by boat, often unseaworthy and overloaded. It is not known how many may have perished at sea either from storms or pirates. There were two waves of **refugee** arrivals: immediately after the fall of the **Republic of Vietnam** and the communist victory and, later, in response to the implementation of the socialist economy as well as the domestic impact of the April 1979 Sino–Vietnamese border war when **China** sought to punish Vietnam for its invasion of **Cambodia**. As the refugees landed in Southeast Asian countries of first asylum, the United Nations High Commissioner for Refugees (UNHCR) played an important role in organizing and managing the refugee camps. The United States was a major financial contributor to the rescue effort. The United States was also prepared to receive the largest number of the "boat people" for resettlement in the United States. The flow of boat people from Vietnam was part of the stimulus for the United States to implement the **Orderly Departure Program (ODP)** for Vietnam.

BOGOR DECLARATION. This was the 15 November 1994 statement by the heads of state of the member countries, including the United States, of the **Asia–Pacific Economic Cooperation (APEC)** forum at its second meeting in Bogor, **Indonesia**. In the declaration, the APEC leaders resolved to liberalize **trade** and **investment** in the Asia Pacific region with a goal of free and open trade by the industrialized economies by the year 2010 and the developing economies by 2020. It was seen essentially as an endorsement of American global trade policy.

BOHLEN, CHARLES E. (1904–1974). Charles "Chip" Bohlen entered the Foreign Service in 1929, to begin a diplomatic career as a Russian specialist. In 1953, he was named ambassador to the Soviet Union after a bruising Senate confirmation battle in which Senator Joseph McCarthy attacked him for his role as an advisor to President Franklin D. Roosevelt at the February 1945 Yalta Conference. As ambassador, Bohlen had serious policy disputes with Secretary of State **John Foster Dulles**. In 1957, Dulles moved him from Russia and Soviet affairs to Manila as ambassador to the **Philippines**, where he served until Dulles's successor **Christian Herter** brought him back to Washington in 1959 as a special assistant on Soviet affairs. He finished his career as ambassador to France. Bohlen's assignment to the Philippines as a kind of exile from the central questions of American foreign policy of the day raised questions about the priority that the Philippines had for the United States and the lack of credibility in Washington of the corrupt government of President **Carlos Garcia**, Garcia's pledges of standing with America in the fight against communism notwithstanding. *See also* BOHLEN–SERRANO AGREEMENTS.

BOHLEN–SERRANO AGREEMENTS. The October 1959 agreements revising the U.S.–Philippines **Mutual Defense Treaty (MDT)** and the **Military Bases Agreement (MBA)** that resulted from negotiations between U.S. ambassador **Charles Bohlen** and Philippine Foreign Affairs Secretary Felizberto Serrano. The agreements provided for the creation of a Mutual Defense Board, the assignment of a Philippine liaison officer to each of the American bases, prior consultation on the introduction of long-range missiles, and operational uses of the bases outside of the MDT and the **Southeast Asia Treaty Organization (SEATO)**. The last had become relevant when it was learned that the **Central Intelligence Agency (CIA)**'s clandestine bombing missions in support of the **PRRI–Permesta** rebels in **Indonesia** had flown from **Clark Air Base**. The agreement also shortened the base lease from 99 years to 25.

BOLKIAH, HASSANAL (1946–). Head of state and the government of **Brunei**, Sultan Haji Hassanal Bolkiah came to the throne in 1967, the 29th in a line going back to the 15th century. The sultan is personally one of the wealthiest men in the world, with a fortune estimated by *Forbes Magazine* in 2004 at $14.3 billion. He is concurrently absolute monarch, prime minister, minister of defense, and finance minister. The sultan had some earlier notoriety in the United States when it was revealed in 1987 that he had been the source of a clandestine $10 million contribution to support the Contras in Central America, illegally solicited by American officials. He met President **George W. Bush** in Washington in December 2002 as the United States sought to mobilize Southeast Asia to support the **war on terror**.

BORDER PATROL POLICE (BPP). Under the control of General **Phao Sriyanond**, **Thailand**'s Border Patrol Police was developed during the 1950s with the assistance of the **Central Intelligence Agency (CIA)**. It was one of the sources of Phao's power in his rivalry with General **Thanom Kittikachorn**. Originally charged with border security, the BPP was also engaged in narcotics trafficking. In the 1970s, it functioned as the primary paramilitary force for internal security and counterinsurgency. Enjoying the patronage King **Bhumibol**, the BPP exercised a high degree of autonomy from other police units. *See also* KMT–BURMA CRISIS; LAIR, JAMES W.; SECRET WAR

BOSWORTH, STEPHEN W. (1939–). A career Foreign Service Officer, Stephen Bosworth had been ambassador to Tunisia and director of the **State Department**'s Policy Planning Office before becoming the U.S. ambassador to the **Philippines** during the critical years 1984 to 1987. Ambassador Bosworth had to position the United States between the mounting opposition to the government of **Ferdinand Marcos** after the 1983 assassination of **Benigno Aquino** and American national interests in a stable Philippines and U.S. basing rights. In the turmoil of the 1986 "people's power" **EDSA revolution**, Ambassador Bosworth warned Marcos against the use of force. He counseled the beleaguered Philippine president that Washington wanted to see a peaceful transition to a new government. In this he was backed by Secretary of State **George Shultz** and Undersecretary of State for Political Affairs **Michael Armacost**, himself a former ambassador to the Philippines. After the installation of President **Corazon Aquino**, Bosworth's task was to demonstrate that the United States unequivocally supported the Aquino government despite the past American support for the Marcos government. Bosworth later served as American ambassador to South Korea. In retirement, he became dean of the Tufts University Fletcher School of Law and Diplomacy.

BOUN OUM (1912–1980). Head of the royal family of Champassak in the southern region of **Laos**, Prince Boun Oum renounced his claim to the throne of a separate principality of Champassak in 1946 in favor of the quasi-autonomous unified Kingdom of Laos, with Luang Prabang's King **Sisavangvong** as head of state. Boun Oum served as the kingdom's prime minister between 1948 and 1950. He became prime minister again in December 1960 when the military forces of U.S.-backed **Phoumi Nosavan** drove the neutralist government of **Souvanna Phouma** from the capital, Vientiane. Boun Oum retired from politics in 1962 with the establishment of the second Laos **coalition government** as part of the implementation of the **Geneva Accords** of 1962 ending the 1960–1962 **Laotian crisis**. He died in Paris exile.

BOWLES, CHESTER B. (1901–1986). A liberal internationalist, Chester Bowles served in various capacities in the administrations of Presidents Franklin D. Roosevelt, **Harry S. Truman**, **John F. Kennedy**, and **Lyndon B. Johnson**. He was twice U.S. ambassador to India (1950–1952 and 1963–1968). During his second India tour, in January 1968, he was sent on a special diplomatic mission to **Cambodia**. There he began discussions with Prince **Norodom Sihanouk**'s government leading to the restoration of diplomatic relations between Cambodia and the United States that had been broken in 1965. The minimum that the Cambodians wanted was a pledge by the United States and its allies to honor Cambodia's borders. The American concern was the presence of **Viet Cong** and People's Army of Vietnam (PAVN) forces in Cambodian sanctuaries. Significantly, during the discussions Sihanouk made an ambiguous unofficial statement about looking the other way if the United States should engage in "hot pursuit." This statement was interpreted by National Security Advisor **Henry Kissinger** in the administration of President **Richard M. Nixon** as permission for the 1969 secret operation "Menu" B-52 bombings of southeastern Cambodia.

BROWN, WINTHROP G. (1907–1987). A career Foreign Service Officer, Winthrop Brown presented his credentials as American ambassador to **Laos** in June 1960. At that time the government was under the control of U.S.-backed military strongman **Phoumi Nosavan**. In August 1960, the **Kong Le** coup restored neutralist **Souvanna Phouma**, the leader of the first Laos **coalition government**, to power. Brown, arguing that a second coalition government was probably the only way to avoid a civil war, counseled support for the new Souvanna government. The United States, although claiming to be technically neutral, cut off the monthly cash subsidy it had been paying the Royal Lao Government. Phoumi installed himself in his southern base in Savannakhet. Following the hard line advocated by former ambassador to Laos **Graham Parsons**, now the **Eisenhower** administration's assistant secretary of state for East Asian and Pacific affairs, the United States began massive assistance to Phoumi's forces. The American military and **Central Intelligence Agency (CIA)** pipeline from **Thailand** to Phoumi was facilitated from the U.S. embassy in Bangkok headed by Ambassador **U. Alexis Johnson**. It was left to Ambassador Brown in Vientiane to make this diplomatically legitimate in a "gentleman's agreement" with Souvanna Phouma in which the United States would resume payments of the cash subsidy to the Souvanna-led Royal Lao Government—on the condition it was used only to support neutralist forces, not the communist **Pathet Lao**—in return for Souvanna's agreement to American delivery of assistance to Phoumi's forces in the south. Brown remained in Laos until July 1962, coincidental with the 1962 **Geneva Accords on Laos** and the formation of the second coalition government. He later served as ambassador to the Republic of Korea.

BRUNEI (NEGARA BRUNEI DARSSALAM). The Sultanate of Brunei, at 2,226 square miles (5,765 square kilometers), is about the size of Delaware. Its population is less then 400,000, the smallest of any Southeast Asian state. The capital is Bandar Seri Begawan. The present state is the territorial remnant of a Brunei maritime empire that in the 17th century reached to Manila Bay. Reduced in size by succession struggles and the depredations of European imperialism, the present boundaries were fixed at the end of the 19th century, when in 1888 Brunei became a British protectorate. In 1959, Brunei became self-governing in domestic affairs. It remained outside of Malaysia in 1963 when Great Britain decolonized its remaining Southeast Asian territories. Brunei became independent in 1984 but retained security ties to Great Britain and Australia. At independence Brunei joined the **Association of Southeast Asian Nations (ASEAN)**, hoping thereby to ease relations with Malaysia and **Indonesia**, both of which Brunei suspected had designs on it. Brunei is governed as a Malay Islamic monarchy. Sultan **Hassanal Bolkiah** is both head of state and prime minister. Although a microstate, Brunei is relatively wealthy. It is the fourth largest oil producer in Southeast Asia and the world's ninth largest exporter of liquefied natural gas. Japan is the main customer for Brunei's resources, although the United States takes 14 percent of the oil exports. Brunei is strategically situated on the east coast of the island of Borneo facing the **South China Sea** and surrounded on land by the Malaysian state of Sarawak.

The first official contact between Brunei and the United States came in 1845 when the USS *Constitution* called at Brunei. Official diplomatic relations between Brunei and the United States were opened in 1850 when the two countries concluded the **Balestier Treaty of Peace, Friendship, Commerce, and Navigation**. An American consulate operated for a brief period between 1865 and 1867. The United States recognized Brunei's independence from Great Britain on 1 January 1984 and opened its embassy in Bandar Seri Begawan in March 1984. The first high-level contact came with a visit to the sultan by Secretary of State **George Shultz** in 1986. In 1994, the United States and Brunei signed a Memorandum of Defense Cooperation and Brunei's armed forces participated in joint exercising, training programs, and other military activities coordinated by the **United States Pacific Command (USPACOM)**. In the framework of the United States **Enterprise for ASEAN Initiative (EAI)**, the **United States Trade Representative (USTR)** concluded a **trade and investment framework agreement (TIFA)** with Brunei in December 2002. It is a participant in the ASEAN dialogue with the United States and ASEAN's cooperation with the United States in counterterrorism and other interest areas of joint concern. Brunei's bilateral and ASEAN activities with the United States were welcomed by President **George W. Bush** when the sultan visited the president in Washington in December 2002.

BRZEZINSKI, ZBIGNIEW (1928–). Sometimes called the Democrat's **Henry Kissinger**, Zbigniew Brzezinski was President **Jimmy Carter**'s national security advisor from 1977 to 1981. In 1978, Brzezinski opposed the process of **normalization of relations with Vietnam** advocated by Secretary of State **Cyrus Vance** and Assistant Secretary of State for East Asia and the Pacific **Richard Holbrooke**. Brzezinski persuaded Carter that such a move would have a negative impact on the more important full normalization of relations with the People's Republic of **China**, which viewed **Vietnam** as a Soviet proxy. This was only one of many foreign policy disagreements between Vance and Brzezinski, which ended with Vance's resignation. At the outbreak of the **Third Indochina War**, Brzezinski encouraged **Thailand**'s promotion of Chinese assistance to the **Khmer resistance**, including the **Khmer Rouge (KR)**. After leaving government, Brzezinski returned to his academic base at Columbia University. *See also* KRIANGSAK CHOMANAN.

BUNDY, MCGEORGE (1919–1996). McGeorge "Mac" Bundy, younger brother of **William Bundy**, was Harvard's youngest dean of arts and science when President **John F. Kennedy** named him special assistant for national security affairs in 1961. He served Kennedy and then President **Lyndon B. Johnson** in that capacity until 1966. He was a central figure in crucial **Vietnam** policy making, strongly supporting escalation and bombing the North. His hawkish position softened, and he advised a more moderate policy after 1966 when he left government to become president of the **Ford Foundation**. When he died, he was working on a book about the **Vietnam War** as a policy mistake.

BUNDY, WILLIAM P. (1917–2000). William "Bill" Bundy was **McGeorge Bundy**'s older brother and **Dean Acheson**'s son-in-law. He spent the years 1951–1961 in the **Central Intelligence Agency (CIA)**, moving to the Defense Department, where he was, first, deputy assistant secretary of defense for international security affairs (1961–1963), and then assistant secretary to March 1964, when he became assistant secretary of state for East Asian and Pacific affairs, until 1969. Although Bundy never reached the highest official level, his influence on **Vietnam** policy under three presidents was deep and pervasive. He was a player in the shaping of the **Tonkin Gulf Resolution**, which gave President **Lyndon B. Johnson** broad war-making authority. Like his brother, he was an early advocate of escalation and bombing, not questioning the decision making leading to involvement. Like so many of his early colleagues, he too had retrospective second thoughts about the war. He would later (in 1989) characterize the **Vietnam War** as a tragedy waiting to happen, which he admitted "was made worse by countless errors along the way in many of which I had a part."

BUNKER, ELLSWORTH (1894–1984). A highly regarded senior American diplomat, Ellsworth Bunker was recruited from private business by his friend, Secretary of State **Dean Acheson**, to be U.S. ambassador to Juan Peron's Argentina. He also served as ambassador to Italy and India. In 1961, President **John F. Kennedy** called on him to moderate the secret talks between **Indonesia** and the Netherlands to resolve the issue of sovereignty in the **West New Guinea dispute**. In April 1965, he was dispatched to **Indonesia** as a special presidential envoy to ease the transition of American ambassadors and policy as Ambassador **Howard Jones** was replaced by **Marshall Green**. In 1967, President **Lyndon Johnson** sent him to Saigon as ambassador to the **Republic of Vietnam**, where he served until 1973. In Saigon he was strongly supportive of American military strategy and was an advocate of carrying the war to **Laos** and **Cambodia**. In the administration of President **Jimmy Carter**, Bunker was called on to negotiate the retrocession of the Panama Canal. He retired in 1978 after the signing of the Panama Canal Treaty.

BURMA (MYANMAR). In American foreign policy, Burma is a pariah state. For political reasons, the United States officially continues to use Burma as the name of the state although it was changed by the Burmese government in 1989 to Myanmar, an English transliteration of its Burmese name. The capital's name was also changed from Rangoon to Yangon, and then in 2005, the capital itself was relocated to Nay Pyi Taw, in the central plain midway between Yangon and Mandalay. The **Association of Southeast Asian Nations (ASEAN)**, the **United Nations (UN)**, other international organizations, and most other nations accept Myanmar as the name of the state. For the United States, Burma has become a **human rights** disaster under harsh military rule for five decades in disregard of its own people and neighbors. Since 1988, the United States has had minimal bilateral functional and diplomatic contacts with Burma, which has also complicated U.S. relations with ASEAN, which embraces Burma as a partner.

About the size of Texas, Burma's 262,000-square-mile (431,206-square-kilometer) territory is bounded by India, **China**, **Thailand**, and Andaman Sea, which has made it an object of strategic competition for its ample resources. It has an estimated population of more than 55 million, but there has been no census since 1983. The ethnic composition is nearly 70 percent Burmese, with numerous minority groups making up the balance. Of these, the Shan at 9 percent and **Karen** at 7 percent are the largest. Although resource rich, the economy has been devastated by misrule and corruption, leaving it one of the Asia's least economically developed countries and its people among the poorest in the region. Economic sanctions imposed by the United States and other Western democracies have negatively affected it as well. New infrastructure **investments** from India, China, and ASEAN countries in resource development, especially natural gas, help to mitigate the downward spiral, although little of the benefits trickle down beyond the needs of the military junta.

For centuries Burma was ruled by Buddhist dynasties often at war with its minorities and Thailand. Its "golden age," a millennium ago, was the Pagan dynasty, whose monumental ruins can be compared to Angkor in **Cambodia**. The Buddhist kingdoms came to an end in the 19th century after three Anglo–Burmese wars that ended in 1885 with the full annexation of Burma to British India. Even as British administration reorganized Burma politically and economically, opposition to colonial rule led to Burmese nationalism. Some of the radical nationalists joined ranks with Japan against the British in World War II.

Prominent among them were **Aung San**, **U Nu**, and **Ne Win**. They broke with the Japanese when Tokyo's promised independence proved a sham and joined the returning British against the Japanese. The British acceded to the postwar Burmese demand for independence once the decision to free India was made. Burma became fully independent in January 1948. From the outset, the state was beset by communist revolutionary and ethnic minority violence as its democratic constitutional system crumbled. In 1958, Prime Minister U Nu, leader of the Anti-Fascist People's Freedom League (AFPFL), called on military chief Ne Win to step in on a temporary caretaker basis to restore peace and order. New elections were held in 1960, bringing U Nu back to power, but two years later Ne Win and the military intervened again, and for good. This set the country on the road to economic destruction and international political condemnation.

The United States had encouraged British decolonization and nominated its first ambassador, J. Klahr Huddle, in October 1947, who presented his credentials in Rangoon on 3 March 1948. American assistance programs came with the embassy establishment minus a military assistance presence. Prime Minister U Nu was staunchly nonaligned, seeking an equidistant position between the two superpowers in the Cold War. This was underlined when, in 1950, Burma, despite American objections, became the first Southeast Asian country to recognize the People's Republic of **China**. U Nu was a co-convener of the 1955 **Asian–African Conference** in which the seeds for the **Nonaligned Movement (NAM)** were laid. American–Burmese relations were exacerbated during the decade of the 1950s by the **KMT–Burma crisis**, in which the United States was providing clandestine assistance to Chinese nationalist forces that had retreated into Burma. U Nu took the U.S. intervention to the United Nations and suspended American assistance and cultural and educational programs. During U Nu's July 1956 visit to the United States, what were described as "frank" discussions between the Burmese prime minister and President **Dwight D. Eisenhower** and Secretary of State **John Foster Dulles** on matters of mutual concern took place.

When General Ne Win took power for the second time in 1962, Burma's nonalignment became self-imposed isolation as Burma became Southeast Asia's hermit nation, withdrawing from the growing networks of global and regional ties. Burma even quit the NAM, of which it was a founder. Ne Win and the military ruled through the Burma Socialist Program Party (BSPP) under a new military-promulgated constitution. The United States resumed low-profile and relatively low-volume programs of developmental and humanitarian assistance. Washington was particularly desirous of halting **narcotics trafficking**. In 1986, President **Ronald Reagan**'s attorney general, Ed Meese, traveled to Burma's Shan States to demonstrate U.S. commitment to the counternarcotics programs. Ne Win's "Burmese road to socialism" became a road to impoverishment for all except the military institution and its favored few. In 1987, the UN declared Burma one of the least developed nations in the world, on a par with the poorest in Africa. Burma stood in sharp contrast to the results that its neighbors in ASEAN were achieving in their market-oriented and foreign **investment**–receptive economic development strategies.

In summer 1988, a clash between students and police turned into revolt as killings by the police spurred antigovernment demonstrations. An 8 August mass rally was met by a military assault that killed more than 1,000 protesters. It was at this point that **Aung San Suu Kyi**, Aung San's daughter, emerged as head of the **National League for Democracy (NLD)** and became the international symbol of Burma's democratic opposition. Military hard-liners responded by a coup against Ne Win's own civilian façade government, declaring martial law and ruling through the **State Law and Order Restoration Council (SLORC)**. Aung San Suu Kyi and other NLD leaders were arrested as the SLORC "restored order" with a violence that left 3,000 demonstrators dead and thousands more fleeing to Thailand or ethnic minority–controlled border areas. American Ambassador **Burton Levin** protested the indiscriminate use of force. He also reported that some of the arrested students were sent to forced labor camps. American embassy contacts with the opposition made it a particular target of the SLORC, which claimed the embassy was being used as a staging ground for the antigovernment movement. The SLORC junta portrayed Aung San Suu Kyi as an American **Central Intelligence Agency (CIA)** and Burmese Communist Party tool, being used to overthrow the Burmese state.

The American response to the SLORC coup and massacre was to suspend all aid to Burma and downgrade the status of the embassy. In May 1990, the SLORC, led by General Saw Maung, felt confident enough in its control over the country to hold what it thought would be managed elections for a People's Assembly to make their rule more legitimate. To the junta's surprise and chagrin, 392 of 485, or more than 80 percent, of the constituencies returned an NLD candidate. The SLORC simply nullified the election and cracked down again on the opposition. Aung San Suu Kyi, winner of the 1991 Nobel Peace Prize, has either been in prison or under house arrest since 1990. For the United States, the NLD's victory in 1990 became the benchmark for democracy in Burma. Since the departure of Ambassador Levin in 1990, there has been no American ambassador in Burma. American official representation is handled by a chargé d'affaires ad interim. In 1992, Gen Tan Shwe replaced Saw Maung as leader of SLORC, which in 1997 changed its name to the **State Peace and Development Council (SPDC)**.

Early in the presidency of **William J. Clinton**, the United States hoped that the SPDC's position might be softening. Deputy Assistant Secretary of State for East Asian and Pacific Affairs **Thomas Hubbard** traveled to Rangoon in November 1994 for the first high-level visit since Ambassador Levin had left. Hubbard presented to the junta the steps it would have to take to restore normal ties with the United States, in what he later called a carrots and sticks formula. He came away hoping that generals would relent on Aung San Suu Kyi and the NLD. Secretary of State **Warren Christopher** called the Hubbard mission a "step that gives us an opportunity to explore whether we should join the other nations in this region in trying to explore constructive engagement." They were to be disappointed. In March 1995, Hubbard noted in a speech the continuing lack of democratic progress and warned of further U.S. actions against the junta. The sanctions came on 20 May 1997, with the issuance of Executive Order 13047 by President Clinton declaring a national emergency with respect to the actions and policies of the Burmese government and invoking a prohibition on new investments in Burma by U.S. persons. He based this on a Burma-related amendment to the FY 1997 appropriations bill and his authority under the International Emergency Economic Powers Act.

The certification of a national emergency with respect to Burma has been renewed every year, with six-monthly periodic reports to Congress by the president on the conditions in Burma . The economic sanctions were expanded on 28 July 2003 in Executive Order 13310, issued by President **George W. Bush** in conformity with the **Burmese Freedom and Democracy Act of 2003**. The measures effectively isolated Burma from U.S. markets. The Bush administration viewed the SPDC as "a xenophobic know-nothing group that maintains its power through sheer force." The sanctions regime was reinforced by the president and Congress in 2007. The problem with the sanctions imposed by the United States is that despite U.S. efforts to get multilateral support, no other country has put in place the same range of measures or shares Washington's seeming belief that sanctions, rather than constructive engagement, will alter the junta's course of action. In July 2007, a rare high-level meeting between U.S. officials headed by Deputy Assistant Secretary of State Eric John and Burmese ministers took place in Beijing, China. The meeting, apparently initiated by the Burmese junta at Chinese prodding, produced a "frank and free exchange" of views. The United States has made it clear that no senior official will visit Rangoon for discussions unless he or she can meet with Aung San Suu Kyi. Burma's announcement in September 2007 of guidelines for a new constitution was denounced by the United States as a "total sham" without any political legitimacy.

In 1997, Burma as an issue in U.S. relations in Southeast Asia took on a new dimension when ASEAN expanded to include Burma. Secretary of State **Madeleine Albright** pressed the ASEAN leaders hard not to accept a government that would only damage ASEAN's international image. Burma's principal supporter in ASEAN, Prime Minister **Mahathir Mohammad** of **Malaysia**, responded scornfully to American protests, saying that "ASEAN must resist and reject such attempts at coercion." The issue of Burma remained an impediment in U.S.–ASEAN relations. The U.S. has consistently raised it in the ASEAN–U.S. dialogue and in the **ASEAN Regional Forum (ARF)**, to which Burma belongs by virtue of its ASEAN membership. When it appeared that Burma would assume the chairmanship of ASEAN through the annual rotation in 2007, it was suggested that the United States would boycott ASEAN that year. Secretary of State **Condoleezza Rice** gave warning of American sentiment when she failed to attend ASEAN's July 2005 postministerial conference (PMC) with the dialogue countries or the annual ARF meeting that followed.

Behind the ASEAN scenes, Burma was quietly persuaded to "voluntarily" postpone its turn. In August 2006, when the U.S.–ASEAN **trade and investment framework agreement (TIFA)** was signed, the United States made it clear that its sanctions regime against Burma was not affected. A proposed U.S.–ASEAN 30th anniversary summit for 2007–2008 was stalled by the American president's unwillingness to participate in a meeting that included a junta leader.

Washington has also carried its campaign to free Aung San Suu Kyi and restore democracy in Burma to the **United Nations (UN)**. In 2006, the United States inscribed Burma on the UN agenda as a threat to the peace. It cited human rights violations, including persecution of minority refugees and forced labor, **trafficking in persons**, trafficking in narcotics, and failure to act to defend against **pandemic and infectious diseases**, particularly HIV/AIDS. The UN General Assembly's Third (Human Rights) Committee censured Burma by a vote of 79 to 28, with 63 abstentions. The only Southeast Asian country to vote with the majority was **East Timor**. Antijunta demonstrations in September 2007 led by Buddhist monks spurred new efforts by the United States and Western European countries to win UN condemnation of the junta's suppression of the Burmese people. *See also* BYROADE, HENRY A.; CHIN; ENVIRONMENTAL ISSUES; REFUGEES.

BURMESE FREEDOM AND DEMOCRACY ACT OF 2003. This legislation became law when signed by President **George W. Bush** on 28 July 2003. Its purpose was to sanction the **State Peace and Development Council (SPDC)**—the military junta—in **Burma**, support the Burmese democratic opposition, and recognize the **National League for Democracy (NLD)** as the only legitimate representative of the Burmese people. The measures adopted expanded the sanctions that had been in place since 1997 by putting a total import ban on Burmese goods. New sanctions included a prohibition on the export of financial services, freezing the assets in the United States of the members of the SPDC and other officials, and barring visas of senior officials. The sanction regime has been extended annually. The act was reinforced by the U.S. Congress in December 2007 when it prohibited the import of gemstones of Burmese origin.

BUSH, GEORGE H. W. (1924–). The 41st president of the United States (1989 –1993), George H. W. Bush was one of the best prepared presidents when he came to office in 1989. He had been U.S. permanent representative to the United Nations, head of the U.S. Liaison Office in **China**, director of the **Central Intelligence Agency (CIA)**, and for eight years President **Ronald Reagan**'s vice president. Bush's foreign policy agenda for Southeast Asia, stewarded by Secretary of State **James Baker** and Assistant Secretary of State for East Asian and Pacific Affairs **Richard Solomon**, had as its regionalist element not just the **Association of Southeast Asian Nations (ASEAN)** but also a wider trans-Pacific regionalism envisioned in the **Asia–Pacific Economic Cooperation (APEC)** format. This meant heading off Prime Minister **Mahathir Mohammad** of **Malaysia**'s push for an exclusive **East Asian Economic Group (EAEG)**. American security policy in the region had to adjust to the loss of the **Philippine** bases. The Bush response was the **East Asia Security Initiative (EASI)**. The Bush administration also continued the process of **normalization of relations with Vietnam** with the presentation of a "road map," which featured the resolution of the **POW/MIA** issue and the termination of the **Third Indochina War**—the Vietnamese invasion and occupation of **Cambodia**. The Bush government also had to deal with the public and congressional fallout on U.S.–**Indonesian** relations caused by the 1991 **Dili massacre** in Indonesian-ruled **East Timor**.

George H. W. Bush only visited the Southeast Asia region once during his presidency, a stopover in **Singapore** between Australia and South Korea in January 1992. He had limited contacts with Southeast Asian counterparts, meeting Malaysia's Mahathir in Boston and President **Suharto** of Indonesia in Washington, and welcoming Philippine President **Corazon Aquino** on a state visit, all in 1989. Bush was defeated in his reelection bid by **William J. Clinton**, who in turn was succeeded in the presidency in 2001 by George H. W. Bush's son, **George W. Bush**. In 2005, the younger Bush named both former presidents Bush and Clinton to represent the U.S. commitment to the **tsunami** relief effort in Southeast Asia.

BUSH, GEORGE W. (1946—). Son of the 41st president, **George H. W. Bush**, George W. Bush, the 43rd president of the United

States, came to office in 2001 with only the governorship of Texas to prepare him to meet challenges in Southeast Asia far greater than any that faced his father. Under the direction of Secretaries of State **Colin Powell** in the first term and **Condoleezza Rice** in the second, there were two main U.S. policy focuses in Southeast Asia: the **war on terror** and balancing the regional rise of **China**. Both were complicated by the impacts of the regionally hugely unpopular American **Iraq War**. After the 11 September 2001 attacks on the United States inspired by **al-Qaeda**, Southeast Asia was identified as the second front in the **war on terror**. President Bush sought to mobilize as quickly as possible Southeast Asian states to mount heightened counterterrorism measures and to support the U.S. wars, first in Afghanistan and then in Iraq.

In the course of the campaign to enlist allies in the war on terror, Bush had more intensive and frequent face-to-face meetings with Southeast Asian counterparts than any previous president. In Washington or New York, he had 18 meetings with presidents or prime ministers between 2001 and 2006. There were three meetings with **Thailand**'s prime minister **Thaksin Shinawatra**; three meetings with **Singapore**'s prime minister Goh Chok Tong and one with his successor, Lee Hsien Loong; two meetings with President **Megawati Sukarnoputri** of **Indonesia** and her successor, **Susilo Bambang Yudhoyono**; two meetings with **Philippine** president **Gloria Macapagal-Arroyo**; a meeting with **Malaysia**'s prime minister **Mahathir Mohammad** and then two with his successor, prime minister **Abdullah Badawi**; and one meeting each with the sultan of **Brunei Hassanal Bolkiah**, **Vietnam**'s prime minister Vo Van Khai, and **Xanana Gusmão**, president of **East Timor**. Traveling to Southeast Asia, he held minisummits with the heads of government of the seven **Association of Southeast Asian Nations (ASEAN)** members attending the **Asia–Pacific Economic Cooperation (APEC)** summits in 2005, 2006, and 2007, as well as bilateral talks with his opposite numbers in Singapore, Indonesia, Vietnam, and the Philippines. In the Philippines in October 2003, President Bush addressed a joint session of the Philippine Congress.

At the regional level, the policy thrust was to bolster the economic and political presence of the United States in Southeast Asia in response to concerns of some policy makers in Southeast Asia and

Washington that a rising China could displace the United States from its position in the regional balance of power. Policy initiatives like the **ASEAN Cooperation Plan (ACP), Enterprise for ASEAN Initiative (EAI)**, and the **ASEAN–United States Enhanced Partnership** were designed to demonstrate continued U.S. commitment to the region. In addition, the Bush administration's **trade** policy was furthered in Southeast Asia by a **free trade agreement (FTA)** with Singapore and FTA negotiations with Thailand, Malaysia, and the Philippines. The first step was taken toward a future U.S.–ASEAN FTA with the conclusion in 2006 of an ASEAN–U.S. **trade and investment framework agreement (TIFA)**. Even as the Bush administration has sought to demonstrate commitment to the region, it is still dogged by U.S. unwillingness to sign the **Treaty of Amity and Cooperation in Southeast Asia (TAC)**. Furthermore, U.S. preoccupation with Iraq and the Middle East sometimes overrides its Southeast Asian interests, as in the cancellation of Secretary Rice's attendance at the 2007 ASEAN postministerial conference (PMC) dialogue and the ASEAN Regional Forum (ARF) and President Bush's cancellation of a 2007 ASEAN–U.S. summit celebrating 30 years of U.S.–ASEAN dialogue. President Bush sought to reclaim some ground at the 2007 APEC summit by inviting the ASEAN heads of government to a Texas summit sometime in 2008 and announcing that he will appoint an American ambassador to ASEAN. The Texas summit proposal was dropped after the September 2007 Burmese crackdown on demonstrating Buddhist monks and their supporters. Disappointed by ASEAN's unwillingness to hold Burma accountable, the White House indicated it would refuse to participate in a meeting that included the junta.

BYROADE, HENRY A. (1913–1993). A West Point graduate, in World War II Henry Byroade fought in the **China–Burma**–India theater of war. He was a military aide to General George C. Marshall on his 1946 mission to China. A brigadier general at the age of 32 in 1946, Byroade was seconded to the **State Department** as deputy and then director of the Bureau of German and Austrian Affairs. He resigned his commission in 1952 to join the State Department as assistant secretary of state for Near East, South Asian, and African affairs, where he was accused of being pro-Arab because of his support of U.S. evenhandedness in the Arab–Israeli conflict. In 1955, he became ambassador to Egypt, only to be moved in 1956 to South Africa, and then to Afghanistan.

Byroade became the U.S. ambassador to **Burma** in October 1963, serving until June 1968, the longest tenure of any American ambassador to Burma. Military strongman **Ne Win** had taken control of the country in 1962, and Byroade saw it as his task to remove the distrust that separated Burma from the United States resulting from the **KMT–Burma** conflict and to convince the Burmese leader that the United States respected Burmese nonalignment. Byroade had good personal relations with the reclusive Ne Win. During Ne Win's state visit to the United States in September 1966, Byroade accompanied him on a golfing holiday to Maui. From his embassy in Rangoon, Byroade had contact with his North Vietnamese counterparts in the Burmese embassy of the **Democratic Republic of Vietnam (DRV)**. His talks with them during the 30-day Christmas 1965 bombing pause were an important element in the failed U.S. multipronged peace overtures at that time.

From Rangoon, Byroade went to the **Philippine** capital, Manila, serving as American ambassador from 1969 to 1973. He was an admirer of President **Ferdinand Marcos**'s efforts to bring discipline to what Byroade saw as a rather ungovernable country. He thought that the first year of Marcos's martial law "was the best government the people ever had." He excused the excesses of the regime as the overzealous acts of Marcos loyalists. He was deeply suspicious of Marcos's principal opponent, **Benigno Aquino**, viewing him as a ruthless seeker of power. Marcos saw his warm relationship with Ambassador Byroade as providing special access to American President **Richard Nixon**. After Manila, Byroade became ambassador to Pakistan.

– C –

CAMBODIA. Since gaining its independence in 1953, the constitutional and institutional forms of the Cambodian state have undergone transformations depending on the political foundations of the governments in power. Alterations in government were products of the three **Indochina Wars**. For the first four decades of U.S. relations with Cambodia, it was that country's role in those wars that shaped American policy toward it. From 1950 to 1970, **Norodom Sihanouk** ruled the Kingdom of Cambodia as king and then prince/ prime minister. From 1970 to 1975, following a coup against Sihanouk, American-backed General **Lon Nol** governed the Republic of Cambodia. From 1975 to 1979, the radical communist **Khmer Rouge (KR)** established **Democratic Kampuchea (DK)**. After a Vietnamese invasion in 1978 expelled the KR, Hanoi put in place a client government, which from 1979 to 1988 was called the **People's Republic of Kampuchea (PRK)**, and then to 1991, the State of Cambodia. The PRK and the State of Cambodia were opposed from exile during the **Third Indochina War** by the **Coalition Government of Democratic Kampuchea (CGDK)**. After a two-year period under the **United Nations Transitional Authority in Cambodia (UNTAC)**, the Cambodian kingdom was restored in 1993 as a democratic constitutional monarchy with the king as ceremonial head of state. Sihanouk was restored to the throne. He abdicated in 2004 in favor of his son, King Norodom Sihamoni.

Cambodia, indigenously known as Kampuchea, is located on mainland Southeast Asia between more powerful **Vietnam** and **Thailand** on its eastern and western borders, respectively. Its territorial area is 69,900 square miles (181,040 square kilometers), about the size of the state of Missouri. The population is 13.6 million (est. 2005), of whom 90 percent are ethnic **Khmer**. The capital is Phnom Penh in south central Cambodia, at the confluence of the **Mekong** and Tonle Sap Rivers. Cambodia is the site of Angkor, one of the great civilizations of ancient Southeast Asia. A representation of the five towers of Angkor Wat adorns the national flag as a nationalist reflection of a past golden age. Over the centuries, the kingdom was menaced from east and west by ambitious Thai and Vietnamese dynasties. Cambodia's geostrategic reality, wedged between historical predators, dominated Cambodia's modern history and in the last half of the 20th century helped influence the substance and quality of U.S.–Cambodia relations. In 1863, to preserve Cambodia's territorial integrity, King Norodom I accepted a French protectorate, and in 1887 Cambodia was incorporated into French **Indochina**. King Norodom died in 1904 and was succeeded by King Sisowath Monivang. Sisowath was the maternal grandfather of Norodom Sihanouk, who became king in 1941. Sihanouk was not only Cambodia's, but one of Southeast Asia's, leading figures for more than half a century and a quixotic adversary of the United States.

In March 1945, under Japanese occupation, King Sihanouk declared Cambodia's independence from France and named a cabinet headed by anti-French nationalist hero **Son Ngoc Thanh**, who a few years later became the leader of the anti-Sihanouk **Khmer Serei**. French rule was restored in October 1945. In 1950, Cambodia received autonomy as an associated state in the projected Indochina federation and French Union. Full independence dates from 9 November 1953. The decolonization of Cambodia took place while the French fought their colonial war in Vietnam—the **First Indochina War**. In Cambodia, the anti-French underground **Khmer Issarak** had links to the **Viet Minh**, who saw the anti-French struggle in Vietnam, **Laos**, and Cambodia as a common cause. Cambodia's international status was secured in the 1954 **Geneva Accords** guaranteeing its neutrality.

United States diplomatic relations with the kingdom began in June 1950 with recognition of Cambodia's autonomous sovereignty. The Hanoi-based nonresident minister accredited to Cambodia, **Donald Heath**, was also accredited to Vietnam and Laos. The Phnom Penh legation was headed by a chargé d'affaires. In 1952, the legation was raised to an embassy but still with a nonresident ambassador. It was not until 1954, after the Geneva Accords ending the First Indochina War, that a resident ambassador, **Robert McClintock**, was accredited. In the early years of the relationship, the United States established a presence built on economic and military assistance to the royal Cambodian government. The assistance was in support of keeping Cambodia in the anticommunist "free world." Although Sihanouk was a domestic anticommunist, being opposed by the Communist Party of Kampuchea (CPK), in foreign policy he was a neutralist, ideologically allying himself with **Indonesia** and **Burma**. He was a cosponsor of the 1955 Bandung **Asian–African Conference**.

In the administration of **Dwight D. Eisenhower**, neutralism was suspect. For Sihanouk, neutralism was a strategy for Cambodian survival, surrounded as it was by historical enemies. Although receiving U.S. military assistance, Sihanouk refused American military trainers. As a demonstration of his neutralism, on a visit to **China** in 1956,

Sihanouk publicly declared his rejection of the **Southeast Asia Collective Defense Treaty** protocol that brought Cambodia under the **Southeast Asia Treaty Organization (SEATO)** umbrella, the centerpiece of U.S. Secretary of State **John Foster Dulles**'s strategy of **containment** in Southeast Asia. Cambodia's 1958 diplomatic recognition of the People's Republic of China further alarmed the United States and its Southeast Asian allies. Anti-American policy machinations by the French establishment in Phnom Penh further complicated the Cambodian–American relationship. For the United States, the central issue was containment of communism. For Sihanouk it was the independence and sovereignty of the kingdom. Cambodia's suspected enemies — Thailand and South Vietnam — were America's allies, which from Sihanouk's vantage point made Washington responsible for its allies' policies toward Cambodia. Schemes such as the **Dap Chhuan plot** and other destabilizing conspiracies and provocations linking Bangkok and Saigon to Cambodian dissidents confirmed for Sihanouk Washington's hostility to Cambodia, despite the constant reassurances flowing from the American embassy.

Senior U.S. policy makers did not fully appreciate how deep and bitter the historical and ethnic antagonisms were complicating U.S. efforts to forge a coherent unified anticommunist strategy for the three countries. In 1959, Deputy Secretary of State for East Asian and Pacific Affairs **J. Graham Parsons**, a former ambassador to **Laos**, was dispatched to the region to try to ease tensions between the neighbors. He concluded that their attitudes toward each other were "psychopathic" and "more thoroughly poisoned with emotion and suspicion than I had comprehended." The question was who was the least pliant: Thai military dictator **Sarit Thanarat**, with Thai irredentist tendencies; **Ngo Dinh Diem** in Saigon, who loathed Sihanouk's neutralism; or Sihanouk, who demanded that the United States restrain the Thai and Vietnamese backers of anti-Sihanouk Cambodian irregular insurgents like Son Ngoc Thanh's Khmer Serei. American, Thai, and South Vietnamese dismay at what they saw as Sihanouk's pro-**Democratic Republic of Vietnam (DRV)**, pro-People's Republic of China version of neutralism was compounded by the fact that communist **Viet Cong** units and elements of the People's Army of Vietnam (PAVN) were carving out sanctuaries in Cambodia's eastern provinces to support their war in South Vietnam.

The steady decline in American–Cambodian relations continued during the administration of President **John F. Kennedy**, who had hoped to cultivate a personal relationship with Sihanouk, meeting him in New York shortly after taking office in 1961. Increasingly, however, the United States saw Sihanouk's efforts to balance America, China, and the DRV as taking sides with the enemy. Cambodia's disavowals of complicity in aiding the Viet Cong and PAVN were not credible in Washington. The **Ho Chi Minh** trail from North Vietnam through Laos had a terminus in Cambodia. Supplies destined for the Viet Cong and PAVN arrived by boat at Sihanoukville, Cambodia's Gulf of Thailand seaport, to be trucked over a highway built with U.S. development assistance and over the Khmer–American Friendship Bridge. The route was known to the Americans as the "Sihanouk trail." Washington viewed Cambodian initiatives to revive the **International Commission for Supervision and Control (ICSC)** or the convening of a new international conference for the neutralization of Cambodia as ploys to end American military support to South Vietnam.

The diplomatic tipping point came in late 1963. The Khmer Serei irritant had become intolerable to Sihanouk, particularly its South Vietnam–located clandestine radio broadcasts. The killing of Ngo Dinh Diem in the anti-**Diem coup** in Saigon proved to him that the Americans could not be trusted and he might be next on the assassination list. Finally, to lessen U.S. influence on the economy and the elite who benefited by it, in the name of Khmer socialism he ordered the suspension of American economic and military assistance. Between 1955 and 1963, U.S. economic grant aid totaled $409.6 million and military assistance $83.7 million. The long-smoldering political hostility between Washington and Phnom Penh burst into flame with the clustered deaths in a period of six weeks of Ngo Dinh Diem, Sarit Thanarat, and President John F. Kennedy. Sihanouk's reaction was to call for national rejoicing since the enemies, including the "great boss" (Kennedy), had departed to meet in hell. After a bitter diplomatic exchange, the respective American and Cambodian diplomatic missions were downgraded. In April 1965, relations were severed. Sihanouk was left alone to deal with China and North Vietnam.

In a domestic context of economic malaise and melting political support, Sihanouk faced the increasing problem of the Viet Cong and PAVN inside Cambodia and the indigenous insurgency of the CPK—

the dreaded **Khmer Rouge** or "Red Khmer"—which went into open revolt in 1968. A mission to Phnom Penh by American ambassador to India **Chester Bowles** in early 1968 began the process of restoring U.S.–Cambodian relations. In June 1969, diplomatic relations were resumed after President **Richard M. Nixon** sent a note to Sihanouk pledging to respect Cambodia's borders. The new American profile was kept low, with no large infusion of economic or military assistance. That Cambodia had become a front in the **Second Indochina War** was clearly demonstrated in 1969 by the beginning of B-52 bombings of targets inside Cambodia. As economic and political unrest grew in Cambodia along with antiethnic Vietnamese popular sentiment, Sihanouk was pushed to the political background. In July 1969, he resigned as head of government and a special congress elected a new, rightist government headed by General Lon Nol as prime minister and **Sirik Matak** as deputy prime minister. It was this government that a few months later deposed Sihanouk while he was abroad; ended the monarchy; and established the Republic of Cambodia, which became an American ally. Sihanouk, with Chinese sponsorship, established a countergovernment in Beijing, the Royal Government of the National Union of Kampuchea (GRUNK), which included CPK members Penn Nouth and **Khieu Samphan** as prime minister and deputy prime minister, respectively. A broader umbrella National United Front of Kampuchea (FUNK) allowed the Khmer Rouge to appropriate Sihanouk's popularity with the people to their revolutionary ends.

The United States hastened to support the Lon Nol government. Backed by Washington, the new government demanded that the PAVN and Viet Cong troops immediately leave Cambodia and followed by launching attacks against them. The Viet Cong–PAVN response was to counterattack. A new land front of the Second Indochina War was opened—sometimes described as a "sideshow" to the main front in Vietnam. In April and May 1970, U.S. and South Vietnamese forces made deep incursions into Cambodia, pushing main force PAVN units westward deeper into Cambodia, where they provided direct support to the Khmer Rouge. American forces were withdrawn from Cambodia in June, but Army of the Republic of Vietnam (ARVN) forces continued to operate across the border. American bombing of Cambodia was unrelenting. The Cambodian incursion provoked strong antiwar reaction in the United States. Congress sought to limit U.S. military actions in Cambodia in the **Church–Cooper amendments**.

The U.S. quickly moved to supply Lon Nol's rapidly expanding army with financing, equipment, and training. **Khmer Krom** troops in South Vietnam from the Khmer Serei and the U.S. Special Forces–trained Civilian Irregular Defense Groups (CIDG) were incorporated into the Cambodian army. Two successive American ambassadors, **Emory Swank** and **John Gunther Dean**, oversaw the diplomatic/political aspects of the alliance relationship while at the same time trying to restrain the growth of the in-country U.S. military mission, the **Military Equipment Delivery Team (MEDT)**. American policy, as formulated in **Henry Kissinger**'s National Security Council, and delivered to Lon Nol repeatedly by Kissinger's deputy **Alexander Haig**, was to keep the anticommunist Phnom Penh government in power and its army in the field. American assistance was to be limited to financial and material support. Between 1970 and 1975, the United States provided the republic with $1.18 billion in military assistance and $503 million in economic assistance. Meanwhile, the American air war against the Viet Cong–PAVN forces continued and went deeper into Cambodia against the Khmer Rouge, until Congress halted it in August 1973.

Even as the internal war in Cambodia was spreading, the United States was negotiating its "peace with honor" with the DRV in Paris. Although no Cambodians were represented, Article 20 of the January 1973 **Paris Agreement** called for the withdrawal of all foreign forces from Cambodia and Laos. This left an emboldened and strengthened Khmer Rouge facing Lon Nol's forces, which had been on the defensive since 1971. No amount of American material support or exhortation from high-level visitors or a conflicted embassy could change the fact that the Cambodian army was poorly led, corrupt, demoralized, and no match for the disciplined and battle-hardened Khmer Rouge. As the noose was tightening around Phnom Penh, American aid was dwindling. A last ditch effort in January 1975 by Secretary of State Kissinger and President **Gerald Ford** to obtain congressional approval for emergency assistance to Cambodia was not acted on, allowing Kissinger to blame Congress for Phnom Penh's fall.

The Khmer Rouge entered Phnom Penh on 17 April 1975. Their first act was to depopulate the cities, beginning a cruel and violent reign that shocked the world, returning Cambodia to what has been called the "year zero." Sihanouk returned to Phnom Penh in September 1975 as ceremonial head-of-state of GRUNK, but soon was shunted aside in the proclamation of Democratic Kampuchea. No longer of use to the Khmer Rouge, he was allowed to go again into exile in 1978. Even as the domestic program of the Khmer Rouge convulsed Cambodian society and culture, Democratic Kampuchea was on a collision course with the DRV, its erstwhile comrade-in-arms. This ended in the Vietnamese invasion and occupation of Cambodia at the end of 1978 and the installation of the new Vietnamese-backed People's Republic of Kampuchea (PRK), led by ex-Khmer Rouge defectors to Vietnam. The Vietnamese invasion resulted in a new wave of Khmer **refugees** streaming into the border region of Thailand, providing a pool of recruits for a **Khmer resistance** movement. The next 12 years of Cambodian international political and diplomatic relations were dominated by the efforts of the resistance, united in the Coalition Government of Democratic Kampuchea (CGDK), supported by the **Association of Southeast Asian Nations (ASEAN)**, the United States, and the People's Republic of China, to force Vietnamese withdrawal from Cambodia and an act of internationally supervised self-determination by the Cambodian people. This was the period of the **Third Indochina War**.

From the evacuation of the embassy on 12 April 1975 to November 1991 and the end of the Third Indochina War and the **comprehensive political settlement of the Cambodia conflict**, there was no U.S. diplomatic mission in Cambodia. The United States extended the trade embargo on the DRV to the DK and PRK. Following the establishment of UNTAC, **Charles Twining**, a State Department Cambodia specialist, was named U.S. representative to the Supreme National Council (SNC), the Cambodian coalition that oversaw government administration under UNTAC. With UNTAC in place, the United States lifted its trade embargo and opposition to international lending to Cambodia. Twining became the first U.S. ambassador when the mission was upgraded to full diplomatic relations on 24 September 1993 with the formation of the new Royal Government of Cambodia. In the government, power was shared between the royalist political party **Funcinpec** and its leader, Norodom Ranariddh, and **Hun Sen**'s Cambodian People's Party. Hun Sen's political roots were in the Khmer Rouge and then the PRK. In a 1997 quasi coup, Hun Sen attempted to eliminate the royalist faction from public life. The United States suspended bilateral assistance to Cambodia and evacuated U.S. citizens. ASEAN was instrumental in resolving the issue, making the 1998 ASEAN-monitored election a condition of Cambodia's membership in the regional grouping. Elections in 1998 and 2003 consolidated the rule of Prime Minister Hun Sen. The United States has pressed his government on issues of democracy, **human rights**, and corruption. In 2006, the American ambassador, Joseph Mussolmeli, publicly criticized the government's prohibition of peaceful assembly and demonstrations. Mussolmeli underlined U.S. support for human rights activism in Cambodia on Human Rights Day in December 2007 by marching shoulder-to-shoulder with the UN special representative for human rights in Cambodia in a demonstration for reform. The United States also has prodded Phnom Penh on its delay in establishing the mechanism for holding the KR accountable for genocide in the **Khmer Rouge trials** process. The government has been cooperative in efforts to account for Americans missing in action **(POW/MIA)**, and the United States has assisted in the removal of **unexploded ordnance (UXO)**.

The legacy of wars, political instability, and corruption has left Cambodia one of the poorest countries in Southeast Asia. On the mainland, only Laos and **Burma** rank lower. Cambodia was admitted into the **World Trade Organization (WTO)** in 2004. The United States executed a **trade and investment framework agreement** (TIFA) with Cambodia in 2006. American bilateral trade with Cambodia is relatively small compared to other ASEAN countries, amounting to $2.26 billion in 2006. The Hun Sen government has depended on a World Bank–coordinated lending consortium of donor nations, the **Consultative Group for Cambodia (CGC)** for 60 percent of its budgetary needs. In 2007, the CGC became the **Cambodia Development Cooperation Forum (CDCF)**. Through the CGC, the United States was Cambodia's second largest donor nation after Japan. In the CDCF, the United States is now third, with **China** in the second position.

CAMBODIA DEVELOPMENT COOPERATION FORUM (CDCF). In 2007, the World Bank–led **Consultative Group for Cambodia (CGC)** aid donor consortium became the Cambodia Development Cooperation Forum. The first CDCF meeting took place in June 2007, at which time a total of more than $689 million was pledged for the first year of a three-year **Cambodian** aid framework. The United States, which had historically been second to Japan as a bilateral aid donor to Cambodia, slipped to third place with a pledge of more than $48 million, behind Japan's $115 million and first-time consortium-member **China**'s $91 million.

CARNEY, TIMOTHY M. (1944–). A Foreign Service Officer (FSO), Timothy Carney began his career, like so many FSOs of his generation, in **Vietnam** and **Cambodia**. He was in Saigon for the Tet Offensive and in Phnom Penh for its evacuation. From Cambodia, he was one of the first to report officially on the nature of **Khmer Rouge (KR)** rule based on the administration of the territories the KR held in eastern Cambodia. Carney also served in the embassy in **Thailand**, monitoring the Thai–Kampuchean border, and in **Indonesia** as the political officer. During the administration of President **George H. W. Bush**, Carney was the senior Asia official on the National Security Council. He returned to Cambodia in 1992 as the senior American in the **United Nations Transitional Authority in Cambodia (UNTAC)**. Following his Southeast Asia career, Carney had ambassadorial postings to Sudan and Haiti. He was recalled from retirement twice: first in 2003 to spend three months with the U.S. occupation government in Baghdad and the then from August 2005 to March 2006 to go back to Haiti as the chargé d'affaires ad interim.

CARTER, JIMMY (JAMES EARL JR.) (1924–). The 39th president of the United States, Jimmy Carter came into office explicitly distancing himself from the policies of the preceding administrations of **Richard Nixon** and **Gerald Ford**, both of whom were served by National Security Advisor and later Secretary of State **Henry Kissinger**. Based largely on Carter's campaign rhetoric, Southeast Asian leaders expressed concern that the Carter administration would downgrade American political and security interests in the

Southeast Asian balance of power. Their anxiety was further heightened by the great priority Carter placed on **human rights** in his foreign policy. The worried leaders in Southeast Asia were wrong. Even though the rhetoric was different, essentially there was continuity in policy under Secretaries of State **Cyrus Vance** and **Edmund Muskie**, supported by Assistant Secretary of State for East Asian and Pacific Affairs **Richard Holbrooke**.

For **Indonesia**, rather than military assistance sanctions because of **East Timor**, the Carter administration expanded weapons sales. In the **Philippines**, a revision of the **Military Bases Agreement** trumped human rights concerns. In both cases, the importance of the bilateral security interest was underlined by the dispatch of Vice President **Walter Mondale** for personal diplomacy with President **Suharto** and President **Ferdinand Marcos**. In the **State Department** turf battles between East Asian and Pacific affairs, represented by Holbrooke, and human rights and humanitarian affairs, represented by **Patricia Derian**, traditional realism won the day. Carter's early desire to hasten **normalization of relations with Vietnam**, signified by the **Woodcock Mission**, was aborted by National Security Advisor **Zbigniew Brzezinski**'s insistence that **China** came first. The Carter administration responded to Vietnam's invasion and occupation of **Cambodia**, which began the **Third Indochina War**, by reaffirming the security commitment to **Thailand**. The United States gave full political and diplomatic backing to the **Association of Southeast Asian Nations (ASEAN)**'s demand for Vietnam's unconditional withdrawal from Cambodia.

Even though Carter's White House had a broad Southeast Asian agenda, President Carter himself had few personal dealings with his counterparts there. He made no trips to the region, not even brief stopovers. The only Southeast Asian leaders he saw in Washington were Prime Minister Hussein Onn of **Malaysia** in September 1997 and **Singapore**'s **Lee Kuan Yew**, whom Carter met twice, in October 1977 and October 1978. The latter was also one of Derian's Southeast Asian human rights targets.

CENTRAL INTELLIGENCE AGENCY (CIA). The Central Intelligence Agency was established by the National Security Act of 1947 during the administration of President Harry S. Truman. This act reorganized U.S. national security capacities. In addition to the CIA, it created the National Security Council (NSC), the U.S. Air Force, and the Department of Defense. The CIA was tasked with the coordination of national intelligence activities and the collection, evaluation, and dissemination to senior government officials of intelligence affecting national security. It was headed by a Director of the Central Intelligence Agency, who was also the Director of Central Intelligence (DCI). The creation in 2004 of a new post of Director of National Intelligence (DNI) reduced the CIA director's bureaucratic authority. The CIA was the successor to the World War II **Office of Strategic Services (OSS)**, headed by General **William Donovan**. As the war ended, Donovan pressed for a postwar intelligence agency against the objections of the **State Department** and the Federal Bureau of Investigation. The OSS was disbanded, but its intelligence groups were housed in the War Department and State Department. Coordination was assigned to a new Central Intelligence Group (CIG). The OSS assets became the core of the new agency.

Although the original mission of the CIA was seen as largely analytical, it was quickly augmented by the NSC's decision to give it a clandestine operational capacity. The covert side of the agency was led by the Deputy Director of Plans (DDP). In 1973, the DDP was succeeded by a Deputy Director of Operations, and in 2004, by a Director of the National Clandestine Services. During the administration of President **Dwight D. Eisenhower** the covert activity of the agency first became an important Cold War tool for the U.S strategy of **containment** of communism in Southeast Asia. Under Director **Allen Dulles**, a former DDP, and his DDP **Frank Wisner**, the CIA picked up momentum, driven in part by the relationship between Allen Dulles and his brother, Secretary of State **John Foster Dulles**. The CIA operated independently from the State Department. CIA station chiefs, although housed in American embassies, were not responsible to the ambassador. This could lead to diplomatic embarrassment when plausible deniability of CIA activity in a country was in fact ignorance about those activities. This was the case in **Burma** during the **KMT–Burma** crisis, when a Burmese general told the American ambassador that he knew more about the CIA's covert activities in support of the Chinese nationalist forces lodged in the country than the ambassador did.

In Southeast Asia, the CIA acted to prop up friendly governments, destabilize unfriendly governments, and seek allies for U.S. policy in the region. In **Vietnam**, CIA operations intensified after the 1954 **Geneva Accords** partitioned the country between North and South Vietnam. Legendary CIA officer **Edward Lansdale** organized sabotage missions and harassment operations in the North and advised South Vietnamese President **Ngo Dinh Diem** as he consolidated his power in 1954–1955. The CIA, through **Lucien Conein**, was the go-between in the 1963 **Diem coup**. As the United States became increasingly involved in the **Vietnam War**, the agency's mission was in direct support of the U.S. military mission. The most publicized of its covert activities was the infamous Phoenix program. This was a CIA-directed effort run by **William Colby**, later a Director of Central Intelligence (DCI), to neutralize the **Viet Cong** infrastructure by identifying and eliminating its cadres through capture, surrender, or killing. As a producer of intelligence on the war for U.S. decision makers, the CIA's estimates were more accurate, and hence less optimistic, than those produced by the military.

The CIA organized and advised the **Hmong** army, led by **Vang Pao**, in the **secret war** in **Laos** against the communist **Pathet Lao** and the **Viet Minh**. The war was organized from the embassy by CIA station chief **Theodore Shackley** and in the field with Vang Pao by case officer **James Lair**. From **Thailand**, the CIA aided in the destabilization of neutralist **coalition governments** in Laos by supporting rightist strongman **Phoumi Nosovan**. CIA case officers trained Thai paramilitary forces like the **PARU** and **Border Patrol Police (BPP)**, which served as "volunteers" in Laos. The CIA was accused by **Cambodia**'s Prime Minister **Norodom Sihanouk** of conspiring with Thai and South Vietnamese groups to overthrow or assassinate him.

In a Dulles brothers' project to destabilize President **Sukarno**'s government in **Indonesia**, the agency provided direct support to the **PRRI–Permesta regional rebellions**. The American involvement was exposed when CIA contract pilot **Allen Pope**, who flew for the CIA proprietary airline **Civil Air Transport (CAT)**, was shot down on a 1958 bombing raid with incriminating papers on him. The agency was accused of providing intelligence support for the Indonesian army's bloody purge of the **Indonesian Communist Party**

(PKI) following the abortive 1965 **Indonesian coup**. In the **Philippines**, CIA officers involved themselves in electoral politics to assist candidates known to be friendly to the United States. The best-known example was the relationship between Edward Lansdale and Philippine President **Ramon Magsaysay**. While Lansdale was working to elect Magsaysay in 1953, American Ambassador **Raymond Spruance** was proclaiming American neutrality in the election. *See also* AIR AMERICA; BISSELL, RICHARD M.; EASTERN CONSTRUCTION COMPANY; FITZGERALD, DESMOND; HELLIWELL, PAUL; HELMS, RICHARD; POE, TONY; SEA SUPPLY CORPORATION; SMITH, JOSEPH BURKHOLDER.

CHILDRESS, RICHARD T. (1942–). A **Vietnam** veteran, Richard Childress joined the administration of President **Ronald Reagan** as deputy director of Asian affairs in the National Security Council with responsibilities for Southeast Asia, becoming director when director **Gaston Sigur** moved to the **State Department**. Childress was the official most deeply involved in seeking a resolution to the **POW/MIA** issue. He was with all delegations to Vietnam as well as talks in New York, Bangkok, and Vientiane. He was the administration's liaison with the **National League of POW/MIA Families**. After leaving government, Childress functioned as an unpaid policy consultant to the League.

CHIN. A minority ethnic group in **Burma**, the Chin number 1.5 million and inhabit the mountainous western border region between Burma and northeast India. Many Chins have adopted Christianity and are now considered by the United States to be of special humanitarian concern because of Burmese efforts to forcibly convert them to Buddhism, as well as acts of violence against churches and preachers. Since 1980, Chin insurgents have harassed government officials. Chin **refugee** communities have been established across the border in India and **Malaysia** and have had immigration restrictions waived by the United States.

CHINA, PEOPLE'S REPUBLIC OF. For the United States, while the military component of containment in Southeast Asia was focused on **Indochina**, the strategic political focus was on the regional ambitions of China. This had two aspects: China's direct support of the **Democratic Republic of Vietnam (DRV)** in **North Vietnam** and Chinese political influence in Southeast Asia through diplomacy and support to local Chinese-backed communist parties and insurgencies. The United States was only partially successful in diplomatically isolating China from Southeast Asia. Both nonaligned **Burma** and **Indonesia** recognized China in the early 1950s. China participated in the 1955 Bandung **Asian–African Conference**, which called for the People's Republic's seating in the United Nations, replacing the Nationalist government on Taiwan. **Cambodia**'s Prince **Sihanouk**, in a snub to the United States, recognized the Beijing government in 1958. In 1967, a strongly anticommunist new military-based Indonesian government suspended relations with China, accusing it of involvement in the 1965 **Indonesian coup**. American diplomatic pressure elsewhere in the region as well as indigenous suspicions about Chinese influence within local overseas Chinese communities and communist insurgencies continued to prevent normal relations with China until the geostrategic landscape shifted in the early 1970s.

The DRV's victory in Vietnam and perceptions of American withdrawal from the region caused China and the Southeast Asian states to view each other through balance of power lenses. The lead was given by the United States in the Nixon–Chou En-Lai 1972 "Shanghai Communiqué" as the first step toward normalization of U.S.–Chinese relations. **Malaysia** acted to recognize China in May 1974, the **Philippines** in June 1975, and **Thailand** in July 1975. It was not until August 1990 that suspended Indonesian–Chinese relations were resumed. **Brunei** followed suit in September 1991. **Singapore**, with its majority Chinese population, waited until all of its **Association of Southeast Asian (ASEAN)** partners were on board before opening diplomatic relations with China in October 1992.

The United States and China were political partners with ASEAN during the **Third Indochina War**—the Vietnamese invasion and occupation of Cambodia. It was a relationship that had more to do with their strategic view of the Soviet Union in the region than interests arising in Southeast Asia itself. Working in concert, the two Great Powers provided political support for ASEAN and the **Coalition Government of Democratic Kampuchea (CGDK)** as well as direct support for the Khmer resistance. China's punitive military incursion into bordering northern Vietnam in February 1979 was ambivalently received in Southeast Asia. Although showing support of frontline state Thailand, it demonstrated China's willingness to use force in Southeast Asia in pursuit of political goals. As part of its political approach to ASEAN, China ceased support to Southeast Asian communist insurgencies.

With peace in Indochina and the incorporation of the Indochinese states into ASEAN, the Cold War context of China's relations to Southeast Asia was transformed. China, in its "peaceful rise to power," has built both on a bilateral basis and through the multilateral agency of ASEAN a network of political and economic partnership links that has made it a major regional actor. As an Asian developing country, China shares many of the same interests with respect to the developed West that the ASEAN nations have. Both China and ASEAN resist the liberal political agenda on democracy and **human rights** pressed by the U.S. and the European Union. Since the end of the **financial crisis of 1997–1998**, while the United States has been preoccupied with the **war on terror**, some analysts see the growing China–ASEAN network as leading to the creation of a China-centric regional system. By 2007, China's **trade** relationships with ASEAN states matched those of the United States. The **ASEAN Plus 3 (APT)** and **East Asia Summit (EAS)** formats, which exclude the United States, give China an unchallenged political field as the regional Great Power. China's impressive military buildup has raised concerns in Southeast Asia about its long-range strategic ambitions and questions about the integrity of the American security commitment to the region. The 2006 U.S. Department of Defense Quadrennial Review states that "the pace and scope of China's military build-up already puts regional military balances at risk."

China and the ASEAN states have moved so rapidly on their agenda that the question has arisen as to whether the United States is ceding its paramount regional position to China. Two former U.S. ambassadors to the **Philippines**, **Morton Abramowitz** and **Stephen Bosworth**, commenting on the regional rise of China, characterized the American policy response as being sporadic and lacking coherence and not commensurate with U.S. interests. Southeast Asian leaders urge the United States to broaden and deepen its engagements in the region to promote important American political, economic, and strategic interests that are more permanent than those in the war on terror. In looking at China, ASEAN realists accept that the United States is no longer a hegemon, nor necessarily the paramount regional power. What they want is for the United States to remain a strong participant in the regional balance of power, if for nothing else, to hedge against the region's uncertain future with China.

CHRISTOPHER, WARREN M. (1925–). Secretary of state from 1993 to 1997 in President **William J. Clinton**'s first term, Warren Christopher had been deputy secretary of state in President **Jimmy Carter**'s administration, in which he was credited for the successful negotiations leading to the release of the American hostages in Iran. Christopher capped the process of **normalization of relations with Vietnam** by leading the American delegation to Hanoi in November 1995 for the official inauguration of diplomatic relations and the opening of the American embassy. Concern was expressed in Southeast Asia when he failed to attend the 1994 **Association of Southeast Asian Nations (ASEAN)** postministerial conference (PMC) in Bangkok after debuting in the region as secretary of state at the 1993 PMC in Singapore. His absence was particularly marked because the 1994 PMC was followed by the first formal meeting of the **ASEAN Regional Forum (ARF)**. ASEAN concerns were allayed when he participated in the 1995 and 1996 PMC and ARF meetings.

CHURCH–COOPER AMENDMENTS. In response to the April 1970 U.S. troop incursions into **Cambodia**, the U.S. Senate passed an amendment sponsored by Senators Frank Church and Sherman Cooper to the **foreign military sales (FMS)** bill, prohibiting American troops in Cambodia after 30 June, American advisors to Cambodian troops, and air operations in support of Cambodian troops. This was not accepted by the House of Representatives. Later Church–Cooper amendments that prohibited the use of U.S. ground troops in Cambodia, **Laos**, and **Thailand** and military advisors in Cambodia did become law on 22 December 1970. The Church–Cooper amendments were the first legislative restrictions ever put on presidential powers as commander in chief while American forces were in combat.

CIVIL AIR TRANSPORT (CAT). In 1950, the **Central Intelligence Agency (CIA)** secretly purchased the Taiwan-based airline Civil Air

Transport, which had been started after World War II by General Claire Chennault of "Flying Tigers" fame. While CAT continued to operate its commercial routes, it also supported the CIA's covert missions in Asia in **China**, **Vietnam**, **Laos**, **Burma**, and **Indonesia**. CAT provided both planes and pilots. In 1959 the name was changed to **Air America** as the CIA proprietary airline became the transport and supply backbone of the **secret war** in Laos. *See also* DIEN BIEN PHU.

CLARK AIR BASE. Clark Air Base in the **Philippines**' central Luzon was the headquarters of the U.S. 13th Air Force, which had command and control of U.S. Air Force operations in the Western Pacific. Its two-mile-long runway, aprons, hangers, and supply and maintenance facilities provided a platform for rapid deployment of forces to the region. It also was an important point in the air link from Hawaii between the North Pacific and Indian Oceans. The associated Crow Valley bombing and gunnery ranges were utilized not just by the American tactical air wing based at Clark but by friendly forces from elsewhere in the region. Together with **Subic Bay Naval Base**, Clark Air Base was considered by the United States to be a vital element in the strategy of **containment**. The future status of Clark was part of the 1990–1991 negotiation of the **Military Bases Agreement (MBA)**, but was decided by the June 1991 cataclysmic eruption of Mt. Pinatubo, which devastated the base.

CLIFFORD, CLARK, M. (1906–1998). A consummate Washington insider, Clark Clifford served four Democratic presidents in various official and unofficial roles in between maintaining a profitable law practice. From 1946 to 1950, he was special counsel to President **Harry S. Truman**. Clifford had input into nearly every decision, including that of aiding France in its colonial war in **Indochina**—the **First Indochina War**—and bringing **containment** to Southeast Asia. He was the foreign policy liaison between incoming president **John F. Kennedy** and the outgoing **Eisenhower** administration. He set the agenda for the Kennedy side and participated in the Eisenhower–Kennedy briefings on Indochina. In the Kennedy administration, Clifford was on the Foreign Intelligence Advisory Board. He served as an informal counsel to President **Lyndon B. Johnson** as well as undertaking special assignments. In the inner circles of both Kennedy's and

Johnson's administrations, Clifford was known as a "hawk" on **Vietnam War** issues. In July 1967, Clifford traveled with General **Maxwell Taylor** to the Pacific region on a mission to consult with American allies on the Vietnam War. Johnson called on Clifford to become secretary of defense in March 1968 after the resignation of **Robert McNamara**. He served for the 10 months remaining in Johnson's term of office, hewing to the president's line on policy. In 1969, Clifford wrote an attention-getting article in the influential journal *Foreign Affairs* favoring the beginning of a withdrawal strategy, adding his voice to the other former administration "hawks" who no longer saw light at the end of the tunnel.

CLINTON, WILLIAM J. (1946–). Elected in 1992, William J. "Bill" Clinton was the 42nd president of the United States. He had two secretaries of state, **Warren Christopher** in the first term and **Madeleine Albright** in the second. With Clinton, U.S. relations in Southeast Asia shifted from their post–World War II Cold War geostrategic focus to a geoeconomic one. This reflected the growing importance of America's interests in trans-Pacific economic relations. Clinton's 1993 call for a **Pacific Community** was matched by policies supporting multilateral structures for cooperation and consultation. At the Blake Island, Washington, gathering of **Asia–Pacific Economic Cooperation (APEC)** heads of governments in 1993, Clinton raised the low-visibility ministerial grouping to the summit level, where it has remained. Clinton also gave the green light to American participation in the **ASEAN Regional Forum (ARF)**, a multilateral security forum that had its first meeting in 1994. This overcame long U.S. resistance to bringing to Asia the Helsinki model of consultation and confidence building. The U.S. dialogue with the **Association of Southeast Asian Nations (ASEAN)** was invigorated. The push for greater attention to an economic dimension to policy and heightened attention to ASEAN came from the bottom up, since Clinton's own foreign policy horizons as a small state governor were experientially limited. Assistant Secretary of State for East Asian and Pacific Affairs **Winston Lord** in the first term and **Stanley Roth** in the second backstopped the administration's initiatives. In his confirmation hearings, Lord listed the promotion of American **trade** and **investment** as the first priority. The other priorities were security and democracy.

The most important bilateral priority in Clinton's first term was the completion of the process of **normalization of relations with Vietnam**. The economic embargo was lifted in February 1994 and diplomatic relations established in July 1995. The Clinton administration faced four crises in the region with mixed results. First, there was the 1997 unraveling of democracy in **Cambodia**. Although a face-saving solution for ASEAN was found, Prime Minister **Hun Sen**, who precipitated the crisis, was left in a stronger position than before. Second, Clinton imposed sanctions on the military junta in **Burma** because of **human rights** violations. The sanctions remain in place but have not altered that government's behavior. Third, the Clinton administration's ambivalent and late response to the **financial crisis of 1997–1998** ignored the political consequences of a policy that was honed by the Treasury Department, not the **State Department**. Finally, the tragedy of **East Timor** revealed again the tensions that had existed since 1975 in U.S. policy toward **Indonesia** in reconciling American real and ideal interests.

The inauguration of the APEC annual summit provided President Clinton with an opportunity to meet both bilaterally and in groups Southeast Asian counterparts on the sidelines. In addition, during his term of office he made state or official visits to **Brunei**, Indonesia, the **Philippines**, and **Thailand**. In Washington, he met with Philippine president **Fidel Ramos** twice (1993, 1998) and with his successor President **Joseph Estrada** (2000). President **Suharto** of Indonesia visited in 1995, as did President **Abdurrahman Wahid** twice (1999, 2000). Prime Minister **Mahathir Mohammad** of **Malaysia** called in 1996, as did Thailand's Chuan Leekpai. In 2005, President **George W. Bush** named former presidents Clinton and **George H. W. Bush** to symbolically head U.S. Southeast Asian **tsunami** relief efforts. Clinton was also appointed by **United Nations** Secretary-General Kofi Annan as his special envoy for the Southeast Asian tsunami recovery effort.

COALITION GOVERNMENT OF DEMOCRATIC KAMPUCHEA (CGDK). The Coalition Government of Democratic Kampuchea was the political framework created in 1982 to unify **Khmer resistance** to **Vietnam**'s invasion and occupation of **Cambodia** and to make it more politically palatable to the United States and other Western democracies. The three factions represented were the National United Front for an Independent, Peaceful, and Cooperative Cambodia (**Funcinpec**), **Khmer People's National Liberation Front (KPNLF)**, and the **Khmer Rouge (KR)**, which as the ruler of **Democratic Kampuchea (DK)** had been the target of the Vietnamese invasion. Funcinpec was the royalist movement loyal to Prince **Norodom Sihanouk**, who was named president of the CGDK. The KPNLF was led by **Son Sann**, a veteran Cambodian politician of **Khmer Krom** ancestry, who became prime minister. **Khieu Samphan**, erstwhile head of the DK state, was named vice president. The creation of a Cambodian coalition government in exile gave the resistance's principal external supporters—the **Association of Southeast Asian Nations (ASEAN), China**, and the United States—legitimate cover for support for an anti-Vietnamese independent Cambodia. It also made the diplomacy of defending the DK as the holder of Cambodia's **United Nations (UN)** seat rather than the Vietnam-sponsored **People's Republic of Kampuchea (PRK)** in Phnom Penh easier. Secretary of State Alexander Haig was caught in a 1981 photo opportunity at the UN shaking hands with Khieu Samphan, a notorious KR leader. The DK flag flew at the UN until it was replaced by the pre-1970 flag.

COALITION GOVERNMENTS—LAOS. During the contest among the right, left, and neutralist forces in **Laos** (1950–1975), there were three coalition governments under the flag of the Kingdom of Laos that tried to bridge the rival factions in one political framework. All three coalition governments were headed by Prince **Souvanna Phouma**. The first coalition government was formed in 1958 against stiff U.S. opposition and collapsed under U.S.-supported rightist pressure in 1958. The second was formed in 1962 as a result of the 1962 **Geneva Accords on Laos** and collapsed in 1963 as the country moved to civil war. The third was created in 1973 as the United States sought to extricate itself from the **Second Indochina War** and was terminated in 1975 by the proclamation of the **Lao People's Democratic Republic (LPDR)**.

COBRA GOLD. The annual Cobra Gold joint/combined military exercise began in 1981 as a bilateral U.S.–Thai exercise demonstrating to

Thailand and the **Association of Southeast Asian Nations (ASEAN)** the vitality of the American commitment to the defense of Thailand, which then was the strategic frontline state in the **Third Indochina War**, following **Vietnam**'s invasion and occupation of **Cambodia**. Cobra Gold's scope has expanded, including since 2002 **Singapore**, and since 2004 the **Philippines** and Mongolia. It has become the largest U.S. military exercise in Southeast Asia. It is a coalition interoperability exercise that goes beyond simply enhancing combat readiness. Since 2002 it has included counterterrorism, and since 2004 peacekeeping operations in conjunction with humanitarian and disaster relief missions. In 2005, with the participation of the Japanese Self Defense Force for the first time, emphasis was given to the lessons learned from the **tsunami** relief effort. Cobra Gold attracts military observers from many other Asian countries, including **Indonesia**, Vietnam, India, and **China**. Despite the suspension of American security assistance to Thailand because of the 2006 military coup there, Cobra Gold 2007 took place as scheduled.

COCHRAN, H. MERLE (1892–1973). A career Foreign Service Officer, Merle Cochran replaced **Coert DuBois** in August 1948 as the American representative on the **United Nations Commission on Indonesia**. He participated in the 1949 Hague Round Table Conference between **Indonesia** and the Netherlands that transferred sovereignty to Indonesia. At the conference he was sympathetic to the Dutch requirement that the newly independent state assume the colonial debt. He became the first U.S. ambassador to independent Indonesia, serving from 1949 to 1953. He was involved in the negotiations with the Indonesian government on the failed **mutual security agreement** that led to the government's fall and the installation of the more radical nationalist government of **Ali Sastroamidjojo**. As ambassador, he tried to cancel the passport of Professor **George Kahin**, founder of the **Cornell University** Modern Indonesia Project, because of Kahin's critical view of Cochran's role in the Round Table Conference. Kahin's view of this is in his memoir, *Southeast Asia: A Testament*.

COLBY, WILLIAM E. (1920–1996). One of the most important Central Intelligence Agency (CIA) officers to work in Southeast Asia during the Indochina wars, William Colby began his lengthy career as a behind-the-lines commando for the **Office of Strategic Services (OSS)** during World War II in Europe. He joined the CIA in 1949. He was station chief in Saigon, 1959–1962, and then chief of the Far Eastern Division in the office of the Deputy Director of Plans (DDP) **Richard Helms** from 1962 to 1967. Colby returned to Vietnam in 1968 holding the rank of ambassador in the embassy headed by Ambassador **Ellsworth Bunker**. Colby was innocuously titled Director of Civil Operations and Rural Development Support. In fact he established and ran the notorious Phoenix program that targeted the **Viet Cong** infrastructure. Colby admitted that the death toll of the Phoenix program exceeded 20,000, but other estimates run as high as 60,000. Colby returned to CIA headquarters in 1971. After a brief tour as Deputy Director for Operations (DDO) (the retitled DDP), Colby was named Director of Central Intelligence (DCI) by President **Richard Nixon** in 1973, replacing James Schlesinger who moved to the Department of Defense. As DCI, Colby presided over an agency that was besieged by Congress. In sworn testimony to Senate and House investigators, he revealed many of the CIA's dirty tricks. This created enemies within the CIA and enraged the American Left. President Gerald Ford essentially fired Colby in 1976, naming in his place **George H. W. Bush**, a possible competitor for the Republican presidential nomination. In 1996, Colby accidentally drowned while canoeing, an incident that sparked conspiracy theories. Colby's autobiography is *Honorable Men: My Life in the CIA*.

COLLINS, J. LAWTON (1896–1987). Known as "Lightning Joe," General J. Lawton Collins was a distinguished career army officer. In World War II, he commanded an infantry division on Guadalcanal and then the VII Corps in the Normandy invasion. He was the Army chief of staff during the Korean War. He was appointed by President **Dwight D. Eisenhower** as the U.S. representative to the North Atlantic Treaty Organization (NATO)'s military committee, but his service there was interrupted by Eisenhower's decision to send him on 3 November 1954 to the **State of Vietnam** as the Special Representative of the President with the personal rank of ambassador. After conferring with outgoing Ambassador **Donald Heath**, Collins was directed to coordinate all operations of U.S. agencies in the country.

Collins was in Vietnam for six months, until 14 May 1955. The next ambassador to the State of Vietnam, **Frederick Reinhardt**, presented his credentials on 28 May. Collins's mission was to manage the new, post-1954 **Geneva Accords** American commitment, particularly military assistance, to what Eisenhower and Secretary of State **John Foster Dulles** were calling "Free Vietnam." Despite Collins's questioning of the suitability and capabilities of Prime Minister **Ngo Dinh Diem**, in February 1955 Eisenhower wrote to Chief of State **Bao Dai** that he was gratified to learn from Gen. Collins of the progress being made by Prime Minister Diem, and that he concurred in Gen. Collins's recommendation to continue and expand support to his government. Collins returned to his NATO post after leaving Vietnam, retiring in 1956.

COMMONWEALTH OF THE PHILIPPINES. This was the institutional framework for the transition of American sovereignty in the **Philippines** to an independent Philippine state. The legal basis was the 1934 **Tydings–McDuffie Act**, which provided for a 10-year transition period. A July 1934 constitutional convention drew up a Commonwealth constitution modeled on the American one. It was approved by the United States in March 1935 and adopted by plebiscite in May 1935. **Manuel Quezon** was elected president in September 1935 and inaugurated on 14 November 1935. His vice president was **Sergio Osmeña**. The Commonwealth was internally self-governing, while foreign policy and defense remained American responsibilities. The United States also attached strings to Commonwealth policies with respect to immigration, **trade**, and currency. Quezon, until his death in 1944, and Osmeña succeeding him, led the Commonwealth government-in-exile from Washington during the Japanese occupation. Osmeña returned to the Philippines in 1944 with General **Douglas MacArthur** to restore the Commonwealth government. He was defeated in the April 1946 presidential election by **Carlos Roxas**, who became the third Commonwealth president and, on 4 July 1946, the first president of the independent Republic of the Philippines. The Commonwealth's constitution became the constitution of the republic.

COMMUNIST PARTY OF KAMPUCHEA (CPK). *See* KHMER ROUGE.

COMMUNIST PARTY OF THE PHILIPPINES/NEW PEOPLE'S ARMY (CPP/NPA). The Maoist-oriented Communist Party of the **Philippines** broke away from the old pro-Soviet Philippine Communist Party in 1968. Its military wing, the New People's Army, was launched in 1969. The CPP's leader from Dutch exile is José Maria Sisson. Its above ground political wing is the National Democratic Front. The Philippine military's alleged use of extrajudicial killings of supposed CPP sympathizers has created a major **human rights** problem for the Philippine government, damaging its security relationship with the United States. The CPP/NPA main bases of operations are in central Luzon and the rural Visayas. The level of violence is low, with sporadic attacks on military, police, politicians, and businessmen.

Once as strong as 25,000–30,000 fighters, its present strength is less than 10,000. It is the only communist insurgency still active in Southeast Asia. Philippine government policy toward the insurgents alternates between offers of negotiations and vows to crush them militarily. The United States has placed the CPP/NPA on its list of **foreign terrorist organizations (FTO)**. This reportedly has cut into the party's fund-raising. As a result, extortion under threat of kidnapping or killing has increased. Since 2004, the CPP/NPA has refused to negotiate with Manila until it is removed from the list. In 2006, President Gloria Macapagal-Arroyo declared all-out war on the NPA, considering it more of a threat to Philippine national security then the Muslim separatists in the south. In mid-2007, senior Armed Forces of the Philippines (AFP) leaders expressed doubt that the president's target of 2010 to eliminate the NPA would be achieved. American cooperation with the Philippines in counterinsurgency has prompted threats that U.S. personnel will be at risk if found in CPP/NPA operational areas.

COMPREHENSIVE POLITICAL SETTLEMENT OF THE CAMBODIA CONFLICT. This was the final act of the **Paris International Conference on Cambodia (PICC)**, adopted on 23 October 1991, officially ending the **Third Indochina War**, which began in 1978 with **Vietnam**'s invasion of **Cambodia**. The terms of the settlement had been worked out by the five permanent members of the **United Nations (UN)** Security Council and adopted by the Security Council and the UN General Assembly. The settlement established a **United Nations Transitional Authority in Cambodia (UN-TAC)** as the implementing agency for a comprehensive peace settlement that would permit free and fair elections, allowing the Cambodian people self-determination in a neutral Cambodia. The decoupling of their alliances in the Third Indochina War from the Great Power relations of China, the Soviet Union, and the United States left the Khmer factions little option but to accept the arrangements. The **Khmer Rouge** refused to compete in the UNTAC framework and remained a problem until amnesties induced rank and file and some leaders to reintegrate into postwar Cambodian society.

CONEIN, LUCIEN E. (1919–1998). A fabled intelligence agent, Lucien Conein began his career with the **Office of Strategic Services (OSS)** in Nazi-occupied Europe, moving to the **Central Intelligence Agency (CIA)** in 1947. In the 1950s, Conein worked for **Edward Lansdale** in the CIA's covert operations against **North Vietnam**. In 1963, Conein was the liaison between the U.S. embassy in Saigon and the Vietnamese military officers plotting the **Diem coup**.

CONFRONTATION. Confrontation, or to use the Indonesian original, *konfrontasi*, is what the undeclared, low-intensity 1964–1966 war waged by **Indonesia** on **Malaysia** was called. The Indonesian goal was to prevent the inclusion of **Singapore** and the British possessions of Sarawak and North Borneo with already independent **Malaya** in the new federal Malaysia state. Indonesia's President **Sukarno** deemed Malaysia an imperialist puppet and promised to crush it. In this he was backed by the **Indonesian Communist Party (PKI)**, which saw "confrontation" as a vehicle to rival the Indonesian army. The United States, alarmed by the prospects of a communist-backed conflict in the rear of the **Second Indochina War**, tried to head it off diplomatically. President **Lyndon B. Johnson** enlisted the assistance of **Robert Kennedy**, who had dealt with Sukarno over the **Allen Pope** case and the **West New Guinea dispute** during his brother **John F. Kennedy**'s administration. When diplomacy failed, the United States backed the British Commonwealth forces in the "undeclared war." The actual fighting took place primarily in the Sarawak–Indonesia jungle border areas. In the aftermath of the post-**Indonesian coup** toppling of the

Sukarno government and the destruction of the PKI, the new military-dominated Indonesian government quickly acted to restore peaceful relations with Malaysia in the framework of the **Association of Southeast Asian Nations (ASEAN)**.

CONSTITUTION, **USS.** In 1844, the U.S. naval frigate *Constitution*, known as "Old Ironsides," already 47 years old, began a two-year circumnavigation to show the flag, search out coaling stations, and investigate trading opportunities. Between January and September 1845, the ship called at ports in Sumatra, **Singapore**, the Borneo coast, Cochin China (Annam [**Vietnam**]), and Manila in Spain's **Philippines**. In **Brunei**, the captain tried unsuccessfully to negotiate a commercial treaty. Calling at Tourane (modern Danang) in Annam, an attempt to free imprisoned French priests resulted in a confrontation with the local population in which shots were fired by the Americans. This has been described as the first historical use of armed force against Vietnam by Western military forces. Five years later, American President Zachary Taylor apologized for the incident to the Annamese emperor in a letter delivered by **Joseph Balestier**.

CONSULTATIVE GROUP FOR CAMBODIA (CGC). This was the multilateral World Bank–led consortium of 18 countries and five international institutions to provide and coordinate economic assistance to **Cambodia**. The CGC grew out of the Japan-led International Committee for Rehabilitation of Cambodia, set up in 1993 to support Cambodia after the **United Nations Transitional Authority in Cambodia (UNTAC)** had finished its job. The CGC had its first meeting in 1996. Until 2002, the CGC's pledging conferences alternated between Tokyo and Paris. Starting in 2002, it met in Phnom Penh. Up to 2007, Japan and the United States were the largest bilateral donors. At the 8th pledging conference in 2006, the United States pledged $61 million and Japan $114 million. The CGI donors have insisted on reform and are particularly concerned about rampant corruption. There has been little effort by the **Hun Sen** government to meet the demands for reform, and in June 2006, funding for some projects was suspended because of corruption in the procurement process. In 2007, the CGC became the **Cambodia Development Cooperation Forum (CDCF)**.

CONSULTATIVE GROUP FOR INDONESIA (CGI). Led by the World Bank and consisting of 20 nations, including the United States, and 14 institutions, the CGI was the primary multilateral framework for donors of developmental economic assistance to **Indonesia** to pledge, coordinate, and cooperate. Begun in 1992, it was the successor to the **Intergovernmental Group on Indonesia (IGGI)**, which was terminated by Indonesia because of Dutch insistence on **human rights** conditionality. After the **financial crisis of 1997–1998**, the CGI broadened the scope of its oversight from macroeconomics and economic development to include issues such as governance, corruption, and legal reform. Indonesia terminated the CGI in 2007.

CONTAINER SECURITY INITIATIVE (CSI). Announced in January 2002, the Container Security Initiative is a port security regime to ensure that all containers that pose a potential risk of terrorism be identified and inspected at foreign ports before they are loaded for shipment on vessels destined for the United States. In Southeast Asia, CSI regimes are in effect in **Singapore**, the **Malaysian** ports of Port Klang and Tanjung Pelapas, and **Thailand**'s Lacm Chabang port. *See also* WAR ON TERROR.

CONTAINMENT. The American global political/military strategy of the Cold War was the "containment" of the expansion of communism by direct or indirect aggression. Most famously articulated by **George Kennan**, the central proposition was that communist pressure against the West "can be contained by the adroit and vigilant application of counterforce at a series of constantly shifting geographical and political points, corresponding to the shifts and maneuvers of Soviet policy." The strategy of containment, together with the **Truman Doctrine**, conceptually underpinned U.S. global policy. That which was to be contained in Southeast Asia was first the Soviet Union and then the People's Republic of **China** or their surrogates: domestic communist parties, insurgent "liberation armies" or proxies. For the United States, the **Indochina Wars** were part of the strategy of containment of communism in Southeast Asia, with the regional focus on, first, the **Democratic Republic of Vietnam** in **North Vietnam**, and after 1975 a unified **Socialist Republic of Vietnam**.

CORNELL UNIVERSITY. Since the early 1950s and the appointment of **George McT. Kahin** as the director of its new Southeast Asia Program, Cornell has been the premier academic center in the United States for Southeast Asia studies. Its multidisciplinary faculty has produced generations of influential Southeast Asian specialists in universities and governments around the world. The Modern **Indonesia** Project, with its journal and publications, has been an important contributor to the study of Indonesian politics. The circulation in 1971 of a so-called white paper on the 1965 **Indonesian coup** seemingly exculpating the **Indonesian Communist Party (PKI)** and indicting the Indonesian army compromised its credibility with **Indonesia**'s **Suharto**-led government, particularly the standing of **Benedict Anderson**, the director of the Indonesia project.

COUNCIL FOR SECURITY COOPERATION IN THE ASIA–PACIFIC (CSCAP). This is an organization that serves as a platform for a structured expert "Track II" nongovernmental dialogue for confidence building and security cooperation among individuals, institutions, and governments in the Asia Pacific region on topics supporting the "Track I" program of the **ASEAN Regional Forum (ARF)**. CSCAP was established in 1993, with member committees in all of the ARF countries. An international steering committee is supported by a secretariat housed in the Malaysian Institute of Strategic and International Studies in Kuala Lumpur. The executive office of the U.S. committee is in the **Pacific Forum/CSIS** office in Honolulu.

– D –

DAP CHHUAN PLOT. In February 1959, General Dap Chhuan, a **Khmer Issarak** veteran with Thai army connections, was the dissident governor of Siem Reap province and military commander in northwest **Cambodia**. His own ambitions linked him to **South Vietnamese** plots to overthrow Prime Minister Prince **Norodom Sihanouk**'s neutralist government, whose relations with Saigon were badly strained. There was credible evidence that the United States was aware of the plotting and even that **Central Intelligence Agency (CIA)** agents in Saigon and Cambodia facilitated the planning and logistics, looking for an alternative to Sihanouk. Sihanouk got wind of the conspiracy via French and Chinese intelligence and sent a military force to take over Siem Reap. South Vietnamese agents were captured at Dap's headquarters. Dap himself was captured trying to escape to **Thailand** and died in captivity. At first, Sihanouk angrily lashed out at the United States for not informing him of the plot and then accused Washington of complicity, protesting in writing to President **Dwight D. Eisenhower**.

DEAN, JOHN GUNTHER (1926–). A career Foreign Service Officer, John Gunther Dean had been a political officer in **Laos** from 1956 to 1958. He returned to Laos as deputy chief of mission (1972–1974). When Ambassador **G. McMurtrie Godley** left Laos in April 1973 to pursue his failed nomination as assistant secretary of state for East Asian and Pacific affairs, Dean served as chargé d'affaires for six months, during which time he gave American support to Prime Minister **Souvanna Phouma**'s negotiations with the **Pathet Lao** for the September 1973 **Laos protocol** establishing the framework for the third **coalition government**. He received a personal letter of thanks from President **Richard Nixon** for his efforts in Laos. In 1974, Dean replaced **Emory C. Swank** as American ambassador to **Cambodia**. Dean's job there was to bolster Cambodia's military defense against the communist **Khmer Rouge (KR)**. He was specifically instructed by National Security Advisor **Henry Kissinger** not to seek a political settlement. On 12 April 1975, as KR troops prepared to enter Phnom Penh, Ambassador Dean, with the embassy's flag folded under his arm, climbed into a helicopter to fly to safety in an evacuation codenamed "**Eagle Pull**." After tours as ambassador in Denmark and Lebanon, Dean returned to Southeast Asia as ambassador to **Thailand** from 1981 to 1985 during the **Third Indochina War**. He finished his career as ambassador to India. In 2007, from retirement in Paris, Ambassador Dean questioned the worth of the planned **Khmer Rouge trials**, saying the budget could be better used for schools and hospitals.

DEMOCRATIC KAMPUCHEA (DK). For 10 months after the victory of the **Khmer Rouge** in **Cambodia**, the Communist Party of Cambodia, headed by **Pol Pot**, worked to transform Cambodian society behind the façade of the Royal Government of the National

Union of Kampuchea (GRUNK), ceremonially headed by Prince **Norodom Sihanouk**. The United States extended its policy of non-recognition and **trade** embargo imposed on the **Democratic Republic of Vietnam (DRV)** to Khmer Rouge–ruled Cambodia. In January 1976, the constitution for Democratic Kampuchea swept Sihanouk away in a flood of unique radical measures by which the revolutionaries in the Angkar—the Organization—at the center of Democratic Kampuchea (DK) could make the leap to a communist society without any transitional period. In a program of societal destruction and reconstruction, the infrastructure of the functioning state and economy was torn down. The middle class and educated elites were the enemies. The Buddhist institutional framework of monks and monasteries was attacked. The time of the great leap backward was described by the French author François Ponchaud as Cambodia's "year zero." It is estimated that 1.5 to 2 million Cambodians died in DK "killing fields," as internal **refugees**, or in the famines of 1977–1978. In December 1978, **Vietnam** invaded and occupied Cambodia, replacing the DK with the **People's Republic of Kampuchea (PRK)**. For a decade during the **Third Indochina War** the Khmer Rouge, under the flag of the **Coalition Government of Democratic Kampuchea (CGDK),** was the military backbone of the **Khmer resistance** to the PRK and its Vietnamese backers, although none of the CGDK's supporters, including the United States, wanted the DK to be restored to rule Cambodia again.

DEMOCRATIC REPUBLIC OF VIETNAM (DRV). The Democratic Republic of Vietnam was the state proclaimed by **Ho Chi Minh** on 2 September 1945 in then **Viet Minh**–controlled Hanoi. The DRV claimed sovereignty over all of French **Vietnam** and fought the French for real independence. This was the **First Indochina War**. In January 1950, after Ho claimed that the DRV was the legal government of Vietnam and called for cooperation with friendly nations, both the People's Republic of **China** and the Soviet Union recognized the DRV as the legitimate government of Vietnam. This, together with Ho's communist background and the revolutionary platform of the Viet Minh, convinced the United States that the DRV was a puppet and stalking horse for international communist expansion and had to be contained. In 1954, the **Geneva Conference**

terminated the French role and temporarily partitioned the country along the 17th parallel of latitude. The United States, pursuing its policy of **containment**, sought to prevent the DRV from uniting the country under its control. This led to the **Second Indochina War**, better known in the United States as the **Vietnam War**. The DRV was the American enemy and then, from 1968 on, the negotiating partner of the United States in the **Paris peace negotiations**. The DRV was succeeded in 1976 in the reunified Vietnam by the renamed **Socialist Republic of Vietnam (SRV)**, a change of names but not regime.

DERIAN, PATRICIA MURPHY (1929–). Named by President **Jimmy Carter** to be the first assistant secretary of state for human rights and humanitarian affairs (1977–1981), Patricia "Pat" Derian made **human rights** a public element of American foreign policy if not the real priority. Active in the Southern civil rights movements, Derian had worked in the George McGovern and **Lyndon B. Johnson** presidential campaigns and was a deputy campaign manager of Carter's campaign. By personally swearing her in as assistant secretary, Carter gave a signal to the **State Department**'s bureaucracy that human rights were to be an important part of the U.S. foreign relations agenda. In fact, Derian and her mission were resisted at all levels of the department. The general feeling was that her aggressively confrontational style on rights issues jeopardized broader U.S. interests in regions and countries. Nowhere was this more evident then in East Asia and the Pacific, where Assistant Secretary for East Asian and Pacific Affairs **Richard Holbrooke** and ambassadors in countries like South Korea, **Singapore**, **Indonesia**, and the **Philippines** pushed for stable bilateral political relations rather than human rights assaults on the regimes respectively of Park Chun Hee, **Lee Kuan Yew**, **Suharto**, and **Ferdinand Marcos**. In the case of Marcos in particular, Assistant Secretary Derian was the only high-level American to visit imprisoned Filipino democratic challenger **Benigno Aquino**. For the foreign policy establishment, the Philippine **Military Bases Agreement**, which Marcos held hostage, was more important.

DEWEY, GEORGE (1837–1917). The only U.S. naval officer to ever hold the rank of Admiral of the Navy, George Dewey was commodore of the navy's Asiatic Squadron at the outbreak of the **Spanish–American War**. Backed by Assistant Secretary of the Navy Theodore Roosevelt, a strong imperialist, Dewy assumed command of the squadron with the express purpose of preparing it to engage the Spanish fleet in Manila Bay in the **Philippines**. He sailed from Hong Kong on 25 April 1898 on board his flagship the cruiser USS *Olympia*, commanded by Captain Charles V. Gridley. Commencing action on 1 May, Dewey uttered the words that became part of American history, "You may fire when you are ready, Gridley." In the span of a few hours, the Spanish fleet and shore installations were destroyed without an American casualty. Dewey's success demonstrated that the United States had to be reckoned with as a naval power in East Asia. Dewey became a national hero. He was promoted to rear admiral on 11 May and then by an 1899 act of Congress was elevated to Admiral of the Navy, a rank that disappeared at his death. Touted as a possible Democratic presidential candidate in 1900, Dewey, after some public relations setbacks, withdrew from competition and eventually endorsed the incumbent Republican president **William McKinley**. At his death, Dewey was still on the active navy list as president of the Navy Board.

DIEM, NGO DINH (1901–1963). Ngo Dinh Diem was president of the **Republic of Vietnam (RVN)** from 1956 until his assassination in a coup on 2 November 1963. Diem came from a prominent Catholic family. Well educated, he became a senior bureaucrat in the French colonial regime, until he quit in 1933. A frustrated nationalist, he spurned collaboration with the Japanese, the French, and **Ho Chi Minh**'s communists. He also refused **Bao Dai**'s first request for him to become prime minister of the French-sponsored **State of Vietnam**. In 1950, Diem went into voluntary exile. In the United States from 1951 to1953, he was sheltered by the Catholic establishment, which brought him to the attention of American Catholic politicians, including Senator **John F. Kennedy**. In 1954, he returned to Vietnam to become prime minister of the State of Vietnam under head-of-state Bao Dai. Although faced with opposition from gangsters, powerful religious sects, the military, and the French, he was able to consolidate his political position with both open and clandestine support form the United States. **Central Intelligence Agency (CIA)** operator **Edward Lansdale**, fresh from working with President **Ramon**

Magsaysay in the **Philippines**, became a close advisor. In February 1955, President **Dwight D. Eisenhower** sent a letter to Bao Dai praising the substantial progress being made in Vietnam under Prime Minister Diem. In October 1955, Diem deposed Bao Dai in a rigged referendum. The State of Vietnam became the **Republic of Vietnam (RVN)**, and under a new constitution Diem became president, a post to which he was reelected in 1961,

Both as prime minister and then as president, Diem rejected the 1954 **Geneva Accords** and the promise of all-Vietnam national elections. In this he was supported by the U.S. government, which saw in Diem's anticommunist nationalism a bulwark of **containment** in Southeast Asia. Diem's nationalist appeal, however, was undermined by the nature of his Catholic minority government: nepotistic, corrupt, and anti-Buddhist. The domestic legitimacy of his government was further damaged by the behavior of his family, particularly his brothers, Ngo Dinh Can and Ngo Dinh Nhu, and Nhu's wife. Madam Nhu became a particular target of Americans outraged by persecution of opposition Buddhist monks. Even as popular support for the Diem regime eroded, the American diplomatic and military establishment continued to support him. It was only when it became apparent that under Diem communism was not going to be contained in Vietnam that critics of the regime in Saigon and Washington either encouraged or passively supported the 1 November 1963 **Diem coup**, which ended in the murder of both Diem and his brother Nhu.

DIEM COUP, 1963. As **Ngo Dinh Diem**'s government of the **Republic of Vietnam (RVN)** became increasingly resistant to reform and unmindful of U.S. advice, critical voices were raised in the administration of President **John F. Kennedy** about its capacity to successfully wage the war against the **Viet Cong**. Diem, once seen by his American backers as the nationalist anticommunist alternative to **Ho Chi Minh**, was becoming a liability rather than an asset in the common struggle. These concerns were shared by a group of senior South Vietnamese military officers, who were in contact with the **Central Intelligence Agency (CIA)**. In reaction to the forceful suppression of Buddhist protests in the spring and summer of 1963, ordered by Diem's brother Ngo Dinh Nhu, Washington, prodded from Saigon by Ambassador **Henry Cabot Lodge**, accepted the need for leadership change in the RVN. On 24 August 1963, a cable was sent to Ambassador Lodge by Acting Secretary of State **George Ball** indicating that the United States would accept a coup outcome. The principal authors of the cable were Undersecretary of State **W. Averell Harriman** and Assistant Secretary of State for East Asian and Pacific Affairs **Roger Hilsman**. Ball had verbally cleared the cable by telephone with Secretary of State **Dean Rusk** and President Kennedy, both of whom were away from Washington. The American position was conveyed to the plotting generals by longtime CIA operative **Lucien Conein**. The coup itself did not take place until 1 November. The next day, to U.S. horror, Diem and his brother Nhu were killed. Rather than ushering in political stability and a new will to win, a series of coups and countercoups followed until General **Nguyen Van Thieu** consolidated his power after the election of 1967. *See also* COLLINS, J. LAWTON; DURBROW, ELBRIDGE; NOLTING, FREDRICK.

DIEN BIEN PHU. In this remote district capital in a mountain valley route linking **North Vietnam** to **Laos**, the French fort at Dien Bien Phu was the site of the climactic battle of the **First Indochina War**. French paratroopers had dropped into Dien Bien Phu in November 1953. The strategic goal was to prevent further **Viet Minh** intrusions into Laos. It was also hoped to draw the main Vietnamese forces into a set-piece battle. By the beginning of March 1954, the French force of 16,000 was encircled by 50,000 of their enemy, who began their assault on 11 March. Paris desperately appealed to the United States to intervene and to have the U.S. Air Force resupply the beleaguered garrison. The administration of **Dwight D. Eisenhower**, unwilling to become officially involved, moved 12 U.S. Air Force C-119 transports to a Hanoi field. American insignia were removed and the French tricolor roundel painted on. The 24 pilots for the planes were supplied from the Taiwan-based **Central Intelligence Agency (CIA)** proprietary company **Civil Air Transport (CAT)**. American Air Force crews maintained the planes at the French air base. Between 13 March and the French surrender of Dien Bien Phu on 7 May, the CAT pilots flew 682 supply missions, with the loss to ground fire of one plane and its two pilots. The fall of Dien Bien Phu took place the day before the opening of the plenary session of the 1954 **Geneva Con-**

ference that resulted in the **Geneva Accords** ending the French war in Indochina. At a February 2005 ceremony at the French embassy in Washington, CAT pilots involved in the Dien Bien Phu missions were recognized as *Chevaliers de la Légion d'Honneur*. Among them was **Allen Pope**, who was shot down over **Indonesia** in 1958 flying a bomber in support of the CIA-backed **PRRI–Permesta** regional rebellions.

DILI MASSACRE. On 12 November 1991, Indonesian troops opened fire point blank into a funeral procession at the Santa Cruz Cemetery in Dili, the capital of **Indonesia**'s **East Timor** province. The crowd was in attendance at a funeral for a Timorese student who had been killed by soldiers at an earlier protest. Along the way the marchers displayed banners calling for East Timor independence and celebrating anti-Indonesian guerrilla leader **Xanana Gusmão**. Casualty figures vary, from the Indonesian official count of 50 killed to what appear to be more reliable figures of up to 270. There were many wounded and a large number of arrests. The eyewitness accounts of foreign journalists and videotapes smuggled out of the province shocked and outraged Western critics of the authoritarian rule of Indonesia's President **Suharto**.

The official American reaction was one of dismay. The **State Department** went on record that nothing could justify the magnitude of the excessive force used by the military and the enormous casualties. The issue was complicated by claims of American complicity because of the close military-to-military relations between Indonesia and the United States, including Indonesian participation in the U.S. **International Military Education and Training (IMET)** programs and **foreign military sales (FMS)** to Indonesia. The **human rights** and democratic activists of the East Timor Action Network (ETAN) bombarded Congress with the charge that U.S.-supplied M-16 rifles were used to kill the Timorese. Congressional pressure forced major restrictions in American arms sales to Indonesia and required a contractual obligation that lethal weapons or helicopters acquired by Indonesia were not to be used in East Timor. While the executive branch of the American government treated the East Timor issue as an Indonesian human rights issue, Congress legislatively identified East Timor as separate from Indonesia.

Over the executive branch's objections, Congress barred Indonesia from IMET in FY 1993, making future participation conditional on Indonesian accountability for the Dili Massacre. The cutoff was extended in 1994 and 1995. However, after 1994, Indonesia was allowed back into the Expanded or E-IMET program with its concentration on human rights and justice. Congressional concerns were raised anew in 1998, when it was revealed that since 1992, U.S. Special Forces had been training Indonesian Special Forces in a series of exercises in a joint combined exchange training (JCET) program. This was barred by Congress in August 1998. Indonesia's reaction was to reject any military relationship conditioned on human rights considerations.

DOMINO THEORY. The domino theory, attributed to President **Dwight D. Eisenhower**, was a statement of the geostrategic consequences for what then was designated the "free world" if **Indochina** should fall to communism. Eisenhower iterated it in a 7 April 1954 news conference in response to a question about the strategic importance of Indochina to the United States. He framed his answer in terms of what he called "the falling domino principle," in which the first falling domino in a row of dominoes will certainly and quickly lead to the fall of the last domino. He enumerated the order as first Indochina and then **Burma**, **Thailand**, the Peninsula (**Malaya** and **Singapore**), and **Indonesia**, with the consequent threat to the defensive island chain from Japan, Taiwan, and the **Philippines**, to Australia and New Zealand. There was nothing novel in the statement as an analysis of the strategic consequences of the failure of **containment** in Southeast Asia. It had been the accepted basis of American support for France in Indochina during the administration of President **Harry S. Truman** as well as the Eisenhower administration. What was new was the domino analogy, which was easily understandable by the wider public.

DONG, PHAM VAN (1906–2000). Second only to **Ho Chi Minh** in the communist hierarchy of the **Democratic Republic of Vietnam (DRV)**, Pham Van Dong became DRV prime minister in 1955, serving in the same role in the successor **Socialist Republic of Vietnam (SRV)** until he retired in 1987. In 1954, he led the DRV delegation to the **Geneva Conference** that ended the **First Indochina War**. During the negotiations to end the **Vietnam War**, it was to Pham Van Dong that President **Richard M. Nixon** addressed his letter promising postwar economic assistance for relief and reconstruction. Pham Van Dong had meetings with the **Woodcock Mission**, sent by President **Jimmy Carter** in 1977, in which the first hopeful signs appeared for possible **normalization of relations with Vietnam**. *See also* NIXON–PHAM VAN DONG MESSAGE.

DONOVAN, WILLIAM J. (1883–1959). Called by President **Dwight D. Eisenhower** the "last hero," William J. "Wild Bill" Donovan was the father of the modern U.S. intelligence establishment. A decorated commander in World War I (DSC and Medal of Honor), despite his Republican politics he was a confidante of President Franklin D. Roosevelt, carrying out secret missions for him, dating back to Roosevelt's time as navy secretary up to the outbreak of World War II. Recalled to active duty, Donovan built and headed the **Office of Strategic Services (OSS)**, the American wartime intelligence agency. When the war ended in 1945, Donovan, now a major general, tried to persuade President **Harry Truman** to maintain the foreign intelligence capabilities that the OSS provided. There was strong bureaucratic resistance to this from J. Edgar Hoover's Federal Bureau of Investigation (FBI) and the **State Department**. Truman terminated the OSS. A core element of OSS veterans, including **Frank Wisner**, continued to work within the State Department. Postwar perceptions of the Soviet Union and the beginnings of the Cold War led in 1947 to the creation of the **Central Intelligence Agency (CIA)**. When **Dwight D. Eisenhower** became president, Donovan lobbied for the job of director of the CIA. He was to be disappointed, as Eisenhower called on his wartime comrade in arms General **Walter Bedell Smith**. Donovan was named ambassador to **Thailand** in 1953, a post he left within a year because of illness. In a ceremony on 8 May 2000 honoring the **Free Thai**, a World War II OSS client, CIA director George J. Tenant said of his legendary predecessor that it was in Thailand that "the General performed his final acts of service, helping to construct the framework for a strong postwar strategic partnership between our countries."

DUBOIS, COERT (1881–1960). A veteran U.S. diplomat, Coert DuBois replaced **Frank Graham** as the American representative on the United Nations **Good Offices Committee in Indonesia** in February 1948. From 1929 to 1932, DuBois had been the U.S. consul general in Batavia, the capital of the Netherlands Indies. He was known to be favorable to the Dutch in the negotiations and had pressed for a federal solution rather than the unitary Republic of **Indonesia**. He asked to be relieved in July 1948 because of illness and was replaced by **Merle Cochran**.

DULLES, ALLEN W. (1893–1968). The longest serving director of the **Central Intelligence Agency (CIA)**, from 1953 to 1961, Allen Dulles worked closely with his brother, Secretary of State **John Foster Dulles** in the **Eisenhower** administration to shape the American response to the perceived threat of communism in Southeast Asia. Like his brother, a lawyer, Allen Dulles began his career as a junior diplomat in Europe after World War I and then joined the law firm of Sullivan and Cromwell, where his brother was a managing partner. Active in the Council on Foreign Relations, he co-authored two books on American foreign policy with its president, Hamilton Fish Armstrong. During World War II, he was recruited to the **Office of Strategic Services (OSS)** by **William J. Donovan**. He ended the war as station chief in Berne, Switzerland, running an espionage network in Germany. In 1948, he headed an intelligence review of the newly formed CIA and in 1951 became Deputy Director of Plans (DDP), the clandestine operations side of the agency. As DDP and director, Dulles favored direct action in support of the policy of **containment**. Not all initiatives were successful. The most public failure was the clandestine intervention in support of the **PRRI–Permesta regional rebellions** in Indonesia in 1958. Although asked to stay on by incoming President **John F. Kennedy**, Dulles retired.

DULLES, JOHN FOSTER (1888–1959). Secretary of state in the administration of President **Dwight D. Eisenhower**, John Foster Dulles was the architect of **containment** in Southeast Asia. His brother was **Allen Dulles**, director of the **Central Intelligence Agency (CIA)**. The Dulles brothers were sons of a Presbyterian minister and had a grandfather who had been secretary of state for President Benjamin

Harrison. Their uncle, Robert Lansing, had been President Woodrow Wilson's secretary of state. An international lawyer by profession, John Foster Dulles's institutional base was the prominent law firm Sullivan and Cromwell, where he was managing partner. From World War I until his death from cancer in 1959, Dulles was deeply involved in U.S. foreign affairs. He was legal counsel to the American delegation to the Versailles Peace Conference ending World War I, and he was a member of the American delegation to the 1945 San Francisco Conference establishing the **United Nations**. He was policy advisor to the failed Republican presidential campaigns of Thomas Dewey in 1944 and 1948. Successful Republican presidential candidate Dwight D. Eisenhower chose Dulles as secretary of state when he took office in January 1951.

Stung by what candidate Eisenhower had called the "loss" of **China** and Chinese intervention in the Korean War, Dulles saw American friends and allies in East and Southeast Asia facing a common single hostile front and believed that the imposition of communism on Southeast Asia by the Soviet Union or the People's Republic of China would be a grave threat to the "free world." Dulles was scornful of neutralism and nonalignment as professed in Southeast Asia by **Burma**, **Cambodia**, and **Indonesia**, describing it as shortsighted and immoral. Dulles saw the 1954 **Geneva Accords** on **Indochina** as a defeat for the West. He promoted the building of a strongly anticommunist regime in **South Vietnam** as an alternative to the communists in the north. He sponsored the **Southeast Asia Collective Defense Treaty (Manila Pact)** and its institutional framework, the **Southeast Asia Treaty Organization (SEATO)**, both as a deterrent and a commitment to forward defense. Dulles viewed with alarm Indonesia's leftward policy course under President **Sukarno**. Hoping to promote a strongly anticommunist Indonesia, either unitary or plural, Dulles signed off on **Central Intelligence Agency (CIA)** covert support to the dissident insurgents in Indonesia's **PRRI–Permesta** regional rebellions. Although the rebels were ultimately unsuccessful, U.S. support only further alienated Sukarno. Dulles's views on resisting communism and in particular the China threat were fully reflected by long-serving Assistant Secretary of State for East Asian and Pacific Affairs **Walter Robertson**.

DURBROW, ELBRIDGE (1903–1997). Elbridge Durbrow was American ambassador to the **Republic of Vietnam** from 1957 to 1961. He became critical of the **Ngo Dinh Diem** government's capacity to make the economic and political changes necessary to broaden its base of support. In 1960, he warned Washington that if the situation in Vietnam should continue to deteriorate, it might become necessary for the United States to consider alternative courses of action and leadership if American goals were to be achieved. He was replaced by the more conciliatory **Frederick Nolting**.

– E –

EAGLE PULL. This was the code name of the operation to evacuate the remaining American establishment in Phnom Penh, **Cambodia**'s capital, on 12 April 1975. A total of 276 persons were lifted by helicopter to aircraft carriers offshore: 82 Americans, including Ambassador **John Dean**; 35 third-country nationals; and 159 Cambodians. To the surprise of the Americans, many Cambodian officials refused the offer to leave. "Eagle Pull" was considered a dress rehearsal for the much more complex **"Frequent Wind"** operation two weeks later that evacuated Americans and Vietnamese from Saigon.

EAST ASIA SECURITY INITIATIVE (EASI). In 1990, during the administration of **George H. W. Bush**, the U.S. Defense Department began planning a gradual and modest reduction of military forces in the East Asian and Pacific region. This was the East Asia Security Initiative. The Philippine Senate's rejection of a new **Military Bases Agreement** hastened the redeployments. The loss of **Clark Air Base** and the naval facilities at **Subic Bay** meant the United States had to find "places," not bases, to give access to facilities for logistical support, training, exercising, and repair. Memorandums of agreement were forged with **Indonesia**, **Malaysia**, **Singapore**, and **Thailand** for access and services. Singapore's cooperation was the most extensive. The willingness of the Southeast Asian states to pick up at least part of the burden rejected by the **Philippines** was politically based on a desire to keep the United States engaged in the region as part of a stable balance of power even in the absence of the perceived threats of the Cold War.

EAST ASIA SUMMIT (EAS). On 14 December 2005, the heads of government of the 10 members of the **Association of Southeast Asian Nations (ASEAN)** and their counterparts from Australia, **China**, India, Japan, South Korea, and New Zealand met in Kuala Lumpur, the capital of **Malaysia**, for an inaugural East Asia Summit meeting. They were joined by Russian president Vladimir Putin as a guest of the EAS. The United States was conspicuously absent, technically excluded since it had not acceded to the **Treaty of Amity and Cooperation in Southeast Asia (TAC)**. The EAS followed as a kind of adjunct to the annual ASEAN summit. The idea of the EAS was mooted in 2004 by Malaysian Prime Minister **Abdullah Badawi** in a visionary concept originally seen as the first step toward an East Asian Community. At the second EAS, postponed to January 2007 at host county **Philippines** request, the first step toward a possible East Asian Community was taken when it was agreed to back a feasibility study for an **East Asian Free Trade Area (EAFTA)**, which also would exclude the United States. The third EAS, which took place in **Singapore** in November 2007, showed little progress toward institutionalization beyond one more "dialogue" opportunity. The U.S. official position on the EAS is that it has no position because EAS is a "black box" and no one knows what it really is.

EAST ASIAN ECONOMIC CAUCUS (EAEC). This was the diluted version of a grander project of an **East Asian Economic Group**, which, as proposed by Prime Minister **Mahathir Mohammad** of **Malaysia**, would exclude the United States. It was supposed to be an ad hoc group within the **Asia–Pacific Economic Cooperation (APEC)** forum. The EAEC never convened. After the **financial crisis of 1997–1998**, Mahathir proposed to institutionalize the EAEC in an East Asia secretariat to be housed in Malaysia's capital Kuala Lumpur, but this too was not accepted.

EAST ASIAN ECONOMIC GROUP (EAEG). In December 1990, **Malaysia's** prime minister **Mahathir Mohammad** proposed the formation of an East Asian Economic Group bringing the **Association of Southeast Asian Nations (ASEAN)**, **China**, the Republic of Korea, and Japan into an alternative consultative structure that would balance the wider U.S.-supported Pacific regionalism represented by the **Asia–Pacific Economic Cooperation (APEC)** forum. The EAEG was designed to exclude the United States. Mahathir argued that APEC was dominated by the United States and functioned as an instrument of American global economic power. The initiative was also a defensive reaction to what Mahathir viewed as the threat of "blocization" in the international economy posed by the European Economic Community (EEC) and the North American Free Trade Area (NAFTA). The United States vigorously opposed the proposal as a retrograde step in liberalizing and expanding **trade** and **investment** in the Asian region. Secretary of State **James Baker** minced no words in opposition. In ASEAN, **Indonesia** took the lead in opposing the EAEG, with President **Suharto** insisting that ASEAN leaders should participate in the 1991 Blake Island, Washington, APEC summit hosted by President **William J. Clinton**. Mahathir boycotted the meeting. As a face-saving gesture to Malaysia, an ASEAN compromise accepted the concept of an **East Asia Economic Caucus** as an ad hoc consultative forum for the East Asian economies within APEC itself. *See also* ASEAN PLUS 3.

EAST ASIAN FREE TRADE AREA (EAFTA). This is a proposal that has been under study since 1998, but was urged by Japan with renewed vigor in 2006, and backed by the **Asian Development Bank (ADB)**. The goal was to create a regional free **trade** area consisting of the ten members of the **Association of Southeast Asian Nations (ASEAN)**, Australia, **China**, India, Japan, New Zealand, and South Korea. Both ASEAN and the **East Asia Summit (EAS)** groupings have agreed to feasibility studies for EAFTA. It is widely viewed as an effort to dilute Chinese economic influence in Southeast Asia. The United States strongly opposes an EAFTA that would draw an economic line down the middle of the Pacific Ocean and that, if realized, could cost the United States as much as $25 billion through trade discrimination and diversion and would have negative impacts on other areas of American relations in Southeast Asia, including security interests. The United States proposed an alternative regional trade grouping through the existing **Asia–Pacific Economic Cooperation (APEC)** framework, to be called the **Asia–Pacific Free Trade Area (APFTA)**.

EAST TIMOR (TIMOR-LESTE). The newest independent state in Southeast Asia, East Timor became an independent republic on 20 May 2002. It is the third smallest state in Southeast Asia, after Singapore and Brunei, with 9,140 square miles (15,007 square kilometers), including the enclave of Oecussi, about the size of Vermont. Its population is estimated at just over one million. The capital is Dili. East Timor's formal independence followed a more than two-year period of authority in the territory by the **United Nations Transitional Administration in East Timor (UNTAET)**. UNTAET was put in place after the 1999 intervention by the Australian-led **International Force in East Timor (INTERFET)** to end the violence following the **East Timor referendum** on independence from **Indonesia**. The United States was represented at the Independence Day celebrations by a delegation led by former president **William J. Clinton**. The American embassy was officially opened by Assistant Secretary of State James Kelly, who recognized former president Clinton's personal interest in the democratic transition of East Timor. Also present was Ambassador **Richard Holbrooke**, who in the Clinton administration had represented the U.S. position on East Timor in the **United Nations** Security Council. Although good relations with the United States are important to the East Timor government, its three most salient bilateral relations are with its former rulers, Portugal and Indonesia, and its southern neighbor, Australia, across the Timor Strait, with whom it shares large seabed oil and gas resources.

For four centuries, until 1974, the eastern half of the island of Timor, deep in the Indonesian archipelago, had been part of the Portuguese colonial realm. Until 1949, the island had been shared between Portugal and the Netherlands East Indies. After 1949, Portuguese Timor's borders were with Indonesia. After the 1974 collapse of Portuguese rule in Timor and a unilateral declaration of independence by East Timorese nationalists, in December 1975 Indonesia invaded and occupied East Timor. For a quarter of a century Indonesia administered East Timor as a province. The repressive nature of its rule and **human rights** violations were widely criticized, particularly after the **Dili Massacre** in 1991, but it was not until the end of the Cold War in Southeast Asia and the toppling of the **Suharto** government in Indonesia that the subsequent government of President **B. J.**

Habibie agreed to the referendum that led to the emergence of independent East Timor.

East Timor is the poorest state in Southeast Asia and one of the 10 poorest countries of the world. Its population is largely involved in subsistence agriculture. Per capita income is less than $536 a year. Until the revenues from oil and natural gas joint development areas with Australia fully come on line, East Timor is essentially a ward of the World Bank and donor nations for both its operating and development budgets. A 50-nation donor conference in December 1999 pledged $522 million for humanitarian aid, reconstruction assistance, and support of UNTAET. Japan, followed by Portugal, Australia, the European Union, and the United States, were the major contributors. Donor-nation funding has had to fill the economic gap created in Timor as a result of the end of the "bubble" effect of UNTAET and, after independence, its successor, the United Nations Mission in Support of East Timor (UNMISET). The UNMISET presence was essentially phased out by 2005. The UN Security Council unanimously supported the maintenance of a smaller United Nations (UN) political office, UN Office in Timor Leste (UNOTIL), in Dili. Renewed violence in 2006 after a military mutiny led to a new Australian-led foreign intervention, the International Stabilization Force (ISF), and a UN Security Council endorsement of a modest UN police mission called the UN Integrated Mission in Timor-Leste (UNMIT). New elections in 2007 made **José Ramos-Horta** president and **Xanana Gusmão** prime minister. Even as another round of violence protesting the new government broke out, the United States quickly welcomed the new government and urged all parties to accept it.

Since independence in 2002, multilateral aid channeled through the World Bank and **Asian Development Bank (ADB)** trust funds has been complemented by bilateral assistance from government-to-government programs. The importance of American assistance to East Timor was signified in May 2001 when Gusmão, then president of Timor's National Council of Timorese Resistance (CNRT) and later (2002–2007) president of East Timor, accompanied by his foreign minister, Nobel Prize winner Ramos-Horta, came to Washington to lobby for long-term, strategically directed U.S. assistance. To this end, Gusmão met with President **George W. Bush**. Through 2005, the United States had provided $154 million in assistance to East

Timor, about 18 percent of the total it has received. The bilateral assistance budget for FY 2007 was $13 million.

The **U.S. Agency for International Development (USAID)** programs in East Timor are directed to economic growth, governance, and public health; democracy building; economic development and job creation; poverty eradication; and basic health services. During the 2006 crisis, USAID worked with other agencies in providing humanitarian assistance to the 150,000 internally displaced East Timorese **refugees**. There has also been a U.S. **Peace Corps** presence, with 57 volunteers in-country in 2005 working in community building and health assistance. The Peace Corps withdrew in 2006 because of the unsettled political conditions. The **Asia Foundation**, supported by USAID, provided voter education and poll monitoring for the August 2001 Constituent Assembly elections and the April 2002 presidential elections. It also provided technical assistance to the Assembly in drafting the constitution. Although traditional security concerns are low on the bilateral priorities, East Timor has negotiated a status of forces agreement (SOFA) covering any U.S. military personnel who might be in-country as well as a bilateral agreement on **International Criminal Court Article 98**, giving impunity to the United States from surrender of its citizens to the International Control Commission (ICC). *See also* INDONESIAN INVASION OF EAST TIMOR.

EAST TIMOR REFERENDUM. In January 1999, Indonesian President **B. J. Habibie** unilaterally announced that **Indonesia** would allow the population of the province of East Timor an opportunity to conduct an act of self-determination. This had been a demand of East Timorese nationalists and international advocates for East Timor since the **Indonesian invasion of East Timor** in 1975. Indonesia had stubbornly resisted allowing an act of self-determination since 1976 despite international condemnation of its **human rights** record and **Fretilin**'s armed liberation struggle, in part fearing this could lead to similar demands elsewhere in the archipelago.

The twin shocks of the **financial crisis of 1997–1998** and the collapse of the **Suharto** government changed the political context within which Indonesia viewed its East Timor problem. President Habibie wanted to remove East Timor from the international agenda so as to garner economic and political support for Indonesia's economic rehabilitation and democratization. In August 1998, **United Nations (UN)**–sponsored talks began between Indonesia and Portugal, which was considered to still be legally sovereign by the UN. The goal was broader autonomy for the territory during a transition period, after which a referendum on its future could be held. Indonesia was being pressured by Australia, the United States, and the European Union to accept the fact that a limited special autonomy would not satisfy the East Timorese. **Consultative Group for Indonesia (CGI)** negotiations for economic assistance to Indonesia had become part of the stakes in the East Timor problem.

Habibie's decision to allow a referendum without a transition period came as a shock to the diplomatic process and to the Indonesian military, which had not been consulted and had not only pride but economic interests invested in East Timor. The format for the referendum was laid out as a "popular consultation" administered by a **United Nations Assistance Mission in East Timor (UNAMET)** authorized by the Security Council. American president **William J. Clinton** and UN ambassador **Richard Holbrooke** strongly urged action. The U.S. provided major funding for UNAMET. The main concern in the run-up to the referendum was security. Already in 1998, the Indonesian military was building prointegration militias in East Timor to thwart any change in the status of the province. Even before the final agreement on 5 May 1998 at the UN establishing the legal basis for the "consultation," the militias were attacking and killing proindependence civilians. In April, both Australia and the United States urged the UN not to take too strong a position on security with the Indonesians for fear of jeopardizing a final agreement. Days before the 30 August ballot, U.S. warnings about the consequences of violence were made by President Clinton to President Habibie, by Secretary of State **Madeleine Albright** to Indonesian Foreign Minister Ali Alatas, and by Secretary of Defense William Cohen to the head of the Indonesian armed forces, General Wiranto.

The citizens of East Timor voted overwhelmingly for independence. This was followed by a terrifying rampage by the militias that killed hundreds of civilians, uprooted a quarter of the population, and destroyed infrastructure. Indonesia was forced to accept a UN Security Council–authorized peacekeeping intervention by the **International Force in East Timor (INTERFET)**. Although not a participant in the field with INTERFET, the United States provided logistic and other support. It also strongly backed the succeeding **United Nations Transitional Administration in East Timor (UNTAET)**. President Clinton, calling what was happening "madness," threatened to cut economic assistance to Indonesia unless it allowed a peacekeeping force, and Congress further restricted U.S.–Indonesian military-to-military relationships in the **Leahy Amendment**.

EASTERN CONSTRUCTION COMPANY. Originally set up in the **Philippines** in 1954 as the Freedom Company, the renamed Eastern Construction Company was established by anticommunist Filipinos with close links to Philippine president **Ramon Magsaysay**. Backed by the **Central Intelligence Agency (CIA)**, it was a vehicle to recruit and deploy Filipinos to the **Republic of Vietnam** and **Laos** for unconventional operations.

EDSA REVOLUTION (Epifano de los Santos Avenue). Known also as the "people's power" revolution, the EDSA revolution was the Catholic Church–supported mass popular revolt against the **Ferdinand Marcos** regime in the **Philippines**. It followed the fraudulent outcome of the February 1986 presidential election, won by **Corazon Aquino** but stolen by Marcos. The EDSA uprising, together with defecting Philippine military leadership and American pressure, led to Marcos's exile in the United States and the assumption of the Philippines presidency by Aquino. EDSA is an acronym for Epifanio de los Santos Avenue, the Manila central highway artery along which the throngs of thousands marched toward military headquarters. The popular demonstrations against Philippine President **Joseph Estrada** in 2001 have been called EDSA II, and the demonstrations in 2006 against President **Gloria Macapagal-Arroyo** suggested a possible EDSA III.

EISENHOWER, DWIGHT D. (1890–1969). Five-star General of the army Dwight D. Eisenhower was the 34th president of the United States (1953–1961). He was a 1915 graduate of West Point who, until he received his first star as a brigadier general in 1941, had had a slow climb through the ranks in staff positions. From 1935 to 1939, he was attached to the staff of General **Douglas MacArthur** in the

Philippines, which he left as a lieutenant colonel. His organizational and logistical skills quickly propelled him upward in wartime circumstances. From the War Department he went to Europe, where, with four stars, he became the commander of U.S. forces in Europe and the supreme commandeer of the Allied invasion forces. He returned to serve as Army Chief of Staff and retired to become president of Columbia University until President **Harry S. Truman** called him back to service in 1950 to become the first supreme commander of North Atlantic Treaty Organization (NATO) forces. Although as a professional army officer Eisenhower was apolitical, he resigned his NATO post in 1952 to run for president on the Republican ticket. His vice presidential running mate was **Richard M. Nixon**. Promising to end the Korean War, Eisenhower won a huge victory over the Democratic candidate, Adlai Stevenson. His foreign policy advisor, **John Foster Dulles**, promised that a Republican victory would "roll back" communism.

As president, Eisenhower was moderate in his domestic policies and cautious in his foreign policy. Although committed to **containment** and faced by Cold War challenges in Europe, Asia, and the Middle East, wherever possible Eisenhower sought relaxation of tension and peaceful resolutions. The hollowness of the bravado of rollback was shown in the failure to support the Hungarian uprising in 1956. A truce and armistice were reached on the Korean peninsula. The Chinese nationalists who had taken refuge on Taiwan were protected by a U.S. security guarantee. In Southeast Asia, the strategy of containment centered on former French **Indochina** and **Indonesia**. Eisenhower's strategic view of the importance of Indochina was captured in his enunciation of the so-called **domino theory**. It was during his presidency that the line of containment was laid in 1954 on the 17th parallel of latitude in **Vietnam**. In Indonesia, the **Central Intelligence Agency (CIA)** assisted the rebel forces in the **PRRI–Permesta** 1958 regional revolt against the government of President Sukarno.

During his presidency, Eisenhower made one trip to Southeast Asia. This was a state visit to the **Philippines** in June 1960 to reinforce the strength of the U.S. commitment to its defense. This returned Philippine president Sergio Garcia's state visit to the United States in June 1959. In 1953, President Eisenhower met with Philippine president

Elpidio Quirino during his official visit to Washington. President **Sukarno** of **Indonesia** was a state guest in May 1956, also addressing Congress. Sukarno had a more informal meeting with Eisenhower in New York during the 1960 **United Nations** General Assembly meeting. America's ally **Thailand** was honored by President Eisenhower's Washington meeting with Prime Minister **Phibul Songgram** in May 1955 and King **Bhumibol**'s state visit in June 1960. Other visiting Southeast Asian heads of government met by Eisenhower were the **Republic of Vietnam**'s **Ngo Dinh Diem** (1957), **Laos**'s **Souvanna Phouma** (1958), and **U Nu** of **Burma** (1956), and although he made no official visits as such, Prime Minister **Sihanouk** of **Cambodia** saw President Eisenhower in 1958 and 1960.

ENTERPRISE FOR ASEAN INITIATIVE (EAI). The Enterprise for ASEAN Initiative was announced in October 2002 by President **George W. Bush** on the sidelines of the Los Cabos, Mexico **Asia–Pacific Economic Cooperation (APEC)** summit meeting. The EAI offered the prospect of bilateral **free trade agreements (FTA)** with members of the **Association of Southeast Asian Nations (ASEAN)** that were committed to economic reforms and openness, were a member of the **World Trade Organization (WTO)**, and had a **trade and investment framework agreement (TIFA)** with the United States. Under the EAI, the United States and individual ASEAN countries will jointly determine when they are ready to move toward an FTA. The standard would be the terms of the U.S.–**Singapore** FTA concluded in 2003. As of the end of 2007, seven ASEAN countries had TIFAs with the United States: **Brunei, Cambodia, Indonesia, Malaysia,** the **Philippines, Thailand,** and **Vietnam**. Only Thailand and Malaysia had moved far enough along the roadmap to begin full negotiations with the United States for an FTA, although initial talks with the Philippines have begun. The goal is to create a network of bilateral FTAs with ASEAN countries. *See also* TRADE

ENVIRONMENTAL ISSUES. The United States has introduced the nontraditional policy goal of promoting environmental safeguards into its economic assistance and **trade** policies in Southeast Asia. This has made U.S. concerns about environmental conservation, degradation, and resource sustainability a condition for American linkage to Southeast Asian economic growth and development strategies. In many of these countries, environmental safeguards are either lacking or poorly enforced. The Trade Act of 2002 requires that American trade policy and environmental protection be mutually supportive and that trade relations promote environmental protection, not weaken or reduce it. The consultative mechanism under U.S. bilateral **trade and investment framework agreements (TIFA)** with Southeast Asian states provides opportunities to address environmental problems. The 2006 U.S.–**Indonesian** agreement on illegal logging is an example. American bilateral **free trade agreements (FTA)** have binding chapters on environmental protections. The U.S.–**Singapore** FTA was the model for the initiation of FTA negotiations with **Malaysia** and **Thailand**. American insistence on environmental safeguards in trade relations as part of its "WTO plus" approach has led to the charge that this is disguised economic protectionism. In trade negotiations, the office of the **United States Trade Representative (USTR)** receives input from the nongovernmental Trade and Environment Policy Advisory Committee. Environmental considerations also go into economic assistance packages administered through the U.S. **Agency for International Development**. Assistance pledged through consultative consortiums like the **Consultative Group for Indonesia** and the **Consultative Group for Cambodia** is also reviewed for environmental impacts. For both trade and aid there remains, however, the problem of monitoring and enforcement.

In the **State Department**, environmental and conservation matters come under a deputy assistant secretary of state for environment in the Bureau of Oceans and International Environmental and Scientific Affairs (OES). OES addresses transboundary environmental issues in regional hubs. The Southeast Asia regional hub is housed in the American embassy in **Thailand**. OES coordinates U.S. policy in international negotiations. American votes in international funding agencies like the World Bank and the **Asian Development Bank (ADB)** for project lending reflect concerns raised by nongovernmental organizations (NGO) and Congress with respect to environmental impacts. In Southeast Asia, large dam projects in **Burma**, **Laos**, **Malaysia**, and **Thailand** have come under scrutiny. The United States has been criticized for forcing its environmental rules on Third

World countries but coming to the defense of American companies and **investment** in cases where local environments have been damaged or regulations violated by American operations. In Indonesia, U.S. mining companies **Freeport–McMoRan** and **Newmont** have been accused of damaging the environment.

ESTRADA, JOSEPH (1927–). President of the **Philippines** (June 1998–January 2001), Joseph Estrada is the only Philippine president to have been impeached. He was the Philippines' most adored movie star when he went into politics, to become first a mayor and then a senator. Popularly known as "Erap," a reverse of the Filipino word *pare,* the slang for "buddy" or "pal," Estrada won an overwhelming plurality of votes, the most any Filipino presidential candidate ever garnered, when he ran for president, succeeding **Fidel Ramos** in 1998. As president, Estrada was a strong proponent of U.S.-Philippine ties and shepherded the U.S.-Philippine **Visiting Forces Agreement (VFA)** through the Philippine Senate in 1999. He was welcomed as a state visitor to the United States by President **William J. Clinton** in 2000. Estrada was a supporter of democracy elsewhere in Southeast Asia. To **Malaysia**'s chagrin, like the United States, he took up the cause of **Anwar Ibrahim**.

A populist politician despised by the Manila elite, Estrada's administration was plagued by accusations of plunder, corruption, and criminality. He was impeached by the Philippine House of Representatives in 2000 and went on trial in the Senate. As the lines were drawn between Estrada's supporters and opponents, the United States made it clear that it would not take sides. The impeachment trial came to an abrupt halt when the prosecution walked out in protest over an 11 to 10 procedural vote that barred certain banking records from being entered in evidence. At that point, Vice President **Gloria Macapagal-Arroyo**'s allies in the opposition took to the streets in what has been called **EDSA** II, a second "people's power" revolution, likening it to the deposition of **Ferdinand Marcos**. The military threw its support behind Arroyo, and with Estrada still in the presidential palace refusing to resign, the Philippine Supreme Court declared the presidency vacant and swore in Arroyo as president on 20 January 2001. Estrada was arrested for corruption. After six years in the courts, a verdict on the corruption charges finally came in September 2007, when he was found guilty of "plunder" and sentenced to life imprisonment. He was quickly pardoned by President Arroyo. Arroyo's irregular, if not illegal, assumption of the presidency in the framework of a thinly disguised coup presented problems for the United States, which recognized that Estrada was a democratically elected, legitimate head of government. American law called for sanctions against a succeeding coup government in such a case. Washington, however, quickly recognized the new Arroyo government. Its justification underlined the fact that no force had been used. Furthermore, the United States accepted the fact that the Supreme Court of the Philippines had made the decision, even though there were no legal or constitutional foundations for declaring the presidency vacant when the duly elected incumbent was still in office. At issue were long-term American interests in the Philippines with a de facto government in power backed by its military. In answering questions about Arroyo's presidency from a skeptical congressional committee, the acting American assistant secretary of state for East Asian and Pacific affairs, **Thomas Hubbard**, stated that "it is in our interest to look to the future, not the past."

– F –

FALINTIL. The Forças Armadas de Libertação Nacional de Timor-Leste (Armed Forces for the National Liberation of **East Timor**) was the military wing of **Fretilin**, the independence movement that carried out at home and abroad the campaign against the Indonesian 1975 takeover of the territory. **Gusmão Xanana** was Falintil's leader until his capture in 1992. Problems of integrating Falintil military elements into the new independent East Timor defense forces led to mutinies and renewed violence in 2006. *See also* INDONESIAN INVASION OF EAST TIMOR.

FARUQ, OMAR AL- (1971–2006). Born in Kuwait of Iraqi parents, Omar al-Faruq became a top agent for **al-Qaeda** in Southeast Asia, building operational ties between it and **Jema'ah Islamiyah (JI)** and other militant Islamic groups in the region. Trained in Taliban-ruled Afghanistan, he began working in Southeast Asia in the 1990s, marrying the daughter of Indonesian militant Haris Fadillah, leader of an anti-Christian militia in Maluku, East Indonesia. Faruq was captured in Jakarta in 2002 while planning bomb attacks against Western embassies. He was turned over to the United States and imprisoned in Afghanistan. He escaped in 2005, but was tracked down in Basra, Iraq, where in September 2006 he was killed in a raid by British forces.

FINANCIAL CRISIS OF 1997–1998. With its currency, the baht, under speculative assault, **Thailand**'s government on 2 July 1997 decided to float it, no longer pegging the baht to the U.S. dollar. This triggered a regional financial shockwave revealing the Asian "miracle" economies to be bubble economies as well. The bubble burst as the cumulative impact of currency speculation, overvalued real estate, underperforming loans, crony capitalism, and corruption left a trail of institutional and political wreckage throughout the Asian region and rippled through financial markets globally. The most severely affected countries were Thailand, **Indonesia**, and South Korea. **Malaysia** did not escape damage. Currencies plunged, financial institutions collapsed, and confidence in leaderships evaporated. The collapse starkly revealed the structural inadequacies and institutional weaknesses that had been concealed by high economic growth rates.

The immediate task facing the afflicted countries was recapitalization and restoring investor confidence. The **International Monetary Fund (IMF)** took the lead in managing the international response. It coordinated a support program of multilateral funding agencies and bilateral assistance packages. The total for Thailand was $17.2 billion and for Indonesia $49.7 billion. Japan was the largest single bilateral donor. In the Thai case, the United States stood aside, with the administration of **William J. Clinton** ruling out a U.S. contribution. American officials thought the Thai problem was isolated and could be contained. The administration also was politically smarting from the domestic political backlash of the controversial 1994 Mexican "bailout." The failure to come to the aid of a longtime ally was a strategic error. It left the impression of an uncaring America as compared to Japan and China and spurred initiatives toward tighter economic ties between Southeast and East Asia, including a currency swap arrangement.

As the contagion spread, the United States did not repeat the Thailand mistake with Indonesia, pledging on 30 October 1997 $3 billion as part of the IMF's "second line of defense" of bilateral aid behind the multilateral rescue package. Japan and **Singapore**, at $5 billion each, were the largest contributors. In both the Thai and Indonesian cases, support programs were contingent on an IMF regime of structural adjustment and adherence to macroeconomic fundamentals of the so-called **Washington consensus**, which was viewed by economic nationalists as a kind of economic pax Americana. The United States played an important role in forcing the IMF's strictures on a resisting Indonesia. On 14 March 1998, Clinton's special envoy, former vice president **Walter Mondale**, was in Jakarta to tell President **Suharto** that the United States would not support Indonesia if it refused the IMF terms. The backlash in Indonesia against the IMF was one of the causes of the 1998 collapse of Suharto's government. The possible negative domestic political consequences of bending to the IMF was also one of the reasons that Prime Minister **Mahathir Mohammad** in Malaysia refused the IMF prescriptions and adopted capital controls and other domestic measures in defiance of the Washington consensus. Thailand paid off its IMF debt by 2003, and Indonesia finished paying back what it owed in 2006.

FIRST INDOCHINA WAR. The First Indochina War is a term denoting the French colonial war against the independence struggle of the **Viet Minh** in **Vietnam**. The Vietnamese nationalism of the anti-French struggle was managed by the Vietnamese Communist Party headed by **Ho Chi Minh**, a veteran Russian-trained agent. At the end of World War II in the Pacific in 1945, and before French forces could get back to Vietnam, Ho Chi Minh declared an independent **Democratic Republic of Vietnam (DRV)**. The Viet Minh were firmly established in Tonkin and northern Annam in Vietnam and had forged close links with the nationalist **Lao Issara** movement in **Laos**. French dominance was restored in Laos and **Cambodia**, but the French and Ho Chi Minh could not reach agreement on a political framework with less than full sovereignty of the DRV over all of Vietnam. A Viet Minh attack on the French in Hanoi on 19 December 1946 was the final precipitant of a war that lasted seven and a half years. Seeking a nationalist alternative to Ho Chi Minh, the French returned the former emperor of Annam, **Bao Dai**, to the head of a unified **State of Vietnam**. Vietnam was united with the other **Indochi-**

nese states, Cambodia and Laos, in a French Union within which the key functions were retained by France. Neither Bao Dai nor his State of Vietnam aroused popular enthusiasm, nor could the state or the French backing it assert control over the swaths of **North Vietnam** held by Ho's forces. Ho himself was assuming a heroic nationalist charisma.

In the earliest stages of the war, the United States evinced little interest in the French Indochina venture. The United States turned down an overture by Ho Chi Minh in 1945 to intervene in the name of democracy, contained in a letter addressed to President **Harry S. Truman**. This had been sent through the **Office of Strategic Services (OSS)** team liaising with the anti-Japanese Vietnamese underground. By 1948, the strategy of **containment** was being fitted to Asia. A tipping point came with the victory of the Chinese Communists over the nationalists and the establishment of the People's Republic of **China** in October 1949, followed by Chinese intervention in the Korean War. Ho Chi Minh's communism loomed much larger in Washington's eyes than Vietnamese nationalism. On 7 February 1950, the United States recognized the State of Vietnam, viewed by many as a French puppet. This followed the recognition of the Democratic Republic of Vietnam by the Soviet Union and other communist states. The First Indochina War had been translated from imperialist versus nationalist to a surrogate war of the "free world" versus communism. This was made explicit in an April 1952 National Security Council memorandum that stated if Indochina was lost to communism, all of Southeast Asia would fall, threatening South Asia and then the Middle East. This definition of the strategic implications of communist victory in Indochina received a later popular formulation by President **Dwight D. Eisenhower** in the **domino theory**.

The armed conflict was largely confined to Vietnam, although the political fate of **Cambodia** and **Laos** was also at stake. Initially using guerrilla tactics, the Viet Minh harassed the French in a war of attrition. With resupply and heavier weaponry from China, by 1952 the Vietnamese moved to larger force action. The French had already suffered more than 90,000 casualties. The conventional war capabilities of the DRV's military were fully demonstrated in the climactic battle of **Dien Bien Phu**, in which a French force of 16,000 was overrun, with 1,500 killed and 4,000 wounded. The United States provided escalating financial and material support to the French as France's capabilities and will to war diminished. **John Foster Dulles**, the uncompromising secretary of state in the administration of President Eisenhower, wanted to keep the French in the field, but not through American unilateral intervention. Without international intervention, however, the human and material costs of the war had become too onerous for France to continue the war. The negotiated way out was the 1954 **Geneva Conference** on Korea and Indochina, which resulted in the **Geneva Accords** ending the First Indochina War, but set the stage for the **Second Indochina War**.

FITZGERALD, DESMOND (1910–1967). A senior **Central Intelligence Agency (CIA)** official, Desmond Fitzgerald's agency roots were in the **Office of Strategic Services (OSS)** during World War II in Asia. He was recruited into the CIA's Far East Division of the Office of Policy Coordination, which became the Directorate of Plans, the clandestine operational side of the agency, headed by Deputy Director of Plans (DDP) **Frank Wisner**, where he worked on operations in Korea, **China**, and **Burma**. He became CIA station chief in the **Philippines** and assisted **Edward Lansdale** and **Ramon Magsaysay** in the campaign against the **Hukbalahap**. As chief of the Far East Division (1957–1962), he oversaw CIA operations in **Laos**, **Vietnam**, and **Indonesia**. In 1962, he took over management of the Cuba problem for the new DDP, **Richard Helms**, and in 1965 he was himself named DDP. He died at age 56 of a heart attack while playing tennis.

FIVE POWER DEFENCE ARRANGEMENT (FPDA). The Five Power Defence Arrangement was established by joint communiqué of the defense ministers of Australia, **Malaysia**, New Zealand, **Singapore**, and Great Britain on 1 November 1971. It provides for consultation for the purpose of deciding on the necessary steps to be taken jointly or separately in response to external aggression or threat of external aggression against Malaysia and Singapore. Before decolonization, Great Britain had been responsible for the defense of **Malaya** and Singapore. After Malaysian independence, an Anglo–Malay defense treaty provided the framework for continued British defense assistance. British, Australian, and New Zealand armed forces joined Malaysia to combat **Indonesia**'s undeclared war (1963–1965), called "**Confrontation.**" With Singapore's separation from the Malaysian federation in 1965 and the 1971 decision by the British government to draw down its security commitments east of Suez, the FPDA was negotiated as a new basis for security collaboration. It provides a useful framework for a Singapore and Malaysian defense relationship despite bilateral political antagonisms. Although Singapore and Malaysia were not part of the U.S. alliance system, the overlapping membership of their Commonwealth security partners in the U.S.-centered **Southeast Asia Treaty Organization (SEATO)**, and of Australia and New Zealand with the United States in the ANZUS Pact, indirectly gave them broader security relations without jeopardizing their nonaligned status.

FORD FOUNDATION. The Ford Foundation, once the largest private philanthropic institution in the world, was established in 1936 and endowed by grants and bequests from Edsel and Henry Ford. It moved its headquarters from Michigan to New York in 1953. It operates a worldwide program of grants and loans to governments, nongovernmental organizations, academic institutions, and individuals to support its mission. The contemporary mission statement focuses on strengthening democratic values, relieving poverty and injustice, promoting international cooperation, and advancing human achievement. Within this broad mission a wide variety of specific programs are supported, ranging from agriculture to art and culture, institutional capacity building, sexuality and reproductive health, gender equity, etc. There are representative offices in **Indonesia** and **Vietnam**. The foundation has operated in Indonesia since 1953, with total grants of more than $125 million. The impact of its programs was most dramatically demonstrated when Indonesian participants in Ford Foundation–supported American university programs became the technocrats—the so-called Berkeley Mafia—who rescued the Indonesian economy in the 1960s after the fall of **Sukarno**. The first grants for Vietnam were made in 1996 from the Bangkok office. In 1998, a representative office was opened in Hanoi and the Bangkok office closed, with **Thai** grants handled from Hanoi. The Manila office was closed in 2003 with the termination of programs in the **Philippines**.

FORD, GERALD R. (1913–2006). Unelected Vice President Gerald
Ford became the 38th president of the United States upon the August
1974 resignation of President **Richard M. Nixon**. President Ford inherited his predecessor's policy of trying to shore up the defenses of
the **Nguyen Van Thieu** government in **South Vietnam** and the **Lon
Nol** government in **Cambodia**. He also inherited and kept on Secretary of State **Henry A. Kissinger**. The continuity of **Indochina** policy, however, was limited by Congress's denial of funds. Ford
presided over the last chapter of the **Vietnam War** with the evacua-
tions of Americans from Vietnam and Cambodia at the fall of Saigon
and Phnom Penh to victorious communist armies in April 1975. Only
a month later, in May 1975, he used military force against the **Khmer
Rouge** in Cambodia in the **Mayaguez incident**, an assertion of power
in Southeast Asia through which he sought to demonstrate that American will to defend its interests by force if necessary had not been crip-
pled by a **"Vietnam syndrome."** The attacks were launched from U.S.
bases in **Thailand** and were not welcomed by the government of Thai
prime minister **Kukrit Pramoj**. Kukrit, who took office in March,
was trying to reorient Thai policy toward rapprochement with its new
communist neighbors and had called for the closure of the bases and
the withdrawal of American forces from Thailand.

Further reinforcement of the continuing U.S. commitment to
Southeast Asia was given in Ford's meetings with President **Ferdinand Marcos** in the **Philippines** and President **Suharto** in **Indonesia** in December 1975. Ford had already met with Suharto in July
1975 at Camp David. The undertakings of American staying power
were formalized in his enunciation of a **Pacific doctrine** in Hawaii
on his way back from Jakarta and Manila. While in the December
meetings with Suharto, Ford and Kissinger were informed of Indonesia's intentions to invade **East Timor** and raised no objections.
Ford was defeated for election to the presidency in November 1996
by **Jimmy Carter**, whose anti-Nixon–Kissinger–Ford foreign policy
campaign and **human rights** rhetoric raised concerns again in Southeast Asia about the possibility of an American "Vietnam syndrome"
at work. *See also* INDONESIAN INVASION OF EAST TIMOR.

FOREIGN MILITARY FINANCING (FMF). This is a U.S. government program of security assistance providing congressionally au-

thorized grants and loans to countries for acquisition of U.S. military articles, services, or training. The funds are allocated by the **State Department**'s Bureau of Political–Military Affairs (PM) and administered by the Defense Security Cooperation Agency. In FY 2007, the **Philippines** was the largest beneficiary, followed by **Indonesia**. **Cambodia** and **East Timor** also received FMF. In FY 2008, Indonesia's proposed budget of $15.7 million will exceed the Philippines' $11 million. **Thailand**, historically a major FMF recipient, had its FY 2007 FMF budget reallocated because of the sanctions prohibiting security assistance, applied by the United States in the wake of the 2006 Thai military coup.

FOREIGN MILITARY SALES (FMS). This is a government-to-government method for selling American military equipment, services, and training. The contracts are authorized by the Directorate of Defense Trade Controls in the **State Department**'s Bureau of Political–Military Affairs and in conformity with the Arms Export Control Act. FMS is administered by the Defense Security Cooperation Agency. The largest customers in Southeast Asia have been **Singapore**, **Thailand**, and the **Philippines**. From 1999 to 2005, **Indonesia** was ineligible because of the **Leahy Amendment** barring FMS to it. The prohibition was waived in 2006, and Indonesia is again eligible.

FOREIGN TERRORIST ORGANIZATION (FTO). The United States secretary of state can designate a foreign organization that meets terrorism criteria as defined by U.S. law as a foreign terrorist organization (FTO). An FTO is an organization that has carried out terrorist acts that threaten the security of the United States, broadly defined as planning or preparing a terrorist act or retaining the capability or intent to carry out such an act. American law prohibits any individual under U.S. jurisdiction from materially assisting or supplying resources to an FTO. Since the list was originated in 1997, three Southeast Asian terrorist groups have been designated FTOs: the **Abu Sayyaf Group (ASG)**, **Jema'ah Islamiyah (JI)**, and the **Communist Party of the Philippines/New People's Army (CPP/NPA)**. The United States was prepared in 2003 to add the **Moro Islamic Liberation Front (MILF)** to the FTO list because it allegedly had been penetrated by **al-Qaeda** and JI elements, but did not do so because the Philippine government was concerned that listing the MILF might scuttle newly initiated peace talks.

FRASER, DONALD M. (1924–). A member of the U.S. House of Representatives from Minnesota (1963–1979), Congressman Donald Fraser, in his role as chairman of the House Committee on International Relations Subcommittee on Foreign Operations, was instrumental in making **human rights** in American foreign policy a major legislative concern. He was the author of the "Fraser amendment" to the 1971 Foreign Assistance Act, which became part of the 1976 Foreign Assistance Act that linked American security assistance to a country to its human rights record. This required the submission of annual human rights country reports to Congress by the **State Department**. In committee hearings in 1977, Fraser accused the United States of complicity in **Indonesia**'s role in **East Timor** by continuing military assistance despite the fact that U.S.-supplied weapons had been illegally used in **Indonesia**'s invasion and occupation of the former Portuguese colony.

FREE ACEH MOVEMENT (GAM). The Free Aceh Movement (Gerakan Aceh Merdeka), founded in 1976, was at the heart of the armed insurgent struggle for independence in **Indonesia**'s Aceh province at the western end of the island of Sumatra. Thousand of lives were lost as the Indonesian army and GAM's guerrillas fought a bitter war in which the civilian populations were the losers. International attention became focused on Aceh after the separation of East Timor from Indonesia in 1999. Many of the same nongovernmental organizations (NGO) that advocated independence for East Timor turned their efforts to Aceh. The consistent official American position had been respect for the territorial integrity of Indonesia, which at independence, unlike East Timor, had included Aceh. This, however, did not preclude official and congressional concern about the **human rights** abuses inflicted during the conflict.

Under President **Megawati Sukarnoputri**, the Indonesian military launched an all-out offensive in 2003 to wipe out GAM once and for all. Megawati, in fact, told the troops not to worry about human rights complaints. The United States had joined with Japan and the

European Union (EU) in a 2002 Tokyo Conference on Peace and Reconstruction in Aceh. As the military confrontation ground toward stalemate, the United States and the other conference conveners issued a Joint Statement on Aceh expressing concern about martial law in Aceh and its impact on the people of the province. What the United States and the international community wanted was a return to a negotiating process that had begun in 2002.

Two events in 2004 catalyzed an Aceh peace settlement. The first was the election of Indonesian President **Susilo Bambang Yudhoyono**, who was determined to end the war. The second was the December 2004 **tsunami** that laid waste to much of Aceh. Now, GAM and the Indonesian government were joined with the international community in a massive relief, rehabilitation, and reconstruction project in the stricken territory, in which the United States played a leading role. An August 2005 GAM–Indonesian government memorandum of agreement put in place a peace process leading to self-government—not independence—for the province. A crucial element of the agreement was Acehnese control over the income from oil and gas exploitation. The implementation of the settlement was monitored by the European Union (EU). In July 2006, the Indonesian parliament granted autonomy to the province. In December 2006, the Acehenese people elected a formerly imprisoned GAM leader, Irwandi Yusuf, a U.S.-trained veterinarian, governor of the province. In September 2007, Governor Irwandi visited Washington and New York seeking economic assistance, **trade**, and **investment**. Coincidentally, in the same month the U.S. Congress passed a resolution praising the Aceh free elections.

FREE PAPUA ORGANIZATION (OPM). The Free Papua Organization (Organisasi Papua Merdeka) is an indigenous Melanesian separatist movement in **Indonesia**'s Papuan provinces. The OPM has fought a low-intensity guerrilla struggle against what it deems Indonesian imperialism since the American-brokered solution of the **West New Guinea dispute** turned the former Dutch colony over to Indonesia in 1962. The OPM has international support from liberationist nongovernmental organizations and **human rights** organizations but not governments. Members of the OPM have been accused of involvement in the 2002 **Timika incident**, in which two American teachers were ambushed and killed. The OPM cause continues to be raised in the U.S. Congress. In 2007, the chair of the House of Representatives Foreign Affairs Committee subcommittee on Asia called for self-determination for Indonesian Papua. Congress made part of the FY 2008 security assistance package to Indonesia conditional on public access to the Papuan provinces.

FREE THAI MOVEMENT (SERI THAI). The Free Thai was the underground anti-Japanese resistance movement in Japanese-occupied **Thailand** during World War II. Its international face was symbolized by **Seni Pramoj** in Washington. In Thailand, liberal politician **Pridi Panomyong** represented domestic above-ground sympathy for the movement. Through the **Office of Strategic Services (OSS)**, the United States liaised with and supported the Free Thai. OSS operatives encouraged the Free Thai's resistance to the imposition of a British hard peace on postwar Thailand. In a tribute on 8 May 2000, the Free Thai were honored by **Central Intelligence Agency (CIA)** director George J. Tenet for their service and sacrifice.

FREE TRADE AGREEMENTS (FTA). A free trade agreement is designed to liberalize international **trade** on a bilateral or multilateral basis by the comprehensive elimination of tariff and nontariff obstacles to the exchange of goods and services between or among the signatories. Unlike a consultative **trade and investment framework agreement (TIFA)**, an FTA is a legally binding agreement and has dispute resolution mechanisms. FTAs have to be consistent with the rules of the **World Trade Organization (WTO)**, but they can go beyond the WTO minimum rules and offer stronger standards in areas such as protection of **intellectual property rights (IPR)**, labor rights, and **environmental** safeguards. These are called "WTO plus." The argument for an FTA is that it helps level the playing field for U.S. business by promoting exports and expands market opportunities in the United States for the foreign contracting parties, enhancing competitiveness. Negotiations for FTAs are difficult since domestic interests seek to protect their positions against foreign imports. This is particularly true in sensitive sectors of agriculture and services.

The U.S. first Asian FTA was with **Singapore**. The United States is Singapore's largest trading partner, and Singapore is the United

States' 12th largest trading partner. The plan for a bilateral FTA was announced by President **William J. Clinton** and Singapore prime minister Goh Chok Tong on the sidelines of the November 2000 **Asia–Pacific Economic Cooperation (APEC)** summit. Negotiations began in December 2000 and, after the change bringing **George W. Bush** to the White House, the agreement was concluded in January 2003 and entered into force after ratification on 1 January 2004. The U.S.–Singapore FTA is deemed the model for future Southeast Asian FTAs that might succeed existing TIFAs. The U.S.–Singapore FTA is "WTO plus," with broad liberalization in market access in goods and services, **investment**, government procurement, intellectual property, and strong cooperation in promoting labor rights and the environment. It is seen as achieving all of the objectives set down by Congress in the Trade Promotion Act of 2002, which gave the president "fast track" **trade promotion authority (TPA)** in trade negotiations.

On 19 October 2003, following his meeting with visiting Prime Minister **Thaksin Shinawatra** of **Thailand**, President Bush announced the launching of negotiations for a comprehensive FTA with Thailand pursuant to the TPA. Thailand was America's 18th largest trading partner. Although strongly supported by a coalition of American businesses, the FTA negotiations were more difficult than with Singapore. The complementarities between the U.S. and Thai economies are different from those with Singapore. Singapore was already a relatively open economy with few sensitive products or services. The main difficulties came from Thai agricultural sectors, some financial services areas, and the generic pharmaceutical industry, which argued that high-cost foreign patented medicines were a threat to public health. The political turmoil in Thailand in 2006 put all Thai trade negotiations on hold until a new democratic government takes office. On 8 March 2006, the United States and **Malaysia** began formal free trade negotiations, although talks had begun in 2004 looking to a future agreement. Malaysia is the U.S.'s 10th largest trading partner. The negotiations were not concluded by the end of March 2007, the deadline for an agreement to be ready before the expiration of the president's "fast track" authority.

FREEPORT–MCMORAN. An American company, Freeport–McMoRan exploits the world's largest open pit gold and copper mine, at Mt. Grasberg, in **Indonesia**'s province of West Papua. With its concession, Freeport is the largest single taxpayer in Indonesia. In Papua for more than 40 years, the company has operated in a lax and corrupt regulatory framework with little official regard to environmental consequences. It has been the target of Indonesian domestic and international environmental nongovernmental organizations and activists. Official U.S. attention was turned on Freeport–McMoRan in 2002 after the murder of two American teachers near **Timika** in the company's concession. The allegations that the killings were the work of Indonesian soldiers upset by a reduction in the payments and other benefits for providing security by the company led to an examination by both the American and Indonesian governments of the legality of the practice. Members of the **Free Papua Organization (OPM)** were tried and convicted in Indonesia for the killings.

FREQUENT WIND. This is the code name of the operation to evacuate U.S. and Vietnamese personnel from Saigon on 29 April 1975 as the People's Army of Vietnam (PAVN) was on the outskirts of the city. From four aircraft carriers standing off shore, in less than 18 hours waves of helicopters lifted out 5,000 refugees from Tan Son Nhut Air Base and 2,100 from the parking lot and roof of the American embassy. Among the last to leave was American Ambassador **Graham Martin**. *See also* EAGLE PULL; VIETNAM.

FRETILIN. The Frente Revolucionária de Timor Leste Independente (Revolutionary Front for the Independence of **East Timor**) was the political organization that combated **Indonesia**'s invasion and occupation of **East Timor**. Its armed wing was **Falintil**. It was represented abroad by **José Ramos-Horta** and underground by **Xanana Gusmão**. Fretilin emerged as the dominant political party after the 2002 elections in the newly independent East Timor. Elections in 2007, however, put it in opposition—sometimes violent—to a coalition government led by former Fretilin hero Gusmão.

FULBRIGHT PROGRAM. The Fulbright program is an educational exchange program named for Senator J. William Fulbright, who authored the 1946 legislation establishing it. Funded by annual appropriations from Congress, it is administered by the **State Depart-**

ment's Bureau of Educational and Cultural Affairs (ECA). For Southeast Asia, from 1949 to 2006 there were 8,057 grants to Southeast Asian nationals coming to the United States and 11,401 grants to Americans going to Southeast Asia, for a total two-way Fulbright exchange of nearly 19,458.

FUNCINPEC. The Front Uni National pour un Cambodge Indépendent, Neutre, Pacifique, et Coopératif (National United Front for an Independent, Neutral, Peaceful, and Cooperative **Cambodia**) is the royalist party created in 1981 as part of the **Khmer resistance** to the 1979 Vietnamese invasion and occupation of Cambodia in the **Third Indochina War**. The head of Funcinpec was Prince **Norodom Sihanouk**, the former king and prime minister, but his son, Prince Norodom Ranariddh, was in charge of the day-to-day operations. Its armed wing was the Armée Nationale Sihanoukiste (ANS, Sihanouk National Army), which probably never exceeded 6,000 men. Funcinpec and Sihanouk's role in the resistance and **Coalition Government of Democratic Kampuchea (CGDK)** helped to overcome politically for the international community the fact of the detested **Khmer Rouge's** inclusion in the coalition. In 1993, Funcinpec contested the **United Nations (UN)**–sponsored elections in the new constitutional monarchy of Cambodia. Although it won, it was forced by the UN to share power in a coalition with **Hun Sen**'s Cambodian People's Party in order to prevent a renewal of violence. In elections in 1998 and 2003, Funcinpec emerged as a minority party in coalition governments. In 2006, Hun Sen maneuvered to oust Ranariddh from government and then from Funcinpec.

– G –

GARCIA, CARLOS P. (1896–1971). Vice president of the **Philippines**, Carlos Garcia succeeded to the presidency on the death of President **Ramon Magsaysay**, who died in a plane crash in 1957. Garcia pledged to carry on the work of his predecessor and was elected in his own right on the Nationalist Party ticket in November 1957. In that election, **Central Intelligence Agency (CIA)** agent **Joseph Burkholder Smith** funneled U.S. clandestine support to his

Liberal Party opponent, José Yulo. Garcia's Nationalist Party running mate for vice president was defeated by the Liberal Party's **Diosdado Macapagal**. Garcia was an economic nationalist, and his "Filipino First" policies were designed to enrich himself and his supporters. If possible, Garcia's presidency was even more corrupt than **Elpidio Quirino**'s. Vice President Macapagal, a self-proclaimed reformist and snubbed by the president, kept the U.S. embassy and CIA apprised of administration malfeasance. Garcia had expertise in international affairs. While Magsaysay's vice president, Garcia served concurrently as secretary of foreign affairs and had presided over the Manila conference leading to the **Southeast Asia Collective Defense Treaty** and the **Southeast Asia Treaty Organization (SEATO)**. He pleased President **Dwight D. Eisenhower**'s administration by outlawing the Communist Party of the Philippines. He also forged close relations with the American-allied government of **Ngo Dinh Diem** in the **Republic of Vietnam**. The **Bohlen–Serrano** revision to the **Military Bases Agreement** was concluded during Garcia's administration. Garcia made a state visit to the United States in 1958, which was reciprocated by President Eisenhower in 1960. He was defeated for reelection in 1961 by Vice President Macapagal.

GELBHARD, ROBERT B. (1944–). A career Foreign Service Officer, Robert Gelbhard was ambassador to **Indonesia** from 1999 to 2001. This was a tumultuous time in Indonesia in the aftermath of the **East Timor referendum** and the election and impeachment of President **Abdurrahman Wahid**, who was succeeded by **Megawati Sukarnoputri**. Ambassador Gelbhard gave strong public voice to issues of democracy, **human rights**, Islamic extremism, and corruption. His diplomatic posture was controversial in Indonesia, and he was accused of interference in Indonesian politics. He had a public falling-out with Indonesia's first-ever civilian minister of defense. A supporter of the U.S. weapons ban on Indonesia, he had difficult relations with the **United States Pacific Command (USPACOM)** and opposed the September 1999 visit to Indonesia by PACOM commander in chief Admiral Denis Blair as sending the wrong message. In November 2000, to Indonesian consternation, Gelbhard closed the embassy for two weeks because of security threats and his view that the Indonesian police were not providing sufficient protection.

GENERALIZED SYSTEM OF PREFERENCES (GSP). The U.S. Generalized System of Preferences is administered by the **United States Trade Representative (USTR)** to promote **trade** for economic growth in the developing world. It provides for preferentially reduced tariffs or duty free import into the United States of more than 4,650 products from 144 countries. The GSP began in 1974 for an initial 10 years and has been reauthorized since. In 2007, five Southeast Asian countries qualified for the GSP: **Cambodia**, **Indonesia**, **East Timor**, the **Philippines**, and **Thailand**.

GENEVA ACCORDS ON INDOCHINA. These were the agreements signed on 21 July 1954 ending the **First Indochina War** and the French colonial role in Southeast Asia. The accords consisted of a Final Declaration of the **Geneva Conference on Indochina** and three armistice agreements for **Vietnam**, **Cambodia**, and **Laos**. Vietnam was provisionally divided at the 17th parallel of latitude for purposes of a cease-fire and regroupment of forces. The division between **North Vietnam** governed by **Ho Chi Minh**'s **Democratic Republic of Vietnam (DRV)** and **South Vietnam**, the territory of the **State of Vietnam**, was to be temporary until elections scheduled for July 1956 could be held allowing "a free expression of the national will." In the Final Declaration the conferees committed themselves to respect the sovereignty, independence, unity, and territorial integrity of Cambodia, Laos, and Vietnam and to refrain from interference in their internal affairs. Neither Vietnam was to join a military alliance or allow foreign bases. Cambodia insisted on its right to request foreign military assistance if its security was threatened. Laos received the same right. Both governments were concerned about the links between the DRV and domestic communist insurgencies. In Laos, the **Pathet Lao** were to be allowed to regroup in the northeast provinces prior to a national election. A national election was also promised for Cambodia.

In the final declaration, signed by none but listing them all, the conference participants accepted the agreements and urged the parties to carry them out. The United States disassociated itself from the final paragraph, which called for consultation with one another on questions of what measures might be necessary to assure respect for the agreements. Speaking for the United States, Under Secretary of

State General **Walter Bedell Smith** took note of the agreements and declared that the United States would not use force to disturb them and would view with grave concern their violation by new aggression. He reserved for the United States complete freedom of action to guarantee the right of the Vietnamese people to territorial unity, independence, and freedom. Similarly, the foreign minister of the State of Vietnam, Tran Van Do, reserved his government's "complete freedom of action to guarantee the sacred right of the Vietnamese people to territorial unity, national independence, and freedom." Three **International Commissions for Supervision and Control (ICSC)** were established to supervise the armistices in the three states. The ICSC members were Canada, India (chairman), and Poland.

GENEVA ACCORD ON LAOS. These were the agreements reached at the 1962 **Geneva Conference on Laos** that closed the **Laotian crisis of 1960–1962**. They were signed on 23 July 1962 and consisted of a Declaration on the Neutrality of Laos and a 20-article implementing protocol. In reaffirming the neutrality of **Laos** that had been part of the 1954 **Geneva Accord** on Laos, the new accords provided for the withdrawal of all foreign advisors and military forces. The Canadian–Indian–Polish **International Commission for Supervision and Control (ICSC)** was charged with overseeing the arrangements. The signatories promised to respect the sovereignty, unity, territorial integrity, and neutrality of Laos. They undertook not to interfere directly or indirectly in Laotian internal affairs and agreed with the Laotian declaration that it did not recognize protection as a **Southeast Asia Treaty Organization (SEATO)** protocol state. Although Laotian neutrality was precarious and would be quickly violated, the agreement did take the Laos problem off the bilateral U.S.–USSR Cold War negotiating table.

GENEVA CONFERENCE ON INDOCHINA, 1954. In May 1954, the foreign ministers of the People's Republic of **China**, France, Great Britain, the United States, and the Soviet Union, together with delegates from **Laos**, **Cambodia**, the **State of Vietnam**, and the **Democratic Republic of Vietnam (DRV)** met in a conference in Geneva seeking to end the **First Indochina War**—the French colonial war in Vietnam. The leader of the DRV delegation was **Pham**

Van Dong, who 20 years later was prime minister during the **Paris peace negotiations** ending the **Vietnam War**. The convening of the conference came from a decision made at the January 1954 Berlin "Big Four" foreign ministers meeting. There, they agreed to an international conference on Korea, which would also include a discussion of the restoration of peace in **Indochina** to which the People's Republic of China would be invited. The conference marked the first recognition of the People's Republic of China as a major power. The invitation to China was not welcomed by the United States. The co-chairs were Britain's Anthony Eden and the Soviet Union's Vyacheslav Molotov. American Secretary of State **John Foster Dulles** had deep reservations about the proceedings. He attended the opening session but quickly departed. Dulles's distaste for the affair was signaled by his refusal to shake hands with Chinese Foreign Minister Zhou Enlai (Chou En-lai). Undersecretary of State **Walter Bedell Smith** was left as the principal American negotiator.

France's premier Pierre Mendes-France was anxious to disengage from the increasingly costly colonial war in Indochina. Although the United States would have liked the French to fight on and was willing to continue to commit financial and material support, it was not willing to intervene militarily. For Dulles, the goal at Geneva was to limit communist gains in a compromise that would keep American options open. Russia and China did not want American intervention in the region to prevent the emergence of communist governments. No power wanted the events in Indochina to escalate to a wider war. The first plenary session on 8 May 1954 took place a day after the fall of the French stronghold at **Dien Bien Phu**. This was the death knell for French power in Asia. It was not until 21 July that a formula was hammered out in three separate armistice agreements for Laos, Cambodia, and Vietnam and a final declaration, collectively known as the **Geneva Accords on Indochina**.

GENEVA CONFERENCE ON LAOS, 1961–1962. As the **Laotian Crisis of 1960–1962** threatened Great Power confrontation in Southeast Asia in spring 1961, both the United States and the Soviet Union sought to deescalate the crisis. Neutralist Prime Minister **Norodom Sihanouk** of **Cambodia** was a key player behind the scenes in bringing the contending Laotian parties together. The formal diplomatic machinery was set in motion on 24 April 1961 by the British and Russian co-chairs, who called for a cease-fire to be verified by the reactivated **International Commission for Supervision and Control (ICSC)**. On 12 May, the ICSC's Indian chairman reported a de facto cease-fire, and on 16 May 1961, the 14-nation Geneva Conference on the Laotian Question formally opened. Assistant Secretary of State for East Asian and Pacific Eastern Affairs **W. Averell Harriman** was the chief U.S. delegate. The membership, originally suggested by Sihanouk, included, in addition to the United States, Great Britain, France, the Soviet Union, the People's Republic of **China**, India, Poland, Canada, **Thailand**, Cambodia, **Laos**, the **Democratic Republic of Vietnam (DRV)**, the **Republic of Vietnam**, and **Burma**.

The United States and the Soviet Union had announced their support for a neutral and independent Laos at the June 1961 Vienna Summit between President **John F. Kennedy** and Soviet Premier Nikita Khrushchev. The mechanics of implementing and verifying a permanent cease-fire were complicated by the issue of **Viet Minh** presence in Laos. Any American willingness to militarily intervene had been dampened by the Cuban Bay of Pigs disaster and mounting congressional opposition to a U.S. troop presence in Laos. Vice President **Lyndon Johnson** had been sent to Southeast Asia shortly before the opening of the conference to reassure American friends and allies about the steadfastness of the U.S. commitment to South Vietnam, Thailand, and the **Philippines**.

The discussions among the Laotian factions were acrimonious with respect to a unified government. The **Phoumi Nosavan**–backed **Boun Oum** government faction and the **Pathet Lao** faction backed by the **Viet Minh** and the DRV could not agree on the terms of a new, second Laos **coalition government**. As the Lao factions squabbled, the Pathet Lao regularly violated the cease-fire, overrunning government positions and gaining control over nearly two-thirds of the kingdom. It was not until the United States withheld its $3 million monthly aid installments to pressure the Royal Lao Government and moved combat troops into Thailand to deter the Pathet Lao that the impasse was broken. In June 1962, the factions negotiated the new neutralist coalition government that took office on 22 June. The conference, which had been recessed for five months, resumed on 2 July, and the **Geneva Accord on Laos** and accompanying protocol were signed on 23 July 1962.

GODLEY, G. MCMURTRIE, II (1917– 1999). Coming straight from the Congo to succeed Ambassador **William Sullivan** in **Laos**, G. McMurtrie "Mac" Godley picked up the support of the **Central Intelligence Agency (CIA)**'s **secret war** from 1969 to 1973. Returning to Washington in mid-1973 as nominee for the post of assistant secretary of state for East Asian and Pacific affairs, he faced a hostile Senate Foreign Relations Committee in his confirmation hearings. For the majority of the senators, Godley's record of support for the American policy in Laos, including B-52 bombings on the **Plain of Jars**, disqualified him. In a rebuke to the administration, the committee refused to confirm his nomination. President **Richard M. Nixon** issued a statement calling the refusal to confirm deplorable and an injustice, adding that it was not in the interest of the Foreign Service or the United States for career officers to be "subject to retribution for diligent execution of their instructions." Godley was posted as ambassador to Lebanon.

GOOD OFFICES COMMITTEE IN INDONESIA. In August 1947, the Indonesian armed struggle for independence from the Netherlands was placed on the agenda of the United Nations (UN) Security Council by Australia and India. The British-brokered 1946 Linggadjati cease-fire had broken down. On 21 July 1947, the Dutch swept out of the area under their control in the first so-called police action, significantly reducing the territory held by the Republic of **Indonesia**. Australia, India, the United States, and Great Britain had all failed in their efforts to mediate with the Dutch, who insisted that it was a matter of domestic jurisdiction. The Security Council's order for a cease-fire was ignored. On 25 August 1947, the Security Council authorized a Consular Commission in Batavia (now Jakarta) to report on the failure of the cease-fire and a Committee of Good Offices to intervene as mediators.

The Good Offices Committee had three members: Australia, named by Indonesia; Belgium, named by the Netherlands; and the United States, agreed to by Australia and Belgium. The United States appointed Dr. **Frank Graham**, president of the University of North

Carolina, as its first representative. He was succeeded by **Coert DuBois** and **H. Merle Cochran**. The committee arrived in Indonesia in October 1947 and facilitated an agreement, signed on board the USS *Renville* on 17 January 1948, known as the **Renville Agreement**. It called for a truce, stand-still, and demilitarized zones. The Good Offices Committee also worked out principles for a permanent political solution. After a year of no progress, the Dutch launched a second "police action" on 24 December 1948, seizing the republican capital of Yogyakarta. On 28 January 1949, the UN Security Council again took action, calling for a cease-fire, release of prisoners, and return of the republican government to Yogyakarta. It changed the Committee of Good Offices into the **United Nations Commission on Indonesia**.

GRAHAM, FRANK P. (1886–1972). Frank Graham was a distinguished North Carolina educator and president of the University of North Carolina from 1930 to 1949. A U.S. Marine officer in World War I, he served on a number of U.S. advisory boards and commissions throughout the Depression and World War II. He was selected by Secretary of State George Marshall to be the initial American delegate on the **Good Offices Committee in Indonesia** in 1947 and as an advisor to the secretary of state on Indonesian affairs. He was appointed to the U.S. Senate from North Carolina in 1949 to fill a vacancy caused by a death but lost the nomination for election to the Senate in 1950. He went on to be a **United Nations (UN)** mediator and UN representative in the Kashmir dispute between India and Pakistan.

GREEN, MARSHALL (1916–1998). Once described as the personification of American policy in Asia from the 1950s to the 1970s, Marshall Green occupied a number of key posts in his career as a Foreign Service Officer. He served twice in Korea, twice in Japan, as ambassador to **Indonesia** (1965–1969), as assistant secretary of state for East Asian and Pacific affairs (1969–1973), and as ambassador to Australia (1973–1975). Green arrived in Indonesia in July 1965 as U.S.–Indonesian relations had reached their nadir under President **Sukarno**. He replaced Ambassador **Howard Jones**, whose efforts to ease bilateral tensions had failed. The new American ambassador was greeted by anti-American demonstrations and the call of "go home

Green." A little more than a month after his presentation of credentials, the failed **Indonesian coup** attempt occurred, setting in motion the events that toppled Sukarno and brought General **Suharto** to power. The coincidence of Green's arrival and the coup led to charges from the political Left that Green—and behind him the **Central Intelligence Agency (CIA)**—had orchestrated the affair. In the initial years of the Suharto government, Ambassador Green and his embassy forged close political and economic support links with Indonesia's new and staunchly anticommunist military rulers. Green's own interpretation of events in Indonesia is his memoir, *Indonesia: Crisis and Transformation*.

In Washington, as assistant secretary of state, Green, an early advocate of rapprochement with **China**, had concerns about the White House's secret management of National Security Advisor **Henry Kissinger**'s policy initiative toward China. Secretary of State **William Rogers** and Assistant Secretary Green were the **State Department** officials traveling with President **Richard M. Nixon** on his 1972 visit to China. Immediately following the trip, Green and Ambassador **John Holdridge** were dispatched to 14 Asian countries to explain and reassure them about the changed U.S.–Chinese relationship.

GRIFFITHS, ANN MILLS. Executive director of the **National League of POW/MIA Families**, Ann Mills Griffiths was a strong advocate for the fullest accounting of American prisoners of war and missing in action **(POW/MIA)** in Southeast Asia. Her personal connection to the issue was her brother, a navy pilot shot down in 1966 over **Vietnam**. Her prominence on the issue came during the administration of President **Ronald Reagan**, which gave the POW/MIA question high priority. She obtained great access to policy makers through **Richard Childress**, the National Security Council's senior staffer charged with the issue. She became an unofficial member of the administration's Interagency Group on POW/MIA Affairs and was an unofficial member of U.S. government delegations to Vietnam as well as League private delegations, which continued into the period after the **normalization of relations with Vietnam**.

GROUP OF 77 (G-77). Now in fact 133, the Group of 77 is the structured political caucus of the developing countries in the **United**

Nations General Assembly (UNGA) and other UN bodies and programs such as the UN Development Program (UNDP). The members of the **Association of Southeast Asian Nations (ASEAN)** are parties to the G-77.

GUAM DOCTRINE. *See* NIXON DOCTRINE.

GULLION, EDMUND A. (1913–1998). A career Foreign Service Officer, Edmund Gullion was U.S. consul general in Hanoi, the senior American diplomat in French **Indochina**, when the **State of Vietnam** was proclaimed on 2 February 1950. The consulate was raised to a legation on 17 February, and Gullion was designated the chargé d'affaires ad interim until the arrival in October of the new minister plenipotentiary, **Donald Heath**, under whom Gullion continued to serve as minister counselor. Gullion was close to the making of the so-called **Bao Dai** solution leading to the creation of the State of Vietnam. He praised the Bao Dai government as one that, with American material support, could defeat the communist **Viet Minh**. As for the French, Gullion thought that they would be effective in containing Communist **China**. He admitted later in retrospect that the Americans put too much faith in French assessments, only to be disappointed. He later served as ambassador to the Congo. In retirement, Gullion became the dean of the Tufts University Fletcher School of Law and Diplomacy. In 1970, he led an unofficial group dispatched by President **Richard M. Nixon** to assess the progress of **Vietnamization**.

GUSMÃO, XANANA (1946–). Born José Alexandre Gusmão, Xanana Gusmão was elected first president of newly independent **East Timor** in April 2002. Educated in Jesuit seminaries, he was a civil servant in the Portuguese colonial administration when he became politically active in 1974, at the time of the collapse of Portuguese rule and East Timor's unilateral declaration of independence. He was on the central committee of **Fretilin**, the Revolutionary Front for an Independent East Timor, and with other Fretilin members he fled to the countryside after the 1975 **Indonesian invasion of East Timor**. From 1981 until his capture in 1992, he was the head of the **Falintil**, the military wing of Fretilin, and also led the umbrella political organization, the National Council of Timorese Resistance

(CNRT). After his capture, he was taken to Jakarta, tried, and sentenced to life imprisonment. Responding to worldwide protest, President **Suharto** reduced the sentence to 20 years. While he was in jail, the Timorese nationalists continued to recognize Gusmão as their leader. In early 1999, he was moved to house arrest in Jakarta in order to participate in the politics and diplomacy leading up to the 1999 August **East Timor referendum**. In March 1999, he met with American secretary of state **Madeleine Albright**. Stepping down from the presidency in 2007, Gusmão formed a new party, the National Congress for the Reconstruction of Timor (CNRT), and after elections formed a coalition government as prime minister, replacing the Fretilin government.

– H –

HABIB, PHILIP (1920–1992). Once described as "the outstanding professional diplomat of his generation," Philip Habib, after serving in **South Vietnam** as political counselor in the Saigon embassy, became a deputy assistant secretary of state for East Asian and Pacific affairs (1967–1969), ambassador to Korea (1977–1974), assistant secretary of state for East Asian and Pacific affairs (1974–1976), and undersecretary of state for political affairs (1976). He came out of retirement twice to serve as special envoy in Central America and the Middle East, for which he received the Presidential Medal of Freedom from President **Ronald Reagan**. For three and a half years (1968–1971), Habib was one of the principal American figures in the **Paris peace negotiations** that eventually led to the 1973 **Paris Agreement**, ending U.S. involvement in the **Second Indochina War**. In 1986, Secretary of State **George Schultz** sent him to the **Philippines** to evaluate the outcome of President **Ferdinand Marcos**'s snap election, won by **Corazon Aquino** but which Marcos tried to steal. Habib supported the reporting of Ambassador **Stephen Bosworth** and added his influential voice to the **State Department** senior officials advising President Reagan that Marcos had to go.

HABIBIE, BACHARUDDIN JUSUF (1936–). In May 1998, with his government crumbling in a political and economic crisis, **Indonesia**'s

President **Suharto** resigned. B. J. Habibie, who had unexpectedly been tapped as vice president only two months earlier, was the constitutional successor as the third president of Indonesia. Habibie was a German-trained aeronautical engineer who had held senior positions in the German aircraft industry until he was called back to Indonesia in 1974 by Suharto to become Indonesia's technology czar and head its defense industries. In February 1999, President Habibie precipitated Indonesia's worst foreign policy crisis since 1975 when, without consultation within his government, he unilaterally announced that Indonesia would permit an **East Timor referendum** on self-determination. Later that year Habibie, mired in a corruption scandal and nationalist anger over the loss of East Timor, was defeated in his effort to become elected president of Indonesia in his own right. He retired from politics and returned to Germany.

HAIG, ALEXANDER M., JR (1924–). In 1969, Colonel Alexander "Al" Haig, a career army officer, was named military assistant to National Security Advisor **Henry A. Kissinger**. A year later he became Kissinger's deputy, serving until 1973. In that four-year span he was promoted to full general. Haig was an important point man for Kissinger and President **Richard M. Nixon** in their dealings with President **Nguyen Van Thieu** in **South Vietnam** and **Lon Nol** in **Cambodia**. In his numerous missions to Saigon and Phnom Penh as Kissinger's surrogate and the president's special representative, it was Haig's job to assure the South Vietnamese officials of American commitment at the same time that the United States was engaged in the **Paris peace negotiations**, trying to extricate itself from the **Vietnam War**. It was Haig who was tasked with telling Thieu to agree to the terms the United States had negotiated with Hanoi or face the cutoff of all American assistance.

In 1973, after a brief tour as army deputy chief of staff, General Haig became President Nixon's chief of staff. Following Nixon's 1974 resignation, Haig returned to active duty and served as supreme commander of the North Atlantic Treaty Organization (NATO) until his retirement in 1978. In 1981, President **Ronald Reagan** named him secretary of state, but he was pushed to resign in 1982. As secretary, he endorsed the American policy of supporting the **Khmer resistance** in the Third Kampuchea as the legitimate government and occupant of Cambodia's seat in the United Nations (UN) and backed the **Coalition Government of Democratic Kampuchea (CGDK)**. An embarrassing photo-op shows Haig shaking hands at the UN with the CGDK's vice president, the notorious **Khmer Rouge** leader **Khieu Samphan**.

HAMBALI (1966–). Hambali (aka Riduan Isamudin), an operational leader of the **Jema'ah Islamiyah (JI)**, was the alleged mastermind of the October 2002 **Bali bombings** as well as the 2003 bombing of Jakarta's Marriot Hotel and other violent anti-West assaults on soft targets, including Christian churches. Some intelligence sources identified him as the only non-Arab member of the **al-Qaeda** leadership. He was described by President **George W. Bush** as "one of the world's most lethal terrorists." Hambali was born in **Indonesia**'s West Java province and as a teenager became involved in radical Islamist activity. From self-imposed exile in **Malaysia** in the 1980s, he went to Afghanistan as a *mujahidin* fighter against the Soviet occupation. After the overthrow of the **Suharto** regime in 1998, Hambali returned to Indonesia. His terrorist reach went beyond Indonesia. **Philippine** authorities claim he was responsible for bombings in Manila killing 22 people, shortly after the Hambali-orchestrated Christmas Eve blasts in Indonesia in 2000. In February 2004, Hambali, Southeast Asia's most wanted terrorist, was arrested by Thai authorities and accused of plotting an attack on the upcoming, Thai-hosted **Asia–Pacific Economic Cooperation (APEC)** summit. **Thailand** turned him over to the United States for interrogation and imprisonment in the facility at Guantanamo, Cuba. The United States refused Indonesia access to Hambali as Jakarta sought to prosecute **Abu Bakar Ba'asyir** in the Bali bombing case. *See also* WAR ON TERROR.

HARE–HAWES–CUTTING PHILIPPINE INDEPENDENCE ACT. This bill, actively lobbied for by Philippine nationalists **Sergio Osmeña** and **Manuel Roxas**, was passed by the U.S. Congress in 1932 but was vetoed by President Herbert Hoover. The veto was overridden, but the act was rejected by the Philippine legislature, led by **Manuel Quezon**. The ostensible reasons for Philippine objections were retention of U.S. military bases, quotas on Philippine exports to the United States, and immigration limits. A new independence act, the **Tydings–McDuffie Act**, was passed in 1934 with only minor differences, for which Quezon could take political credit in the **Philippines**. *See also* COMMONWEALTH OF THE PHILIPPINES.

HARRIMAN, W. AVERELL (1891–1986). Averell Harriman had a very long career as a senior American diplomat as well as politician. He had been ambassador to the Soviet Union during World War II. After the war, he was secretary of commerce in President **Harry S. Truman**'s cabinet. He was elected governor of New York (1955–1958). President **John F. Kennedy** named Harriman assistant secretary of state for East Asian and Pacific affairs in 1962. He headed the U.S. delegation that negotiated the **Geneva Accord of 1962**, which, on paper at least, renewed the guarantee of neutrality to **Laos** that had been negotiated in the **Geneva Accords of 1954**. From 1963 to 1965, Harriman was undersecretary of state for political affairs. It was Harriman, with **Roger Hilsman**, who composed the 24 August 1963 telegram that authorized Ambassador **Henry Cabot Lodge** in Saigon to inform Vietnamese army plotters that the U.S. would not object to a coup against **Ngo Dinh Diem**. In March 1965, Harriman became ambassador at large. He pressed for a diplomatic framework for a political settlement of the **Vietnam War** that could be negotiated from the strength of the American forces in place in **Vietnam**. He opposed escalation but did not want to lose the bargaining chip that withdrawal would have meant. After the administration of President **Lyndon B. Johnson** decided in 1968 to seek a negotiated disengagement, Harriman, together with **Cyrus Vance**, opened the **Paris peace negotiations** with the **Democratic Republic of Vietnam (DRV)** in May 1968, to be replaced in the incoming administration of President **Richard M. Nixon** by Ambassador Lodge.

HARRIS, TOWNSEND (1804–1878). Townsend Harris, a New York businessman in the China trade, is best known as the first American envoy to Japan. Appointed by President Franklin Pierce in 1855, Harris negotiated the first American treaty with Japan in 1858. He also negotiated a new treaty with **Siam** on his way to Japan, the 1856 **Harris Treaty**.

HARRIS TREATY, 1856. Townsend Harris, en route as the first U.S. envoy to Japan, stopped in **Siam,** where he negotiated a new Treaty of Amity and Cooperation, signed on 29 May 1856. This replaced the 1833 **Roberts Treaty.** The Harris treaty was modeled on the other "unequal" treaties forced on Siam by Western trading nations and contained provisions for extraterritoriality that were not lifted until the **Siam–U.S. Treaty and Protocol of 1920.**

HEATH, DONALD R. (1894–1981). A veteran diplomat whose career had begun in the consular service in Europe in the 1920s, in 1950 Donald Heath became the first American minister and then ambassador to the former French colonies in **Indochina** that had been given independent identities as associated states in the French Union. He was posted from Bulgaria, where he was ambassador. Prior to Heath's arrival in Saigon, the senior American diplomat in French Indochina was **Edmund A. Gullion,** consul general in Saigon. Heath was accredited to the **State of Vietnam** and the kingdoms of **Laos** and **Cambodia.** He was resident in Saigon, with chargé d'affaires in the legations in Vientiane and Phnom Penh. With the signing of the **Geneva Accords** terminating the **First Indochina War,** Heath was superseded in Cambodia in October 1954 by a resident ambassador, **Robert McClintock,** and in Laos in November 1954 by **Charles V. Yost.** Ambassador Heath ended his tour in Vietnam on 14 November 1954. Between then and the presentation of credentials by his successor, **G. Frederick Reinhardt,** on 28 May 1955, the senior American official in the State of Vietnam was General **J. Lawton Collins,** serving as personal representative of President **Dwight D. Eisenhower.** Heath headed three more embassies before he retired in 1961, after 40 years of service.

HELLIWELL, PAUL L. E. (1915–1976). A lawyer, Paul Helliwell became a high-ranking **Office of Strategic Services (OSS)** agent during World War II. After President **Harry S. Truman** disbanded the OSS in 1945, Helliwell remained in the Strategic Services Unit in the War Department as chief of the Far East Division until the establishment of the **Central Intelligence Agency (CIA)** in 1947. In 1951, he was sent to Taiwan to support Chiang Kai Shek's Kuomintang government in its continuing struggle against the communist People's Republic of **China**, now in control of the mainland. Helliwell was instrumental in the creation of two CIA proprietary companies, **Civil Air Transport (CAT)** in Taiwan and **Sea Supply Corporation** in Bangkok. He later operated from Miami, Florida, in support of CIA operations against Castro's Cuba. *See also* KMT–BURMA CRISIS.

HELMS, RICHARD M. (1913–2002). Described as "the man who kept the secrets," Richard Helms headed the **Central Intelligence Agency (CIA)** from June 1966 to February 1973, a tenure exceeded only by **Allen Dulles**. Helms came to the **Office of Strategic Services (OSS)** from the U.S. Navy in 1943 and from the OSS to the CIA in 1947. He served as deputy to **Frank Wisner**, the Deputy Director of Plans (DDP)—the clandestine side of the agency. When Wisner was replaced in 1959, Helms was passed over for the DDP post by Dulles, who named **Richard Bissell**. Helms continued as Bissell's deputy until Bissell left the CIA after the Bay of Pigs disaster in 1962. Helms succeeded Bissell as DDP at a time of deepening engagement of the CIA in the wars in Indochina. When President **Lyndon Johnson** made Admiral Thomas Raborn Director of Central Intelligence (DCI) in 1965, Helms became the deputy director. During Raborn's contentious 14-month DCI tour, Helms kept the agency on track. Succeeding Raborn in 1966, Helms was constantly pressed by President **Richard Nixon** and Secretary of State **Henry Kissinger** to have the agency do more in Vietnam, Laos, and Cambodia. His collision with the Nixon administration came over his resistance to the White House effort to involve the CIA in the Watergate scandal. Nixon dismissed Helms, sending him off as ambassador to Iran. In 1975, Helms was forced to testify before the U.S. Senate Select Committee to Study Governmental Operations with Respect to Intelligence Activities (the Church Committee) where he was less than fully forthcoming about the CIA's covert activities. This led to his conviction for perjury in 1977 and a sentence of two years suspended and a $2,000 fine. Helms kept his secrets until late in life when in the post-Cold War era he told some of them in his posthumously published autobiography *A Look over My Shoulder: A Life in the Central Intelligence Agency*.

HERTER, CHRISTIAN A. (1895–1996). Undersecretary of state (1957–1959), Christian Herter succeeded Secretary of State **John Foster Dulles**, who died in 1959. Herter served until the end of President **Dwight D. Eisenhower**'s term of office. Herter had been a Massachusetts Republican congressman (1943–1952) and then governor of Massachusetts (1953–1957). As secretary of state, Herter continued the administration's policy of bolstering the **Ngo Dinh Diem** government in the **Republic of Vietnam** while at the same time pressing for reform. As the administration was ending, the most immediate problem in Southeast Asia was the growing crisis in **Laos**. Herter, well aware that the **Southeast Asia Treaty Organization (SEATO)** did not guarantee military or political support for Laos, preferred a political solution, but if that failed, he understood that the United States had to support the anticommunists. In the administration of President **John F. Kennedy**, Herter, a committed internationalist, was named special representative for trade negotiations.

HILSMAN, ROGER (1919–). During World War II, Roger Hilsman, a West Point graduate, fought with Merrill's Marauders in **Burma**. He then went to the **Office of Strategic Services (OSS)**. He completed a Ph.D. in international relations at Yale University in 1951. As head of the foreign affairs division of the Library of Congress Legislative Reference Service, he was noticed by Senator **John F. Kennedy**, who, when president, made Hilsman the head of the **State Department**'s Bureau of Intelligence and Research (INR) from 1961 to 1963. Hilsman was a strong supporter of counterinsurgency as the proper tactic in **Vietnam** and argued against conventional military tactics. He became assistant secretary of state for East Asian and Pacific affairs in April 1963. He is best known as being one of the principal authors of the 24 August 1963 telegram to Ambassador **Henry Cabot Lodge** signaling that the U.S. government would not oppose the **Diem coup**. Hilsman became an early "dove," but his ability to argue against policy that was supported by more senior advisors, including his boss, Secretary of State **Dean Rusk**, did not survive the Kennedy administration. He resigned in February 1964.

HIV/AIDS. *See* PANDEMIC AND INFECTIOUS DISEASES.

HMONG. The Hmong, also called Meo (Miao), are an ethnic minority spread over the mountainous border region of southwest **China**, northern **Vietnam**, and northeastern **Laos**. In Laos, a Hmong army under General **Vang Pao** was the backbone of the **Central Intelligence Agency (CIA)**'s **secret war** against the **Pathet Lao** and its **Viet Minh** ally. After 1975, tens of thousands of Hmong people fled to **refugee** camps in **Thailand**. Thousands were resettled in the United States, from where support was generated for cross-border incursions by Hmong guerrilla groups, which impeded normalization of Thailand–Laos and U.S.–Lao relations. The Thai efforts to close the refugee camps by forcible repatriation of Hmong refugees to Laos was supported by the administration of President **William J. Clinton**, but because of congressional protest from senators and representatives with Hmong constituents, a new U.S. intake of Hmong refugees was approved, with the last 15,000 arriving in 2004. In 2007, more than 7,000 Hmong refugees still remained in Thailand, threatened with involuntary repatriation.

HO CHI MINH (1890–1969). Founder of the Indochinese Communist Party (ICP) in 1930 and the League for the Independence of Vietnam (**Viet Minh**) in 1941; proclaimer of the **Democratic Republic of Vietnam (DRV)** in 1945; and head of the Vietnam Communist Party—the "Workers Party" (*Lao Dong*)—until his death, Ho Chi Minh was the most prominent 20th-century communist leader in Southeast Asia. Named Nguyen Tat Thanh at birth, Ho Chi Minh was the last and most famous of the aliases the veteran communist organizer and leader had used in his career. He left **Vietnam** in 1911 as a cook's helper on ocean liners, settling in Paris after World War I. There, in 1920, as Nguyen Ai Quoc, he became a founding member of the French Communist Party. He went to the Soviet Union in 1923. After training, he returned to Asia as an agent of the Comintern. The ICP was organized in Hong Kong. As Ho Chi Minh, he clandestinely returned to Vietnam in 1940 and assumed leadership of the ICP and the Viet Minh. During World War II, while Ho was building the Viet Minh's political capacity and the beginnings of a military force, he cooperated with the United States against the occupying Japanese, liaising with the **Office of Strategic Services (OSS)**. It was through the OSS that **Ho Chi Minh's letter to President Harry S. Truman**

asking for American support for Vietnam's independence was sent. In declaring the independence of the DRV in 1945, Ho quoted the American Declaration of Independence. After more than a year of abortive negotiations with the returning French, full-scale war broke out in December 1946. Ho was the visible political leader of the DRV against the French in the **First Indochina War** and, until his death, against the Americans in the **Vietnam War**. He was loved as "Uncle Ho" by the Vietnamese people. Against his stated wishes, his body was embalmed and placed in a grand mausoleum in the heart of Hanoi.

HO CHI MINH LETTER TO PRESIDENT HARRY S. TRUMAN. In a letter dated 28 February 1946 addressed to American president **Harry S. Truman**, **Ho Chi Minh**, the communist leader of the **Democratic Republic of Vietnam (DRV)**, requested American assistance in ending French aggression. The letter was delivered to Washington via the **Office of Strategic Services (OSS)** liaison with the **Viet Minh**. In the letter, Ho noted the alliance with the United States against their common Japanese enemy, American democratic principles, and United Nations principles. He asked that the United States help Vietnam achieve what America had "graciously" given to the **Philippines**. He ended by calling for future cooperation between the two countries. Ho's letter went unanswered.

HO CHI MINH TRAIL. This was the name used for the land route through **Laos** on the western side of the mountain range bordering Laos and **Vietnam** to the eastern **Cambodia–South Vietnam** border region. The trail was used by the People's Army of Vietnam (PAVN) to move men, weapons, and supplies from north to south. From a network of paths and forest trails, it was developed over time for wheeled vehicles and even had a pipeline running along it. It was a major target for American bombing during the **Vietnam War**, and defense of it provided the strategic background of the heavy PAVN presence in Laos.

HOLBROOKE, RICHARD C. A. (1941–). Assistant secretary of state for East Asian and Pacific Affairs in the administration of President **Jimmy Carter** (1977–1981), Richard Holbrooke is the only

American diplomat to have been assistant secretary for two different regions in two administrations, becoming the assistant secretary of state for Europe and Canadian affairs (1992–1996) in the first administration of President **William J. Clinton**. In Clinton's second administration, Holbrooke was U.S. permanent representative to the **United Nations (UN)** (1999–2000). His career began as a junior Foreign Service Officer in **Vietnam**. He was part of the American mission at the **Paris peace negotiations** that ended the war. Before joining the Carter administration, Holbrooke was the editor of the journal *Foreign Policy*. Working for Secretary of State **Cyrus Vance**, Assistant Secretary Holbrooke was instrumental in the **State Department's** efforts to get **normalization of relations with Vietnam** on track. He was the principal in a series of negotiations with Vietnamese counterparts in 1977–1978. In the end, however, the president's national security advisor, **Zbigniew Brzezinski**, influenced the president to put **China** before Vietnam. Holbrooke also worked to maintain stability in U.S.–Southeast Asian relations as the **human rights** issues raised by Assistant Secretary of State for Human Rights and Humanitarian Affairs **Patricia Derian** politically threatened relations with key allies. Despite the congressional uproar over the **Indonesian invasion of East Timor**, Holbrooke kept a military supply link open to Jakarta. In Manila, he sought to prevent the rights issue from damaging American security ties to the **Philippines**, especially negotiations on revisions in the U.S.–Philippine **Military Bases Agreement (MBA)**. During the **Third Indochina War**, Holbrooke acted to reassure the Southeast Asian states that the United States stood behind their resistance to Vietnam's invasion and occupation of **Cambodia**. As American representative to the UN in the Clinton administration, Holbrooke worked diligently for the **East Timor referendum** and then UN intervention to restore order after the postreferendum violence. His Asian interests continued out of government as chairman of the executive committee of the **Asia Society**.

HOLDRIDGE, JOHN H. (1924–2001). A talented Chinese language officer, John Holdridge was National Security Advisor **Henry Kissinger's** senior staff member for East Asia. He was involved in the planning and execution of Kissinger's and President **Richard M. Nixon's** policy initiatives toward **China**. He accompanied Kissinger on his 1969 secret trip to China and was with the party on President Nixon's 1972 trip to China. Immediately following that, he and Assistant Secretary of State for East Asian and Pacific Affairs **Marshall Green** were dispatched to 14 Asian nations to explain the changed U.S.–Chinese relationship. Holdridge was the deputy chief of the U.S. Liaison Mission in China when it opened in 1973. From there, he went to **Singapore** as American ambassador (1975–1978), to reassure Prime Minister **Lee Kuan Yew** of American staying power in Southeast Asia.

After serving for three years as assistant secretary of state for East Asian and Pacific affairs (1981–1983), Holdridge took up the post of ambassador to **Indonesia**. His presentation of credentials to President **Suharto** in February 1983 was important for the bilateral relationship. Since the departure of Ambassador **Edward Masters** in November 1981, the United States had been represented by Masters's former deputy, John C. Monjo, as chargé d'affaires ad interim for 13 months. The first American nominee for ambassador, **Morton Abramowitz**, was not acceptable to the Indonesians. The Indonesian government did not understand the delay in the nomination and confirmation of another nominee. Rightly or wrongly, Jakarta interpreted it as either a mark of displeasure at the handling of the Abramowitz nomination or a downgrading of Indonesia's importance to the United States. To give a special emphasis to it, Holdridge's nomination was announced by President Ronald Reagan at a state dinner honoring President Suharto of Indonesia during his November 1982 visit to Washington. Holdridge's accomplished diplomatic background reassured Jakarta that Indonesia still counted. Monjo went on to a distinguished Foreign Service career as ambassador to **Malaysia** (1987–1989), Indonesia (1989–1992), and Pakistan (1992–1995).

HONASAN COUPS. Colonel Gregorian Honasan was a charismatic Philippine army officer at the center of military plots against the **Philippine** government of President **Corazon Aquino**. Nicknamed "Gringo," he led a coup attempt in 1987 that shook the government and led to both reforms in and purges of the military. In December 1989, another coup attempt inspired by Honasan involved elite military units, which seized important government strongholds, along with air attacks on the presidential palace. The army wavered in its allegiance to the government. Leading figures from the previously deposed government of **Ferdinand Marcos** were at work behind the scenes. The United States, anxious to defend both the new democratic government and its security interests in Philippine stability, intervened with a show of force approved by President **George H. W. Bush**. American Air Force jet fighters out of **Clark Air Base** flew over Manila, grounding the Philippine propeller-driven T-28s flown by the rebels. The American display did not immediately end the coup, but it indicated to the Philippine military that the United States stood behind the Aquino government, which ultimately prevailed. In legal politics, Honasan became a senator. Honasan was also alleged to again be a coup plotter during the presidency of **Gloria Macapagal-Arroyo**. After months in hiding, he was arrested in 2006, but was reelected to the senate in 2007.

HUBBARD, THOMAS C. (1943–). Thomas Hubbard joined the Foreign Service in 1965. Originally trained as a Japanese language officer, his later career was Southeast Asia–oriented, particularly toward the **Philippines**. He was a Philippine country desk officer in the State Department (1985–1987) before going to **Malaysia** as the deputy chief of mission. From 1990 to 1993, he was the deputy chief of mission in the Philippines. During the administration of President **William J. Clinton**, Hubbard served first as deputy assistant secretary of state for East Asian and Pacific affairs. In that post, in 1994 he had the first high-level bilateral contact with **Burma** since 1990. He was named ambassador to the Philippines and concurrently Palau in 1996. His major accomplishment in Manila was the negotiating of the new **Visiting Forces Agreement (VFA)** that renewed the basis for Philippine–U.S. military cooperation. He was also a vigorous and visible advocate for Philippine **trade** liberalization, making the American embassy a focal point for antiglobalism, anti-**International Monetary Fund (IMF)**, and anti-American demonstrations. Hubbard left the Philippines in July 2000 as Philippine opposition to President **Joseph Estrada** was mounting. Back in Washington, he served as acting assistant secretary of state for East Asian and Pacific affairs in the four-month interregnum between the ending of the Clinton administration and President **George W. Bush**'s appointment of a new assistant secretary. In that role, Hubbard defended the incoming Philippine administration of

Gloria Macapagal-Arroyo as being committed to reform. Hubbard's final positing was as ambassador to South Korea (2001–2004).

HUKBALAHAP. This was a Filipino revolutionary peasant movement in the post–World War II years. It had its origins as a guerrilla resistance force during the Japanese occupation of the **Philippines** (1942–1945), hence its name, Anti-Japanese People's Army (*Hukbo ng Bayan Laban sa Hapong*). Led in postwar Philippines by radical leftists and communists, the Huks fed on the deep-rooted poverty and social discontent of the rural Filipino peasants, long suffering under oppressive landlordism. Controlling large swaths of Central Luzon, the Huks were more than agrarian reformers. They challenged the legitimacy of the newly independent **Philippine** state and its continuing ties to the United States. The Huks, renamed the People's Liberation Army (*Hukbong Magpalayang Bayan*), became strong enough in 1949 to threaten Manila. Political corruption and a demoralized, poorly led army seemed to promise the collapse of the government.

The government of **Elpidio Quirino**, who, after a violent and corrupt campaign, was elected in 1949, turned to the United States for greater assistance. President **Harry S. Truman** dispatched a survey commission led by a former undersecretary of the treasury, Daniel Bell, to see what could be done to strengthen the Manila government. For the United States this was to be the first test of its policy of **containment** of communism in Southeast Asia. The **Bell Economic Survey Mission**'s report recommended that aid for the Philippines should be conditional on economic and social reform.

Quirino named former anti-Japanese guerrilla leader and rising politician **Ramon Magsaysay** as secretary of national defense, giving him a free hand to combat the Huks. Magsaysay worked closely with the Joint United States **Military Assistance Advisory Group (MAAG)**, and especially Colonel **Edward Lansdale**, to reorganize and retrain the army and to take the political initiative away from the Huks. The turning point came in October 1950 with the capture in Manila of the communist's politburo, a blow that fragmented the revolutionary movement.

HUMAN RIGHTS. One of the most contentious issues in U.S. relations in Southeast Asia is the political weight to be given to human rights in the substance and quality of American relations with the countries of the region. Ever since U.S. representative **Donald Fraser** focused Congress's legislative attention on human rights in the mid-1970s, they have been an important part of U.S. foreign policy in the region. Not only are human rights issues a question of bilateral state-to-state relations; they figure in the dialogue between the American executive and the Congress in the conduct of foreign relations, particularly in security assistance decisions.

The global human rights regime has its roots in the Charter of the United Nations and the 1948 Universal Declaration of Human Rights. To these founding documents, more than a hundred treaties and other international instruments have added a normative framework setting standards by which a government's treatment of its own peoples can be measured by other governments. In the United States, these universal norms are interpreted in the context of American political history and ideology, with an emphasis on civil and political rights. Leaders in Southeast Asia have perceived the American preoccupation with these categories of rights as ignoring economic, social, and cultural rights and different expressions of historical processes. The most sophisticated counterargument to the American insistence on the universality of an essentially Western conception of human rights found expression in the so-called **Asian values** debate. Furthermore, Southeast Asian states are jealous of their sovereignty. They resist external pressures about issues that the governments consider to be matters of domestic jurisdiction.

The lead agency in the U.S. government for human rights in American foreign policy is the **State Department**'s Bureau of Democracy, Rights, and Labor (DRL), headed by an assistant secretary. Its bureaucratic origin is the Bureau of Human Rights and Humanitarian Affairs, created in 1977 by President **Jimmy Carter**, reacting to what he saw as the moral shortcomings of the realpolitik, clandestine excesses of **Henry Kissinger**'s foreign policy. Carter picked Assistant Secretary of State **Patricia Derian** to make human rights advocacy a central feature of American foreign policy. Derian aggressively pursued a human rights agenda in dealings with the governments of President **Ferdinand Marcos** in the **Philippines**, Prime Minister **Lee Kuan Yew** in **Singapore**, and President **Suharto** in **Indonesia**. The State Department's congressionally mandated annual Human Rights Country Reports and the complementary Religious Rights Country Reports arouse ire in the countries singled out for negative evaluations. The data used in making official evaluations of the rights situation in specific countries are derived not only from U.S. government sources, but also from nongovernmental organizations such as Human Rights Watch and Amnesty International.

From the outset, the U.S. human rights agenda has collided with real political and security interests in Southeast Asia represented by the strategic value placed by the United States on its relations with its friends in the Cold War environment of Southeast Asia. In the **Philippines**, the **Military Bases Agreement (MBA)** trumped the human rights record of Ferdinand Marcos's government. It was only when Marcos's determination to hang on to power threatened Philippine political stability that the United States reluctantly shifted its support to the democratic opposition so that American security interests might survive regime change. In Indonesia, for nearly a quarter of a century the U.S. perception of Indonesia's strategic importance overrode human rights concerns about the Indonesian army's cruel and corrupt rule in **East Timor**.

No country in Southeast Asia has escaped American human rights scrutiny. **Thailand** was angered by criticism of widespread extrajudicial killings that were part of Thai Prime Minister **Thaksin Shinawatra**'s war against drug trafficking. The American ambassador to **Cambodia** has spoken out publicly about the antidemocratic quality of Prime Minister **Hun Sen**'s rule. The treatment of Laotian ethnic minorities, particularly the **Hmong**, has been censured. **Permanent normal trade relations (PNTR)** with **Vietnam** were held hostage by Congress to its status as a country of particular concern (CPC) for denial of **religious** rights. The harsh internal security acts in Singapore and **Malaysia** have been criticized as tools to suppress legitimate dissent and political opposition. In the case of Malaysia, the bilateral issue came to a head over the imprisonment of **Anwar Ibrahim** in 1998. The principal official rights focus in Southeast Asia has been on **Burma**, with the detention of **Aung San Suu Kyi** at the symbolic center. Even America's closest security ally in Southeast Asia, the **Philippines**, is not immune from criticism. Both the State Department and Congress have decried the extrajudicial killings carried out by the Philippine military.

American direct diplomacy in support of human rights is largely rhetoric and persuasion, what is sometime called "constructive engagement." Indirectly, the United States, through support to programs fostering the building of civil society institutions, seeks to expand democratic political space. Coercive measures such as sanctions to force compliance with U.S. demands for reform have rarely been employed. Limitations on military assistance to Indonesia because of its behavior in **East Timor** were put in place after the 1991 **Dili Massacre**. These were reinforced by the **Leahy Amendment** after the 1999 violence following the **East Timor referendum**, but they have since been waived. It is only against the military junta in **Burma** that the United States has imposed a full economic sanctions regime. Beginning in 1997 and expanded in 2003, the sanctions prohibit all economic and financial dealings between the United States and Burma.

HUMPHREY–TRUONG ESPIONAGE CASE. Ronald Humphrey, an employee of the U.S. Information Agency, was discovered by the Federal Bureau of Investigation (FBI) in 1977 passing classified **State Department** cables and documents to Vietnamese immigrant David Truong. Truong in turn delivered the secret material to **Vietnam**'s **United Nations (UN)** mission and the Vietnamese embassy in Paris. The courier, a Vietnamese woman, was an FBI informant. A wiretap on Truong revealed the Humphrey connection. Humphrey's incentive was the repatriation from Vietnam of his common-law wife and her children. Humphrey and Truong were indicted on six counts of espionage, tried, convicted, and sentenced to 15 years each. The Vietnamese ambassador to the UN, Dinh Ba Thi, was named an unindicted co-conspirator and expelled from the United States. While no important secrets were lost, the case temporarily chilled American official attitudes toward the negotiations for **normalization of relations with Vietnam**.

HUN SEN (1951–). Prime minister of **Cambodia**, Hun Sen is the longest serving elected head of government in Southeast Asia and one of the most controversial. He joined the revolutionary movement in Cambodia in 1970, becoming a field commander in **Pol Pot**'s **Khmer Rouge (KR)**. He was wounded shortly before Phnom Penh fell in April 1975, losing sight in an eye. After the KR victory he was sent to the eastern regions adjoining **Vietnam**. As a split in the KR between the Pol Potists and those who wanted to maintain good relations with Vietnam widened, Hun Sen, fearing a purge and possible execution, defected to Vietnam in 1977. After proper indoctrination, Hun Sen and other pro-Vietnam Cambodians came back to Phnom Penh in 1979 with the Vietnamese forces, whose invasion began the **Third Indochina War**. The returning Cambodians became the officials of the **People's Republic of Kampuchea (PRK)**. Hun Sen at age 28 was named foreign minister. In 1981, he added deputy prime minister to his folio, and in 1985, he became prime minister and leader of the ruling party, the People's Revolutionary Party. As prime minister and foreign minister he conducted the negotiations for the PRK that ended with the **comprehensive political settlement of the Cambodia conflict**.

In the **United Nations (UN)**–sponsored elections of 1993, Hun Sen's party, now renamed the Cambodian People's Party, finished second to the royalist **Funcinpec** Party, but with UN-backing forced its way into a coalition government. Hun Sen and the royalist party's leader, Norodom Ranariddh, became co-prime ministers. The power sharing arrangement was shattered in 1997 when Hun Sen's security forces turned on Funcinpec and Ranariddh in anticipation of the 1998 elections. The **Association of Southeast Asian Nations (ASEAN)** put off Cambodia's entry into ASEAN, and economic assistance from donor nations, including the United States, was suspended. ASEAN, with the assistance of Japan, arranged for a new internationally monitored election, which was held in 1998. This was narrowly won by Hun Sen's party. Despite allegations of voting fraud and government intimidation, the outcome was accepted by ASEAN and the international community. Hun Sen emerged as the sole prime minister and unrivaled dominant political actor in Cambodia. Elections in 2003 followed a predictable course given Hun Sen's authoritarian command of the electoral machinery. The antidemocratic quality of Hun Sen's rule led American ambassador to Cambodia Joseph Mussolmelio to voice in 2006 U.S. concerns about the government's suppression of democratic opposition. When the UN Special Representative for **Human Rights** reported in 2006 about the "abuse of law and a politics of impunity" in Cambodia, Hun Sen's retort was that the UN official was "deranged." It has also been alleged that Cambodia's stalling on establishing the mixed Cambodian-international tribunal for the **Khmer Rouge trials** was in part because of Hun Sen's own KR background.

– I –

INDOCHINA. This is a French designation—*l'Indochine*—which was both a geographic and political expression of France's colonial and imperial possessions in continental Southeast Asia: the colony of Cochin China and protectorates in Annam and Tonkin—the three making up modern **Vietnam**—and protectorates in **Cambodia**, and the principalities of **Laos**. French policy treated the region as a political and economic unit. A French governor general stood at the administrative apex that included a governor of Cochin China and a resident in each of the protectorates. The entire area was covered by political and economic councils that advised the governor general. The political—but not cultural—unity of the area was expressed as well in the 1930 founding of the Indochinese Communist Party (ICP) in Hong Kong by Comintern agent Nguyen Ai Quoc, better known as **Ho Chi Minh**. Primarily Vietnamese in membership, the ICP claimed the nationalist revolutionary mantle for Cambodia and Laos as well. After France gave up the last of its claims to sovereignty in the 1954 **Geneva Accords** ending the **First Indochina War**, Indochina became a collective term for the independent states of Vietnam, Cambodia, and Laos, comprising a subregion of Southeast Asia.

INDOCHINA WARS. This is a collective term covering the three historically connected conflicts in **Cambodia**, **Laos**, and **Vietnam** that were the focus of American political and security policy in the Southeast Asian region from 1950 to 1990. *See* FIRST INDOCHINA WAR; SECOND INDOCHINA WAR; THIRD INDOCHINA WAR.

INDONESIA. The Republic of Indonesia, the pre–World War II Netherlands East Indies, is an archipelagic nation of more than 17,000 islands and islets stretching nearly 3,000 miles athwart the equator from Sumatra to West Papua. The total land area is 707,188 square miles (1,826,440 square kilometers), and its total area, including territorial seas, is 741,100 square miles (1,919,440 square kilometers), about three times the size of Texas. Its command of the vital straits linking East Asia to the Middle East has since its independence defined Indonesia's strategic interest to the United States. Indonesia's population of nearly 250 million makes it the fourth most populous country in the world. Nearly 90 percent of the population professes Islam, which makes it the world's largest Muslim country. Since 2001 and the beginning of the war on terror, its Islamic quality has also become an important U.S. interest. Since at least the end of the **Second Indochina War**, the United States has identified Indonesia as the linchpin of security and stability in the Southeast Asian regional international order.

American engagement with Indonesia began during the decolonization of the Netherlands East Indies, when the Republic of Indonesia was proclaimed by nationalist leader **Sukarno** on 17 August 1945, two days after the Japanese surrender in World War II. The claimed independence was met by the Netherlands' determination to reassert sovereignty in the territory. Through negotiation and military action, the returning Dutch tried to defeat the republic or, if that were not possible, to at least to limit its territorial extent and keep it in a political framework of union under the Dutch crown. The Dutch found themselves stalemated on the ground and under great international pressure to grant Indonesia full independence. Bilateral pressures on The Hague included threats by influential U.S. congressmen to cut off postwar Marshall Plan aid to the Netherlands, which they claimed was offsetting the costs of the Dutch colonial war. The **United Nations (UN)** Security Council became involved in the situation in 1947 after a first attempt at negotiated settlement broke down. This had led to the first "police action," a Dutch euphemism for military attacks on republican forces. Calling for a cease-fire and renewed negotiations, the Security Council named a **Good Offices Committee (GOC)** of Australia, Belgium, and the United States. The GOC brokered another agreement, signed on board the USS *Renville* in January 1948, hence the **Renville Agreement**. A second "police action" in December 1948 captured the republican capital of Yogyakarta. An aroused Security Council demanded that the republican government be reinstated and charged its **United Nations Commission on Indonesia (UNCI)**, the successor to the GOC, to assist in negotiations leading to a transfer of sovereignty to the Republic of the United States of Indonesia in December 1949. Although at first a federal state, within a few months it became a unitary Republic of Indonesia. Remaining outside of the new state, however, was the Dutch possession of West New Guinea, the source of later frictions as Indonesia demanded its inclusion in the republic.

The first U.S. ambassador to Indonesia, **H. Merle Cochran**, presented his credentials to independent Indonesia's president **Sukarno** on 30 December 1949. Cochran was suspect to the Indonesians because as a member of the UNCI he had seemed sympathetic to Dutch negotiating positions. The ideological basis of the new Indonesian state's foreign policy was laid out in terms of "free and active," not wishing to have to choose between the United States and the Soviet Union during the Cold War. The **Eisenhower** administration, however, tried to force choice by linking desperately needed assistance to a **mutual security agreement** that would commit Indonesia to the "free world." Nationalist and leftist protest against what was claimed as a compromise of Indonesia's Cold War nonalignment led to the parliamentary collapse of the government negotiating with the United States. It was succeeded in 1953 by a government led by **Ali Sastroamidjojo**, who began what the United States considered the radicalization and leftward drift of Indonesian foreign policy. With President Sukarno, Ali was a convener of the 1955 **Asian–African Conference**, the precursor of the **Nonaligned Movement (NAM)** that was anathema to American secretary of state **John Foster Dulles**. American concerns about Sukarno's politics became so great that in 1955 the White House instructed the **Central Intelligence Agency (CIA)** to undertake covert activies to keep Indonesia from going communist.

In 1957, Sukarno declared martial law and ended parliamentary democracy in Indonesia, then two years later put in place a "guided democracy" that gave a place in government to the **Indonesian Communist Party**—the Partai Kommunis Indonesia (PKI). He also threatened to use force to bring Dutch-controlled West New Guinea into the republic. The **Eisenhower** administration was convinced that Sukarno was a crypto-communist or at least a PKI sympathizer. The United States attempted to overthrow or destabilize the Sukarno regime through CIA support of the **PRRI–Permesta** regional revolts in 1957–1958. The U.S. role was exposed when CIA contract pilot

Allen Pope was shot down on a bombing run over the island of Ambon on 18 May 1958.

Even though there was no political warmth in the bilateral relationship, American economic and military assistance continued to flow to Indonesia. There was fear that a back door was opening to communism in Southeast Asia behind the **containment** shield the United States was putting in place in **Indochina**. The U.S. government particularly wanted to maintain ties to the Indonesian army, viewing it as a counterweight to the growing domestic power of the PKI. American military attachés, particularly Colonel **George Benson**, were important links between the U.S. embassy and senior Indonesian military officers. In 1962, the incoming administration of President **John F. Kennedy** tried to improve relations by brokering a resolution of the **West New Guinea dispute** favorable to Indonesia, utilizing the diplomatic skills of Ambassador **Ellsworth Bunker**. Washington did not want to see an armed conflict between the Netherlands and Indonesia that could only benefit the PKI. Kennedy's ambassador to Indonesia, **Howard Jones**, pressed a policy of accommodation with Indonesia, only to be politically and personally humiliated by Sukarno.

In soaring revolutionary rhetoric, Sukarno called for a **Jakarta–Phnom** Penh–Hanoi–Beijing–Pyongyang axis of the world's "New Emerging Forces" to fight imperialism wherever it occurred. For Sukarno, Indonesia's front in that battle was the campaign called *Konfrontasi* ("**Confrontation**") to crush **Malaysia**, which Sukarno described as a British imperialist puppet. This meant in 1964–1965 low-intensity armed conflict with Great Britain, Australia, and New Zealand, Malaysia's Commonwealth allies who had come to its defense. The action took place primarily along the East Malaysian Sarawak state border with Indonesia. When Malaysia became a nonpermanent member of the UN Security Council, Sukarno took Indonesia out of the United Nations, becoming the only nation ever to quit the world organization. With Ambassador Jones in the audience, he said "to hell" with American aid. To Washington, Sukarno seemed to be moving the country inexorably into the Sino–Soviet orbit and preparing to deliver the government to the PKI.

Whatever concerns the United States may have had about a communist future for Indonesia were allayed by the climactic events of

1965–1966. The collapsing economy had led to even greater polarization of domestic politics. In the context of *Konfrontasi*, an emboldened PKI pushed for a "fifth force" of armed peasants and workers outside of the Indonesian military establishment. Islamic leaders were fearful of an imminent communist seizure of power. To the volatile mix of social, economic, and political antagonisms, in August 1965 concerns and rumors about Sukarno's health were added. On the night of 30 September 1965, an abortive coup, attributed by the army to the PKI, decisively reshaped Indonesian politics and foreign policy, particularly relations with the United States. In the wake of the 1965 **Indonesian coup** the PKI was destroyed in a bloody purge, Sukarno forced from his office through constitutional maneuvers, and a military-based government led by General **Suharto** installed. Although there is no credible evidence that the United States was involved in the coup, it certainly welcomed it.

In the years from 1966 to 1968, as Suharto progressed from acting with Sukarno's authority, to acting president, to president, Indonesia's policies underwent dramatic change. Confrontation with Malaysia was ended. Indonesia rejoined the United Nations. Relations with China were frozen. With its Southeast Asian partners, it helped found the **Association of Southeast Asian Nations (ASEAN)**. The United States responded with new economic assistance programs tailored to recovery and development. This was carried out in a multilateral framework of the U.S.-inspired **Intergovernmental Group on Indonesia (IGGI)**. The military assistance program was reestablished, with a Defense Liaison Group (DLG) dispatched for delivery and training.

The new security ties to the United States were built within the continuing broader framework of Indonesian nonalignment, even though, as Ambassador **Marshall Green** reported to President **Richard M. Nixon**, Suharto and his generals, with their antipathy toward communism and China, were much less nonaligned than the official position portrayed by the Foreign Ministry. As vice president, Nixon had already met Suharto in Indonesia before becoming president and was favorably impressed. Nixon had National Security Advisor **Henry Kissinger** establish a special back-channel of communication with the Indonesian military leadership to facilitate bilateral military relations. At American behest, Indonesia transferred AK-47 arms and ammunition to **Lon Nol**'s forces in **Cambodia**. Indonesia also provided diplomatic support for anticommunist Cambodia.

After the 1975 victories of the communist armies in Indochina, the United States viewed Suharto's Indonesia as the key player in the Southeast Asian regional balance of power. Throughout the decade of the 1980s, the United States favored Indonesia as a bulwark of stability in Southeast Asia and the untitled leader of ASEAN. Indonesian officials were conscious of this appreciation and sensitive to any perceived slight. In April 1984, for example, when President **Ronald Reagan** canceled his scheduled visit to the **Philippines** after the assassination of **Benigno Aquino**, in order to soften the blow to President **Ferdinand Marcos**, a scheduled stop in Indonesia was also canceled. The Indonesians viewed this as a downgrading of their importance, particularly since visits to Japan and South Korea on Reagan's trans-Pacific itinerary went on as scheduled.

American geostrategic interest in its security relationship with the Suharto government and the impressive economic gains it had made pushed to the official background concerns about the authoritarian nature of the regime. In the first decade of the new relationship, two **human rights** issues in particular challenged the official priorities. The first was accountability for the anticommunist bloodletting in 1965–1966 and any American complicity in it. Related to that was the fate of allegedly communist political prisoners. The official U.S. approach preferred "quiet diplomacy," which led to charges by human rights advocacy groups of American indifference. After the December 1975 **Indonesian invasion of East Timor** and its forcible incorporation into Indonesia, Jakarta's human rights record in the new province became an issue for American policy. The American official de facto recognition of the new status quo was challenged by advocacy groups and congressional critics. Of particular concern was the continued flow of military assistance to Indonesia in a military-to-military relationship that Indonesia's opponents alleged enabled ongoing abuses. Congressional efforts to limit the security relationship were thwarted or circumvented even during the administration of President **Jimmy Carter**. The 1991 **Dili massacre**, however, changed the policy priorities, and Congress put in place the first significant limitations on the U.S.–Indonesian security relationship, over the objections of the administration of **George H. W. Bush**.

Presidential candidate **William J. Clinton** declared on the campaign trail that American policy on East Timor was "unconscionable," but his presidential administration essentially followed the same policy as his predecessors, trying to not allow congressional anger about human rights violations to damage the broader array of American interests. One of those interests was to head off Malaysian Prime Minister **Mohammad Mahathir**'s efforts to create an **East Asian Economic Group (EAEG)** that would exclude the United States. In this, Clinton had an ally in Suharto. Despite Mahathir's call for a boycott, Suharto led the rest of the ASEAN leaders to the first **Asia–Pacific Economic Cooperation (APEC)** summit meeting, hosted by President Clinton. It was not until after the collapse of the Suharto administration in the wreckage of the **financial crisis of 1997–1998** that U.S. policy toward East Timor became more proactive. In low profile, Washington supported the 1999 **East Timor referendum**, the peacekeeping of the **International Force in East Timor (INTERFET)**, and the **United Nations Transitional Administration in East Timor (UNTAET)**. Congress, demanding accountability for Indonesian military responsibility for the violence after the referendum, enacted the **Leahy Amendment**'s tough new restrictions on U.S. security ties to Indonesia. These were only lifted in 2005.

With the issue of East Timor's fate behind them, U.S.–Indonesian relations entered a new phase in the post-Suharto era. Washington was still interested in a politically stable Indonesia in the regional balance of power. Now, however, stability was to be achieved by fostering democratic transition and economic reform rather than strongman rule. Indonesia's first three post-Suharto presidents—**B. J. Habibie**, **Abdurrahman Wahid**, and **Megawati Sukarnoputri**—did not have the capacity to effect great institutional change. Habibie was brought down by East Timor and corruption; Wahid by erratic behavior and illness; and Megawati by inattention, personality, and bad advice. The American democratization priority was overtaken in 2001 by the **war on terror**. It was only with the election of **Susilo Bambang Yudhoyono** in 2004 that Indonesia had a government that seemed to have a serious commitment to democratic consolidation, institutional reform, and the war on terrorism. Despite the domestic political constraints of operating in a Muslim-majority nation, President Yudhoyono intensified counterterrorism cooperation with the

United States. Both governments speak of the new bilateral relationship in terms of a strategic partnership. The 2005 waiver of the last restriction on the military-to-military relationship fully restored a normal security relationship with Indonesia to complement the political and economic dimensions of the partnership. In 2006, initial discussions began within the **trade and investment framework agreement (TIFA)** consultative framework for a future U.S.–Indonesian **free trade agreement (FTA)**. *See also* TRADE.

INDONESIAN COMMUNIST PARTY (PKI). Under the leadership of D. N. Aidit, the Indonesian Communist Party (Partai Kommunis Indonesia [PKI]), with party and front-group membership of 27 million Indonesians, grew to be **Indonesia**'s largest political party and the third largest communist party in the world after the USSR's and **China**'s. The PKI's strategy of choosing cooperation with President **Sukarno** in his 1959 framework of "guided democracy" led to its domestic political ascendancy, which challenged the anticommunist Indonesian army. While the United States was seeking to contain communism in **Vietnam**, the PKI threatened to come to power by acclamation in Indonesia. The failed 30 September 1965 **Indonesian coup** led to an anticommunist purge and bloodbath that wiped out the party and its leadership.

INDONESIAN COUP. On 30 September 1965, an abortive coup d'état was launched in Jakarta that allegedly sought to preempt a coup by anticommunist army generals. In **Indonesia** the coup is called GESTAPU, an acronym for the Indonesian Gerakan September Tiga Puluh—the 30 September Movement (G30S). It was launched by a group of army officers with links to the **Indonesian Communist Party (PKI)**. In the course of the night and the following morning, six senior generals were murdered. The coup leaders announced over the seized state radio the formation of a Revolutionary Council with a new cabinet. President **Sukarno** wavered in his reaction, since the coup seemed to be pro-Sukarno. He irrevocably compromised himself by taking refuge at Halim Air Force Base with PKI head D. N. Aidit and air force commander Omar Dhani, who had endorsed the Revolutionary Council. Rallied by General **Suharto**, commander of the Indonesian Army Strategic Reserve (KOSTRAD), the primary military combat units, the army struck back and quickly crushed the coup, sidelining Sukarno, who was thought to be complicit. In the wake of the coup's failure, the army sponsored a violent assault on the PKI and its sympathizers down to the village level. Aidit was tracked down in Central Java and extrajudicially executed. Muslim youth groups were in the vanguard of mass killings numbering hundred of thousands, a number only to be exceeded a decade later by the **Khmer Rouge** in **Cambodia.** Hundreds of other alleged PKI sympathizers were arrested, with many sent into decades-long imprisonment on Buru, a remote East Indonesian island.

The extent of PKI involvement in the coup has been a matter of controversy. The official Indonesian version puts the PKI at the center, orchestrating the affair. This was rebutted by the claim that it was an internal army affair, an interpretation that gained credibility from a "white paper" by **Cornell University** Indonesian program scholars. An even more radical interpretation suggests that Suharto himself engineered the coup. Also controversial is the question of U.S. involvement. There is no question but that the United States throughout the period of Sukarno's "guided democracy" saw the Indonesian army as a bulwark against a communist takeover of Indonesia. There is no evidence, however, to support the more radical claims that the coup was a **Central Intelligence Agency (CIA)**–backed provocation or that the purge of the PKI was directed by the American embassy headed by **Marshall Green**. The embassy did provide intelligence and material support as the Suharto-led military consolidated its power. A list of known PKI members compiled by political officer Robert Martens was given to the army on the authority of senior political officer **Edward Masters** and Ambassador Green. Former CIA director **William Colby** later favorably compared the roll-up of the PKI to the notorious Phoenix program he had headed in Vietnam that targeted the Viet Cong infrastructure.

INDONESIAN INVASION OF EAST TIMOR. On 7 December 1975, Indonesian troops armed with American-supplied weapons invaded the former Portuguese colony of **East Timor**. This act forcibly ended months of intra-Timorese elite conflict and Indonesian subversion that followed the collapse of Portuguese rule in April 1974. The Indonesian attack took place only hours after the end of a two-day (5–6 December) visit to Jakarta by U.S. president **Gerald R. Ford** and secretary of state **Henry Kissinger**. Ford had met with Suharto at Camp David in July 1975, and was returning the Indonesian president's visit. Documents released in 2001 show that during the course of the discussions, President Suharto warned that events in East Timor might make it necessary to take rapid or drastic action. This would have come as no surprise since, as declassified documents show, the National Security Council and **Department of State** were fully aware of Indonesia's intentions to incorporate East Timor, by force if necessary. American ambassador **David Newsom** had already warned Indonesia of a probable negative congressional reaction, requesting that they not act until after Ford had left the country. Not unexpectedly, President Ford responded that he understood the problem and Indonesia's intention and would not press the issue. Kissinger added that whatever Indonesia did should succeed quickly. Whether this was an American "green light" for Indonesia's invasion is arguable, suggesting as it does that the United States had veto power. It did signal, however, at the highest level, that the longer term Cold War strategic relationship between Indonesia and the United States would not be disturbed by the invasion.

Indonesia decided to use force after it became clear that the indigenous East Timor political movement, **Fretilin** (Revolutionary Front for the Independence of East Timor), was the strongest of the competing domestic political groups. Its goal was independence, not absorption into Indonesia. Indonesia represented Fretilin to the United States as communist-inspired. It did not help Fretilin that its cause was championed by the People's Republic of **China** and the newly triumphant **Democratic Republic of Vietnam (DRV)**. The last straw for Indonesians was Fretilin's unilateral declaration of independence on 28 November 1975. Indonesia, with its forces and battle plan in place, acted swiftly to prevent the possibility of international recognition of a new state in the archipelago or an appeal to the **United Nations (UN)**. Once the capital city, Dili, and main towns were secured, Indonesia integrated East Timor into the republic in early 1966 as its 27th province.

This did not end the struggle. In East Timor, a low-intensity guerrilla war led by Fretilin's military wing, **Falintil**, continued. Indonesia reacted with brutal suppression. The UN General Assembly regularly called for an internationally supervised act of self-determination for the East Timorese people. Most governments, however, including the United States, while decrying **human rights** violations, accepted the de facto integration of East Timor. It was not until the end of the Cold War that the West and the United States would begin to look at the Indonesian occupation of Timor through a democratic lens.

Even though the invasion of East Timor did not present Kissinger and the U.S. government with a moral problem, it did leave a legal problem. There is no question but that Indonesian military forces used U.S.-supplied equipment and weapons in the invasion. The end-use agreement covering the transfer of American military equipment to Indonesia called for it to be used only in defense. Kissinger was made aware of the possibility that the congressional prohibition could be breached five months before the invasion. After a temporary suspension of certification of new military equipment deliveries to Indonesia, the programs were renewed. This led to the continuing issue of whether the United States was assisting Indonesia in its "pacification" of East Timor. This was addressed in the section on "Responsibility of the United States of America" in the massive report of the East Timor Commission for Reception, Truth and Reconciliation (CAVR) on Indonesian rule and human rights abuses, presented to UN Secretary-General Kofi Annan 20 January 2006. It states that even though the United States was aware that military equipment supplied by it to Indonesia was being used in the East Timor invasion, Washington turned a blind eye.

INTELLECTUAL PROPERTY RIGHTS (IPR). Issues having to do with the protection of intellectual property rights have become an important part of the **United States Trade Representative's (USTR)** negotiations of **trade and investment framework agreements (TIFA)** and **free trade agreements (FTA)** in Southeast Asia. The Trade Act of 1974 as amended requires the USTR to promote effective protection of U.S. intellectual property and fair and equitable market access for U.S. products. Furthermore, since the end of the **World Trade Organization (WTO)** 1986–1994 Uruguay Round of negotiations, there is for the first time a broad-based multilateral agreement, Trade-Related Aspects of Intellectual Property Rights (TRIPS), that provides minimum standards for IPR protection and a mandatory dispute settlement process.

The counterfeiting and piracy of media products, software, pharmaceuticals, and other patented products is rife in Southeast Asia, although not as great a problem for the USTR as **China**. The demand for lower cost drugs is driven in part by the spread of **pandemic and infectious diseases** in the region. As mandated by Section 301 of the Trade Act, the USTR publishes an annual review detailing the adequacy and effectiveness of IPR protection in 87 countries. In 2007, **Indonesia**, **Malaysia**, the **Philippines**, and **Vietnam** were on the Section 301 "Watch List," and **Thailand** was on the "Priority Watch List" because of the overall deterioration of IPR protection there. In 2007, the Thai government unilaterally issued compulsory licenses for generic versions of two patented drugs from American pharmaceutical companies. *See also* TRADE.

INTERGOVERNMENTAL GROUP ON INDONESIA (IGGI). The Intergovernmental Group on Indonesia was a forum established by development assistance donor nations to **Indonesia** in 1967 at U.S. urging and under the leadership of the Netherlands. IGGI's purpose was to pledge and coordinate economic assistance to Indonesia in a multilateral framework. The United States was an important member but not the largest aid donor; that was Japan. Indonesia terminated IGGI in 1992 because of Dutch insistence that **human rights** become a condition of assistance to Indonesia. Moving from Amsterdam to Paris, the donor consortium was reconstituted, minus the Netherlands, as the **Consultative Group for Indonesia (CGI)**.

INTERNATIONAL COMMISSION FOR CONTROL AND SUPERVISION (ICCS). Set up as the mechanism for monitoring implementation of the 1973 **Paris Agreement** ending the **Vietnam War**, the International Commission for Control and Supervision consisted of Hungary, Poland, Canada, and **Indonesia**. Unlike its historical predecessor, the **International Commission for Supervision and Control (ICSC)**, set up by the 1954 **Geneva Accords**, the ICCS had no "neutral" member. Mistrusted by both Vietnamese sides, the ICCS, if anything, was even less effective in its task than the ICSC, since it required unanimity to act. Canada soon quit, calling it a "charade," and was replaced by Iran.

INTERNATIONAL COMMISSION FOR SUPERVISION AND CONTROL (ICSC). Set up as the monitoring mechanism for implementation of the 1954 **Geneva Accords**, the ICSC—often abbreviated to International Control Commission (ICC)—consisted of Canada, Poland, and India (chair). ICSCs were established for **Vietnam, Laos**, and **Cambodia**. The ICSC had no enforcement authority. It could inspect and investigate and report to the co-chairs of the **Geneva Conference**, Great Britain and the Soviet Union. Cooperation with the ICSC was grudging and limited. It could also be used as a backchannel vehicle for communication between combatant parties.

INTERNATIONAL CRIMINAL COURT (ICC), ARTICLE 98 AGREEMENTS. In 1998, an international diplomatic conference adopted a treaty known as the Rome Statute to create an International Criminal Court to prosecute war crimes and crimes against humanity. The United States voted against the treaty, but signed it on 31 December 2000. President **William J. Clinton** did not forward it to the Senate for ratification, feeling it was fundamentally flawed. The administration of President **George W. Bush** shared that view, finding the treaty unacceptable to U.S. sovereignty and the protection of American military personnel overseas, who could be subjected to courts whose jurisdiction the United States did not recognize. Based on the administration's interpretation of Article 98 of the Rome Statute—which has yet to be tested—the United States has pressed for bilateral nonsurrender agreements, in which the signatory promises not to deliver U.S citizens to the ICC. The agreement is a condition of U.S. military assistance unless a waiver is granted. By 2007, 104 such bilateral agreements had been signed. All Southeast Asian nations except **Burma, Malaysia**, and **Indonesia** have signed one, but the latter two are still security assistance recipients because they have not yet ratified the Rome Statute and thus are not yet parties to the ICC. *See also* HUMAN RIGHTS.

INTERNATIONAL FORCE IN EAST TIMOR (INTERFET). This was the **United Nations (UN)**–approved multinational military force led by Australia that intervened in **East Timor** in September 1999 in the violent aftermath of the **East Timor referendum** on independence from **Indonesia**. Its task was to restore order and prepare the way for UN peacekeepers and a **United Nations Transitional Administration in East Timor (UNTAET)**. At its strongest in November 1999, INTERFET's strength was 11,000 troops, with contributions from 22 countries. The United States, both in the UN Security Council and in its bilateral advice to the Indonesian government of President **B. J. Habibie**, strongly backed the deployment of INTERFET. In addition to its diplomatic support, the United States provided what the Australian commander called "niche capabilities." The 385 noncombatant American troops on the ground were in communications, intelligence, and civil affairs. A thousand U.S. marines stood offshore. Perhaps most important, the United States provided "lift" for the other forces.

INTERNATIONAL MILITARY EDUCATION AND TRAINING (IMET). The IMET program brings foreign military officers to American military and Department of Defense schools and training centers for enhancement of professional skills. Congressionally appropriated funds are allocated by the **State Department**'s Bureau of Political and Military Affairs (PM) and administered by the Defense Security Cooperation Agency (DSCA). All Southeast Asian countries, with the exception of **Brunei**, **Burma**, and **Singapore**, were IMET participants in 2007, with the **Philippines** and **Indonesia** having the largest number of participants. Indonesia was barred from IMET from 1993 to 2005 because of congressional concerns over human rights abuses in **East Timor** after the **Dili massacre** in 1991 and the militia violence after the 1999 **East Timor referendum**. Beginning in FY 1990, an Expanded or E-IMET began as a separate program to share U.S. democratic values with foreign militaries. E-IMET's emphasis is on military justice in the context of **human rights** and respect for the principle of civilian control of the military.

INTERNATIONAL MONETARY FUND (IMF). The International Monetary Fund is an international financial institution created after World War II to promote foreign exchange stability and assist in member countries' balance of payments difficulties. It has become an important lending agency for the financial rescue of failing economies. Its loans are conditional on reform measures of fiscal discipline, free markets, and privatization, reflecting the economic preferences of the so-called **Washington consensus**. The United States is the largest shareholder in the IMF, with 16.97 percent of the institution's voting power, followed by Japan with 6.06 percent. The IMF was a leading actor in reacting to the Asian **financial crisis of 1997–1998**, providing critical assistance to **Thailand** and **Indonesia**. **Malaysia**'s prime minister **Mahathir Mohammad** refused rescue by the IMF, attacking the conditionality of its loans as a form of Western neoimperialism.

INVESTMENT. The United States is second only to Japan as a source of foreign direct investment (FDI) to the countries of Southeast Asia. After recovering from the **financial crisis of 1997–1998** and adjusting to the competition for FDI posed by **China**, the flow of investment to the **Association of Southeast Asian Nations (ASEAN)** rebounded. In 2007, total U.S. FDI in the ASEAN region was more than $90 billion. The greatest part of that has gone to five states. Highly developed **Singapore** has attracted more than a third of that investment. American investment in **Thailand** is estimated at $21 billion, second only to Japan. The United States is **Malaysia**'s largest single source of FDI, with a cumulative total of more than $10 billion. The figure for the **Philippines** is $7 billion. **Vietnam**'s share of U.S. FDI is growing rapidly, from $4 billion in 2006 to an expected $8 billion in 2008.

It is not just opportunities that operate to constrain investment. The investment climate in a number of ASEAN countries is disturbed by domestic conditions. Political instability, regulatory laxness, and weak legal systems inhibit investment or present unacceptable risk. American **trade and investment framework agreements (TIFA)** provide consultative structures to address some of these kinds of issues. In the context of U.S. domestic law, for American investors in particular, the problem of corruption is an obstacle to investment. On indexes of corruption, **Cambodia**, **Indonesia**, the Philippines, and Vietnam are at or near the bottom.

IRAQ WAR. The United States and its allies invaded Iraq on 18 March 2003. The multinational force was termed the "Coalition of the Willing." Among the willing in Southeast Asia were the **Philippines**, **Singapore**, and **Thailand**. Their contributions were symbols of support for U.S. policy and the desire to protect their own security relationships with the United States. Philippine President **Gloria Macapagal-Arroyo**, noting that "we are part of a long-standing alliance," deployed a noncombatant force numbering 51 medics, engineers, and other support personnel. The contingent was prematurely withdrawn on 15 July 2004 after a Filipino contract laborer was kidnapped by terrorists, with Philippine force withdrawal as the condition for his release. Singapore sent 192 soldiers, plus transport aircraft, and a naval vessel for duty in the Persian Gulf. The army element was withdrawn on 31 July 2004. Singapore also provided transit and access for U.S. military deployments based on a 1990 U.S.–Singapore memorandum of understanding. Thailand, under Prime Minister **Thaksin Shinawatra**, after hesitation also joined the coalition, with a 423-strong Thai Humanitarian Assistance Force that completed its tour on 10 September 2004. Technically, the Southeast Asian coalition forces left after the war and occupation was over and authority handed over to the successor Iraqi state on 28 June 2004.

Among the unwilling in Southeast Asia, the Muslim majority states were the most visible opponents of the Iraq War. Not accepting Washington's linkage of Iraq to the **war on terror**, **Malaysia** condemned the invasion from the outset. The government argued that without a specific **United Nations (UN)** resolution authorizing the invasion, it was illegal. Prime Minister **Mahathir Mohammad** used what the American ambassador to Malaysia called "blunt and intemperate remarks" to denounce American imperialism and unilateralism. Mahathir repeatedly connected the issue of Iraq to American support of Israel, accusing the United States of making war on Islam, even calling President **George W. Bush** a war criminal. Mahathir's more moderate successor, **Abdullah Badawi**, acknowledged some differences on Iraq and Palestine during his July 2004 White House visit, but emphasized that the foundations of the bilateral relationship have remained firm. In **Indonesia**, demonstrations against the war at one point forced the American embassy to close temporarily. The government, however, couched its criticism of the war in a diplomatically lower key. The Indonesian concern was that aroused anti-American feeling on the issue would play into the hands of Islamic extremists. Importantly for the United States, neither Indonesia nor Malaysia allowed disagreement over the Iraq War to hinder their bilateral cooperative efforts in the war on terror. Because of the policy gulf between the American allies and the Muslim majority states, the **Association of Southeast Asians Nations (ASEAN)** was unable to formulate a collective stance on the issues of the war.

ISAMUDDIN, RIDUAN. *See* HAMBALI.

– J –

JACKSON–VANIK AMENDMENT. Sponsored by Senator Henry Jackson and Representative Charles Vanik, the Jackson–Vanik amendment to the 1974 Trade Reform Act prohibits the granting of **normal trade relations (NTR)** status to nonmarket economies that prohibit the free emigration of their people. Originally designed to pressure the Soviet Union on Jewish emigration, it has been applied in Asia to **China**, **Vietnam**, and **Laos**. In order to apply NTR, the president must annually request a waiver from Congress. For a country to "graduate" from Jackson–Vanik requirements and achieve **permanent normal trade relations (PNTR)** status, the president must certify to Congress that it is in compliance. PNTR was granted to Laos in December 2004. Vietnam was granted PNTR in November 2006. *See also* TRADE.

JEMA'AH ISLAMIYAH (JI). This is an **Indonesia**-based network of militant Southeast Asian Muslims who have adopted terrorist violence to advance their objective of extirpating Western influence and uniting all Muslims in Southeast Asia under Islamic law. Jema'ah Islamiyah—literally meaning Islamic Community—has its roots in a failed Islamic revolt in the first decade of Indonesia's independence. During the **Suharto** period, a number of fundamentalist Islamic teachers either were jailed or fled into Malaysian exile. In the democratization process following the overthrow of Suharto in 1998, political space was opened for them to return. Above ground, the radical message was carried by the Indonesian Mujahidin Council (Majelis Mujahidin Indonesia) inspired by the JI's **Wahabist** spiritual leader **Abu Bakar Ba'asyir**. The **Bali bombings** on 12 October 2002, which killed over 200 people, and other attacks or planned attacks on American and other "soft" Western targets, put the JI at the top of America's enemy's list in the Southeast Asian theater of the **war on terror**. It is one of the three Southeast Asian groupings officially designated by the United States as a **foreign terrorist organization (FTO)**.

The JI terrorist network was covertly managed by a number of operatives who had their ideological and military skills honed as volunteers with the Taliban in Afghanistan. There they forged lasting links with other militant groupings, particularly **al-Qaeda**. A senior al-Qaeda operative, **Omar al-Faruq**, liaised with JI and other militants from the 1990s until his capture in Indonesia in 2002. The operational leader of JI was **Hambali**, who was captured in Thailand in 2002 and was turned over to the United States to be imprisoned in the American detention facility at its Guantanamo, Cuba, naval base. The JI connection and JI cells stretch to **Malaysia**, southern **Thailand**, and especially the southern **Philippines**, where JI and al-Qaeda training has taken place within the **Moro Islamic Liberation Front (MILF)** and the **Abu Sayyaf Group (ASG)**. By 2007, the arrests of top JI leaders had effectively decapitated the organization although diffused and fragmented cells continue to exist.

JOHNSON, LYNDON B. (1908–1973). The administration of Lyndon B. Johnson, the 35th president of the United States, was consumed by the **Vietnam War**. Sworn in as President **John F. Kennedy**'s vice president in January 1961, he became president after Kennedy's assassination in November 1963. In May 1961, Kennedy sent Vice President Johnson on a Southeast Asian tour of friends and allies to reassure them that the United States did not intend to withdraw from the region. In Saigon, he promised **South Vietnamese** prime minister **Ngo Dinh Diem** continued American support, but at the same time pressed him for domestic reform. Back in Washington, Johnson reported the need to stand strongly behind South Vietnam. President Johnson inherited and continued the policies of his predecessors, and his advisors were largely those who had worked with Kennedy.

In a major speech at Johns Hopkins University in April 1965, and already under domestic political fire for beginning bombing in **North Vietnam**, Johnson laid out his view of the war, which he saw as defining the future of Southeast Asia. His justification for American intervention was placed squarely in the context of **containment** and included honoring the pledges that had been made since 1954 to defend the independence of South Vietnam. Furthermore, he cautioned that America's role in a peaceful world order was at stake as its credibility as an ally was being tested. This was set against the prospect of further aggression in Southeast Asia, with **China** looming as the future threat. Johnson reasserted that the United States would do everything necessary and would not be defeated in its defense of freedom in Southeast Asia. Holding out to North Vietnam a vision of a peaceful Southeast Asia, he pledged a contribution of $1 billion to a Lower **Mekong River** development plan that would economically benefit all of Southeast Asia.

In doing everything necessary, President Johnson, responding to the requirements of his commander in the field, General William Westmoreland, managed an escalation of American forces to nearly half a million by the end of 1967. He pressured U.S. allies for "more flags" for Vietnam, which led to **Philippines**, **Thailand**, South Korea, Australia, and New Zealand contingents in the field. Johnson personally lobbied for this in an October 1966 meeting in the Philippines with the heads of governments of the allied states. As the domestic antiwar movement built up momentum and congressional support wavered, Johnson began to seek ways to disengage but not lose the war. On 31 March 1968, he announced he would not run for reelection and that the United States was ready to talk peace with the enemy at any time, in any place.

JOHNSON, U. ALEXIS (1908–1997). In a career that spanned 42 years, U. Alexis Johnson was an important participant in Southeast Asia policy decision making in four presidential administrations. He was American ambassador to **Thailand** from 1958 to 1961. In Thailand he worked closely with the **Sarit Thanarat** government, coordinating the Thai–U.S. policy of political and military support to the anticommunist forces of **Laos** military strongman **Phoumi Nosavan**. While encouraging Thai interventionist policies toward Laos, Johnson sought to limit Thai provocations to **Cambodia**. Picked to be assistant secretary of state for East Asian and Pacific affairs in 1961, he was instead named deputy undersecretary of state for political affairs from 1961 to 1964, where he coordinated political/military affairs with other agencies, including the Defense Department and the **Cen-**

tral Intelligence Agency (CIA). He spent a year (1964–1965) in Saigon as the deputy ambassador to the Republic of Vietnam—a post unique to Vietnam in the war years. He returned to the post of deputy undersecretary for political affairs for a year and then became ambassador to Japan (1966–1969). From 1969 to 1973, he was undersecretary of state for political affairs, the top-ranked post in the State Department for a career Foreign Service Officer. From 1973 to his retirement in 1977, he was an ambassador at large and led the U.S. negotiations in the strategic arms limitations talks (SALT).

JOINT CASUALTY RESOLUTION CENTER (JCRC). An organization unique in American military history, the Joint Casualty Resolution Center was dedicated to locating, recovering, and repatriating the remains of Americans killed or missing in action in Indochina during the Vietnam War. It was activated in Saigon on 23 January 1973 on the basis of an article in the U.S.–Democratic Republic of Vietnam (DRV) Paris Agreement calling for cooperation and information in resolving the issues of missing personnel. Vietnamese willingness to cooperate was a factor in the progress of U.S. normalization of relations with Vietnam. The JCRC's work was extended to Laos and Cambodia. Its field headquarters was in Thailand and its forensic lab in Hawaii. In 1992, the JCRC was folded into the Joint Task Force–Full Accounting (JTF–FA).

JOINT SPECIAL OPERATIONS TASK FORCE–PHILIPPINES (JSOTF–P). In January 2002, as part of Operation Enduring Freedom–Philippines (OEF–P), the U.S. Special Operations Command Pacific (SOCPAC) deployed Joint Task Force 510 to the southern Philippines to conduct counterterrorist operations with Armed Forces of the Philippines (AFP). JTF 510 redeployed in August 2002, leaving behind military elements in a Joint Special Operation Task Force–Philippines to continue to support the AFP. The JSOTF–P mission was to increase the counterterrorism capacity of the AFP in its battle with the Abu Sayyaf Group (ASG) and related Islamist insurgent groups with links to al-Qaeda or the Jema'ah Islamiyah (JI) as part of the war on terror. The JSOTF–P assists and advises at the strategic and operational level in tactics, intelligence, and psychological warfare. It also is active in local humanitarian and civic action projects. The JSOTF–P has been credited with helping the AFP make significant gains in its southern campaigns. Its presence in the Philippines, however, has been criticized by Filipino nationalists as being in violation of the 1987 constitution, Article 18, section 25, which states that after the 1991 expiry of the U.S. bases agreement, foreign military bases, troops, or facilities shall not be allowed in the Philippines except under a treaty ratified by the Philippine Senate or, if required, by a majority vote in a national referendum. The Philippine government position is that JSOFT–P is covered by the U.S.–Philippines **Mutual Defense Treaty (MDT)**. *See also* MILITARY BASES AGREEMENT; MUTUAL LOGISTICS SUPPORT AGREEMENT; VISITING FORCES AGREEMENT.

JOINT TASK FORCE–FULL ACCOUNTING (JTF–FA). Headquartered in Hawaii, the JTF–FA was established in 1992 to resolve cases of prisoners of war/missing in action **(POW/MIA)** in the Southeast Asian wars. The JTF–FA and its Central Identification Laboratory grew out of the 1973 **Joint Casualty Resolution Center (JCRC)**. Since October 2003, the Task Force has been folded into the Joint POW/MIA Accounting Command (JPAC), whose mandate covers all wars, not just the **Second Indochina War**. It has detachments in Bangkok, Hanoi, and Vientiane, and regularly dispatches field investigation teams to possible recovery sites.

JONES ACT. Sponsored by Representative William A. Jones of Virginia, the 1916 Jones Act was the first legislative act by the U.S. Congress providing an organic law for the gradual decolonization of the **Philippines** under U.S. democratic tutelage. Officially known as the Philippine Autonomy Act, it replaced the 1902 Philippines Organic Act. The Jones Act provided for Filipinization and political participation at all levels of the Philippine government. The stated expectation was the eventual independence of the Philippines. The framework of the Jones Act provided a political arena in which Philippine nationalists like **Manuel Quezon**, **Sergio Osmeña**, and **Manuel Roxas** wrestled with American governors-general in the Philippines over control of the political process and pace of change, with the governor-general holding an ultimate veto.

JONES, HOWARD P. (1899–1973). Howard Jones was the longest serving American ambassador to **Indonesia**, from February 1958 to May 1965. Prior to that, he had been director of the U.S. **Agency for International Development** mission in Jakarta. In the administration of President **Dwight D. Eisenhower**, it fell to Jones to explain away to Indonesian president **Sukarno** American clandestine support for the **PRRI-Pemesta** rebellion. As ambassador during the **Kennedy** years, Jones pursued an accommodationist line toward the radicalizing government of President Sukarno, arguing that a U.S. tilt toward Indonesia in the **West New Guinea dispute**, American economic assistance, and good personal relations could attract Sukarno toward the United States. The pro-Sukarno posture was contentious within the embassy and the **State Department** and ultimately failed personally for Jones. The discredited Jones approach was replaced by a lower profile embassy, a policy change signaled to Sukarno in April 1965 by visiting special presidential envoy **Ellsworth Bunker** and to be implemented by new U.S. Ambassador **Marshall Green**. Jones's defense of his Indonesia mission is his memoir, *Indonesia: The Possible Dream*.

– K –

KAHIN, GEORGE MCTURNAN (1918–2000). From his academic base at **Cornell University**, George McT. Kahin became one of the most influential American scholars of contemporary politics and international relations in Southeast Asia. The programs he developed at Cornell became a model for Southeast Asian area studies curriculum elsewhere. Kahin pioneered modern Indonesian studies. His field work in **Indonesia** during the Indonesian revolution led to the publication in 1951 of his Johns Hopkins University Ph.D. dissertation, *Nationalism and Revolution in Indonesia*, the first major study by an American of the forces of nationalism in Southeast Asia. The critical mass of students, researchers, and faculty he brought together in the Modern Indonesian Project shaped the academic and policy discourse on Indonesia. During the **Second Indochina War**, Kahin was a trenchant critic of U.S. policy in Southeast Asia. Kahin's personal critique of American policy is his memoir, *Southeast Asia: A Testament.*

KAMPUCHEA. *See* CAMBODIA.

KAREN. The Karens are a minority group in **Burma**, numbering more than seven million. Under the banner of the Karen National Union (KNU) and the Karen National Liberation Army, a decades-long struggle for autonomy has been carried out against the Burmese government. In 2004, the Burmese junta and the KNU entered into a temporary cease-fire, but no durable peace ensued. More than 100,000 ethnic Karens have fled to camps in Thailand, from which resettlement in the United States has been offered to those who meet the U.S. requirements. *See also* REFUGEES.

KENNAN, GEORGE F. (1904–2005). A singularly influential American diplomat, George Kennan was a specialist in Soviet affairs. In 1947, while director of the **State Department**'s policy planning staff, he authored pseudonymously the famous "Mr. X" article, "The Sources of Soviet Conduct," in *Foreign Affairs*, laying out the political and strategic underpinnings of American **containment** policy in the Cold War. Although known as the "father of containment," Kennan later vigorously criticized its militarization in Southeast Asia.

KENNEDY, JOHN F. (1917–1963). John F. Kennedy, the 35th president of the United States, was a committed cold warrior. As a U.S. senator, Kennedy had championed the cause of **Ngo Dinh Diem** as a future leader of **Vietnam**. He inherited the American policies toward **Indochina** from his predecessor, President **Dwight D. Eisenhower**, and essentially continued them. President Kennedy's backing of **containment** was made clear in his inaugural address, when he announced: "[L]et every nation know, whether it wishes us well or ill, that we shall pay any price, bear any burden, meet any hardship, support any friend, oppose any foe to assure the survival and the success of liberty." He found the test of the fulfillment of this vow in the **Vietnam War**, which received its first major escalation of U.S. military presence with his decision to break through the **Geneva Accords** ceilings on foreign military presence in **Indochina**. In this, he was following the advice of his advisors, **Maxwell Taylor** and **W. W. Rostow**. Kennedy's willingness to draw the line in Vietnam did not extend to **Laos**, where, during the **Laotian Crisis of 1960–1962**, when confronted by the possibility of collision with the Soviet Union, he accepted the terms of the 1962 **Geneva Accords on Laos**.

Kennedy had few opportunities to practice personal diplomacy with Southeast Asian leaders. He met only **Indonesia**'s president **Sukarno** and Prime Minister Norodom **Sihanouk** of **Cambodia**. In neither case did charm and style change the negatives of the bilateral relationships. Sihanouk, in fact, celebrated Kennedy's murder. President Kennedy also angered Philippine president Diosdado Macapagal by supporting the creation of **Malaysia** that included **Sabah**, the former British North Borneo colony, as opposed to Philippine sovereign claims to Sabah.

KENNEDY, ROBERT F. (1925–1968). Brother of President **John F. Kennedy** and attorney general of the United States, Robert Kennedy played a major role in U.S efforts to end the **West New Guinea dispute**. In February 1962, he traveled to Jakarta and The Hague to urge bilateral negotiations under the **United Nations**. Kennedy suggested to the Indonesians that an agreement would end satisfactorily for **Indonesia** and that the United States would use its influence in favor of a transfer of sovereignty of the territory to Indonesia. While in Jakarta, Kennedy also sought the release of **Allen Pope**, an American **Central Intelligence Agency (CIA)** pilot who had been shot down in 1958 while bombing Ambon in the **PRRI–Permesta regional rebellions**.

KHIEU SAMPHAN (1931–). The leading intellectual in the ranks of the **Khmer Rouge (KR)**, Khieu Samphan was the titular president of **Democratic Kampuchea** from 1976 to 1979. **Pol Pot** was the effective ruler as prime minister. When the **Coalition Government of Democratic Kampuchea (CGDK)** was created in 1981 as the rival (in exile) of the **Vietnam**-sponsored **People's Republic of Kampuchea (PRK)**, Khieu Samphan became the CGDK's vice president in charge of foreign affairs. By keeping Pol Pot in the background, it was hoped that condemnation of the KR would not prevent the CGDK from diplomatically engaging the international community. Khieu Samphan was the public face of the KR in the diplomacy ending the **Third Indochina War**. He returned to Phnom Penh in 1991, only to flee back to the KR territorial area in the west after facing angry mobs. He surrendered to the Cambodian government in 1998. In 2007, charged with crimes against humanity, he was arrested to face the tribunal conducting the **Khmer Rouge trials**.

KHMER. This term denotes the indigenous inhabitants of **Cambodia** and affiliated ethnic minorities in **Thailand** and **Vietnam**.

KHMER ISSARAK. After World War II and the Japanese occupation, the Khmer Issarak (Independent Khmer), an originally **Thailand**-backed irregular force of anti-French and anti-King **Norodom Sihanouk** Cambodians, operated in the western Cambodian provinces of Battambang and Siemreap provinces that Thailand had been forced to retrocede to **Cambodia**. The movement was loosely structured, with no central command authority. One leftist faction allied itself with the communist-led **Viet Minh**. This later became a source of recruitment for the **Khmer Rouge**. In 1952, **Son Ngoc Thanh** took the Khmer Issarak partisans into the anticommunist, antimonarchy **Khmer Serei**. After 1953 and full independence, a number of Khmer returned to the fold of the kingdom.

KHMER KROM. This was the name of the ethnic Khmer (Cambodian) minority in **South Vietnam**. They were a pool for recruitment by U.S. Special Forces into South Vietnam's Civilian Irregular Defense Groups (CIDG) as well as the anti-**Sihanouk Khmer Serei**, led by **Son Ngoc Thanh**. After 1970, Khmer Krom from the CIDG and the Khmer Serei supported **Lon Nol** against the **Khmer Rouge** and the People's Army of Vietnam (PAVN).

KHMER PEOPLE'S NATIONAL LIBERATION FRONT (KPNLF). The KPNLF, established by **Son Sann**, were with the royalist **Funcinpec** and the **Khmer Rouge** the elements of the **Khmer resistance** to the 1978 Vietnamese invasion and occupation of **Cambodia**. Anti–Khmer Rouge and vaguely republican, the KPNLF was forced into the tripartite **Coalition Government of Democratic Kampuchea (CGDK)** as a condition of military and other assistance from the **Association of Southeast Asian Nations (ASEAN)**, the United States, and **China** in the **Third Indochina War**. The KPNLF's armed strength was estimated at between 12,000 and 15,000 men. By the mid-1980s, its military commanders, many of whom had served under former rightist strongman **Lon Nol**, were trying to limit Son Sann's political meddling in military affairs.

KHMER RESISTANCE. This was the **Thailand**-based military force that carried out low-intensity warfare in **Cambodia** during the **Third Indochina War**. The Khmer resistance complemented on the ground the political and diplomatic efforts of the **Association of Southeast Asian Nations (ASEAN)**–backed **Coalition Government of Democratic Kampuchean (CGDK)**. The armed strength of the resistance may have reached 60,000–70,000 fighters, the backbone and best equipped of which were the 40,000–50,000 strong **Khmer Rouge**. There was little central command authority, with the units of the three CGDK factions—Khmer Rouge, **Son Sann**'s **Khmer People's National Liberation Front (KPNLF)**, and the royalist **Funcinpec**'s Armée Nationale Sihanoukiste (ANS)—largely operating independently. **China** was a major supplier of weapons to the Khmer Rouge. Although pressed by Thailand and **Singapore**, the United States officially provided only nonlethal assistance to the Khmer resistance. There is a question, however, of whether some of the increased volume of U.S. military assistance to the Thai army may have been clandestinely transferred to Khmer resistance forces. A problem for the postwar **United Nations Transitional Authority in Cambodia (UNTAC)** and the new Cambodian government was disarming the Khmer Rouge ensconced in the country's west.

KHMER ROUGE (KR). Khmer Rouge (Red Khmer) was the popular designation for the Communist Party of **Cambodia** (CPK), which launched an armed struggle against Prime Minister **Norodom Sihanouk** and then, after Sihanouk's overthrow in 1970, the American-supported government of **Lon Nol**. Under the leadership of **Pol Pot**, the KR occupied Phnom Penh on 17 April 1975, ending the Cambodian front of the **Second Indochina War**. The KR's roots are in the history of Indochinese communism. Originally mentored by the Vietnamese, by the time Pol Pot became head of the CPK in 1963, Cambodian Marxism–Leninism was being transformed by a chauvinistic and nihilistic radicalism that insisted on the total destruction of the old culture and society in order to build a new one. Once in power the KR, now known as the *angkar* (the "organization") and governing **Democratic Kampuchea (DK)**, embarked on a horrific assault on its own people. During *angkar*'s four years in power, between 1.5 and 2 million Cambodians died in what has been described as a genocide that can be compared only to the Holocaust. The relationship with **Vietnam** quickly soured, and in December 1978, Vietnam invaded and occupied Cambodia, installing a pro-Vietnam government headed by KR defectors. From exile bases in **Thailand**, the KR became the backbone of the coalition **Khmer resistance** to Vietnam in the **Third Indochina War**. The end of the war saw the KR marginalized by the **United Nations Transitional Authority in Cambodia (UNTAC)**. The remnants of the KR—its leaders **human rights** pariahs—occupied bases in northwestern Cambodia and supported themselves by illegal trade with Thailand. Under amnesty, the rank and file gradually returned to Cambodia's new society. Beginning in 1997, a decade-long process got underway to try the leaders of the Khmer Rouge for genocide and crimes against humanity. *See also* KHMER ROUGE TRIALS.

KHMER ROUGE TRIALS. Despite the reluctance of the government of **Cambodia**, its international donors, including the United States, insisted that the surviving leaders of the **Khmer Rouge (KR)** be held accountable for their crimes against humanity. The Cambodian hesitation was in part because Cambodian prime minister **Hun Sen** and other members of the government were once members of the KR themselves. Negotiations for a tribunal began in 1997 but progressed slowly because of differences over the mix of Cambodian and international participation in the court. It was not until 2005 that the **United Nations (UN)** could begin to establish the logistics for the court. In addition to jurisdictional disputes and disagreements over the legal standards to be applied, financing issues delayed the court, with Cambodia insisting that foreign donors should pay all of the costs, estimated at more than $56 million. It was not until mid-2007 that the joint Cambodian–foreign prosecuting team was prepared to submit cases to the tribunal. The first to be indicted was Kang Kek Ieu, known as Duch, the chief of the infamous Tuol Sleng prison, where thousands of prisoners were killed. Other KR leaders brought to the tribunal bar included **Khieu Samphan**, former president of **Democratic Kampuchea (DK)**, Nuon Chea, second in command to **Pol Pot**, and Ieng Sary, Pol Pot's brother-in-law and the DK foreign minister.

In the UN proceedings leading up to the court, the United States strongly backed initiatives to create an international tribunal but was prohibited by Congress from pledging funds for a tribunal established by Cambodia. American government agencies have, however, been the major financial supporters of the independent Documentation Centre of Cambodia (DC-CAM), whose database on the KR is invaluable. The DC-CAM itself is a spin-off from the Yale University Cambodian Genocide Program, which was funded by the Office of Cambodian Genocide Investigations in the **State Department**'s Bureau of East Asian and Pacific Affairs (EAP), as authorized by the congressional Cambodian Genocide Act of 1994. State Department coordination of U.S. government support for war crimes accountability is in the Office of War Crimes Issues (WCI).

KHMER SEREI. The Khmer Serei (Free Khmer) in **Cambodia** was an anticommunist, anti-**Sihanouk** political/military grouping based in both **Thailand** and **South Vietnam**. The nominal leader was **Son Ngoc Thanh**, who enjoyed a collaborative relationship with Thai and American intelligence and logistics infrastructure. The Khmer Serei's roots were in the anti-French underground and the **Khmer Issarak** movement. The Khmer Serei's most effective weapon was propaganda broadcasts from transmitters in both Thailand and South Vietnam. Among the events leading to the final severing of relations between the United States and Cambodia in 1965 was Sihanouk's demand that the United States shut down the Khmer Serei radio, something that Washington either would not or could not do.

KINGDOM OF LAOS. *See* LAOS.

KISSINGER, HENRY A. (1923–). National security advisor (1969–1973) and then secretary of state (1973–1974) in the administration of President **Richard M. Nixon** and continuing as secretary of state (1974–1977) during the administration of President **Gerald Ford**, Henry Kissinger controlled the policies and diplomacy that ended the **Vietnam War**. Emigrating from Germany to the United States as a teenager, he became an American citizen in 1943. After serving in the U.S. Army in World War II, Kissinger attended Harvard and then served on its faculty. A towering strategic thinker, he consulted with American government agencies and was an advisor to presidential aspirant Nelson Rockefeller. He became Nixon's special assistant for national security affairs in 1969 and centralized critical decision making in foreign policy in the White House, eclipsing the **State Department** and Secretary of State **William Rogers**. Policy in this period is often described as Nixon–Kissinger policy.

Nixon was elected with the promise of ending the Vietnam War. Kissinger's task was to extricate the United States from Vietnam without acknowledging defeat. Even as the war was widening in **Cambodia** and **Laos**, Kissinger pursued a negotiated settlement in Vietnam, continuing the **Paris peace negotiations** begun by the **Johnson** administration in 1968. Kissinger sought to fashion a proper mix of incentives and pressures that would wring concessions and compromises from the **Democratic Republic of Vietnam (DRV)**. The goal for the Nixon administration was "peace with honor." To achieve this, the war continued with punitive bombings, to force the DRV to make political concessions, even though it was cynically understood that the political arrangements for South Vietnam would not be carried out. Kissinger achieved in the 1973 **Paris Agreement** his real goal: a diplomatic framework for U.S. disengagement even if it left the **Republic of Vietnam** to face the enemy alone. For that, Kissinger and his Vietnamese interlocutor in Paris, **Le Duc Tho**, were nominated for a Nobel Peace Prize.

The three volumes of Kissinger's memoirs give no indication of any real interest in Southeast Asia as a policy area beyond the framework of ending the Vietnam War. With the war over, however, Kissinger sought to demonstrate that the United States was not withdrawing from the region but rather bringing American commitment and interests into a new balance. At President Ford's side in Jakarta, Indonesia, in December 1975, he expressed tacit American acceptance of the planned **Indonesian invasion of East Timor**. In the **Philippines**, he initiated an eventually unsuccessful new round of military base negotiations following President Ford's brief visit to Manila in December 1975.

KMT–BURMA CRISIS. As Chinese nationalist resistance to Mao Ze-dong's People's Liberation Army crumbled in **China** in 1948, ele-ments of the Nationalist Fifth Army, loyal to their general, Li Mi, re-treated from Yunnan Province into the Shan states of northeastern **Burma** near the **Thai** border. They were known as KMTs, an abbre-viation of Nationalist President Chiang Kai-Shek's Kuomintang (KMT) or National People's Party, which had fled to Taiwan. By 1953, Li Mi's forces were 16,000 strong. Calling themselves the Yun-nan Anti-Communist National Salvation Army, they challenged Ran-goon's control of large swaths of territory, aiding ethnic separatism and becoming involved in **narcotics production and trafficking**. General Li Mi used his Burmese sanctuaries for provocative raids into Yunnan Province, confronting Burma's Prime Minister **U Nu**'s neutralist government with the prospect of Chinese retaliation after China had warned its neighbors about harboring KMT refugees. Li Mi maintained political and material supply ties to Taiwan. Regular flights were made from Taiwan into the KMT airstrip at Mong Hsat in Kengtung state by the **Central Intelligence Agency (CIA)**'s pro-prietary **Civl Air Transport (CAT)**, and weapons were funneled to the KMT forces by **Sea Supply Corporation**, another CIA propri-etary company. **Desmond Fitzgerald**, a future chief of the clandes-tine side of the CIA, cut his operational teeth in the Li Mi support ac-tivity. The CIA role was facilitated by Thai police chief general **Phao Sriyanond**, who through his American-supported **Border Patrol Po-lice (BPP)** ensconced himself in the Burmese opium trade.

When the Soviet Union charged in 1952 that the United States was using KMT troops in Burma to mount operations against China, an alarmed Burma, fearing being trapped in the Cold War, denied any in-volvement beyond the Republic of China on Taiwan. The mainland Chinese government was forbearing, apparently preferring that the Burmese persuade both Taiwan and their American allies to cease sup-port to the KMT forces. Even though the American involvement in support of Li Mi was an open secret in Rangoon, the American am-bassador was instructed by Assistant Secretary of State for East Asian and Pacific Affairs **Dean Rusk** to deny it. In 1953, after two failed mil-itary campaigns against the KMTs, Burma's neutralist prime minister **U Nu** formally took the issue of the Republic of China's "aggression" to the **United Nations (UN)** General Assembly, calling for a resolution to condemn the Republic of China. Before going to the UN, U Nu's government officially terminated U.S. aid programs in Burma, believing that business as usual would weaken their case. A watered-down resolution that did not mention the Republic of China was passed by a vote of 59–0, with Taiwan's abstention. It deplored the foreign forces in Burma and called for their disarmament, internment, and departure. A joint military commission of representatives from Burma, the Republic of China on Taiwan, the United States, and Thailand was established to deal with the situation. It was only after the Burmese army captured the Mong Hsat airfield in 1954 that the bulk of the KMTs could be repatriated by a U.S. airlift. Several thousand remained in the Burmese–Thai border regions, a continuing source of friction between Burma and Thailand. In the administration of President **John F. Kennedy**, Secretary of State **Dean Rusk** pressed Taipei to repatriate the remainder. In 1961, President Kennedy assured U Nu that Taiwan had promised that the KMT irregulars would be withdrawn. After further American diplomatic intervention, a Chinese nationalist airlift repatriated another 4,000 KMTs from Thailand. An unknown number simply settled down with local wives to go into the opium business along the mountainous border between Kengtung and Thailand's Chiang Rai Province.

KONG LE (1934–). On the morning of 8 August 1960, 26-year-old paratrooper captain Kong Le led his 2nd Paratroop Battalion in a surprise neutralist coup against the rightist **Laos** government, restoring to power Prime Minister **Souvanna Phouma**. Kong Le was a popular neutralist who called for an end to Lao internal conflict and to foreign interference. His coup revealed the deep divisions in the Royal Lao Army (FAR). The **Central Intelligence Agency (CIA)**–sponsored right-wing leader **Phoumi Nosovan** prepared a counter coup as the leftist **Pathet Lao** declared support for Kong Le. In December 1960, when Phoumis's American and **Thai**-backed forces retook the capital, Vientiane, Kong Le's troops retreated to the **Plain of Jars**, held by the Pathet Lao. Weakened by defections to the Pathet Lao, Kong Le tried to reconcile with the Lao military under the post-1962 **Geneva Accords** second **coalition government**. He was distrusted by the United States and Lao rightists, who excluded him. He resigned as commander of the neutralist forces and in 1967 left for exile in France.

KRIANGSAK CHOMANAN (1917–2003). Prime minister of **Thailand** (1977–1980), General Kriangsak Chomanan came to power through a coup. Recognizing Thailand's altered strategic framework as a result of communist victories in **Indochina** and a perception of a loss of American interest in post–**Vietnam War** Southeast Asia, Kriangsak initially pursued a policy of reconciliation with Thailand's neighbors. This changed with the December 1978 Vietnamese invasion of **Cambodia** and the installation of its client government, the **People's Republic of Kampuchea (PRK)**. With the Vietnamese army on Thailand's Cambodian border and fear of an expansion of the **Third Indochina War**, Kriangsak traveled to both Washington and Beijing in 1979 seeking bilateral assistance and support. President Jimmy Carter's National Security Advisor **Zbigniew Brzezinski** encouraged the Thai prime minister's overtures to **China**. It is believed that Kriangsak negotiated a Chinese supply line to the anti-Vietnamese **Khmer resistance** based in Thailand in return for a cessation of Chinese support for the Communist Party of Thailand's insurgency. By opening a Chinese strategic window into Southeast Asia, Kriangsak set the stage for a new Chinese political role in the region. Kriangsak's de facto Chinese alliance was balanced by reinvigorated security ties with the United States.

KUKRIT PRAMOJ (1911–1995). Prime minister of **Thailand** (1975–1976) Kukrit Pramoj was a British-educated Thai politician and influential intellectual. He was the younger brother of **Seni Pramoj**. Kukrit became prime minister during a wave of anti-American protests following the bloody overthrow of the **Thanom Kittikachorn** dictatorship in 1973. With an eye to the impending communist victories in **Indochina** as well as domestic anger about U.S. support for the Thanom regime, immediately on taking office in March 1975, Kukrit demanded the withdrawal of all American forces from Thailand. In July 1975, he led a delegation to **China** for the normalization of Sino–Thai relations. Thai military and police elements viewed Kukrit as appeasing Thai leftists. This led to political conflict that brought down his government after only 14 months. Kukrit was known to American movie audiences for playing the role of the prime minister of Sarkhan opposite Marlin Brando in the 1963 movie version of *The Ugly American*.

– L –

LAIR, JAMES W. (1924–). For over a decade James "Bill" Lair was the point man in the field for the **Central Intelligence Agency (CIA)**'s **secret war** in **Laos**. He saw combat in Europe in World War II as an enlisted man. After the war he attended Texas A & M, and joined the CIA in 1950. He was posted to **Thailand** in 1951, where he created an elite parachute-trained Thai paramilitary police unit, the Police Arial Reinforcement Unit (**PARU**), to support the **Border Patrol Police (BPP)**, both under the command of General **Phao Sriyanond**. Phao conferred on Lair the rank of a Thai police special colonel, the equivalent to an American brigadier general. PARU units introduced clandestinely into Laos became trainers of **Hmong** guerrillas, who were to be a stay-behind force on the **Plain of Jars**. When at one point CIA financing for the PARU was threatened at the branch level of the CIA, the head of the Far Eastern Division, **Desmond Fitzgerald**, intervened to save it. Lair was the CIA liaison with Hmong general **Vang Pao**, headquartered at **Long Tieng**, his mountain redoubt in Central Laos. In a meeting with Lair in December 1959, Vang Pao proposed expanded American support for a Hmong army. This was verbally outlined to Fitzgerald by Lair when the division chief stopped in Vientiane en route to Saigon. Fitzgerald asked Lair to draft a proposal and send it to Washington. The seed of the secret war had been planted. In 1966, CIA Laos station chief **Theodore "Ted" Shackley** moved Lair to the CIA command post for Laos paramilitary operations at the Thai Air Force base in Udorn. He was replaced by his deputy, Lloyd "Pat" Landry, in 1968.

LANGLEY, JAMES M. (1894–1968). A New Hampshire newspaper publisher, James M. Langley was active in the presidential campaign of **Dwight D. Eisenhower**. In 1955, he led the American delegation that negotiated the **Laurel–Langley Agreement** with the **Philippines** revising the 1946 **Bell Act**. Langley served as ambassador to Pakistan from 1957 to 1959.

LANSDALE, EDWARD G. (1908–1987). Edward Lansdale created a legendary persona in the 1950s and 1960s as an intelligence officer, psychological warfare warrior, and counterinsurgency specialist, first in the **Philippines** and then in **Vietnam**. Lansdale joined the **Office of Strategic Services (OSS)** in 1942 as a civilian and then on active military service as an army intelligence officer in 1943. In 1947, he transferred to the Air Force, where he remained until his retirement in 1968 with the rank of major general. From the very beginning of his military career, however, he was tasked by the OSS and its successor, the **Central Intelligence Agency (CIA)**.

In the late 1940s, as a major, Lansdale was sent to the **Philippines** as an intelligence officer to assist in building a Philippine intelligence service. He returned to the United States in 1948, where, promoted to lieutenant colonel, he lectured on intelligence and counterinsurgent warfare at the Air Force's Strategic Intelligence School. In 1950, through a mutual friend he met visiting Philippine secretary of national defense **Ramon Magsaysay**. Magsaysay asked that Lansdale be assigned to the Joint U.S. **Military Assistance Advisory Group** (JUSMAAG) in the Philippines. This led to a close personal relationship between the two, lasting until Magsaysay's death in a plane crash in 1957. The Lansdale–Magsaysay connection became a major vehicle for American advice and assistance in the defeat of the **Hukbalahap** communist insurrection.

Although designated the JUSMAAG's G-2 (intelligence), Lansdale was given great autonomy both from his military superiors in Manila and the CIA's Far East chief **Desmond Fitzgerald**. He became a personal military and political advisor to Magsaysay. Because of threats to his life, Magsaysay even moved into the MAAG compound with Lansdale. The two men traveled the country together searching for ways to upgrade the professionalism of the Philippine military and attack the social and economic causes of popular revolt. They also planned a psychological warfare campaign to separate the Huks from the people. Lansdale and Magsaysay understood that building morale in the defense forces and support for the government's commitment to economic and social development was essential to defeat the Huks. Lansdale and his team worked behind the scenes in Magsaysay's successful 1953 presidential campaign, in which he defeated the incumbent, President **Elpidio Quirino**. Lansdale was recalled to the United States in late 1953 to prepare for assignment to the **Republic of Vietnam**, but Magsaysay asked President **Dwight D. Eisenhower** to allow Lansdale to return. Lansdale was back in Manila in early 1954 but continued on to Vietnam in May, where he began a new chapter in his career as America's leading counterinsurgency specialist.

In Vietnam, Lansdale held a variety of posts, beginning with chief of the Saigon Military Mission (SMM), the "dirty tricks" department. He became an advisor to President **Ngo Dinh Diem**. He came back to Washington, to become in 1961 assistant secretary of defense for special operations. His opposition to plans for the **Diem coup** diminished his influence in the administration of President **John Kennedy**. Lansdale retired in 1963 but returned to Saigon in 1965 as a special assistant to Ambassador **Henry Cabot Lodge**. The job was ambiguously defined and with little real influence. He left Vietnam and the U.S. government in 1968. Lansdale was fictionally immortalized as Alden Pyle in Graham Greene's *The Quiet American* and Col. Hillandale in William Lederer's and Eugene Burdick's *The Ugly American*. Lansdale's own memoir is *In the Midst of Wars*.

LAO ISSARA. The Lao Issara, or "Free Lao," was an anticolonial movement that at the end of World War II asserted national independence from France for a unified Laos. Led by Prince **Phetsarat Ratnavongsa**, the Lao Issara was an uneasy coalition that linked politically the **Lao Serai**, collaborationists in the Japanese-sponsored Royal Lao Government, historically rival clans, communists, and royalists. In the wake of the Japanese surrender, it formed a government in September 1945 that resisted the French reassertion of sovereignty. Driven from Vientiane in 1946 by French military superiority, the leaders went into exile in Thailand, where they attempted to mobilize international support and began cross-border military raids.

The movement splintered in 1949 after the French accepted Laotian semiautonomy within the French Union. The Lao Issara dissolved itself. Moderates, under Prince **Souvanna Phouma**, returned to Laos to work within the new political framework. Radicals and communists went into revolt under Prince **Souphanouvong**, establishing themselves in alliance with the **Viet Minh** in northeastern Laos. Phetsarat remained in self-imposed exile until 1957. *See also* THAILAND.

LAO PEOPLE'S DEMOCRATIC REPUBLIC (LPDR). *See* LAOS.

LAO SERAI. This was an anti-Japanese underground resistance movement of young Lao nationalists during World War II. It was a spin-off of the **Free Thai** underground with U.S. **Office of Strategic Services (OSS)** support. The Lao Serai, with their OSS contacts, became part of the anti-French **Lao Issara** movement.

LAOS. The country of Laos has been ruled since 1975 as the Lao People's Democratic Republic (LPDR). From 1950, in the framework of the Kingdom of Laos, authority in the state was contested by U.S-backed anticommunists, neutralists, and communists. The communist-led **Pathet Lao** was supported by the **Democratic Republic of Vietnam (DRV)** and behind it the Soviet Union. It was this struggle that made Laos a theater of the **Second Indochina War**. In Laos, however, the war was a "**secret war**," since the neutralization of the country in the 1954 and 1962 **Geneva Accords** theoretically excluded external military intervention in Laotian affairs. For more than two decades, Laos was a focus of U.S. military and political attention, second only to **Vietnam** in Southeast Asia.

Southeast Asia's only landlocked county, Laos covers 91,400 square miles (236,800 square kilometers), about the size of Oregon. It is bounded by **Thailand**, **Cambodia**, **Vietnam**, **China**, and **Burma**, making it a cockpit for competing economic and political interests of more powerful states. The capital is Vientiane (Viang Chan). The population of 6,200,000 (July 2005 est.) is ethnically diverse, with perhaps as many as 50 distinct identities grouped in three large categories. The dominant group is the Tai-speaking Lao Loum, "lowland" Lao, making up two-thirds of the population, The second grouping is the Lao Theung, the "upland" Lao, comprising over 20 percent of the population. The third and smallest grouping is the Lao Sung or "mountain" Lao. The latter reflects the movement in the past two centuries of Tibeto–Burmese-speaking ethnic groups into the mountainous north. The most numerous among this population are the **Hmong**, a major recruitment source for the **Central Intelligence Agency (CIA)**'s secret war.

France created the outline for modern Laos with the extension of its imperial reach westward from **Vietnam** at the end of the 19th century. Before that, the political map of the territory consisted of competing principalities focused on Luang Prabang in the north, Vientiane in the center, and Champassak in the south. These states were caught between hegemonic claims of subordination from their Siamese and Vietnamese neighbors. In 1893, the French coerced **Siam** (Thailand) into ceding all of its Laotian territories east of the **Mekong River**. The French did not think of Laos as a single entity, and administration was divided between the directly ruled south (Lower Laos) and the protectorate of the Kingdom of Luang Prabang (Upper Laos) with the French capital in Vientiane, all within the geopolitical framework of French **Indochina** that included Vietnam and Cambodia.

After the defeat of France in World War II, officials loyal to the collaborationist Vichy government were allowed to continue to administer Laos under watchful Japanese eyes. Japan also rewarded Thailand for its peaceful acceptance of Japanese domination by forcing France to retrocede the lost trans-Mekong territories of Luang Prabang. The decline of French prestige, anti-Vietnamese sentiments, and concerns about Siamese ambitions spurred a sense of nationalism in the anti-Japanese **Lao Issara** movement, led by Prince **Phetsarat Ratnavongsa**. On 8 April 1945, the Japanese forced the pro-French King **Sisavangvong** to declare Luang Prabang's independence from France. Phetsarat and his Lao Issara colleagues formed a government which, after the Japanese surrender six months later, reinforced the April declaration with its own 15 September 1945 declaration of independence of a unified Laos. The returning French forced the Lao Issara into exile in Thailand. The French, at war in Vietnam, sought a new political context for Laos. In 1947, a constitution was adopted for an autonomous Kingdom of Laos within the French Union. In this framework, the French still maintained significant influence and veto powers. Continued nationalist resistance and the expansion of the **First Indochina War** led to a July 1949 Franco–Lao convention granting greater independence. The Lao Issara factionalized, with the **Viet Minh**–allied **Pathet Lao** going into revolt and the moderates returning to Vientiane to make independence real. A formal transfer of power to the Royal Lao Government took place on 6 February 1950.

On the day after the declaration of formal independence, the new government, led by Prime Minister **Phoui Sananikone**, was recognized by the United States. A nonresident minister, **Donald Heath**, was credentialed (resident in Saigon) and a legation was opened on 22 August 1950 under a chargé d'affaires. After the 1954 Geneva Accords, the legation was upgraded in 1955 to an embassy with a resident ambassador. The first American ambassador to Laos was **Charles W. Yost**. Like the French, U.S. interest in Laos was derivative. From the outset, Washington viewed American relations with Laos through the prism of **containment** of communism in Southeast Asia, seeing it as the extension of the battlefield in Indochina. One strategic objective was to defend the Mekong Plain, and therefore Thailand, against the advance of the Pathet Lao and their Vietnamese backers. Laos also was a front in the American war in Vietnam as the United States sought to interdict the flow of men and material from **North Vietnam** to **South Vietnam** along the **Ho Chi Minh trail** running inside of Laos. American diplomatic policy was to maintain an anticommunist government in Laos. Militarily, the United States sought to bolster the capabilities of the Royal Lao Army (Forces Armées Royale [FAR]) and keep in the field the ethnic minority forces of the secret war.

The U.S. grand strategy overlay a complicated domestic Lao conflict that in cross-cutting cleavages pitted royalists against republicans, clan against clan, southerners against northerners, rightists against leftists, and neutralists in confused patterns of coalitions, coups, and countercoups. Three main contending groupings emerged. Phetsarat's brother Prince **Souvanna Phouma** and half-brother Prince **Souphanouvong** were the poles of the neutralists and the Pathet Lao leftists, respectively. From the south, the U.S.- and Thai-backed rightists led by **Phoumi Nosavan** were firmly anticommunist, antineutralist, and anti-Vietnamese. Souvanna Phouma led the first elected government from 1951 to 1954. His goal was to bring the Pathet Lao back into the kingdom's fold. During 1953, the Viet Minh made deep incursions into Laos as the First Indochina War was coming to a climax. Souvanna's vision of a unified Laos was dimmed by the 1954 **Geneva Accord on Laos**, which essentially turned the two northeastern-most provinces of Phongsali and Huaphan, bordering North Vietnam, over to the Pathet Lao for regroupment prior to integration. Rather than integrating, the northeast became a bastion for the Pathet Lao, the Viet Minh, and eventually the People's Army of Vietnam (PAVN).

Souvanna's government fell in late 1954, but after the 1955 elections called for by the Geneva Accord, Souvanna sought to form a government that would include the Pathet Lao in a neutralist framework. The

U.S. embassy worked to obstruct this. The American position was that to compromise with the Pathet Lao would be the first step to a communist takeover. The first **coalition government** took office in November 1957. American ambassador **J. Graham Parsons**, who replaced Yost in 1956, told Congress in 1959 that he had done all he could to prevent an agreement. To demonstrate his neutrality, Souvanna visited Beijing and Hanoi and in January 1958, President **Dwight D. Eisenhower**. While Souvanna was negotiating with the Pathet Lao, the United States was consolidating its position in Laos, to the discomfiture of the French, who still had a military training role. A U.S. Operating Mission (USOM) was opened in 1955 to funnel American economic and military assistance to Laos. American funding built up the FAR. An innocuously named Programs Evaluation Office (PEO) was embedded in USOM, made up of U.S. military advisors not using rank nor wearing uniforms.

The first coalition government lasted only eight months. In addition to the parliamentary and extraparliamentary battling of Left and Right, the United States made its displeasure known in July 1958 by cutting off support to the Lao currency, the kip, and withholding aid disbursement. The government collapsed and a new government, led again by Phoui, abandoned neutralism and forged closer political and military ties to the United States. Prominent leftists were arrested and the FAR, led by Phoumi Nosavan, began to campaign against the Pathet Lao. As the country lurched toward civil war, a coup d'état in August 1960 by FAR captain **Kong Le** briefly put Souvanna Phouma back in power but led to a crisis that brought a Cold War confrontation in Laos between the United States and Soviet Union. The diplomatic resolution of the **Laotian Crisis of 1960–1962**—the 1962 **Geneva Accords**—led to the second coalition government, again led by Souvanna and including an ever stronger Pathet Lao element.

The international circumstances were changing, however, as the **Vietnam War** was intensifying. The second coalition government collapsed in April 1963. Neutralism as a policy no longer was relevant as Laos was caught between the strategic needs of the United States and the DRV. Lao elites were polarized between Left and Right—the Pathet Lao and the elite who looked to the United States for the defense of the still technically neutral Royal Lao Government, led by Souvanna Phouma for the next 12 years. During that period, critical decision making for Laos was done at the American embassy in Vientiane and in Washington and carried out by the managers of the secret war. Even though the secret war was an open secret, public denial was the only shred of neutrality left to Souvanna. He did keep his lines of communication to the Pathet Lao open, but any negotiations to constitute a unified government for Laos depended on the outcome of the U.S.–DRV negotiations to end the Vietnam War.

In 1972, as Secretary of State **Henry Kissinger** and his Vietnamese counterpart **Le Duc Tho** were closing in on the **Paris Agreement**, Souvanna Phouma and Souphanouvong began their own negotiations, leading to a February 1973 cease-fire. In September the **Laos Protocol** set the terms of an agreement on the formation of a third coalition government, which took office in April 1974. With the United States no longer committed to containment in Indochina, the defeat of the **Republic of Vietnam** by the DRV in April 1975, and the victory of the **Khmer Rouge** in **Cambodia**, there was little resistance from the remaining rightists in Laos to the takeover of the government by the Pathet Lao. On 2 December 1975, the monarchy was abolished and the Lao People's Democratic Government was proclaimed. The name reflected the parallelism of the socialist revolution of Laos with that of the DRV.

After the forced abdication of King **Savangvatthana**, Souphanouvong became president and head of state. Souvanna Phouma was named to a ceremonial post of supreme advisor to the new government. Real power, however, was in the hands of Prime Minister Kaysone Phomvihan, the head of the Lao People's Revolutionary Party (Communist Party). In accordance with the provisions of the Foreign Assistance Act of 1961, the United States terminated all assistance to Laos on 26 June 1975. Unlike the cases of Vietnam and Cambodia, however, U.S.–Lao diplomatic relations were not broken. A small American mission, limited to 12 persons, remained in Vientiane. It was headed from August 1975 to 9 June 1987 by a chargé d'affaires ad interim and from 10 June 1987 to 6 August 1992 by a chargé d'affaires. On 6 August 1992, the last chargé, Charles B. Salmon, became the first American ambassador to the LPDR. The upgrading of the mission reflected a Lao assertion of a degree of independence within the constraints of its "special relationship" with Vietnam; Lao cooperation with the United States on prisoners of war and missing in action **(POW/MIA)** issues, beginning with **Joint Casualty Resolution Center (JCRC)**'s first MIA recovery mission in 1985; and the ending of the **Third Indochina War**. In May 1995, an economic assistance relationship was renewed. Modest in scope, it is primarily delivered through nongovernmental organizations and focused on humanitarian concerns, including the removal of **unexploded ordnance (UXO)**. In 2004, Laos was accorded **permanent normal trade relations (PNTR)** with the United States, and a bilateral **trade** agreement followed in 2005. Bilateral trade between the United States and Laos in 2006 totaled only $15.6 million. The move from NTR to PNTR status had to overcome Wisconsin's senators' sensitivity to the concerns of their large Hmong ethnic constituency about a permanent waiver of the **Jackson–Vanik amendment**'s requirement on free emigration.

Laos is one of the poorest countries in Southeast Asia, with a per capita income in 2006 of $572 and a workforce still primarily involved in agriculture. It is a second-tier country in the **Association of Southeast Asian Nations (ASEAN)**'s multilateral economic arrangements. Laos's most important natural resource is its river systems, with their great hydroelectric generating potential. Of concern are the **environmental issues** raised by impacts of the necessary dam building. Contemporary U.S. interests in Laos include its role as a member of the ASEAN, countering **narcotics production and trafficking**, and continued accounting for American MIAs. The bilateral relationship is exacerbated by anti-LPDR activities in the exile Hmong community in the United States. In 2007, U.S. agents broke up a California-based Hmong coup plot against the LPDR, with nine arrests, including Hmong leader **Vang Pao**.

LAOS PROTOCOL. This is the September 1973 agreement between the Laotian government of Prime Minister **Souvanna Phouma** and the **Pathet Lao**, establishing the framework for a third **coalition government**. The United States, in the process of extricating itself from **Vietnam** in the **Paris peace negotiations**, strongly supported neutralist Souvanna Phouma's efforts to terminate the Laos theater of the **Second Indochina War**. American diplomat **John Gunther Dean**, chargé d'affaires in the U.S. embassy, played a facilitating and mediating role in the negotiations leading to the protocol. Dean faced down an attempted right-wing military putsch against the prime minister in August 1973, warning its leaders that all American assistance would be cut off. Dean received the personal thanks of President **Richard M. Nixon** for his role in Laos.

LAOTIAN CRISIS, 1960–1962. On 9 August 1960, army paratroop captain **Kong Le**'s surprise coup in Vientiane against the pro-West government led by rightist **Phoui Sananikone** installed the neutralist government of Prince **Souvanna Phouma**. Souvanna's previous **coalition government** had been undermined in 1958 by the United States in favor of a rightist government with close American ties. American Ambassador **Winthrop Brown** counseled support for the new government but was opposed by the U.S. military and the **Central Intelligence Agency (CIA)**. In December 1960, rightist forces under General **Phoumi Nosavan** drove Kong Le and his paratroopers out of the capital and installed as prime minister the head of the hereditary Champassak southern royal house, Prince **Boun Oum**. This government was recognized and supported by Thailand and the United States. In 1961, the United States took the wraps off its covert military advisory team in the Programs Evaluation Office (PEO) of the aid mission and established a formal **Military Assistance Advisory Group (MAAG)** for Laos. Souvanna fled to **Pathet Lao**–held Xiang Khuang on the **Plain of Jars** and set up a rival government, recognized by the Soviet Union, the People's Republic of **China**, and the **Democratic Republic of Vietnam (DRV)**. Spearheaded by the Pathet Lao, the pro-Souvanna Phouma forces mounted a military campaign that threatened to overwhelm the Vientiane government's forces. The Soviet Union directly intervened by airlifting to Souvanna's Xiang Khuang base personnel, weapons, and fuel. Hanoi, too, provided men and material in support of the Pathet Lao.

President **Dwight D. Eisenhower** viewed the contest in Laos as critical, holding it to be the key to all of Southeast Asia. He handed it off to incoming president **John F. Kennedy**, warning his successor that Laos could be the next "domino." This was the position that the Kennedy administration initially endorsed. On 23 March 1961, on American national TV Kennedy threatened military intervention in Laos. The **Southeast Asia Treaty Organization (SEATO)** Council, meeting only a few days later, while noting its "grave concern," only agreed to "take action appropriate in the circumstances," leaving the question of what might be appropriate up in the air. The British and French did not want to confront the Soviet Union over Laos. **Thailand**, alarmed by the Pathet Lao advance toward its **Mekong River** border with Laos, was given a bilateral U.S. defense commitment in the **Rusk–Thanat agreement**. The threat of an American–Soviet confrontation in Laos or the widening of a Laotian civil war spurred a search for a diplomatic solution that led to the convening of an international conference on Laos, which opened in Geneva on 16 May 1961.

The Kennedy administration's support for the 1962 **Geneva Conference** on Laos reflected a break with the previous administration's support of Laotian rightists. The new policy, especially pressed by Assistant Secretary of State for East Asia and the Pacific **W. Averell Harriman**, was to support a truly neutralist government—which meant Souvanna Phouma—as the alternative to a communist government. This required overcoming or ignoring the objections of Phoumi Nosavan, who felt betrayed. In a statement at the June summit meeting in Vienna between U.S. president Kennedy and soviet premier Nikita Khrushchev, the two agreed on the importance of a neutral and independent Laos in the framework of international agreements and an effective cease-fire. The problem of the Geneva conference was to bring the Laotian parties into agreement. **Cambodia**'s Prince **Sihanouk** mediated among Souvanna Phouma, the Pathet Lao's Souphanouvong, and Phoumi Nosavan. In May 1962, the Pathet Lao launched a new attack, strengthening its bargaining position. President Kennedy ordered 5,000 marines to Thailand, both as a reassurance to Bangkok and as a deterrent to further Soviet or DRV intervention. In June 1962, the administration was seriously considering putting as many as 40,000 U.S. troops across the Mekong into Laos. The mounting international pressure on the Laotian parties finally led to the formation of a Provisional Government of National Union—the so-called second coalition government—led by Souvanna Phouma with rightist General Phoumi Nosavan and the Pathet Lao's Souphanouvong as deputy prime ministers, the three with co-equal veto powers. This was the Lao government that signed the **Geneva Accord** of 1962, ending the immediate crisis, but not the struggle for Laos.

LAUREL, JOSÉ P. (1891–1959). When occupying Japan forced a declaration of independence from the United States by the **Philippines** on 14 October 1943, José P. Laurel became its president. Laurel was a member of the Philippine political elite who stayed behind to deal with the Japanese occupation after the surrender of U.S. forces in 1942. In 1944, Laurel was forced to declare war on the United States. At war's end, the Japanese brought him to Japan, where he was taken into custody by the Americans. Returned to the Philippines, he was charged with 132 counts of treason. Before Laurel could be brought to trial, he was freed in an April 1948 general amnesty offered by Philippine President **Manuel Roxas**. In 1949, Laurel was the Nationalist Party's candidate for president and was narrowly defeated by the incumbent Liberal Party's standard bearer, **Elpidio Quirino**. Despite American concern about the corruption of the Quirino government and its inability to meet the challenge posed by the revolutionary **Hukbalahap** movement, Quirino was seen as preferable to Laurel, who was tainted by collaboration and embittered anti-Americanism. Laurel was elected to the Philippine Senate in 1951, and in 1953 ceded Nationalist Party leadership to **Ramon Magsaysay**, who went on to defeat Quirino in the 1953 presidential election. In 1955, Laurel led the Philippine mission that negotiated the **Laurel–Langley** revision of the 1946 **Bell Act**.

LAUREL–LANGLEY AGREEMENT. This was a 1955 revision of the 1946 **Bell Act**, negotiated on behalf of the **Philippines** by Senator **José P. Laurel** and for the United States by **James M. Langley**. Among other things, the agreement made parity rights reciprocal, freed the peso from the dollar, allowed the imposition of quantitative restrictions on a reciprocal basis, and permitted the Philippines to levy export taxes. The U.S. Congress amended the Bell Act to allow the president to sign an executive agreement with these provisions on 6 September 1955. The Laurel–Langley Agreement expired in 1974, and U.S.–Philippine **trade** relations were normalized within the framework of the General Agreement on Tariffs and Trade (GATT), which has been succeeded by the trade rules of the **World Trade Organization (WTO)**.

LAXALT, PAUL D. (1922–). A U.S. senator from Nevada from 1974 to 1986, Paul Laxalt was a close political confidante of President

Ronald Reagan. In October 1985, as the United States became increasingly concerned about the situation in the **Philippines**, Reagan sent Laxalt to Manila to press Philippine president **Ferdinand Marcos** for reforms. Laxalt continued to stay in touch with Marcos. On 24 February 1986, as the Marcos regime was crumbling, at Reagan's behest Laxalt called Marcos to counsel restraint, advising the Philippine leader "to cut and cut cleanly." He let Marcos know from Reagan that he would be welcomed in the United States if he should see fit to leave.

LEAHY AMENDMENT. Named for Senator Frank Leahy (D-VT), the Leahy amendment was attached as an amendment to Congress's Foreign Operations Appropriation act in FY 2000 and subsequent years. It prohibited weapons sales and military assistance to **Indonesia** until the president could certify to Congress that the government of Indonesia had held accountable those officials and members of the military responsible for the violence and **human rights** abuses after the **East Timor referendum**. In a post–11 September 2001 reassessment of U.S. security interests in Indonesia in the **war on terror**, Congress allowed Indonesia back into the **International Military Education and Training (IMET)** program. However, after the murder of two American teachers in the **Timika incident**, allegedly by Indonesian soldiers, Congress stripped the FY 2004 authorization bill of IMET money for Indonesia until the president could certify that Indonesia was effectively investigating and prosecuting those responsible. The congressional ban on a normal military-to-military relationship was viewed by the executive branch as a major obstacle to American–Indonesian joint efforts to combat terrorism and support their common regional security interests. In May 2005, President **George W. Bush** and Indonesian president **Susilo Bambang Yudhoyono** jointly declared that normal military relations were in the interest of both countries and that they would work toward that objective. IMET was resumed in February 2005 based on Secretary of State **Condoleezza Rice**'s assessment of Indonesian cooperation in investigation of the Timika incident. In May 2005, Secretary Rice announced the decision to restore nonlethal **foreign military sales (FMS)** to Indonesia. In November 2005, Secretary Rice used her authority under the act to waive the legislative restrictions on **foreign**

military financing (FMF) and lethal equipment export licenses for Indonesia, declaring that it was in the national interest.

LEE KUAN YEW (1923–). A third generation **Singapore** Chinese, Lee Kuan Yew is the founding father of the Singapore state. Educated in English in Singapore, he studied law at Cambridge University. Returning to Singapore to practice law, he plunged into the politics of decolonization, becoming the general-secretary of the new People's Action Party (PAP). With the PAP as his political vehicle, and with extraordinary ability, pragmatism, and ruthlessness, Lee became the prime minister of self-governing Singapore in 1959 and prime minister of independent Singapore in 1965. Lee is credited with the vision and the drive that made Singapore an economic powerhouse, a model of uncorrupt capitalist development, a bastion of political stability, and a steadfast friend of the United States. Along the way—to the dismay of democrats—he curtailed civil and political rights, preaching an "Asian Way," the roots of which were embedded in **Asian values.** Despite the outward form of a Westminster parliamentary democracy, Lee Kuan Yew's Singapore was a scholar-bureaucrat meritocracy in which opponents were scorned as riff-raff.

Lee moved into the official background in 1990, ceding the government to "second generation" leadership. He took the title senior minister. His successor, Prime Minister Goh Chok Tong, became senior minister in 2004, when he stepped down in favor of Lee Kuan Yew's son, Lee Hsien Loong. The elder Lee then became minister mentor, still having extraordinary influence and still a fierce political combatant. His successive American counterparts viewed Lee as the preeminent international relations intellect in Southeast Asia, cultivating his approval for U.S. policy in the region. In balancing the international forces at work in the Southeast Asian region, Lee Kuan Yew was the master of pragmatic political realism.

LEVIN, BURTON (1930–2006). A career Foreign Service Officer, Burton "Burt" Levin was one of the **State Department**'s most accomplished Chinese language officers. From 1981 to 1987, he was the U.S. consul general in Hong Kong, one of the most important windows the United States had on **China.** He had also served in Hong Kong earlier in his career as well as in Taiwan. Prior to becoming the principal officer in Hong Kong, Levin had been the deputy chief of the U.S. mission in **Thailand**. In 1987, he was named U.S. ambassador to **Burma**, where he served until 1990. This was the period when the civilian façade for military rule collapsed under popular revolt, followed by a harsh martial law regime. Levin constantly pressed the junta's **State Law and Order Restoration Council (SLORC)** to return to civilian rule and an elected government. He aroused the SLORC's ire by embassy contacts with opposition leaders of the **National League for Democracy (NLD)**, including **Aung San Suu Kyi**. The SLORC charged Levin with interfering in Burma's domestic affairs and accused him of having **Central Intelligence Agency (CIA)** links. After retirement from the Foreign Service in 1990, Levin headed the **Asia Soci**ety office in Hong Kong.

LIPPO-GATE. The Lippo Group was one of **Indonesia**'s largest financial conglomerates, with close connections to the **Suharto** family and access to President **William J. Clinton**'s White House. Lippo founder Mochtar Riady and his son James utilized their entrée to the Clinton administration to bolster their business interests in Indonesia and **China**. Directly and through intermediaries they channeled millions of dollars in illegal campaign contributions to Clinton's 1992 and 1996 presidential campaigns. In 2001, James Riady pleaded guilty to unlawful reimbursement of campaign donations with foreign corporate funds and was fined $8.6 million, the highest amount ever for campaign finance fraud.

LODGE, HENRY CABOT, JR. (1902–1985). Henry Cabot Lodge was born into a distinguished Massachusetts political family. He was elected to the U.S. Senate in 1936, and after serving in the army in World War II was elected again in 1946. **John F. Kennedy** defeated him for reelection in 1952. Lodge became President Dwight D. Eisenhower's U.S. ambassador to the United Nations from 1953 to 1960 and **Richard M. Nixon**'s unsuccessful vice-presidential running mate in 1960. President Kennedy appointed him ambassador to the **Republic of Vietnam** in June 1963, replacing **Frederick Nolting**. Extremely critical of the **Ngo Dinh Diem** government, Lodge pressed for change at the top, reporting to Washington that there was no way the war could be won under the Diem administration.

Lodge's assessments were at odds with the optimism of General Paul Harkins, the U.S. military commander. Lodge, telling Washington there was no turning back, strongly supported the November 1963 **Diem coup**, which toppled the government. Lodge returned to the United States in 1964 to seek (unsuccessfully) the Republican presidential nomination. He was back in Saigon again as U.S. ambassador in 1965–1967. He was committed to winning the war in Vietnam and strongly backed escalation and bombing in the north. When the Nixon administration took office in January 1969, Lodge replaced **W. Averell Harriman** as head of the American delegation at the Paris peace talks.

LON NOL (1913–1985). General, marshal, prime minister, and president of **Cambodia**, Lon Nol engineered the 18 March 1970 coup d'état that overthrew Prince **Norodom Sihanouk**. In power, Lon Nol invited military assistance from the United States, thus ending Cambodia's technical neutralism and opening a new front for the United States in the **Second Indochina War**. A civil servant in the French protectorate, Lon Nol entered the army as a lieutenant in 1946 to fight the **Viet Minh**. He became chief of the Cambodian police and then in 1960 defense minister. In 1966, he was named prime minister but resigned in 1967 for reasons of health. Despite not fully trusting him, Sihanouk made him prime minister again in 1969. One of the many issues leading to the coup was Sihanouk's tolerance of the **Viet Cong** and People's Army of Vietnam (PVAN) sanctuaries in Cambodia's eastern provinces. Lon Nol conspired with **Sirik Matak**, his deputy prime minister, and on 18 March 1970, in a bloodless coup, the national assembly removed Sihanouk from power while he was abroad in the Soviet Union. This was followed by deadly antiethnic Vietnamese rioting. Abolishing the monarchy, Lon Nol, despite having suffered a stroke in 1971, took total control of the state in March 1972 by concurrently holding the offices of president, prime minister, and defense minister.

By openly allying the government on the American side of the Second Indochina War, and with the United States freely bombing Viet Cong and PAVN targets inside Cambodia, Lon Nol widened the scope of the civil war in Cambodia. The Vietnamese now gave direct assistance to the communist Khmer Rouge, whereas previously out of deference to Sihanouk they had been more discreet. Despite generous American military assistance and advice to the new Cambodian government, the Khmer Rouge made steady advances against it. Lon Nol's government was unpopular, corrupt, and divided. Lon Nol's military leadership was indecisive and incompetent. Support of Lon Nol became an issue within the American embassy and between the embassy and National Security Advisor **Henry Kissinger**. Ambassador **Emory Swank** pictured Lon Nol to Washington as mentally and physically a sick man. Swank was replaced by **John Gunther Dean**. On 1 April 1975, with the Khmer Rouge just outside of Phnom Penh, Lon Nol fled the country for the United States, using the excuse of seeking medical assistance.

LONG TIENG. A remote **Hmong** village in north-central **Laos**, Long Tieng became the headquarters of General **Vang Pao**'s Hmong army in the **Central Intelligence Agency (CIA)**'s **secret war**. It was supplied by **Air America**, flying in and out of one of the most dangerous fields in Laos. The CIA's operational center was located here and, as Lima Site 20A, it was an important post for the "Ravens," the American forward air controllers of the air war in Laos. In 1971, it was accidentally bombed by an American F-4, whose pilot mistook his target. In May 1975, Long Tieng was evacuated using overloaded Air America C-46s, which flew out more than 12,000 Hmong refugees for internment in Thai camps.

LORD, WINSTON (1937–). A senior policy planner and career diplomat, Winston Lord was best known for his expertise on **China**. He was an aide to National Security Advisor **Henry Kissinger** from 1969 to 1973, accompanying Kissinger in 1969 on his secret trip to Beijing, and in 1972 accompanying President **Richard M. Nixon** to China. Lord was American ambassador to China from 1985 to 1989. In 1993, he was named assistant secretary of state for East Asian and Pacific affairs in President **William J. Clinton**'s first term. Assistant Secretary Lord helped shape Clinton's vision of a **Pacific Community** and American participation in the **Asia–Pacific Economic Cooperation (APEC)** forum. He was very involved in the last stages of the process of **normalization of relations** with the **Socialist Republic of Vietnam (SRV)**. In July 1993, following up on Special Emissary **John Vessey**'s April 1993 trip, Lord co-led a high-ranking delegation to Hanoi that emphasized to the SRV President Clinton's insistence on continuing progress on the missing in action (**POW/MIA**) problem and **human rights**. Lord returned to Hanoi in December 1993 and reported that tangible progress had been made in these areas of concern. This became part of the basis for Clinton's decision in 1994 to end the embargo against Vietnam.

LUGAR, RICHARD G. (1932–). A Republican U.S. Senator from Indiana, Lugar, as chairman of the Senate Foreign Relations Committee, headed an official American delegation sent by President **Ronald Reagan** to observe the February 1986 snap election in the **Philippines** called by President **Ferdinand Marcos**. Lugar played a pivotal role in persuading President Reagan that Marcos was "cooking the results" and that **Corazon Aquino** had in fact won the election. Senator Lugar was the author in 2006 of legislation calling for the appointment of an American ambassador to the **Association of Southeast Asian Nations (ASEAN)**.

– M –

MACAPAGAL, DIOSDADO (1910–1997). Unlike most Philippine politicians, Diosdado Macapagal had humble roots, rising to the highest office in the land, president of the **Philippines**, from 1961 to 1965. His popular image as an honest and reformist legislator led to his election in 1957 as vice president on the Liberal Party ticket to the Nationalist Party's **Carlos Garcia**. Excluded from real power in the corrupt administration of Garcia, Macapagal was close to the **Central Intelligence Agency (CIA)**'s Manila embassy station. When it came time to face Garcia in the 1961 presidential election, the CIA, perhaps looking for another **Ramon Magsaysay**, provided advice and financial support. Although Macapagal may have wanted reform, it was business as usual in his administration by the entrenched political and bureaucratic interests. The warm embrace that the United States had given Garcia cooled for Macapagal in the administration of **John F. Kennedy**. President Kennedy did not support legislation for an additional $73 million in war claims for the Philippines, which led Macapagal to cancel a scheduled trip to the United States. It was also on Macapagal's initiative that Philippine Independence Day was switched from 4 July to 12 June, the day **Emilio Aguinaldo** declared independence in 1898. In 1965, in a hugely expensive and nasty campaign, Macapagal was defeated in his reelection bid by **Ferdinand Marcos**. One of his legacies was his daughter, Gloria Macapagal, who as **Gloria Macapagal-Arroyo** became president of the Philippines in 2001.

MACARTHUR, ARTHUR (1845–1912). Father of General **Douglas MacArthur**, Arthur MacArthur, a career soldier, won the Medal of Honor in the Civil War, fought Indians in the American West, participated in the invasion of Cuba in 1898, commanded a division against **Emilio Aguinaldo's** Philippine "insurrectionists" in 1899, and was military governor of the **Philippines** in 1900–1901. After Aguinaldo's capture in March 1901, MacArthur allowed him to have his freedom after taking an oath of allegiance to the United States, rather than exiling him to Guam as desired by **William Howard Taft**, who would succeed MacArthur as the first civilian governor.

MACARTHUR, DOUGLAS (1889–1964). One of America's most famous professional soldiers, Douglas MacArthur is also the American who left the greatest personal imprint on the **Philippines**. He was the son of General **Arthur MacArthur**, who, while Douglas was at West Point, had been military governor of the Philippines. Young MacArthur graduated in 1903 at the top of his class and was posted to an engineering battalion on the island of Panay in the Philippines' Visayan region, from where he moved to a staff position in Manila. It was there that Lieutenant MacArthur first met **Manuel Quezon** and **Sergio Osmeña**, with both of whom he would work in the future when they became presidents of the **Commonwealth of the Philippines**. MacArthur's first Philippine tour was abbreviated by malaria, and after traveling in Southeast and South Asia with his father, then the U.S. military attaché in Japan, he returned to the United States. During World War I, Colonel MacArthur distinguished himself in France as the chief of staff of the Rainbow Division and was promoted to the rank of brigadier general.

It was after World War I that MacArthur's career became firmly connected to the Philippines. In 1922, he was named commanding general of the District of Manila, and a year later commander of the 23rd Infantry Brigade. In 1925, he was promoted to the rank of major general, the youngest in the army. After a tour back in the United States as commander of the Washington district, he returned to Manila in 1928, becoming the senior American military officer as commanding general of the Department of the Philippines. In 1930, he returned to the United States as a full general and chief of staff of the U.S. Army, completing the tour in 1935. Rather than retiring at the peak of a peacetime military career, MacArthur returned to the Philippines at the behest of Manuel Quezon, who headed the new Commonwealth government. Reverting to his permanent rank of major general, MacArthur became the chief military advisor to the government as it began planning for its own military forces. In 1937, MacArthur retired from active duty in the U.S. Army with the rank of general on the retired list. He continued to work as a quasi civilian on building a Philippine army, not only for future independence but for a possible impending Pacific War. President Quezon made him a field marshal, the only American to ever hold that rank. His personal ties with Quezon were cemented in a uniquely Filipino way when Quezon became godfather to MacArthur's son, born in 1938.

As war with Japan loomed, in July 1941 MacArthur was recalled to active duty as a general commanding the U.S. Armed Forces in the Far East (USAFFE). At the outbreak of the war in December 1941, MacArthur, given a fifth star as General of the Army, led the defense of the Philippines from the island bastion of Corregidor until President Franklin D. Roosevelt ordered him to Australia to command Allied Forces in the Pacific. In March 1942, MacArthur left the Philippines, together with President Quezon and Vice President Osmeña, prior to the surrender of the Filipino–American forces. When he arrived in Australia he uttered the words that are immortalized in Philippine history, "I came out of Bataan and I shall return." From Allied headquarters in Brisbane, Australia, MacArthur commanded the campaign against the Japanese northward through the Southwest Pacific. He returned to the Philippines with the landings at Leyte in the Visaya Islands on 29 October 1944, where he waded ashore, accompanied by President Sergio Osmeña, who had succeeded the late

President Quezon. The Allied forces fought a bitter campaign northward, and it was not until March 1945 that Manila was retaken, after house-to-house fighting. Japanese resistance continued on Luzon until the end of the war in August 1945.

MacArthur left the Philippines to oversee the Japanese occupation and then to take command of **United Nations** forces in the first year of the Korean War, until he was removed from command for insubordination by President **Harry S. Truman**. No matter how controversial he may have become in the United States, in the Philippines he was a hero. In 1961, he made what he called a "sentimental journey" back to the Philippines, where he was received by adulatory crowds as a liberator. President **Carlos Garcia** bestowed on him the Philippine "Legion of Honor" and the honorary rank of chief commander.

MAGSAYSAY, RAMON (1907–1957). Ramon Magsaysay was president of the **Philippines** from 1954 to his death in a plane crash in 1957. In his 1953 presidential campaign against incumbent President **Elpidio Quirino**, Magsaysay had behind-the-scenes financial and political support from the United States, funneled through his American advisor, **Edward Lansdale**. Magsaysay was the first nonlawyer to occupy the presidency. During the Japanese occupation of the Philippines (1942–1945), he led a guerrilla resistance group. Magsaysay began his political career as a congressman in 1946, the start of a meteoric rise to the presidency. In 1949, Quirino named him secretary of defense. In that office, Magsaysay reoriented the struggle against the communist **Hukbalahap** insurrection. His success, with American support, in defeating the Huks gave him great political prominence, which together with his charm and charisma made him a national hero. He was elected president with the largest number of votes ever won by a candidate. Part of Magsaysay's strategy to defeat the Huks was to offer amnesty and to resettle with land titles thousands of Luzon's landless to Mindanao, changing the balance between Christians and Muslims and sowing the seeds for the later Muslim revolts. Although a strong ally of the United States, Magsaysay was conscious of the Philippines' Asian colonial legacy. He urged the adoption of the anti-imperialist **Pacific Charter** at the

1954 **Manila Conference**, which created the **Southeast Asia Treaty Organization (SEATO)**.

MAHATHIR MOHAMMAD (1925–). Prime minister of **Malaysia** from 1981 to 2003, Mahathir Mohamad, by training a medical doctor, was once an outcast in his own party, the United Malays National Organization (UMNO), because of his Malay ethnic chauvinism. He became Malaysia's prime minister in 1981 in the wake of the Malay–Chinese riots after the election and suspension of the constitution. As prime minister, Mahathir championed Malay rights in a plural community with Chinese and Indian minorities. He was the author of the New Economic Policy (NEP), which in its various iterations was an economic affirmative action program for Malays. After more than two decades, Mahathir stepped down in 2003 in favor of Prime Minister **Abdullah Badawi.**

Mahathir was a strong leader and in the Third World, a vocal, and to American ears radical, spokesman for economic and social grievances against the developed West. He was critical of the American global role, characterizing it as imperialism. During the regional **financial crisis of 1997–1998**, he spurned the **International Monetary Fund (IMF)**, which he saw as an instrument for American expansive capitalism. He unsuccessfully promoted an **East Asian Economic Group (EAEG)** that would have excluded the United States, as an alternative to what he saw as the American-dominated **Asia–Pacific Economic Cooperation (APEC)** consultations. He championed the **Association of Southeast Asian Nations (ASEAN)**'s relations with **China** in the **ASEAN Plus 3 (APT)** grouping of ASEAN, **China**, Japan, and the Republic of Korea. In **Nonaligned Movement (NAM)** summit meetings he condemned American unilateralism and its global police role. He vehemently denounced the American war in Iraq. He was outspokenly critical of the U.S. democracy and **human rights** agenda, characterizing it as discriminatory and aimed at slowing the economic progress of developing economies. Underneath the public displays of opposition to U.S. policies, it was very much business as usual in economic and other functional state-to-state relations. President **George W. Bush**, ignoring Mahathir's past rhetoric, warmly welcomed him to the White

House in May 2002 as an ally in the **war on terror**. Out of office, Mahathir became a vocal and biting critic of his successor.

MAJOR NON-NATO ALLY (MNNA) STATUS. In 2003 President **George W. Bush** designated the **Philippines** and **Thailand** as Major Non-NATO Allies of the United States, reaffirming their positions as U.S. treaty allies. In Asia, the two Southeast Asian countries joined South Korea, Japan, and Australia in this expression of a close working security relationship with the United States. The granting of MNNA was in part recognition of their contribution to the coalition forces in the **Iraq War**. In addition to its symbolic implications, the status provides for priority for delivery of excess defense articles, participation in cooperative research and development projects for conventional defense and counterterrorism, stockpiling of U.S. defense articles, and bidding on contracts for maintenance and repair of Department of Defense equipment outside of the United States. MNNA status does not entail the same mutual defense and security guarantees afforded to North Atlantic Treaty Organization (NATO) members. In April 2007, a bill was introduced in Congress to strip Thailand of its MNNA status because of the 2006 military coup.

MALAYA. This was the British colonial possession on the Malay Peninsula. It became independent in 1957. In 1962, it became the core of the Federation of **Malaysia**, which included as well British North Borneo (**Sabah**), Sarawak, and **Singapore**. Malaya's independence was delayed by a communist insurrection known as the "Emergency," which was fought from 1948 to 1962 by British, Australian, New Zealand, and Malay forces against a largely ethnic Chinese revolutionary movement. At independence Malaya was closely tied to Great Britain and British Commonwealth associated nations. Its major security framework was the 1957 Anglo–Malayan Defense Agreement, which in 1963 became the Anglo–Malaysian Defense Agreement (AMDA) and in 1971 the **Five Power Defence Arrangement (FPDA)**.

MALAYSIA. Malaysia was formed in 1963 by the incorporation into a federal system of already independent **Malaya** and the British decolonized territories of **Singapore**, Sarawak, and **Sabah** (North Borneo). Singapore was forced from the federation in 1965 and became an independent state. **Brunei**, Great Britain's last dependency in Southeast Asia, remained outside of the Malaysian state and became independent only in 1984. Peninsular Malaysia, the two states of East Malaysia, and the federal territory of Labuan at the head of Brunei Bay are separated by 370 miles of South China Sea waters. The total land area is 127,316 square miles (329,749 square kilometers), slightly larger than New Mexico. The 2006 population was 29.6 million. Its capital is Kuala Lumpur. The creation of Malaysia was opposed by **Indonesia** and an undeclared war was fought, called by Indonesia "**Confrontation**," requiring intervention by British, Australian, and New Zealand allies of Malaysia.

Malaysia has emerged as one of the economic powers in Southeast Asia. American economic relations with it have made the United States an important bilateral partner. Malaysia has become the United States' 10th largest trading partner, with two-way **trade** totaling $49 billion in 2006, which was 16 percent of Malaysia's total global trade. The United States is Malaysia's largest source of foreign direct **investment (FDI)**, with a 2006 cumulative value of more than $10 billion. The 2004 bilateral **trade and investment framework agreement (TIFA)** provided the basis for negotiations beginning in May 2006 for a bilateral **free trade agreement (FTA)**, which if completed would make Malaysia the largest U.S. trading partner with an FTA outside of the North America Free Trade Agreement (NAFTA). A deadline of 31 March 2007 for an agreement before the expiration of President **George W. Bush**'s trade promotion authority was not met. The negotiations were complicated by U.S. linkage of the proposed FTA to a Malaysian company's $16 billion energy deal with Iran.

Even as Malaysia and the United States were forging strong economic ties, Malaysia's long-time prime minister **Mahathir Mohammad** sought to avoid economic dependencies on the Western developed economies by "looking East" and advocating tighter economic ties with Japan, South Korea, and **China**. In the 1990s, Mahathir began urging the creation of an **East Asian Economic Group (EAEG)** composed of the **Association of Southeast Asian Nations (ASEAN)** and the three Northeast East Asian countries to rival North American- and European-centered economic blocs. This was vigorously opposed by the United States. According to a former American ambassador to

Malaysia, a bitter personal feud between Mahathir and American Secretary of State **James Baker** ensued. At one point Mahathir refused to accept a phone call from President **George H. W. Bush**. Mahathir viewed the U.S. promotion of its version of a liberalizing trade agenda in the **Asia–Pacific Economic Cooperation (APEC)** format as a disguise for American capitalist imperialism. During the **financial crisis of 1997–1998**, Mahathir scorned the conventional wisdom of the U.S.-backed **International Monetary Fund (IMF)** reform agenda, resorting instead to controversial capital controls and blaming the crisis on capitalist **George Soros** and Jews.

During the administration of President **William J. Clinton**, **human rights**, not economics, headed the list of Mahathir's policy grievances with the United States. Although there were deep bilateral policy differences on appropriate responses to the Asian financial crisis, U.S. policy in the Middle East, and the U.S. sanctions regime against **Burma**, the major disruption in the civility of the relationship came over the arrest and imprisonment of Malaysian deputy prime minister **Anwar Ibrahim** in 1998. The United States regularly criticized aspects of Malaysia's domestic political system with respect to **religious rights**; the lack of an independent judiciary; and especially the use of the draconian Internal Security Act (ISA), inherited from the British colonial administration. The United States charged that the ISA was used against political opponents. Mahathir, a defender of **Asian values**, bristled at Washington's criticism, launching counterattacks on the moral collapse of the United States: institutionalized racism, crime, drug addiction, and homelessness. The Anwar case, however, was seized upon by the United States as an example of Malaysia's human rights violations. Mahathir's fury at U.S. intervention reached its peak when U.S. Vice President Al Gore made a 1998 speech in Kuala Lumpur, Malaysia's capital, seeming to incite pro-Anwar Malaysian demonstrators. Despite the antagonism, the functional interdependencies in the bilateral relationship meant no major diplomatic breach occurred.

From the outset, the fundamental political policy differences between the United States and Malaysia have been on questions of the Middle East. Malaysia is a Muslim majority country and under Mahathir was a strident advocate of Muslim causes around the world. Malaysia is an activist member of the **Organization of the Islamic**

Conference (OIC). Kuala Lumpur believes that the United States enables Israeli aggression and occupation of the West Bank and permits the suppression of the Palestinian people. Malaysia has consistently argued that there can be no peace in the Middle East until the United States stops supporting Israel. Malaysia opposed the **Persian Gulf** and **Iraq Wars**. Malaysia's position on Middle East questions was little different from that of many other Muslim-majority states, but during the Mahathir years the quality of the U.S.–Malaysian dialogue was soured by his inflammatory language. He accused the United States of making war on Islam. He claimed that Washington is dominated by Jews and called President George W. Bush a war criminal. Since Mahathir retired, the official rhetoric has been toned down, even though the ex-prime minister fires occasional salvos from the sidelines.

Underneath the verbal outbursts and unbridgeable policy gulf on the Arab–Israeli conflict, a low-visibility U.S. security relationship with Malaysia has been in place. Since independence, Malaysia has been nonaligned. Its only formal Western security tie is within the framework of the 1971 **Five Power Defence Arrangement (FPDA)** with Singapore, Great Britain, Australia, and New Zealand. In the ASEAN framework, nonaligned Malaysia was the most vigorous promoter of both the Southeast Asia **Zone of Peace, Freedom, and Neutrality (ZOPFAN)** and the **Southeast Asia Nuclear Weapons Free Zone (SEANWFZ)**. Nevertheless, even without the kind of tight security relations that the United States has with its Southeast Asian allies, the United States and Malaysia have friendly military-to-military links. An agreement on naval exercises dates back to 1984. Malaysian officers are enrolled in **International Military Education and Training (IMET)** programs. Malaysian military and civilian defense personnel attend courses and conferences at the **Asia Pacific Center for Strategic Studies (APCSS)**. American naval ships regularly make port calls in Malaysia. Mahathir once visited on board the USS *Blue Ridge*, the flag ship of the U.S. 7th Fleet, when it called at Port Klang. Also, since the 1992 closure of the U.S. naval base at **Subic Bay** in the **Philippines**, there has been repair and maintenance work done on U.S. vessels in Malaysian yards. Malaysia has allowed American military flyovers and provides a base for U.S. military jungle training. Malaysia also participates with the United

States in joint exercises. In a 2002 speech detailing the scope of bilateral security cooperation between Malaysia and the United States, the Malaysian defense minister characterized it as an "all too well-kept secret." The **war on terror** raised U.S. security cooperation with Malaysia to a new level. Malaysia hosts the **Southeast Asian Regional Center for Counterterrorism (SEARCCT)**, for which the United States provides the largest number of trainers.

The transfer of authority in Malaysia in 2003 from Mahathir to **Abdullah Badawi** did not necessarily lead to a closer relationship, since Malaysian interests have not changed. What did change was the willingness to manage the relationship differently at the highest executive level. This was evident in Abdullah's July 2002 Washington visit. He accepted President Bush's assurances that the United States was committed to the development of a Palestinian state that can live side-by-side with Israel in peace. He said that Malaysia was ready to contribute to the reconstruction of Iraq. Abdullah's bottom line was that the bilateral relationship was "very, very, very strong."

MANILA CONFERENCE. The United States, alarmed by the French defeat in **Indochina** and the 1954 **Geneva Accords** ending the **First Indochina War**, moved in consultation with Great Britain to create a collective defense system in Southeast Asia. The planning for a forward deterrent against communist aggression in Southeast Asia began even before the **Geneva Conference**. Even though there was no support from **Burma** and **Indonesia** and stiff Indian opposition, the United States pressed ahead, convinced, as Secretary of State **John Foster Dulles** was, of the need to contain communism "to bring security to the free peoples of Southeast Asia." In September 1954, two months after the Geneva agreements had been signed, a conference was convened in the **Philippine** capital, Manila, to construct a regional collective security system. In addition to the host nation, the participants included the United States, Great Britain, Australia, New Zealand, **Thailand**, France, and Pakistan. While the latter two may have seemed somewhat tangential, the French wished to maintain a political presence as a regional power despite the Geneva Accords, and Pakistan's eye was on India. The formal result of the conference was the **Southeast Asia Collective Defense Treaty** or Manila Pact. The Philippine host, President **Ramon Magsaysay**, concerned by the imperialist tinge of some members of the conference, pushed for a kind of conference anticolonial addendum known as the **Pacific Charter**. *See also* CONTAINMENT.

MANILA PACT. *See* SOUTHEAST ASIA COLLECTIVE DEFENSE TREATY.

MARCOS, FERDINAND E. (1917–1989). President of the Republic of the **Philippines** from 1966 until he was deposed in 1986, Ferdinand Marcos was born in the northern Philippine Ilocos region. His father was a lawyer and politician. Marcos had two early distinctions, when in 1939 he earned the highest score on the national bar examination and had his conviction for the murder of a political opponent of his father overturned on appeal. His more extravagant claims of being a heroic guerrilla leader against the Japanese during the 1942–1945 occupation have been challenged. After the war, he established a firm political base in Luzon's northern regions, battling for veterans' benefits. He was elected to the House of Representatives in 1949 and reelected in 1953 and 1957. In 1959, he was the leading vote getter in a race for the Philippine Senate. In 1954, he married **Imelda Romualdez Marcos**. As a legislator he had a modest reputation as a reformer. He ran on the Liberal ticket and expected to gain the Liberal nomination for president in 1961. This went, however, to **Diosdado Macapagal**, who though a Liberal had been vice president to the nationalist president **Carlos Garcia**. In the election Macapagal defeated Garcia, and in 1965 when Macapagal decided to seek a second term, Marcos, switching parties, won nomination as the nationalist candidate and easily defeated Macapagal.

Marcos's first constitutional term began with policy decisions that seemed directed to immediate domestic economic and social problems, including land reform. Even though the economic situation began to worsen and domestic violence increased, Marcos remained popular. He and his wife presented a glamorous façade, as if modeled on **John F. Kennedy**'s Camelot. They were a popular couple in the United States as well, being as close an ally as President **Ramon Magsaysay** had been a decade earlier. Their 1966 state visit to Washington was a public relations triumph, during which Marcos bargained with the **Johnson** administration for greater economic support for the Philippines in return for Philippine forces in **Vietnam**. This was the **Philippine Civic Action Group (Philcag)**. The Philippine president was given the rare opportunity of addressing a joint session of Congress. In the 1969 presidential election, Marcos crushed the Liberal candidate, Sergio Osmeña, by a margin of two million votes, and his nationalists won seven of the eight contested Senate seats and 80 percent of the House seats.

Despite or perhaps because of the concentration of authority in Marcos's hands, protest and opposition spread as organized violence by the **Communist Party of the Philippines/New People's Army (CPP/NPA)**, Muslim separatists, and local warlords threatened regional anarchy. In a lame duck second term, constitutionally barred from a third term and unlikely to be able to promote his wife to her own presidency, Marcos looked for alternative leadership formats. He articulated a need for constitutional change and a "New Society." The 1971 off-year legislative elections rejected pro-Marcos candidates and indicated that the Liberals, led by **Benigno Aquino**, would defeat any nationalist candidate in presidential elections. Marcos had publicly said he would do anything to prevent Aquino, whom he accused of being a communist, from becoming president. A 1971–1972 Marcos-inspired constitutional convention failed to deliver an amendment that would allow a third term. After a staged attack on Defense Minister Juan Ponce Enrile's automobile on 23 September 1972, Marcos declared martial law, citing rebellion as the legal justification. American ambassador **Henry Byroade**, who was personally close to Marcos and his wife, had alerted Washington to the possibility of martial law more than a week earlier. President **Richard M. Nixon**'s administration treated martial law as a fait accompli. The American concern was the status of the U.S. bases, which Marcos promised not to disturb. The presidential couple was again warmly received in Washington during a 1980 state visit, during which President **Ronald Reagan** praised Marcos for sharing the American values of liberty, democracy, justice, and equality.

Martial law, with its arrests and suspension of civil liberties, lasted until 17 January 1981, to be replaced by the structures and institutions of constitutional authoritarianism, under which Marcos was elected to a new six-year presidential term. The political and economic excesses of the undemocratic regime undermined its legitimacy, particularly the corruption and wealth of the Marcos and Romualdez families and their supporters. In 1983, there was widespread belief that Marcos was seriously ill. It was at this point that Aquino decided to return from the United States to Manila, where he was assassinated, triggering the political turmoil that climaxed in the **EDSA revolution**, Marcos's flight from the Philippines, and the 1986 presidency of Aquino's widow, **Corazon Aquino**. Marcos died in Hawaii on 28 September 1989. His embalmed body was returned to the Philippines, where it lies in a glassed-in refrigerated crypt in Laoag City in his home province of Ilocos Norte.

MARCOS, IMELDA ROMUALDEZ (1929–). Wife of Philippine president **Ferdinand Marcos**, Imelda Marcos was a former beauty queen and tireless campaigner who enhanced Marcos's political career. She was born on the island of Leyte and came from a politically prominent Visayan family. She reigned as the **Philippines'** first lady for two decades, amassing great wealth. Her extravagance helped undermine the legitimacy of the regime. With the authority of her husband's position, she accumulated both bureaucratic and psychological power. She was minister of human settlements and governor of Metro Manila and controlled a large patronage network. She was unofficial Philippines ambassador to the world, eclipsing the foreign minister. Her brother, Kokoy Romualdez, was named ambassador to Washington and managed her trips to Washington and New York, where she was the center of media attention. She has long been thought complicit in the plot to assassinate **Benigno Aquino** on his return to the Philippines in 1983. She went into exile in Hawaii with her husband in 1986, returning to the Philippines in 1991 to become one of the unsuccessful candidates in the 1992 presidential electoral field of six, won by **Fidel Ramos**. The Philippine government has been singularly unsuccessful in U.S. and other foreign courts in repatriating the alleged overseas fortunes of the Marcos family or holding Imelda Marcos accountable for her alleged illegal excesses. The family remains politically potent nationally.

MARTIN, GRAHAM A. (1919–1990). Graham Martin was the last U.S. ambassador to the **Republic of Vietnam**, from 1973 to the surrender of Saigon on 30 April 1975. He had previously been ambassador to

Thailand, from 1963 to1967, where he successfully resisted utilizing American troops in the Thai counterinsurgency campaign and negotiated agreements for U.S. bases in Thailand. Between serving in Bangkok and Saigon, he had been ambassador to Italy. Martin was sent to Saigon to mitigate the damage that the **Paris Agreement** ending the American military role in Vietnam had done to the Republic of Vietnam's cause. In Saigon and Washington Martin tried to put the best face on a deteriorating situation, not wishing to add further to the fear that the United States was abandoning Vietnam. To critics, it was a question whether his optimism was diplomatic or real. In the chaos of the 29–30 April 1975 fall of Saigon, Martin tried to keep the last minute helicopter evacuation of remaining Americans and at-risk Vietnamese going as long as possible. Martin returned to the State Department, where he remained in a kind of limbo until his retirement in 1976. A very negative picture of Martin's Saigon embassy was painted in Frank Snepp's book, *Decent Interval*.

MASTERS, EDWARD E. (1924–). A career Foreign Service Officer, Edward Masters was political counselor in the American embassy in Indonesia, headed by Ambassador **Marshall Green**, at the time of the 1965 **Indonesian coup**. He became deputy chief of mission of the American embassy in **Thailand** and then ambassador to Bangladesh. Masters returned to Indonesia as ambassador (1978–1981) during the administration of President **Jimmy Carter**. Like other American ambassadors in the region, he was caught in the crossfire in the **State Department** by the contest for influence between Assistant Secretary of State for East Asia and the Pacific **Richard Holbrooke** and Assistant Secretary of State for Human Rights and Humanitarian Affairs **Patricia Derian**. Two **human rights** issues were high on the Jakarta embassy's agenda: the status of the hundreds of alleged communist political prisoners held without trial on the remote island of Buru in East Indonesia and the plight of the East Timorese under Indonesian military occupation after the 1975 invasion of **East Timor**. Masters's "quiet diplomacy," while obtaining results in terms of prisoner release and humanitarian assistance, did not satisfy human rights activists, who criticized him for not doing enough. In retirement, Masters was the founding president of the **United States–Indonesia Society (USINDO)**.

MAYAGUEZ INCIDENT. On 12 May 1975, the American container ship *Mayaguez* was seized off the coast of **Cambodia** and its crew of 39 taken ashore as prisoners at Koh Tang by soldiers of the new **Khmer Rouge** regime. President **Gerald R. Ford** ordered helicopter gunships and U.S. marines to the rescue. They met heavy resistance on the beach, and Ford unleashed a crushing bombing attack on Cambodian shore installations. Unknown to Washington, the *Mayaguez*'s crew had been taken to Phnom Penh, where they were released. President Ford seized on the American display of force as a new indicator of American confidence after the Vietnam War.

MCCLINTOCK, ROBERT M. (1909–1976). The first U.S. ambassador to independent **Cambodia**, Robert McClintock served from 1954 to 1956. McClintock did not have a good relationship with King **Norodom Sihanouk**. He belittled the king behind his back, calling him the "little king." It was also McClintock who bestowed the demeaning nickname "Snooky" on Sihanouk. McClintock's disregard of court protocol gave the anti-American French advisors of Sihanouk ammunition to feed the hostility the royal palace felt toward the American embassy. McClintock went on to become ambassador to Lebanon, Argentina, and Venezuela.

MCKINLEY, WILLIAM (1843–1901). Twenty-fifth president of the United States (1897–1901), William McKinley managed the acquisition of American empire in the Pacific following the **Spanish–American War**. Although the **Philippines** had not been the focus of the conflict, Commodore **George Dewey**'s success in Manila Bay and the insurrection of Philippine nationalists against Spanish rule created the condition that was later described as "contingent necessity"; that is, if the United States did not acquire the Philippines, another country would. Already shut out of the imperialist scramble for China, McKinley saw commercial advantage for the United States as well as public support for American imperialism. He made cession of the Philippines one of the terms of the Treaty of Paris that ended the war. The strategic and economic factors were cloaked in an American version of the "white man's burden," a "civilizing mission" of "benevolent assimilation." The political interpretation of this meant putting American institutions in place to prepare the Philippines for self-government.

MCNAMARA, ROBERT S. (1916—). Robert McNamara was secretary of defense from 1961 to 1968 in the **Kennedy** and **Johnson** administrations. He was a key participant in decision making on the **Vietnam War**. During World War II, he was an Army Air Corps officer working in operations and planning. After the war he worked for the Ford Motor Corporation, becoming president in 1960. Tapped by newly elected President Kennedy for the defense cabinet post, McNamara brought in civilian systems analysis to reorganize the management of the American military. McNamara was an early promoter of widening the war in Vietnam. For antiwar protesters, the conflict was tagged "McNamara's war." As the number of troops in South Vietnam escalated and the bombing of **North Vietnam** did not seem to impress the foe, he began quietly to question whether the war could be won at an acceptable cost. While never publicly breaking with the administration's policy, his slow transition into a "dove" distanced him from the president. His personal post mortem of the war is his 1995 memoir, *In Retrospect: The Tragedy and Lessons of Vietnam*. McNamara left government in 1968 to become president of the World Bank, a post he held until 1981.

MCNUTT, PAUL V. (1891–1955). Lawyer and Democratic politician Paul McNutt, a governor of Indiana, was named high commissioner to the **Commonwealth of the Philippines** in 1937, where he served until 1939. Although the **Philippines** was in transition from commonwealth status to independence, McNutt angered the Philippine leadership by questioning the Philippines' preparedness for independence. At the same time, he worked with Commonwealth president **Manuel Quezon** to facilitate the immigration of Jewish refugees from Europe to the Philippines. During World War II, passed over as vice-presidential candidate for President Franklin D. Roosevelt's third term, he served the administration as head of the Federal Security Agency and director of the War Manpower Commission. In 1946, President **Harry S. Truman** sent him back to Manila as high commissioner and then named McNutt as the first American ambassador to the Philippines. He left in 1947. After retirement, he chaired the Philippine–American Trade Council.

MEGAWATI SUKARNOPUTRI (1947–). The second child and eldest daughter of **Indonesia**'s first president, **Sukarno**, Megawati

Sukarnoputri ("daughter of Sukarno") came into anti-**Suharto** politics in the 1990s as the figurehead leader of the Indonesian Democratic Party of Struggle. She had no real political or governmental experience but was the symbol of traditional Indonesian nationalist politics. She became Indonesia's fifth president in July 2001, when as vice president she succeeded the impeached president, **Abdurrahman Wahid**. In her eyes, she had been cheated out of the presidency in 1999, when, despite the fact that her party had won the plurality of seats in the parliament, backroom maneuvering had made Wahid president. The United States welcomed the change from Wahid. Megawati was bitterly disappointed again in 2004, when in Indonesia's first direct presidential election her candidacy was crushed by **Susilo Bambang Yudhoyono** by a margin of 61 to 39 percent of the vote.

As president, Megawati's public persona was carefully scripted and in many respects stolidly enigmatic. Although perhaps a relief from the off-the-cuff eccentricity of Wahid, unlike her father a generation earlier, she seemed unable to make the presidency a bully pulpit to move the nation. Her seeming irresolution in the face of the challenges of political instability, decentralization, corruption, ethnic conflict, separatist struggles of the **Free Aceh Movement (GAM) in Aceh** and **Free Papua Organization (OPM)** in Papua, and the **war on terror** left those who had placed great hope in her assumption of office disheartened. President Megawati was the first foreign leader to visit President **George W. Bush**, one week after the terrorist attacks of 11 September 2001. In the United States she pledged support for the war on terror. Returning home, her support for the United States was lukewarm and her government in seeming denial about terrorist threats in Indonesia.

MEKONG RIVER. The Mekong River is the central artery of mainland Southeast Asia, running more than 3,000 miles from its source in Tibet, through western **China**, touching **Laos**, **Burma**, **Thailand**, and **Cambodia** before draining into the **South China Sea** through its mouths in **Vietnam**'s southern delta. It is the 12th longest river in the world, and in volume of flow it is the world's 10th greatest river. Trans-Mekong ethnic and state rivalries have made the river's drainage basin a historical cockpit of conflict. In modern times, the Mekong River as the strategic border between Thailand and its **Indochina** neighbors gave it geopolitical significance in American policy. It was the Laos–Thailand Mekong border that was the focus of U.S. defense guarantees to Thailand during the **Second Vietnam War**. The economic development of the Lower Mekong was the centerpiece of the vision of a peaceful Southeast Asia laid out by President **Lyndon B. Johnson** in a major speech at Johns Hopkins University in April 1965.

MILITARY ASSISTANCE ADVISORY GROUP (MAAG). A military assistance advisory group is a unified U.S. military command in a country receiving U.S. security assistance. Its reporting line is military, ultimately to the secretary of defense. The MAAG is responsible for administering U.S. military assistance planning and programming in the host country. It monitors delivery and end use of assistance. The first MAAG in Southeast Asia was established in the **Philippines** in 1947. Beginning in 1950, an **Indochina** MAAG worked with first the French and then the **Republic of Vietnam**. It was folded into the U.S. **Military Assistance Command, Vietnam (MACV)** in 1962, as the United States became more directly engaged in the war. A MAAG **Laos** operated from 1955 to 1962, when it was ended because of the terms of the 1962 **Geneva Accords**. This did not terminate American security assistance to Laos in the **secret war**. A MAAG **Cambodia**, but without trainers, operated from 1955 until Prime Minister **Norodom Sihanouk** closed down all U.S. assistance in 1963. In 1950, the Joint United States Military Advisory Group (JUSMAG) arrived in **Thailand**, where it is still active in the framework of Thai–American security cooperation. Even where for political or legal reasons a MAAG as such does not exist in a country receiving security assistance, an organization with a different name but functioning like a MAAG will be in place. For example, in Cambodia from 1971 to 1975, it was a **Military Equipment Delivery Team (MEDT)** and in **Indonesia** from 1966, the U.S. Defense Liaison Group (USDLG).

MILITARY ASSISTANCE COMMAND, VIETNAM (MACV). This was the headquarters controlling all U.S. forces in Vietnam, established 8 February 1962 and terminated 29 March 1973. It was headed successively by U.S. Army generals Paul Harkins, William Westmoreland, Creighton Abrams, and Fredrick Weyand.

MILITARY BASES AGREEMENT (MBA). The 1947 Military Bases Agreement between the United States and the Republic of the **Philippines** was central to the so-called special relationship between the two countries. The American bases were a vital element in the U.S. policy and strategy of the **containment** of communism in Asia. The agreement gave the United States the right to retain the use, free of rent for 99 years, of 16 military bases and another 7 if military necessity required it. The 99-year duration could be extended by agreement of both parties. No third state would be allowed to acquire bases in the Philippines without the consent of both parties, and neither party could unilaterally abrogate the treaty. Of the specified bases, the **Subic Bay Naval Base** and **Clark Air Base** were the most important. Although the bases were to be provided "rent free," both sides understood that U.S. financial and material security assistance to the Philippines could be considered compensation.

As the United States and the Philippine **Commonwealth** government in exile negotiated the restructuring of a postindependence relationship between the two countries, the bases were an important part of the complex of economic, political, and security issues at hand. In June 1944, a joint resolution was passed by the American Congress authorizing the president to keep and hold bases he might consider necessary for the protection of the Philippines and the United States. A parallel resolution was passed by the Commonwealth Congress in July 1945. A preliminary statement outlining the principles of an agreement had already been signed by American president **Harry S. Truman** and his Philippines counterpart, **Sergio Osmeña**, on 14 May 1945.

In the Treaty of General Relations between the United States and the Republic of the Philippines that was part of the 4 July 1946 independence package, the United States gave up all rights of possession, control, jurisdiction, or sovereignty in the Philippines, with one exception: the use of bases and the rights incident to the use that might be agreed to between the two countries. The Philippine Senate ratified the MBA on 26 March 1947 by a vote of 18–0, with three senators absent. The Philippines' acceptance of the derogation of sovereignty represented by the bases was a tradeoff for the American security presence and economic assistance. The implicit defense relationship inherent in the base agreement was made explicit in 1951 by the U.S.–Philippines **Mutual Defense Treaty (MDT)**.

From the outset of the negotiations—and for the life of the agreement—a central issue was that of criminal jurisdiction over American personnel on or off the bases. A compromise was reached in which the United States would have exclusive jurisdiction over offenses committed on base, including over Filipinos, unless both the offending and offended parties were Filipinos. Off base, the United States had extraterritorial jurisdiction in cases in which both the offender and offended were American personnel or the offense had been committed in the performance of actual military duties. In the event that the Philippines had off-base jurisdiction, the accused American military person would be turned over to the nearest base commander to be held pending trial and judgment. The U.S. claim of criminal jurisdiction in the MBA was more expansive than that in the North American Treaty Organization (NATO) Status of Forces Agreement (SOFA) or the Japan SOFA. This confirmed for Filipino nationalists the inequalities in their military relations with the United States.

In subsequent years, numerous modifying amendments and clarifications were made to the MBA as the bases became more strategically important to the United States and Philippine nationalist opposition grew. On 3 July 1956, in a joint statement Philippine president **Ramon Magsaysay** and visiting U.S. vice president **Richard M. Nixon** stated that the United States fully recognized the sovereignty of the Philippines over the bases. In 1957, the United States allowed the Philippine flag to fly alongside the American flag on the bases as a symbolic expression of that sovereignty. In 1958, negotiations between Philippine secretary of foreign affairs Felixberto Serrano and U.S. ambassador **Charles Bohlen** led to the creation of a Mutual Defense Board to deal with issues arising under the MBA. It also provided for the stationing of a Philippine liaison officer at each base as an advisor to the base commander concerning observance of Philippine law and issues arising from Philippine nationals on base, and as a point of contact with Philippine officials.

In 1959, the **Bohlen–Seranno** talks produced further agreements, although not fully official until the exchange of notes between U.S. secretary of state **Dean Rusk** and his Philippine counterpart, Narciso Ramos, in 1966. The United States agreed to consult with the Philippines on operational use of the bases for military combat actions outside of the terms of the MDT or the **Southeast Asia Collective De-**

fense Treaty. Clark Air Base had been covertly used by the **Central Intelligence Agency (CIA)** during the **PRRI–Permesta regional revolts** in Indonesia. The United States also agreed that no long-range missiles would be introduced into the Philippines without prior consultation. Most importantly for the future, the duration and termination requirements of the MBA were amended. It had been agreed to reduce the length of the agreement from 99 to 25 years, but the 25-year clock did not start until the Rusk–Ramos notes were exchanged on 16 September 1966. This made 15 September 1991 a critical date. In a Philippines environment inflamed by killings on the bases and an American concern about Philippine support in the **Vietnam War**, the MBA was amended by executive agreement, bringing the MBA criminal jurisdiction provisions more into line with the NATO and Japanese defense treaty SOFAs.

During the years of the **Ferdinand Marcos** government, questions of status of forces, sovereign Philippine presence, compensation in the form of U.S. assistance, and other details of the relationship continued to be addressed at the working and policy levels. Despite nationalist opposition in the Philippines and dismay at the quality of the Philippine government as expressed in the 1996 **Symington Committee** hearings, the fundamental underpinning seemed secure even though negotiations in 1971, 1974, and 1976 could not fully resolve the questions of jurisdiction and compensation amount or mix. During President **Jimmy Carter**'s administration, the question of **human rights** was introduced into the bilateral dialogue with President Carter's pledge that human rights would be an integral part of the U.S. foreign policy process. This collided with the American desire to maintain the bases in the Philippines. President Marcos made it clear that there could be no successful base negotiation if human rights issues were involved. In the United States, the bases–human rights linkage pitted Assistant Secretary of State for East Asia and the Pacific **Richard Holbrooke** against Assistant Secretary of State for Human Rights and Humanitarian Affairs **Patricia Derian**. American strategic concerns were heightened by an increased Russian naval presence in East Asia and its access to the former U.S. facilities at Cam Ranh Bay in Vietnam. In 1978–1979, negotiations involving Holbrooke and his Filipino counterpart, Secretary of State **Cyrus Vance** and his counterpart, and Vice President **Walter Mondale** and

Imelda Marcos, led to a 1979 amendment to the MBA in which the principles of respect for Philippine sovereignty and unhampered American operational control of the bases were spelled out, along with an increase in the compensation package to $500 million over five years. In order to reach the agreement, the question of criminal jurisdiction was put aside.

Early in the **Reagan** administration, both Vice President **George H. W. Bush** and Defense Secretary Casper Weinberger, on visits to Manila, emphasized the importance of the bases to American strategy and Philippine security. In 1982, President Marcos made a state visit to the United States, and he and President Reagan agreed to hold a new round of base negotiations in 1983. This went more smoothly than in the previous administration, perhaps because the 1979 amendment had removed many contentious issues. The United States agreed to prior consultation on combat operations and agreed to inform the Philippine government on level of forces and weapons systems. Interestingly, the United States also promised to take measures to ensure that any American military, civilians, or dependents would refrain from participating in any political activity in the Philippines. After the assassination of **Benigno Aquino,** the Marcos government went into decline. A stream of senior American officials came to Manila to warn that if reform did not take place, Congress would not vote for the security and economic assistance programs tied to the bases. When the 1984 security assistance budget was passed in Congress, it was in fact reduced and accompanied by a concurrent resolution making future assistance conditional on fair and honest elections. The fraudulent 1986 elections and the popular uprising against Marcos forced the United States to counsel Marcos to leave.

One of the first acts of the new government of President **Corazon Aquino** was to draft a new democratic constitution, which was approved by a margin of 80 percent in a February 1987 referendum. Article II, Section 8, and Article XVIII, Section 25, of the constitution directly related to the bases. The former declared, consistent with its national interest, a Philippine policy of freedom from nuclear weapons in its territory. The latter stated that after the September 1991 expiration of the MBA, any foreign military bases, troops, or facilities shall not be allowed, unless by treaty ratified by the Philippine Senate. Aquino herself had indicated that after 1991 she would keep her options open. This was the background to the 1988 base review, which the United States, looking to the negotiation for the MBA renewal, tried to keep limited. In particular, the United States wished to avoid the nuclear weapons question. An interim agreement was reached that called for a substantial increase in compensation to nearly a half billion dollars a year. The Philippine side called it "rent," but Washington did not accept this interpretation.

The final negotiations on the MBA took place in 1991. The deadline date was 15 September. Special presidential envoy **Richard Armitage** was the American principal, with Foreign Minister Raul Manglapus acting for the Philippines. The urgency that the United States had historically felt about the value of the bases had been eased. The Cold War was over, and Great Power tensions had been reduced. The eruption of Mt. Pinatubo had essentially rendered Clark Air Base unusable for the U.S. Air Force, and the United States took it off the negotiating table while cutting the proposed compensation package by more than a third. Weighing in for the American negotiators was the enormous economic value of the bases to the Philippines. Next to the Philippine government, the United States was the second largest employer in the country. Almost 3 percent of the Philippine gross national product was derived from the bases. To overcome nationalist charges of selling out to American neocolonialism, the government sought $825 million a year in compensation, more than four times what the United States would offer—$203 million for Subic Bay Naval Base. A 10-year agreement was reached essentially on the American terms. This was rejected by the Philippine Senate 12 to 11, after an emotional debate focusing on sovereignty, pride, the non-nuclear constitution, American past support for the Marcos regime, American intervention in the 1989 **Honasan coup**, and the size of the compensation. The government presented the United States with a three-year phase-out program. This was shortened by the Americans to one year, the end of 1992.

MILITARY EQUIPMENT DELIVERY TEAM (MEDT)– CAMBODIA. This was the in-country structure for American military assistance to the National Cambodian Army (FANK). Although the **Church–Cooper amendments** prohibited American military advisors in **Cambodia**, the law required that the delivery of military assistance be monitored. Although lodged in the American embassy, the commander of the MEDT reported to the Commander in Chief Pacific Forces (CINCPAC) in Hawaii. From an original 60 men in January 1971, the MEDT ballooned to over a thousand by 1973. Although technically barred from operational activities, the work took the team members into the field with Cambodian units. Together with a swelling group of military attachés, the U.S. defense establishment in Cambodia came functionally to resemble a **Military Assistance Advisory Group (MAAG)**, even though it could not legally be one.

MONDALE, WALTER F. (1928–). Vice president of the United States (1977—1981) during the administration of President **Jimmy Carter**, Walter "Fritz" Mondale had already served two terms in the U.S. Senate representing Minnesota. In May 1978, Carter sent Mondale to Southeast Asia to reassure a nervous region that the United States still considered it an important interest area. In the **Philippines**, Mondale pressed for the conclusion of the ongoing negotiations for amendments to the U.S. **Military Bases Agreement**. In Indonesia, although **human rights** and **East Timor** were on his agenda, the continuing American security connection and a deal for A-4 airplanes for Indonesia had priority. In **Thailand**, he reaffirmed the American commitment to the obligations of the **Southeast Asia Collective Defense Treaty**. Defeated by President **Ronald Reagan** in the 1984 presidential campaign, Mondale became President **William J. Clinton**'s ambassador to Japan in 1993–1997. In March 1998, Clinton dispatched Mondale to **Indonesia** to press President **Suharto** to fully adopt the restructuring plan demanded by the **International Monetary Fund (IMF)** as part of its support package for Indonesia in the Southeast Asian **financial crisis of 1997–1998**.

MONTGOMERY, GILLESPIE V. (1920–2006). Usually called "Sonny," G. V. Montgomery was a Mississippi Democratic member of the U.S. House of Representatives from 1967 to 1997. He championed the interests of American military veterans of all wars, chairing for 14 years the House Veteran Affairs Committee. From 1975, he became deeply involved in the **Indochina POW/MIA** question. He chaired the House Select Committee on Prisoners of War and Missing in Action, sometimes called the Montgomery Commission, which was the first extra-Pentagon, full-scale investigation into the fate of missing Americans in Indochina. Perhaps its most important finding was that no Americans were being held as prisoners in Indochina. He was a member of the 1977 **Woodcock Mission**, which opened the door to negotiations on the **normalization of relations with Vietnam**. Montgomery made 14 trips to Southeast Asia.

MORO. This was a Spanish label—from "moor"—for the Muslim population, now numbering more than five million, in the **Philippines'**-southern region of Mindanao and the Sulu Archipelago. During Spanish rule, it was the frontier in the battle between Christianity, represented by the Catholic Church, and Islam. After annexation of the Philippines by the United States, and only after years of bitter fighting, the Moro region was "pacified" and brought within the civil law framework of the American administration. Since Philippine independence, the changing demographic balance as northern migrants moved into Moro regions, plantation agriculture, lumbering, and mining all disturbed Moro customary law and traditional land rights as well as adding to religious tensions. The grievances of the Moro People—the **Bangsamoro**—have been politically expressed through separatist movements like the **Moro National Liberation Front (MNLF)** and the **Moro Islamic Liberation Front (MILF)**. They have been further fueled by awareness of the wider Islamic world, including connections to Libya and Islamic radical terrorist groups like **al-Qaeda** and **Jema'ah Islamiyah**, whose tactics have been echoed in the Moro region by the **Abu Sayyaf Group (ASG)**. The Moro insurgencies since the founding of the MNLF in 1969 have claimed more than 120,000 lives.

MORO ISLAMIC LIBERATION FRONT (MILF). The Moro Islamic Liberation Front is the main **Philippine** Muslim separatist organization. It was founded by Salamat Hashim after splitting in 1984 from the mainstream **Moro National Liberation Front (MNLF)**. The MILF rejected the MNLF's willingness to accommodate to a less than independent status in an Autonomous Region of Muslim Mindanao (ARMM). The MILF also professes a more fundamentalist Islamic agenda then the MNLF. The MILF enjoys the support of the majority of the **Moro** people (**Bangsamoro**). Salamat died in 2003 and was succeeded by Al Haj Murad Ebrahim. Since 1997, the MILF has engaged in an on again, off again cease-fire, punctuated by negotiations for a peace agreement with Manila based on Moro self-determination. These have been brokered by **Malaysia** acting for the **Organization of the Islamic Conference (OIC)**. Although the MILF has claimed to oppose international terrorism, both the Philippine government and the United States have accused elements of the MILF of harboring and training **Jema'ah Islamiyah (JI)** and **Abu Sayyaf** terrorists as well as having ties to **al-Qaeda**. In 2003, the United States threatened to officially label the MILF a terrorist organization on its **Foreign Terrorist Organization (FTO)** list. Washington retreated, however, at Manila's behest, recognizing that the consequences would be a breakdown in peace negotiations and a full-scale renewal of the war in the south against the 12,500-man MILF force. Instead, the United States promised full diplomatic and financial support to the peace process if the MILF cut its ties to terrorists. The U.S. **State Department** has also funded the **United States Institute of Peace (USIP)** from 2003 to 2007 to provide support for the peace negotiating process. In a December 2007 Libya-brokered agreement, the MILF agreed to reconcile with the rival MNLF. *See also* WAR ON TERROR.

MORO NATIONAL LIBERATION FRONT (MNLF). The Moro National Liberation Front (MNLF) was the first paramilitary Muslim separatist movement in the southern Philippines. It was established in 1969 and led by Nur Misuari. The MNLF was recognized by the **Organization of the Islamic Conference (OIC)** as the legitimate representative of the **Moro** people (**Bangsamoro**) and enjoyed as well the political support of Libya and the sympathy of the Philippines' Muslim neighbors, **Indonesia** and **Malaysia**. A 1976 peace agreement brokered in Tripoli during the administration of **Ferdinand Marcos** collapsed. In 1987, during the administration of **Corazon Aquino**, a new agreement, the "Jeddah Accord," was reached. Finally, in 1996, during the administration of President **Fidel Ramos**, a peace agreement that reflected the substance of the failed Tripoli agreement was initialed between the Philippine government and the MNLF, with Indonesia facilitating the negotiations for the OIC. Even as the MNLF negotiated with Manila, hard-line conservatives broke away from Nur

Misuari's leadership and formed the **Moro Islamic Liberation Front (MILF)** in 1984. While the MNLF was being pacified, the MILF carried on the armed struggle and eclipsed the MNLF as the standard bearer for the Bangsamoro. After 2001, President **Gloria Macapagal-Arroyo** targeted the MILF as the primary interlocutor for the Moros and, supported by the United States, since 2003 has pursued peace negotiations with it. A lower level tripartite dialogue among Manila, the MNLF, and the OIC has been stymied by the increasing militancy of some factions of the MNLF, which allegedly have been penetrated by the **Jema'ah Islamiyah (JI)** and the **Abu Sayyaf Group (ASG)**. Indonesia still chairs the OIC effort to implement the 1996 pact. Nur Misuari's own influence over the course of events seems diminished. He finished third in the 2007 election for governor of Sulu Province. In a December 2007 Libya-brokered agreement, the MNLF agreed to reconcile with the rival MILF. *See also* WAR ON TERROR.

MUSKIE, EDMUND S. (1914–1996). A U.S. senator from Maine, Edmund "Ed" Muskie resigned his seat in 1980 when asked by President **Jimmy Carter** to fill the secretary of state vacancy created by the resignation of **Cyrus Vance**. Muskie had been the losing Democratic vice-presidential candidate in 1968 and had unsuccessfully tried for the Democratic presidential nomination in 1972. He served as secretary of state for eight months. In that time, however, he left an imprint on U.S. relations in Southeast Asia by forcing the Carter administration to move further and faster on support for **Thailand** and the **Association of Southeast Asian Nations (ASEAN)** in the **Third Indochina War**. Against White House and **State Department** advice, he attended the June 1980 ASEAN foreign ministers meeting, which was very much concerned about the Thai–Vietnamese standoff on the **Cambodia** border. Denouncing the Vietnamese "aggression," Muskie gave Thailand an unqualified pledge of American support if **Vietnam** invaded Thailand. He also promised speedy delivery of an enhanced American military assistance package. He placed American political support squarely behind ASEAN's efforts to prevent the international community from recognizing the legitimacy of the Vietnam-installed **People's Republic of Kampuchea (PRK)** government in Phnom Penh. This firm American line was maintained and amplified in the succeeding **Reagan** administration.

MUTUAL DEFENSE TREATY (MDT), U.S.–PHILIPPINE. The 1951 U.S.–Philippine Mutual Defense Treaty was designed to assuage **Philippine** concerns about the Japanese Peace Treaty, which Manila felt might pave the way for Japanese remilitarization. Its terms were parallel to the collective mutual defense treaty signed by the United States, Australia, and New Zealand—the ANZUS pact. Both Australia and New Zealand had similar worries about a future Japan, with which the United States was also signing a mutual defense treaty. In the Philippines MDT, each party agreed that an armed attack in the Pacific area on either of the parties would be dangerous to its own peace and safety. This was further defined to include an armed attack on the metropolitan territory of the parties or on the island territories under its jurisdiction in the Pacific or on its armed forces, public vessels, or aircraft in the Pacific. In case of attack, they declared that they would act to meet the common dangers in accordance with their constitutional processes. The treaty was indefinite in duration. Either party could terminate it upon one year's notice. The MDT was different from the ANZUS pact and the U.S.–Japanese defense treaty in that in those instruments termination had to be agreed upon by all parties.

For implementation purposes the United States has defined the Philippine metropolitan territory as the land areas and adjacent waters ceded to the United States by Spain in the **Treaty of Paris** (1898) and subsequent Treaty of Washington (1900). For the United States, this excluded Philippine claims to **Sabah**, the British North Borneo territory that later was incorporated in **Malaysia**. It seemingly leaves ambiguous whether the contemporary Philippine claims in the **South China Sea** dispute are covered by the MDT as island territories under Philippine jurisdiction or whether clashes between Philippine naval or air units in the South China Sea zone are covered. Even though the U.S.–Philippine **Military Bases Agreement (MBA)** was terminated in 1991, the MDT remains in force and is one of the juridical bases of the **Balikatan** U.S.–Philippine military exercises, since it called for the parties separately or jointly in self-help or mutual aid to maintain and develop their individual and collective military capacities to resist armed attacks. The presence since 2002 of the American **Joint Special Operations Task Force–Philippines (JSOTF–P)** has also been justified by reference to the MDT.

MUTUAL LOGISTICS SUPPORT AGREEMENT (MLSA), U.S.–PHILIPPINE. In 2002, the United States and the Philippines signed a five-year Mutual Logistics Support Agreement (MLSA) that provides for reciprocal provision of logistic support, supplies, and services for joint training purposes. It allows the prepositioning of U.S. supplies and equipment and provides access to Philippine transport, repair facilities, and other requirements to enhance greater interoperability, readiness, and effectiveness. As such, according to the Philippines defense secretary, it enhanced the capability of the Philippines to cope with threats to national security and to fight terrorism. The Philippine MLSA was viewed as complementing the **Visiting Forces Agreement** and as such caused a storm of protest from the same opponents. It was condemned as a first step toward new American bases in the Philippines and unconstitutional. President **Gloria Macapagal-Arroyo**'s government insisted that the MLSA was rooted in the 1951 **Mutual Defense Treaty (MDT)**, and since it was not a separate treaty, it did not have to be submitted to the Philippine Senate. Secretary of State **Colin Powell** in Manila in August 2002 addressed the furor, categorically denying that the United States was looking for bases or a new permanent presence in the Philippines or Southeast Asia.

MUTUAL SECURITY AGREEMENT. During the Cold War the terms and conditions for the provision of American military assistance were contained in bilateral mutual security agreements. An article in these agreements required that U.S. assistance was to be used by the recipient for the "development of its own defensive strength and the defensive strength of the free world." For the United States the "free world" meant the countries enlisted in the effort to contain communist expansion. The agreements also provided for American military personnel to be in-country to facilitate and monitor the use of the assistance. These were **military assistance advisory groups (MAAG)**. The negotiation of such an agreement caused the collapse of a government in **Indonesia** in 1953 and was burdensome for the post-1954 neutralized governments of **Cambodia** and **Laos**. *See also* CONTAINMENT.

MYANMAR. *See* BURMA.

– N –

NARCOTICS PRODUCTION AND TRAFFICKING. Southeast Asia has long been a problem area for the United States as a major source of narcotics production and trafficking. A congressionally mandated annual *International Narcotics Control Strategy Report* (*INCSR*), prepared by the **State Department**'s Bureau of International Narcotics and Law Enforcement Affairs (INL), assesses the efforts of foreign nations to combat the illicit drug trade and related money laundering. In Southeast Asia the historic concern has been poppy cultivation, the opium from which is processed into heroin. Since the 1990s, the explosive growth of the manufacture of methamphetamines, particularly in the Burmese border areas, has given new urgency to the U.S. cooperative efforts in the region to eliminate production and interdict transit in the illicit drug trade.

The major poppy growing areas in Southeast Asia have been concentrated in the tri-border region of **Burma**, **Laos**, and **Thailand**, the so-called Golden Triangle. Burma is Southeast Asia's largest producer of opium. It is estimated that more than 90 percent of Southeast Asia's heroin comes from Burma. Although locally significant, it is a relatively small share of global production, being, for example, only 8 percent of Afghanistan's production. The cultivators of poppy are largely minority ethnic groups whose single largest source of income is opium. Opium production was the source of the wealth that kept Burmese drug lord Khun Sa's Shan United Army in the field against the Burmese army. The middlemen have been Thailand- and Yunnan-based smugglers. American efforts to work with the Burmese government on the elimination of poppy cultivation and heroin production are hampered by the fact that American counternarcotics assistance to Burma was suspended after the imposition of sanctions in 1988. Indirect support is given by U.S. funding contributions to the United Nations Office of Drug Control (UNODC) programs in Burma.

Laos ranks behind Burma in opium production but has made substantial inroads in local production through its crop eradication programs. During the **secret war** in Laos, opium trade became part of the funding for General **Vang Pao**'s ethnic **Hmong** troops in the field against the **Pathet Lao** and **Viet Minh**. Critics of the war charged the **Central Intelligence Agency (CIA)** and particularly its proprietary airline, **Air America**, with facilitating the transit of opium. Bilateral counternarcotics cooperation with Laos began in 1989. Up to 2005, the United States has contributed $41 million to the Lao government's counternarcotics efforts through the State Department counternarcotics program as well as the U.S. contributions to fund UNODC programs. Even as opium production has been substantially reduced, it is feared that Laos will become a new center for methamphetamine transit.

Large-scale opium production in Thailand has been eradicated. Thailand has cooperated with the United States in trying to stem the flow of methamphetamines from Burma since its own public is at risk. A mid-1990s American–Thai joint counternarcotics operation, code named "Tiger Trap," on the Thailand–Shan State border seriously disrupted Khun Sa's operation. The drug center moved to the Wa and Kokang minorities, with new transit routes through **China**. The United Wa State Army became the largest single producer of opium in Burma and the largest manufacturer of methamphetamines in Southeast Asia. In 2002, a tablet form of Wa-produced methamphetamine called "yaba" appeared in the United States. The middlemen were Lao and Thai nationals, with distribution networks in Southeast Asian ethnic minority communities resettled in the United States. In January 2005, eight Wa drug kingpins were indicted in a New York federal court for their activities. A 2003 Thai "war on drugs" by the **Thaksin Shinawatra** government forced some Thai-based activities back into Laos. The extrajudicial killings of alleged drug dealers in the Thai counternarcotics campaign became a **human rights** issue in Thailand's relations with the United States.

The Department of Justice Drug Enforcement Agency (DEA) is the principal U.S. field force in counternarcotics activities. It has offices for intelligence collection and enforcement cooperation throughout Southeast Asia, with agents in Bangkok, Chiang Mai and Udorn in Thailand, Vientiane, Kuala Lumpur, Singapore, Manila, and Yangon (Rangoon). According to the DEA, its Burmese counterparts have been extremely cooperative. The DEA admits that the goals of its mission in Burma cannot be met because of U.S. law and policy toward Burma—the sanction regime. In the annual *Presidential Determinations on Major Drug Transit or Major Illicit Drug Producing Countries*, required since 2003 by Congress, Laos and Burma were the only Southeast Asian countries listed in 2006. Burma was one of two countries singled out as having "failed demonstrably" in meeting their obligations to fight drug trafficking.

NATIONAL LEAGUE FOR DEMOCRACY (NLD). The National League for Democracy is the umbrella democratic opposition movement to the ruling military junta in **Burma**, the **State Peace and Development Council (SPDC)**. Arising amid the antimilitary violence of 1988 in Burma, with **Aung San Suu Kyi** as its leader it swept the 1990 legislative elections. The junta retaliated by nullifying the elections and jailing hundreds of opposition figures, including Aung San Suu Kyi. Many other NLD activists fled to **Thailand** to organize international resistance to the junta. In 2006, estimates were that there were still more than a thousand political prisoners in Burma. The junta considers the NLD to be illegal and shut it out of the new constitutional drafting process that began in 2003. The United States accepts the results of the 1990 election to be a valid expression of Burmese democratic will and insists that the NLD must participate in the restoration of democracy in Burma. In expanding economic sanctions against the military regime, the U.S. Congress, in the **Burmese Freedom and Democracy Act of 2003**, recognized the NLD as the legitimate representative of the Burmese people.

NATIONAL LEAGUE OF POW/MIA FAMILIES. Led by long-serving executive director **Ann Mills Griffiths**, the National League of POW/MIA families is the oldest and most influential private group seeking the fullest accounting of American prisoners of war and missing in action **(POW/MIA)** in Southeast Asia. Founded in the early 1960s as an ad hoc support group for the families of MIAs, the League incorporated and became an important lobby pressing the government to make the POW/MIA issue central to U.S. policy toward relations with postwar **Vietnam** and **Laos**. During the administration of President **Ronald Reagan**, the League became a virtual partner of the government through its liaison with **Richard Childress**, the point man on the issue in the National Security Council. In the postnormalization of relations with Vietnam, the League has continued to press both Washington and Hanoi to maintain the commitment to resolve outstanding POW/MIA cases.

NATIONAL LIBERATION FRONT (NLF). This is the common acronym for the National Front for the Liberation of South Vietnam (NFLSV), the communist-organized and -directed united front group in **South Vietnam**, which claimed to be an indigenous movement of South Vietnamese anti-imperialists and nationalists. Emerging in December 1960, it presented an ostensibly independent southern leadership alternative to the U.S.-backed **Republic of Vietnam**. Although claiming political autonomy and tactical control over the **Viet Cong** guerrillas, the NLF worked in close coordination with the communist leadership in the north and the People's Army of Vietnam (PAVN). In 1969, the NLF was replaced as a negotiating tool in the **Paris peace negotiations** by the **Provisional Revolutionary Government (PRG)** of South Vietnam.

NEWMONT MINING CORPORATION. In August 2005, American executives of the Denver, Colorado-based Newmont Mining Corporation were put on trial in Menado, **Indonesia**. The company, the world's largest gold miner, was charged with polluting Buyat Bay in North Sulawesi with toxic wastes from its mining operation and poisoning local villagers. The mine had operated from 1996 until it closed in August 2005. The fact that an indictment was drawn chilled potential investors in Indonesian mining. It reflected both a new concern for **environmental issues** and the changed legal framework in Indonesia after decentralization of authority as part of democratization. In 2006, Newmont settled a $133 million civil suit lodged by the Indonesian government for $30 million, paid out over 10 years. A criminal trial against Newmont executives ended in an acquittal in 2007.

NEWSOM, DAVID D. (1918–). A career Foreign Service Officer (FSO), David Newsom began his career in 1947 and retired in 1981 as undersecretary of state for political affairs, the highest post for an FSO. Between 1974 and 1977, he was U.S. ambassador to **Indonesia**. It was his task to manage in Jakarta the problem created for the United States by the 1975 **Indonesian invasion of East Timor**. At stake in the immediate aftermath of the communist victories in **Indochina** was the vitality of American security interests in Indonesia. As it became clear that Indonesia was preparing to incorporate the former Portuguese territory of East Timor by force, Newsom advised Secretary of State **Henry Kissinger** that the United States should maintain policy silence. He informed the Indonesian government that the use of American-supplied weapons would violate American law and could provoke congressional reaction. He explained, however, that the administration understood Indonesia's position. In advance of the visit to Jakarta by President **Gerald Ford** and Kissinger, Newsom asked that any attack not take place until after they had left the country. When the predicted congressional furor occurred and sanctions were threatened, Ambassador Newsom began contingency planning to circumvent any congressional ban on military assistance to Indonesia. After Indonesia, Newsom went to the **Philippines** (1977–1978) before returning to Washington. After leaving the State Department, Ambassador Newsom was a professor and director of the Institute for the Study of Diplomacy at Georgetown University and a professor at the University of Virginia.

NE WIN (1911–2002). Military strongman General Ne Win seized power in **Burma** in 1962, toppling the second, democratically elected, **U Nu** government. Ne Win was one of the Burmese "30 comrades," including **Aung San** and U Nu, who slipped out of British Burma for military training in Japan. As one of the leaders of the Burma Independence Army, Major Ne Win came back with the invading Japanese in 1942. He went into revolt against the Japanese in 1944. At independence from Great Britain in 1948, he was named army head and defense minister. His forces were engaged in constant warfare against communist and ethnic insurgents. In 1958, elected prime minister U Nu stepped down, and Ne Win became a caretaker prime minister until a new government could be elected. U Nu came back in 1960, only to be ousted by Ne Win. Since then, Burma has been ruled by the military. Ne Win instituted the "Burmese way to socialism," which became a way to poverty and oppression in a one-party state with the military as its foundation. Forced to the background in 1988 by an internal army coup, his "retirement" was met by antigovernment, prodemocracy demonstrations that were crushed by the military and prompted the emergence of **Aung San Suu Kyi** as the symbol of Burmese democratic resistance. In early 2002, an ailing Ne Win saw members of his family arrested, tried, and sentenced to death for corruption and plotting a coup.

NIXON, RICHARD M. (1913–1994). Inaugurated as 37th president of the United States in 1969, Richard M. Nixon resigned the office in the wake of the Watergate Scandal on 9 August 1974. First a California congressman (1947–1950) and then a senator (1951–1952), Nixon was elected and served two terms as vice president during the administration of President **Dwight D. Eisenhower**. In 1956, Vice President Nixon was sent to the **Philippines** and the **Republic of Vietnam** to reinforce the administration's message of **containment** in Southeast Asia. In 1960, he was the Republican nominee for president but was defeated by **John F. Kennedy**. In running against Democratic candidate Hubert Humphrey, President **Lyndon B. Johnson**'s vice president, in 1968, Nixon capitalized on the mounting American opposition to the course of the **Vietnam War**, claiming he had a plan to end it.

Nixon chose **Henry A. Kissinger** as his national security advisor. Kissinger centralized critical decision making in the White House, relegating Secretary of State **William P. Rogers** to the background. In a clear break with the Vietnam War strategy of his predecessor, the enunciation of the **Nixon doctrine** set limits on American security commitments to friends and allies. Even while claiming to shift the burden of military defense to the Republic of Vietnam through the process of **Vietnamization**, the Nixon administration was anxious to demonstrate that it would remain a credible security partner. Washington was particularly solicitous of **Thailand**'s crucial role of support for the United States in the **Vietnam War** and the **secret war** in Laos. Nixon traveled to Thailand in July 1969 to assure the Thais of America's commitment to their defense. The United States was sympathetic to Thai requests for greater military and economic assistance as well as import relief for the Thai textile industry. The **Philippines** also received special attention as part of the U.S.–Philippine "special relationship." Early in his first term Nixon, with Rogers and Kissinger, traveled to Manila to meet with President **Ferdinand Marcos** and his wife, **Imelda Marcos**. As criticism of the Marcos presidential dictatorship mounted in Congress, Nixon rallied behind the

Philippine couple. Before he became president, Nixon had already met **Indonesia**'s President **Suharto** on a private visit arranged by U.S. Ambassador **Marshall Green**. The Nixon administration spearheaded the financial rescue of Indonesia after the fall of **Sukarno** in the organization of the **Intergovernmental Group on Indonesia (IGGI)**. At Nixon's urgings, and through a Kissinger back-channel, the Suharto government supported U.S. diplomacy backing the **Lon Nol** government in **Cambodia**. *See also* NIXON–PHAM VAN DONG MESSAGE; PARIS PEACE NEGOTIATIONS; VIETNAM.

NIXON DOCTRINE (GUAM DOCTRINE). On 25 July 1969, on the first leg of a Pacific trip to the **Philippines, Thailand, Vietnam, Indonesia**, India, and Pakistan, President **Richard M. Nixon** announced a new strategy for American security commitments. It consisted of three statements of policy: The United States will keep its treaty commitments; the United States will provide a shield in the event a nuclear power threatens an ally or a nation whose survival is vital to the security of the United States and the security of the region as a whole; and in case of other types of aggression, the United States, when requested, will furnish appropriate military and economic assistance, but will look to the nation directly threatened to assume the primary responsibility for its defense. The doctrine provided a principled justification for the policy of **Vietnamization**, that is, the replacement of American combat forces with Vietnamese. The context was the American public's frustration over the **Vietnam War**. An unintended consequence was to create in Southeast Asia apprehensions about U.S. resolve.

NIXON–PHAM VAN DONG MESSAGE. In a message dated 1 February 1973, President **Richard M. Nixon** secretly communicated to Vietnamese Prime Minister **Pham Van Dong** the terms of U.S. participation without any political conditions in the postwar reconstruction of **Vietnam**, as promised in Article 21 of the **Paris Agreement**. The message was declassified and released in May 1977. Nixon stated U.S. willingness to undertake programs falling in the range of $3.25 billion of grant aid over five years, and food and commodity aid in the range of $1 to 1.5 billion. In the initial diplomatic phases of the process of **normalization of U.S. relations with Vietnam**, the

Vietnamese government insisted that the U.S. assistance was reparations for the war and linked delivery of the assistance to cooperation
on the prisoner of war/missing in action (**POW/MIA**) issue, a position Washington rejected.

NOLTING, FREDERICK E. (1911–1989). Frederick "Fritz" Nolting,
a career Foreign Service Officer, had no Asian experience when sent
by President **John F. Kennedy** to be U.S. ambassador to **South Vietnam** in 1961 to replace Ambassador **Elbridge Durbrow**, who had
been critical of the **Ngo Dinh Diem** regime. Nolting was unwilling to
press the regime for reform. The fact that Nolting's optimistic reporting on the situation in Vietnam was in sharp variance to that of
the international press led to antagonistic relations between the
American embassy and the press corps. Nolting's conciliatory approach to the shortcomings of the Diem government, particularly the
roles of Diem's brother-in-law Ngo Dinh Nu and his wife, was mir-
rored by the military optimism of U.S. military commander General
Paul Harkins. After the Buddhist crisis of spring 1963 destroyed the
credibility of the embassy's position, Nolting left Saigon, to be replaced by **Henry Cabot Lodge**, who supported the coup that toppled
Diem. Nolting later remarked that the initial failure in Vietnam was
American connivance in the **Diem coup**, leading the United States
into a "military trap." In retirement, Nolting was on the faculty of the
University of Virginia, of which he was an alumnus. Nolting's defense of his Vietnam mission is his memoir, *From Trust to Tragedy*.

NONALIGNED MOVEMENT (NAM). Formally established at the
1961 Belgrade first nonaligned summit meeting of 25 nations, the
NAM's roots are in the Bandung, **Indonesia, Asian–African Conference** in 1955. Its original ideological cement grew out of the experience of decolonization and the desire to avoid involvement in the
Great Power politics of the Cold War through alliance, security agreements, or bases. Its program institutionalized the **Bandung Principles**. From its outset, the United States viewed the NAM with suspicion. Secretary of State John Foster Dulles considered it to be a
stalking horse for the Soviet Union. **Burma**, **Cambodia**, and **Indonesia** were founding members, represented respectively by **U Nu**,
Norodom Sihanouk, and **Sukarno**. As its membership grew and

seemed dominated by members sympathetic to the Soviet Union's international positions in the Cold War, the original cohesion disappeared. The fact that Cuba and **Vietnam**, with their security ties to the USSR, were among the leaders of the NAM, indicated a double standard for nonalignment. Burma, in fact, quit the NAM. The NAM was seriously fractured by the Soviet invasion of Afghanistan in 1979 and the socialist bloc's support for Vietnam's invasion and occupation of Cambodia in the **Third Indochina War**.

In the post–Cold War era, the NAM grew to 116 members. All 10 **Association of Southeast Asian Nations (ASEAN)** members belong, including American allies and security partners the **Philippines**, **Thailand**, and **Singapore**. When Indonesia chaired the movement between 1992 and 1995, President **Suharto**, searching for a new relevance for the organization, shifted its emphasis from politics to economic and social development. Programmatically, there is little to distinguish the NAM from the even larger United Nations caucus of the "**Group of 77**"—actually 133—in terms of the agenda. The triennial summits, however, still provide a platform to oppose American policies. Prime Minister **Mahathir Mohammad** of **Malaysia**, hosting the 2003 summit, opened it with a blistering attack on U.S. "coercive unilateralism," declaring to his approving audience that "no single nation shall be allowed to police the world."

NORMAL TRADE RELATIONS (NTR). This is the term used since 1998 in place of "most favored nation" (MFN) treatment. It means that the United States applies the same nondiscriminatory tariff on products imported from all countries with NTR status, which are basically the member countries of the **World Trade Organization (WTO)**.

NORMALIZATION OF RELATIONS WITH VIETNAM. For more than 20 years after the 23 January 1973 signing of the **Paris Agreement** ending the **Vietnam War**, the United States and the **Socialist Republic of Vietnam (SRV)** were engaged in a process of defining their postwar relationship. The stakes for Vietnam were high. As long as the United States refused to recognize it in a normal diplomatic fashion and maintained the punitive economic sanctions of an embargo, frozen assets, and barriers to access to international financial institutions (IFI), Vietnam's reconstruction and economic development would be severely handicapped. During the process of normalization, fundamental changes in the regional geostrategic structure—the collapse of the Soviet Union, the rise of China, and the regional focus on the **Association of Southeast Asian Nations (ASEAN)**—further disadvantaged Vietnam in its posture toward the United States. From the outset of negotiations, two fundamental issues dogged the prospects for a quick reconciliation: the prisoner of war/missing in action **(POW/MIA)** question and the Vietnamese demand for reparations.

In the Paris peace agreement, the United States undertook "to contribute to the healing of the wounds of war and to postwar reconstruction of the Democratic Republic of Vietnam and throughout Indochina." The terms of U.S. assistance were spelled out by President **Richard M. Nixon** in a secret message to Vietnamese prime minister **Pham Van Dong**. The total package of proposed assistance was more than $5 billion. This was the basis of the Vietnamese demand for the payment of the "reparations" as a precondition to assistance in accounting for the POW/MIAs. From the U.S. point of view, Vietnam's massive violations of the agreement negated any moral obligation that might be implied by the Nixon promise. Furthermore, a hostile Congress specifically prohibited any economic assistance to Vietnam, **Laos**, or **Cambodia**. The United States also prevented the SRV from taking a seat in the **United Nations (UN)** in 1976.

In 1977, the incoming administration of President **Jimmy Carter** started afresh. It withdrew American objections to the SRV in the United Nations. In March 1977, President Carter sent to Hanoi a high-level delegation led by **Leonard Woodcock** to try to convince the Vietnamese that it would be in their interest to be forthcoming on the POW/MIA question. The **Woodcock mission** returned feeling that the Vietnamese had become more flexible on the reparations issue. A month later, Assistant Secretary of State for East Asian and Pacific Affairs **Richard Holbrooke** found that this was not in fact the case. Meeting in Paris with his Vietnamese opposite number, Holbrooke was confronted again by the reparations demand. When the Vietnamese subsequently published the **Nixon–Pham Van Dong** correspondence, Congress made it clear that there would be no money for Vietnam. Negotiations were also compromised by the unmasking of a

Vietnamese spy who was passing information on the U.S. positions to the Vietnamese in the UN and Paris. By the end of 1977, the Carter initiative had reached a dead end, stymied by Vietnamese preconditions and National Security Advisor **Zbigniew Brzezinski**'s concern that normalization of relations with Vietnam would jeopardize the more important **China** relationship. Vietnam deputy foreign minister **Nguyen Co Thach** made one last effort in September 1978. Meeting Assistant Secretary of State Holbrooke in New York, he dropped all preconditions to normalization. But the China card was played by Brzezinski.

The Vietnamese invasion and occupation of **Cambodia** in December 1978—the **Third Indochina War**—added new American conditions to normalization. In addition to President **Ronald Reagan**'s commitment to a full accounting for the POW/MIAs, his administration tied normalization to the future of Cambodia. A breakthrough on the POW/MIA question was signaled after a 1987 visit to Hanoi by the **Vessey Mission**. Vietnamese cooperation with the work of the **Joint Casualty Resolution Center (JCRC)** was more forthcoming. In April 1989, Vietnam announced that all of its troops would be out of Cambodia by September. In September 1990, U.S. secretary of state **James Baker** met his counterpart, Nguyen Co Thach, in New York to discuss Cambodia and the POW/MIA question. In 1991, Assistant Secretary of State for East Asia and Pacific Affairs **Richard Solomon** presented Vietnam with a "road map" to normalization. It promised a gradual relaxation of the **trade** embargo and steps toward an eventual normalization of diplomatic relations, contingent on continued Vietnamese cooperation on POW/MIA questions; acceptance and implementation of the Cambodian peace plan, endorsed by the five permanent members of the UN Security Council; and Hanoi's influence on the Vietnam-backed government in Phnom Penh to sign off on it.

As the political impediments to normalization were being overcome by the adoption of the **comprehensive political settlement in Cambodia**, a gradual thawing of the bilateral U.S.–Vietnamese relationship occurred, despite hard-line opposition from some POW/MIA interest groups. The U.S. steps, implicitly if not formally, conformed to the "road map." A new impetus on the U.S. side came from the American business community, which did not want to be shut out of Vietnam as new resources became available to Vietnam through international sources of assistance. In November 1991, the administration of President **George H. W. Bush** eased travel restrictions to Vietnam for Americans. A year later, the Bush administration responded to new positive acts by Vietnam on the POW/MIA question by allowing American companies to open representative offices in Vietnam and to sign contracts for implementation after the embargo was lifted. It was left, however, for President **William J. Clinton** to finish the process of normalization. Holding to the "road map" and pressing Hanoi on the POW/MIA question, he continued to relax economic sanctions. In July 1993, he approved IFI financing for Vietnam, and in September he allowed U.S. companies to participate in development projects funded by IFIs. Recognizing that "tangible results" had been achieved on the POW/MIA question, and with congressional approval, President Clinton lifted the Vietnam embargo on 3 February 1994. An agreement on liaison offices in their respective capitals was reached by the two countries on 4 May. The offices were opened in December. On 11 July 1995, President Clinton and Prime Minister Vo Van Kiet of Vietnam announced that diplomatic relations had been established. *See also* CHILDRESS, RICHARD; HUMPHREY–TRUONG ESPIONAGE CASE; LORD, WINSTON; NATIONAL LEAGUE OF POW/MIA FAMILIES; NIXON–PHAM VAN DONG MESSAGE; SIGUR, GASTON.

NORTH VIETNAM. For purposes of the 1954 armistice in the **First Indochina War**—the French colonial war—the 1954 **Geneva Conference** geographically divided Vietnam between north and south on the line of the 17th parallel of latitude and created a demilitarized zone (DMZ). This was not conceived of as a permanent territorial boundary, but rather only as a temporary one for cessation of hostilities and regroupment of forces prior to a national election that would unify the country. The election never happened, and the line became a de facto international boundary between two competing states: in the north, the **Democratic Republic of Vietnam (DRV)**, and in the south, the **Republic of Vietnam (RVN)**. In the course of the **Vietnam War**, or **Second Indochina War**, the geographic division was identified with the political division, so North Vietnam became synonymous with the DRV and **South Vietnam** with the RVN, the terms being used interchangeably. In territorial size, North Vietnam had an area of 61,293 square miles (158,750 square kilometers), slightly smaller than the south, encompassing the old French divisions of Tonkin and the northern part of Annam.

– O –

OFFICE OF STRATEGIC SERVICES (OSS). The Office of Strategic Services was the U.S. World War II intelligence and covert special operations agency, established in June 1942. Headed by **William J. Donovan**, the OSS had operational units in all theaters of the war. In the China–Burma–India Theater and the Ceylon-headquartered Southeast Asia Command, the OSS supported behind the lines guerrilla resistance in **Burma** and **Malaya**. Its "Mission Deer" liaised with **Ho Chi Minh**'s **Viet Minh** anti-Japanese guerrillas in northern **Vietnam**. It was through the OSS that **Ho Chi Minh** made his 1945 overtures to the United States, including **Ho Chi Minh's letter to President Harry S. Truman**. In **Thailand**, OSS agents promoted contacts with the underground **Free Thai** movement and provided intelligence assistance to American diplomacy that sought to soften the Anglo–Thai peace settlement. The OSS Research and Analysis branch, staffed by academics and country experts, perfected the tools of strategic intelligence. They produced the first comprehensive analyses of nationalist and insurgent forces in Southeast Asia. President **Harry S. Truman** terminated the OSS at the end of 1945. Some elements remained intact in the War Department until the 1947 creation of the **Central Intelligence Agency (CIA)**.

OPEN SOCIETY INSTITUTE. The **George Soros**–backed Open Society Institute is a private grant-making foundation that has 50 programs. The mission is to shape public policy to promote democracy; **human rights**; and legal, social, and economic reform. It has grant-making activity in eight Southeast Asian countries. **Indonesia** has the greatest funding priority, with more than half of the regional grants going to Indonesian programs in justice, human rights, local governance, pluralism, media, and capacity building. Even though the Open Society Institute cannot work in **Burma**, its Burma Project, supporting advocacy efforts to promote democratic change, is second only to Indonesia in priority.

OPERATION ENDURING FREEDOM (OEF). This was the name given to the American-led multinational coalition, counterterrorist military response to the 11 September 2001 attacks on the World Trade Center and the Pentagon. Initiated in October 2001, the major combat objective was Afghanistan. The United States also sought global cooperation in disrupting terrorist networks in the **war on terror**. In Southeast Asia, U.S. counterterrorism assistance to the **Philippines** was deployed under the rubric Operation Enduring Freedom–Philippines (OEF–P).

ORDERLY DEPARTURE PROGRAM (ODP). The Orderly Departure Program began in 1979 with the cooperation of the **Socialist Republic of Vietnam (SRV)** to provide safe and legal exit from Vietnam for immigration into the United States, even as waves of Vietnamese **refugees**, the so-called **boat people**, were flowing into Southeast Asia. The ODP operated from the U.S. embassy in Bangkok and an office in Ho Chi Minh City (previously Saigon). The Bangkok office closed in 1999. More than a half million Vietnamese processed by the ODP left for the United States as refugees, immigrants, or parolees. Family reunification was a major criterion of eligibility. Other groups included Amerasian children and immediate family, former U.S. government employees and immediate families, and released detainees from "reeducation" camps. The Humanitarian Resettlement Section of the U.S. consulate in Ho Chi Minh City continues the work begun under the ODP, with new legislative authority.

ORGANIZATION OF THE ISLAMIC CONFERENCE (OIC). The organization of the Islamic Conference is a 57-member intergovernmental organization of Islamic or Muslim majority states that seeks to speak with a single voice on issues affecting Muslims worldwide. Established in 1969, its secretariat is located in Jeddah. The Southeast Asian member nations are **Brunei**, **Malaysia**, and **Indonesia**. **Thailand** has observer status. The OIC's primary organs are the triennial Conference of Kings and Heads of States and Governments—the so-called Islamic Summit—and the annual Islamic Conference of

Foreign Ministers. The OIC's agenda in Southeast Asia includes the ongoing Muslim insurgencies in Thailand and the **Philippines**.

OSMEÑA, SERGIO, SR. (1878–1961). Sergio Osmeña was second only to **Manuel Quezon** in the quest for Philippine independence. He was a member of the first Philippine Assembly from 1907 to 1922 and from 1916 its speaker. He was elected to the Philippine Senate in 1923. With **Manuel Roxas**, Osmeña had been an advocate of the 1932 **Hare–Hawes–Cutting** independence bill. With **Manuel Quezon** in opposition, it was defeated in the Philippine Congress. It was superseded by the only slightly changed 1934 **Tydings–McDuffie Act**, which Quezon took credit for. In 1935, Osmeña was elected **Commonwealth of the Philippines** vice president while Quezon was president. In February 1942, Osmeña left the Philippines with Quezon and General **Douglas MacArthur**. He succeeded to the presidency of the commonwealth government in exile on President Manuel Quezon's death in 1944. Returning to the Philippines, President Osmeña faced Roxas in the 1946 presidential election. Roxas, who had been personally cleared by MacArthur of the charge of collaborationist activities during the Japanese occupation, won the election.

– P –

PACIFIC CHARTER, 1954. In addition to the **Southeast Asia Collective Defense Treaty (Manila Pact)**, the September 1954 **Manila Conference**, at the urging of **Philippine** president **Ramon Magsaysay**, adopted the Pacific Charter. Dated 8 September 1954, its signatories were Australia, France, New Zealand, Pakistan, the **Philippines**, **Thailand**, Great Britain, and the United States. Magsaysay had been concerned about the imperialist backgrounds of some of the signers of the defense agreement. In the Charter, the parties pledged to uphold the principles of equal rights and self-determination of peoples and the promotion of self-government and independence of all countries, "whose peoples desire it and are able to undertake its responsibilities." The last condition had not been part of the Philippines' original draft and was inserted at the insistence of Britain, France, Australia, and New Zealand.

PACIFIC COMMUNITY. On 7 July 1993, in a speech at Tokyo's Waseda University, the new American president, **William J. Clinton**, announced a vision of a Pacific Community, reflecting the post–Cold War international environment in East Asia and the Pacific, in which the United States would be at the center of a trading system whose growth would determine the stability and prosperity of the region. For the United States, the historic geostrategic importance of the Asia Pacific was now matched by its geoeconomic significance. President Clinton stated that the architecture of such a community rested on three pillars: economic growth, democracy, and security. These three interest areas provided a context for American relations in the region, replacing the conflict scenario of the Cold War. The building blocks for a Pacific Community, whether structural, such as the **Asia–Pacific Economic Cooperation (APEC)** forum or the **ASEAN Regional Forum (ARF)**, or conceptual, required the participation of the Southeast Asian nations, which in the **Association of Southeast Asian Nations (ASEAN)** were already community building in their regional domain. It was the second pillar of the American vision—democracy—that became most problematic for Southeast Asia. With the rise of **China** to regional economic and political prominence, the notion of a Pacific Community has been overshadowed since 2004 by the Japanese-driven idea of an **East Asian Free Trade Agreement (EAFTA)**. Concerns about U.S. exclusion prompted the **Bush** administration in 2006 to advance a proposal for an **Asia Pacific Free Trade Agreement (APFTA)** as a new first step toward community. *See also* EAST ASIA SUMMIT; TRADE.

PACIFIC DOCTRINE. On 7 December 1975, returning from a Pacific region trip including the **Philippines** and **Indonesia**, President **Gerald Ford** enunciated his "Pacific Doctrine" in a speech at the University of Hawaii. The doctrine rested on five premises: American strength, partnership with Japan, normalization of relations with the People's Republic of **China**, the U.S. stake in the security and stability of Southeast Asia, and resolution of outstanding conflict. With respect to Southeast Asia, Ford added that the United States shared the political and economic concerns of the five (at that time) members of the **Association of Southeast Asian Nations (ASEAN)**, with which the United States was actively engaged.

PACIFIC FORUM/CSIS. The Honolulu-based Pacific Forum was founded as an autonomous foreign policy research institution centered on U.S.–Pacific nations' relations. It later became the Pacific arm of the Washington, D.C., think tank the Center for Strategic and International Studies (CSIS). The Pacific Forum carries out an extensive program of conferences and publications, including an e-journal, *Comparative Connections*, which includes a quarterly discussion and chronology of U.S.–Southeast Asian relations. The Pacific Forum is the administrative link between the U.S. participants and the network of institutions and individuals in the "Track II" **Council for Security Cooperation in the Asia–Pacific (CSCAP).**

PANDEMIC AND INFECTIOUS DISEASES. In the era of globalization and increasing interdependencies, the occurrence of pandemic and infectious diseases has become a foreign policy issue as well as one of public health and humanitarian assistance. The implications are caught up in the term "biosecurity," which takes in not only naturally occurring disease but also bioterrorism. The idea of partnership, which has become a major thrust of U.S. bilateral and regional relations in Southeast Asia, includes making available to afflicted countries not just U.S. financial resources but scientific and technical support through the **Agency for International Development (USAID),** the Department of Health and Human Services and its Centers for Disease Control and Prevention, the Department of Agriculture, the Defense Department, and other relevant agencies. American programs operate both bilaterally and through multilateral agencies such as the World Health Organization (WHO). The 2002–2003 SARS (severe acute respiratory syndrome) epidemics in the region were a wakeup call to Southeast Asia's vulnerabilities to the spread of disease as the region became more integrated. There was an increasing awareness of the need for collective action to prevent, detect, and coordinate responses. This was recognized at the 2003 **Asia–Pacific Economic Cooperation (APEC)** leaders' meeting, which launched the U.S.-driven Health Security Initiative to improve the region's preparedness. As a first step, the United States and **Singapore** established a joint Regional Emerging Disease Intervention Center (REDI).

The emerging diseases of concern are avian and pandemic influenza. The U.S. diplomatic response to this threat is coordinated in the **State Department**'s Avian Influenza Action Group. The most recent and destructive H5NI strain of the avian virus has been detected in **Indonesia**, **Burma**, **Laos**, **Thailand**, and **Vietnam**. It has the highest mortality rate and can be transmitted to humans. The United States has sought to be proactive in establishing an International Partnership on Avian and Pandemic Influenza, to which through 2005 it had contributed $392 million. The most serious disease problem in Southeast Asia is HIV/AIDS, the incidence of which is still growing. The WHO reported in 2006 that 7.8 million Southeast Asians are HIV-infected, of whom 2 million are women. The State Department's Office of the U.S. Global AIDS Coordinator is responsible for coordinating all of the U.S. bilateral assistance programs in the U.S. Emergency Plan for AIDS Relief, operating in 123 countries in cooperation with government public health agencies and nongovernmental organizations (NGO). In 2005, the plan was to cost $10 billion over five years. In Southeast Asia, bilateral and regional assistance is being provided to HIV/AIDS programs in every country except **Brunei**, **Malaysia**, and **Singapore**. Vietnam is one of the 14 countries worldwide that has been singled out as a country of focus for American assistance because of the severity of the problem. Burma's inaction in combating HIV/AIDS is one of the justifications used by the United States in accusing it of threatening regional security. A vexing problem for U.S. **trade** relations and the protection of **intellectual property rights (IPR)** is the demand in Southeast Asia for lower cost generic drugs even if in violation of patents. In 2007, Thailand violated American-owned patents on two HIV/AIDS drugs.

PARIS INTERNATIONAL CONFERENCE ON CAMBODIA (PICC). Chaired by **Indonesia** and France, the Paris International Conference on Cambodia was a multilateral effort to end the **Third Indochina War** and bring peace to **Cambodia**. It took place in two sessions. The first phase was from 30 July to 30 August 1989. In addition to the co-conveners, the participants were the Cambodian factions in the **Coalition Government of Democratic Kampuchea (CGDK)–Funcinpec**, the **Khmer People's National Liberation Front (KPNLF)**, and the **Khmer Rouge**–the People's **Republic of Kampuchea (PRK)**; the 10 members of the **Association of Southeast Nations (ASEAN)**—Australia, Canada, **China**, India, Japan,

Laos, the Soviet Union, Great Britain, the United States, and **Vietnam**; Zimbabwe (chair of the **Nonaligned Movement (NAM)**; and Secretary-General of the **United Nations** Pérez de Cuéllar. American secretary of state **James Baker** made the opening statement for the United States. Baker outlined the American position that a settlement had to have a meaningful role for the noncommunist Cambodian parties headed by Prince **Norodom Sihanouk**. The PICC was suspended when it was unable to agree on issues of a new constitution for Cambodia, power sharing during transition to a new government, and international verification of Vietnamese troop withdrawal from Cambodia. It reconvened two years later, 21–23 October 1991, to ratify the **comprehensive political settlement on the conflict in Cambodia**, which had been fashioned by the five permanent members of the Security Council and adopted by the Security Council and General Assembly of the United Nations.

PARIS PEACE NEGOTIATIONS, 1968–1973. By early 1968, the **Democratic Republic of Vietnam**'s **(DRV)** Tet Offensive and the human costs of the battle of Khe San demonstrated an emerging battlefield stalemate in **Vietnam**, further eroding American public support for the **Vietnam War**. In his 31 March 1968 speech declaring that he would not run for president again, President **Lyndon B. Johnson** announced a bombing halt north of the 20th parallel and a willingness to negotiate with the enemy at any time and any place. The DRV agreed to the talks on 3 April. At the initial talks that began in Paris on 13 May 1968, **W. Averell Harriman** represented the United States. The DRV was represented by former foreign minister Xuan Thuy. Early in the negotiations, however, senior Communist Party politburo member **Le Duc Tho** appeared as an "advisor" to the Vietnamese delegation and effectively became the primary Vietnamese negotiator. The **Republic of Vietnam (RVN)** and the DRV's front in the south, the **Provisional Revolutionary Government of South Vietnam (PRG)**, joined the talks in October 1968. After President **Richard M. Nixon** took office in 1969, Ambassador **Henry Cabot Lodge** took Harriman's place, but it was not until Le Duc Tho and National Security Advisor **Henry A. Kissinger** began their private talks in February 1970 that the serious bargaining began.

The negotiating gulf between the United States and the DRV was great. The United States was politically committed to a "Two Vietnams" solution. The DRV's goal was reunification of the North and South, as called for in the 1954 **Geneva Accords**' "temporary" partition of the country. On the battlefield, the United States called for symmetrical withdrawal of U.S. forces and the People's Army of Vietnam (PAVN). The DRV demanded unilateral U.S. troop withdrawal, the end of American support to the government of **Nguyen Van Thieu** in South Vietnam, and a coalition government in place of the Thieu government. Without guarantees for the future of the southern government, this was tantamount to American surrender.

While the talks went on, so did the fighting, including U.S. and Army of the Republic of Vietnam (ARVN) incursions into Cambodia and Laos and PAVN's 1972 failed "Easter Offensive." At the same time, Kissinger's policy of détente with the Soviet Union and the beginning of the normalization of U.S.–**Chinese** relations threatened to undermine the DRV's strategic ties to its communist allies. By February 1972, the DRV had modified its position on imposing a political settlement on the south and the United States had given up on symmetrical military withdrawals. By 11 October, a compromise draft agreement was ready. The main elements provided for a U.S. troop withdrawal and a PAVN standstill in the areas it controlled. The future of South Vietnam would be worked out in negotiations between the DRV-sponsored PRG and the Thieu government, leading to eventual reunification "through peaceful means."

When presented with the agreement, RVN president Thieu refused to sign, denouncing it as a sellout. The DRV blamed the United States for Thieu's recalcitrance. Kissinger, who on 31 October had jubilantly claimed "peace is at hand," saw the agreement unraveling. The U.S. response was twofold. It tried to reassure Thieu of continued backing by providing a massive infusion of weapons and munitions, including aircraft and armor, and a promise by Nixon to Thieu that the United States would come to his assistance with "full force" should the DRV violate the terms of the agreement. The United States also pressed the DRV to accept changes demanded by Thieu in the agreed-upon draft. Hanoi's unwillingness to do so provoked the United States to launch the heaviest bombing campaign of the war,

18 to 29 December 1972, concentrated on the Hanoi–Haiphong corridor. The Vietnamese delegation in Paris, now led by Vice Foreign Minister **Nguyen Co Thach**, walked out, but in January 1973 the two sides quickly picked up the pieces. On 13 January, a new draft of a **Paris Agreement** was ready. The principal elements of the October agreement remained in place, with only cosmetic changes.

PARIS AGREEMENT, 1973. The "Agreement on Ending the War and Restoring Peace in Vietnam" was signed in Paris on 27 January 1973 by U.S. secretary of state **William P. Rogers** and **Democratic Republic of Vietnam (DRV)** foreign minister Nguyen Duy Trinh. Also signing were the ministers of foreign affairs for the **Republic of Vietnam (RVN)** and the **Provisional Revolutionary Government of the Republic of South Vietnam (PRG)**. In the agreement itself, the two South Vietnamese signatories were only identified as the "parties" to the agreement. The fashioning of the instrument, however, was largely the work of President **Richard M. Nixon**'s national security advisor, **Henry A. Kissinger**, and DRV senior politburo member **Le Duc Tho**.

The agreement consisted of 23 articles in 9 chapters. A preamble acknowledged the South Vietnamese people's right to self-determination. In Chapter I, the United States asserted its respect for the independence, sovereignty, unity, and territorial integrity of Vietnam as recognized by the 1954 **Geneva Accords**. Chapter II dealt with the cessation of hostilities and withdrawal of troops. It called for a cease-fire in place for all forces; the withdrawal of U.S. forces in 60 days, to be supervised by a four-power joint military commission; and the cessation of U.S. military involvement and intervention in the internal affairs of **South Vietnam**. Chapter III provided for the exchange of prisoners. Chapter IV set out the PRG and RVN mechanisms for national reconciliation, including a Council of National Reconciliation and Concord through which internal affairs of South Vietnam would be regulated in preparation for free and democratic elections. Chapter V called for a step-by-step reunification process through peaceful means. Chapter VI dealt with the establishment of a four-party military commission to oversee the cease-fire and withdrawal of the United States as well as a new **International Commission of Control and Supervision (ICCS)** to monitor the implementation of the agreement. In Chapter VII, the parties agreed to respect the neutrality of **Cambodia** and **Laos**.

Chapter VIII covered future U.S.–DRV relations. In Article 21, the United States promised to contribute to the reconstruction of the DRV and throughout **Indochina**. Chapter IX provided for the agreement to enter into force.

The final agreement was not substantially different from the draft reached the previous October in the **Paris peace negotiations** and rejected by South Vietnam. Two issues in particular had concerned Saigon: the People's Army of Vietnam (PAVN) forces that remained in South Vietnam and recognition of the division of Vietnam at the 17th parallel in the demilitarized zone (DMZ). With respect to the first, President Nixon told RVN President **Nguyen Van Thieu** that the DRV rejected any change but that he believed the problem of the North Vietnamese troops was manageable under the agreement. The DRV did accept a reference to the DMZ line, but this was qualified with the words that it was "only provisional and not a political or territorial boundary."

Even though the agreement was imperfect and disadvantageous, Thieu had little choice but to acquiesce. In a 5 January 1973 letter to him, Nixon made it clear that the United States would sign with or without the RVN. He warned that if Thieu split with the United States, the "survival" of South Vietnam would be "gravely jeopardized." This was reinforced by Kissinger, who sent his deputy, **Alexander Haig**, to Saigon to inform Thieu that if the RVN did not sign, it faced a cut-off of American assistance. As it was, the RVN did not survive. Thieu was correct. The agreement left the RVN politically and militarily vulnerable, with basically unworkable provisions about reconciliation. It provided legitimacy for the PRG as a coequal in determining the South's future with the PAVN still in place. It accomplished for the United States the purpose of providing a negotiated basis for extraction of U.S. forces from Vietnam while leaving the RVN intact to face the DRV without the United States. This was from the American vantage point a "peace with honor."

PARIS, TREATY OF, 1898. The Treaty of Paris, signed on 10 December 1898, terminated the **Spanish–American War**. In it, Spain ceded its territories in the **Philippines** to the United States. In return, the United States paid Spain $20 million. A subsequent Treaty of

Washington in 1900 included in the cession the Sulu Islands west to Sibutu and Cagayan de Sulu, for an additional payment of $100,000.

PARSONS, J. GRAHAM (1907–1991). A career Foreign Service Officer from 1936 to 1972, Parsons was U.S. ambassador to **Laos** in 1956–1958. He represented at the diplomatic level Secretary of State **John Foster Dulles**'s policy, which frowned on neutralism, which in Laos was the program of Prime Minister **Souvanna Phouma**. Parsons struggled against the formation of and then worked to undermine the first Lao **coalition government**, which brought Prince **Souphanouvong**'s communist **Pathet Lao** movement into the government. Parsons became deputy assistant secretary of state for Far Eastern affairs in 1958, and in 1959 was hand-picked by retiring Assistant Secretary **Walter Robertson** to succeed him. In that role Parsons, like his predecessor, saw **China** as an enemy and in Southeast Asia continued to orchestrate from Washington the American anti-Souvanna Phouma policy as well as the other aspects of regional **containment**. When the 1960 **Kong Le** coup brought Souvanna back to power, Parson's goal was clear: Souvanna had to go. His instrument was the rightist military strongman **Phoumi Nosavan**. Souvanna's assessment of Parsons was that he was "the most nefarious and reprehensible of men."

PARU (POLICE AERIAL REINFORCEMENT UNIT). Created by the **Central Intelligence Agency (CIA)**'s **James W. Lair**, the PARU was an elite special force in the **Thai** police designed for quick deployment to border areas and guerrilla warfare. It was innocuously named the Police Aerial Reinforcement Unit in order to avoid friction with the Thai army. It was controlled by the powerful and corrupt police commander, General **Phao Sriyanond**. The PARU became the model for the initial training of General **Vang Pao**'s **Hmong** forces in **Laos**. PARU "volunteers" also took part in the **secret war** in Laos.

PATHET LAO. Translated as "Lao Nation" or "Land of Laos," Pathet Lao is the name of the communist movement that fought from 1950 onward against the French, the royalists, and the U.S.-backed governments of **Laos** until its seizure of power in April 1975. Its roots were in the immediate post–World War II **Lao Issara** movement.

From secure bases in Sam Neua and Phong Saly provinces, awarded to it as regroupment areas by the 1954 **Geneva Accord**, the Pathet Lao, led by Prince **Souphanouvong**, waged its political and military campaigns in alliance with the **Viet Minh** and the People's Army of Vietnam (PAVN). The communist People's Party was the core of the Pathet Lao. In 1972, the People's Party became the Lao People's Revolutionary Party (LPRP).

PEACE CORPS. Senator **John F. Kennedy**'s 1960 presidential campaign challenge to students to serve the country in the cause of peace by volunteering to live and work in developing countries found its institutional form in President Kennedy's creation of the Peace Corps in 1961. Since then, more than 187,000 Peace Corps volunteers have served around the world. At its height in 1966, there were 15,000 in the field. In 2007, there were Peace Corps programs in three Southeast Asian countries, the **Philippines**, **Thailand**, and **Cambodia**. The Philippines program was the second to get underway, with the first group of volunteers arriving in October 1961. To 2007, more than 8,100 volunteers have worked in the Philippines. The Thailand program has been in place since 1962, with 4,700 volunteers having served there. The Cambodia program began in 2007. A program in **East Timor** with 57 volunteers began in 2002, but withdrew in 2006 because of the unsettled and violent political situation. Programs once existed in **Indonesia** (1962–1964) and **Malaysia** (1962–1983), but became casualties of the wider bilateral political relationship.

PEOPLE'S REPUBLIC OF KAMPUCHEA (PRK). This was the name adopted by the government installed in **Cambodia** by **Vietnam** after its 1978 invasion beginning the **Third Indochina War**. The PRK was proclaimed immediately upon the Vietnamese invasion so as to preempt charges of Vietnamese occupation. The Cambodian members of the government were primarily dissident members of the old Communist Party of Kampuchea (CPK) and ex-**Khmer Rouge** members now organized as the Khmer People's Revolutionary Party. The PRK under Vietnamese tutelage was organized on the Vietnamese socialist model. In 1985, **Hun Sen** became prime minister, a post he still held in 2007 in the restored Cambodian democracy. The PRK had limited diplomatic recognition. To the **Association of**

Southeast Asian Nations (ASEAN), **China**, the United States, and a majority of the United Nations, it was a Vietnamese puppet state. ASEAN termed it the Heng Samrin regime after the People's Revolutionary Party's leader. In 1988, in order to move negotiations along and attenuate the Vietnamese link, the People's Republic became the **State of Cambodia**.

PERMANENT NORMAL TRADE RELATIONS (PNTR). In cases of nonmarket economies that are not members of the **World Trade Organization (WTO)**, **normal trade relations (NTR)** status can be negotiated with the United States on a conditional basis subject to an annual congressional renewal. NTR status qualifies for nondiscriminatory and generalized most-favored-nation trading regulations. NTR status can become permanent with the conclusion of a bilateral trade agreement and the waiver of the annual congressional review if the president can certify compliance with the **Jackson–Vanik amendment** to the Trade Reform Act of 1974 with respect to free emigration. NTR or PNTR does not mean that exceptions to nondiscriminatory trade rules cannot be imposed. This is the case with U.S. trade sanctions against **Burma** because of its **human rights** violations. **Vietnam** was the last of **Association of Southeast Asian Nations (ASEAN)** members to win PNTR status. Normal U.S.–Vietnamese trade relations were achieved in 2001 with a bilateral trade agreement and its reciprocal provision for NTR status. Negotiations for PNTR status were continued through 2006, with Congress finally giving legislative approval on 9 December 2006.

PERSIAN GULF WAR. In March 1991, during the administration of **George H. W. Bush**, the United States led a multinational force with **United Nations (UN)** authorization into Iraq to liberate Kuwait after Iraq invaded and occupied it. A 34-nation coalition waged a lightning 45-day assault. There were no Southeast Asians among the countries that contributed to the UN-backed forces, but both the **Philippines** and **Singapore** supported the United States through their basing and access agreements for U.S. military deployment and supply. Singapore's interest in particular was the international defense of the sovereignty of a small country against aggression by a larger power. Singapore's staunch support of the United States was criticized by

Malaysia, which viewed stronger Singapore defense ties with the United States in the context of its own troubled relationship with Malaysia. Malaysia had opposed the run-up to the war, arguing that sanctions had to be given a longer time to work. Malaysia was a nonpermanent member of the UN Security Council at the time. Malaysia angered the United States when it linked the question of sanctions against Iraq to U.S. support of Israel on the Palestine question. When it came time to vote on Security Council resolution 678 authorizing the use of force, U.S. secretary of state **James Baker**, in a cool and tense meeting with his Malaysian opposite number, made it clear that the vote was very important for the United States and that how Malaysia voted would influence future bilateral relations. Malaysia voted for the resolution, which passed 12 to 2 (Cuba and Yemen voting against and **China** abstaining.

PETERSON, DOUGLAS J. (1935–). When diplomatic relations were opened in 1995 between the United States and the **Socialist Republic of Vietnam (SRV)**, the appointment by President **William J. Clinton** of Douglas J. "Pete" Peterson as the first American ambassador had great significance. Pete Peterson, a three-term Florida congressman and a former U.S. Air Force officer, had been shot down over Vietnam on 6 September 1966. Badly injured after parachuting, he was captured and imprisoned until his release on 4 March 1973. Peterson's words on taking up his post expressed the sentiments of the Clinton administration at the new start of relations: "I want to heal the wounds between the United States and Vietnam. It's a tragic history that we've shared as two peoples. No one can change that, but there is a great deal we can all do about the future. And that's why I am in Vietnam." Peterson served for more than four years, leaving his post for an unsuccessful bid in 2002 for the Florida governorship.

PHAO SRIYANOND (1910–1960). As director of **Thailand**'s police from 1951 to 1957 in the government of Field Marshal **Phibul Songgram**, General Phao Sriyanond was a brutal and ruthless partner of Phibul and rival of General **Sarit Thanarat** for power and influence. He was heavily involved in the illegal narcotics trade. Phao facilitated the **Central Intelligence Agency (CIA)**'s resupply of Chinese nationalist forces in **Burma**, which in return gave him access to

Burmese opium sources. Phao used the material support of the American military establishment and the CIA to build a police paramilitary force as his own army, including the **Border Patrol Police (BPP)** and the **PARU** (Police Arial Reinforcement Unit). Phao was forced into exile in Switzerland after Sarit's lightning coup in 1957. *See also* KMT–BURMA CRISIS; LAIR, JAMES.

PHETSARAT RATNAVONGSA (1890–1959). Prince Phetsarat was the leading early Laotian nationalist politician. As viceroy of the Kingdom of **Laos**, his lineage and popularity rivaled and competed with those of the king. Long suspect by the French because of his nationalism, Phetsarat led the **Lao Issara** government, which after the Japanese surrender declared independence from France in September 1945. He and his colleagues fled to exile in **Thailand** in December 1946 after the French military reclaimed power. He was an elder brother of **Souvanna Phouma** and a half-brother of **Souphanouvong**, the twin poles of Lao politics for nearly three decades. Phetsarat returned from exile in 1957 after the reconciliation of his brothers in the first **coalition government**, which he had advocated, but in which he played no role.

PHIBUL SONGGRAM (1897–1964). French military trained, Field Marshal Phibul Songgram was the dominant military figure in **Thailand** in the mid-20th century. He was instrumental, together with civilian leader **Pridi Panomyong**, in the overthrow of the absolute monarchy in 1932. Restive under civilian governments, the military seized power in 1939, with Phibul as prime minister. Phibul allowed the bloodless occupation of Thailand by Japan and in 1942 declared war against the United States and Great Britain. As Japan was losing the war, Phibul was forced from office in 1944 but seized power again in another military coup in November 1947. As prime minister, he forged the Thai alliance relationship with the United States. He made an official visit to the United States on 2–6 May 1955. He was driven from power by the **Sarit Thanarat** coup in 1957 and ended his days in exile in Japan.

PHILIPPINE AUTONOMY ACT OF 1916. *See* JONES ACT.

PHILIPPINE CIVIC ACTION GROUP (PHILCAG). This was a noncombatant military force deployed from the **Philippines** to the **Republic of Vietnam (RVN)** in 1966–1969. Prior to that, the **Central Intelligence Agency (CIA)**–sponsored Filipino company, the **Eastern Construction Company** (originally named the Freedom Company), had recruited Filipinos for covert activity in **Laos** and **Vietnam** as well as military logistics. In 1964, Philippine president **Diosdado Macapagal** had authorized negotiations with the United States for a larger overt program for Philippine participation in Vietnam, but this was opposed in the Philippine Senate headed by Macapagal's political opponent, **Ferdinand Marcos**. The next year, as president, Marcos requested the Philippine Congress to appropriate funds to send a 2,000-man-strong noncombatant force to the RVN in support of its fight against communism. The turnabout cemented the Marcos–U.S. security axis. The Philippine Congress authorized $8 million, and the United States provided $39 million for training and support. The Philcag comprised engineering and medical units, with combat forces for security, and was sent in III Corps to Tay Ninh province, the site of heavy combat between the United States and the **Viet Cong** and the People's Army of Vietnam (PAVN). The enemy of the Americans rarely engaged the Filipinos, who were not in combat roles. In 1969, the termination of the Philcag mission became an issue in Philippine politics, including Filipino demands that the United States pay more to support it, embarrassment over the negative assessments of the **Symington Committee**, and anger over the U.S. failure to back Manila in its claim to **Sabah** (former British North Borneo).

PHILIPPINE INDEPENDENCE ACT OF 1934. *See* TYDINGS–MCDUFFIE ACT.

PHILIPPINE REHABILITATION ACT OF 1946. This law, signed by President **Harry S. Truman** on the same day as the Philippine Trade Act **(Bell Act)**, provided for compensation to persons and businesses for war damage, assistance in restoring and improving public infrastructure, and technical training. It authorized $620 million. While recognizing the economic needs of the Philippines, it also was a kind of compensation to ease the political pain of the Bell Trade Act. On the other hand, no claims over $500 would be honored unless the Philippines accepted the trade act.

PHILIPPINE TRADE ACT OF 1946. *See* BELL ACT.

PHILIPPINES. The Philippines is the Southeast Asian country with which the United States has had the closest and deepest historical, cultural, political, security, and economic ties. Once an American possession and today an ally, the Philippines enjoyed what was called a "special relationship" with the United States that set it apart from the rest of Southeast Asia. The Philippines is an archipelagic nation of over 7,000 islands stretching more than 1,100 miles north to south and separating the South China Sea from the Philippine Sea and Pacific Ocean. Its area is 112,187 square miles (300,000 square kilometers), a little smaller than New Mexico, with a population estimated in 2007 at 89 million. The capital is Manila on the Island of Luzon.

In 1521, Ferdinand Magellan, in the first circumnavigation of the world, reached the Philippines and claimed it for Spain. For years Spanish rule impressed Roman Catholicism on the population while suppressing a retreating Muslim minority in Mindanao and other southern islands. In the second half of the 19th century, indigenous nationalist aspirations among Spanish-educated Filipino elites led to revolt in 1896, which was interrupted when Commodore **George Dewey** sailed into Manila Bay on 1 May 1898 during the **Spanish–American War**. Spanish rule came to an end in 1898, when Spain ceded the Philippines to the United States in the **Treaty of Paris**. On 12 June 1898, the Filipino revolutionaries declared Philippine independence. Under the leadership of **Emilio Aguinaldo**, the revolt against Spain became a war for independence, labeled by the United States an insurrection. It was only after the American capture of Aguinaldo that peace was officially proclaimed, on 4 July 1902. A brutal war against American control continued in the southern Muslim territories for another decade.

As military control of the Philippines gave way to civilian administration, a framework of American rule was erected that had as its goal the establishment of self-government through political institutions modeled on those of the United States. In 1916, an explicit promise of future independence was given to the Philippines in the **Jones Act**. The political dynamic that evolved pitted aspiring Filipino nationalists seeking to expand autonomy against American governors-general defending American rights and sovereignty. The Filipino side was rife with rivalries and competition for status and privilege, and the American side had ambivalent backing from presidents and Congress, unsure of U.S. best interests. A major concern for the United States after 1904 and the Russo–Japanese War was the problem and costs of defending the Philippines from Japanese expansion. In the course of diplomacy, the United States tried to both placate Tokyo—through the **Taft–Katsura Agreement** and **Root–Takahira Agreement**—and limit its strategic reach—through the **Washington Naval Conference**. In the Philippines, the United States built bases and fortifications—the most impressive being the bastion of Corregidor guarding the entrance to Manila Bay—and raised a Filipino military force as an auxiliary to U.S. troops stationed in the islands. In this area of activity, the towering figure of General **Douglas MacArthur** looms large in Filipino–American relations.

A framework for Philippine independence was established by Congress in 1934 in the **Tydings–McDuffie Act**, a slightly revised version of the 1933 **Hare–Hawes–Cutting** bill, which had been rejected by the Philippine Congress, in part because of provisions for U.S. postindependence military basing. In addition to the work and lobbying of Filipino nationalists, American agricultural interests and labor unions in the throes of the Depression feared competition from island products and immigration. Furthermore, the exposed strategic position of the Philippines to Japanese expansion led to calls for American defensive withdrawal to Hawaii. The independence measure provided for a 10-year transition in the institutional framework of a **Commonwealth of the Philippines**. **Manuel Quezon** and **Sergio Osmeña** were elected president and vice president, respectively. The Commonwealth period was interrupted by the outbreak of World War II in the Pacific. In the Philippines, the war started on 8 December 1941, with the first Japanese bombings, 10 hours after the attack on Pearl Harbor. Manila was declared an open city and occupied on 2 January 1942, and the final surrender of American–Filipino forces was in April. MacArthur, together with Quezon and Osmeña, left for Australia from Corregidor.

During the Japanese military occupation of the Philippines, some Filipinos collaborated under duress, while others in guerrilla bands resisted Japanese rule. A puppet Japanese-constructed republic was headed by **José P. Laurel**. Political collaboration became an issue after the war, with it being defended as shielding the people from an even harsher Japanese administration and criticized as opportunism. One of the leading politicians charged with collaboration was **Manuel Roxas**, a friend of MacArthur, who personally cleared him. Roxas became the independent Philippines' first president and in 1948 issued a blanket amnesty to accused collaborators. Another was **Claro Recto**, who became the most acerbic and trenchant critic of the postwar "special relationship" and American bases.

The U.S.–Philippine relationship became one of sovereign equals on 4 July 1946. The transfer of sovereignty was embedded in a legal framework of political and economic treaties and agreements that to Filipino nationalists encumbered the country's newly independent status. Through the 1947 **Military Bases Agreement (MBA)** and Military Assistance Agreement, followed by the 1951 **Mutual Defense Treaty (MDT)**, the Philippines became the keystone of U.S. Cold War security architecture in East Asia and the Pacific. The MBA, with its legal immunities for American personnel, became the central focus of the bilateral political relationship. Over the next four decades, different Philippine governments sought greater control over the bases, while the United States insisted on unrestricted use. The postindependence U.S.–Philippine economic relationship had as its centerpiece the 1946 Philippine Trade Act, better known as the **Bell Act**, which had a parity clause providing for equality of economic rights for American citizens with Filipinos. This was denounced by nationalists as neocolonialism. It was only after the expiration in 1974 of the **Laurel–Langley agreement** that superseded the Bell Act that **trade** relations were normalized within the framework of the global General Agreement on Tariffs and Trade (GATT).

As the United States and the Philippines were adjusting to the new bilateral relationship, the Philippines was challenged from within by the growing communist-led **Hukbalahap** insurgency, the roots of which were in agrarian unrest. The governments of Roxas and his successor, **Elpidio Quirino**, with their elite roots, were ineffectively corrupt as politicians and bureaucrats scrambled for the spoils of independence. The United States, committed to Philippine postwar rehabilitation, economic development, and American security interests, pressed hard for reform. Following up the 1950 **Bell Economic Survey**, the United States tried to make aid conditional on reform. At the same time, in 1953 the United States promoted new leadership within the Philippines through **Central Intelligence Agency (CIA)** connections, particularly Colonel **Edward Lansdale**, with the rising political star of **Ramon Magsaysay**. Reforms under President Magsaysay, backed by the United States, blunted the Hukbalahap's threat. Magsaysay was killed in a plane crash in 1957.

Magsaysay's successors, **Carlos Garcia** and **Diosdado Macapagal**, were a return to the pre-Magsaysay political establishment's corruption and drift. American economic leverage on reform, however, was limited by the leverage the Philippines had on the United States as host of the military bases deemed by Washington as vital to U.S. security and its **containment** policy in Asia. President Macapagal's cancellation in 1962 of a scheduled trip to the United States was an expression of growing Philippine frustration about what was seen as American highhandedness on agricultural issues and Philippine war claims. Macapagal, who had aggressively asserted a Philippine claim to **Sabah** (British North Borneo) and opposed its incorporation into **Malaysia**, was upset that not only would the United States not support the Philippines, but President **John F. Kennedy** had said that Malaysia would be the best hope for security in the region.

In 1965, events outside and inside the Philippines coincided that transformed the quality of U.S.–Philippine relations. The American role in **Vietnam** deepened with the **Tonkin Gulf Resolution** and military escalation, and Filipinos elected **Ferdinand Marcos** as president. For more than 20 years, the United States and Marcos were paired in a dance to the tune of American security interests, as represented by the bases and the repressive nature of the Marcos regime. Following two elected terms of office, on 21 September 1972 Marcos declared martial law and began a presidential dictatorship. During the Marcos regime, a rebellion by the Maoist-inspired Communist Party of the Philippines and its **New People's Army (CPP/NPA)** and the **Moro National Liberation Front (MNLF)** Muslim separatist insurgency in the south challenged the capabilities of the Armed Forces of the Philippines (AFP). Growing concern in the United

States about Marcos's regime and its **human rights** abuses was balanced by the reality of the need for the military bases and Marcos's political support in the Cold War. The administration of President **Richard M. Nixon** and its ambassador, **Henry Byroade**, saw no alternative to Marcos.

When confronted by President **Jimmy Carter**'s stance on human rights, President Marcos made it clear that the United States could not sanction the Philippines because of human rights and expect to keep the bases. When Marcos visited Hawaii in 1980, his first visit to the United States since his 1964 election, President Carter sent former secretary of state **Dean Rusk**—who had had no official position in the government since the **Johnson** administration—as the U.S. government's official greeter. This was interpreted as a snub. The tenseness of the Marcos–Carter period did not prevent the two countries from initialing a revised base agreement after negotiations that had begun in 1971.

A new cordiality came with the inauguration in the United States of President **Ronald Reagan**. In 1981, Vice President **George H. W. Bush** signaled the change from Carter in a Manila visit during which he praised Marcos, saying "we love your adherence to democratic principles and to the democratic process." Bush's comment was derisively greeted in the Philippines and criticized by human rights advocates in the United States. Before a 1982 state visit to the United States, Marcos preemptively raised the bases issue when he stated that the "usefulness of the bases to Philippine security should be reexamined." During the visit, President Reagan was less effusive than his vice president when praising Marcos as "a recognized force for peace and security in Southeast Asia." While the Americans had the MBA in mind, Marcos wanted to demonstrate U.S. support for his administration.

The new warmth in the relationship began to cool during the political turmoil in the Philippines following the August 1983 murder of Filipino opposition leader **Benigno Aquino**, which was blamed on Marcos's military. Reagan canceled a planned visit to the Philippines, but angered President **Suharto** in **Indonesia** by canceling an Indonesian visit as well to make it appear that Marcos was not being singled out. As opposition to the Marcos regime mounted in Manila, voices in the **State Department** and the American embassy in

Manila warned that U.S. interests were being put at risk if Marcos continued his course. Marcos responded by calling a snap election in January 1986. Aquino's widow, **Corazon Aquino**, won the election, but Marcos tried to steal it, triggering mass demonstrations in Manila. This was the **EDSA** "people's power" revolution. The United States was faced by a future without Marcos but burdened in a future democratic Philippines by its association and support of Marcos in the past. The Reagan administration cut its political ties to Marcos, providing him with a safe exile, while endorsing and promoting President Aquino and supporting her against attempted military coups.

While Filipinos were primarily concerned with reestablishing democracy, the American agenda focused on the upcoming 1991 expiration of the MBA. Although negotiations for a renewed MBA were successful, the Philippine Senate rejected the treaty. A withdrawal of all U.S. forces was completed in November 1992. The post–U.S. bases relationship with the Philippines, which coincided with the post–Cold War era in Southeast Asia, was one in which until 11 September 2001 the focus was on economic and commercial ties rather than the former "special relationship." Aquino's 1992 presidential successor, **Fidel Ramos**, sought to burnish relations with the United States and at the same time broaden the Philippines' ties with the **Association of Southeast Asian Nations (ASEAN)** and other friendly nations as the country moved away from what nationalist critics argued was a passive dependence on the United States.

After the 1991 termination of the MBA, the 1951 MDT remained the legal underpinning of the security relationship, but defense cooperation was limited. Negotiations for a **Visiting Forces Agreement (VFA)** were initiated during Ramos's term of office and completed in 1999 during the presidency of his successor, **Joseph Estrada**. The VFA provided the framework for the United States and the Philippines to resume an active program of cooperation and exercises, the largest being the **Balikatan** series. Led on the Philippine side by President **Gloria Macapagal-Arroyo**, the Philippines was described in 2002 by U.S. secretary of state **Colin Powell** as being in the forefront of leadership in Southeast Asia in the global **war on terror**. The United States has designated the Philippines a Major Non-NATO Ally and in 2002 signed a **Mutual Logistics Support Agreement (MSLA)**. The Philippines has also received increased security assistance, with U.S.

foreign military financing (FMF) for the Philippines at more than $80 million between 2005 and 2008. The U.S. **International Military Education and Training (IMET)** program for the Philippines is the largest in Asia and the second largest in the world. The burgeoning new security relationship was tarnished in 2007 when U.S. congressional concern was expressed over the Philippine military's involvement in extrajudicial killings of alleged Filipino leftists. When asked in a March 2007 U.S. Senate committee hearing whether military assistance to the Philippines should be suspended, Deputy Assistant Secretary of State for East Asian and Pacific Affairs Eric John responded that it would be "counterproductive" to U.S. efforts to influence change. Congress, nevertheless, made a portion of its FY 2008 security assistance package for the Philippines contingent on the Arroyo government's holding accountable those responsible for the killings.

Although the old "special relationship" between the Philippines and the United States are no longer in place, major elements of it persist. The United States still plays an important role in the Philippine economy. In 2006, 18 percent of Philippine exports went to the United States and 16 percent of its imports were from the United States. The Philippines is the U.S.'s 26th largest export market and 30th largest supplier of imports. The United States has had a **trade and investment framework agreement (TIFA)** with the Philippines since 1989, and the Philippines is eligible for the U.S. **Generalized System of Preferences (GSP)**. The United States is the single largest source of foreign **investment** for the Philippines. American economic assistance to the Philippines since 1946 exceeds $5 billion. During base negotiations, the Philippine government considered the aid as rent for the bases, a contention the United States never accepted. Although aid dropped considerably after 1991—in 1997–1998 it was $57 million—it began to climb again in 1999, and in 2006 it was $70 million.

The rehabilitation of the security ties in the war on terror was symbolized by regular invocations by Filipino and American officials and diplomats of shared histories, battlefields, political systems, and cultures. Thousands of Filipinos receive benefits from the U.S. Veterans Affairs and Social Security Administrations, and there are three million Philippine Americans. The strengthened ties of friendship have been a theme during the state visits to the United States by President Aquino in 1989, President Ramos in April 1998, President Estrada in 2000, and President Arroyo in August 2002. These visits were reciprocated by the state visits to the Philippines of U.S. presidents **William J. Clinton** in November 1994 and **George W. Bush** in October 2003. During his visit, Bush became the first U.S. president since **Dwight D. Eisenhower** to address a joint session of the Philippine Congress.

PHOUMI NOSAVAN (1920–1985). An important military and political player in the politics of **Laos**, anticommunist Phoumi Nosavan was an opponent of the first and second **coalition governments**, helping to bring down the first coalition. He rose from the rank of colonel in the Royal Lao Armed Forces (FAR) in 1958 to commander in chief in 1959. With close ties to the U.S. **Central Intelligence Agency (CIA)**, Phoumi was the American balance to the neutralism of **Souvanna Phouma**. Phoumi, with his American ties and his own animosity toward Souvanna Phouma, accelerated the polarization between Left and Right in Laos, driving neutralists into the welcoming embrace of the communist **Pathet Lao**. As the country plunged into civil war, the **Laotian crisis of 1961–1962** threatened to involve Great Power confrontation. In a shift of policy, the United States tried to persuade Phoumi, the power behind rightist prime minister **Boun Oum**, to accept a new coalition government. This was spurned, despite direct appeals by President **John F. Kennedy** and a face-to-face meeting between Phoumi and Assistant Secretary of State for East Asian and Pacific Affairs **W. Averell Harriman**, who was accompanied by Thai prime minister **Sarit Thanarat**, a distant relation of Phoumi. Frustrated by Phoumi's stubborn refusal to deal, President Kennedy cut off military and economic assistance to Laos. Still Phoumi refused to bend, using Laotian opium traffic to keep his army in the field. It was only when the FAR was routed by the Pathet Lao in the battle of Nam Tha in May 1962, and the United States suggested that he was politically replaceable, that Phoumi assented to the terms of the second coalition government, the centerpiece of the 1962 **Geneva Accords** on Laos. Phoumi became a deputy prime minister in the coalition, but without American and Thai patronage his role was diminished. In 1965, inter-FAR conflict over spoils of drug trafficking and smuggling forced him to take refuge in **Thailand**, where he was involved in Lao exile resistance movements until his death. *See also* NARCOTICS PRODUCTION AND TRAFFICKING.

PHOUI SANANIKONE (1903–1983). Prime minister of Laos twice and also twice foreign minister, Phoui Sananikone was a moderate anticommunist, anti-Vietnamese rightist. He was prime minister from 1950 to 1951 and, more importantly, from 1958 until overthrown by the **Kong Le** coup in 1960. He had been the speaker of the National Assembly before becoming prime minister in 1950. As foreign minister, he led the Lao delegation to the 1954 **Geneva Conference** that produced the **Geneva Accord** neutralizing Laos. As prime minister in 1958, he turned the government away from the neutralism of his predecessor, **Souvanna Phouma**, and associated Laos with the United States, opening relations with U.S. allies the **Republic of Vietnam** and Taiwan. He fled Laos in May 1975. Sentenced to death by the new communist government of the **Lao People's Democratic Republic (LPDR)**, he organized a government in exile in France dedicated to the overthrow of the LPDR.

PLAIN OF JARS. This is a strategically important plateau in northern **Laos**. The city of Xieng Khuang, which was a **Pathet Lao** stronghold, is in its center. The name comes from the prehistoric urns dotting it. It was battled over by the American-backed **Hmong** army of General **Vang Pao** and the Pathet Lao and its North Vietnamese allies during the **secret war**. Beginning in 1970, it was heavily bombed by U.S. B-52s and is littered with **unexploded ordnance (UXO)**.

POE, TONY (ANTHONY POSHEPNY) (1924–2003). Notorious **Central Intelligence Agency (CIA)** paramilitary case officer Tony Poe was reputedly the model for the crazed Colonel Kurtz in the film *Apocalypse Now*. A Hungarian refugee, Poe saw combat in the Pacific as a Marine enlisted man during World War II. Recruited out of college by the CIA, after training Poe was sent to Korea and then to **Thailand** with the cover provided by **Sea Supply Corporation**. Together with Lloyd "Pat" Landry, he liaised for the agency with Indonesian dissidents during the **PRRI–Permesta** revolt, and with Landry had to be exfiltrated from Sumatra in 1958 by a U.S. Navy submarine. His next assignment was training Tibetan Khmba tribesman, who in 1959 helped the Dali Lama escape to India. In 1961, he joined the **secret war** in **Laos** to work under **William "Bill" Lair** supporting **Vang Pao**'s **Hmong** forces on the **Plain of Jars**, with headquarters at **Long Tieng**. Poe married a niece of Touby Ly-foung, a Hmong leadership rival of Vang Pao. Poe's own relations with Vang Pao were troubled. There was reportedly at least one fist-fight. In 1965 Poe, a heavy drinker, was moved to the Nam Yu base in Northwestern Laos to lead another ethnic minority CIA-supported force. It was there that he won his bloodthirsty reputation. He re-warded the delivery of the severed ears of **Pathet Lao** fighters with cash payments and permitted decapitated heads to be staked. In 1970, he was sent to the rear as a training officer at a Thai base. Chafing at being sidelined, Poe left the agency in 1975, having twice earned the CIA's highest decoration. With his wife and three daughters he re-mained in Thailand until 1992, when he returned to live in Sonoma, California. At his death, he was praised as one of the finest case offi-cers the CIA had ever produced.

POL POT (1928–1998). Born Saloth Sar to a land-owning rice farmer in **Cambodia**, Pol Pot was the leader of the Communist Party of Kampuchea (CPK), infamously known as the **Khmer Rouge**. A mediocre student, he went to France for further study. There, with other young Cambodian nationalist intellectuals, he developed com-munist contacts and joined the Cambodian section of the French Communist Party. Returning to Cambodia in 1953, he became active in Cambodian and Vietnamese communist politics along with other members of the "Paris student group." His association with the Vietnamese-dominated **Viet Minh** convinced him that Cambodians had to make their own Cambodian revolution. He worked his way up the leadership of the communist organization, with its different names: Khmer People's Revolutionary Party, Khmer Worker's Party, and finally the Communist Party of Kampuchea. In 1963, he became the general-secretary of the party and, with his close allies from the "Paris students' group," began to prepare the party for revolt. He traveled along the **Ho Chi Minh trail** to Hanoi in 1965, where he was advised to be patient, and then in 1966 to **China**, where he was impressed by the Cultural Revolution. The 1970 **Lon Nol** coup that overthrew Prince **Norodom Sihanouk** propelled Pol Pot's Khmer Rouge toward power. Facing a corrupt and incompetent American-backed unpopular government, and now backed by the **Democratic Republic of Vietnam (DRV)**, the KR swept through the country to surround and eventually occupy Phnom Penh in April 1975.

It was what happened after the victory that made the name Pol Pot a global synonym for horror. The four-year reign of brutal terror that destroyed Cambodia's social infrastructure and took up to two million Cambodian lives was ended by the Vietnamese invasion and occupation of Cambodia in December 1978. While the Khmer Rouge was a prominent part of the **Khmer resistance** in the **Third Indochina War**, Pol Pot himself stayed in the background, not wishing to compromise the resistance in the eyes of its foreign supporters. The postwar KR, unwilling to participate in the internationally brokered new political system for Cambodia, withdrew to its northwestern Cambodian strong points. Major defections to the government and recriminations of elitism led in 1997 to Pol Pot's arrest by the KR's military leader, Ta Mok. Ill and without support, he was put on trial by his former comrades and sentenced to death. His death in April 1998, however, was reportedly of natural causes. Even as other KR leaders are dying natural deaths, a few are still awaiting trial for genocide. *See also* KHMER ROUGE TRIALS.

POPE, ALLEN L. (1928–). A former U.S. Air Force lieutenant, Allen Pope was a pilot with the **Central Intelligence Agency (CIA)**'s proprietary **Civil Air Transport (CAT)**. He was among the pilots decorated by the French government in 2002 for flying supplies to the besieged defenders of **Dien Bien Phu** in 1954. In 1958, Pope was flying bombing raids supporting the CIA's clandestine backing of Indonesian rebels in the **PRRI–Permesta regional rebellions**. On 18 May, his B-26 bomber was shot down over Ambon in East **Indonesia**. Pope, injured, parachuted and was captured with papers on him implicating the United States in support of the anti-**Sukarno** forces. To recover from a broken leg, he was first held at Kaliurang, a hill station above the Central Java city of Yogyakarta, the home of Gadjah Mada State University, where three American-funded teaching teams were on the faculty at the time. When recovered, he was transferred to Jakarta, tried, and sentenced to death. Disowned by the American embassy, Pope became a pawn in U.S.–Indonesian relations. In 1962, after successful conclusion of negotiations sponsored by President **John F. Kennedy**'s administration on the **West New Guinea dispute** and a personal request by Kennedy conveyed to Sukarno in Jakarta by his brother **Robert F. Kennedy**, Pope was released after four years of imprisonment. Pope went back to flying for CIA clandestine airlines in the Caribbean.

POWELL, COLIN L. (1937–). Secretary of state during President **George W. Bush**'s first term (2001–2005), Colin Powell already had been distinguished in a military career that carried him from an ROTC-commissioned second lieutenant to a four-star general and chairman of the Joint Chiefs of Staff (JCS). As chair of the JCS (1989–1993) under President **George H. W. Bush**, he was responsible for the military conduct of the **Persian Gulf War**. Before that (1987–1989) Powell had been President **Ronald Reagan**'s national security advisor. From George W. Bush's State Department, Powell had two related major tasks after the 11 September 2001 terrorist attack on the United States. The first was to mobilize friendly nations to join the United States in the **war on terror**. The second was to make the case against Iraq and its alleged development of weapons of mass destruction. Although he did not travel as often as his predecessors, during his four years as secretary of state he attended four **Association of Southeast Asian Nations (ASEAN)** postministerial dialogues and sessions of the **ASEAN Regional Forum (ARF)**. In the ASEAN context, he sought to balance the alliance interests of American's traditional security partners—the **Philippines**, **Singapore**, and **Thailand**—against the sensitivities of overwhelmingly Muslim **Brunei**, **Malaysia**, and **Indonesia**. The United States was able to get consensus on a U.S.–ASEAN declaration on cooperation against terrorism but not on the **Iraq War**.

In perhaps the most intense policy campaigning in Southeast Asia of any American secretary of state, in mid-2002 Powell visited in order Thailand, Malaysia, Singapore, Brunei, Indonesia, and the Philippines. Powell viewed Indonesia as a critical actor in the war on terror. He felt that a resumption of U.S.–Indonesian military-to-military relations, which had been severed since 1999 by the Leahy Amendment, was a necessary element in developing Indonesian counterterrorist capabilities. At the conclusion of his 2002 visit, he said that he thought the United States and Indonesia were starting down the path to normal defense relations, but then the **Timika incident** threw up another road block. In the Philippines, as the United States forged deeper bilateral security ties after the ratification of the **Visiting Forces Agreement (VFA)**, Secretary Powell emphatically denied that America was interested in new basing rights. In his last trip as secretary in January 2005, Powell traveled to Phuket Island in Thailand and Indonesia's Aceh Province to assess **tsunami** damage and relief efforts and then represented the United States at a leaders' meeting in Jakarta on tsunami recovery and reconstruction.

POW/MIA. One of the legacies of the **Vietnam War** was accounting for American prisoners of war (POWs) or those listed as missing in action (MIA) and recovery of the remains of the killed in action (KIA) in **Laos**, **Cambodia**, and **Vietnam**, many of them pilots or crewmen lost in the air war. From its beginnings in January 1973, the **Joint Casualty Resolution Center (JCRC)** was tasked with the search for and recovery of remains. A Department of Defense **Joint Task Force–Full Accounting (JTF–FA)** took over the task in 1992. This was merged in 2003 into the Joint POW/MIA Accounting Command (JPAC). The office of deputy assistant secretary of defense for POW/MIA affairs continues to exist in the Defense Department. From 1973 to 2006, more than 700 sets of remains from the war were returned for identification. That still leaves more than 1,800 MIA unaccounted for in **Indochina**, 1,400 in Vietnam alone, including airmen downed at sea.

Cooperation by the **Socialist Republic of Vietnam (SRV)** in a full accounting for POW/MIAs became a prerequisite for the United States in the 20-year-process of **normalization of relations with Vietnam**. The issue was complicated by the widely held belief in the United States that Americans were still being held as prisoners. Even though there were questionable live sightings of American prisoners, no credible evidence could be produced. In 1993, the U.S. Senate Select Committee on POW/MIAs reported that "there is no compelling evidence that proves that any American remains alive in captivity in Southeast Asia." This simply repeated what Representative **G. V. "Sonny" Montgomery**'s House committee had already reported in

1976. An early effort by President **Jimmy Carter** to resolve the problem with Vietnam failed when the hope raised by the 1977 **Woodcock Mission** was dashed by Vietnamese intransigence and the priority of **China** in American foreign policy.

President **Ronald Reagan** made the MIAs the centerpiece of his administration's stance on recognition of the SRV. In this he was backed not only by popular opinion and Congress, but by the politically potent **National League of POW/MIA Families**. The League became a de facto stakeholder in negotiations with Hanoi, with executive director **Ann Mills Griffiths** participating in official missions. Vietnam, anxious to end its isolation, became more forthcoming. It consistently denied that it held any prisoners. In the mid-1980s, without preconditions, the Vietnamese invited Department of Defense officials to come to Vietnam to take possession of the remains of presumed American war dead. A series of official visits to Hanoi by Deputy Assistant Secretary of Defense **Richard Armitage** and National Security Council official **Richard Childress** prepared the way for President Reagan to send the **Vessey Mission** to Hanoi in 1987. The result was an agreement to accelerate efforts to find U.S. MIAs in Vietnam. Beginning in 1992, joint American–Vietnamese field investigations demonstrated the seriousness of Vietnam in resolving a humanitarian issue that had become a primary political issue delaying normalization of relations. Similar field investigations began in Laos and Cambodia. In 1995, officials in the administration of President **George H. W. Bush** could report to Congress and the public that Vietnam was fully cooperating with the United States. The actual cost of the investigations was pumping up to $11 million a year into Vietnam's economy. It was left to the administration of President **William J. Clinton** to overcome domestic anti-Vietnam opposition and close the MIA question as the block to normalization even as the process of recovery of remains continues.

PRIDI PANOMYONG (1900–1983). Known as the father of democratic government in **Thailand**, Pridi, a French-trained lawyer, led the civilian elements in the 1932 revolution that ended the absolute monarchy. As the leader of the People's Party, Pridi's programs clashed with the more conservative military forces led by General **Phibul Songgram**. In 1942, at Japan's behest, Prime Minister

Phibul's government declared war on the United States. The anti-Japanese Pridi refused to accede to it. He left the government to accept the post of regent for the absent king. As regent he maintained clandestine contacts with the **Office of Strategic Services (OSS)**–supported **Free Thai** movement led from Washington by **Seni Pramoj**. In July 1944, as it was becoming clear that Japan was losing the war, Phibul was forced from office. Although not holding the prime minister's office, Pridi was the dominant political figure as the Free Thai intensified their preparations to throw off the Japanese occupation. On 16 August 1945, Pridi acting as regent proclaimed the declarations of war against the United States and Great Britain null and void and repudiated all treaties and agreements made under Japanese duress. Pridi became prime minister in 1946 and was at the center of the political turmoil surrounding the death of the young king Ananda Mahidon. Rightist military elements considered Pridi to be a socialist or even a communist and accused him of complicity in regicide. A November 1947 military coup backed by Phibul forced Pridi into exile. After a failed prodemocracy countercoup in 1949, Pridi took refuge in the People's Republic of **China** before finally retiring to Paris, where he died.

PROLIFERATION SECURITY INITIATIVE (PSI). Announced by President **George W. Bush** in May 2003, the Proliferation Security Initiative is an informal voluntary global effort to halt the shipment of weapons of mass destruction, their delivery systems, and related materials. In September 2003, 11 core nations adopted a Statement of Interdiction Principles. Since then 80 countries have supported the objectives of the PSI either as members or observers. In Southeast Asia, **Singapore** is a founding participant in the PSI although not one of the original core nations. **Thailand**'s Prime Minister **Thaksin Shinawatra** in a 2005 meeting with President Bush pledged to explore cooperation in the PSI. **Malaysia** is an observer.

PROVISIONAL REVOLUTIONARY GOVERNMENT (PRG). In June 1969 the Provisional Revolutionary Government of **South Vietnam** superseded the **National Liberation Front (NLF)** as the political organization of the communist revolutionary movement. As a claimed shadow government in waiting, it was formally accorded a place at the **Paris peace negotiations** along with the **Republic of South Vietnam**. Like its predecessor, the PRG was essentially an instrument of the **Democratic Republic of Vietnam (DRV)**. The PRG disappeared during the reunification of Vietnam following the communist military victory in 1975. Huynh Tan Phat, president and a former NLF leader, became one of seven deputy prime ministers in the postunification **Socialist Republic of Vietnam (SRV)**.

PRRI–PERMESTA REGIONAL INDONESIAN REBELLIONS. In 1958, dissident Indonesian army officers and politicians in Sumatra and Sulawesi rebelled against **Indonesia**'s central government. Although two separate movements, the Pemerintah Revolusioner Republik Indonesia (PRRI; Revolutionary Government of the Republic of Indonesia) and Permesta (Perjuangan Semesta Alam [Total Struggle]) jointly challenged what they saw as the corrupt, Left-leaning, and Java-centric government of President **Sukarno**. The administration of **Dwight D. Eisenhower** saw an opportunity to weaken and perhaps even topple the Sukarno government, which was viewed by Secretary of State **John Foster Dulles** and the president as procommunist.

At the direction of its head, **Allen Dulles**, the **Central Intelligence Agency (CIA)**, under Deputy Director of Plans (DDP) **Frank Wisner**, began a massive program, coordinated from **Singapore**, of covert support to the Indonesian insurrectionists involving financing, training, propaganda, and direct liaison with CIA agents. A **Philippine**-based PRRI–Permesta virtual air force was managed and staffed through **Civil Air Transport (CAT)**, with eight B-26 Invader bombers and six ex-Philippine Air Force F-51 Mustang fighters. It was the use of Clark Air Base to launch air raids against Indonesia that caused the Philippine government to insist in the 1959 **Bohlen–Serrano Agreements** that prior consultation was required for combat operations outside of the scope the U.S.–Philippine **Mutual Defense Treaty (MDT)** or **Southeast Asia Collective Defense Treaty**. Marked-over Taiwanese CAT transport planes brought supplies including munitions to Permesta forces through Menado in northern Sulawesi, which was held by the rebels. The U.S. secret effort came to an embarrassing end when **Allen Pope**, an American pilot flying out of the U.S. **Clark Air Base** in the Philippines, was shot down on a bombing raid and captured in May 1958 on the island of Ambon in East Indonesia. Pope had on him incriminating evidence of the American connection. As the U.S. link was exposed, CIA case officiers **Tony Poe** and Lloyd "Pat" Landry were exfiltrated from Sumatra by submarine. The rebellions were fully suppressed by 1962 through firm and forceful counteraction by the Indonesian military loyal to the unitary republic. While the Indonesian government downplayed the depth of the U.S. involvement, not wishing to irreparably damage its ties to the United States, the failed covert campaign against the Sukarno government strained U.S.–Indonesian relations to the end of the Eisenhower presidency. It was left to the incoming administration of President **John F. Kennedy** to try to restore normal relations, marked by the 1962 release of Pope from Indonesian imprisonment.

– Q –

QUEZON, MANUEL L. (1878–1944). Elected president of the **Commonwealth of the Philippines** in 1935, Manuel Quezon had been a leading advocate for Philippine independence from his 1907 entrance into national politics as a member of the first Philippine Assembly and its floor leader. Quezon's close association with American politicians and officials with interests in the Philippines began while he was in Washington from 1909 to 1916 as a resident commissioner to the U.S. House of Representative, where he lobbied for the **Jones Act**, which promised eventual independence for the Philippines. Quezon was elected to the first Philippine Senate and served as its president. Together with, and sometimes in rivalry with, **Sergio Osmeña**, he battled in Manila and in Washington against Filipinos and Americans who wanted to retain the islands as an American possession. Quezon's political skills in Washington were tested in shaping the final version of the 1934 **Tydings–McDuffie Act** (Philippine Independence Act), which established the framework for a 10-year transition to independence. In its constitution, the presidential term was set at six years without reelection, but it was amended, allowing Quezon to be reelected in November 1941. He and Vice President Osmeña were forced to flee the Philippines with General **Douglas MacArthur** in January 1942, after the Japanese invasion. Quezon headed the Philippine government in exile until his death. He was buried in Arlington National Cemetery, but after the war his remains were ceremonially returned to the Philippines for reburial.

QUINN, KENNETH M. (1942–). A career Foreign Service Officer (FSO), Kenneth Quinn was closely associated with **Vietnam** and **Cambodia**. His first six years of service were in Vietnam. Along with **Timothy Carney**, he recognized early the true nature of **Pol Pot**'s **Khmer Rouge**. (His 1982 University of Maryland Ph.D. dissertation was titled "The Origins of Radical Cambodian Communism.") During the administration of **George H. W. Bush**, Quinn served as deputy assistant secretary of state of East Asian and Pacific affairs. In that post he participated in the negotiation and implementation of the **comprehensive political settlement of the conflict in Cambodia**, in preparing the "road map" for **normalization of relations with Vietnam**, and in the closing of the American bases in the Philippines. For four years he chaired the Inter-Agency Task Force on **POW/MIA**s. In 1995, President **William J. Clinton** nominated Quinn to be U.S. ambassador to **Cambodia**, where he served from 1996 to 2000. Those were tumultuous years of coups, countercoups, violence, and terrorism that unraveled the coalition government cobbled together by the United Nations, leaving Prime Minister **Hun Sen** in the ascendancy. The American embassy was the site of demonstrations and even a rocket attack. Secretary of State **Madeleine Albright** singled out Quinn's direction of the mission for special commendation. At retirement, he was one of the most decorated FSOs of his generation.

QUIRINO, ELPIDIO (1890–1956). President of the **Philippines** from 1948 to 1953, Elpidio Quirino was vice president when **Manuel Roxas** died in April 1948. In 1949 he was elected to a full term but was defeated for reelection in 1953 by **Ramon Magsaysay**, who had been his secretary of national defense. Quirino was a lawyer and long-time Liberal Party politician, having served in the Philippines House and Senate and as a **Commonwealth of the Philippines** cabinet officer. During his presidency, he was challenged by the economic and social conditions that had led to the **Hukbalahap** rebellion. The United States viewed with dismay the graft and corruption that marked his administration, fearing that more than a billion dollars of U.S. aid was being abused and wasted. With the **Bell Mission**'s 1950 report in hand, the administration of President **Harry S. Truman** made any further aid grants conditional on major reforms. In 1953, the administration of **Dwight D. Eisenhower** turned loose the **Central Intelligence Agency (CIA)**'s principal operator in the Philippines, **Edward Lansdale**, to assist the Nationalist Party candidate Magsaysay win the presidential election.

– R –

RAMOS, FIDEL V. (1928–). A West Point–educated Philippine army officer, Fidel Ramos was president of the **Philippines** (1992–1998), succeeding President **Corazon Aquino**. Ramos had loyally served President **Ferdinand Marcos** for more than 20 years, rising to head the Philippine Constabulary. At a climactic moment in the 1986 **EDSA revolution** that drove Marcos from office, Ramos abandoned Marcos and brought critical military support to Aquino's "people's power" revolution. In the Aquino administration, Ramos served as chief of staff of the Philippine Armed Forces and concurrently minister of defense. In those roles, he was instrumental in quashing at least seven coup attempts. In the succeeding presidential race with six candidates, Ramos narrowly won a plurality, with 23.5 percent of the popular vote.

Ramos's major tasks as president were consolidating the democratic transition from the Marcos regime and restoring the relationship with the United States, which had been damaged by the failure of the new **Military Bases Agreement (MBA)** to win ratification by the Philippine Senate in 1991. He sought to transform the long-time U.S.–Philippine "special relationship," which radical nationalists had viewed as a neocolonial relationship, into a normal relationship in which the United States would continue to assist the Philippines economically and militarily as it sought to consolidate the new democracy, bring about domestic reform, and make efforts at national reconciliation. Ramos emphasized the fact that the Philippine–U.S. **Mutual Defense Treaty (MDT)** continued to contribute to regional peace and security. To underline the strength of the bilateral relationship, President Ramos decreed 4 July 1996 to be Philippines–America Friendship Day commemorating the 50th anniversary of Philippines independence. His feelings of friendship were reciprocated during his 1998 visit to the United States.

Limited by the new Philippine constitution to one six-year presidential term, Ramos was succeeded by **Joseph Estrada**, who was overthrown in the 2001 extraconstitutional **EDSA** II "people's power" revolt that brought Vice President **Gloria Macapagal-Arroyo** to power. Former president Ramos defended what many saw as an Arroyo coup. In public and private communications to influential Americans, he tried to interpret it in democratic terms, arguing that it was an "assertion of the sovereign people's ultimate right to intervene—when political institutions fail—to undertake a last effort to make democracy work the way it should." Ramos once had an exchange on democracy with **Singapore**'s **Lee Kuan Yew**, an advocate of **Asian values**. Lee argued that "the exuberance of democracy" leads to disorder and lack of development. Ramos's answer was, "without democracy we cannot truly win development."

RAMOS-HORTA, JOSÉ (1949–). A founder of **Fretilin** (Revolutionary Front for the Independence of East Timor), from exile José Ramos-Horta became the leading international spokesperson for **East Timor**'s independence from **Indonesia** after the 1975 **Indonesian invasion of East Timor**. In 1996, he shared the Nobel Peace Prize with East Timor's Catholic Bishop Carlos Belo. At independence in 2002, Ramos-Horta was named East Timor's foreign minister. In 2006, he served as prime minister, and in 2007 he was elected president. He was a major voice for reconciliation with Indonesia.

REAGAN, RONALD (1911–2004). The 39th president of the United States (1981–1989), Ronald Reagan was a conservative anticommunist who came to office pledging to restore America's self-confidence and pride after what he described as the post–**Vietnam War** "age of decline." An advocate of "peace through strength," in Southeast Asia he sought to bolster the American security presence in order to reassure American friends and allies in the region that the United States intended to remain a major actor. Reagan was particularly concerned with the growth of Russian naval strength in the region and its basing rights at Cam Ranh Bay in **Vietnam**. In this, he was seconded by **Singapore** prime minister **Lee Kuan Yew**—Southeast Asia's ultimate anticommunist realist—who, unprecedented for a Southeast Asian leader, visited Reagan four times for private talks in Washington during his presidency (1981, 1982, 1985, and 1988). An element of idealism in Reagan's approach can be seen in his nomination acceptance speech, in which he underlined America's role as a place of refuge for the suffering people of the world seeking freedom, mentioning among them Southeast Asia's "**boat people**."

Early in Reagan's tenure, it became clear that the **human rights** emphasis in the preceding administration of President **Jimmy Carter** would not receive the same priority. In addition to his close relationship with Prime Minister Lee—who had been on the Carter administration's human rights violators list—in 1982 President Reagan warmly welcomed the state visit of Philippine president **Ferdinand Marcos** and his wife, **Imelda Marcos**. Reagan's relationship with the Marcos couple began before his presidency. He had been their guest in Manila in 1969. Reagan praised the economic and social progress made by the **Philippine** administration and underlined the two countries' common security interests. This was while looking forward to renewed **Military Bases Agreement (MBA)** negotiations in 1983. Under the prodding of the **State Department**, a distancing from Marcos began after the assassination of **Benigno Aquino**. This was signaled by Reagan's reluctant cancellation of a Philippine stopover en route to **China** in April 1984. To soften the blow, however, he canceled as well a stop to see President **Suharto** in **Indonesia**. Although President Reagan was prepared to accept the fact that there were problems with democracy in the Philippines, he asked, "What is the alternative?" and answered, "It is a large communist movement." It was only as the Marcos regime was collapsing in 1986 under the assault of **Corazon Aquino**'s "people's power" **EDSA revolution** that Reagan, at the urging of his advisors, withdrew American support for Marcos and counseled him to leave. When Aquino, as Philippine president, made a state visit to the United States in September 1986, Reagan praised her for her peaceful revolution leading to the restoration of democracy in the Philippines. At the same time, the underlying reality for the administration remained the security of the bases, which Reagan saw as threatened by the Philippine communist insurgency. He pledged U.S. assistance for the rebuilding of the Philippines armed forces to meet that threat.

Reagan's consistent major focus in Southeast Asia was on **Vietnam** and the **POW/MIA** question. The head of the Asian directorate of the National Security Council, **Gaston Sigur**, and his staff, especially **Richard Childress**, were instructed by the White House to pursue this issue vigorously. The diplomacy of the **Third Indochina War** added new resolution to the Reagan administration's firm line on the preconditions to **normalization of relations with Vietnam**. In 1988, public utterances by Sigur, then assistant secretary of state for East Asian and Pacific affairs, adding verifiable Vietnamese troop withdrawal from **Cambodia** as a precondition, prompted Vietnam temporarily to cease cooperation with the United States on resolution of POW/MIA cases.

In August 1986, President Reagan made his only official visit to Southeast Asia, traveling to Bali, Indonesia, for an **Association of Southeast Asian Nations (ASEAN)** ministerial meeting while en route to a G-7 meeting in Tokyo. Reagan pronounced ASEAN "one of the most successful and admirable regional groupings in the developing world," pointing out the mutual benefits that could be derived in the U.S.–ASEAN relationship and setting the tone for American future engagement with the group. In Bali, Reagan met President Suharto, overcoming Indonesian disappointment at the cancellation of Reagan's planned 1984 visit and adding further political cement to a relationship established during the Indonesian president's state visit to the United States in October 1982. The Bali visit was marred, however, by a flap over press freedom. Indonesia, angry at an Australian newspaper article suggesting that Suharto would go the way of Marcos, barred Australian reporters from the meeting and expelled the *New York Times* correspondent. Negative press coverage about this overshadowed the substance of the Reagan–Suharto meeting.

RECTO, CLARO M. (1890–1960). Ardent nationalist, jurist, and legislator, Philippine senator Claro M. Recto was one of the most articulate and influential critics of the Philippine–American relationship in the first decade and a half of **Philippine** independence. Before World War II, as a senator he was engaged in the independence negotiations with the United States leading to the **Tydings–McDuffie**

Act. He was president of the constitutional convention in 1935 that drew up the **Commonwealth of the Philippines** constitution. During the Japanese occupation, he served in the cabinet of the Japanese-sponsored government led by **José Laurel**. After the war, he wrote a spirited, and to many, convincing defense of the patriotism of Filipino elite collaborators who sought to use their positions to shield the people from the worst practices of the Japanese. Recto condemned the treaty relationship with the United States and Philippine official subscription to the U.S. **containment** policy in Asia as not being in the Philippine national interest and perpetuating dependence on the Americans. He derided the Filipino supporters of the "special relationship" with the United States as having in their "submission" to the United States a "colonial mentality." He was particularly outraged by the **Military Bases Agreement (MBA)**, which he saw as degrading Philippine security by making it a possible target for the USSR. Recto ran for president against **Carlos Garcia** in 1957 on a minor party ticket, placing fourth with 8.6 percent of the vote. The election results do not reflect the lasting impression Recto's principled positions had on radical Filipino nationalists and the "Left." Thirty years after his death, Recto's attacks on the U.S.–Philippine alliance were echoed in the debates over the new MBA that was defeated in 1991 by the Philippine senate.

REFUGEES. A human legacy of the **Indochina Wars** has been the displacement of hundreds of thousands of people as refugees. A Comprehensive Plan of Action for Indochinese refugees was established in 1989 as a multilateral framework to resolve the outflow of people from **Indochina**. This ended in Southeast Asia in 1996. Since 1975, 1.3 million Southeast Asian refugees have been resettled in the United States, from either countries of first asylum or in-country processing programs. Responsibility for U.S. refugee assistance and admission programs rests in the **State Department**'s Bureau of Population, Refugees, and Migration (PRM), headed by an assistant secretary of state. The U.S. willingness to accept the largest number of Indochinese refugees for permanent resettlement is only in part an expression of humanitarianism. There is also a sense of responsibility and obligation, and for some nongovernmental organizations (NGO) groups a sense of guilt. To this can be added to the diplomatic reality presented by the adamant Southeast Asian countries of first asylum that the refugees could not stay. This is particularly true of **Thailand**, which had the heaviest refugee burden, and which presented the unacceptable alternative of involuntary forced repatriation.

The great majority—more than 900,000—of the refugees were Vietnamese. The first Vietnamese intake was the 135,000 mainly ex-military, government officials, or others who worked with the Americans and who fled with American official sponsorship after the fall of Saigon. Since then, hundreds of thousands have come from the refugee camps in the first asylum countries in Southeast Asia where the "**boat people**" landed and ended up in United Nations High Commissioner for Refugees (UNHCR) camps or by processing from **Vietnam** through the **Orderly Departure Program (ODP)**. After the ending of the ODP program, a Resettlement Opportunity for Vietnamese Returnees and a Humanitarian Resettlement program continued to process from the U.S. Consulate General in Ho Chi Minh City applicants who would have been eligible for the ODP program before registration closed in September 1994. The last Vietnamese refugees—approximately 1,500—who had been in the **Philippines** since 1989 without hope of integration, were cleared for admission to the United States in 2005.

The **Khmer Rouge (KR)**'s 1975 victory in **Cambodia** brought a first wave of 34,000 Cambodian refugees who were associated with the old American-supported government, most of whom were quickly accepted by the United States and other countries, in which they often had existing ties. The fearful rule of the KR sent another wave of Cambodians westward, so by 1978, 150,000 were in UNHCR camps in **Thailand**. After the Vietnamese invasion, a third wave arrived—another 150,000—many of whom were KR. By 1980, an estimated 300,000 refugees were in supervised camps in Thailand. In addition, there were at least another 200,000 unsupervised uprooted Cambodians along the Thai–Cambodian border. Those refugees were unregistered and ineligible for processing for resettlement. Most of them eventually voluntarily returned to Cambodia or were involuntarily repatriated by Thai authorities. Between 1978 and 1985, when the Cambodian flow of refugees eligible for resettlement slowed to a trickle, the United States had accepted for resettlement 150,000 Cambodians.

In addition to Vietnamese and Cambodians, a large refugee population fled **Laos** to Thailand after 1975. Perhaps a third of them were ethnic **Hmong**, who fought with the United States in the **secret war**. The Hmong continued to arrive as a Hmong low-level insurgency against the new regime provoked government counterinsurgent tactics, described by Hmong advocates as genocide. The Thais, however, treated the latecomers as illegal economic migrants. The United States accepted for resettlement 90,000 Hmong refugees. Even though the major programs have ended, the processing of refugees continues. The final groups of more than 15,000 Hmong arrived in the United States in 2004 and 2005. There remained, however, some 7,000–8,000 Hmong in camps in northern Thailand, whose prospects for resettlement were dim and who were under threat of forcible repatriation to Laos.

As the flood of Indochinese refugees receded, U.S. refugee admission programs in Southeast Asia focused on 100,000 refugees from **Burma**, particularly the **Karen** ethnic minority people who have fled to Thailand and the **Chin** minority people who have taken refuge in India and **Malaysia**. Given the persecution these peoples have suffered from the Burmese military, the United States considers them as being of special humanitarian concern. In 2006, the United States, working with the UNHCR, prepared to welcome 10,800 Burmese minority refugees, 9,300 Karen from Thailand and 1,500 Chin from Malaysia. However, new **war on terror**–related restrictions in U.S. immigration law delayed the filling of the quota. American law bans entry to anyone who belongs to or provides material support to armed rebel groups. This included the Karen National Defense Organization (KNDO) as well as Chin rebels. The State Department, in cooperation with the Department of Homeland Security, waived the restriction for the Chin and Karen so long as all other criteria for eligibility were met, including not posing a danger to the safety and security of the United States. A much smaller group of Southeast Asian refugees is made up of an estimated 2,000 Vietnamese tribal Montangards, mostly Christian, who fled from Vietnam's highlands into Cambodia in 2004 after violent protests against claimed persecution were met by Vietnamese force. Tripartite negotiations between Cambodia, the UNHCR, and Vietnam led to the voluntary repatriation of the majority. The UNHCR granted refugee status to nearly 700 of them, 260 of whom were admitted to the United States.

REINHARDT, G. FREDERICK (1911–1971). A career Foreign Service Officer, Frederick Reinhardt came from Paris, where he had been counselor of the embassy, to become the American ambassador to first the **State of Vietnam** and then the **Republic of Vietnam** (1955–1957). Technically he succeeded Ambassador **Donald Heath**, but in political fact he followed President Dwight D. Eisenhower's personal representative General **J. Lawton Collins**, who held the personal rank of ambassador but was not diplomatically accredited to Vietnam. This was the period when Prime Minister **Ngo Dinh Diem** was consolidating his control over the country after defeating the sects and deposing **Bao Dai**. Reinhardt was instructed by Secretary of State **John Foster Dulles** to provide Diem full support and assistance. After Vietnam, Reinhardt served as ambassador to Egypt and Italy.

RELIGIOUS FREEDOM. Religious freedom has been an official part of U.S. foreign policy since the Religious Freedom Act of 1998. There is an Office of International Religious Freedom in the **State Department**'s Bureau of Democracy, Rights, and Labor (DRL), which produces an annual International *Religious Freedom Report* that is submitted to Congress. There is also a U.S. Ambassador at Large for Religious Freedom. This office cooperates with the U.S. Commission on International Religious Freedom, created by the same legislative mandate. The issuance of the annual report can provoke angry reactions. **Malaysia**, for example, takes strong exception to criticism of government policies favoring Islam. **Brunei** and **Indonesia** also have been cited for discrimination against non-Muslims.

Countries found to be engaged in systematic, ongoing, and egregious violations of religious freedom are designated "countries of particular concern" (CPC) and can become subjects of sanctions. In Southeast Asia, **Burma** and **Vietnam** have been designated CPC because of their "severe violations" of religious freedom. Burma, a CPC since 1999, refuses to discuss the issues with the United States. Vietnam went on the list in 2004. Extensive negotiations between Washington and Hanoi led to Vietnam's pledge to improve its record. This was connected to its desire to be accorded **permanent normal trade relations (PNTR)** status by the United States. The issue was on the agenda of the June 2005 meeting between President **George**

W. Bush and Vietnam prime minister Vo Van Khai. Vietnam's CPC status was finally lifted in November 2006, recognizing, according to the State Department, "significant improvements towards advancing religious freedom" in the country. Politically, it was connected to the failed efforts by President Bush's administration's to get congressional approval of PNTR for Vietnam prior to his visit to Hanoi for the 2006 **Asia–Pacific Economic Cooperation (APEC)** summit. Burma, however, remained a CPC. *See also* HUMAN RIGHTS.

RENVILLE AGREEMENT, 1948. This was an agreement that was signed on 17 January 1948 on board the USS *Renville* between representative of the Netherlands and the Republic of **Indonesia** for a truce in the so-called Dutch police action, witnessed by the delegates on the **United Nations** Security Council's **Good Offices Committee in Indonesia**.

REPUBLIC OF VIETNAM (RVN). On 26 October 1955, **Ngo Dinh Diem** proclaimed the Republic of Vietnam. Diem had been prime minister of the **State of Vietnam** headed by French nominee **Bao Dai**, the last emperor of Annam. Diem deposed Bao Dai by referendum. In 1956, under a new constitution, an elected National Assembly confirmed Diem as president. The American ambassador, **G. Frederick Reinhardt**, was instructed to assure Diem that American support to the republic would continue. The political impact of the establishment of the new government was to cement the de facto partition of Vietnam between north and south, with two governments claiming international personality, recognition, and international support. It put the nail in the coffin of the national election called for by the 1954 **Geneva Accords**. From the American strategic point of view, support for the RVN was part of a policy of **containment** of communism in Southeast Asia. The new structure of the state gave the alliance a new political quality. This was put baldly in 1965 in the **State Department** White Paper, *Aggression from the North*, in which the **Vietnam War** was characterized as aggression from the communist state in **North Vietnam** to conquer a sovereign people in a neighbor state.

While the U.S. military faced the **Viet Cong** and later the regulars of the People's Army of Vietnam (PAVN) in the field, the American foreign policy establishment in Washington and the embassy in Saigon worked to keep the RVN government fully engaged with the United States. Five secretaries of state and seven ambassadors and their staffs and advisors wrestled for two decades with an RVN political establishment that was both unable and seemingly unwilling to mobilize the necessary resources and commitment. The essentially undemocratic, semiauthoritarian regimes that after the 1963 **Diem coup** were products of military maneuverings and conspiracies seemed mired in corruption and ineptitude. The American establishment was constantly frustrated by its inability to wring what it deemed necessary reforms from the RVN's leadership.

On 30 April 1975, two years after the signing of the **Paris Agreement** and American withdrawal from Vietnam, the PAVN entered Saigon. President **Nguyen Van Thieu** had already resigned nine days earlier, fleeing the country. General Duong Van Minh, one of the key figures in the 1963 **Diem coup** and a rival of Thieu, became the RVN's last president. A PAVN tank battered down the gate to the presidential palace. Minh was confronted in the palace by a PAVN colonel, to whom he surrendered. The RVN had been extinguished and, after three decades, **Ho Chi Minh**'s revolution had been completed. *See also* VIETNAM; VIETNAM WAR.

RICE, CONDOLEEZZA (1954–). President **George W. Bush**'s national security advisor in his first term, Condoleezza Rice became secretary of state in 2005 at the beginning of Bush's second term, replacing **Colin L. Powell**. Her involvement in Southeast Asian affairs got off to a rocky start when she snubbed the July 2005 **Association of Southeast Asian Nations (ASEAN)** postministerial conference (PMC) with its dialogue partners and the subsequent annual meeting of the **ASEAN Regional Forum (ARF)**. Fairly or not, this was interpreted by some ASEAN officials as indifference to Southeast Asia even as the United States was trying to engage the region in the **war on terror**. Although blamed by the **State Department** on scheduling problems, another explanation was that it was a sign of American unhappiness at the prospect of **Burma** becoming chair of ASEAN in 2006. To take some of the sting out of her absence, Rice made an 18-hour stop in Phuket, **Thailand**, in July 2005 on her way to Beijing and Tokyo, ostensibly to assess **tsunami** relief efforts. In September

2005, she met the ASEAN foreign ministers in New York during the **United Nations** General Assembly session to reassure them of U.S. commitments in the region. Her 2006 Southeast Asia agenda reflected this. In May, she traveled to **Indonesia** to underline visibly the full normalization of U.S.–Indonesian security ties. In July, she appeared at the 2006 ASEAN PMC and ARF sessions. At the PMC, she and her ASEAN counterparts unveiled the "Framework Document" for the **ASEAN–U.S. Enhanced Partnership**. The glow of the new engagement was slightly dimmed, however, in 2007 when Secretary Rice again failed to appear at the ASEAN PMC and the ARF, pleading Middle East business.

ROBERTS, EDMUND (1784–1836). Owner of a Portsmouth, New Hampshire, shipping business, Edmund Roberts was sent by President Andrew Jackson as an envoy to **Siam** (**Thailand**), Muscat, and Annam (**Vietnam**) to further American trade interests. The British had negotiated a treaty with Siam in 1826 following the first Anglo–Burmese War, and the United States sought equal footing. Arriving in Siam in 1833 on the U.S. naval sloop *Peacock*, Roberts concluded a "Treaty of Amity and Commerce." He was less successful with the king of Annam. The Siam treaty was deemed important enough for Roberts to voyage back to Siam in 1836 to exchange the ratifications. Edmunds died in Macao returning from Siam. *See* ROBERTS TREATY.

ROBERTS TREATY, 1833. Negotiated by **Edmund Roberts** with the Kingdom of **Siam**, the Roberts "Treaty of Amity and Commerce" was the first U.S. treaty with an Asian state. Its effects were limited, as no special rights were granted and there was no permission to open a consulate. In 1849, American envoy **Joseph Balestier** sought to strengthen the Roberts Treaty, but it was not until more than two decades later that the **Harris Treaty** placed the United States on the same footing in Siam with its British commercial rivals.

ROBERTSON, WALTER S. (1893–1970). A noncareer appointee, Walter S. Robertson was perhaps the most influential assistant secretary of state for East Asian and Pacific affairs who has ever served. From 1953 to 1959, Robertson was the right-hand Asia man for his friend, Secretary of State **John Foster Dulles**, in the administration of President **Dwight D. Eisenhower**. A Virginia investment banker and student of the Chinese economy, Robertson was a major contributor to the architecture of American Cold War engagement in Asia. He mapped out the course of **containment** in Korea, Taiwan, and Southeast Asia, backing Syngman Rhee, Chiang K'ai Shek, and **Ngo Dinh Diem**. Robertson was guided by one principle: "resisting the power and influence of Communist **China**." A proponent of the so-called **domino theory** of the strategic consequences of failure in **Vietnam**, he championed full support for the Diem regime to help it eradicate communist subversion and influence. Ailing, he tried to retire in 1957, but Secretary Dulles told him, "You can't leave. I need you for policy."

ROGERS, WILLIAM P. (1913–2001). Secretary of state from 1969 to 1973, William P. Rogers was a well-connected lawyer and Republican activist who had been attorney general in President **Dwight D. Eisenhower**'s second administration. He was personally close to **Richard M. Nixon** who, despite Rogers's lack of foreign policy expertise, made him secretary of state. In that post, he was overshadowed by National Security Advisor **Henry A. Kissinger** operating from the White House. In the critical years of the diplomacy ending the **Vietnam War**, Rogers was frozen out of the policy-making loop. He was out of synchronization with Kissinger from the beginning of the Nixon administration, when he advocated an early American cease-fire and called the U.S. decision to draw down its forces in Vietnam through the process of **Vietnamization** "irreversible." He dutifully carried out his official functions, representing the United States at **Southeast Asia Treaty Organization (SEATO)** Council meetings and accompanying the president on his state visits to Southeast Asia. It was Rogers who signed the 24 January 1973 **Paris Agreement** ending the **Vietnam War** for the United States. Rogers was unwilling to support Nixon in the Watergate scandal and was forced to resign, to be succeeded by Kissinger.

ROMULO, CARLOS P. (1899–1995). The **Philippines**' most famous diplomat, Carlos Romulo was also a major literary figure, becoming in 1942 the first Asian to win a Pulitzer Prize. During the period of the **Commonwealth of the Philippines**, he was the Philippine delegate to the U.S. Congress. As an aide to General **Douglas MacArthur**, he came ashore at Leyte with MacArthur and Commonwealth President **Sergio Osmeña** in 1944. From 1944 to Philippine independence in 1946, he was the resident commissioner of the Philippines in Washington. He signed the Charter of the **United Nations (UN)** on behalf of the Philippines and served as president of the UN General Assembly in 1949–1950. In addition to being a Philippine ambassador to the United States, Romulo served three Philippine presidents as minister/secretary of foreign affairs: **Elpidio Quirino** (1950–1952), **Diosdado Macapagal** (1963–1964), and **Ferdinand Marcos** (1968–1984). In tribute to Romulo's "long and close association with the United States," President **Ronald Reagan** awarded him the Presidential Medal of Freedom in 1984.

ROOT–TAKAHIRA AGREEMENT, 1908. In 1908, as the United States and Japan seemed to be drifting toward war, both countries resolved to preserve good relations by asserting their intention to maintain the status quo in the Pacific. In a 30 November 1908 agreement between Secretary of State Elihu Root and Japan's ambassador in Washington, Takahira Kogoro, the two countries agreed to respect each other's territorial possessions, with the United States accepting both Japan's right to annex Korea and its special position in Manchuria.

ROSTOW, WALT WHITMAN (1916– 2003). A Yale Ph.D. and Rhodes Scholar, Walt Rostow was perhaps the most "hawkish" of Presidents **John F. Kennedy**'s and **Lyndon B. Johnson**'s senior civilian advisors on **Vietnam**. Rostow came into the Kennedy administration in 1961 as deputy to **McGeorge Bundy**, the president's special assistant for national security affairs. During World War II, he had served in the **Office of Strategic Services (OSS)**. A political economist, from 1950 to 1960 he was on the faculty of the Massachusetts Institute of Technology. He was the author of *The Stages of Economic Growth: A Non-Communist Manifesto*, an influential study of developmental economics. In 1960, he joined Senator Kennedy's presidential campaign. He was the intellectual guru of the Kennedy administration's approach to "nation building." From the outset of his official service, Rostow advocated carrying the war to **North Vietnam**. He accompanied General **Maxwell Taylor** on the October 1961 **Taylor–Rostow mission** to Saigon, which led to the recommendation to intensify the American military commitment to the defense of **South Vietnam**. He moved over to the **State Department** at the end of 1961 to become the head of the Policy Planning Council. Although out of the decision-making loop, he continued to argue for a forceful response to North Vietnamese aggression. He came into the presidential circle again in 1966 when Johnson named him to replace Bundy as national security advisor. His unwavering commitment to the course of the war earned him the opprobrium of his fellow academics in the northeast, and on leaving government he took a post at the University of Texas in the Lyndon B. Johnson School of Public Service.

ROTH, STANLEY O. (1954–). Named assistant secretary of state for East Asian and Pacific affairs in President **William J. Clinton**'s second term (1997–2001), Stanley Roth brought a new focus to the post. He felt that not enough attention had been given to Southeast Asia and consciously sought to raise the region's bureaucratic profile. On his first trip to his area of responsibility, he included the **Philippines** and **Indonesia**. He also brought to the office an appreciation of congressional sensibilities. From 1978 to 1982, he had been a legislative aide to Representative **Stephen Solarz** and went with Solarz to the House Subcommittee on East Asia and the Pacific, where he served as director and consultant from 1983 to 1992, while Solarz chaired it. In the first Clinton administration he was a deputy assistant secretary of defense for East Asia and the Pacific and then the senior officer for Asian affairs on the National Security Council. He began his tour as assistant secretary of state as the **financial crisis of 1997–1998** threatened political stability in the region and finished it in the struggle to build an independent **East Timor**. In between, he dealt with the final touches in the normalization of relations with **Vietnam**, the coup in **Cambodia**, the **Joseph Estrada** impeachment and irregular succession of **Gloria Macapagal-Arroyo** in the Philippines, diplomatic efforts to mount a multilateral front against the junta in **Burma**, and the democratic political transition in post-**Suharto** Indonesia. At the end of the Clinton administration, Roth left government for the private sector as vice president for international relations for the Boeing Company. His continued interest in Indonesia was reflected in his membership on the Board of Trustees of the **United States–Indonesia Society (USINDO)**.

ROXAS, MANUEL (1892–1948). Manuel Roxas was first president of the independent Republic of the **Philippines** (1946–1948). He died in office and was succeeded by Vice President **Elpidio Quirino**. Roxas's political career began in 1917, when he was elected a municipal councilor in Capiz (now named Roxas). He became a member of the Philippine House of Representatives and was its speaker. During the Japanese occupation, Roxas cooperated with the collaborationist government headed by **José Laurel**. Faced with the possibility of trial after the war, Roxas was completely exonerated by his friend, General **Douglas MacArthur**. In the 1946 presidential election, he defeated **Sergio Osmeña**, who had become **Commonwealth of the Philippines** president when President **Manuel Quezon** died during the war. Two months after his inauguration as commonwealth president, Roxas became president of the independent Philippine state, on 2 July 1946. In January 1948 he extended a general amnesty to all Filipinos who had been arrested for collaboration with the Japanese. Roxas's term of office was marked by corruption and the rise of the **Hukbalahap** rebellion. He was criticized by Philippine nationalists for granting the United States special rights in the package of agreements that tied the Philippines closely to the United States including the **Military Bases Agreement (MBA)** and the **Bell Act**. These, however, appeared to be the American conditions for large inputs of U.S. economic assistance for postwar Philippine rehabilitation.

ROY, J. STAPLETON (1935–). One of the **State Department**'s premier Asia hands, Stapleton Roy had already served as ambassador to **Singapore** (1984–1986) and the People's Republic of **China** (1991–1994), as well as earlier postings to Taiwan and **Thailand**, before he was sent as ambassador to **Indonesia** from 1996 to 1999. His tenure coincided with the final years of President **Suharto**'s government, the **financial crisis of 1997–1998**, Suharto's resignation, and new President **B. J. Habibie**'s decision to hold the **East Timor ref-**

erendum. In the political uncertainties of the moment, Roy represented American support for the Indonesian democratization process.
He warned the Indonesian military of the bilateral consequences if
there were intervention against the civilian government. Roy's embassy was a forceful advocate for American companies threatened by
cancellation of possibly corrupt contracts made with companies connected to Suharto. He argued that the sanctity of contracts trumped
corruption. Ambassador Roy's insistence on a firm, consistent policy
was complicated by the public damage of "**Lippo-gate**," the illegal
contributions from James Riady to the Democratic Party and President **William J. Clinton** in the 1994 and 1996 American elections.
Returning from **East Timor** after an inspection of preparations for
the referendum, Ambassador Roy expressed his concerns about Indonesia's responsibility for providing security. He also warned the international community not to use East Timor to exacerbate separatism elsewhere in Indonesia. Back in Washington in 1999, Roy was
named assistant secretary of state for intelligence and research. On
retirement in 2001, he became a managing partner in Kissinger As-
sociates. Ambassador Roy epitomized American policy toward Indonesia in a statement attributed to him and widely circulated by advocates of East Timorese rights: The dilemma, he said, "is that
Indonesia matters and East Timor doesn't."

RUSK, DEAN (1909–1994). Named secretary of state by President
John F. Kennedy in 1961, Dean Rusk served in that capacity to the
end of the administration of President **Lyndon B. Johnson** in 1969.
Only Cordell Hull had a longer tenure as secretary of state. An alumnus of Davidson College, as a Rhodes Scholar at Oxford University
he was in the room when the Oxford Union cast its famous vote in favor of appeasing Nazi Germany. Rusk was an Army intelligence officer during World War II, serving first in the China–Burma–India
theater and ending as a colonel in the War Department, where he
helped draw the 38th parallel line separating the Soviet and American postwar zones in Korea. He joined the **State Department** in
1946. As assistant secretary of state for Far Eastern affairs under
Dean Acheson in 1950, he helped manage American diplomacy in
the first years of the Korean War as well as the initial fallout from
U.S. support to Chinese nationalist general Li Mi's forces in Burma

in the **KMT–Burma crisis**. Already a trustee of the Rockefeller Foundation in 1950, Rusk left government in 1952 to become president of the foundation, until Kennedy selected him to head the State Department.

Somewhat overshadowed in the Kennedy administration by National Security Advisor **McGeorge Bundy**, Rusk came into his own in the Johnson administration. A staunch anticommunist and implacably hostile to the People's Republic of **China**, he was among the most "hawkish" of the presidential advisors during the **Vietnam War**. He supported escalation and carrying the war to **North Vietnam**. He believed that American military power would win the United States a position of strength from which to force the **Democratic Republic of Vietnam (DRV)** to yield. When the United States began its bombing campaign against the North, Rusk noted that to stop the bombing "all they had to do is to leave the South alone." His uncompromising support of the war, even as American public opinion was turning against it, made him a favorite target of antiwar protesters, including his son Richard, from whom he became estranged only to reconcile later—but without changing his mind. Unlike many of his colleagues, Rusk never doubted the correctness of his course, remarking only that he had underestimated the tenacity of the enemy and overestimated the patience of the American people.

RUSK–THANAT COMMUNIQUÉ. On 6 March 1962, U.S. secretary of state **Dean Rusk** and **Thai** foreign minister Thanat Khoman issued a joint communiqué that bilateralized the obligations of Article IV of the **Southeast Asia Collective Defense Treaty** (Manila Pact), creating the **Southeast Asia Treaty Organization (SEATO)**. In the statement the United States declared that its obligation to help Thailand in the event of a "communist armed attack" was "individual as well as collective." Furthermore, it affirmed that the stated obligation did not depend on prior agreement by other SEATO members. It was asserted that the United States had the "firm intention" of helping Thailand resist direct and indirect communist subversion and aggression. In policy terms, the Rusk–Thanat interpretation of SEATO obligation placed U.S.–Thai security relations on a basis similar to the **Philippines**, which had a **Mutual Defense Treaty (MDT)** with the United States. The context for the statement was Bangkok's apprehensions over the continuing advances of the communist **Pathet Lao** in Laos toward the Thai–Lao **Mekong River** border and Thai doubts of the value of SEATO's multilateral commitment. The Rusk–Thanat formulation was reaffirmed by successive Thai and American governments and became the underpinning of the Thai–U.S. alliance in the **Vietnam War**. In 1969, for example, Secretary of State **William P. Rogers** expressly stated that the Rusk–Thanat agreement was a "valid restatement" of U.S. responsibilities in SEATO. The same obligations were expressed during the **Third Indochina War**, as **Vietnam**'s army on the Thai–Cambodian border seemed poised to pursue the **Khmer resistance** in their Thailand sanctuaries.

– S –

SABAH. The former British crown colony of North Borneo, Sabah was incorporated into the Federation of **Malaysia** at its creation in 1962 over the objections of the **Philippines**. The Philippine claim is based on inheritance of the territorial rights of the Sultanate of Sulu, now part of the modern Philippine state. Originally part of **Brunei**, to which the Sulu sultan was theoretically subject, the territory was leased in 1865 for 10 years by the American consul in Brunei, who in turn transferred it to an American trading company. In 1882, the lease passed to the British North Borneo Company. After World War II, the North Borneo Company transferred its interest to the British crown, which then in 1962 ceded the territory to the new Malaysian state. The Philippines insisted that Great Britain did not have sovereign rights to cede and that with British withdrawal North Borneo remained part of the Philippines, which had inherited the Sultan of Sulu's rights. The Sabah dispute continues to plague Malaysian–Philippine relations. Washington's position on the issue is neutrality, although while the United States was sovereign in the Philippines, it understood that the status of North Borneo was a leased territory. Support by President John F. Kennedy's administration for the inclusion of Sabah in Malaysia as contributing to regional stability did not sit well in Manila. The United States has made it unambiguously clear that its security obligation to the defense of the Philippines does not extend to Sabah.

SARIT THANARAT (1908– 1963). Field Marshal Sarit Thanarat replaced **Phibul Songgram** as **Thailand**'s military strong man in a 1957 lightning coup. Prime Minister Sarit expanded the close relationship with the United States fostered by Phibul. This won large amounts of U.S. economic and military assistance. He initiated Thailand's first Five Year Plan, geared to an export-oriented economic strategy. Politically, he embraced a traditional Thai identity of nation, king, and religion, emphasizing the king's ceremonial role in the Thai state. Washington applauded his suppression of domestic leftists and communists, many of whom fled into exile, to resurface as part of the Thai communist insurgency in the early 1960s. Sarit's government collaborated with the American embassy, headed from 1958 to 1961 by **U. Alexis Johnson**, in the efforts to destabilize the neutralist government of **Laos** headed by Prime Minister **Souvanna Phouma**. Sarit was a distant relative of American-favored Laotian rightest strong man **Phoumi Nosavan**. Sarit's government also facilitated dissident Cambodian groups seeking to overthrow **Cambodia**'s Prime Minister **Norodom Sihanouk**. Sarit was seconded in power by General **Thanom Kittikachorn**, who led a peaceful transition of authority on Sarit's death.

SAVANGVATTHANA (1907–1978). Second and last ruler of the independent Kingdom of **Laos**, King Savangvatthana ascended the throne de jure at the death of his father, King **Sisavangvong**, in 1959. He had acted as regent during the old king's illness. Savangvatthana was never ceremonially installed as ruler, waiting for the end of the civil wars. The revolutionary regime of the **Pathet Lao** forced his abdication on 1 December 1975. He, his wife, and his son, the crown prince, died under mysterious circumstances in a prison camp in 1978.

SAYRE, FRANCIS B. (1885–1972). Francis "Frank" Sayre was the son-in-law of President Woodrow Wilson. He went to Bangkok in 1923 as an advisor on foreign affairs to the king of **Siam (Thailand)**. Working from the model of the 1920 **Siam–U.S. treaty**, he advised the Ministry of Foreign Affairs as its diplomats worked to revise the unequal treaties with other Western powers. By 1927, Siam had freed itself from the burdens of special **trade** concessions and consular courts. Sayre was held in high regard, and the king awarded him the title of

"Lord of Good Friendship." A street in Bangkok running alongside the Foreign Ministry building is named for him. Between 1933 and 1939, Sayre served as an assistant secretary of state dealing with Far Eastern affairs. In 1937, he co-chaired the Philippine–American Commission to examine the problems of preparation for **Philippine** independence. In 1939 President Roosevelt sent him to the **Commonwealth of the Philippines** as American high commissioner, where he had to defend a U.S. policy that deemed the Philippines strategically expendable. He escaped from the Philippines by submarine before its fall to the Japanese.

SEA SUPPLY CORPORATION. The Overseas Southeast Asia Supply Corporation, better known as Sea Supply, was a **Central Intelligence Agency (CIA)** proprietary company established in Bangkok, **Thailand**, by **Paul Helliwell**. It functioned to provide weapons and ammunition to the Chinese nationalist forces in **Burma** and to support CIA activities in Thailand and **Laos**. *See also* KMT–BURMA CRISIS; SECOND INDOCHINA WAR; SECRET WAR; VIETNAM WAR.

SECOND INDOCHINA WAR. This is the term used to describe the complex of conflicts in **Vietnam**, **Laos**, and **Cambodia** between 1954 and 1975. In these countries the United States, implementing its policy of containment of **communist** expansion, engaged in direct and indirect military intervention to sponsor and defend anticommunist governments against what America called communist aggression. The Vietnam front is better known as the **Vietnam War**. *See also* KHMER ROUGE; PATHET LAO; SECRET WAR.

SECRET WAR. This is the name given to the war funded and managed in **Laos** by the **Central Intelligence Agency (CIA)** from 1961 to 1972 and waged by the **Hmong** army of General **Vang Pao**, against the communist **Pathet Lao** and its North Vietnamese **Viet Minh** and People's Army of Vietnam (PAVN) allies. At the Laotian national level of conflict, the war was to prevent the Pathet Lao from defeating the noncommunist neutralist government of the Kingdom of Laos. For the Americans, the war was the Laotian front of the **Vietnam War**. The strategic goal was to disrupt and interdict North

Vietnamese lines of supply and communication between north and south along the **Ho Chi Minh trail**. The Hmong were defending their ethnic identity and traditional patterns of life. **Thailand**, under the leadership of first **Sarit Thanarat** and then **Thanom Kittika-chorn**, viewed the defense of Laos's **Mekong River** plain as vital to its own security and provided basing and "volunteer" support for the secret war. The reason it was "secret" is because the 1962 **Geneva Accords on Laos** had guaranteed the country's neutrality and limited any foreign military presence.

Overt U.S. military activity in Laos was in place in 1954, embedded in the United States Operating Mission (USOM) in the form of a Program Evaluation Office (PEO) responsible for delivering military assistance to the Royal Lao Army (FAR). The United States displaced the French from their advisory role to the Lao military, and by 1959, American Special Forces advisors disguised as civilians were operating in 12 mobile training teams. In 1961, the American military presence was officially signaled by the establishment of a U.S. **Military Assistance Advisory Group (MAAG)**. While uniformed Americans were officially working with FAR, American CIA civilians were clandestinely training ethnic Hmong. The model was the Thai paramilitary **PARU** special police units that had been built up by CIA case officer **James W. "Bill" Lair**. Lair's PARU training of the Hmong took place on both sides of the Lao–Thai border.

As the situation in Laos grew "confused," to use President **Dwight D. Eisenhower**'s characterization, the need to mount a stronger anticommunist military capability without direct American involvement led to the decision to arm and train the Hmong. American ambassador to Laos **Leonard Unger**, who successfully resisted a plan to introduce more uniformed American soldiers, supported an expanded Hmong program. In order to keep the political damage of possible failure limited, he had all of the support functions done from Thai facilities under a secret agreement with Thailand. The CIA's military control of the war operated from Udorn Air Base, where the CIA-commanded 4802nd Joint Liaison Detachment was based. In Laos, a group of nine American CIA case officers and 99 Thai PARU went to work. Beginning with a force of 1,000 in 1961, by 1963 President **John F. Kennedy** had authorized an expansion to 20,000 armed Hmong to harass new PAVN forces coming into Laos, who were attacking FAR posts as well as Vang Pao's Hmong. The CIA's airline, **Air America**, supplied the Hmong and provided troop mobility. The Hmong guerrillas were also used by the Studies and Observation Group (SOG), a U.S. Special Forces unit that carried out reconnaissance and harassment in Laos along the **Ho Chi Minh** trail. SOG activities in Laos ran from 1965 to 1971.

In the first years of the secret war, the Hmong guerrillas were engaged in a seasonal see-saw battle across the **Plain of Jars** that saw the Pathet Lao and PAVN on the offensive against the Hmong in the dry season, and the Hmong striking back in the rainy season. After 1966, when **Theodore "Ted" Shackley** became CIA station chief in Laos, the Hmong were pressured to shift from guerrilla tactics to a more conventional posture and began taking heavy casualties. In 1968, new PAVN main force units undertook the dry season offensive. As the PAVN became more entrenched on the Plain of Jars, U.S. air sorties increased. In 1969, backed by American air power, Vang Pao reclaimed the Plain of Jars, only to lose it to two fresh PAVN divisions in early 1970. By then the United States was using B-52 bombers not just to interdict the Ho Chi Minh trail, but also in support of Vang Pao. In northwest Laos's Nam Tha Province, a smaller CIA-organized paramilitary force of Yao, Lahu, and Akha tribesmen, with a few Wa from **Burma**, operated from a base at Nam Yu. Commanded first by William Young and after 1965 by **Tony Poe**, the force was engaged in intelligence collection in **China**'s contiguous Yunnan Province as well as harassment of Pathet Lao units.

Strategic headquarters for the secret war was in the American embassy in Vientiane. Two American ambassadors in particular, **William Sullivan** (1964–1969) and **G. McMurtrie Godley** (1969–1973), acted as proconsuls, running the war and propping up the government of **Souvanna Phouma** who, although a neutralist, only had the Americans between him and a Pathet Lao victory. He could go to the ambassadors to call in air strikes to defend government-held lines, but he was largely kept in the dark about the secret war or SOG activities along the Ho Chi Minh trail. The secret war in Laos paralleled the **Vietnam War** but with independent lines of command. The political line from Vientiane ran ultimately to National Security Advisor and Secretary of State **Henry Kissinger**. The overt military line ran back to the Hawaii headquarters of the **United States Pacific Command**.

The CIA tactical command ran from the station chief back to CIA headquarters in Washington. Both Sullivan and Godley carefully managed the war so as to maintain diplomatic deniability. The independence of the American ambassador in Vientiane from the U.S. military command in Saigon in putting restrictions on activities by U.S. ground forces in Laos like the SOG was a point of friction. While tactical command was in Vientiane. Shackley moved Lair from Vang Pao's **Long Tieng** headquarters to Udorn in 1966 to head up the CIA's 4802nd. When Lair left in 1968, his deputy, Lloyd "Pat" Landry, took over. Landry was a veteran of the CIA intervention in Indonesia's **PRRI–Permesta** revolt who, like Poe, had escaped capture by submarine.

To bolster Vang Pao's weakened forces, 1971 saw the increasing deployment of Thai "volunteer" military units sponsored by the CIA. In early 1972, Long Tieng itself was threatened by a Vietnamese assault. Even with American air support, it was clear that the Vietnamese had gained the strategic advantage in northeast Laos. As the American Vietnam War ended on 27 January 1973, Souvanna Phouma and the Pathet Lao signed their own cease-fire agreement in February 1973. The cease-fire did not hold, and American B-52 strikes continued until 17 April. Reconnaissance flights providing intelligence on Pathet Lao and Vietnamese troop movements ended on 4 June 1974, when the U.S. Congress prohibited any American funds to be used for military activities in **Indochina**. Vang Pao's army now stood alone against the Pathet Lao, who threatened genocide. The Hmong continued to fight on. In the face of a major Pathet Lao and PAVN assault in May 1975, the CIA persuaded Vang Pao to withdraw from Long Tieng, and on 15 May 1975 to be air lifted out of Laos. He was among the tens of thousand Hmong who fled the country in justified fear of retaliation. The last Hmong mountain stronghold fell to the Vietnamese in 1977. Although the precise figure will never be known, it is estimated that over 10,000 Hmong warriors died in the secret war. *See also* REFUGEES.

SENI PRAMOJ (1905–1997). Thai statesman and politician Seni Pramoj was **Thailand**'s minister to the United States in 1942, when under Japanese influence the Thai government of **Pibul Songgram** declared war on the United States. Seni refused to deliver the declaration and, acting independently of Bangkok, enlisted American support for the **Free Thai** underground anti-Japanese movement. At the end of the war, Seni returned to Thailand, to become prime minister and negotiate the terms of peace with the Western allies. He led three short and ill-fated democratic governments in 1975 and 1976. Seni was an older brother of **Kukrit Pramoj**.

SHACKLEY, THEODORE (1927–2002). Nicknamed the "blond ghost," Theodore "Ted" Shackley was a key official of the **Central Intelligence Agency (CIA)**. Coming to the agency from U.S. Army counterintelligence in 1953, he was quickly involved in covert operations. From Guatemalan and Cuban operations, he moved in 1966 to **Laos**, where as CIA station chief in Ambassador **William Sullivan**'s American embassy he directed the **secret war** against the **Pathet Lao** and their North Vietnamese allies. In 1969, he moved to Saigon as station chief and under **William Colby** ran the Phoenix program of directed assassinations in the **Viet Cong** infrastructure. Critics of the CIA's activities have alleged that during his years in Southeast Asia, Shackley helped finance operations by involvement in the drug trade. He returned to Washington to head the Western Hemisphere division and then became associate deputy director for operations, second-in-command for covert operations. He was retired in 1979 as part of President **Jimmy Carter**'s shakeup of the CIA. Shackley's posthumous autobiography is *Spymaster: My Life in the CIA*.

SHULTZ, GEORGE P. (1920–). Secretary of State George Shultz served in the administrations of President Ronald Reagan from July 1982 until the end of the second term in January 1989. He replaced Alexander Haig, who basically had been fired after 18 months in office. Shultz was more than prepared for the job. A trained economist, Shultz came into the highest levels of government in President **Richard M. Nixon**'s administration from being dean of the University of Chicago Graduate School of Business. He was labor secretary and then secretary of the treasury under Nixon. Between the Nixon and Reagan administrations, Shultz headed the Bechtel Corporation. For his Asian responsibilities, he was supported in the first term by Assistant Secretary of State for East Asian and Pacific Affairs **Paul Wolfowitz** and in the second term by **Gaston Sigur**. Reversing the patterns of the Nixon and **Carter** administrations, Shultz wrested control of foreign policy back from the National Security Council to the **State Department**.

In Southeast Asia, Secretary Shultz gave due diligence to the concerns of the **Association of Southeast Asian Nations (ASEAN)**, attending all of the grouping's annual meetings from 1983 to 1989. Shultz believed that ASEAN's evolution was an example of peaceful cooperation for the world. To his ASEAN counterparts, he pressed an economic agenda of market forces, limited government intervention, and trade liberalization. With respect to ASEAN's immediate regional political concerns, Shultz reiterated American policy of support for ASEAN in the **Third Indochina War**, advising the members to keep the pressure on Hanoi. Aware of the burdens that Indochinese **refugees** were placing on the countries of first asylum, the secretary assured them of American commitment to resettle refugees and provide humanitarian relief. The special security and refugee needs of **Thailand** were addressed in meetings in Bangkok with Thailand's Prime Minister Prem Tinsulanonda in 1988, capped by a visit to a Cambodian refugee camp. During his time in office, in addition to the ASEAN meetings Shultz met twice with Prime Minister **Lee Kuan Yew** in **Singapore** (1984 and 1986), visited President **Suharto** in **Indonesia** (1988), and called on Sultan **Hassanal Bolkiah** in **Brunei** in 1986. Shultz had two meetings in **Malaysia** with Prime Minister **Mahathir Mohammad** (1984 and 1988), during which the differences in the two countries' regional economic and political perspectives were displayed.

The greatest bilateral attention to Southeast Asia during Shultz's time in office was given to the **Philippines**. Shultz had traveled to Manila to meet with President **Ferdinand Marcos** in June 1983, only weeks before the assassination of **Benigno Aquino**, which triggered the crisis that led to Marcos's downfall. In the turmoil following the disputed January 1986 snap election called by Marcos, Shultz agreed with senior State Department advisors that Marcos had to go. The problem was convincing President Reagan of that. After Reagan reluctantly agreed, Shultz, whose closeness to the president had been part of his strength as secretary of state, worried that his personal relationship might have been irreparably damaged. The next task was to bolster the new democratic Philippine government of President **Corazon Aquino**. Shultz visited Aquino in the Philippines three times, in 1986, 1987, and 1988, to demonstrate the vitality of the "unique" American interest in the Philippines. In 1987, he unveiled in Manila an emergency package of economic assistance, which was valued at $325 million. While proving that the United States was a reliable ally, Washington also sought to overcome the resentment against its long association with the Marcos government and look to the future, which included the most vital of the American interests, the renegotiation of the **Military Bases Agreement (MBA)**.

SIAM. The country now known as **Thailand** was known until 1939 as Siam and its citizens as Siamese. The etymology of the word Siam is obscure. The historical origins of the Siamese kingdoms are in the prehistoric movement of ethnic T'ai people from southern **China** into the river valleys and plains of northern continental Southeast Asia. The name Siam does not appear as a name among any of the T'ai states and principalities that eventually arose. One theory is that Siam is a dialectical variant of an originally Chinese word, *xiān*, referring to the Shan, who are ethnic T'ai. The two most important T'ai kingdoms before the modern state were Sukhothai, founded in the 13th century, and Ayutthia (Ayudhya), founded in the 14th century. From the first Western contacts at the end of the 16th century, the ruler of Ayutthia was known as the king of Siam. Ayutthia was sacked by the Burmese in 1767. In 1782, Siam's modern Rattnakosin era began, called after the island location in Bangkok—today's "old city"—where King Rama I founded the Chakri dynasty. The king of Siam encountered by American envoy **Edmund Roberts**, who negotiated the first U.S.–Siamese treaty in 1833, was Rama III (Nangklao), grandson of the dynastic founder. Diplomatic intercourse with the Kingdom of Siam continued until 1939, when extreme nationalist prime minister **Phibul Songgram** officially renamed the state Muang Thai, or Thailand (Land of the Free), with its play on T'ai ethnicity. The postwar government, repudiating the Phibul regime, reverted to the name Siam, but when Phibul returned to power in 1949, the name Thailand was restored for good. Informally, Siam and Thailand and Siamese and Thai are both still used synonymously.

SIAM–U.S. TREATY AND PROTOCOL OF 1920. This instrument replaced **Townsend Harris**'s treaty of 1856. The United States gave up its rights of extraterritoriality and special **trade** rights. It recognized Siam's new place in the international system as a signatory to the Treaty of Versailles and member of the League of Nations, as well as the modernization of the Siamese state. On the advice of **Francis B. Sayre**, the American advisor to the Siamese Ministry of Foreign Affairs, the new U.S. treaty set the pattern for the revision of Siam's unequal treaties with other Western trading nations.

SIGUR, GASTON J., Jr. (1924–1995). A distinguished academic expert on Japan and East Asian international relations at George Washington University, Gaston Sigur had been director of the university's Sino–Soviet Center when he joined the administration of President **Ronald Reagan**. During Reagan's first term (1981–1985), he was director of Asian affairs in the National Security Council, moving in the second term (1985–1989) to the post of assistant secretary of state for East Asian and the Pacific affairs. He had responsibilities at the working level for the development of American policy toward **normalization of relations with Vietnam** and the prisoners of war/missing in action (**POW/MIA**) issues as well as support for the resistance of the **Association of Southeast Asian Nations (ASEAN)** to the Vietnamese invasion and occupation of **Cambodia** in the **Third Indochina War**. After leaving government, Sigur returned to George Washington University, where the university's Center for Asian Studies is now named for him.

SIHANOUK, NORODOM (1922–). King of **Cambodia**, prime minister, prince, president, "head of state," and king again, Norodom Sihanouk had the longest and most variegated official public life in modern Southeast Asia. At the death of King Sisowath Monivang in 1941, the French passed over his eldest son in favor of 19-year-old Sihanouk, a maternal grandson, in the hope of getting a more pliable figurehead ruler. After World War II, Sihanouk expressed the nationalist aspirations that were being urged elsewhere in **Indochina**. By 1953, enjoying popular traditional deference as a **Khmer** king, Sihanouk helped win independence from France. Two years later, in 1955, Sihanouk shocked the nation by abdicating in favor of his father, Norodom Suramarit, so that he could rule as prime minister and not be bound by the ceremonies and obligations of the court.

Sihanouk defined Cambodia's international role as neutralist and was a convener of the Bandung **Asian–African Conference** and a founder of the **Nonaligned Movement (NAM)**. Sihanouk sought in neutralism protection against U.S. allies **Thailand** and the **Republic of Vietnam**, both of which he felt had designs on Cambodia. The reporting to Secretary of State **John Foster Dulles** on the significance for the United States of Sihanouk's position on Vietnam from Ambassador **Carl Strom** in Phnom Penh and **Elbridge Durbrow** in Saigon was markedly different. The latter, however, gained a more attentive hearing. To the dismay of the United States, Sihanouk's neutralism involved closer relations with the Soviet Union and, particularly, the People's Republic of **China**. Sihanouk's hostility to the United States grew with his suspicions that Washington and the **Ngo Dinh Diem** government in South **Vietnam** were conspiring to overthrow or even assassinate him. Ultimately, his anger caused a breach in diplomatic relations in 1965 that was not repaired until 1969.

Sihanouk faced domestic opposition from democrats, anticommunist rightists, and communists. On 18 March 1970, while he was out of the country, a coup in Phnom Penh deposed him. From exile in Beijing, he rallied a National United Front of Cambodia (FUNK) against the American-supported **Lon Nol** government. Fronting for the **Khmer Rouge**, he returned to Phnom Penh in 1975 as head of state in the Royal Government of the National Union of Kampuchea (GRUNK). In 1976, the Khmer Rouge (KR), in total control in **Democratic Kampuchea (DK)**, forced him to resign and held him in semihouse arrest. In 1978, he was allowed to go into exile again in Pyongyang and Beijing. During the **Third Indochina War**, Sihanouk was the titular head of the **Coalition Government of Democratic Kampuchea (CGDK)**, the political face of the **Khmer resistance** against the Vietnamese invasion and occupation of Cambodia. He returned to Cambodia in 1993 as a ceremonial constitutional monarch and "head of state for life" of the new Cambodian state. Ageing and ill, Sihanouk abdicated in 2004 in favor of King Norodom Sihamoni, his eldest son by his sixth wife, the Italian–Cambodian Queen Monique, passing over his eldest son, Norodom Ranariddh, who had led the royalist party **Funcinpec** in the CGDK during the Third Indochina War and then in the political competition of the post-1993 Cambodian state.

SINGAPORE. An island city-state at the tip of the Malay Peninsula, Singapore, at 265 square miles (685 square kilometers), with a population of 4.7 million people (est. 2007), is the smallest territorial state in Southeast Asia, but in U.S. policy is one of the most important regional states. Singapore became independent in 1965, and with the establishment of diplomatic relations became a close political, economic, and military friend of the United States. Prior to independence, Singapore, founded in 1819, had been a British crown colony until it was folded into federal **Malaysia** in 1963. The difficulties of politically absorbing ethnic Chinese-dominated Singapore into the Malay-dominated Malaysia led to the separation of Singapore from Malaysia two years later. From 1959, when it became internally self-governing, to the general election of 2007, Singapore has been ruled by the People's Action Party (PAP), which, while bringing political stability and economic prosperity to its citizens, has been characterized as "soft authoritarian." During the administration of President **Jimmy Carter**, the antidemocratic quality of the PAP's rule in Singapore was criticized.

The commanding political figure in Singapore is **Lee Kuan Yew**, who was prime minister to 1990; senior minister from 1990 to 2004 while Goh Chok Tong was prime minister; and since 2004, minister mentor in the cabinet of his son, Prime Minister Lee Hsien Loong. The elder Lee is Southeast Asia's ultimate foreign policy realist. To offset Singapore's geostrategic vulnerability between **Indonesia** and Malaysia, Lee pursued a strategy of becoming an economic powerhouse, building a high-technology military force and forging political and security links with external partners, in particular the United States.

Singapore's economic success has attracted American direct investment and businesses. It is the financial services and information technology center in Southeast Asia. More then 1,500 American companies do business in Singapore, and U.S. direct **investment** totals more than $61 billion, making it Singapore's largest single source of foreign direct investment (FDI). Singapore is the U.S.'s 15th largest **trade** partner. The United States and Singapore signed a **free trade agreement (FTA)** in 2003 that went into force on 1 January 2004. This comprehensive agreement, which covers trade in goods, services, **intellectual property**, labor rights, **environmental** matters and other areas, making it a **World Trade Organization (WTO)** "plus" agreement, has become the model for American FTA negotiations with other Southeast Asian nations in the **ASEAN–United States Enhanced Partnership**.

Singapore's conviction that a strong U.S. security presence is necessary for a stable balance of power in Southeast Asia led it to become a "place," not a "base," to fill some of the defense holes left by the termination of the U.S.–Philippine **Military Bases Agreement (MBA)** in 1991. In 1990, the U.S. and Singapore initialed a memorandum of understanding (MoU) allowing American military access to naval and air facilities in Singapore. The U.S. Navy's Western Pacific logistic command is headquartered in Singapore, and more than 100 U.S. naval vessels call there each year. In 1999, the MoU was amended to include berthing facilities for aircraft carriers at a new dock completed in 2001. Singapore—to the consternation of Malaysia—backed the United States in the **Persian Gulf War**, with its sympathies being with Kuwait, a small state victimized by its larger neighbor. Singapore has also strongly backed the United States in the **war on terror**. It has joined the **Proliferation Security Initiative (PSI)** and the **Container Security Initiative (CSI)**. Its port is the second largest containerized port in the world. Singapore also made a modest contribution to support the U.S.-led coalition in the Iraq War. Because of Singapore's concerns about potential strategic threats to the **Strait of Malacca**, it has encouraged U.S. support for the littoral nations' efforts to upgrade security measures. In July 2005, President **George W. Bush** and Prime Minister Lee Hsien Loong affirmed a strategic framework agreement between their two nations that had been in the works since October 2003. Singapore has been designated a Major Security Cooperation Partner by the United States, which together with the "strategic framework" makes it a de facto ally of the United States.

SIRIK MATAK (1914–1975). A Cambodian prince and cousin of **Norodom Sihanouk**, Sirik Matak was the political brain behind the 1970 coup against Sihanouk. Some accounts have it that he forced **Lon Nol** at the point of a gun to sign the decree deposing Sihanouk. He served as deputy prime minister in Lon Nol's pro-American government. He was offered asylum in the United States in April 1975 by Ambassador **John Gunther Dean** as the **Khmer Rouge (KR)** forces prepared to enter Phnom Penh. Like most of the Lon Nol government's senior officials, he declined, saying, "I have only committed the mistake of believing in you, the Americans." Sirik Matak was executed by the KR.

SISAVANGVONG (1885–1959). Last king of Luang Prabang and first ruler of the Kingdom of **Laos**, King Sisavangvong came to the throne in Luang Prabang in 1909. Pro-French, he resisted Lao nationalism, but became the constitutional ruler of the Kingdom of Laos on its proclamation in 1945 and recognition by France in 1947. On his death, he was succeeded by his son, King **Savangvatthana**.

SMITH, JOSEPH BURKHOLDER (1918–). A veteran operative of the **Central Intelligence Agency (CIA)**, "Little" Joe Smith, as distinguished from another CIA agent named Joseph Smith, was based in **Singapore** while involved in the 1958 clandestine efforts to destabilize President **Sukarno**'s government in **Indonesia**. In the Philippines in 1958, he worked without success to defeat President **Carlos Garcia**'s election bid. He later served as CIA station chief in Malaysia and Indonesia as well as director of the Far East division of the agency's clandestine office of the Deputy Director of Plans (DDP).

SMITH, WALTER BEDELL (1896–1961). Soldier–diplomat Walter Bedell Smith served as General **Dwight D. Eisenhower**'s chief-of-staff in Europe from 1942 to 1945. After the war, he was U.S. ambassador to the Soviet Union (1946–1949) and director of the **Central Intelligence Agency (CIA)** (1950–1953). He ended his government service as undersecretary of state (1953–1954), in which post Secretary of State **John Foster Dulles** left Smith as the principal American negotiator at the 1954 **Geneva Conference**, which led to the settlement of the **First Indochina War** in the 1954 **Geneva Accords**.

SOCIALIST REPUBLIC OF VIETNAM (SRV). This was the name adopted to replace the old **Democratic Republic of Vietnam (DRV)** upon the official reunification of North and South Vietnam in July 1976. It did not signify any discontinuities in the ideology, policies, or political structure of the state. The politburo of the Vietnamese Communist Party (*Lao Dong* or "Workers Party") still controlled the SRV. While most countries of the world recognized the SRV, U.S. recognition did not come until the process of **normalization of relations with Vietnam** was completed in 1995. *See also* VIETNAM.

SOLARZ, STEPHEN J. (1940–). A member of the U.S. House of Representatives from New York from 1975 to 1993, Solarz served from 1981 on the House International Relations Committee and chaired its Subcommittee on Asian and Pacific Affairs. He was a vocal critic of the government of **Ferdinand Marcos** in the **Philippines**. His 1983 hearings on U.S.–Philippine relations gave an important American platform to Marcos's opponent, **Benigno Aquino**. Solarz also was a major congressional voice in U.S. policy toward **Cambodia**, urging in the mid-1980s direct American assistance to the **Khmer resistance** in the **Third Indochina War**. Solarz's principal staffer on the subcommittee had been **Stanley Roth**, who later served as assistant secretary of state for East Asian and Pacific affairs in the administration of President **William J. Clinton**. In 1997, Solarz was President Clinton's special envoy on Cambodia to coordinate U.S. policy toward the **Hun Sen** coup, and he also headed the U.S. delegation to monitor the 1998 Cambodian elections.

SOLOMON, RICHARD H. (1937–). A specialist in East Asian politics at the Rand Corporation, a government contracting think tank, Richard Solomon was assistant secretary of state for East Asian and the Pacific affairs (1989–1992) during the administration of President **George H. W. Bush**. Solomon was the U.S. principal in the negotiations of the **United Nations** Security Council's permanent five members for the **comprehensive political settlement for Cambodia** that ended the **Third Indochina War**. He was also involved in the establishment of the **Asia–Pacific Economic Cooperation (APEC)** forum as well as the **normalization of relations with Vietnam**. In 1992–1993, he was the U.S. ambassador to the **Philippines**, coordinating the closing of the U.S. military bases in the Philippines and establishing a new framework for bilateral relations. Since 1993, Solomon has been the president of the **United States Institute of Peace (USIP)**.

SON NGOC THANH (1908–1977). Son Ngoc Thanh, a **Khmer Krom**, was an anti-French nationalist hero. During World War II, from exile in **Thailand** and then Japan, he advocated independence for Cambodia. He returned from Japan to become first foreign minister and then prime minister in King **Norodom Sihanouk**'s short-lived independent government of **Cambodia** in 1945. After the restoration of French authority, he was sent into exile and detention. Thanh returned to Cambodia in 1951, where his popularity overshadowed Sihanouk's. In 1952, suspected by both Sihanouk and the French of opposition politics, he left Phnom Penh to join the **Khmer Issarak** and then led the antimonarchical **Khmer Serai**. As an enemy of Sihanouk, Thanh's Khmer Serai was facilitated by Thailand and the U.S. **Central Intelligence Agency (CIA)**. After the 1970 coup against Sihanouk, he returned to Phnom Penh, to briefly become a largely powerless member of the **Lon Nol** government. In 1972, he left Cambodian politics for good and retired to South Vietnam, where he died.

SON SANN (1911–2000). A leading political figure in **Cambodia**, Son Sann served in a variety of governments from the 1950s to the 1990s. He was Prince Sihanouk's prime minister in 1967–1968. After the **Lon Nol** coup in 1970, Son Sann went into exile, first in Beijing and then Paris. In exile, he rallied anticommunist Cambodians against the **Khmer Rouge**, and after 1978, the Vietnamese. Building on the pool of Cambodian refugees in Thailand, he created the **Khmer People's National Liberation Front (KPNLF)**. As head of the KPNLF, he became the prime minister in the tripartite **Coalition Government of Democratic Kampuchea (CGDK)** during the **Third Indochina War**. After the war, he competed in the first **United Nations**–sponsored free elections and was a minority member of the first Cambodian coalition government. He left Cambodia for Paris in 1997, where he died in 2000. He was given a state funeral in Phnom Penh.

SOROS, GEORGE (1930–). Born in Hungary, George Soros immigrated to the United States in 1950. A Wall Street entrepreneur, Soros set up the Quantum Fund in 1975, one of the earliest hedge funds. His financial dealings earned him great wealth, which he turned to philanthropy. During the Asian **financial crisis of 1997–1998**, he was demonized by **Malaysia**'s prime minister **Mahathir Mohammad** as the symbol of Jewish capitalist imperialism that sought to prevent Malaysia's economic success. Soro's network of foundations operates under the umbrella of the **Open Society Institute (OSI)**, which is active in Southeast Asia.

SOUPHANOUVONG (1909–1995). A Lao prince, Souphanouvong was the leader of the communist **Pathet Lao** forces which, in alliance with the **Viet Minh**, battled for two decades to establish a communist government in **Laos**. He was the younger half-brother of the neutralist prince **Souvanna Phouma**, and like Souvanna was educated in France as an engineer and received his nationalist political baptism in the anti-French **Lao Issara** movement. He was in contact with the Viet Minh as early as 1945 and had a Vietnamese wife. Souphanouvong was in and out of fragile **coalition governments** as the balance of forces in Laos teetered among the rightists, neutralists, and radical leftists, with the United States clandestinely determining outcomes. By 1963, Souphanouvong and the Pathet Lao were operating from their northeastern Laos strongholds in concert with North Vietnamese forces lodged in Laos. After the 1973 **Paris Agreement** ending the U.S. war in Vietnam, the **containment** of communism in Laos was no longer the imperative for American intervention, and the Pathet Lao moved back into a coalition government in 1974 and seized power from within in 1975. Souphanouvong became president of the renamed **Lao People's Democratic Republic (LPDR)**, stepping down after illness in 1991. His elevation to the presidency, a largely ceremonial post, raised questions about his role in the Pathet Lao and the communist Lao People's Revolutionary Party (LPRP). He was the most popular and prestigious figure in the movement and may have been fronting for the hard-line Marxist managers of the party. *See also* SECOND INDOCHINA WAR; SECRET WAR; VIETNAM WAR.

SOUTH CHINA SEA. The South China Sea, lying between continental and maritime Southeast Asia, is a kind of geopolitical lake. Competing and overlapping claims to territory, continental shelves, and maritime jurisdictions have produced a complex web of rivalries and conflict within the **Association of Southeast Asian Nations**

(**ASEAN**) and between ASEAN and **China** centered on the islets, reefs, and rocks of the Spratly Islands at the sea's center. The prospect of seabed oil and natural gas reserves has only raised the stakes. The United States has remained aloof from the local contests, taking no position on the legal merits of the individual claims to sovereignty or jurisdiction, calling only for the peaceful resolution of disputes. Washington has welcomed the efforts by the claimant parties to develop a "Code of Conduct" for their relations in the contested zones. The major American interest has been expressed by U.S. insistence on strategic access and freedom of navigation, including for its nuclear powered and armed warships. This was the basis of one of the U.S. objections to the **Southeast Asian Nuclear Weapons Free Zone (SEANWFZ)**. American oil companies have exploration interests in the region, which have been stalled by tensions. In 2007, ConocoPhillips pulled out of a joint development project with British Petroleum and **Vietnam**'s Petrovietnam in a disputed concession, in the face of Chinese armed threats.

The U.S. position on the contested claims in the South China Sea is complicated by ambiguities in its mutual defense relationship with the **Philippines**, whose claims in the Spratlys dating from the 1950s have been resisted by China, Vietnam, and **Malaysia**. Legally the U.S. obligations to the defense of the Philippines do not extend beyond the boundaries of the **Treaty of Paris** ending the **Spanish–American War**, which did not include the Spratlys. Nevertheless, the United States in 1999 indicated that it would come to the aid of the Philippines if it were attacked in the South China Sea. This was reinforced by a 2004 statement by Philippines president **Gloria Macapagal-Arroyo**, who said that before the **war on terror**, U.S.–Philippine cooperation in the framework of the new U.S.–Philippine **Visiting Forces Agreement (VFA)** had been focused on the South China Sea. *See also* STRAIT OF MALACCA.

SOUTH VIETNAM. For purposes of the 1954 armistice in the **First Indochina War**—the French colonial war—the **Geneva Conference** geographically divided **Vietnam** between north and south on the line of the 17th parallel of latitude. This was not conceived of as a permanent territorial boundary, but rather only as transitional for the cessation of hostilities and regroupment of military forces prior to a national election. The election never happened, and the line became a de facto international boundary between two competitive states: in the south, the **Republic of Vietnam (RVN)**, and in the north, the **Democratic Republic of Vietnam (DRV)**. In the course of the **Vietnam War** the geographic division was identified with the political division, so South Vietnam became synonymous with the RVN and **North Vietnam** similarly with the DRV, the terms being used interchangeably. In territorial size, South Vietnam had an area of 67,108 square miles (173,809 square kilometers), slightly larger than North Vietnam, encompassing the old French divisions of Cochin China and most of Annam. At partition, the population in the south was slightly less than the north.

SOUTHEAST ASIA COLLECTIVE DEFENSE TREATY (MANILA PACT), 1954. The Manila Treaty, signed on 8 September 1954, was the formal result of the September 1954 **Manila Conference**, hosted by Philippine President **Ramon Magsaysay**. It was convened at the urging of U.S. secretary of state **John Foster Dulles** following the signing of the July 1954 **Geneva Accords** ending the **First Indochina War**. The signatories to the treaty were Australia, France, New Zealand, Pakistan, the **Philippines**, **Thailand**, Great Britain, and the United States. Through overlapping memberships, the Manila Pact was the multilateral keystone of an overarching regional network of security agreements and arrangements. The Philippines and the United States were already allied in their bilateral **Mutual Defense Treaty (MDT)**. Australia and New Zealand were allies of the United States in the ANZUS pact. Great Britain and its Commonwealth partners Australia and New Zealand backed the security of **Malaya** (later **Malaysia**), a relationship formally structured in 1971 in the **Five Power Defence Arrangement (FPDA)**, which included **Singapore**.

The parties to the Manila Treaty recognized that an armed attack against any party or state or territory in the treaty area that the parties unanimously might later designate would endanger its own peace and security. They agreed in that event to meet the common danger in accordance with constitutional processes. In the event of indirect aggression, the parties would consult on steps for common defense. To both the cases of direct and indirect aggression, the United States attached its understanding that its obligations under the treaty applied only to communist aggression. This significantly reduced the value of the pact for Pakistan, although not fully relieving nonaligned India of its Cold War concerns about the treaty. By protocol, the parties extended the treaty's coverage to **Laos**, **Cambodia**, and the **State of Vietnam**. This got around the Geneva Accords neutralization of the three Indochina states, which by that agreement could not join the Manila system. The treaty area was defined to exclude Taiwan and British Hong Kong. At the time of signing, Malaya, Singapore, and the British colonies of Sarawak and North Borneo (**Sabah**) came under the treaty area, but after their independence Malaya and later Malaysia and Singapore did not accede to the treaty. In 1956, Cambodia's prince Prime Minister **Sihanouk** renounced the Manila security umbrella. The neutralization of Laos in the 1962 **Geneva Accords** nullified its status as a protocol state. During the **Vietnam War**, one of the major arguments used by the United States in justifying its role in the war was its treaty obligations under the Manila treaty. In the 1962 **Rusk–Thanat communiqué**, the United States and Thailand agreed that the pact's obligations extended to their bilateral security relationship. The institutional structure for implementing the Manila Pact was the **Southeast Asia Treaty Organization (SEATO)**.

SOUTHEAST ASIA NUCLEAR WEAPONS FREE ZONE (SEANWFZ). The treaty on the Southeast Asia Nuclear Weapons Free Zone was signed by the 10 Southeast Asian heads of government at the 15 December 1995 **Association of Southeast Asian Nations (ASEAN)** Bangkok Summit. The parties to the treaty were the six ASEAN states at that time and the candidate members **Cambodia**, **Laos**, **Burma**, and **Vietnam**. The treaty came into force with the deposit of the 7th (**Indonesia**) ratification in March 1997. In the treaty, the parties agreed not to develop, manufacture, base, or transport nuclear weapons nor allow other states to do so inside their zonal territories. They also agreed not to dispose of radioactive materials at sea or in the atmosphere. Disposal on land would be in accordance with the standards and procedures of the International Atomic Energy Agency (IAEA). The treaty did not prejudice the parties' rights to use nuclear energy for economic development and social progress.

The origin of the SEANWFZ was paragraph 8 of the 27 November 1971 Kuala Lumpur Declaration of a **Zone of Peace, Freedom, and Neutrality (ZOPFAN)**, which took note of the 1963 Tlatelolco Treaty for a Latin American nuclear-free zone and the 1970 Lusaka Declaration proclaiming an African nuclear-free zone. The ZOPFAN was reiterated in the first ASEAN Summit's Bali Declaration of ASEAN Concord on March 1976. A further model for a SEANWFZ was the 1984 Treaty of Rarotonga establishing a South Pacific Nuclear Free Zone (SPNFZ). Although pushed by **Malaysia** and Indonesia, the Cold War environment and **Thai** and **Philippine** alliances with the United States meant that it was not until the 17th ASEAN Ministerial Meeting in 1984 that ASEAN formally revived the idea in the ASEAN Task Force on ZOPFAN. What the 1992 ASEAN summit's "Singapore Declaration" delicately called "changing circumstances"—the end of the Cold War, collapse of the Soviet Union, and normalization of relations with **China**—allowed ASEAN to move to the completion of negotiations on the drafting of the 1995 SEANWFZ treaty.

The treaty left open by protocol provision for signature by the existing nuclear weapons states, specified as China, Great Britain, France, Russia, and the United States. No nuclear weapons state has acceded to the protocol, although in 2000 China said it would. In 2006, China again said it was ready to sign at an unspecified early date. By the time of the first meeting of the SEANWFZ Commission in July 2007, the first since the treaty came into force, China had not yet signed. Even without accession, the treaty called on the nuclear weapons states to respect the SEANWFZ and not to contribute to any act that could constitute a violation of the treaty by its parties. This meant that, like the ZOPFAN, the full implementation of a SEANWFZ would require voluntary compliance by external nuclear weapons states.

In the drafting and coming into force of the SEANWFZ, Washington had opposed key provisions of the treaty. The United States remained vitally interested in the transit of nuclear powered and armed ships and planes through Southeast Asian air and sea space in support of its global strategy. Washington insisted that the treaty could not impose restrictions on rights recognized under international law, including high seas freedom, the right of innocent passage through territorial and archipelagic seas, the right of transit passage through international straits, and the right of archipelagic sea lanes passage through archipelagic waters. The United States objected to the coverage of the zone extending beyond the territorial waters of the Southeast Asian states out to the 200-mile boundary of their Exclusive Economic Zones (EEZ) and the width of their respective continental shelves. Also, as some of the functions once performed at the Philippine **Subic Bay Naval Base** were shifted, the United States did not want to jeopardize naval access and port calls elsewhere in the region, especially Singapore. In practice, the SEANWFZ, despite occasional local protest, did not interfere with the strategic and tactical missions of the U.S. military or military cooperation, including joint and combined exercises between the U.S. Navy and Air Force and friendly forces in Southeast Asia.

SOUTHEAST ASIA TREATY ORGANIZATION (SEATO). This was the implementing structure of the 1954 **Southeast Asia Collective Defense Treaty (Manila Pact)**, signed by Australia, France, Great Britain, New Zealand, Pakistan, the **Philippines**, **Thailand**, and the United States. The executive authority was the SEATO Council of Foreign Ministers, which met annually in a capital of one of the members to determine the policy of the organization. The first meeting took place on 23 February 1955. At that meeting, Bangkok was selected as SEATO headquarters and the distinguished Thai statesman Pote Sarasin was named secretary-general. The Council was advised by a Military Advisors Group at the theater commanders or chiefs of staff level. Below the foreign ministers there was a Council of Representatives at the ambassadorial level, located in Bangkok, which gave policy guidance and coordinated nonmilitary cooperation. A Military Planning Office was also established in Bangkok.

SEATO cannot be compared to the North Atlantic Treaty Organization (NATO). The collective defense commitments set forth in the founding treaties were different. There was no SEATO unified command. There were no standing forces or national forces designated for SEATO. It did provide a multilateral framework for training exercises; headquarters planning; communications standardization; and other military areas, including intelligence that would enhance interoperability if future combined or joint operations became necessary. SEATO also provided a larger political umbrella for bilateral military cooperation and assistance. In the SEATO framework, educational and economic initiatives were undertaken and bilateral aid programs were "SEATO-ized."

As a military alliance, SEATO could not meet the test of common defense interests with respect to the founding treaty's protocol states, **Cambodia**, **Laos**, and **South Vietnam**. SEATO's response to **Pathet Lao** advances in **Laos** in 1960 and 1961 and to Thailand's threat perceptions was ambiguous and indecisive. A disappointed Thailand, faced with the prospect of trans-**Mekong River** direct and indirect aggression, questioned the value of the SEATO commitment. The 1962 **Rusk–Thanat communiqué**'s interpretation of the Manila Pact as being a bilateral obligation gave the Thais what they had really wanted in the first place—an implicit American bilateral defense agreement. The United States utilized its obligations under the Manila Pact to maximum legal and rhetorical effect in justifying its military effort in defense of the **Republic of Vietnam** in the **Vietnam War**. Organizationally, however, SEATO was on the sidelines. The presence of troops from Australia, New Zealand, Thailand, and the Philippines in Vietnam was not the result of a SEATO decision.

In the wake of the 1975 communist victories in Vietnam, Laos, and Cambodia, both the Philippines and Thailand felt it necessary to adopt more equidistant postures vis-à-vis their communist neighbors and the United States and agreed to a phase out of SEATO. The organization went out of existence in 1976, even though its treaty basis remained in effect. This was emphasized by U.S. vice president **Walter Mondale** during a Bangkok visit in May 1978, when he stated that, "circumstances have changed, but our commitments of both a regional and bilateral nature under the Manila Pact are still valid."

SOUTHEAST ASIAN REGIONAL CENTER FOR COUNTER-TERRORISM (SEARCCT). The **Malaysia**-based Southeast Asian Regional Center for Counterterrorism operates under the Malaysian Ministry of Foreign Affairs. It provides a framework for cooperation among the members of the **Association of Southeast Asian Nations (ASEAN)** for counterterrorism training, capacity building, and public awareness in the regional **war on terror**. From July 2003, when it was set up, to 2007, SEARCCT had conducted 39 training courses with nearly 1,400 participants. President **George W. Bush** had promoted the establishment of such a regional institution on the sidelines of the 2002 **Asia–Pacific Economic Cooperation (APEC)** meeting, but sensitivity to U.S. visibility by Muslim Malaysia, particularly after the March 2003 invasion of Iraq, prevented any formal American partnership. The United States has, however, been a key provider of resources for the Center.

SOUVANNA PHOUMA (1901–1984). From 1951 to 1973, Prince Souvanna Phouma was the leading neutralist political figure in **Laos** in the three-way contest among the anticommunist rightists, the neutralists, and the communist-backed **Pathet Lao**. In that contest, the United States—backing the anticommunists—was both diplomatically and, in the **secret war**, militarily deeply involved. Souvanna was Laos's prime minister five times. Both Souvanna Phouma and his half-brother, Prince **Souphanouvong**, leader of the **Pathet Lao**, were scions of the second-most influential royal family. He was the younger brother of leading nationalist Prince **Phetsarat Ratnavongsa**. Educated in France as an engineer, Souvanna Phouma had a French wife. His political roots were in the **Lao Issara** nationalist movement led by Phetsarat.

Souvanna Phouma became prime minister of the French-dependent Royal Lao government in 1951. He was forced from office in 1954 by rightists, becoming prime minister again in 1957 in the first **coalition government** with the Pathet Lao, only to be forced again from office by American pressure in 1958. He was restored by the **Kong Le** coup in 1960, but driven out of Vientiane by rightist forces of **Phoumi Nosavan** five months later. This initiated the **Laotian crisis of 1960–1962**, which ended in the **Geneva Accords of 1962**, establishing the second coalition government led by Souvanna. After the Pathet Lao went into open opposition in 1964 as the neutralists were undermined by the rightist Royal Lao Army (FAR), Souvanna became a symbol of neutralism. His government operated in a de facto alliance with the United States in its **secret war** against the Pathet Lao and the North Vietnamese forces in Laos. As that war closed out in the wake of the termination of the American **Vietnam War**, a third coalition government was formed with Souvanna as prime minister, which was transformed by mid-1975 into a Pathet Lao government. Souvanna's last official post was "counselor" to that government.

SPANISH–AMERICAN WAR, 1898. The Spanish–American War, a so-called hundred days' war, had its origins in American outrage over the excesses of Spanish rule in Cuba and sympathy for Cuban insurrectionists within the context of a growing imperialist urge in an American vision of "manifest destiny." A reluctant President **William McKinley** was forced into action by the sinking of the battleship *Maine* in Havana harbor. McKinley's declaration of "neutral intervention" was followed by three acts of Congress tantamount to a declaration of war. The war officially began with President McKinley's signing on 20 April 1898 of the congressional joint resolution calling for war. Poised in Hong Kong, Commodore **George Dewey** and his fleet sailed to Manila Bay, arriving on 1 May 1898. Dewey forced the surrender of the Spanish flotilla there and seized the city. The formal occupation of the city by U.S. forces took place on 13 August 1898. At first allied with the Philippine insurrectionists led by General **Emilio Aguinaldo**, who had declared **Philippine** independence, once American intentions to acquire the Philippines became clear, U.S. forces came into conflict with the Filipino nationalists. The Spanish–American War was officially terminated by the 1900 **Treaty of Paris**, which ceded the Philippines to the United States. The war against the Philippine nationalists continued into 1902, and even longer against the Muslim **Moro** resistance to American rule in the south.

SPRATLY ISLANDS. *See* SOUTH CHINA SEA.

SPRUANCE, RAYMOND A. (1886–1969). Admiral Raymond Spruance was a senior U.S. Navy officer in the Pacific theater of World War II. He retired from the navy in 1948. In 1952, President **Harry S. Truman** called him out of retirement to become U.S. ambassador to the **Philippines**, where he served until 1955. He took up his post in Manila during the term of Philippine president **Elpidio Quirino**, whose administration was marked by corruption and threatened by the **Hukbalahap** insurrection. During the 1953 Philippine presidential campaign that pitted Quirino against **Ramon Magsaysay**, while Ambassador Spruance was publicly asserting American neutrality in the election, the **Central Intelligence Agency (CIA)**, spearheaded by **Edward Lansdale**, was working to elect Magsaysay. Spruance was later criticized for "false and misleading" statements about illegal interference in Philippine domestic affairs. As ambassador, however, he was only echoing the denials of involvement by President **Dwight D. Eisenhower** and Secretary of State **John Foster Dulles**.

STANTON, EDWIN F. (1901–1968). An "old China hand," Ambassador Edwin F. Stanton headed the U.S. mission to **Thailand** for more than seven years, presenting his credentials in April 1946 as minister and then a year later as ambassador, ending his mission in June 1953. This was the period when the United States became Thailand's most important bilateral partner. There are conflicting views of his success. President **Dwight D. Eisenhower** wrote in 1954, apparently reflecting the view of ambassador to the **Philippines Raymond A. Spruance**, that "[Stanton] served American interests so poorly that our position in the region was at an all time low when he left." A senior Foreign Service Officer, on the other hand, commented that Stanton was "probably one of the most effective ambassadors in Southeast Asia."

STATE DEPARTMENT. The U.S. Department of State is the lead agency for American official relations with foreign nations and international organizations. The career professional diplomatic personnel of the department are Foreign Service Officers (FSO), who staff American embassies around the world and hold policy positions in Washington. The State Department has responsibilities for the formulation, implementing, and representation of American foreign policy goals to other nations. The department is headed by the secretary of state, a cabinet-level officer confirmed by the Senate of the United States. In 2005, **Condoleezza Rice** became the 66th American secretary of state. The secretary is supported by a deputy secretary of state and an undersecretary for political affairs. Below the senior executive level there are a number of offices and bureaus with functional and geographic responsibilities. Southeast Asia as a geographic region comes under the Bureau of East Asian and Pacific Affairs (EAP), headed by an assistant secretary of state. In EAP, there are a number of deputy assistant secretaries of state, one of whom is tasked with

Southeast Asia. Under him or her are the Office of Maritime Southeast Asia (EAP/MTS) and the Office of Mainland Southeast Asia (EAP/MLS), each headed by a director. In these offices there are country officers for each Southeast Asian state. Elsewhere in EAP, its Office of Regional and Security Policy Affairs has separate officers for the **Association of Southeast Asian Nations (ASEAN)** and the **ASEAN Regional Forum (ARF)**. The United States maintains embassies in all 11 Southeast Asian states, with all but **Burma** having ambassadors accredited to them. The great majority of U.S. ambassadors to Southeast Asian nations have been career FSOs. American interests in Burma are represented by a chargé d'affaires. In 2006, a bill was introduced in Congress to name an ambassador to ASEAN. President **George W. Bush** announced in a meeting with ASEAN heads of government on the sidelines of the 2007 **Asia–Pacific Economic Cooperation (APEC)** meeting that an ambassador would be so named.

Outside of EAP, matters concerning Southeast Asian affairs and U.S. relations are dealt with in other departmental bureaucratic structures. Security assistance is handled by the State Department's Bureau of Political–Military Affairs (PM). **Human rights** fall under the Bureau of Democracy, Rights, and Labor (DRL). The State Department's links for the **war on terror** are through the Coordinator for Counterterrorism. Nontraditional matters of diplomatic concern with Southeast Asian manifestations, such as **refugees, narcotics production and trafficking, pandemic disease**, and **trafficking in persons**, are located in appropriate bureaus and offices. (The State Department's unclassified phone book, available on its website, has a complete organizational chart.) Overlapping jurisdictions within the department and between the State Department and other departments and agencies, such as the Departments of Defense, Treasury, Justice, and other departments and agencies with international responsibilities, mean that a major task is interdepartmental and interagency consultation and coordination.

STATE OF VIETNAM. This was a French political creation officially proclaimed on 2 February 1950 to present the semblance of independence to **Vietnam** as a nationalist alternative to the **Viet Minh**'s Democratic **Republic of Vietnam (DRV)**. Together with the "associated states" of **Cambodia** and **Laos**, the State of Vietnam was incorporated into the French Union. The head of state was **Bao Dai**. The same day, Secretary of State **Dean Acheson** sent a memo to President **Harry S. Truman** recommending that the United States recognize the State of Vietnam. Truman approved it. With U.S. recognition came American political and economic assistance. Although supporting what was called the "Bao Dai solution," Washington continued to press the reluctant French to grant full independence to the associated states. Bao Dai's government was ineffective, inefficient, and corrupt. In June 1954, as the French cause became a lost one at the **Geneva Conference** and the United States even more concerned about the **containment** of communism in Southeast Asia, Bao Dai turned to the anti-French, anticommunist, ardent Catholic **Ngo Dinh Diem**, to try to salvage the sinking ship of state. With a broad grant of authority and political skill, Diem consolidated power. On 23 October 1955, while Bao Dai was in France, Diem held an outrageously rigged national referendum in which **South Vietnam**'s electorate was asked to choose between Bao Dai or Diem—a French-backed ex-monarch or a democratic republic. Diem won more than 98 percent of the vote. Bao Dai was deposed. On 26 October 1955, the **Republic of Vietnam** was proclaimed with Ngo Dinh Diem installed as its first president. The United States, although concerned by possible negative international reaction to the blatant unfairness of the referendum, willingly accepted the outcome as promising a stronger partner in the **containment** of communist expansion. *See also* COLLINS, J. LAWTON; GULLION, EDMUND.

STATE LAW AND ORDER RESTORATION COUNCIL (SLORC). This was the name assumed by the military junta that declared martial law and ruled **Burma** after the 1988 popular revolt against General **Ne Win**'s military-backed Burmese Socialist Program Party (BSPP)'s regime. The SLORC was headed first by General Saw Maung and then from 1992 by General Tan Shwe. The SLORC changed its name in 1997 to the **State Peace and Development Council (SPDC)**, but the junta was the same.

STATE PEACE AND DEVELOPMENT COUNCIL (SPDC). This was the name adopted in 1997 by **Burma**'s ruling military junta to replace the **State Law and Order Restoration Council (SLORC).** The new label was cosmetic, designed to be more internationally attractive as Burma edged toward membership in the **Association of Southeast Asian Nations (ASEAN).** There was no regime change, and General Tan Shwe remained in charge.

STRAIT OF MALACCA. Running 500 miles, the Malacca Strait separates **Indonesia**'s island of Sumatra from peninsular **Malaysia.** With the connecting Singapore Strait, it is the strategic link between the **South China Sea** and the Indian Ocean and the shortest route to and from Asia from the Indian Ocean and the North Pacific. More than 60,000 vessels, carrying a third of global trade and 75 percent of China's, Japan's, and Korea's oil imports, traverse the Singapore and Malacca Straits annually, making them one of the world's most vital strategic sea lanes of communication. Historically, the Malacca Strait has been considered an international waterway, but where it is less than 24 nautical miles wide its waters are now the territorial waters of Indonesia and Malaysia. At its narrowest, at the entrance to the Singapore Strait, it is only two miles wide. A 1970 Indonesian–Malaysian treaty drew their 12-mile territorial maritime boundary in the strait along a centerline. A 1971 joint statement by the two countries claimed their sovereign jurisdiction over their territorial waters in the straits and responsibility for safety and regulation of navigation.

The issue for the United States at that time was free, unimpeded passage of not only commercial vessels but warships. This was very important for the deployment of the U.S. Seventh Fleet, headquartered in Japan and with its major repair facility at **Subic Bay Naval Base** in the **Philippines.** In the new Malaysian–Indonesia navigation regime, warships were subject to the rules of "innocent passage," by which Malaysia and Indonesia claimed to require prior notification and other restrictions on warships. The United States and the Soviet Union had similar interests in pressing for more liberal navigation rules covering international straits in the Third Law of the Sea Conference (UNCLOS III), which began in 1973 and ended with the adoption of the Law of the Sea Convention in 1982. Rather than "innocent passage," a new legal right of passage was created called "transit passage." This is the right of freedom of navigation solely for the continuous and expeditious transit of the strait between one area of high seas or economic zone to another, warships and aircraft not excepted.

The vulnerability of the Straits of Malacca and Singapore to threats to the security of ships navigating them has become a major interest of the maritime states utilizing the route. The region is rife with piracy and is viewed by regional security managers as subject to possible terrorist attack. Countries with major commercial interests like Japan or strategic interests like the United States want to guarantee that transit is not compromised by the inability of the littoral states to provide security. In 2004, the commander of the **United States Pacific Command** proposed a Regional Maritime Security Initiative (RMSI) that would provide U.S. Special Forces or marines on a flotilla of high-speed boats to conduct surveillance and interdiction in the straits. Although welcomed by **Singapore**, the idea was quickly rejected by Indonesia and Malaysia as a violation of their sovereignty. **China** darkly warned of an American strategic design to get control of the straits. Washington quickly dropped the idea. In a joint statement in August 2005, the littoral states reasserted their sovereign rights and responsibility for security. International concern has forced Indonesia and Malaysia to greater cooperation with Singapore and Thailand on maritime security, with the technical and funding support of Japan, the United States, and Australia. The security of the Malacca and Singapore Straits has become an important part of the United States National Strategy for Maritime Security (NSMS), signed by President **George W. Bush** in September 2005.

STROBEL, EDWARD H. (1855–1908). A Harvard-trained lawyer and diplomat, Edward H. Strobel served as U.S. minister to Ecuador and to Chile before becoming Bemis Professor of International Law at Harvard in 1898. In 1903, he became foreign policy advisor to **Siam**'s King Chulalongkorn (Rama V). At that time, Siam was being hard pressed by France to retrocede the provinces of Battambang and Angkor to the French **Cambodia** protectorate. Strobel, who had great influence with the king, persuaded him that it would be in Siam's interest to liquidate all frictions with the French since after the 1904 signing of the Anglo–French *entente cordiale* Great Britain was no longer a dependable counterweight to France in defending Siam's territorial integrity. Strobel was one of the principal drafters of the Siam–France Treaty of 22 April 1907, which returned the contested territory to **Cambodia**. Strobel died in Bangkok.

STROM, CARL W. (1899–1969). A career diplomat, Carl Strom was American ambassador to **Cambodia** from 1956 to 1959, a period of deteriorating U.S.–Cambodian relations. A critical point was reached in 1958 after South Vietnamese troop incursions into eastern Cambodia. Cambodia's prime minister Sihanouk demanded that the United States restrain Saigon. It fell to Ambassador Strom, under personal instructions from Secretary of State **John Foster Dulles**, to tell Prime Minister **Sihanouk** that the United States would not interfere in the bilateral dispute between Cambodia and **South Vietnam**. At the same time, Strom advised him that the use of U.S.-supplied arms against the South Vietnamese could lead to a cut off of American military assistance to Cambodia. American unwillingness to intervene triggered Cambodia's recognition of the People's Republic of **China**. Dulles was deeply suspicious of Sihanouk's neutralism. Sihanouk viewed American allies **Thailand** and the **Republic of Vietnam** as potential enemies. Ambassador Strom warned Washington that the tension between Saigon and Phnom Penh damaged the U.S. goal of denying Southeast Asia to communism. While Strom argued that Cambodia had legitimate grievances against **South Vietnam**, his counterpart in Saigon, Ambassador **Elbridge Durbrow**, whose antipathy toward Sihanouk's neutralism was as strong as that of Dulles, held Cambodia responsible for the poor state of Cambodian–South Vietnamese relations. After the **Dap Chhuan plot** against Sihanouk, Strom urged that U.S. pressure be put on Thailand and Vietnam to cease interfering in Cambodia in order to maintain Cambodia as a neutral buffer against communist expansion. Strom's advice ran counter to the **State Department**'s animus against Sihanouk.

SUBIC BAY NAVAL BASE. The jewels of American military bases in the **Philippines** were Subic Bay Naval Base and its adjacent Cubi Point Naval Air Station, which together with **Clark Air Base** were the major platforms for American forward deployment in Southeast Asia and the military component of what the United States called its contribution to the regional balance of power. Subic Bay also played a crucial role in U.S. global maritime strategy. Situated on the southwestern tip of Luzon's Bataan Peninsula, it is strategically located on the **South China Sea** maritime routes connecting East Asia to the Southwest Pacific. The Subic Bay Naval Base was the largest U.S. naval complex outside of the United States. Its ship repair facility was the largest west of Hawaii. Subic Bay was intensively used by the U.S. Seventh Fleet for training, resupply, and repair. The United States left Subic Bay in 1992 after the Philippine Senate rejected the new Philippine–U.S. **Military Bases Agreement (MBA)**.

SUHARTO (1921–2008). The second president of **Indonesia** (1967–1998), General Suharto, commanding the Indonesian Army's Strategic Reserve (K0STRAD), its principle combat units, crushed the 1965 **Indonesian coup** attributed by the army to the **Indonesian Communist Party (PKI)**. Parallel to the bloody purge of the PKI, Suharto and his army colleagues methodically dismantled the "guided democracy" of his predecessor, President **Sukarno**. Suharto became acting president in 1967 and president in 1968. Managed elections every five years from 1971 onward in an essentially one-party state resting on a military oligarchy led to his reelection as president until he was forced to step down in 1998.

Suharto was a professional soldier whose original military training was in the Japanese-raised "Fatherland Defense Force." He distinguished himself in the independence war against the Dutch during the recapture of the republican capital of Yogyakarta in March 1949. His rise in the army was relatively rapid, even though, unlike many of his peers, he had no foreign training. In 1960—then a major general—he was named to head the Mandala Command, a special force to wrest Dutch New Guinea from the Netherlands. Although no invasion was launched, Indonesian military pressure contributed to the diplomatic settlement of the **West New Guinea dispute**. In 1962, Suharto commanded the Central Java–based Dipanegara Division, and in 1963 he took command of KOSTRAD.

Loyalty and support of the army was the basis for Suharto's presidential authority in a state where economic and social gains were achieved at the expense of political and **human rights**. Growing discontent with the authoritarian state was fueled as well by the expanse and depth of its corruption, much of it centered on the president's immediate family. In May 1998, in the crisis surrounding regime survival, army commander General Wiranto let it be known that the army would not use force to keep Suharto in power. Suharto agreed to retire in a peaceful transfer of authority to his vice president, **B. J. Habibie**. In the democratic turmoil following the collapse of the Suharto government, angry voices were raised calling for his arrest and trial for corruption and human rights violations. Suharto escaped accountability when the courts found him too ill to stand trial.

SUKARNO (1901–1970). Indonesia's first president (1945–1967), Sukarno was the most prominent leader of the pre–World War II Indonesian nationalist movement in what was then the Dutch East Indies. Calling for noncooperation with colonial authority and eventual independence, Sukarno articulated a secular ideology of social and economic justice in an independent state. In the 1930s, Sukarno's message and mass popularity led to his arrest, imprisonment, and eventual banishment, first to the island of Flores and then to Bengkulu in Sumatra. During the Japanese occupation (1942–1945), he headed a Japanese-sponsored administration that, while mobilized for the Japanese war effort, furthered the propagation of the nationalist message. Collaboration was rewarded in 1945 when, under a benign Japanese eye, Indonesian delegates prepared an Indonesian constitution. Indonesia's independence was proclaimed by Sukarno and Mohammad Hatta on 17 August 1945, two days after the Japanese surrender. Sukarno was named president and Hatta vice president.

Sukarno's role in the initial years of his presidency was first limited by the politics of the war against the Dutch and then by a vulnerable and stalemated parliamentary democracy. On 14 March 1957, backed by the army, he declared martial law, ending parliamentary democracy. For the United States, Sukarno's new "Guided Democracy" was a disguise for creeping communism and to be resisted. During a May 1956 state visit to Washington, Sukarno was lectured on the immorality of nonalignment. Sukarno's personal dealings with Americans were preceded by his reputation for flamboyance and womanizing. On an unofficial visit to the Oval Office in October 1960, he surprised President **Dwight D. Eisenhower** by bringing along the head of the **Indonesian Communist Party (PKI)**, D. N. Aidit.

American–Indonesian relations reached a nadir in the aftermath of the Eisenhower administration's intervention in the **PRRI–Permesta regional revolts**. Although charmed by President **John F. Kennedy** during an unofficial visit in April 1961, Sukarno remained undeterred in his ever more extreme radical course. To the United States he said "to hell with your aid." He opposed the creation of **Malaysia** and in the policy of "**confrontation**" sought to crush it. To his countrymen, caught in a downward spiral of impoverishment, he inveighed "eat stones" in a sacrifice for the revolution. The unreality of his self-proclaimed Jakarta–Phnom Penh–Hanoi–Beijing–Pyongyang Axis was evident in the fact that when at his command Indonesia stormed out of the **United Nations**, no other country followed.

As Sukarno sought to polarize an imperialist–anti-imperialist world, Indonesia's domestic politics became polarized between the PKI and the Indonesian army. On 30 September 1965, a failed **Indonesian coup** attempt began a course of army political reaction. In the aftermath, Sukarno was methodically stripped of power and office while the PKI was destroyed. On 11 March 1966, Sukarno was forced to transfer presidential authority to General **Suharto**, who had led the countercoup. A year later, the provisional constitutional parliament named Suharto acting president and in March 1968 confirmed him as president. President Suharto formally absolved ex-President Sukarno of complicity with the PKI in the coup, but Sukarno remained under virtual house arrest until his death from natural causes in 1970. He was buried without state ceremony at Blitar in East Java. Two decades later, his daughter, **Megawati Sukarnoputri**, rehabilitated his memory in her own political career.

SULLIVAN, WILLIAM H. (1922–). A career Foreign Service Officer, William Sullivan was deeply involved in **Indochinese** affairs. He worked for Assistant Secretary of State **W. Averell Harriman** on Laotian affairs and the 1962 **Geneva Accords** on **Laos**. He followed Harriman as a special assistant when Harriman became undersecretary of state for political affairs in 1963. In 1964, Sullivan became a special assistant for **Vietnam** affairs in the office of the secretary of state. That same year, he spent five months in Saigon assisting Ambassador **Maxwell Taylor**. Sullivan was designated U.S. ambassador to Laos at the end of 1964, succeeding **Leonard Unger**, and served until 1969. In Laos, he took personal charge of the conduct of the **secret war**, trying to maintain the fiction of the Geneva Accords. Against Sullivan's opposition, however, South Vietnamese troops led by U.S. Special Forces expanded covert cross-border operations into Laos in the effort to cut the **Ho Chi Minh trail**. Returning to the United States, Sullivan continued to work on Indochina as a deputy assistant secretary of state for East Asian and Pacific affairs and was involved in the **Paris peace negotiations**. He was named U.S. ambassador to the **Philippines** from 1973 to 1977. Following the Philippines, Sullivan became ambassador to Iran, leaving after the Islamic revolution. In retirement, Sullivan was a founder of the U.S.–Vietnam Trade Council. His autobiography is *Obligato, 1939–1979: Notes on a Foreign Service Career*.

SWANK, EMORY C. (1922–). A career Foreign Service Officer, Swank was U.S. ambassador to **Cambodia** in 1970–1973. Although supportive of military assistance to the **Lon Nol** government in its war against the **Khmer Rouge (KR)**, Swank tried to hold down the size of the in-country U.S. **Military Equipment Delivery Team (MEDT)**. This led to tensions between the embassy and the military chain of command. After the **Paris Agreement** of January 1973 and the armistice in **Vietnam**, Swank questioned the prolongation of the war in Cambodia. Leaving his post in September 1973, he described the Cambodian conflict as **Indochina**'s "most useless war." Out of Secretary of State **Henry Kissinger**'s favor, Swank's reward was a kind of diplomatic Siberia as political advisor to the North Atlantic Fleet in Norfolk, Virginia.

SYMINGTON COMMITTEE. This was the U.S. Senate Foreign Relations Committee ad hoc Subcommittee on U.S. Security Agreements and Commitments Abroad, chaired by Senator W. Stewart Symington from 1969 to 1973. The committee's hearings were often classified, with only censored versions made public. Between 30 September and 3 October 1969, hearings on the **Philippines** were held that questioned the value of the American military bases there and gave exposure to the seamy side of the regime of President **Ferdinand Marcos** and unaudited transfer of U.S. funds to the Marcos government. The testimony was angrily received in Manila both by

Marcos and American Ambassador **Henry Byroade**, who recommended withholding the contents of the committee's report until after the Philippine presidential election, in which the embassy supported Marcos.

– T –

TAFT, WILLIAM HOWARD (1857–1930). President of the United States (1909–1913) and later chief justice of the Supreme Court (1923–1929), William Howard Taft, a lawyer and politically connected administrator, was named in 1900 by President **William McKinley** to chair the Philippine Commission sent out to Manila to study and make recommendations for the civil administration of the newly annexed territory. His conciliatory approach contrasted sharply with that of the military governor, General **Arthur MacArthur**. Named in 1901 to be the first civilian governor of the **Philippines**, Taft was generally sympathetic and tolerant within the paternalistic racial attitudes of the day. He left Manila in 1904 to become the secretary of war in Theodore Roosevelt's cabinet. His record in the Philippines was reformist and progressive, setting the pattern for future policy and governors.

TAFT–KATSURA AGREEMENT. After the conclusion of the Russo–Japanese War, President Theodore Roosevelt, concerned about the possibilities of further Japanese aggressiveness and the security of the **Philippines**, sent Secretary of War **William Howard Taft** to Tokyo for consultations with Japanese Prime Minister Taro Katsura. The result was a secret "agreed memorandum," dated 29 August 1905, in which Japan confirmed that it had no aggressive designs on the Philippines and the United States accepted that a Japanese protectorate over Korea would contribute to the stability of East Asia. Roosevelt subsequently endorsed the bargain. It was abrogated by the 1923 Nine Power Treaty, signed during the **Washington Naval Conference**, and only became public in 1924.

TAYLOR, MAXWELL D. (1901–1987). A professional soldier, Taylor graduated from West Point in 1922. He was army chief of staff from 1955 to 1959. As a military thinker, he was an advocate of "flexible response" as opposed to the doctrine of "massive retaliation" prevailing in the administration of President **Dwight D. Eisenhower**. He supported building a counterinsurgent military capacity for unconventional warfare and became an advocate of special warfare operations. He retired from the army in 1959 at the rank of general. President **John F. Kennedy** called on Taylor for advice on **Laos** and **Vietnam** based on his counterinsurgency expertise as well as familiarity with the military issues in Southeast Asia. In October 1961, Kennedy dispatched him, together with **Walt Rostow**, to Saigon to survey the situation and make recommendations on a future course of action. The **Taylor–Rostow Mission's** report was the underpinning for the first American escalation of the **Vietnam War**. Kennedy recalled Taylor to active duty in 1962 as chairman of the Joint Chiefs of Staff, from which post he was bullish on the course of the war in Vietnam. In 1964, **President Lyndon B. Johnson** sent Taylor to Saigon to replace **Henry Cabot Lodge** as American ambassador. Taylor resigned in July 1965 and was replaced by a returning Lodge. Taylor continued as one of the principal advisors to Johnson on the war. Together with **Clark Clifford**, he traveled to the Pacific region in mid-1967, consulting with America's allies in the war on future courses of action.

TAYLOR–ROSTOW MISSION, 1961. President **John F. Kennedy** dispatched General **Maxwell Taylor** and Deputy National Security Advisor **Walt W. Rostow** to **Vietnam** to survey the situation there and make recommendations for American policy. This was a response to President **Ngo Dinh Diem**'s request through Ambassador **Frederick Nolting** for increased military assistance. In the country from 18 October to 2 November 1961, the Taylor–Rostow mission reported that only a major effort by the U.S. military to retrain the Army of the Republic of Vietnam (ARVN) and reorient it to counterinsurgency warfare could turn the tide in Vietnam. They recommended sending as many U.S. advisors as necessary to accomplish this. The political and military risks of a deepening of the American involvement were recognized, including escalation, but the alternative was viewed as leading to an erosion of American credibility as an ally and the possible loss of all of **Indochina** to the communists.

The administration responded by upping the U.S. military presence from under 1,000 in 1961 to nearly 17,000 at the end of 1962, shredding the external force ceiling of the 1954 **Geneva Accords**.

THACH, NGUYEN CO (1923–1988). Nguyen Co Thach was foreign minister of the **Socialist Republic of Vietnam (SRV)** from 1980 to 1991. He was the formal and informal point of contact in Hanoi for the United States on matters of **normalization of relations with Vietnam**, including resolution of the **POW/MIA** question. Beginning in 1987, he had numerous meetings with U.S. special emissary General **John Vessey**. In September 1990, Thach became the first high-level Vietnamese official to visit the United States, where he held talks with American secretary of state **James Baker**. Thach also was Vietnam's diplomatic face in the negotiations to end the **Third Indochina War**. He fell out of favor in Hanoi in part because he was unable to win the sought-after diplomatic ties with the United States. Also, as Vietnam moved to normalize relations with **China**, Beijing made known its displeasure with him as a negotiator in the Third Indochina War.

THAILAND. The Kingdom of Thailand, at 198,114 square miles (513,115 square kilometers), is a France-sized nation of 65 million people located at the continental center of Southeast Asia. Its capital is Bangkok, with a population of 10 million. Until 1939, the kingdom's name was **Siam**. From 1939 to 1946, it was Thailand. It became Siam again from 1946 to 1949, when the name Thailand was restored. Thailand is a constitutional monarchy. The current ruler is King Rama IX (King **Bhumibol Adulyadej**), ninth in the line of the Chakri Dynasty that was founded in 1792. King Bhumibol was born in the United States, where his father was studying at Harvard Medical School. The United States helped celebrate the 50th anniversary of the king's ascension to the throne by the November 1996 visit of President and Mrs. **William J. Clinton**. Former president **George H. W. Bush** represented the United States in 2006 at the celebration of the 60th anniversary of the king's ascension to the throne.

Thailand is unique in Southeast Asia in that it never became a colonial domain of a Western power. **Burma** to its west and **Malaya** in the south became part of Great Britain's Southeast Asian domains.

Laos and **Cambodia** to its north and east were incorporated into the French empire. Thailand's uneasy independence functioned in a balance of power between France and Great Britain. The British and French did appropriate Thai dependent territories and traditional vassals at the margins of the kingdom's core. Caught between the two European powers, Siam appointed American international lawyer **Edward H. Strobel** in 1903 to be the king's foreign policy advisor to help ease tensions between Thailand and France over Cambodia's western provinces. Bilateral treaties with France in 1907 and Great Britain in 1909 guaranteed the sovereignty of the state in what are essentially its present borders. Thailand was also subject to a Western **trade** and jurisdictional regime in which special rights were granted to the Western powers, including the United States.

Thailand (then Siam) was the first Southeast Asian country with which the United States had diplomatic intercourse. The first American merchant ships reached Bangkok in 1821, and American missionaries had been in Siam since 1831. In 1833, during the presidency of Andrew Jackson, **Edmund Roberts** concluded a Treaty of Amity and Commerce between the United States and Siam. This was the first U.S. treaty with an Asian state. In 1849, American envoy **Joseph Balestier** unsuccessfully sought Siamese implementation of the **Roberts Treaty**. The Roberts Treaty was replaced in 1856 by a treaty negotiated by **Townsend Harris**, who was en route to Japan become the first American consul. The **Harris Treaty** was an "unequal" treaty along the lines of the treaty regime forced on **China** by the Western powers. Stephen Mattoon, a Presbyterian missionary, was named the first U.S. consul in Siam. In 1881, James A. Halderman became the first officially appointed consul general, and two years later Halderman opened an American legation as resident minister. The Harris Treaty was revised in 1920 by a new **Siam–U.S. Treaty and Protocol** that eliminated extraterritoriality. This treaty became the pattern for revision of Thailand's other unequal treaties. American advisor **Francis Sayre** played an important role in this. In 1937, the United States and Siam signed a new Treaty of Amity, Commerce, and Navigation, which again set a pattern of equality in bilateral relations for all of Thailand's trading partners. It was not until 1946 that the diplomatic status of the U.S.–Thai relationship was raised from legation and minister to embassy and ambassador.

Thailand's absolute monarchy was overthrown in 1932. The succeeding constitutional monarchy was dominated by military strongmen, the first of whom, **Phibul Songgram**, was prime minister when World War II broke out. Pressured by Japan, Phibul declared war on the United States. His government took back, with Japanese approval, claimed Thai territories lost to the French and British. The Thai minister in Washington, **Seni Pramoj**, refused to deliver the declaration of war and continued to represent **Free Thai** interests independent of the Japanese-influenced regime in Bangkok. The **Office of Strategic Services (OSS)** maintained contact with the Free Thai underground movement. On 8 May 2000, the Free Thai were honored at **Central Intelligence Agency (CIA)** headquarters by Director George Tenet. At the end of the war, the United States did not treat Thailand as defeated enemy nation and worked to ease the peace terms demanded of Thailand by the French and British, although Thailand was forced to retrocede the territories seized during the war.

Up to 1941, U.S. interests in Thailand were largely commercial. The kingdom's political and strategic significance were matters for the British, French, and Japanese. Thailand's historical foreign policy was to bend like a bamboo stalk in the wind as it maneuvered in the regional balance of power. In the new postwar distribution of power, under a Phibul government that came to power by coup in 1947, Thailand opted not for balance but for alliance with the United States. Along with the American alliance came chronic Thai concerns about the strength of the American commitment to Thai security. The Bangkok view of the threat posed by **China**-backed communist aggression coincided with Washington's. For the United States, Thailand was a crucial Southeast Asian **domino** and key to American regional security strategy. American economic and military assistance was a material and political resource for the Thai military's authoritarian anticommunism and efforts to re-create Thai spheres of influence in its neighboring states. Phibul was backed by the powerful, ruthless, and corrupt police General **Phao Sriyanond**, who had close ties to the CIA.

The foundations for a U.S.–Thai security alliance that persists to the present were laid during the mission of long-serving (1946–1953) Ambassador **Edwin F. Stanton**. A Thai–U.S. Military Assistance Agreement was signed in 1950, and a U.S. **Military Assistance**

Advisory Group (MAAG) arrived to work with Thai military counterparts. Thailand was one of the 16 **United Nations (UN)** members to provide military forces to the U.S.-led UN command in the Korean War. It also supplied more than 40,000 tons of rice for Korean relief. Sharing American alarm caused by the French defeat in the **First Indochina War** and the prospects of further communist expansion in Southeast Asia, Thailand accepted with alacrity the American proposal for a regional security structure. Together with the **Philippines**, Thailand was one of the two Southeast Asian nations that signed the 1954 **Southeast Asia Collective Defense Treaty (Manila Pact)** establishing the **Southeast Asia Treaty Organization (SEATO)**. The Thai government was happy to host SEATO's headquarters. In 1955, Prime Minister Phibul made an official visit to the United States. He was awarded the Legion of Merit by President **Dwight D. Eisenhower** and addressed a joint session of the U.S. Congress, where he affirmed Thailand's commitment to its American ally.

Phibul was forced from office in a 1957 coup led by Field Marshal **Sarit Thanarat** and his deputy, Field Marshal **Thanom Kittikachorn**, who succeeded Sarit in 1963. The policy of alliance with the United States continued, with the Thai side seeking constant reassurances from Washington that America would come to Thailand's defense. The Thai strategic eye was on **Laos**, where the forces of the **Viet Minh**–backed **Pathet Lao** threatened to reach the **Mekong River** plain and the Thai border. During the **Laotian Crisis of 1960–1962**, President **John F. Kennedy** dispatched 5,000 marines to Thailand both as a deterrent and a clear signal to the Thais that the United States was unequivocally committed to Thailand's defense against communism. This promise was given political form in the 1962 **Rusk–Thanat communiqué** bilateralizing SEATO obligations. This did not prevent some official second-guessing among the Thai elite about American steadfastness, with some discussion of whether Thailand should return to its traditional foreign policy of balancing and hedging. Nevertheless, the Manila Pact, with its Rusk–Thanat understanding, was the basis for even closer future Thai security collaboration with the United States. State visits to Thailand in 1966 by President **Lyndon B. Johnson** and in 1969 by President **Richard M. Nixon** during the Thanom government were designed to give Thailand assurance of the American commitment to its defense. What the

United States would not give Thailand was a separate bilateral defense treaty similar to that between America and the Philippines.

In 1963, a special logistic agreement was signed allowing prepositioning of U.S. war supplies in Thailand. Thai military support for the CIA's **secret war** in Laos was critical. It is estimated that more than 15,000 Thai troops were in Laos by 1973. The Thai government directly supported the United States in the **Vietnam War**. The Thai military force in Vietnam numbered over 11,000 men at its peak in 1969. Thailand's most important contribution, however, was to allow basing for 500 U.S. combat aircraft and 45,000 American military at seven airfields. These rights were on the basis of unsigned secret agreements negotiated by American ambassador **Graham Martin**. The Thais also were engaged in clandestine cross-border activities in Burma and Cambodia. The alleged Thai–American link to Cambodian dissidents became a serious issue for American relations with Cambodia's Prime Minister **Norodom Sihanouk**. After 1964, Thailand faced its own low-intensity communist insurgency in its northeastern and northern provinces. President Nixon, visiting Thailand in July 1969, unambiguously promised that "the United States will stand proudly with Thailand against those who might threaten it from abroad or from within." The United States supported the expansion of Thailand's counterinsurgency capability but did not commit American forces.

With the outcome of the **Vietnam War** in doubt, the Thais sought to balance their American alliance with closer relations with other noncommunist Southeast Asian states. Thailand was a founding member of the **Association of Southeast Asian Nations (ASEAN)** in 1967 and a party to ASEAN's **Zone of Peace, Freedom and Neutrality (ZOPFAN)** and **Southeast Asian Nuclear Weapons Free Zone (SEANWFZ)**. Like the Philippines, Thailand insisted that its ASEAN engagements did not alter its security relationship with the United States. With the 1975 communist victories in Vietnam, Laos, and Cambodia, Thailand faced a drastically altered strategic and foreign policy environment. The **Nixon doctrine**, combined with what was seen as the American abandonment of its South Vietnamese ally, suggested that Thailand had to adjust to the reality of potentially threatening communist neighbors without an American guarantee. In 1973, military strongman Thanom's American-allied government was ousted. The most wrenching adjustment came in 1975 during the relatively brief and coup-ended government of civilian Prime Minister **Kukrit Pramoj**, who recognized the People's Republic of **China** and demanded that the U.S. bases be terminated and American military forces leave Thailand. The American withdrawal was completed by mid-1976. Also in 1975, Thailand and the Philippines agreed to the phasing out of SEATO, but retaining the obligations of the Manila Pact.

The Vietnamese invasion and occupation of Cambodia in 1978 made Thailand the frontline state in the **Third Indochina War** and reinvigorated Thai–U.S. security ties. The diplomacy of the Third Indochina War was channeled through the multilateral structure of ASEAN and supported by the United States and China. At the bilateral level, Vice President **Walter Mondale**, in Bangkok in May 1978, tried to reassure the government of Prime Minister **Kriangsak Chomanan** that the administration of President **Jimmy Carter** was not abandoning Southeast Asia. Shortly after the Vietnamese invasion of Cambodia, Kriangsak traveled to Washington in February 1979 to meet with Carter. The White House reaffirmed the de facto alliance of the 1962 Rusk–Thanat communiqué. More immediately important, as Vietnamese military forces pressed close to the Thai border, President Carter expedited military equipment deliveries, including F-5E aircraft, tanks, armored personnel carriers, and weapons. **Foreign military sales (FMS)** credits for Thailand jumped from $4 to $40 million. The United States also reauthorized a limited military grant aid program that had been ended in 1969. In February 1979, Assistant Secretary of State for East Asian and Pacific Affairs **Richard Holbrooke** promised very active U.S. support for Thailand if Vietnamese forces should cross the border. Secretary of State **Cyrus Vance** carried Carter's message of support to the ASEAN foreign ministers, meeting them in July 1979. An even stronger expression of American support was conveyed the next year by Secretary of State **Edmund Muskie**.

The policy set in the Carter administration was followed in the succeeding **Reagan** administration. In 1981, the first of the annual **Cobra Gold** Thai–American joint/combined military exercises began. This gave a new, highly visible vitality to the bilateral defense relationship. But Thailand was not always in lockstep with the United

States. In 1986, it joined, "with a very heavy heart," the **United Nations** vote condemning the American air attack on Libya. Although Washington warned that it might cut off assistance to "so-called friendly countries" who voted against it, in fact military assistance to Thailand increased, and a long-discussed U.S.–Thai war reserve weapons pool was agreed to in 1987. In 1994, however, Thailand refused to allow the United States to place a floating supply depot in Thai waters. Thailand also suffered the greatest impact from the immense flow of Indochinese **refugees**. The United States was a major contributor to the international efforts for, first, humanitarian relief and, then, resettlement.

In the post–Cold War era and the integration of the Indochinese states into the cooperative framework of ASEAN, the political/security issues of that earlier period no longer drive Thai–American relations, but security is still an important interest area. The United States had access to Thai ports and airfields for logistic support of the 1991 **Persian Gulf** and 2003 **Iraq Wars**. Thailand made a symbolic deployment of troops to Afghanistan and Iraq. Thailand under Prime Minister **Thaksin Shinawatra** became a close ally in the **war on terrorism**. A Counterterrorism Intelligence Center was established in Thailand to facilitate intelligence sharing shortly after the 11 September 2001 attacks. In October 2003, President **George W. Bush** designated Thailand a **Major Non-NATO Ally (MNNA)**. Thailand and the United States also have had cooperative counter**narcotics production and trafficking** activities as well as programs to combat **pandemic and infectious diseases**. Thailand's Utapao air base and Sattahip naval base were the hubs of U.S. relief operations in the wake of the 2004 **tsunami** disaster. The bilateral relationship has been sporadically irritated by U.S. **human rights** concerns in Thailand.

The United States also has pressured Thailand on democratization. This was the case after a short-lived military coup in 1991 and a September 2006 military coup overthrowing the government of Thaksin Shinawatra. An interim government backed by a military junta in a martial law regime wrote a new constitution that would assure a continued Thai army voice in government, even though new elections for a parliament were promised. As required by American law, the United States suspended military assistance to Thailand and pressed the government to return to democracy. Unlike after coups elsewhere, however, no serious interruption of friendly U.S.–Thai relations occurred, and Cobra Gold 2007 went ahead as scheduled. New elections, generally deemed free and fair, took place in December 2007 with the political party allied with the exiled former Prime Minister Thaksin emerging with a large plurality. Although Thailand was unhappy that the United States was not forthcoming with assistance during the **financial crisis of 1997–1998**, U.S.–Thai **trade** and economic relations have become an important part of the bilateral relationship as Thailand has recovered from the regional economic downturn. In 2006, the United States was Thailand's second largest trading partner after Japan, and Thailand had become the 20th largest goods trading partner of the United States. The United States was the second largest investor in Thailand. Thailand remained eligible for the U.S. **Generalized System of Preferences (GSP)**. The 2002 U.S.–Thai **trade and investment framework agreement (TIFA)** led to the initiation in 2004 of negotiations for a **free trade agreement (FTA)**. Negotiations were suspended in 2006 after Prime Minister Thaksin was forced from office. Even though the U.S. economic stake in Thailand continues to increase, its relative position is changing as a rising China forges close commercial ties with Thailand.

THAKSIN SHINAWATRA (1949–). Prime minister of **Thailand** from 2001 to 2006, Thaksin Shinawatra came to office on a populist platform, and his Thai Rak Thai Party won the largest number of parliamentary seats any Thai party ever had. Thaksin himself was a telecommunications multimillionaire. He allied Thailand with the United States in Afghanistan and Iraq, the **war on terror**, and the liberalization of **trade** in a proposed Thai–U.S. **free trade agreement (FTA)**. In two meetings at the White House with President **George W. Bush**—in 2003 and 2005—Prime Minister Thaksin affirmed the importance of the historical Thai–American alliance. While enjoying Washington's confidence, at home Thaksin was criticized by opposition politicians for heavy-handed rule and corruption. After winning an election in 2006 boycotted by the opposition, he was forced by massive protests in Bangkok to call for new elections. Fearing Thaksin's party would win again, his government was forcefully terminated by a military coup in September 2006, prompting a suspension of American military assistance to Thailand. New elections were held in December 2007 in which a party allied with Thaksin won a huge plurality.

THANOM KITTIKACHORN (1912–2004). A Thai military dictator, Field Marshal Thanom Kittikachorn was deputy to Field Marshal **Sarit Thanarat** in their coup against Prime Minister **Phibul Songgram** in 1957. Thanom served briefly as prime minister in 1958, when Sarit was in the United States for medical treatment, and then succeeded Sarit as prime minister upon his death in 1963. Thanom ruled Thailand with an iron hand, abolishing the constitution in 1971. Like his predecessors, he maintained close ties to the United States. He was overthrown and forced into temporary exile in 1973 after a bloody student uprising and the intervention of King **Bhumibol**. The popular protests against Thanom's tyrannical unconstitutional rule were also used by Thai leftists to attack Thai–American relations and the American bases in Thailand.

THIEU, NGUYEN VAN (1924–2001). Nguyen Van Thieu was president of the **Republic of Vietnam (RVN)** from 1967 until its fall in April 1975. One of the most professional of the generals who were involved in the 1963 **Diem coup**, he was elected president in 1967 and, eclipsing his rivals, firmly established himself as a stubborn and, if necessary, repressive ruler. Even as domestic politics in the United States was forcing President **Lyndon B. Johnson** and then **Richard M. Nixon** to find an exit strategy from the Vietnam War, Thieu believed that it could be won. He opposed the **Paris peace negotiations** and was aghast at the terms of the January 1973 **Paris Agreement** that left North Vietnamese forces in **South Vietnam** while the United States withdrew. He signed them only when Washington threatened to cut off all military assistance. Through 1973–1974, Thieu balked at the implementation of the armistice, continuing military operations and ignoring the political framework. He believed that there would be a last-minute American intervention if the armistice collapsed. On 21 April 1975, as the People's Army of Vietnam (PAVN) advanced, pummeling and then crushing the resistance of the Army of the Republic of Vietnam (ARVN), Thieu, embittered by what he saw as the American betrayal, resigned his presidency. Saigon surrendered nine days later. Thieu went into exile to Taiwan, London, and finally, in 1990, the United States.

THIRD INDOCHINA WAR, 1978–1991. On 26 December 1978, the **Socialist Republic of Vietnam (SRV)**'s People's Army invaded **Khmer Rouge (KR)**–ruled **Democratic Kampuchea (DK)(Cambodia)**. This was the beginning of the Third Indochina War. For **Vietnam**, with its security tie to the USSR, its action meant the elimination of a threat of Chinese encirclement through Beijing's ties to the DK. For the **Association of Southeast Asian Nations (ASEAN)**, however, Cambodia had become the first Southeast Asian **domino** to fall to a militarily strong communist state. The war did not officially end until nearly 13 years later, with the signing on 21 October 1991 of the **comprehensive political settlement of the Cambodia conflict**. Although the United States was not a battlefield partner of the **Khmer resistance** forces that fought the Vietnamese and their **People's Republic of Kampuchea (PRK)** client government, America was an important political, diplomatic, and economic supporter of the Khmer exile coalition—the **Coalition Government of Democratic Kampuchea (CGDK)**—and its ASEAN sponsors, in particular **Thailand**, ASEAN's frontline state and long time American ally. Vietnam's role in Cambodia added a new obstacle to American **normalization of relations** with it. The People's Republic of **China** also came to the support of ASEAN and the Khmer resistance. For both the United States and China, there were Great Power strategic implications as well as local ones since Vietnam's alliance partner was the Soviet Union.

Vietnam's goal was to make its fait accompli in establishing the PRK irreversible and to have a compliant neighbor to its west. ASEAN, branding the PRK illegitimate, called for the withdrawal of Vietnamese forces, a **United Nations (UN)** peacekeeping force, and UN-organized and -supervised elections in which the Cambodian people could exercise their democratic right to self-determination. Neither the United States nor ASEAN wanted an outcome that would bring the KR back to power. The ASEAN position was endorsed by the UN. In 1980, the UN General Assembly (UNGA) called for the convening of a special conference on Cambodia. The UN International Conference on Kampuchea (ICK) took place in July 1981. Over the objections and even boycott by the communist bloc and its friends, the ICK issued a declaration that essentially endorsed ASEAN's call for a comprehensive settlement under the supervision of the UN that would guarantee Cambodia's independence and self-determination for its people. The terms of the ICK declaration were subsequently overwhelmingly endorsed in annual UNGA resolutions. For several years the western reaches of Cambodia became a kind of Vietnam's "Vietnam," with its forces unable to extinguish the Khmer resistance forces. Different perceptions within ASEAN of the implications of a more intense Sino–Soviet competition in the region and Vietnam's awareness of the wasting nature of its Cambodia adventure worked to move the parties toward negotiations.

ASEAN solidarity was tested by the flexibility of individual members. **Indonesia** opened a bilateral channel to Hanoi in 1984, and in 1988 Thai prime minister Chatichai Choonhaven accepted the administrative reality of the PRK regime. The carrot offered to Vietnam by ASEAN was eventual ASEAN membership. The U.S. sweetener was progress toward normalization of relations. The stick was the Khmer resistance. Two Jakarta informal meetings (JIM I and II) in 1988 and 1989 between the Khmer parties, Vietnam, and ASEAN set the stage for the 1989 19-nation **Paris International Conference on Cambodia (PICC)**, which deadlocked. The logjam was freed when a Great Power consensus was reached in the UN Security Council on a formula for a **comprehensive political settlement of the Cambodia conflict**, which was endorsed by the reconvened PICC in October 1991.

THO, LE DUC (1910–1986). Le Duc Tho was a founding member of the Indochinese Communist Party (ICP) in 1930 and became one of the most powerful members of the Vietnamese Workers Party's (Communist Party) politburo. In September 1968, he became an "advisor" to the **Democratic Republic of Vietnam (DRV)**'s delegation to the **Paris Peace negotiations**, but in fact led the negotiations from the DRV side. He was the primary negotiator with U.S. National Security Advisor **Henry Kissinger** in reaching the 1973 **Paris Agreement**. Together with Kissinger, Tho was awarded the 1973 Nobel Peace Prize. Tho declined the award because peace in fact had not been won in South Vietnam.

TIMIKA INCIDENT. In October 2002, near the town of Timika in the **Freeport–McMoRan** mining concession in **Indonesia**'s Papua province, a road convoy carrying eight Americans was attacked by armed men. Two of the Americans, teachers in a company school, were killed. The gunmen were allegedly Indonesian soldiers, although the Indonesian authorities claimed they were members of the indigenous **Free Papua Organization (OPM).** The attack complicated U.S.–Indonesian relations when Congress added it to the **human rights** abuses that had provoked the **Leahy Amendment** prohibiting normal U.S.–Indonesian military-to-military relations. The American insistence on a full investigation of the shootings, aided by the Federal Bureau of Investigation (FBI), was publicly lobbied for at high official levels in both governments by Patsy Spier, the widow of one of the victims, who personally met with Indonesia's President **Susilo Bambang Yudhoyono**. In January 2006, the FBI arranged for the surrender of 12 OPM supporters, including one who had been indicted by a Washington, D.C., grand jury. Six were put on trial in Jakarta and found guilty. The verdict and long sentences brought vows by the OPM of reprisals against the United States and Indonesia. Despite the official closure of the case, the question of Indonesian military involvement remained open, with one theory being that the military were disgruntled by a reduction of payments to soldiers who provided security to the Freeport–McMoRan operation.

TIMOR LESTE. *See* EAST TIMOR.

TONKIN GULF INCIDENT. On 2 August and 4 August 1964, two U.S. destroyers, the *Maddox* and *Turner Joy*, allegedly came under attack by North Vietnamese torpedo boats while patrolling in what the United States claimed were international waters. It is likely that the ships were on reconnaissance missions in support of a covert program of assault and intelligence-gathering landings on the North Vietnamese coast. The dispute over whether or not there had actually been attacks on the American ships surfaced again in 2005, when declassified documents showed that U.S. signals intelligence had been deliberately altered to indicate North Vietnamese hostile activity. President **Lyndon B. Johnson** ordered retaliatory air strikes against North Vietnamese naval targets and fuel storage facilities, the first

U.S. bombings north of the 17th parallel. More significantly, the incident was the trigger for the Johnson administration to seek a congressional mandate to widen the war in the **Tonkin Gulf Resolution**. *See also* VIETNAM WAR.

TONKIN GULF RESOLUTION. The "Southeast Asia Resolution," better known as the Tonkin Gulf Resolution, was a joint resolution of Congress passed on 7 August 1964 by a vote of 416–0 in the House and 88–2 in the Senate. It was precipitated by the **Tonkin Gulf incident**, but such a resolution had already been drafted by the White House, only awaiting a proper time to introduce it. It approved the president's determination to take all necessary measures, including the use of force to repel any armed attack against the forces of the United States and to prevent any further aggression. It also authorized the president to take all necessary steps, including the use of armed force, to assist any member or protocol state of the **Southeast Asia Treaty Organization (SEATO)** requesting assistance in defense of its freedom. In retrospect, the Tonkin Gulf Resolution has been viewed as a blank check to wage the undeclared **Second Indochina War** not only in **Vietnam**, but in **Cambodia** and **Laos** as well. The resolution was repealed by Congress on 24 June 1970.

TRADE. Trade between the United States and Southeast Asia is rapidly expanding. In 2003, two-way trade was valued at $127 billion; in 2004, $136 billion; in 2005, $148 billion; and in 2006, $160 billion, making the **Association of Southeast Asian Nations (ASEAN)** region the fourth-largest U.S. trading partner. **China**'s two-way trade in 2006 with Southeast Asia was also valued at $160 billion. The continuing rapid growth of China–Southeast Asia trade since China's 2001 **World Trade Organization (WTO)** membership and its 2004 **free trade agreement** with **ASEAN** mean that China's share of Southeast Asian trade will exceed that of the United States in 2007. Trade promotion is an important activity in the economic sections of U.S. embassies. All but a small portion of the ASEAN trade comes from the more developed ASEAN core five members. **Malaysia** is the United States' largest single ASEAN trading partner, with two-way trade in 2006 totaling $49 billion or more than 30 percent of the ASEAN total. Malaysia is the United States' 10th largest market.

Singapore ranked second, with 2006 two-way trade at $42 billion, and **Thailand** third, with 2006 two-way trade with the United States valued at $30 billion. Four Southeast Asian countries have U.S. **Generalized System of Preferences (GSP)** qualified status: **Cambodia**, **Indonesia**, the **Philippines**, and Thailand. The United States has imposed strict trade sanctions on **Burma (Myanmar)** because of continuing Burmese violations of **human rights**.

The United States has brought to Southeast Asia its global trade policy of expansion and liberalization. In this, it has had to overcome protectionist sentiment both in the United States and in the Southeast Asian countries. With the great economic advances made by ASEAN's members, U.S. trade policy focus has broadened to include regional as well as bilateral engagements. As early as 1984, in the **Reagan** administration, **United States Trade Representative (USTR)** William Brock offered to discuss regional economic cooperation, with ASEAN including a possible free trade area. Since 1989, the U.S. regional trade agenda has been promoted through the **Asia–Pacific Economic Cooperation (APEC)** structure. As well as protectionism, the United States has also had to resist exclusionary regionalism, represented by the thwarted **East Asian Economic Group (EAEG)** and a possible **East Asian Free Trade Area (EAFTA)**.

Since 2002, trade negotiations with Southeast Asian states have been spurred by the U.S. **Enterprise for ASEAN Initiative (EAI)**. The USTR has the responsibility for negotiations. The EAI had as its goal the negotiation of bilateral **trade and investment framework agreements (TIFA)** as first steps toward bilateral **free trade agreements (FTA)**. TIFAs have been executed with **Brunei**, Cambodia, Indonesia, Malaysia, the Philippines, Thailand, and Vietnam. Singapore graduated in 2003 from a TIFA to an FTA with the United States. Negotiations for an FTA with Thailand and Malaysia were ongoing in 2006 and announced for the Philippines. However, the expiration in 2007 of the president's "fast track" **trade promotion authority (TPA)** meant that Congress will have to enact legislation to renew the TPA before negotiations can be successfully concluded. Preliminary discussions looking to a future Indonesian FTA also were started in 2005. At a meeting with the heads of government of seven ASEAN member states at the 2005 APEC meeting, President **George W.**

Bush committed the United States to an **ASEAN–U.S. Enhanced Partnership** that had as a short range goal an ASEAN–U.S. TIFA as a first step toward a U.S.–ASEAN FTA. The TIFA was signed in August 2006. The United States has also proposed for the future an **Asia–Pacific FTA** within the APEC framework. *See also* BURMESE FREEDOM AND DEMOCRACY ACT; TRADING WITH THE ENEMY ACT.

TRADE AND INVESTMENT FRAMEWORK AGREEMENT (TIFA). A trade and investment framework agreement, or TIFA, establishes a consultative mechanism through which the United States can work with bilateral or multilateral partners to liberalize and facilitate the development of **trade** and **investment** for the promotion of mutually beneficial economic growth under the regulatory umbrella of the **World Trade Organization (WTO)**. In a TIFA structure, a joint council meets regularly to review the trade and investment relationship and specific trade problems. The **United States Trade Representative (USTR)** is the negotiating agent for the United States. As of 30 June 2007, in Southeast Asia America had bilateral TIFAs with the **Philippines** (1989), **Indonesia** (1996), **Brunei** (2002), **Thailand** (2002), **Malaysia** (2004), Cambodia (2006), and **Vietnam** (2007). Initial negotiations for a TIFA had begun with **Cambodia**. A TIFA is viewed as a precursor to a **free trade agreement (FTA)**. The U.S.–Singapore FTA is the only one that the United States had in Southeast Asia. Negotiations for an FTA have been underway with Malaysia, Thailand, and the Philippines. Since the presidential announcement in October 2002 of the **Enterprise for ASEAN Initiative (EAI)**, TIFAs and other U.S. efforts to promote and facilitate trade and investment in Southeast Asia have been placed in a regional context of the **Association of Southeast Asian Nations (ASEAN)**. The planning for the **ASEAN–U.S. Enhanced Partnership** announced in November 2005 called for a regionwide TIFA. The ASEAN–U.S. TIFA was signed on 25 August 2006.

TRADE PROMOTION AUTHORITY (TPA). This gave the president so-called fast track trade promotion authority (TPA) to negotiate **free trade agreements (FTA)** with other countries, which when presented to Congress would be subject to an up or down vote within 90 days without amendment. The "fast track" under the TPA was used for the U.S.–**Singapore** FTA and was the basis of FTA negotiations in 2006 with **Malaysia** and **Thailand**. The negotiating benefit is that other countries can have confidence that the agreements they negotiate will not be subject to future renegotiation depending on congressional intervention. The president's TPA expired on 30 June 2007. Legislation was introduced in February 2007 to renew and expand it but had not been acted on before expiration of the existing TPA.

TRADING WITH THE ENEMY ACT (TWEA). Originally enacted in 1917, the Trading with the Enemy Act, as amended, has been used by American presidents since Woodrow Wilson to restrict economic and commercial intercourse with countries deemed hostile to the United States It is the source of authority for the presidential economic sanctions in Southeast Asia. Based on the TWEA, a trade and financial embargo was placed on the **Democratic Republic of Vietnam (DRV)** in 1964. It was extended to all of **Vietnam** and **Cambodia** in 1975. The Cambodian sanctions were lifted in 1992. TWEA sanctions required annual determinations and renewals and could be amended and waived. The gradual loosening of TWEA restrictions was part of the U.S. strategy to encourage Vietnam to be more forthcoming on American prisoners of war/missing in action (**POW/ MIA**) during the process of **normalization of relations** with Vietnam. The embargo on Vietnam was lifted in 1994.

TRAFFICKING IN PERSONS. Since 2000, the problem of trafficking in persons has become an official part of U.S. relations in Southeast Asia, as elsewhere in the world. It is estimated that annually as many as a quarter of a million people are trafficked in Southeast Asia. The Trafficking Victims Protection Act, which has been reauthorized by successive Congresses, is designed to combat trafficking in women, men, and children for purposes of sexual exploitation, slavery, and involuntary servitude. It also addresses the issue of violence against women. The **State Department**'s Office to Monitor and Combat Trafficking in Persons (G/TIP) compiles an annual congressionally mandated "Trafficking in Persons" report covering 150 source, transit, and destination countries. An interagency coordinating body was set up to monitor the antitrafficking programs of the different participating U.S. agencies. Both the report and the programs funded by the United States depend heavily on cooperation with local nongovernmental organizations (NGOs) working on women's issues.

The annual trafficking report assigns countries to three tiers of compliance with antitrafficking standards. In 2005, no Southeast Asian country was listed at the first tier, full compliance. The second tier, countries that did not fully comply but were making significant efforts to do so, included **East Timor**, **Indonesia**, **Laos**, **Malaysia**, **Singapore**, **Thailand**, and **Vietnam**. The **Philippines** was placed on a Tier II "watch list" because of inadequate efforts to enforce its antitrafficking laws. The third tier, on which **Burma** and **Cambodia** were placed, consists of those countries not in compliance and not making a significant effort to do so. In the case of Burma, the military's use of women and children in forced labor has been singled out for condemnation. Cambodia was identified as a source for trafficking in women to Thailand and Malaysia as well as a transit point for women from Vietnam. Its systemic corruption and inadequate legal system meant no real effort had been made in combating trafficking in persons. By Presidential Determination, Tier III countries can be denied certain economic or security assistance funding. The changing dynamics of the problem in terms of domestic legislation, enforcement, and protection is illustrated by the fact that in the 2006 trafficking report Singapore had been promoted to Tier I and the Philippines to Tier II; Indonesia was demoted to the Tier II "watch list" along with Malaysia; Cambodia was promoted to the Tier II "watch list"; and Laos dropped back into Tier III. Burma remained in Tier III. In 2007, there were no Southeast Asian countries in Tier I. Singapore had been dropped back to Tier II; Indonesia was taken off the Tier II "watch list"; Cambodia was promoted from the Tier III to Tier II "watch list"; and Malaysia was placed with Burma in Tier III. **Brunei** is a separate case because of lack of reliable information and is not assigned a tier placement. *See also* HUMAN RIGHTS.

TREATY OF AMITY AND COOPERATION IN SOUTHEAST ASIA (TAC). The 24 February 1976 Treaty of Amity and Cooperation was produced by the second **Association of Southeast Asian Nations (ASEAN)** summit held in Bali, Indonesia. It was a reaction to the American defeat in **Indochina** and the emergence of communist governments in **Vietnam**, **Laos**, and **Cambodia**. It expressed a new political solidarity among the five member states, with a willingness to legally commit themselves to peaceful dispute settlement and the nonuse of force in regional relations. With a view to Indochinese states, the TAC was open for accession by other Southeast Asian signatories willing to accept the regulative norms of ASEAN. Accession to TAC became a requirement for membership as ASEAN expanded from the core five to the present ten.

In 1998, the TAC was amended to open it to states outside of Southeast Asia, but without membership in ASEAN. A number of states have signed on: Australia, Bangladesh, **China**, France, India, Japan, New Zealand, Pakistan, Papua New Guinea, Russia, Sri Lanka, and South Korea. Despite ASEAN urging, the United States has refused to accede. In the vision statement of the 2005 **ASEAN–U.S. Enhanced Partnership**, however, America stated that it respects the spirit and principles of the TAC as a code of conduct governing international relations in Southeast Asia. Accession to the TAC is a requirement to participate in the **East Asia Summit**, but not a guarantee of invitation. In the lead-up to the July 2007 ASEAN ministerial meeting, the **State Department** disclosed that the United States was looking closely at the treaty. This reflected U.S. desire to demonstrate its strong interest in ASEAN as well as Washington's concerns about being excluded from wider East Asian regionalism including the East Asia Summit (EAS).

TRUMAN, HARRY S. (1884–1972). Upon the death of President Franklin D. Roosevelt in 1945, Vice President Harry S. Truman became the 33rd president of the United States. The imperatives of the Cold War, which began during his administration with the **Truman Doctrine**'s definition of America's role in the world and the strategy of **containment**, were carried into Southeast Asia. Although, according to his special counsel **Clark Clifford**, Truman had little interest in Southeast Asia, it was Truman who made the first economic and political commitments to the three-decade-long U.S. effort to prevent the victory of communism in **Indochina**. **Ho Chi Minh's letter**, dated 28 February 1946, asking for U.S. recognition of the **Democratic Republic of Vietnam (DRV)**, was never answered. During the

Truman administration, support was pledged and delivered to the French, who sought to restore their colonial authority in the **First Indochina War**. The victory of the Chinese communists in 1949 convinced the Truman administration that the front line of containment of communism in Southeast Asia was in **Indochina**.

Elsewhere in Southeast Asia, the Truman administration was frustrated by the corruption of the Philippine governments of Presidents **Manuel Roxas** and **Elpidio Quirino**, which wasted economic assistance and undermined democratic stability. Truman, like American presidents succeeding him, was held hostage by U.S. security interests in the **Philippines** in the defeat of the **Hukbalahap** communist insurgents and maintenance of the U.S. military bases. There was, as well, a sense of responsibility for postwar reconstruction and rehabilitation. The sympathy shown by the Truman administration for **Indonesia**'s independence struggle was in part an appreciation of the anticommunist credentials the nationalists had demonstrated in crushing an abortive communist revolt as well as public and congressional expressions of support for Indonesian independence.

TRUMAN DOCTRINE. The Truman Doctrine was enunciated on 17 March 1947 in a speech by President **Harry S. Truman** to a joint session of the U.S. Congress. The occasion for the speech was a call for assistance for Greece and Turkey, which were seen as imminently threatened by USSR-backed communism. The specific threat and the requirements for U.S. policy, however, were generalized globally and together with the strategy of **containment** became the conceptual underpinnings of American policy in the Cold War. In the speech, Truman asserted that direct and indirect threats to free peoples by totalitarian aggression (i.e., communism) were a threat to international peace and the security of the United States. In the case of such threats, the United States was the only nation willing and able to come to the assistance of nations threatened by such aggression.

TSUNAMI. On 26 December 2004, a magnitude 9 deep sea earthquake in the Indian Ocean off **Indonesia**'s island of Sumatra triggered a devastating tsunami, with massive destruction across six countries. Indonesia's Aceh province was the hardest hit, with more than 170,000 dead or missing, 500,000 displaced, and devastation along nearly 500 miles of coastline. Peninsular **Thailand**'s Andaman Sea coast was also severely affected. The largest international humanitarian rescue and relief operation since World War II was mobilized to provide assistance, with a total of nearly $7 billion for relief and reconstruction raised worldwide. The support provided by elements of the **United States Pacific Command (USPACOM)** was crucial to the first response to the disaster. It was, in the words of the Indonesian defense minister, the "backbone of the logistical operations providing assistance to all afflicted." The multination response to the emergency was coordinated by a U.S.-led Combined Support Force headquartered at the Royal Thai Naval Air Base at Utapao, with **Singapore** a key staging area for supplies. The USS *Abraham Lincoln* Carrier Strike Group sailed from Hong Kong and the USS *Bonhomme Richard* Expeditionary Strike Group sailed from Guam. The 13 ships and thousands of sailors and marines they carried spearheaded the immediate relief effort in Aceh. They were joined by the hospital ship USNS *Mercy*. The PACOM response was a dramatic illustration of the "soft power" potential of the U.S. presence in the Southeast Asian region.

Continued U.S. commitment to tsunami recovery was symbolized by President **George W. Bush**'s dispatch in 2005 of former presidents **George H. W. Bush** and **William J. Clinton** to the stricken area. More concretely, for the humanitarian and recovery stages of the tsunami relief effort, the United States committed over $300 million. Congress appropriated another $631 million for reconstruction, of which $400 million was destined for Indonesia. Former presidents Bush and Clinton jointly headed a public drive for funds. The **United Nations** Global Consortium for Tsunami Recovery was chaired by former president Clinton, who was designated UN Special Envoy for Tsunami Recovery.

TWINING, CHARLES J. (1940–). In the late 1970s, Foreign Service Officer Charles Twining was a **Cambodia** specialist based in the U.S. embassy in **Thailand**. After that he became director of the **Laos**, Cambodia, **Vietnam** office at the State Department. In 1991, with the ending of the **Third Indochina War**, Twining became the first U.S. diplomatic representative to Cambodia since Ambassador **John Gunther Dean** evacuated the embassy in 1975. Twining first headed a representative mission from 1991 to 1993, then became the first American ambassador to the restored Kingdom of Cambodia. His subsequent career was centered on Africa. In 2003, Twining was with the U.S. mission to the **United Nations**, where he worked on establishing the framework for the UN-sponsored **Khmer Rouge trials**.

TYDINGS–MCDUFFIE ACT. The Philippine Independence Act of 1934 is named for Senator Millard Tydings (D-MD), Chairman of the Senate Insular Affairs Committee, and Representative John McDuffie (D-AL), Insular Affairs Committee counterpart in the House. The legislation enabled a Philippine constitutional convention to draft a basic law for a **Commonwealth of the Philippines** government in preparation for independence from the United States. The law provided for a 10-year transition period before the **Philippines** would become sovereign. The transition was interrupted by the outbreak of World War II and the Japanese occupation of the Philippines. The major difference between the Tydings–McDuffie Act and the defeated **Hare–Hawes–Cutting Act** was the absence of a provision for postindependence U.S. Army bases in the Philippines.

– U –

U NU (1907–1995). A devout Buddhist and Burmese nationalist, U Nu was prime minister of **Burma** in 1948–1956, 1956–1958, and 1960–1962. He was an exponent of equidistant neutralism for Burma in the Cold War and was critical of the American-sponsored **Southeast Asia Treaty Organization (SEATO)**. U Nu's Burma was the first Southeast Asian country to recognize the Peoples' Republic of **China**. One of the conveners of the 1955 **Asian–African Conference**, U Nu was also a founding father of the **Nonaligned Movement**. In 1953, Burmese–U.S. relations soured over the presence of remnants of Chinese Nationalist (KMT) army forces in Burma—the **KMT–Burma crisis**. The United States was accused of clandestinely supporting the KMT troops. Despite American diplomatic efforts, U Nu took the matter to the **United Nations** General Assembly. U Nu visited the United States in July 1956 and had "frank" discussions with President **Dwight D. Eisenhower** and Secretary of State **John**

Foster Dulles. After the 1962 military intervention by General **Ne Win**, U Nu spent time under house arrest and in exile. After the elections of 1988, which were overturned by the military junta, U Nu set up a parallel government, was arrested, and was released in 1992.

UNEXPLODED ORDNANCE (UXO). The **Indochina wars** left a legacy of unexploded ordnance in **Laos**, **Vietnam**, and **Cambodia**. The problem is particularly severe in northeastern Laos, with heavy UXO contamination. There is a Laotian national UXO program funded by a **United Nations** Development Program (UNDP) trust fund and annual pledges by donor nations. Although not accepting responsibility for the problem of UXO in Laos, the United States, through the **State Department**'s Office of Weapons Removal and Abatement in the Bureau of Political and Military Affairs (PM), has contributed to UXO Laos and U.S. Special Operations Forces soldiers have trained Lao UXO clearance teams. The UNDP also works in Cambodia with donor support from Japan, France, and Great Britain. In Vietnam, since 1975, 38,000 people have been killed and 64,000 wounded by UXO. In 2000, the United States provided Vietnam with a $1.75 million grant for mine and UXO clearance equipment. In 2003, the Department of State funded a Vietnam Veterans of America Foundation program for data collection on mines and UXO. A first phase clearance program was carried out in 2004 and 2005. Agreement for a second phase was signed in November 2006.

UNGER, LEONARD S. (1917–). A career Foreign Service Officer, Leonard Unger was U.S. ambassador to **Laos** from 1962 to 1964, during the early years of the **secret war**, and ambassador to **Thailand** from 1967 to 1973 while Thailand was an ally of the United States in the **Vietnam War**. Between the posts in Vientiane and Bangkok, in 1965–1966, he was deputy assistant secretary of state for East Asian and Pacific affairs and chaired the Vietnam Coordination Committee in the **Department of State**. In that capacity he prepared the concept paper for the reorganization of the Vietnam pacification program. From Bangkok, Unger went to Taiwan as the last American ambassador to the Republic of China. After retirement, he was associated with the Tufts University Fletcher School of Law and Diplomacy helping to develop its Southeast Asia program.

UNITED NATIONS (UN). The United Nations organization was created by treaty at the June 1945 San Francisco United Nations Conference on International Organization. The Charter of the United Nations was signed by its 51 founding members on 26 June 1945, and it came into legal existence on 24 October 1945 with the last of the ratifications of the Charter. The **Philippines**, still in its **Commonwealth of the Philippines** status, was the only Southeast Asian founding member. The UN's World War II roots are in the 1942 war aims set forth in the "Declaration of the United Nations" by the 26 allies in the war against the Axis powers. It is considered to be the successor to the interwar League of Nations. In its more than six decades, UN membership by 2007 had grown to 192 nation states. Only one member, **Indonesia**, has ever voluntarily quit the organization. This was during the period of **confrontation** with **Malaysia** when President **Sukarno** protested Malaysia's seating on the Security Council. Indonesia returned to the UN after the Sukarno government was replaced by the **Suharto** government following the 1965 **Indonesian coup** and countercoup. All of the **Association of Southeast Asian Nations (ASEAN)** member states are members of the UN. In that body, in addition to their ASEAN political identification, they are also considered to be part of the Asia geographic grouping and, as appropriate, part of the **Group of 77**, **Nonaligned Movement (NAM)**, and **Organization of the Islamic Conference (OIC)** groupings.

The purpose of the UN as set forth in its charter is to maintain international peace and security and promote economic and social development. Its security mechanism is collective security, in which the members promise not to use force in international affairs except in self-defense or in carrying out UN-authorized missions. The UN's principal organs are the General Assembly (GA), the Security Council (SC), the Economic and Social Council (ECOSOC), and the Trusteeship Council. The organs of the UN are serviced by the Secretariat, headed by the secretary-general. Over the years, numerous specialized agencies, funds, and programs have expanded the UN system to 30 major bodies, not to mention subsidiary bodies of the principal organs themselves. The work of agencies like the World Health Organization (WHO), the Food and Agriculture Organization (FAO), the Economic and Social Commission for Asia and the Pacific (ESCAP), and the United Nations Development Program (UNDP) are just a few examples of the many UN agencies whose developmental and humanitarian work on a regional and bilateral basis are carried out throughout Southeast Asia. The United States has been supportive of the United Nations High Commissioner for Refugees (UNHCR), especially the work with Indochinese **refugees** and ethnic minorities in Southeast Asia.

For U.S. political relations in Southeast Asia, it is primarily in the General Assembly, the Security Council, and the Secretariat that Washington interacts with the Southeast Asian states on regional issues that have been raised to the global level of diplomacy. All UN members are represented in the General Assembly on a one-country, one-vote basis. In 2006, the overall UNGA voting coincidence with the United States was 23.6 percent. ASEAN's voting coincidence with the United States was only 20 percent, reflecting a continuing decline since 1995 similar to that of Third World geographic or political groups as a whole. The United States identified 13 votes as important. On only one of those votes did an ASEAN state—the **Philippines**— vote the same way the United States did. All of the other ASEAN members voted differently, abstained, or were absent. One ASEAN state—Indonesia—voted differently than the United States on all 13 votes. The policy differences are marked on questions of the Middle East, arms control, and **human rights**. ASEAN votes are similar to those of their geographic neighbors, India and **China**. In matters affecting the vital interests of an ASEAN state, the other states act in solidarity with it. This has been particularly frustrating for the United States with respect to the issues of democracy and human rights in **Burma**. There is no correlation between ASEAN voting in the General Assembly and the quality of U.S. bilateral relations with the ASEAN states and ASEAN itself. In the 15-member Security Council, ASEAN states have to compete with other Asian nations for a nonpermanent, two-year seat. Voting dynamics in the Security Council are very different. The members make every effort to fashion a resolution that can be accepted by all, or at the most draw an abstention. In the 2005 Security Council in which the Philippines was a member, there were 71 votes on which no negative votes were cast.

Issues of importance to the United States originating from Southeast Asia that have been matters of General Assembly concern have included the **KMT–Burma** crisis, the **West New Guinea dispute**, the **Indonesian invasion and occupation of East Timor**, and **Vietnam**'s invasion of **Cambodia** in the **Third Indochina War**. In the Security Council, one of the first problems came from **Indonesia** and the Dutch military efforts to prevent Indonesian independence. The SC authorized the **United Nations Commission on Indonesia (UNCI)**, which facilitated the Dutch transfer of sovereignty to Indonesia. The five permanent members of the SC were able to agree to the formula to end the Third Indochina War and put in place the **United Nations Transitional Authority in Cambodia (UNTAC)**. Similarly, consensus was reached for peacekeeping and a **United Nations Transitional Administration in East Timor (UNTAET)**.

UNITED NATIONS COMMISSION ON INDONESIA (UNCI). The **United Nations (UN)** Commission on Indonesia was the 1949 successor to the Security Council's **Good Offices Committee**. The latter had brokered the **Renville Agreement** truce, broken by the Netherlands' second "police action' during **Indonesia**'s struggle for independence. Dr. **Frank Graham** remained the American member of the three-nation commission (Australia, Belgium, and the United States). He was succeeded by **Coert DuBois** and **Merle Cochran**. American policy was supportive of Indonesia's aspirations. The skillful diplomacy of Indonesian representatives played on American anti-imperialism and democratic values in foreign policy elite and congressional circles. Senior U.S. senators warned of a cutoff of American Marshall Plan aid to the Netherlands if it were used to offset the costs of the colonial war in Indonesia. The UNCI was tasked with carrying out the UN Security Council's decisions. On 31 March 1949, the Council called again for a cease-fire and the restoration of the republican government to its Yogyakarta capital. It instructed the UNCI to assist the Dutch and Indonesians in agreeing on a date and place for a Round Table Conference to reach a political settlement. The Round Table opened in The Hague, the Netherlands, on 23 August 1949, with the Dutch and Indonesian representatives joined by the members of the Commission, including American diplomat Merle Cochran, whose sympathy for the Dutch upset the Indonesians. The Round Table Conference ended on 2 November 1949 with the instruments for the transfer of sovereignty from the Netherlands to independent Indonesia. The formal transfer took place on 27 December 1949.

UNITED NATIONS ASSISTANCE MISSION IN EAST TIMOR (UNAMET). **United Nations (UN)** Security Council Resolution 1246 established the UN Mission in East Timor on 11 June 1999 to organize and conduct the "popular consultation" on the future of **East Timor**. This had been agreed to on 5 May by **Indonesia** and Portugal, who entrusted the UN to carry out the "popular consultation." The **United Nations Transitional Administration in East Timor (UNTAET)** took over the UN role in East Timor on 25 October 1999. This was after attacks on East Timorese civilians and UNAMET by Indonesian Army–sponsored militias protesting the outcome of the "consultation" prompted the intervention of the **International Force for East Timor (INTERFET)**. The United States, a permanent member of the UN Security Council, had strongly promoted the creation of UNAMET and voluntarily contributed $10 million to its initial $52 million estimated cost. This made it, with Portugal, Australia, and Japan, followed by the European Union, one of the largest funding supporters of UNAMET. The final cost of $80 million dollars was made up by UN assessment based on the regular UN proportional assessment schedule. The United States was part of a "Core 5" group, including Security Council member Great Britain, as well as Australia, Japan, and New Zealand, that provided practical and day-to-day diplomatic support to the secretary-general and UNAMET.

UNITED NATIONS TRANSITIONAL ADMINISTRATION IN EAST TIMOR (UNTAET). **United Nations (UN)** Security Council Resolution 1272 established the UN Transitional Administration in East Timor on 25 October 1999 as an interim government of **East Timor** for purposes of peacekeeping and preparing the territory for independence from **Indonesia**. Its mission ended on 20 May 2002. In its place, a United Nations Mission to Support East Timor (UNMISET) continued to function in the newly independent state. UNTAET was organized in the wake of the violence following the **East Timor referendum** and the intervention by the **International Force in East Timor (INTERFET)**. In the United Nations and in bilateral U.S.–Indonesian contacts, the U.S. government strongly urged the creation of UNTAET. American direct participation in UNTAET was limited to three military observers and a handful of civilian police. The United States provided 27 percent of the budget. In addition, the United

States was a major contributor to the World Bank trust fund for East Timor as well as bilateral assistance through the U.S. **Agency for International Development (AID)**. Although outside of UNTAET's chain of command, a 20-man, rotating U.S. military detachment, the U.S. Support Group East Timor, carried out humanitarian actions.

UNITED NATIONS TRANSITIONAL AUTHORITY IN CAMBODIA (UNTAC). Authorized by the **United Nations (UN)** Security Council as the implementing agency of the 1991 **comprehensive political settlement of the Cambodia conflict**, the UN Transitional Authority in Cambodia operated from February 1992 to September 1993 when, after UNTAC-supervised elections, a new Cambodian government was installed. At its maximum strength, UNTAC had nearly 20,000 peacekeeping forces and civil administrators in the field. They were drawn from 46 countries including the United States. The senior American was **State Department Cambodia** specialist **Timothy Carney**. At the time, it was the UN's largest Peacekeeping Operation (PKO). The budget was $1.7 billion, of which the United States was assessed nearly a third, more than the 30 percent it was willing to be assessed. At the termination of UNTAC's mission there was an American arrearage of $11.4 million that remains on the books.

UNITED STATES–ASEAN BUSINESS COUNCIL. The U.S.–ASEAN Business Council is the American private sector link to governments, organizations, and businesses in the 10 countries of the **Association of Southeast Asian Nations (ASEAN)**. It is headquartered in Washington, D.C., with representative offices in several ASEAN countries. Its objective is to expand markets in the region through liberalization of **trade** and **investment**. Under its organizational umbrella country-specific groups work, such as the U.S.–Vietnam WTO Coalition, the U.S.–Malaysia FTA Business Coalition, and the U.S.–Thailand FTA Business Coalition.

UNITED STATES–INDONESIA SOCIETY (USINDO). Established in 1996, USINDO acts to promote U.S.–Indonesian relations. It is a binational organization with co-chairs from each country and a representative board. Its outreach is to corporations, foundations, and academic institutions, as well as governments. Its founding president was a former U.S. ambassador to Indonesia, **Edward E. Masters**.

UNITED STATES INSTITUTE OF PEACE (USIP). Established and funded by Congress in 1984, the United States Institute of Peace's mission is to help prevent and resolve international conflict and promote stability and democracy. Its president since 1993 has been former assistant secretary of state for East Asia and Pacific **Richard Solomon**. USIP's research, analysis, publications, and outreach are global. In mid-2003, Deputy Secretary of State **Richard Armitage** tasked USIP with an unofficial effort to help the contending parties in the separatist conflict in the **Philippines** to reach an "equitable and durable" peace agreement. This work was designed to support Malaysia's promotion of negotiations between the Philippine government and the **Moro Islamic Liberation Front (MILF)**. Eugene Martin, a former deputy chief of mission in the U.S. embassy in the Philippines, was named USIP's director of the Philippines facilitation project. The State Department ceased funding the project in 2007.

UNITED STATES PACIFIC COMMAND (USPACOM). The Pacific Command is the largest unified U.S. military command. Headquartered in Honolulu, it covers the Pacific Basin and Indian Ocean. Its force structure includes six aircraft carrier battle groups, two-thirds of the total U.S. Marine Corps combat strength, 14 Air Force fighter squadrons, and two infantry divisions. A third of its 300,000 personnel are forward deployed, maintaining a credible overseas presence. Elements of the command routinely show the flag in Southeast Asia, often the Seventh Fleet flagship, the USS *Blue Ridge.* In 2003, the guided missile frigate USS *Vandegrift*, calling at Ho Chi Minh City, became the first U.S. Navy ship to visit **Vietnam** since the end of the **Vietnam War**. PACOM forces provided critical initial humanitarian support in response to the 2004 **tsunami** disaster in Southeast Asia.

A robust program of bilateral and multilateral military exercises with allied and friendly regional armed forces enhances combat readiness, combined planning, and interoperability between U.S. forces and their Pacific partners. In addition, they demonstrate continuing

American commitment to regional security. Activities in Southeast Asia include the annual **Cobra Gold** exercise, begun in 1981, the largest joint/combined military exercise in Southeast Asia, linking **Thailand, Singapore**, the **Philippines**, and Mongolia with the United States. The annual trilateral Cope Tiger, begun in 1994, with the United States, Singapore, and Thailand, is the largest joint combined air exercise in the Southeast Asian region. **Malaysia** and **Singapore** also participate in the 12 nation Cooperative Cope Thunder air combat training exercise, which takes place in the Alaskan bombing and firing range. A bilateral series of Cooperation Afloat Readiness and Training (CARAT) exercises began in 1996. CARAT links the United States to the armed forces of **Brunei, Indonesia**, Malaysia, Singapore, and Thailand. The U.S.–Philippine **Balikatan** annual joint/combined exercise is the largest of the cooperative bilateral activities that take place under the Philippines–U.S. **Mutual Defense Treaty (MDT)**. Since 11 September 2001, counterterrorism has become an element of military-to-military relations. In 2004, for example, an at-sea counterterrorism exercise named Southeast Asia Cooperation against Terrorism (SEACAT) was held. Navy liaison officers from **Brunei**, Indonesia, Malaysia, the Philippines, Singapore, and Thailand were on board U.S. Navy vessels to share techniques involving tracking and boarding rogue merchant ships.

UNITED STATES TRADE REPRESENTATIVE (USTR). The United States Trade Representative is the principal international **trade** negotiator and advisor to the president. The office is within the Executive Office of the President. Although technically not a member of the cabinet, the USTR holds a cabinet-level position requiring Senate confirmation. The USTR is responsible for negotiating American bilateral **trade and investment framework agreements (TIFA)** and **free trade agreements (FTA)** in Southeast Asia and in 2005 was given responsibility with the secretary of state to plan and implement the **ASEAN–United States Enhanced Partnership**. Since the early 1980s, the USTR has played an important role in the protection of American **intellectual property rights (IPR)**, an important area of concern in U.S. trade relations with Southeast Asia.

– V –

VANCE, CYRUS (1917–2002). Cyrus Vance was secretary of state from 1977 to 1980 in the administration of President **Jimmy Carter**. He resigned after the failure of the Teheran hostage rescue operation, which he had opposed. He was secretary of the army in President **John F. Kennedy**'s administration and deputy secretary of defense in President **Lyndon B. Johnson**'s administration. Like many of his colleagues, his support for the **Vietnam War** had weakened by 1967. Together with ambassador at large **W. Averell Harriman**, Vance, with the title ambassador, represented the United States in 1968 in the first months of the **Paris peace negotiations** with the **Democratic Republic of North Vietnam (DRV)**. As President Carter's secretary of state, he often clashed with National Security Advisor **Zbigniew Brzezinski**. Vance's influence with Carter waned as Brzezinski marginalized the State Department's input on critical issues, including **normalization of relations with Vietnam**, which Vance favored and Brzezinski feared would prevent normal relations with **China**. To the consternation of the **Association of Southeast Asian Nations (ASEAN)**, in 1978 Secretary Vance missed the first opportunity for an American secretary of state to participate in an official dialogue with ASEAN at a postministerial conference (PMC) dialogue. He did travel to Bali, Indonesia, the next year for the July 1979 PMC, where he consulted with ASEAN foreign ministers on American support for ASEAN in the **Third Indochina War** and the problem of dealing with the Vietnamese "**boat people**" flooding Southeast Asia.

VANG PAO (1925–). Vang Pao was a charismatic ethnic **Hmong** chief in **Laos** who, with the guidance and support of the **Central Intelligence Agency (CIA)**, led the Hmong forces in the **secret war** against the **Pathet Lao** and North Vietnamese intruders. His initial CIA link was with **William Lair**. In 1959, Vang Pao, a colonel in the Royal Lao Armed Forces (FAR), commanded an infantry battalion on the **Plain of Jars**. He was already known to the Americans in Laos, having been selected in 1957 for a six-month counterinsurgency course in the **Philippines**. As the strength of the Soviet-supplied and **Viet Minh**–advised Pathet Lao grew, Vang Pao ordered the evacuation of the Hmong population to the mountainous region south of the Plain of Jars. With headquarters at **Long Tieng**, Vang Pao's forces, numbering up to 30,000 men, provided the first line of defense against what was defined as the communist enemy. As the CIA closed out its presence in Laos in 1975, Vang Pao was flown out to **Thailand** and from there to the United States, where he became the preeminent figure in the Wisconsin Hmong expatriate community. He remained fiercely opposed to the communist regime in Laos, organizing from exile the United Lao National Liberation Front. In 2007, he was arrested in California as a suspect in a conspiracy to mount an armed coup against the **Lao People's Democratic Republic (LPDR)**.

VESSEY, JOHN W., JR. (1922–). General John W. Vessey Jr. retired from the U.S. Army in 1985 after serving as chairman of the Joint Chiefs of Staff (JCS). He was the last four-star general who had seen combat in World War II. In 1987, President **Ronald Reagan** sent him as special emissary to the **Socialist Republic of Vietnam (SRV)** to open a dialogue on American prisoners of war/missing in action **(POW/MIA)** in the **Vietnam War**. He continued in this role for President **George H. W. Bush**. By October 1992, he had made six visits to Hanoi. President **William J. Clinton** called on Vessey again, dispatching him to Vietnam in April 1993 as special emissary on POW/MIA affairs to press for further progress as part of the accelerating process of **normalization of relations with Vietnam**. Vessey's work as a special emissary was the basis for the **Joint Task Force–Full Accounting** and a resident American POW/MIA mission in Hanoi. *See also* VESSEY MISSION.

VESSEY MISSION. In August 1987, President **Ronald Reagan** sent a special mission to the **Socialist Republic of Vietnam (SRV)** to discuss the **prisoners of war/missing in action (POW/MIA)** issue, a primary obstacle to the U.S. **normalization of relations with Vietnam**. The mission was headed by General **John W. Vessey Jr.**, a former chairman of the Joint Chiefs of Staff (JCS) and a Vietnam veteran. The mission followed up on informal contacts in which the SRV indicated interest in better cooperation with the United States. The Vessey mission had three plenary sessions with Vietnamese counterparts and four private meetings with SRV foreign minister **Nguyen**

Co Thach. The Vietnamese agreed to accelerate their efforts to help find American MIAs. On the American side, the U.S. delegation agreed to look into "humanitarian concerns" that the Vietnamese had that were part of the fallout from the war. The first specific outcome was to assist the Vietnamese with a prosthetics program. While the substantive outcome was limited by the official agenda, the Vessey mission opened the window to a broader dialogue between Washington and the SRV.

VIET CONG. This was the name given to the communist-led insurgents in **South Vietnam**, ostensibly under the direction of the **National Front for the Liberation of South Vietnam (NLF)**, **North Vietnam**'s political agency in South Vietnam fighting the **Republic of Vietnam (RVN)**. "Viet Cong" is an abbreviation of *Viet Nam Cong San*—Vietnamese communist—a label applied to the guerrillas by the South Vietnamese government. For their North Vietnamese backers and international sympathizers, the Viet Cong were the People's Liberation Armed Forces (PLAF).

VIET MINH. The League for the Independence of Vietnam (*Viet Nam Doc Lap Dong Minh*), or Viet Minh, was the movement created in 1941 by the Indochinese Communist Party (ICP) when it went underground. The Viet Minh was conceived of as a broad anti-Japanese, anti-French united front of Vietnamese nationalists. Guided by the Communist Party, it was the nationalist umbrella of the Vietnamese independence struggle against the French. The Viet Minh saw itself as the elder brother of like nationalist/communist movements in **Laos** and **Cambodia**. Its ability to influence the programs of the related movements was limited by anti-ethnic Vietnamese sentiments of the populations of those countries. *See also* FIRST INDOCHINA WAR; HO CHI MINH; KHMER ISSARAK; LAO ISSARA.

VIETNAM. The country of Vietnam is now ruled as the Socialist Republic of Vietnam (SRV). This name was adopted in 1976 after the reunification of the country following the **Vietnam War**, which pitted the **Democratic Republic of Vietnam (DRV)** in **North Vietnam** against the **Republic of Vietnam (RVN)** in **South Vietnam** and its ally, the United States. With an area of 127,243 square miles

(332,224 square kilometers), the size of Ohio, Kentucky, and Tennessee combined, Vietnam stretches from **China** to the **South China Sea**. It is bordered on the east by the Tonkin Gulf and on the west by **Laos** and **Cambodia**. The population of 85 million is upward of 90 percent ethnic Vietnamese. From prehistoric times, a main thread of Vietnamese history was the southward push of the ethnic Vietnamese from a South China homeland, with behind them the expanding Chinese empire. While historically resisting Chinese political dominance, Vietnamese kingdoms and culture were sinicized. The political history was one of dynastic wars with alternating periods of unification under strong rulers, some of whom carried their authority into **Laos** and **Cambodia**. The last great unifier at the beginning of the 19th century was Gia Long of the Nguyen dynasty, who called his empire Nam Viet, reversed to Viet Nam.

Gia Long administered his kingdom in three parts. Annam was at the center, with its capital, Hué, the seat of Gia Long's rule. Viceroys ruled in Tonkin to the north and Cochin China in the south. Between 1856 and 1881, this domain fell to French imperialism. Cochin China was annexed. Annam and Tonkin became protectorates. France also claimed inheritance of Vietnamese claims to sovereignty in Cambodia and Laos. Eventually all were linked in the structure of French **Indochina**, headed by a governor-general based in Hanoi. French rule was interrupted by World War II in the Pacific. The Japanese occupied French Indochina. A façade of nominal French rule was maintained by the Japanese for their Vichy-French ally until 1944, when Japan sized power.

In Vietnam, Laos, and Cambodia, prewar nascent nationalism was mobilized to anti-Japanese and anti-French resistance. The most potent of these groups was the **Viet Minh** in Vietnam, led by **Ho Chi Minh** and in its vanguard the Communist Party. Upon the Japanese collapse in August 1945, the Viet Minh prepared to seize power. On 14 August Hanoi was in their hands. On 2 September, Ho proclaimed the founding of the DRV. The Viet Minh were caught between the returning French and Nationalist Chinese army forces, who took the Japanese surrender north of the 16th parallel. Ho Chi Minh was forced to negotiate. With no prospect of genuine full independence from France and faced with growing French military pressure, the Viet Minh saw no hope for a peaceful transfer of power. On 13 December 1946, the Viet Minh attacked the French in Hanoi as a reaction to a French order to disarm. This was the beginning of what for the Vietnamese was a 30-year war for independence; for the French a colonial war that lasted until 1954; for the historian, the **First Indochina War**; and for Americans, the beginning of an involvement in Vietnam that dominated U.S. relations in Southeast Asia for nearly half a century.

From 1947 to 1954, the U.S. engagement in Vietnam was in support of the French effort to defeat the Viet Minh's military effort to expel the French and establish a communist state. The policy, begun under President **Harry S. Truman**, was one of **containment** of communism. American assistance to France was financial and material. Despite French pleas, President **Dwight D. Eisenhower**'s administration resisted direct intervention. Even while backing the French war, the United States constantly pressed Paris to give greater independence to the Vietnamese. Washington welcomed the creation of the **State of Vietnam** in 1950 with the last Annamite emperor **Bao Dai** as head. The United States viewed a French victory as a crucial element in **containment** in Southeast Asia. The most manifest aspect of the communist threat was the People's Republic of **China**, a major supporter of the DRV. By 1953, French politicians and the French public were wearied by the human and budgetary cost of a war that seemed to have no end. The United States, unwilling to commit itself militarily to the struggle, had to accede to the negotiated framework for French withdrawal from the war that was set forth in the 1954 **Geneva Accords**. By the Geneva settlement, Vietnam was partitioned at the 17th parallel between North and South Vietnam, to be unified through national elections in 1956. The elections were never held, largely because the regime in South Vietnam, backed by the United States, feared the possible outcome. This left the 17th parallel as a de facto border between two hostile, competitive Vietnamese governments: the DRV in the north and the State of Vietnam in the south. In the south, the State of Vietnam was replaced in September 1955 by the **Republic of Vietnam (RVN)**, whose first president was **Ngo Dinh Diem**, the erstwhile prime minister of the State of Vietnam who had deposed Bao Dai.

The Geneva Accords signifying the end of the First Indochina War did not change the strategic equation for the United States. The problem still was to contain the DRV, viewed as the forward wedge of communist expansion in Southeast Asia. For the Eisenhower administration, this meant giving the fullest possible assistance—short of direct military involvement—to what the administration called "Free Vietnam." This was promised to Prime Minister Diem in an October 1954 letter from President Eisenhower assuring him that American aid would come directly to Vietnam. A heightened American presence in South Vietnam was underlined by the dispatch of General **J. Lawton Collins** in late 1954 as a personal representative of President Eisenhower to put firmly in place an American assistance infrastructure to replace the French. A key element in this was an agreement that transferred the training of the South Vietnamese military from the French to the United States. The U.S. efforts to build a politically strong anticommunist bulwark in South Vietnam rested on a weak foundation. Diem's RVN government was suppressive, corrupt, and increasingly unpopular. It resisted the urgent advice of American ambassadors and high-level visitors, direct appeals of secretaries of state, and presidential interventions calling for reform and democratization. The growing opposition to the Diem government spurred an expanded communist insurgency, for which the conventionally trained Army of the Republic of Vietnam (ARVN) was little prepared.

When President **John F. Kennedy** took office in January 1961, he was handed a deteriorating political and military situation in Vietnam. At the same time, Vietnam had become the key to both U.S. strategy and political commitment underpinning containment in Southeast Asia. In October 1961, Kennedy dispatched the **Taylor–Rostow mission** to appraise the situation. The commission reported back in November, calling for critical reforms in the Diem government, even the placement of U.S. advisors in the government. Diem turned a deaf ear to this. American official disenchantment with Diem led to American support for, or at least not discouragement of, a military coup against Diem on 1 November 1963. Of even greater import for future U.S.–RVN relations was the Taylor–Rostow recommendation for the introduction of U.S. combat forces and the reorientation of the ARVN from conventional warfare capability to counterinsurgency. This would involve massive retraining, requiring as many American counterinsurgent advisors and experts as necessary to do the job. President Kennedy rejected the recommendation for combat forces, but in National Security Action Memorandum (NSAM) no. 111, dated 22 November 1961, authorized a huge expansion of U.S. advisors. At the beginning of 1961 there were about 900 U.S. military personnel in U.S. **Military Assistance Advisory Group (MAAG)** for Vietnam. By the end of the year, the number had jumped to 3,200, breaking through the Geneva Accords MAAG ceilings. By mid-1962, the number of U.S. military in Vietnam had risen to over 12,000, and the MAAG had been subsumed in the newly formed U.S. **Military Assistance Command, Vietnam (MACV)**. The U.S. advisors were authorized to accompany their Vietnamese units into the field. For some analysts, NSAM 111 marked a fateful watershed in U.S.–Vietnamese relations and the American role in Southeast Asia. The United States had moved from assistance to the RVN to what appeared to be an irrevocable commitment to participation as a full partner in the armed struggle over the future of Vietnam. For Americans, this new phase of the relationship is known as the **Vietnam War**. In its broader context, which includes Cambodia and Laos, it can be called the **Second Indochina War**.

The American Vietnam War lasted until the **Paris Agreement** of January 1973, arrived at after more than four years of intermittent negotiations. As the **Paris peace negotiations** went on, the fighting continued as ferociously as ever. A beleaguered RVN government constantly sought reassurance of the U.S. commitment, knowing, however, that the United States was looking for an exit strategy. Washington was concerned that any peace agreement should not be seen as a sell-out of the South. This idea was captured by President **Richard M. Nixon**, who spoke of "peace with honor." National Security Advisor **Henry Kissinger**, who did not shrink from merciless bombings punctuating negotiations, later expressed the view, which many officials of four administrations held in 20/20 hindsight, that, "Vietnam was a great tragedy. We should never have been there at all. But it's history."

The Paris Agreement was a fragile cover for U.S. withdrawal. Its framework for peaceful cohabitation of the DRV and the RVN working toward reunification was unrealistic. The implementation of the international monitoring and verification instruments was dysfunctional. Both Vietnamese sides, seeking the advantage, repeatedly violated the cease-fire provisions. While morale and will were being hollowed out of the RVN, the DRV mobilized for a final campaign, launched at the end of 1974. With surprising speed, the North's People's Army of Vietnam (PAVN) forces advanced against the crumbling defenses of the South. Although the United States continued to provide military assistance, it could not provide leadership and will. Nor did it provide what President Nixon had promised in his letter of 5 January 1973 to RVN President **Nguyen Van Thieu**: that the United States would respond with full force should the settlement be violated by North Vietnam. From Saigon's vantage point, the American "peace with honor" with the DRV had been a betrayal that ended in defeat on 20 April 1975. Congress's refusal to make a final massive infusion of assistance to the South in 1975 as the PAVN advanced against a crumbling ARVN resistance was seized upon by Kissinger to blame Congress for the loss of Vietnam.

Within a year North and South Vietnam were officially united as the Socialist Republic of Vietnam (SRV), winning general international recognition and acceptance—except by the United States. The economic sanctions imposed by the United States against the DRV were extended to the SRV, blocking it not only from the American economy but international funding institutions (IFI) in which the United States had an influential voice. The United States also blocked the SRV's first bid for membership in the **United Nations**. For the next two decades, the issue for the United States in bilateral and multilateral contacts was the problem of **normalization of relations with Vietnam**. Opinion in the United States about normalization was divided. At one pole were those individuals and groups that wanted to punish the SRV and make its victory costly. At the other pole were calls for speedy reconciliation. Many in the latter group were in or sympathized with the antiwar movement. As reflected in the diplomacy of four U.S. successive American administrations—**Jimmy Carter**, **Ronald Reagan, George H. W. Bush**, and **William J. Clinton**—the controlling official opinion rested on cost-benefit analyses of what would best serve U.S. interests in a normal state-to-state relationship with Vietnam.

Hanoi initially framed its approach to the United States as a demand for reparations based on Article 21 of the **Paris Agreement** and President Nixon's message to SRV Prime Minister **Pham Van Dong** spelling out what the United States would contribute to Vietnamese reconstruction. This was rejected out of hand by Congress. Hanoi had abandoned that demand by 1978. For many Americans the most important issue was full accounting for American prisoners of war and missing in action (**POW/MIA**) in Vietnam. The Vietnamese at first insisted that the United States had to recognize the SRV before they would cooperate on the POW/MIA question. For President Reagan, the POW/MIA question was the most important policy issue in Southeast Asia. A breakthrough came in 1987 with General **John Vessey**'s first humanitarian mission to Vietnam. His subsequent trips to Hanoi for Presidents Reagan, George H. W. Bush, and Clinton were important in finally allowing President Clinton to report in 1994 that "tangible progress" had been made in resolving the POW/MIA issue.

Vietnam's position in the broader U.S. strategic equation also was in play. President Carter's initial tentative moves toward normalization were derailed by fear that this would block the U.S.–Chinese normalization negotiations. Isolation from the United States and a perceived Chinese threat pushed Vietnam closer to the USSR for material and political support, cemented in 1978 by a de facto SRV–Soviet military alliance. For the Reagan White House this confirmed its conviction that the SRV was a communist threat to Southeast Asia. This was translated to the noncommunist members of the **Association of Southeast Asian Nations (ASEAN)** in December 1978, when Vietnam invaded and occupied Cambodia, making it in Southeast Asian eyes the first "**domino**." This was the beginning of the **Third Indochina War**. Vietnamese withdrawal from Cambodia was added to the normalization agenda on the "road map" the United States presented to the Vietnamese. The 1991 **comprehensive political settlement of the conflict in Cambodia**, negotiated by the Great Powers, and continued Vietnamese cooperation on resolution of the POW/MIA issue were matched in the Bush and Clinton administrations by step-by-step legal and political acts leading to full normal relations between the United States and the Socialist Republic of Vietnam on 11 July 1995.

The normalization of the bilateral relationship was exemplified by President Clinton's official visit to Vietnam in November 2000. This was reciprocated by Prime Minister Vo Van Khai's state visit to the

United States in June 2005. He and President **George W. Bush** promised further bilateral and multilateral cooperation. President Bush went to Vietnam in November 2006 in connection with the **Asia–Pacific Economic Cooperation (APEC)** summit meeting. A very high political priority for the United States in its new relationship was the continuation of joint efforts to achieve the fullest possible accounting of American missing and unaccounted for in Indochina. The United States has also engaged Vietnam in dialogues on **human rights** and regional security. In 2006, both the American secretary of defense and the commander in chief of the **United States Pacific Command (USPACOM)** were guests of Vietnam. The human rights dialogue has led to progress on **religious freedom** in particular. Vietnam was delisted as a country of particular concern (CPC) for religious freedom in 2006. Vietnam has also cooperated on **refugee** emigration issues through the **Orderly Departure Program (ODP)** and its successors. The United States has financially supported clearance of **unexploded ordinance (UXO)** in Vietnam. Perhaps the greatest benefit of normalization of relations for Vietnam has been in **trade**. In 2001, the United States and Vietnam signed a bilateral trade agreement giving Vietnam **normal trade relation (NTR)** status, clearing the way for Vietnam to negotiate entry into the **World Trade Organization (WTO)**. In 2006, Congress granted Vietnam **permanent normal trade relations (PNTR)** status, putting U.S.–Vietnamese economic relations on the same basis as those of the other ASEAN states. In 2006, two-way trade between Vietnam and the United States was valued at more than $ 9 billion. President George W. Bush visited Vietnam in 2006, and 2007 saw the first postnormalization visit of an SRV head of state, President Nguyen Minh Triet, to the United States. During the visit, a U.S.–SRV **trade and investment framework agreement (TIFA)** was signed. *See also* JOINT CASUALTY RESOLUTION CENTER; JOINT TASK FORCE–FULL ACCOUNTING (JTF-FA).

VIETNAM SYNDROME. In foreign policy, a term used to describe the reluctance of the American executive and Congress to use, and limits on the use of, American military force abroad because of the human, economic, and political costs of the lost **Vietnam War**.

VIETNAM WAR. The Vietnam War—or **Second Indochina War**—was the armed conflict in which the United States and its ally, the **Republic of Vietnam (RVN)**, sought to defend the political and territorial integrity of **South Vietnam** from forced incorporation into a unified Vietnam under the authority of the communist North Vietnamese **Democratic Republic of Vietnam (DRV)**. The DRV received material and political support from the Soviet Union and the People's Republic of **China**.

The boundary between **North Vietnam** and South Vietnam had been drawn along the 17th parallel in the 1954 **Geneva Accords** that ended the **First Indochina War**—the French colonial war. For the United States, anticommunist South Vietnam was the first strategic **domino** that had to be defended if there were to be **containment** of communism in Southeast Asia. The DRV was allied in the south with the **National Front for the Liberation of South Vietnam (NLF)**, which later was renamed the **Provisional Revolutionary Government of South Vietnam (PRG)**. The NLF's guerrilla armed forces in the south were the **Viet Cong**, or People's Liberation Armed Forces (PLAF), and the regular forces from the north were the People's Army of Vietnam (PAVN). The ground war was in the south, but the north suffered heavily from U.S. bombing campaigns. Both the air and ground wars spilled over into **Cambodia** and **Laos**, where American-backed governments were under attack from indigenous communist movements, the **Khmer Rouge** and the **Pathet Lao**, respectively.

By 1959, a full-scale, DRV-backed insurgency had broken out in South Vietnam against the American-backed government of **Ngo Dinh Diem**, who was viewed by the communists as a puppet of the American imperialists. Until 1962, the U.S. role in Vietnam had been confined to political support for the anticommunist government of the RVN and massive economic and military assistance. A relatively small number of U.S. military personnel—fewer than 1,000—were engaged in military equipment delivery and training. The threat had originally been viewed as a conventional attack from the north. In order to turn the Army of the Republic of Vietnam (ARVN) around to face a southern insurgency, President **John F. Kennedy** authorized a large increase in U.S. advisors and trainers. By the end of 1962, 12,000 American military personnel were in country, some of whom went into combat as advisors. By 1964, the number of advisors had reached 23,000. Despite the American input and superior fire power, the ARVN could not hold on to the initiative, and the insurgents' strength grew with new local recruits as well as infiltrators from the north. Even as the security situation in the south continued to deteriorate, there was civil and political strife at the RVN's center, culminating in the November 1963 **Diem coup**, which ended in Diem's murder.

An increase in DRV military assistance to its southern forces brought warnings from the United States that this could lead to attacks on North Vietnam. The **Tonkin Gulf incident** in August 1964 involving North Vietnamese patrol boats and American naval vessels led to retaliatory U.S. air strikes north of the 17th parallel. Washington interpreted the affair as an act of "unprovoked warfare" and acted accordingly. Congress, in a flush of nationalism, on 7 August 1964, in the **Tonkin Gulf Resolution** gave President **Lyndon B. Johnson** a blank check to fight a war against communism in Southeast Asia. Once the November 1964 elections were over, President Johnson was prepared to react to increasingly bold Viet Cong and PAVN thrusts. The consistent official American justification for its military support of the RVN was U.S. obligations as a **Southeast Asia Treaty Organization (SEATO)** partner to help defend the RVN against the "aggression from the north." Underlying the official position was the perception that U.S. will and credibility in its global security strategy were being tested.

The trigger for massive escalation of U.S. force was a February 1965 attack on an American airfield at Pleiku in South Vietnam's central highlands. Immediate retaliatory air strikes against targets in southern North Vietnam were ordered, followed by a bombing campaign that inaugurated sustained bombings of North Vietnam. As the air campaign was launched, U.S. Marine and Army combat forces arrived in Vietnam to defend American air bases, and in June 1965 General William Westmoreland, the American military commander in Vietnam, was given authority to commit U.S. forces to combat. At the end of 1965, there were more than 180,000 American troops in Vietnam. As the ground war went on, the escalation of the American force level was matched by a growing antiwar movement in the United States. By the end of 1966, the number of American troops in

Vietnam was 380,000, and by the end of 1967, 480,000. Also in the field were Australians, New Zealanders, Koreans, Filipinos, and Thais, in relatively small numbers in relation to U.S. strength but responsive to their American ally's pressure for "more flags."

The course of the war seemed to be leading to a protracted stalemate, with both sides bleeding. The United States had prevented the PAVN and Viet Cong from conquering the south, but it had not dislodged them from their strongholds. In January–February 1968, the PAVN and Viet Cong launched a surprise general attack against large cities and provincial capitals—the Tet offensive coincident with the Vietnamese lunar New Year. This demonstrated that despite years of war and huge casualties, the enemy still had the capability to strike with great force throughout the country. Although the U.S. forces and ARVN successfully counterattacked, inflicting great losses on the enemy, the fact that such an attack could be mounted shocked the American public. The DRV achieved a political and psychological victory. Even as the United States was reinforcing its troop strength in Vietnam—peaking in 1969 at more than half a million—the search for an exit began. On 31 March 1968, President Johnson announced that he would not seek reelection and was ready to talk about peace. The Vietnam War had entered a new phase. Military confrontation was paired with diplomatic confrontation, talking and fighting.

Five days after President **Richard M. Nixon** was inaugurated on 20 January 1969, the first plenary session of the **Paris negotiations**, begun six months earlier, took place. In June, Nixon met with his RVM counterpart, **Nguyen Van Thieu**, on Midway Island to inform him of a planned phased withdrawal of 25,000 U.S troops. This was the preamble to the administration's strategy of **Vietnamization**, that is, turning the frontline burden over to the ARVN while the United States equipped and trained a strengthened ARVN with greater capabilities. The strategic task was to prevent the DRV from gaining the initiative on the battlefield, which would allow it to negotiate from strength and, if not overwhelming the RVM, at least force a coalition government on the south. This meant the United States had to remain in the field, if for nothing else, to coerce the north into concessions.

The antiwar movement in the United States was galvanized by the U.S. military incursion into Cambodia in May 1970 and the killing of four protesting students at Kent State University by national guardsmen. Congress initiated legislation prohibiting American ground troops in **Laos**, Cambodia, and **Thailand**. By the end of 1971, U.S. forces had ceased offensive actions, and fewer than 160,000 American military personnel remained in Vietnam. The foreign-flagged forces had also withdrawn. The bombing of North Vietnam continued. As the United States and the DRV continued to talk, the PAVN made advances against the ARVN, winning large swaths of the northern part of South Vietnam. American forces continued to be drawn down and, by mid-1972, the force level was under 70,000, with U.S. combat capability essentially ended. By October 1972, a framework for peace had been worked out. Although objecting, President Thieu had to accept the **Paris Agreement** in January 1973 or be faced with a cut-off of continued American assistance. For the United States, at least, the Vietnam War was over; for Vietnam, it continued another two years until the DRV's final victory in April 1975.

The human costs of the Vietnam War were heavy for all the combatants. For the United States the official casualty figures were over 58,000 dead and more than 300,000 wounded. The Vietnam Veterans Memorial Wall in Washington had 58,249 names on it in 2006. To the American dead, more than 5,000 Korean, Australian, New Zealand, Thai, and Filipino combat deaths can be added. The American "body count" of the enemy of nearly 700,000 is probably low. Hanoi has used the figure of nearly a million and a half dead or missing from 1954 to 1975. The estimate of South Vietnamese combat deaths exceeds 200,000. The total number of Vietnamese deaths—north and south, soldier or civilian—exceeds two million. Beyond the human costs, there was enormous physical destruction caused by bombing, rocketing, artillery, defoliants, and the other tools of war. For the United States, the economic costs of the war were great and the political costs, both domestic and international, continue to be paid. The total cost was summed up in the immediate postwar foreign and security policy promise of "no more Vietnams," which has been called the **Vietnam syndrome**.

VIETNAMIZATION. This is the term used to describe President **Richard M. Nixon**'s phased withdrawal of U.S. troops from **Vietnam** beginning in mid-1969, and turning the battlefield over to a strengthened army of the **Republic of Vietnam**. It was an initial step in implementing the **Nixon doctrine**. *See also* VIETNAM WAR.

VISITING FORCES AGREEMENT, U.S.–PHILIPPINE (VFA). On 14 January 1998, the United States and the **Philippines** initialed a Visiting Forces Agreement negotiated during the administration of Philippine president **Fidel Ramos**. The agreement was attacked by nationalist and leftist domestic political groups in the Philippines. The VFA was sent to the Philippine Senate by President **Joseph Estrada**, where it was ratified by a vote of 23 to 5 on 17 May 1999. When the Philippine Senate in 1991 refused to ratify the revised **Military Bases Agreement (MBA)**, it meant that in the absence of a status of forces agreement (SOFA) regularizing the legal status for an American military presence, U.S.–Philippine military-to-military relations were limited. The combined exercises and training that took place under the rubric **Balikatan** or "Shoulder-to-Shoulder" were suspended in 1995. With the VFA in place, the Balikatan exercises resumed in 2001. The VFA, complemented by the 2002 **Mutual Logistics Support Agreement (MLSA)**, provided the framework of enhanced security relations with the Philippines, including cooperation in the **war on terror**.

Nationalist sentiments against the VFA were rekindled in 2005 when four American Marines accused of rape were not turned over to the Philippine authorities pending trial. As a mark of displeasure, Philippine president **Gloria Macapagal-Arroyo** abolished the office in charge of Balikatan, threatening abrogation of the VFA and the renegotiation of a new agreement. However, the scheduled Balikatan 2006 was carried out as planned. The trial was held in 2006. Three marines were acquitted and one convicted and sentenced to 40 years in jail. President Arroyo's spokesman said that, "the outcome of this case will not in any way affect Philippine–U.S. relations for it is not about diplomatic relations but about universal justice and the rule of law." When the court refused to turn the convicted marine over to U.S. custody pending appeal, as required by the agreement, the United States announced cancellation of the upcoming 2007 Balikatan exercise, claiming that the Philippines was in violation of the terms of the VFA. For the sake of the strategic alliance, President Arroyo intervened and transferred the marine to the custody of the U.S. embassy.

– W –

WAHABISM. Named after Islamic scholar Ibn Abd al Wahab (1703–1792), Wahabism is a fundamentalist Sunni Islamic stream that aggressively seeks to restore Islam to its original purity of belief and practice. Wahabists describe themselves as Salafis, following the Salaf, the way of the forefathers. The prominence of Wahabism, in addition to its ideological appeal as the strictest form of Islam, is due to its promotion by Saudi Arabia, whose royal house of Saud has historically adhered to it. The Wahabist inclinations of Southeast Asia's radical Islamic movements have led to terrorism and calls for holy war against nonbelievers, Western culture in general, and the United States in particular. *See also* AL-QAEDA; BA'ASYIR, ABU BAKAR; JEMA'AH ISLAMIYAH; WAR ON TERROR.

WAHID, ABDURRAHMAN (1941–). A distinguished moderate Indonesian Muslim leader, Abdurrahman Wahid was elected **Indonesia**'s fourth president in October 1999. A nationalist and democrat, he commanded a wide following among traditionalist Muslims and had sounded a voice of political reason in the politics of opposition to President **Suharto**'s rule. Popularly known as Gus Dur, Wahid headed Indonesia's largest Islamic organization, the Nahdlatul Ulama. He was indirectly elected president in a contest that pitted him against **Megawati Sukarnoputri**, whose party had been the largest vote getter in the national election. Megawati was named vice president and succeeded to the presidency in July 2001 after Wahid's impeachment. Gus Dur came to the high office with serious physical disabilities. He was a partially blind diabetic who had suffered a stroke. In office, he was autocratic, eccentric, and erratic. He was removed from office for incompetence. During his presidency, U.S.–Indonesian relations reached a very low point. Gus Dur seemed to go out of his way to tweak the eagle's beak. He reasserted Indonesia's "free and active" foreign policy by constant overseas traveling, making his first official vista to the People's Republic of **China** to demonstrate solidarity against Western domination. He traveled to Cuba to show that Indonesia would not be "colonized" by the United States, repeating this only three days after meeting President **William J. Clinton**. When Wahid left office, Indonesian foreign policy was in disarray regionally and globally, having, as one Indonesian commentator put it, "lost its soul."

WAR ON TERROR. The 11 September 2001 (9/11) terrorist attacks by agents of **al-Qaeda** on New York's World Trade Center's twin towers and the Pentagon in Washington galvanized President **George W. Bush** to declare a worldwide war on terror. The United States mobilized a multinational military response under the name **Operation Enduring Freedom (OEF)**. The immediate target of that war was Osama bin Laden's al-Qaeda forces, embedded in Taliban-led Afghanistan. American officials identified Southeast Asia as a second front in the war on terror because it was the home of radical Islamist groups whose political agendas and tactics of violence complemented al-Qaeda's. The United States pointed to the direct and indirect links between al-Qaeda and local terrorists to demonstrate an identity of American and Southeast Asian interests in combating a common enemy. The focus in Southeast Asia has been on the **Indonesia**-based **Jema'ah Islamiyah (JI)**, spiritually inspired by Indonesian cleric **Abu Ba'asyir**. JI agents are known to have penetrated radical Muslim groups throughout the region and have operated terrorist training camps in the Mindanao–Sulu Archipelago regions of the **Philippines'** south, held by the **Moro Islamic Liberation Front (MILF)**, the **Moro National Liberation Front (MNLF)**, and the **Abu Sayyaf Group (ASG)**. Intelligence has shown that al-Qaeda and JI have had a presence in **Malaysia** and plotted terrorist attacks on U.S. and other Western targets in **Singapore**. There is evidence that JI has infiltrated the spreading Muslim separatist insurgency in south **Thailand**.

Since 9/11, the United States has carried out an intensive diplomatic campaign at both the bilateral and multilateral levels of international relations to mobilize its allies and friends in Southeast Asia to the common cause of fighting the war on terror. The issue of terrorism and how to combat it have become a regular agenda item for the **Association of Southeast Asian Nations (ASEAN)**, the **ASEAN Regional Forum (ARF)**, and the **Asia–Pacific Economic Cooperation (APEC)** meetings. President Bush and Secretaries of State **Colin Powell** and **Condoleezza Rice** pressed the need for cooperation against terrorism at every opportunity with their counterparts in

Southeast Asia. Between 9/11 and the end of 2006, President Bush had 18 meetings with Southeast Asian presidents or prime ministers, a more extensive regional summitry than any of his predecessors. The **United States Pacific Command (USPACOM)** has reoriented its exercising and training programs with allied and friendly Southeast Asian militaries toward counterterrorism. Washington's task of mobilizing allies in the war on terrorism in Southeast Asia was complicated by the **Iraq War**. The American-led invasion and occupation of Iraq was unpopular in the Muslim populations of Southeast Asia. Even so-called moderate Muslims opposed the Iraq War and were sympathetic to the charge that the United States was making war on Islam. This allowed radical Islamists to link their attacks on American targets to the defense of Islam. This had a political impact on decision making in Indonesia and Malaysia about what kind of counterterrorism cooperation with the United States that would be domestically politically acceptable.

At the ASEAN level, a consensus was developed that was expressed in the August 2002 ASEAN–United States Joint Declaration for Cooperation to Combat International Terrorism. It is at the bilateral level, however, that the most productive results in terms of engaging the terrorist enemy have been achieved. Philippine President **Gloria Macapagal-Arroyo** was the first ASEAN leader to contact President Bush after 9/11, pledging assistance in the war on terror. The United States became a vital partner of the Philippines in its domestic struggle against terrorism. American military assistance has been hugely expanded to increase the capabilities of the Armed Forces of the Philippines (AFP). Joint training and exercising have concentrated on counterterrorism. The Philippine Army's successes in 2006 against the ASG were backstopped by the U.S. **Joint Special Operations Task Force–Philippines (JSOTF–P)**. In Indonesia, the 2002 **Bali bombings** brought home to the government the fact of domestic terrorism. Since then, with the new resolution of President **Susilo Bambang Yudhoyono** and behind-the-scenes police and intelligence assistance from the United States and Australia, the government has made more than 200 arrests and has driven the JI to ground. A new confidence in the bilateral U.S.–Indonesian security partnership was shown by the 2005 waiver of the last U.S. restrictions on military-to-military relations.

Cooperation between the United States and Thailand led to the capture and transfer to U.S. custody of the al-Qaeda/JI bombing mastermind **Hambali**. Malaysia and Singapore have used their already very efficient internal security structures and laws (ISA) to good effect against suspected terrorist activities. An important element in Southeast Asian–U.S. cooperation in the war on terror has been the increased willingness to share intelligence and the application of technical means of gathering information. The United States was a behind-the-scenes partner of the Malaysia-based **Southeast Asian Regional Center for Counterterrorism (SEARCCT)**. With the exception of the Philippines, however, no country wants a counterterrorist U.S. military presence. An insistence on sovereignty was made clear by the refusal of Malaysia and Indonesia to entertain the idea of a U.S. Marines or Special Forces presence in guarding the **Strait of Malacca**, which was tentatively mooted in USPACOM's 2004 Regional Maritime Security Initiative (RMSI).

WASHINGTON CONSENSUS. This term refers to the policy recommendations adopted by national and international lending institutions (IFI), particularly the United States and the Washington-based **International Monetary Fund (IMF)** and World Bank, following the Latin American debt crisis in the 1980s. The policy prescriptions include liberalized markets, small budget deficits, deregulation, and privatization. They became a matter of controversy with Southeast Asian economic nationalists as they were applied as conditions for assistance during the **financial crisis of 1997–1998**. Prime Minister **Mahathir Mohammad** of **Malaysia** in particular objected to what he denounced as economic imperialism.

WASHINGTON NAVAL CONFERENCE, 1922. Convened by the United States, the Washington conference resulted in three treaties—the Four Power Treaty, the Five Power Treaty, and the Nine Power Treaty. The primary American goal was to restrict Japanese naval expansion in the Western Pacific and potential threats to the **Philippines** and Hawaii. Japan's seizure of Germany's Pacific territories in World War I had sparked unease about Japan's ultimate intentions. The Four Power Treaty—United States, Great Britain, Japan, and France—froze the status quo in the Pacific, with the signatories promising not to seek further territorial expansion and pledging respect for the territory of the others. The agreement prohibited the construction of new fortifications in their Pacific realms. The Five Power Treaty, which added Italy, sought to prevent a naval arms race by establishing a ratio of capital ships to 20:20:12:7:7, effectively for the United States, Great Britain, and Japan a ratio of 5:5:3. The Nine Power Treaty—the five plus Belgium, **China**, the Netherlands, and Portugal—reaffirmed the open-door principles in China. While alleviating immediate concern about an expensive arms race, the Washington "system" strategically advantaged Japan. The United States had a two-ocean navy and Great Britain a global navy. Japan's interest was the Pacific. The prohibition on new fortifications, while not applying to Hawaii, meant that Philippine defenses could not be built up against possible future Japanese attack. A subsequent 1930 naval conference in London continued the Washington system, but in 1934 Japan gave two-year notice of withdrawal. Effectively, however, Japan had already broken out of the restrictions by building battleships, heavy cruisers, and aircraft carriers that exceeded the tonnage limitations of the treaties.

WASHINGTON SPECIAL ACTIONS GROUP (WSAG). The Washington Special Actions Group was one of the six subunits set up in the National Security Council (NSC) during the administration of President **Richard M. Nixon** and chaired by National Security Advisor **Henry Kissinger**. Its charge was crisis management and covert activities. Its membership was composed of high-ranking officials of the NSC, **Department of State**, **Central Intelligence Agency (CIA)**, Department of Defense, and Joint Chiefs of Staff. In Southeast Asia it had oversight of the **secret war** in **Laos**, clandestine bombings in **Cambodia**, the evacuation of the American embassies in Phnom Penh and Saigon, and other **Indochina**-related activities. The minutes of its meetings can be found in the Nixon and President **Gerald Ford** presidential libraries and the Nixon/Ford presidential years in the 1969–1976 volumes of the State Department's Foreign Relations series.

WEST NEW GUINEA DISPUTE. In 1961, a long-festering dispute between the Netherlands and **Indonesia** over the sovereignty of the western part of the island of New Guinea was moving toward war. The Indonesian government, disappointed in its failure to secure a two-thirds majority vote in support of its claims in the **United Nations** General Assembly, was preparing to use force to occupy the territory. The seeds of the crisis went back to Indonesia's independence in 1949, when the issue of the status of Dutch New Guinea was left for future negotiations. With Indonesia adamantly committed to the rounding out of its country with all of the former Dutch regional colonial possessions, bilateral compromise was impossible. Indonesia's President **Sukarno** had made acquisition of what Indonesia called West Irian (Irian Barat) a centerpiece of Indonesian nationalism. As the Dutch began militarily reinforcing their position, the Indonesians created a special military command under Major General **Suharto** and began clandestine landing of Special Forces in West New Guinea.

The United States was faced with serious policy questions. The Netherlands was a North Atlantic Treaty Organization (NATO) ally. Another ally, Australia, was sympathetic to Dutch sovereignty. On the other hand, the United States was opposed to colonialism and supportive of Asian nationalism. Furthermore, the United States had been actively engaged in securing Indonesian independence from the Dutch. The administration of President **Dwight D. Eisenhower** insisted that America remain neutral, which was interpreted by Sukarno as being pro-Dutch. In 1961, the incoming American administration of **John F. Kennedy** reviewed the dispute and American policy. The administration became positively engaged, communicating to both the Dutch and the Indonesians its desire for a peaceful settlement. It was on the agenda of U.S. Attorney General **Robert F. Kennedy**, the president's brother, when he visited Jakarta and The Hague in 1961. Washington was worried about the strategic consequences of an armed clash. Of particular concern was the American fear that the escalation of the dispute could bolster the strength of the **Indonesian Communist Party (PKI)** and strengthen the influence of the Soviet Union in Indonesia. In a kind of reverse **domino theory**, Kennedy's security advisors counseled that the loss of Indonesia would make the defense of mainland Southeast Asia difficult. The Kennedy administration was already wrestling with the problem of the **Vietnam War**.

The emerging U.S. position was to seek an agreement that would ultimately lead to Indonesia's accession of West New Guinea but would allow the Dutch to disengage without embarrassment. The United States named Ambassador **Ellsworth Bunker** as special representative to facilitate secret talks between the two sides. The talks began in March 1962 in Middleburg, Virginia. Bunker's role was technically under U Thant, secretary-general of the **United Nations (UN)**, and thus independent of the United States. The talks quickly broke down. They were resumed after direct intervention by President Kennedy through letters to Sukarno and the Dutch prime minister. By May, Bunker had presented American proposals that were welcomed by the Indonesians and U Thant, although the Dutch were critical of them. Nevertheless, the Bunker proposals became the basis for the final settlement embodied in the 15 August 1962 bilateral "Treaty of New York" which was endorsed by the UN General Assembly on 21 September.

The settlement established an interim United Nations Temporary Executive Administration (UNTEA), to which the Dutch transferred authority. The UNTEA transferred administrative authority on 1 May 1963 to an Indonesian administration that was committed to conduct an act of self-determination for the Papuans by the end of 1969. The UN-mandated "Act of Free Choice," often derided as an "Act of No Choice" consisted of a coerced decision by specially selected tribal chiefs for incorporation into Indonesia as its 26th province. Within the province, indigenous Melanesian nationalists demanding independence began a low-level insurgency under the banner of the **Free Papua Organization (OPM)**, which continues to enjoy the support of **human rights** advocacy groups and has been the subject of congressional hearings. The American mining company **Freeport–McMoRan** operates the world's largest open pit gold and copper mine in what is now Indonesia's West Papua province.

WISNER, FRANK G. (1910—1965). Deputy Director of Plans (DDP) for the **Central Intelligence Agency (CIA)** from 1952 to 1959, Frank Wisner has been characterized as the man who was most responsible for creating a covert action capability for the United States in the post–World War II era and opening years of the Cold War. By education a lawyer, Wisner was a veteran of the **Office of Strategic**

Services (OSS), serving in the European theater of World War II. After President **Harry S. Truman** terminated the OSS, Wisner ran an Office of Special Projects based in the Department of State, which became the nucleus of an Office of Policy Coordination (OPC) in the newly established CIA in the Directorate of Operations headed by **Allen Dulles**. After Dulles became CIA director in August 1951, Wisner in 1952 merged the OPC with the Office of Special Operations in the Directorate of Plans. Wisner became the DDP responsible for clandestine intelligence collection and covert operations.

A protégé of Dulles, Wisner seemed a likely future CIA head after successes in the overthrow of Mohammad Mossadegh in Iran (1953) and Jacobo Arbenz in Guatamala (1954). He was held responsible, however, for the failure of the CIA's support of the 1957–1958 **PRRI–Permesta regional rebellions** against **Sukarno** in **Indonesia**. Wisner, who said in 1956, "I think it's time to hold Sukarno's feet to the fire," personally directed the U.S. intervention in Indonesia. He set up a forward headquarters in Singapore, backed by **Desmond Fitzgerald**, a future DDP. The capture of American pilot **Allen Pope**, shot down over Indonesia, and the military successes of the Indonesian army dashed any hopes that the American clandestine intervention could lead to the ouster of Sukarno. In 1959, Wisner was replaced as DDP by **Richard Bissell**, who himself was later held accountable for the Bay of Pigs fiasco and was replaced as DDP by Wisner's operations chief, **Richard Helms**. Frank Wisner, fighting depression, tragically took his own life at the age of 55.

WOLFOWITZ, PAUL D. (1923–). A University of Chicago Ph.D. and former member of the Yale University faculty, Paul Wolfowitz was best known as a conservative hawk as deputy secretary of defense—the department's number two man—in the first years of the **war on terror** and the **Iraq War** in the administration of President **George W. Bush**. He had already seen long official service in the administrations of Presidents **Jimmy Carter**, **Ronald Reagan**, and **George H. W. Bush**. In the Carter government, he was the deputy assistant secretary of defense for regional policy. From 1983 to 1986, in the Reagan administration, he was assistant secretary of state for East Asian and Pacific affairs, managing diplomatic support to the **Association of Southeast Asian Nations (ASEAN)** in the **Third Indochina War**—the resistance to the

Vietnamese invasion of Cambodia. Working closely with Undersecretary **Michael Armacost**, he helped coordinate American policy toward the **Philippines** in the critical years of transition from the dictatorship of **Ferdinand Marcos** to the more democratic government of Corazon **Aquino**. Named ambassador to **Indonesia** (1986–1989), Wolfowitz went on to become one of America's most successful ambassadors in Southeast Asia, vigorously supporting American economic policy interests, especially **intellectual property rights**, while being viewed in Indonesia as a highly visible friend. Like American ambassadors to Indonesia before and after him, Wolfowitz was criticized by advocacy nongovernmental organizations (NGO) for not being vocal enough about Indonesian **human rights** abuses or the situation in **East Timor**. That was not his policy charge from Secretary of State **George Shultz**. Behind the scenes, however, he was in contact with a broad political spectrum of Indonesians, making a special effort to reach out to Muslim community leaders like **Abdurrahman Wahid**. As he prepared to leave Indonesia in 1989, Wolfowitz made two speeches that shocked the regime. In one, he criticized the government's corruption. In the other, he called for greater political openness. Suharto himself later acknowledged that these remarks "intensified and aggravated" political debate in the country.

Wolfowitz returned to Washington in 1989 to become undersecretary of defense for policy during the administration of George H. W. Bush. From 1993 to 2001, he was the dean of the Johns Hopkins School of Advanced International Studies (SAIS). At SAIS, he strengthened the Southeast Asia program. Wolfowitz maintained his interest in Indonesia and was a founding member of the **United States–Indonesia Society (USINDO)**. Back at the Defense Department as deputy secretary in the George W. Bush administration, he reached out to Indonesia and other Southeast Asian moderate Muslims for a better understanding of America's policies in the war on terror and the Iraq War. In 2005, Wolfowitz was named president of the World Bank. He was forced to resign from the bank in 2007 as a result of alleged improper personnel decisions favoring a woman with whom he had a personal relationship.

WOOD, LEONARD (1860–1927). A Harvard-trained M.D., Leonard Wood was the only medical doctor ever to rise to the rank of U.S.

Army chief of staff (1910–1912). Wood fought in the Indian wars in the American West, was personal physician to Presidents Grover Cleveland and **William McKinley**, and rode with Theodore Roosevelt's Rough Riders in Cuba during the **Spanish–American War**. In 1902, as a major general, he was sent to the **Philippines** to command the Philippines Division. From 1903 to 1906, he was the first governor of the **Moro** province, where he sought to impose by whatever force necessary American administration and law on the resistant Muslim population. He lost the U.S. field command in World War I to General John J. Pershing. A Republican who once held presidential ambitions himself, he was sent by President Warren Harding back to the Philippines as governor-general, serving from 1921 until his death in 1927. Governor-General Wood saw his task as tightening American authority and had a stormy relationship with Philippine nationalist leader **Manuel Quezon**. Quezon accused Wood of breaking the American pledge of giving the Philippines the greatest measure of self-government. Wood, in turn, accused the nationalists of challenging American sovereignty.

WOODCOCK, LEONARD (1911–2001). Longtime labor unionist and president of the United Auto Workers, Leonard Woodcock was chosen by President **Jimmy Carter** in 1977 to lead a presidential mission to **Vietnam** to resolve the issue of American prisoners of war/missing in action **(POW/MIA)** in a bid to open the door to **normalization of relations with Vietnam**. A year later, as head of the U.S. liaison mission to the People's Republic of **China**, Woodcock, siding with National Security Advisor **Zbigniew Brzezenski**, opposed normalization of relations with Vietnam.

WOODCOCK MISSION. In March 1977, President **Jimmy Carter** dispatched a high-level delegation to Hanoi, led by **Leonard Woodcock**, to open negotiations on the accounting for American prisoners of war/missing in action **(POW/MIA)**, hoping to start a process of **normalization of relations with Vietnam**. The delegation included America's most senior professional diplomat, Ambassador **Charles Yost**; Senator Mike Mansfield; Congressman **G. V. "Sonny" Montgomery**; and civil rights advocate Marian Edelman, founder of the Children's Defense Fund. After a pro forma demand for reparations, the Vietnamese agreed that issues of U.S. assistance could be separated from the POW/MIA question. As a humanitarian gesture of good faith, Vietnam turned over to the delegation the remains of 12 American servicemen. The Vietnamese indicated that the United States could reciprocate in a humanitarian fashion by aiding in Vietnamese reconstruction. Prime Minister **Pham Van Dong** told the group that Vietnam and the United States could resolve their problems in the new spirit that President Carter had initiated. Woodcock came away from the meeting with the Vietnamese feeling that the prospects for normalizing U.S.–Vietnamese relations had been improved. Improving relations with **China**, however, had a higher priority for National Security Advisor **Zbigniew Brzezinski**.

WORLD TRADE ORGANIZATION (WTO). The World Trade Organization came into existence in 1995 as the institutional successor to the post–World War II General Agreement on Tariffs and Trade (GATT). In the forum of the WTO a number of other agreements have been negotiated regulating the international **trade** relations of its 184 member states. The central tenet is nondiscrimination based on **permanent normal trade relations (PNTR)**, what used to be GATT's most favored nation (MFN) principle. To become a member, a state must conform to the rules and standards set by the WTO. **Brunei, Burma, Indonesia, Malaysia**, the **Philippines**, and **Singapore** were founding members of the WTO. **Cambodia** became a member in 2001. **Vietnam** began negotiating membership in 2002, but was accepted only in 2006 after completing difficult negotiations with major trading partners, including the United States. Congress embarrassed President **George W. Bush** by not giving Vietnam PNTR status until after Bush traveled to Hanoi for the 2006 **Asia–Pacific Economic Cooperation (APEC)** summit hosted by Vietnam. **Laos** began negotiating its WTO accession in 2004. WTO member nations' multilateral and bilateral trade agreements and **free trade agreements (FTA)** must be consistent with the WTO but in promoting liberalization can exceed them—that is "WTO plus." This includes the U.S.–**Singapore** FTA and the proposed U.S. FTAs with **Malaysia** and **Thailand**. The WTO's dispute resolution mechanisms are meant to enforce the obligations that the member states have undertaken.

– Y –

YOST, CHARLES W. (1907–1981). A distinguished career ambassador, the highest rank in the Foreign Service, Charles Yost's first ambassadorial posting was to newly fully independent **Laos** in 1955, where he served until 1957. In 1969, President **Richard Nixon** called him out of retirement to become the U.S. permanent representative to the **United Nations**. He retired again in 1971. At President **Jimmy Carter**'s request he became part of the **Woodcock Mission** to Vietnam in 1977, an early effort in the process of **normalization of relations with Vietnam** after the **Vietnam War**.

YUDHOYONO, SUSILO BAMBANG (1949–). Elected sixth president of Indonesia in 2004, President Yudhoyono, familiarly known as SBY, defeated President **Megawati Sukarnoputri** in Indonesia's first-ever direct presidential election. A former four-star general, he retired from the army in 1999 and entered politics. He served in Presidents **Abdurrahman Wahid**'s and Megawati's cabinets as coordinating minister for political and security affairs. His political party, the Democrat Party, was a minority party in the parliament, and his government was a coalition government. With a large popular mandate, President Yudhoyono impressed the United States as a reformist president attacking corruption, Islamic extremism, and terrorism. During his presidency, the police seriously disrupted the terrorist network of the **Jema'ah Islamiyah**. He strongly backed the negotiated peace with the **Free Aceh Movement (GAM)**. Indonesian–U.S. relations markedly improved during SBY's presidency, one sign of which was the normalization in 2005 of U.S.–Indonesian military-to-military links, previously banned by the **Leahy Amendment**. During his state visit to the United States in May 2005, SBY established a cordial personal relationship with President **George W. Bush**, of whom President Yudhoyono said, "We both see eye to eye on things." President Bush returned the visit in November 2006. Meeting again at the 2007 **Asia–Pacific Economic Cooperation (APEC)** summit, President Bush expressed admiration for President Yudhoyono's leadership and strength of character. SBY in turn said he was thankful for President Bush's role and leadership in fostering American–Indonesian friendship and cooperation.

– Z –

ZONE OF PEACE, FREEDOM, AND NEUTRALITY (ZOPFAN). The **Association of Southeast Asian Nations (ASEAN)**'s first avowedly political regional initiative was the 1971 Kuala Lumpur Declaration, in which the foreign ministers of the five noncommunist member governments agreed to make the necessary efforts "to secure recognition of, and respect for, Southeast Asia as a Zone of Peace, Freedom and Neutrality free from any form or manner of interference by outside powers." It referenced the norms in the Charter of the **United Nations** and the **Bandung Principles** as the regulative basis of the Southeast Asia ZOPFAN.

A Malaysian initiative, the ZOPFAN was prompted in part by a reassessment of the integrity of the passive American security umbrella following the 1969 announcement of the **Nixon doctrine** and the uncertainties about the U.S. efforts to end the **Vietnam War**. Also, the rapprochement between the United States and **China** raised questions about the future power balance in Southeast Asia. The ZOPFAN was proactive as a regional strategy that would not be threatening to the **Indochina** states, particularly the **Democratic Republic of Vietnam (DRV)**. ASEAN's inability to give substance to the ZOPFAN beyond a rhetorical declaration reflected a lack of consensus in the group about the conditions of a ZOPFAN. American allies **Thailand** and the **Philippines** insisted on their rights to maintain alliances and foreign military bases. **Malaysia** and **Singapore** were associated with Australia, Great Britain, and New Zealand in the **Five Power Defence Arrangement (FPDA)**. ASEAN considered the post–Cold War 1995 Bangkok treaty establishing a **Southeast Asia Nuclear Weapons Free Zone (SEANWFZ)** as the first concrete building block of an ASEAN ZOPFAN. No nuclear-armed Great Power acceded to it.

Appendix A:
United States Presidents and
Secretaries of State, 1950–2007

President	Secretary(ies) of State
Harry S. Truman, 1945–1953	James F. Byrnes, July 1945–January 1947
	George C. Marshall, January 1947–January 1949
	Dean G. Acheson, January 1949–January 1953
Dwight D. Eisenhower, 1953–1961	John Foster Dulles, January 1953–April 1959
	Christian A. Herter, April 1959–January 1961
John F. Kennedy, January 1961–November 1963	Dean Rusk, 1961–1963
Lyndon B. Johnson, November 1963–January 1969	Dean Rusk, 1963–1969
Richard M. Nixon, 1969–1974	William P. Rogers, January 1969–September 1973
	Henry A. Kissinger, September 1973–August 1974
Gerald Ford, 1974–1977	Henry A. Kissinger, August 1974–January 1977
Jimmy Carter, 1977–1981	Cyrus Vance, January 1977–April 1980
	Edmund Muskie, May 1980–January 1981
Ronald Reagan, 1981–1989	Alexander Haig Jr., January 1981–July 1982
	George P. Shultz, July 1982–January 1989

George H. W. Bush, 1989–1993

James A. Baker III, January 1989–August 1992

Lawrence S. Eagleburger (Acting), August 1992–January 1993

William J. Clinton, 1993–2001

Warren M. Christopher, January 1993–January 1997

Madeleine Albright, January 1997–January 2001

George W. Bush, 2001–

Colin L. Powell, January 2001–January 2005

Condoleezza Rice, January 2005–

Appendix B:
Assistant Secretaries of State for East Asian and Pacific Affairs, 1950–2007

Dean Rusk (March 1950–December 1951)
John M. Allison (February 1952–April 1953)*
Walter S. Robertson (April 1953–June 1959)
J. Graham Parsons (July 1959–March 1961)
Walter P. McConaughy (April 1961–December 1961)*
W. Averell Harriman (December 1961–April 1963)
Roger Hilsman Jr. (May 1963–March 1964)
William P. Bundy (March 1964–May 1969)
Marshall Green (May 1969–May 1973)*
Robert Stephen Ingersoll (January 1974–July 1974)
Philip C. Habib (September 1974–June 1976)*
Arthur W. Hummel Jr. (July 1976–March 1977)*
Richard C. Holbrooke (March 1977–January 1981)
John H. Holdridge (May 1981 –December 1982)*
Paul D. Wolfowitz (December 1982–March 1986)
Gaston J. Sigur Jr. (March 1986–February 1989)
Richard H. Solomon (June 1989–July 1992)
William Clark Jr. (July 1992–April 1993)*
Winston Lord (April 1993–February 1997)
Stanley O. Roth (August 1997–January 2001)
James Andrew Kelly (May 2001–January 2005)
Christopher R. Hill (April 2005–)*

---

*Denotes Foreign Service Officer.

Bibliography

CONTENTS

I. INTRODUCTION

This bibliography is designed to support the historical entries by reference to a representative collection of major English-language published sources. The criterion for inclusion was the work's relevance to U.S. relations in the Southeast Asian region generally and the 11 countries in it. The entries are heavily weighted by virtue of historical policy interests to the Indochina states of Cambodia, Laos, and Vietnam; Indonesia; and the Philippines. Books on the military aspects of the Vietnam

War are not included. For that we refer the reader to the bibliography in Edward Moïse, *Historical Dictionary of the Vietnam War*. The bibliography also excludes works dealing with Southeast Asian nations' relations with other powers such as China or Japan, except where a triangular relationship with the United States is a particular focus. Chapters in books, journal articles, research papers, and fugitive materials have not been included because of space limitations.

For primary documentation, the State Department's *Foreign Relations of the United States* series has reached the year 1972 in published volumes. Future volumes will be published electronically. Congressional hearings are under the appropriate regional or country heading. For a survey of Southeast Asia's international relations in general, see Donald E. Weatherbee, *International Relations in Southeast Asia: The Struggle for Autonomy*. For a broad interpretive overview of U.S. relations in Southeast Asia since 1945, Robert J. McMahon, *Limits of Empire: The United States and Southeast Asia since World War II*, is recommended. For the earliest postwar period, Gary Hess, *The United States Emergence as a Southeast Asia Power, 1940–1950*, is good. For the most recent years, James B. Tyner, *America's Strategy in Southeast Asia: From the Cold War to the Terror War* (2007) is the most up to date.

For political background on U.S. relations with some of the individual countries, the following works are useful: for Burma, David I. Steinberg, *Burma: The State of Myanmar*; for Cambodia, Keith J. Clyman, *The United States and Cambodia, 1960–2000: A Troubled Relationship*; for Indonesia, Paul F. Gardener, *Shared Hopes, Separate Fears: Fifty Years of U.S.–Indonesia Relations*; for Laos, Perry Stiegletz, *In a Little Kingdom: The Tragedy of Laos, 1960–1980*; for Malaysia, R. S. Milne and Diane K. Mauzey, *Malaysian Politics under Mahathir*; for the Philippines, Stanley Karnow, *In Our Image: American Empire in the Philippines*; for Thailand, Sean Randolph, *The United States and Thailand: Alliance Dynamics*; and for Vietnam, Garry R. Hess, *Vietnam and the United States: Origins and Legacy of War*. Southeast Asia as a region and U.S. bilateral relations with the countries in the region are also dealt with in the volumes on specific periods in U.S. diplomatic history in the series Historical Dictionaries of U.S. Diplomacy, in which this volume appears, published by Scarecrow Press.

For contemporary official data on U.S.–Southeast Asian relations, the State Department's website at www.state.gov has links to its bureaus and offices, country data, embassy websites, and the office of the historian. Its keyword search engine sorts by date or relevance. The official statements, releases, communiqués, etc., of the current presidential administration can be accessed at www.whitehouse.gov. Its news links date back to January 2001. For previous administrations, the collections of the presidential libraries from Harry S. Truman to William J. Clinton are the primary policy research repositories. Their documentary records are supplemented by rich oral history collections. An overview of these libraries and research availability can be found in links to the libraries at www .whitehouse.gov/history/liblinks.html. The online unclassified versions of the Central Intelligence Agency's "Studies in Intelligence" are indexed and linked at www.cia.gov/center-for-the-study-of-intelligence/index .html. The National Security Archive housed at George Washington University has several online document collections relevant to U.S.–Southeast Asia relations. The website is at www.gwu.edu/~nsarchiv/. Association of Southeast Asian Nations (ASEAN)'s documents, including relations with the United States, are available online at www.asean.org. American academic centers with major Southeast Asia research collections are at Arizona State University, Cornell University, Northern Illinois University, Ohio University, University of California–Berkeley, University of Michigan, University of Washington, University of Wisconsin–Madison, and Yale University. The Vietnam archive at Texas Tech University specializes in the war years. In Southeast Asia, the Institute of Southeast Asian Studies in Singapore has a comprehensive library collection on modern Southeast Asian politics and international relations.

II. DOCUMENT COLLECTIONS AND OFFICIAL PUBLICATIONS

Barrett, David M. *Lyndon B. Johnson's Vietnam Papers: A Documentary Collection*. College Station: Texas A & M University Press, 1997.

Bunker, Ellsworth. *The Bunker Papers: Reports to the President from Vietnam, 1967–1973*. Berkeley: University of California Institute of East Asian Studies, 1990.

Gettleman, Marvin, H., Bruce Franklin, Jane Franklin, and Marilyn Young, eds. *Vietnam and America: A Documented History*. rev. ed. New York: Grove Press, 1995.

Porter, Gareth, ed. *Vietnam: The Definitive Documentary of Human Decisions.* 2 vols. New York: E. M. Coleman, 1979.

United States Central Intelligence Agency. *World Fact Book.* Various years.

United States Department of Defense. *United States–Vietnam Relations, 1945–1967.* 12 vols. Washington, D.C.: U.S. Government Printing Office, 1971. [*The Pentagon Papers*]

United States Department of State. Bureau of Democracy, Human Rights, and Labor. *Country Reports on Human Rights Practices.* Annual, 1977– .

———. *Report on International Religious Freedom.* Annual. 1998– .

United States Department of State. Bureau of International Narcotics and Law Enforcement Affairs. *International Narcotics Control Strategy Report.* Annual. 1996– .

United States Department of State. Office of the Historian. *Foreign Relations of the United States.* Washington. D.C.: U.S. Government Printing Office.

1945–1953 [President Harry S. Truman]
  1945 Vol. VI: *The Far East and China*
  1946 Vol. VII: *The Far East*
  1947 Vol. VI: *The Far East*
  1948 Vol. VII: *The Far East and Australasia*
  1949 Vol. VII: *The Far East and Australasia*
  1950 Vol. VI, Part 1: *East Asia and the Pacific*
  1951 Vol. VI, Parts 1 and 2: *East Asia and the Pacific*
1953–1961 [President Dwight D. Eisenhower]
  1952–1954 Vol. XII, Parts 1 and 2: *East Asia and the Pacific*; Vol. XII: *Indochina*; Vol. XVI: *The Geneva Conference: Korea and Indochina*
  1955–1957 Vol. 1: *Vietnam*; Vol. XV: *South and Southeast Asia*; Vol. XVI: *East Asia Regional, Laos, Cambodia*; Vol. XVII: *Indonesia*
  Microfiche Supplements—Vols. XV/XVI, Part 1: *Brunei, Malaysia-Singapore, East Asia Regional, Cambodia.* Part 2: *Laos*; Vols. XVII/XVIII: *Indonesia, Japan, Korea*
1961–1963 [President John F. Kennedy]
  Vols. I–IV: *Vietnam*
  Vol. XXII: *Southeast Asia*
  Vol. XXIV: *Laos Crisis*
  Microfiche Supplement—Vols. XXII/XXIV: *Northeast Asia/Laos*
1964–1968 [President Lyndon B. Johnson]
  Vols. I–II: *Vietnam*
  Vol. XXVI: *Indonesia, Malaysia, Singapore, Philippines*
  Vol. XXVII: *Mainland Southeast Asia, Regional Affairs*
  Vol. XXVIII: *Laos*

1969–1976 [Presidents Nixon and Ford]
    Vol. VI: *Vietnam, July 196 July 1970*
    Vol. XX: *Southeast Asia, 1969–1972* (Thailand, Philippines, and Indonesia)

III. BIOGRAPHY AND MEMOIRS

Acheson, Dean. *Present at the Creation: My Years in the State Department.* New York: W.W. Norton, 1969.

Albright, Madeleine. *Madam Secretary: A Memoir.* New York: Hyperion Publishers, 2003.

Baker, James A. *The Politics of Diplomacy: Revolution, War and Peace, 1989–1992.* East Rutherford, N.J.: Putnam, 1995.

Ball, George W. *The Past Has Another Pattern.* New York: W.W. Norton, 1982.

Bissell, Richard. *Reflections of a Cold Warrior: From Yalta to the Bay of Pigs.* New Haven, Conn.: Yale University Press, 1996,

Bohlen, Charles E. *Witness to History, 1929–1969.* New York: W.W. Norton, 1973.

Brown, Winthrop. *Postmark Asia: Letters of an American Ambassador Written to His Family from India, Laos, and Korea, 1957–66.* n.p.: Author, 1967.

Brzezinski, Zbigniew. *Power and Principle: Memoirs of the National Security Advisor, 1977–1981.* New York: Farrar, Straus & Giroux, 1983.

Carter, Jimmy. *Keeping Faith: Memoirs of a President.* New York: Bantam, 1982.

Christopher, Warren. *Chances of a Lifetime.* New York: Scribner's, 2001.

Clifford, Clark J., with Richard Holbrooke. *Counsel to the President.* New York: Random House, 1991.

Clinton, William J. *My Life.* New York: Alfred A. Knopf, 2004.

Collins, J. Lawton. *Lightning Joe: An Autobiography.* New York: Presidio Press, 1994.

Colby, William E. *Honorable Men: My Life in the CIA.* New York: Simon and Schuster, 1978.

Eisenhower, Dwight D. *The White House Years: Mandate for Change, 1953–1956.* Garden City, N.Y.: Doubleday, 1963.

Green, Marshall. *Indonesia: Crisis and Transformation, 1965–1968.* Washington, D.C.: Compass Press, 1990.

Haig, Alexander M., Jr. *Inner Circles: How America Changed the World: A Memoir.* New York: Warner Books, 1992.

Helms, Richard with William Hood. *A Look over My Shoulder: A Life in the Central Intelligence Agency.* New York: Random House, 2003.

Johnson, Lyndon B. *The Vantage Point*. New York: Holt, Rinehart & Winston, 1971.

Johnson, U. Alexis. *The Right Hand of Power*. Englewood Cliffs, N.J.: Prentice Hall. 1984.

Jones, Howard P. *Indonesia: The Possible Dream*. New York: Harcourt Brace Jovanovich, 1971.

Kahin, George McT. *Southeast Asia: A Testament*. London: RoutledgeCurzon, 2003.

Kissinger, Henry. *White House Years*. Boston: Little, Brown, 1979.

———. *Years of Upheaval*. Boston: Little, Brown, 1983.

Lansdale, Edward G. *In the Midst of Wars: An American Mission to Southeast Asia*. New York: Harper & Row, 1971.

McNamara, Robert S. *In Retrospect: The Tragedy and Lessons of Vietnam*. New York: Random House, 1995.

Nixon, Richard M. *RN: The Memoirs of Richard Nixon*. New York: Grosset and Dunlap, 1989.

Nolting, Fredrick E. *From Trust to Tragedy: The Political Memoirs of Frederick Nolting, Kennedy's Ambassador to Diem's Vietnam*. Westport, Conn.: Greenwood, 1988.

Powell, Colin. *My American Journey*. New York: Random House. 1995.

Rusk, Dean, with Richard Rusk. *As I Saw It*. New York: Norton, 1990.

Shackley Ted with Richard A. Finney. *Spymaster: My Life in the CIA*. Dulles, Va.: Potomac Books, 2005.

Shultz, George P. *Turmoil and Triumph: My Years as Secretary of State*. New York: Scribner's, 1993.

Smith, Joseph Burkholder. *Portrait of a Cold Warrior*. New York: Putnam, 1976.

Stanton, Edwin F. *Brief Authority: Excursions of a Common Man in an Uncommon World*. New York: Harper, 1956.

Sullivan, William H. *Obbligato, 1939–1979: Notes on a Foreign Service Career*. New York: W.W. Norton, 1984.

Taylor, Maxwell C. *Swords and Plowshares*. New York: W.W. Norton, 1972.

Truman, Harry S. *Memoirs.* New York: New American Library, 1965.

Vance, Cyrus. *Hard Choices: Critical Years in America's Foreign Policy*. New York: Simon & Schuster, 1983.

IV. REGIONAL EAST ASIA AND U.S. RELATIONS

Aggarwal, Vinod, and Charles Morrison, eds. *Asia Pacific Crossroads: Regime Creation and the Future of APEC*. New York: St. Martin's Press, 1998.

Aldrich, Richard J., Garry D. Rawnsley, and Ming-Yeh T. Rawnsley, eds. *The Clandestine Cold War in Asia, 1945–65*. London: Frank Cass, 2000.

Armacost, Michael H., and Stephen Bosworth. *Chasing the Sun: Rethinking East Asia Policy*. New York: Century Foundation Press, 2006.

Bird, Kai. *The Color of Truth: McGeorge Bundy and William Bundy: Brothers in Arms*. New York: Simon & Schuster, 1998.

Blum, Robert M. *Drawing the Line: The Origins of the American Containment Policy in East Asia*. New York: Norton, 1982.

Buckley, Roger. *The United States in the Asia-Pacific since 1945*. New York: Cambridge University Press, 2002.

Bundy, William. *A Tangled Web: The Making of Foreign Policy in the Nixon Presidency*. New York: Hill and Wang, 1998.

Cohen, Warren I., and Nancy Bernkopf Tucker, eds. *Lyndon Johnson Confronts the World: American Foreign Policy, 1963–1968*. New York: Cambridge University Press, 1994.

Devine, Robert A. *Eisenhower and the Cold War*. New York: Oxford University Press, 1981.

Haig, Alexander M., Jr. *Caveat: Realism, Reagan, and American Foreign Policy*. New York: Scribner's, 1984.

Hellman, Donald C., and Kenneth B. Pyle, eds. *From APEC to Xanadu*. New York: M.E. Sharpe, 1997.

Hersh, Seymour. *The Price of Power: Kissinger in the Nixon White House*. New York: Summit Books, 1983.

Hilsman, Roger. *To Move a Nation: The Politics of Foreign Policy in the Administration of John F. Kennedy*. New York: Doubleday, 1967.

Iriye, Akira. *The Cold War in Asia: An Historical Introduction*. Englewood Cliffs, N.J.: Prentice Hall, 1974.

Kunz, Dianne B., ed. *Diplomacy of the Crucial Decade: American Foreign Policy During the 1960s*. New York: Columbia University Press, 1994.

Marks, Frederick W., III. *Power and Peace: The Diplomacy of John Foster Dulles*. Westport, Conn.: Praeger, 1972.

McGlothlen, Donald L. *Controlling the Waves: Dean Acheson and U.S. Foreign Policy in Asia*. New York: W.W. Norton, 1993.

McInnes, Colin, and Mark G. Rolls. *Post-Cold War Security Issues in the Asia-Pacific Region*. Ilford, Essex, UK: Frank Cass, 1994.

Newsom, David. *The Imperial Mantle: The United States, Decolonization, and the Third World*. Bloomington: Indiana University Press, 2001.

Pempel T. J., ed. *The Politics of the Asian Economic Crisis*. Ithaca, N.Y.: Cornell University Press, 1999.

Ravenhill, John. *APEC and the Construction of Pacific Rim Regionalism*. New York: Cambridge University Press, 2002.

Schlesinger, Arthur J., Jr. *A Thousand Days: John F. Kennedy in the White House*. Boston: Houghton Mifflin, 1965.

Schoenbrum, Thomas J. *Waging Peace and War: Dean Rusk in the Truman, Kennedy, and Johnson Years*. New York: Simon & Schuster, 1988.

Shavit, David. *The United States in Asia: A Historical Dictionary*. New York: Greenwood, 1990.

Sorenson, Theodore. *Kennedy.* New York: Harper & Row, 1965.

Statler, Kathryn C., and Andrew L. Jones, eds. *The Eisenhower Administration, the Third World, and the Globalization of the Cold War*. Lanham, Md.: Rowman & Littlefield, 2006.

Sutter, Robert. *The United States and East Asia: Dynamics and Implications*. Lanham, Md.: Rowman & Littlefield, 2003.

Thomas, Evan. *The Very Best Men: The Daring Early Years of the CIA*. New York: Simon & Schuster, 1991.

Thomason, James C., Peter W. Stanley, and Johns C. Perry. *Sentimental Imperialists: The American Experience in East Asia*. New York: Harper & Row, 1981.

U.S. Congress. Senate. Committee on Foreign Affairs. Subcommittee on East Asian and Pacific Affairs. *The Emergence of China throughout Asia: Security and Economic Consequences, Hearing.* 109th Cong., 1st sess., 7 June 2005. Washington, D.C.: U.S. Government Printing Office, 2006.

Weiner, Tim. Legacy of Ashes: *The History of the CIA*. New York: Doubleday, 2007.

Yahuda, Michael. *The International Politics of the Asia Pacific, 1945–1995*. London: Routledge, 1996.

V. REGIONAL SOUTHEAST ASIA

Abuza, Zachary. *Militant Islam in Southeast Asia: Crucible of Terror*. Boulder, Colo.: Lynne Rienner, 2003.

Arndt, H. W., and Hal Hill, eds. *Southeast Asia's Economic Crisis: Origins, Lessons and the Way Forward.* Singapore: Institute of Southeast Asian Studies, 1999.

Bert, Wayne. *The United States, China, and Southeast Asia: A Changing of the Guard?* New York: Palgrave Macmillan, 2003.

Bresnan John. *From Dominos to Dynamos: The Transformation of Southeast Asia*. New York: Council on Foreign Relations Press, 1994.

Colbert, Evelyn. *Southeast Asia in International Politics, 1941-1956*. Ithaca, N.Y.: Cornell University Press, 1977.

Eldridge, Philip H., ed. *The Politics of Human Rights in Southeast Asia*. London: RoutledgeCurzon, 2000.

Ellings, Richard, and Sheldon Simon, eds. *Southeast Asian Security in the New Millennium.* Armonk, N.Y.: M.E. Sharpe, 1996.

Esterline, John H., and Mae Esterline. *How the Dominoes Fell: Southeast Asia in Perspective.* Lanham, Md.: Rowman & Littlefield, 1986.

Fifield, Russell H. *Americans in Southeast Asia: The Roots of Commitment.* New York: Crowell, 1973.

———. *Southeast Asia in United States Policy.* New York: Praeger, 1963.

Finklestein, Lawrence S. *American Policy in Southeast Asia.* New York: American Institute of Pacific Relations, 1950.

Gregor, A. James. *In the Shadow of Giants: The Major Powers and the Security of Southeast Asia.* Stanford, Calif.: Hoover Institution Press, 1990.

Gurtov, Melvin. *Southeast Asia Tomorrow: Problems and Prospect for U.S. Policy.* Baltimore, Md.: Johns Hopkins University Press, 1970.

Heiner, Hanggi. *ASEAN and the ZOPFAN Concept.* Singapore: Institute of Southeast Asian Studies, 1991.

Henderson, William. *Southeast Asia: Problems of American Foreign Policy.* Cambridge, Mass.: M.I.T. Press, 1963.

Hess, Gary. *The United States' Emergence as a Southeast Asian Power, 1940–1950.* New York: Columbia University Press, 1987.

Institute of Southeast Asian Studies, various eds. *Southeast Asian Affairs.* Singapore: Institute of Southeast Asian Studies. Annual. 1974– .

King, John Kerry. *Southeast Asia in Perspective: The Political Economy of a Dynamic Region.* Cambridge, Mass.: M.I.T. Press, 1963.

Levine, Alan J. *The United States and the Struggle for Southeast Asia, 1945–1975.* Westport, Conn.: Praeger, 1995.

Lyon, Peter. *War and Peace in Southeast Asia.* London: Oxford University Press, 1969.

McCoy, Alfred. *The Politics of Heroin in Southeast Asia.* New York: Harper & Row, 1972.

McMahon, Robert J. *Limits of Empire: The United States and Southeast Asia Since World War II.* New York: Columbia University Press, 1999.

Morrison, Charles E. *Japan, the United States and a Changing Southeast Asia.* Lexington, Mass.: University Press of America/Asia Society, 1985.

Narine, Shaun. *Explaining ASEAN: Regionalism in Southeast Asia.* Boulder, Colo.: Lynne Rienner, 2002.

Neher, Clark. *Southeast Asia in the New International Era.* Boulder, Colo.: Westview Press, 1991.

Ramakrishna, Kumar, and See Seng Tan, eds. *After Bali: The Threat of Terrorism in Southeast Asia.* Singapore: World Scientific Publishing, 2003.

Rotter, Andrew J. *The Path to Vietnam: Origins of the American Commitment to Southeast Asia.* Ithaca, N.Y.: Cornell University Press, 1987.

Simon, Sheldon. *Neutralism and U.S. Foreign Policy*. Washington, D.C.: American Enterprise Institute for Public Policy Research, 1975.

Smith, Paul J., ed. *Terrorism and Violence in Southeast Asia: Transnational Challenges to States and Regional Stability.* Armonk, N.Y.: M.E. Sharpe, 2005.

Sokolsky, Richard, Angel Rabasky, and C. R. Neu. *The Role of Southeast Asia in U.S. Strategy towards China*. Santa Monica, Calif.: Rand Corporation, 2000.

Thayer, Philip W., ed. *Southeast Asia in the Coming World*. Baltimore, Md.: Johns Hopkins University Press, 1953.

Tilman, Robert O. *Southeast Asia and the Enemy Beyond*. Boulder, Colo.: Westview Press, 1987.

Tyner, James A. *America's Strategy in Southeast Asia: From the Cold War to the Terror War*. Lanham, Md.: Rowman & Littlefield, 2007.

U.S. Congress. House. Committee on International Relations. *Asian Free Trade Agreements: Are They Good for the U.S.A.? Hearing.* 109th Cong., 2nd sess., 20 July 2006. Washington, D.C.: U.S. Government Printing Office, 2006.

US Congress. House. Committee on International Relations. Subcommittee on Asia and the Pacific. *Recent Developments in Southeast Asia, Hearing.* 108th Cong., 1st sess., 10 June 2003. Washington, D.C.: U. S. Government Printing Office, 2003.

———. *Southeast Asia After 9/11: Regional Trends and U.S. Interests, Hearing.* 107th Cong., 1st sess., 12 December 2001. Washington, D.C.: U.S. Government Printing Office, 2002.

———. *The United States and Southeast Asia: Developments, Trends, and Policy Choices, Hearing.* 109th Cong., 1st sess., 21 September 2005. Washington, D.C.: U.S. Government Printing Office, 2006.

———. *U.S. Policy towards Southeast Asia, Hearing.* 108th Cong., 1st sess., 20 March 2003. Washington, D.C.: U.S. Government Printing Office, 2003.

Vandenbosch, Amry, and Richard Butwell. *Southeast Asia among the World Powers*. Lexington: University of Kentucky Press, 1958.

Weatherbee, Donald E. *International Relations in Southeast Asia: The Struggle for Autonomy.* Lanham, Md.: Rowman & Littlefield, 2005.

Wurfel, David A., and Bruce Burton, eds. *The Political Economy of Foreign Policy in Southeast Asia.* New York: St. Martin's Press, 1990.

———. *Southeast Asia in the New World Order*. New York: St. Martin's Press, 1996.

VI. REGIONAL INDOCHINA

Brown, Frederick Z. *Second Chance: The United States and Indochina in the 1990s*. New York: Council on Foreign Relations, 1989.

Cable, James. *The Geneva Conference of 1954 on Indochina*. New York: St. Martin's Press, 1986.

Chanda, Nayan. *Brother Enemy: The War after the War*. New York: Harcourt, Brace Jovanovich, 1986.

Dommen, Arthur J. *The Indochina Experience of the French and the Americans: Nationalism and Communism in Cambodia, Laos, and Vietnam*. Bloomingon: Indiana University Press, 2002.

Duiker, William J. *U.S. Containment Policy and the Conflict in Indochina*. Stanford, Calif.: Stanford University Press, 1991.

Eliot, David W. P., ed. *The Third Indochina Conflict*. Boulder, Colo: Westview Press, 1981.

Farley, Miriam. *United States Relations in Southeast Asia with Special Reference to Indochina, 1950–1958*. New York: American Institute of Pacific Relations, 1958.

Hawley, Thomas. *The Remains of War: Bodies, Politics, and the Search for the Remains of American Soldiers Unaccounted for in Southeast Asia*. Durham, N.C.: Duke University Press, 2004.

Irving, Ronald E. *The First Indochina War: French and American Policy, 1945–1954*. London: Croon Helm, 1975.

Kimball, Jeffrey P., ed. *To Reason Why: The Debate about the Causes of U.S. Involvement in the Vietnam War*. New York: McGraw-Hill, 1990.

Lacouture, Jean, and Philippe Devillers. *End of a War: Indochina 1954*. New York: Praeger, 1969.

Poole, Peter. *Eight Presidents and Indochina*. Melbourne, Fla.: Krieger Publishing, 1978.

Ross, Robert. *The Indochina Tangle*. New York: Columbia University Press, 1988.

Solomon, Richard H. *Exiting Indochina: U.S. Leadership of the Cambodian Settlement and Normalization of Relations with Vietnam*. Washington, D.C.: United States Institute of Peace Press, 2000.

U.S. Congress. House. Committee on Foreign Affairs. Subcommittee on Asian and Pacific Affairs. *Resolving the POW/MIA Issue: A Status Report, Hearing*. 102nd Cong., 1st sess., 17 July 1991. Washington, D.C.: U.S. Government Printing Office, 1992.

———. *U.S. Policy towards Indochina since Vietnam's Occupation of Kampuchea, Hearings*. 97th Cong., 1st sess., 15, 21, and 22 October 1982. Washington, D.C.: U.S. Government Printing Office, 1982.

U.S. Congress. House. Committee on International Relations. Subcommittees on Asia and the Pacific and International Operations and Human Rights. *Indochinese Refugees: Comprehensive Plan of Action, Joint Hearing*. 104th Cong., 1st sess., 25 July 1995. Washington, D.C.: U.S. Government Printing Office, 1996.

U.S. Congress. House. Committee on Veterans Affairs. *Americans Missing in Southeast Asia.* Committee Print. 100th Cong., 2nd sess., 5 August 1988. Washington, D.C.: U.S. Government Printing Office, 1988.

U.S. Congress. Senate. Foreign Relations Committee. Subcommittee on East Asian and Pacific Affairs. *U.S. Policy toward Indochina, Hearing.* 101st Cong., 1st sess., 2 October 1989. Washington, D.C.: U.S. Government Printing Office, 1990.

U.S. Congress. Senate. Select Committee on POW/MIA Affairs. *Hearings on the Paris Peace Accord.* 102nd Cong., 2nd sess., 21, 22, and 24 September 1992. Washington D.C.: U.S. Government Printing Office, 1993.

Weatherbee, Donald E., ed. *Southeast Asia Divided: The ASEAN–Indochina Crisis.* Boulder, Colo: Westview Press, 1985.

Young, Marilyn B. *The Vietnam Wars, 1945–1950.* New York: HarperCollins, 1991.

Zasloff, Joseph J., ed. *Postwar Indochina: Old Enemies and New Allies.* Washington: U.S. Department of State, Foreign Service Institute Center for the Study of Foreign Affairs, 1988.

Zasloff, Joseph J., and MacAlister Brown. *Communist Indochina and U.S. Foreign Policy: Postwar Realities.* Boulder, Colo: Westview Press, 1978.

VII. CAMBODIA

Bradey, Christopher. *United States Foreign Policy towards Cambodia, 1977–1992: A Question of Realities.* New York: St. Martin's Press, 1999.

Brown, Frederick Z. *Cambodia and the Dilemmas of United States Foreign Policy.* New York: Council on Foreign Relations, 1991.

Carney, Timothy M. *Communist Party Power in Kampuchea (Cambodia): Documents and Discussion.* Cornell University Southeast Asia Program data paper no. 106. Ithaca, N.Y.: Cornell University Press, 1977.

Chandler, David P. *The Tragedy of Cambodian History: Politics, War and Revolution since 1945.* New Haven, Conn.: Yale University Press, 1991.

Chandler, David, and Ben Kiernan, eds. *Revolution and Its Aftermath: Eight Essays.* New Haven, Conn.: Yale University Southeast Asian Studies, 1983.

Clymen, Keith J. *The United States and Cambodia, 1960–2000: A Troubled Relationship.* London: RoutledgeCurzon, 2004.

Corefield, Justin J., and Laura Summers. *Historical Dictionary of Cambodia.* Lanham, Md.: Scarecrow Press, 2003.

Deak, Wilfred P. *Road to the Killing Fields: The Cambodian War of 1970–75.* College Station: Texas A & M University Press, 1992.

Guilmartin, John F., Jr. *A Very Short War: The Mayaguez and the Battle of Koh Kang*. College Station: Texas A & M University Press, 1995.

Haas, Michael. *Cambodia, Pol Pot, and the United States: The Faustian Pact*. New York: Praeger, 1991.

Issacs, Arnold. *Without Honor: Defeat in Vietnam and Cambodia, 1973–1975*. Baltimore. Md.: Johns Hopkins University Press, 1983.

Jackson, Karl D., ed. *Cambodia 1975 –1978: Rendezvous with Death*. Princeton, N.J.: Princeton University Press, 1989.

Leifer, Michael. *Cambodia: The Search for Security*. London: Pall Mall, 1967.

Ponchaud, François. *Cambodia: Year Zero*. London: Penguin Press, 1978.

Rowan, Roy. *The Four Days of the Mayaguez*. New York: W.W. Norton, 1975.

Shawcross, William. *Sideshow: Kissinger, Nixon and the Destruction of Cambodia*. New York: Simon & Schuster, 1979.

Sihanouk, Norodom. *My War with the CIA*. London: Penguin Press, 1973.

Smith, Roger M. *Cambodia's Foreign Policy*. Ithaca, N.Y.: Cornell University Press, 1965.

Sutter, Robert G. *The Cambodia Crisis and U.S. Policy Dilemmas*. Boulder, Colo.: Westview Press, 1990.

U.S. Congress. House. Committee on Foreign Affairs. Subcommittee on International Political and Military Affairs. *Seizure of the Mayaguez, Hearings*. 94th Cong., 1st sess., 14 May 1975. Washington, D.C.: U.S. Government Printing Office, 1975.

U.S. Congress. House. Subcommittee on Asian and Pacific Affairs. *The Democratic Kampuchea Seat at the United Nations and American Interests, Hearing*. 97th Cong., 2nd sess., 15 September 1982. Washington, D.C.: U.S. Government Printing Office, 1983.

———. *Familiar Ground: The Breakdown of Democracy in Cambodia and Implications for U.S. Foreign Policy, Hearing*. 105th Cong., 1st sess., 16 July 1997. Washington, D.C.: U.S. Government Printing Office, 1997.

———. *Kampuchea and American Foreign Policy Interests, Hearing*. 97th Cong., 1st sess., 23 July 1981. Washington, D.C.: U.S. Government Printing Office, 1982.

———. *The Paris Peace Conference on Cambodia: Implications for U.S. Policy, Hearing*. 101st Cong., 1st sess., 14 September 1989. Washington, D.C.: U.S. Government Printing Office, 1990.

———. *Shattered Dream, the Uncertain State of Democracy in Cambodia, Hearing*. 105th Cong., 2nd sess., 26 February 1998. Washington, D.C.: U.S. Government Printing Office, 1998.

U.S. Congress. Senate. Committee on Foreign Relations. Subcommittee on East Asian and Pacific Affairs. *Cambodia, Post-Elections and U.S. Policy Options, Hearing.* 105th Cong., 2nd sess., 2 October 1998. Washington, D.C.: U.S. Government Printing Office, 1999.

———. *Cambodian Peace Negotiations: Prospects for Settlement, Hearing.* 101st Cong., 2nd sess., 10 July and 19 September, 1990. Washington, D.C.: U.S. Government Printing Office, 1992.

Whitaker, Donald P., ed. *Cambodia: a Country Study.* 2nd ed. Washington, D.C.: Foreign Area Studies, The American University, 1983.

VIII. LAOS

Castle, Timothy. *At War in the Shadow of Vietnam.* New York: Columbia University Press, 1993.

Conboy, Kenneth, and James Morrison. *Shadow War: The CIA's Secret War in Laos.* Boulder, Colo.: Paladin Press, 1995.

Dommen, Arthur. *Conflict in Laos: The Politics of Neutralization.* New York: Praeger, 1971.

Fall, Bernard. *Anatomy of a Crisis: The Laotian Crisis of 1960-1961.* New York: Doubleday, 1969.

Goldstein, Martin. *American Foreign Policy towards Laos.* Rutherford, N.J.: Fairleigh Dickinson University Press, 1973.

Hamilton-Merritt, Jan. *Tragic Mountains: The Hmong, The Americans, and Secret Wars for Laos.* Bloomington.: Indiana University Press, 1993.

Morrison, Gayle. *Sky Is Falling: An Oral History of the CIA's Evacuation of the Hmong from Laos.* Jefferson, N.C.: McFarland, 1999.

Stevenson, Charles. *The End of Nowhere: American Policy towards Laos since 1954.* Boston: Beacon Press, 1973.

Stieglitz, Perry. *In a Little Kingdom: The Tragedy of Laos, 1960–1980.* Armonk, N.Y.: M.E. Sharpe, 1990.

Stuart-Fox, Martin. *Historical Dictionary of Laos.* Lanham, Md.: Scarecrow Press, 2001.

———. *A History of Laos.* Cambridge: Cambridge University Press, 1997.

———. *Buddhist Kingdom, Marxist State.* Bangkok: White Lotus Press, 2002.

U.S. Congress. Senate. Committee on Foreign Relations. Subcommittee on United States Security Agreements and Commitments Abroad. *AID Activities in Laos, Hearing.* 92nd Cong., 2nd sess., 13 April 1972. Washington, D.C.: U.S. Government Printing Office, 1972.

Warner, Roger. *Backfire: The CIA's Secret War in Laos and Its Links to the War in Vietnam.* New York: Simon & Schuster, 1995.

——. *Shooting at the Moon: The Story of America's Clandestine War in Laos*. South Royalton, Vt.: Steerforth Press, 1996.

IX. VIETNAM

Anderson, David L. *Trapped by Success: The Eisenhower Administration and Vietnam, 1953–1961*. New York: Columbia University Press, 1991.

Arnold, James R. *The First Domino: Eisenhower, the Military, and America's Intervention in Vietnam*. New York: W. Morrow, 1991.

Austin, Anthony. *The President's War*. New York: Lippincott, 1971.

Bain, Chester A. *Vietnam: The Roots of Conflict*. Englewood Cliffs, N.J.: Prentice Hall, 1967.

Bartholomew-Feis, Dixee R. *The OSS and Ho Chi Minh: Unexpected Allies in the War against Japan*. Lawrence: University Press of Kansas, 2006.

Blair, Anne E. *Lodge in Vietnam: A Patriot Abroad*. New Haven, Conn.: Yale University Press, 1998.

Colby, William E. with James McCargar. *A First Hand Account of America's Sixteen-Year Involvement in Vietnam*. Chicago, Ill.: Contemporary Books, 1990.

Cooper, Chester L. *The Lost Crusade. America in Vietnam*. New York: Dodd Mead, 1970.

DiLeo, David L. *George Ball, Vietnam, and the Rethinking of Containment*. Chapel Hill: University of North Carolina Press, 1991.

Dillard, Walter Scott. *Sixty Days to Peace: Implementing the Paris Peace Accords, Vietnam 1973*. Washington, D.C.: National Defense University, 1982.

Fisher, Ross A., John N. Moore, and Robert F. Turner, eds. *To Oppose Any Foe: The Legacy of U.S. Intervention in Vietnam*. Durham, N.C.: Carolina Academic Press, 2006.

Gardner, Lloyd C. *Approaching Vietnam: From World War II through Dienbienphu*. New York: W.W. Norton, 1988.

Gelb, Leslie H., and Richard K. Betts. *The Irony of Vietnam: The System Worked*. Washington, D.C.: The Brookings Institution, 1979.

Gurtov, Melvin. *First Vietnam Crisis: Chinese Communist Strategy and United States Involvement, 1953–1954*. New York: Columbia University Press, 1968.

Halberstam, David. *The Making of a Quagmire: America and Vietnam during the Kennedy Era*. New York: McGraw-Hill, 1988.

Haycraft, William R. *Unraveling Vietnam: How American Arms and Diplomacy Failed in Southeast Asia*. Jefferson, N.C.: McFarland, 2005.

Herring, George. *America's Longest War: The United States and Vietnam, 1950–1975*. 3rd ed. New York: McGraw-Hill, 1996.

Herrington, Stuart. *Peace with Honor? An American Reports on Vietnam, 1973–1975*. Novato, Calif.: Presidio, 1983.

Hess, Gary R. *Vietnam and the United States: Origins and Legacy of War*. Boston: Twayne Publishers, 1998.

Holbrooke, Richard. *Prelude to Tragedy: Vietnam, 1960-1965*. Annapolis, Md.: U.S. Naval Institute Press, 2000.

Hoopes, Townsend. *The Limits of Intervention*. New York: McKay, 1969.

Hunt, Michael. *Lyndon Johnson's War*. New York: Hill & Wang, 1996.

Hurst, Steven. *The Carter Administration and Vietnam*. New York: St. Martin's Press, 1996.

Isaacs, Arnold. *Without Honor: Defeat in Vietnam and Cambodia, 1973–1975*. Baltimore, Md.: Johns Hopkins University Press, 1983.

Jacobs, Seth. *Cold War Mandarin: Ngo Dinh Diem and the Origins of America's War in Vietnam, 1950–1963*. Lanham, Md.: Rowman & Littlefield, 2006.

Kahin, George McT. *Intervention: How America Became Involved in Vietnam*. New York: Knopf, 1986.

Kahin, George McT., and John Lewis. *The United States in Vietnam*. New York: Delta, 1967.

Kaiser, David. *American Tragedy: Kennedy, Johnson, and the Origins of the Vietnam War*. Cambridge, Mass.: Harvard University Press, 2000.

Kattenburg, Paul M. *The Vietnam Trauma in American Foreign Policy, 1945–75*. New Brunswick, N.J.: Transaction Books, 1980.

Kimball, Jeffrey. *Nixon's Vietnam War*. Lawrence: University Press of Kansas, 1998.

Lewy, Gunter. *America in Vietnam*. New York: Oxford University Press, 1978.

Lind, Michael. *Vietnam: The Necessary War*. New York: Simon & Schuster, 1999.

Lockhart, Bruce M., and William J. Duiker. *Historical Dictionary of Vietnam*. Lanham, Md.: Scarecrow Press, 2006.

Lodge, Henry Cabot. *The Storm Has Many Eyes*. New York: W.W. Norton, 1973.

Logeville, Frederick. *Choosing War: The Lost Chance for Peace and the Escalation of War in Vietnam*. Berkeley: University of California Press, 1999.

McCargo, Duncan, ed. *Rethinking Vietnam*. London: RoutledgeCurzon, 2004.

Miller, Robert Hopkins. *The United States and Vietnam, 1787–1941*. Honolulu: University Press of the Pacific, 2005.

——. *Vietnam and Beyond: A Diplomat's Cold War Education*. Lubbock: Texas Tech University Press, 2002.

Moïse, Edwin E. *Historical Dictionary of the Vietnam War*. Lanham, Md.: Scarecrow Press, 2002.

Morley, James W., and Masashi Nishihara, eds. *Vietnam Joins the World*. Armonk, N.Y.: M.E. Sharpe, 1997.

Newman, John M. *JFK and Vietnam: Deception, Intrigue, and the Struggle for Power*. New York: Random House, 1964.

Olson, James S., and Randy Roberts. *Where the Dominos Fell: America and Vietnam, 1945–1995*. New York: St. Martin's Press, 1996.

Patti, Archimedes. *Why Vietnam: Prelude to America's Albatross*. Berkeley: University of California Press, 1980.

Rust, William J. *Kennedy in Vietnam*. New York: Scribner's, 1988.

Schulzinger, Robert D. *A Time for War: The United States and Vietnam, 1941–1975*. New York: Oxford University Press, 1997.

Snepp, Frank. *Decent Interval: An Insider's Account of Saigon's Indecent End Told by the CIA's Chief Strategy Analyst in Vietnam*. New York: Vintage Books, 1978.

Stern, Lewis M. *Defense Relations between the United States and Vietnam: The Process of Normalization, 1977 –2003*. Jefferson, N.C.: McFarland, 2005.

Thayer, Carl, and Ramses Amer, eds. *Vietnam Foreign Policy in Transition*. New York: St. Martin's Press, 1999.

Thies, Wallace. *When Governments Collide: Coercion and Diplomacy in the Vietnam Conflict, 1964–1968*. Berkeley: University of California Press, 1980.

U.S. Congress. House. Committee on Foreign Affairs. Subcommittee on Asian and Pacific Affairs. *The Vessey Mission to Hanoi, Hearings*. 100th Cong., 1st sess., 10 September 1987.

U.S. Congress. House. Committee on International Relations. Subcommittee on Asia and the Pacific. *U.S. Vietnam Relations, Hearing*. 105th Cong., 1st sess., 18 June 1997. Washington, D.C.: U.S. Government Printing Office, 1997.

U.S. Congress. House. Committee on International Relations. Subcommittees on Africa, Global Human Rights and International Operations and the Subcommittee on Asia and the Pacific. *The Human Rights Dialogue with Vietnam: Is Vietnam Making Significant Progress? Joint Hearing*. 109th Cong., 2nd sess., 29 March 2006. Washington, D.C.: U.S. Government Printing Office, 2006.

U.S. Congress. House. Committee on International Relations. Subcommittees on Asia and the Pacific and International Economic Policy and Trade. *Prelude to New Directions in United States–Vietnam Relations: The 2000 Bilateral Trade Agreement, Joint Hearing*. 106th Cong., 2nd sess. 19 September 2000. Washington, D.C.: U.S. Government Printing Office, 2001.

U.S. Congress. Senate. Committee on Foreign Relations. *The Plight of the Montangards, Hearing*. 105th Cong., 2nd sess., 10 March, 1998. Washington, D.C.: U.S. Government Printing Office, 1998.

X. BURMA (MYANMAR)

Butwell, Richard. *U Nu of Burma*. Stanford, Calif.: Stanford University Press. 1969.

Johnstone, William C. *Burma's Foreign Policy: A Study in Neutralism*. Cambridge, Mass.: Harvard University Press, 1963.

Liang, Chih-shad. *Burma's Foreign Relations: Neutralism in Theory and Practice*. New York: Praeger, 1990.

Lintner, Bertil. *Burma in Revolt: Opium and Insurgency since 1948*. Boulder, Colo.: Westview Press, 1994.

Renard, Ronald D. *The Burmese Connection: Illegal Drugs and the Making of the Golden Triangle*. Boulder, Colo.: Lynne Rienner, 1996.

Rotberg, Robert I. *Burma: Prospects for a Democratic Future*. Washington, D.C.: Brookings Institution, 1998.

Seekins, Donald. *The Disorder of Order: A Political History of Modern Burma*. Bangkok: White Lotus, 2000.

——. *Historical Dictionary of Burma (Myanmar)*. Lanham, Md.: Scarecrow Press, 2006.

Smith, Martin. *Burma: Insurgency and the Politics of Ethnicity*. 2nd ed. London: Zed Books, 1999.

Steinberg, David I. *Burma: The State of Myanmar*. Washington, D.C.: Georgetown University Press, 2001.

U.S. Congress. House. Committee on International Relations. Subcommittees on Human Rights and International Organizations and on Asian and Pacific Affairs. *The Crackdown in Burma: Suppression of the Democracy Movement and Violation of Human Rights, Joint Hearings*. 101st Cong., 1st sess., 13 September 1989. Washington, D.C.: U.S. Government Printing Office, 1989.

U.S. Congress. House. Subcommittees on Africa, Global Human Rights, and International Operations and on Asia and Pacific of the Committee on International Relations. *Human Rights in Burma: Where We Are Now and What Do We Do Next? Joint Hearing*. 109th Cong., 2nd sess., 7 February 2006. Washington, D.C.: U.S. Government Printing Office, 2006.

U.S. Congress. House. Subcommittees on International Terrorism, Nonproliferation, and Human Rights and on Asian and Pacific Affairs. *Human Rights in Burma: Fifteen Years Post-Military Coup, Joint Hearings*. 108th Cong., 2nd sess., 1–2 October 2003. Washington, D.C.: U.S. Government Printing Office, 2004.

U.S. Congress. Senate. Committee on Banking, Housing, and Urban Affairs. *The Burma Freedom and Democracy Act of 1995, Hearing*. 104th Cong., 2nd sess., 22 May 1996. Washington, D.C.: U.S. Government Printing Office, 1996.

U.S. Congress. Senate. Committee on Foreign Relations. Subcommittee on East Asian and Pacific Affairs. *A Review of Development of Democracy in Burma, Hearing.* 108th Cong., 1st sess., 18 June 2003. Washington, D.C. U.S. Government Printing Office, 2003.

———. *U.S.–Burma Relations, Hearing.* 109th Cong., 2nd sess., 29 March 2006. Washington, D.C.: U.S. Government Printing Office, 2006.

XI. EAST TIMOR (TIMOR LESTE)

Cotton, James. *East Timor, Australia, and Regional Order: Intervention and Its Aftermath in Southeast Asia.* New York: RoutledgeCurzon, 2004.

Fox, James J., and Dionisio Babo Soares, eds. *Out of the Ashes: Destruction and Reconstruction of East Timor.* Adelaide, South Australia: Crawford House, 2000.

Hainsworth, Paul, and Stephen McCloskey, eds. *The East Timor Question: The Struggle for Independence from Indonesia.* London: I.B. Tauris, 2000.

Martin, Ian. *Self-Determination in East Timor: The United Nations, the Ballot, and International Intervention.* Boulder, Colo.: Lynne Rienner, 2001.

Smith, Michael G. *Peacekeeping in East Timor: The Path to Independence.* Boulder, Colo.: Lynne Rienner, 2001.

Tanter, Richard, Mark Selden, and Stephen R. Shalom, eds. *Bitter Flowers, Sweet Flowers: East Timor, Indonesia, and the World Community.* Lanham, Md.: Rowman & Littlefield, 2001.

Taylor, James G. *Indonesia's Forgotten War: The Hidden History of East Timor.* London: Zed Books, 1991.

U.S. Congress. House. Committee on International Relations. Subcommittee on Asia and the Pacific and Senate Committee on Foreign Relations, Subcommittee on East Asian and Pacific Affairs. *East Timor: A New Beginning? Joint Hearing.* 106th Cong., 2nd sess., 10 February 2000. Washington, D.C.: U.S. Government Printing Office, 2000.

———. *East Timor: Instability and Future Prospects, Hearing.* 109th Cong., 2nd sess., 28 June 2006. Washington, D.C.: U.S. Government Printing Office, 2006.

U.S. Congress. House. Committee on International Relations. Subcommittee on International Operations and Human Rights. *The Humanitarian Crisis in East Timor, Hearing.* 106th Cong., 1st sess., 30 September 1999. Washington, D.C.: U.S. Government Printing Office, 2000.

U.S. Congress. House. Committee on International Relations. Subcommittees on International Organizations and on Asian and Pacific Affairs. *Human Rights in East Timor and the Question of the Use of U.S. Equipment by the*

Indonesian Armed Forces, Hearing. 95th Cong., 1st sess., 23 March 1977. Washington, D.C.: U.S. Government Printing Office, 1977.

U.S. Congress. House. Committee on International Relations and Senate Committee on Foreign Relations Subcommittees on East Asian and Pacific Affairs. *The Political Futures of Indonesia and East Timor, Joint Hearing.* 106th Cong., 1st sess., 9 September 1999. Washington, D.C.: U.S. Government Printing Office, 2000.

U.S. Congress. Senate. Committee on Foreign Relations. *Crisis in East Timor and U.S. Policy towards Indonesia, Hearings.* 102nd Cong., 2nd sess., 17 February and 6 March 1991. Washington, D.C.: U.S. Government Printing Office, 1992.

XII. INDONESIA

Anwar, Dewi. *Indonesia in ASEAN: Foreign Policy and Regionalism.* Singapore: Institute of Southeast Asian Studies, 1994.

Agung, Ide Anak Augung Gde. *Twenty Years of Indonesian Foreign Policy, 1945–65.* Yogyakarta, Indonesia: Duta Wacana University Press, 1990.

Bresnan, John. *Managing Indonesia,* New York: Columbia University Press, 1993.

——, ed. *Indonesia: The Great Transition.* Lanham, Md.: Rowman & Littlefield, 2004.

Conboy, Kenneth, and James Morrison. *Feet to the Fire: Covert CIA Operations in Indonesia, 1957–1958.* Annapolis, Md.: Naval Institute Press, 2002.

Cribb, Robert, and Audrey Kahin. *Historical Dictionary of Indonesia.* Lanham, Md.: Scarecrow Press, 2004.

Emmerson, Donald, ed. *Indonesia Beyond Suharto: Economy, Society, and Transition.* Armonk, N.Y.: M.E. Sharpe, 1998.

Forrester, Geoff, and R. J. May. *The Fall of Soeharto.* Bathhurst, NSW, Australia: Crawford House Press, 1998.

Frederick, William H., and Robert L. Worden. *Indonesia: A Country Study.* Washington, D.C.: Federal Research Division, Library of Congress, 1993.

Friend, Theodore. *Indonesian Destinies.* Cambridge, Mass.: The Belknap Press of the Harvard University Press, 2005.

Gardner, Paul F. *Shared Hopes, Separate Fears: Fifty Years of U.S.–Indonesia Relations.* Boulder, Colo.: Westview Press, 1997.

Glasius, Marlie. *Foreign Policy on Human Rights: Its Influence in Indonesia Under Suharto.* Antwerp. Belgium: Intersentia-Hart, 1999.

Gouda, Frances, with Thijs Brocades Zeeberg. *American Visions of the East Indies/Indonesia: U.S. Foreign Policy and Indonesian Nationalism, 1920–1949.* Amsterdam: Amsterdam University Press, 2002.

Harvey, Barbara.S. *Permesta: Half a Rebellion*. Ithaca, N.Y.: Cornell Modern Indonesia Project, 1977.

Kahin, George McT. *Nationalism and Revolution in Indonesia*. Ithaca, N.Y: Cornell University Press, 1952.

Kahin, George McT., and Audrey Kahin. *Subversion as Foreign Policy: The Secret Eisenhower and Dulles Debacle in Indonesia.* New York: The New Press, 1995.

King, John Kerry. *West New Guinea: The Dispute and Its Settlement*. South Orange, N.J.: Seton Hall University Press, 1973.

Legge, John D. *Sukarno: A Political Biography*. New York: Praeger, 1972.

Leifer, Michael. *Indonesia's Foreign Policy*. London: Allen & Unwin, 1983.

Mackie, J.A. C. *Konfrontasi: The Indonesia–Malaysia Dispute, 1963–1966*. Kuala Lumpur, Malaysia: Oxford University Press, 1974.

McMahon, Robert J. *Colonialism and the Cold War: The United States and the Struggle for Indonesian Independence, 1945–1949*. Ithaca, N.Y.: Cornell University Press, 1981.

Orentlicher, Dianne F. *Human Rights in Indonesia and East Timor*. New York: Human Rights Watch, 1988.

Osborne, Robin. *Indonesia's Secret War: The Guerilla Struggle in Irian Jaya*. Sydney, New South Wales, Australia: Allen & Unwin, 1985.

Pringle, Robert. *Indonesia and the Philippines: American Interests in Island Southeast Asia*. New York: Columbia University Press, 1980.

Roadnight, Andrew. *United States Policy towards Indonesia in the Truman and Eisenhower Years.* London: Palgrave Macmillan, 2002.

Saltford, John. *United Nations and the Indonesian Takeover of West Papua, 1962–1969: The Anatomy of a Betrayal*. London: RoutledgeCurzon, 2004.

Smith, Anthony L. *Strategic Centrality: Indonesia's Changing Role in ASEAN*. Singapore: Institute of Southeast Asian Studies, 2000.

Suryadinata, Leo. *Indonesia's Foreign Policy under Suharto: Aspiring to International Leadership*. Singapore: Times Academic Press, 1996.

United States Central Intelligence Agency. *Indonesia 1965: The Coup that Backfired*. Washington, D.C.: Author, December 1968.

U.S. Congress. House. Committee on International Relations. Subcommittee on Asia and the Pacific. *Indonesia: Confronting the Political and Economic Crises, Hearing*. 106th Cong., 1st sess., 16 February 2000. Washington, D.C.: U.S. Government Printing Office, 2000.

———. *Indonesia in Transition: Implications for U.S. Interests, Hearing*. 107th Cong., 1st sess., 18 July 2001 (Serial No. 107-35). Available at www.house.gov/international–relations.

———. *U.S. Policy Options toward Indonesia: What We Can Expect; What We Can Do, Hearing*. 105th Cong., 2nd sess., 4 June 1998. Washington, D.C.: U.S. Government Printing Office, 1998.

U.S. Congress. Senate. Committee on Foreign Relations. *Crisis in East Timor and U.S. Policy Towards Indonesia, Hearings.* 102nd Cong., 2nd sess., 27 February and 6 March 1992. Washington, D.C.: U.S. Government Printing Office, 1992.

U.S. Congress. Senate. Subcommittee on Asian and Pacific Affairs. *U.S.–Indonesian Relations, Hearing.* 109th Cong., 1st sess., 15 September 2005. Washington, D.C.: U.S. Government Printing Office, 2006.

Vatikiotis, Michael. *Indonesia Under Suharto: Order, Development, and Pressure for Change.* London: Routledge, 1993.

XIII. BRUNEI, MALAYSIA, AND SINGAPORE

Abdullah, Datuk Ahmad. *Tengku Abdul Rahman and Malaysian Foreign Policy, 1963–1970.* Kuala Lumpur, Malaysia: Berita Publishing, 1985.

Bedlington, Stanley. *Malaysia and Singapore: The Building of New States.* Ithaca, N.Y.: Cornell University Press, 1978.

Chan Heng Chee. *Singapore: The Politics of Survival.* Singapore: Oxford University Press, 1971.

Chin Kin Wah. *The Defense of Malaysia and Singapore: The Transformation of a Security System.* New York: Cambridge University Press, 1983.

Dickens, Peter. *SAS: Secret War in South-East Asia.* New York: Greenhill Books, 2003.

Ganesan, N. *Realism and Interdependence in Singapore's Foreign Policy.* London: Routledge, 2005.

Gould, James W. *The United States and Malaysia.* Cambridge, Mass.: Harvard University Press, 1969.

James, Harold, and Denis Shiel-Small. *The Undeclared War: The Story of the Indonesian Confrontation, 1962–1966.* Lanham, Md.: Rowman & Littlefield, 1971.

Jones, Matthew. *Conflict and Cooperation in Southeast Asia: Britain, the United States, and the Creation of Malaysia.* Cambridge: Cambridge University Press, 2002.

Kaur, Amarjit. *Historical Dictionary of Malaysia.* Lanham, Md.: Scarecrow Press, 2001.

Lepoer, Barbara Leitch, ed. *Singapore: A Country Study.* Washington, D.C.: Federal Research Division, Library of Congress, 1991.

Leifer, Michael. *Singapore's Foreign Policy: Coping with Vulnerability.* New York and London: Routledge, 2000.

Mackie, J. A., and C. Konfrontasi. *The Indonesia–Malaysia Dispute, 1963–1966.* New York: Oxford University Press, 1974.

Milne, R. S., and Diane K. Mauzey, *Malaysian Politics Under Mahathir*. New York: Routledge, 1999.

Mulliner, K., and Lian The-Mulliner. *Historical Dictionary of Singapore*. Metuchen, N.J.: Scarecrow Press, 1991.

Murugusu, Pathmanathan. *Winds of Change: The Mahathir Impact on Malaysia's Foreign Policy*. Kuala Lumpur, Malaysia: Eastview, 1984.

Singh, D. S. Ranjit, and Jatswan S. Sidhu. *Historical Dictionary of Brunei Darussalam*. Lanham, Md.: Scarecrow Press, 1997.

Sodhy, Pamala. *The U.S.–Malaysian Nexus: Themes in Superpower–Small State Relations*. Kuala Lumpur, Malaysia: Institute of Strategic and International Studies, Malaysia, 1991.

Vreeland, Nina, ed. *Malaysia: A Country Study*. Washington, D.C.: Foreign Area Studies, American University, 1977.

U.S. Congress. House. Committee on Foreign Affairs. Subcommittee on Human Rights and International Organizations. *Recent Developments in Malaysia and Singapore, Hearings*. 100th Cong., 2nd sess., 2 July and 22 September 1988. Washington, D.C.: U.S. Government Printing Office, 1988.

U.S. Congress. House. Committee on International Relations. Subcommittee on Asia and the Pacific. *Malaysia, Assessing the Mahathir Agenda, Hearing*. 106th Cong., 1st sess., 16 June 1999. Washington, D.C.: U.S. Government Printing Office, 1999.

U.S. Congress. Senate. Committee on Finance. *Implementation of the U.S. Bilateral Free Trade Agreement with Singapore and Chile, Hearing*. 108th Cong., 1st sess., 17 June 2004. Washington, D.C.: U.S. Government Printing Office, 2004.

XIV. PHILIPPINES

Abueva, José B. *Ramon Magsaysay: A Political Biography*. Manila: Solidaridad, 1971.

Bain, David Harward. *Sitting in Darkness: Americans in the Philippines*. New York: Houghton Mifflin, 1984.

Berry, William E., Jr. *U.S. Bases in the Philippines: The Evolution of the Special Relationship*. Boulder, Colo.: Westview Press, 1989.

Blackburn, Robert M. *Mercenaries and Lyndon Johnson's "More Flags": Hiring of Korean, Filipino, and Thai Soldiers in the Vietnam War*. Jefferson, N.C.: McFarland, 1994.

Blanchard, William H. *Neocolonialism American Style, 1960–2000*. Westport, Conn.: Greenwood Press, 1996.

Blitz, Amy. *The Contested State: American Foreign Policy and Regime Change in the Philippines.* Lanham, Md.: Rowman & Littlefield, 2000.

Bonner, Raymond. *Waltzing with a Dictator: The Marcoses and the Making of American Policy.* New York: Time Books, 1987.

Brands, H. W. *Bound to Empire: The United States and the Philippines.* New York: Oxford University Press, 1992.

Bresnan, John, ed. *Crisis in the Philippines: The Marcos Era and Beyond.* Princeton, N.J.: Princeton University Press, 1966.

Buell, Thomas. *The Quiet Warrior: A Biography of Admiral Raymond A. Spruance.* Annapolis, Md.: Naval Institute Press, 1957.

Bunge, Fredrica M., ed. *The Philippines: A Country Study.* Washington, D.C.: U.S. Government Printing Office, 1984.

Burton, Sandra. *Impossible Dream: The Marcoses, the Aquinos, and the Unfinished Revolution.* New York: Warner Books, 1989.

Buss, Claude A. *The United States and the Philippines.* Stanford, Calif.: Hoover Institution, 1977.

Colbert, Evelyn. *The United States and the Philippine Bases.* Lanham, Md.: Rowman & Littlefield, 1988.

Cullather, Nick. *Illusions of Influence: The Political Economy of the United States–Philippines Relations, 1942–1960.* Palo Alto, Calif.: Stanford University Press, 1994.

Currey, Cecil B. *Edward Lansdale: The Unquiet American.* Boston: Houghton Mifflin, 1988.

Friend, Theodore. *Between Two Empires.* New Haven, Conn.: Yale University Press, 1965.

Greene, Fred, ed. *Philippine Bases: Negotiating for the Future.* New York: Council on Foreign Relations, 1988.

Guillermo, Artemio R., and May Kyi Win. *Historical Dictionary of the Philippines.* Lanham, Md.: Scarecrow Press, 2005.

Karnow, Stanley. *In Our Image: America's Empire in the Philippines.* New York: Random House, 1989.

Kerkvliet, Benedict J. *The Huk Rebellion: A Study of Peasant Revolt in the Philippines.* Berkeley and Los Angeles: University of California Press, 1977.

Kirk, Donald. *Looted: The Philippines after the Bases.* New York: St. Martin's Press, 1998.

Lande, Carl, ed. *Rebuilding a Nation: Philippine Challenges and American Policy.* Washington, D.C.: Washington Institute Press, 1977.

Manchester, William L. *American Caesar: Douglas MacArthur, 1880–1964.* New York: Dell Publishing, 1978.

Meyer, Milton W. *A Diplomatic History of the Philippine Republic.* Honolulu: University of Hawaii Press, 1965.

Miller, Stuart Creighton. *Benevolent Assimilation: The American Conquest of the Philippines, 1898–1903.* New Haven, Conn.: Yale University Press, 1962.

Poole, Fredrick R. *Revolution in the Philippines: The United States in a Hall of Cracked Mirrors.* New York: McGraw-Hill, 1984.

Pringle, Robert. *Indonesia and the Philippines: American Interests in Island Southeast Asia.* New York: Columbia University Press, 1980.

San Juan, E., Jr. *After Post –Colonialism: Remapping Philippines–United States Confrontation.* Lanham, Md.: Rowman & Littlefield, 2000.

Shalom, Stephen. *The United States and the Philippines: A Study of Neo-colonialism.* Quezon City, Philippines: New Day Publishers, 1986.

Stanley, Peter A. *A Nation in the Making: The Philippines and the United States, 1899–1921.* Cambridge, Mass.: Harvard University Press, 1984.

——, ed. *Reappraising an Empire: New Perspectives on Philippine-American History.* Cambridge, Mass.: Harvard University Press, 1984.

Steinberg, David J. *The Philippines: A Singular and Plural Place.* Boulder, Colo.: Westview Press, 1982.

Taylor, George A. *The Philippines and the United States.* New York: Praeger, 1964.

Thompson, W. Scott. *Unequal Partners: Philippine and Thai Relations with the United States, 1965–1975.* Lexington, Mass.: Lexington Books, 1975.

——. *The Philippines in Crisis.* New York: St. Martin's Press, 1992.

Tyner, James A. *Iraq, Terror, and the Philippines' Will to War.* Lanham, Md.: Rowman & Littlefield, 2005.

U.S. Congress. House. Committee on Foreign Affairs. Subcommittee on Asian and Pacific Affairs. *Hearings on United States-Philippines Relations and the New Base and Aid Agreement.* 98th Cong., 1st sess., 17, 23, and 28 June 1983. Washington, D.C.: U.S. Government Printing Office, 1983.

U.S. Congress. House. Committee on Foreign Affairs. Subcommittee on Human Rights and International Organizations. *Human Rights in the Philippines, Hearings.* 98th Cong., 1st sess., 22 September 1983. Washington, D.C.: U.S. Government Printing Office, 1983.

U.S. Congress. House. Committee on Foreign Affairs. Subcommittees on Asian and Pacific Affairs and on Human Rights and International Organizations. *U.S. Policy toward the Philippines, Hearing.* 97th Cong., 1st sess., 19 November 1981. Washington, D.C.: U.S. Government Printing Office, 1982.

U.S. Congress. Senate. Committee on Foreign Relations. Subcommittee on East Asian and Pacific Affairs. *Extra-judicial Killings in the Philippines: Strategies to End the Violence, Hearings.* 110th Cong., 1st sess., 13 March 2007.

——. *The Philippine Bases Treaty, Hearings.* 102nd Cong., 2nd sess., 25 September 1991. Washington, D.C.: U.S. Government Printing Office 1992.

——. *The Philippines: Present Political Status and Its Role in the New Asia, Hearings.* 107th Cong., 1st sess., 6 March 2001. Washington, D.C.: U.S. Government Printing Office, 2001.

XV. THAILAND

Alagappa, Muthiah. *The National Security of Developing States: Lessons from Thailand.* Dover, Mass.: Auburn House, 1982.

Aldrich, Richard J. *The Key to the South: Britain, the United States, and Thailand during the Approach of the Pacific War, 1929–1942.* New York: Oxford University Press, 1993.

Blackburn, Robert M. *Mercenaries and Lyndon Johnson's "More Flags": Hiring of Korean, Filipino, and Thai Soldiers in the Vietnam War.* Jefferson, N.C.: McFarland., 1994.

Caldwell, Alexander. *American Economic Aid to Thailand.* Lexington, Mass.: Lexington Books, 1974.

Darling, Frank C. *Thailand and the United States.* Washington, D.C.: Public Affairs Press, 1965.

Fineman, Daniel. *A Special Relationship: The United States and Military Governments in Thailand, 1947–1958.* Honolulu: University of Hawaii Press, 1997.

Galasser, Jeffrey D. *The Secret Vietnam War: The United States Air Force in Thailand, 1961–1975.* Jefferson, N.C.: McFarland, 1995.

Indorf, Hans N. *Thai–American Relations in Contemporary Affairs.* Singapore: Executive Publications, 1982.

Jackson, Karl, ed. *United States–Thailand Relations.* Berkeley: University of California Institute of East Asian Studies, 1986.

Lomax, Louis E. *Thailand: The War That Is, the War That Will Be.* New York: Random House, 1967.

Muscat, Robert J. *Thailand and the United States: Development, Security, and Foreign Aid.* New York: Columbia University Press, 1990.

Neher, Clark D., and Wiwat Mungkandi, eds. *U.S.–Thailand Relations in a New International Era.* Berkeley: University of California Institute of East Asian Studies, 1990.

Ramsey, Ansel, and Wiwat Mungkandi, eds. *Thailand–U.S. Relations: Changing Political, Strategic, and Economic Factors.* Berkeley: University of California Institute of East Asian Studies, 1988.

Randolph, Sean R. *The United States and Thailand: Alliance Dynamics.* Berkeley: University of California Press, 1986.

Reynolds, E. Bruce. *Thailand's Secret War: OSS, SOE, and the Free Thai Underground during World War II*. Cambridge: Cambridge University Press, 2005.
Smith, Harold E., Gayla S. Nieminen, and May Kyi Win. *Historical Dictionary of Thailand*. Lanham, Md.: Scarecrow Press, 2005.
Thompson. W. Scott. *Unequal Partners: Philippine and Thai Relations with the United States, 1965–1975*. Lexington, Mass.: Lexington Books, 1975.

XVI. INTERNET RESOURCES

Asia-Pacific Economic Cooperation, www.apec.org
Asian Development Bank, www.adb.org
Association of Southeast Asian Nations, www.seansec.org
Central Intelligence Agency, www.cia.gov
Trade Stats Express, www.tse.export.gov
U.S. Department of State, www.state.gov
U.S. Trade Representative, www.ustr.gov
White House, www.whitehouse.gov
World Bank, www.worldbank.org
United Nations, www.un.org

About the Author

Donald E. Weatherbee is the Donald S. Russell Distinguished Professor Emeritus at the University of South Carolina, where he specialized in the politics and international relations of Southeast Asia. A graduate of Bates College, he holds an M.A. and Ph.D. from the Johns Hopkins School of Advanced International Studies.

In addition to the University of South Carolina, Prof. Weatherbee has taught at Wilson College, the University of Rhode Island; Gajah Mada University in Indonesia; Chulalongkorn University in Thailand; University Kebangsaan in Malaysia; and the Free University of Berlin. He has held major research grants at the Institute of Southeast Asian Studies in Singapore and the Institute of Strategic and International Studies in Bangkok. He has lectured at and consulted with official and academic institutions throughout Southeast Asia. Prof. Weatherbee spent three years at the U.S. Army War College (1974–1977) as the Henry L. Stimson Professor and was awarded the Army's Distinguished Civilian Service award for his work on the post–Vietnam war profile of Southeast Asia, "guiding senior army planners in the redefinition of United States national strategy." In 2004 Prof. Weatherbee was in the Philippines as the Fulbright-Sycip Distinguished Lecturer in American Studies, where he presented a series of lectures on American foreign policy in Southeast Asia.

Prof. Weatherbee is past president of the Southeastern Conference of the Association of Asian Studies, past editor for Southeast Asia of *Asian Affairs*, past member of the editorial board of *Asian Survey*, and past member of the Contemporary Affairs Committee of the Asia Society. He is currently on the Board of Advisors of the United States–Indonesian Society, a director of the American–Indonesian Cultural and Educational Foundation, and a participant in the Columbia University Southeast Asia Seminar. He continues as a consultant to public and private agencies with Southeast Asian interests.

Prof. Weatherbee has a lengthy publications record, beginning with his first monograph, *Ideology in Indonesia: Sukarno's Indonesian Revolution* (1966). His most recent book is *International Relations in Southeast Asia: The Struggle for Autonomy*, published in 2005. A second revised edition is planned for 2008. His other recent major publications include the chapters "Indonesian Foreign Policy: A Wounded Phoenix," in *Southeast Asian Affairs 2005*; "Strategic Dimensions of Economic Interdependence in Southeast Asia," in *Strategic Asia 2006–2007*; "Southeast Asia in 2006: Déjà vu All Over Again" in *Southeast Asian Affairs 2007*; "Political Change in Southeast Asia: Challenges for U.S. Strategy" in *Strategic Asia 2007–2008*; and "ASEAN's Identity Crisis" in *Legacies of Change in Southeast Asia,* forthcoming in 2008.